Modern Law of Contracts and Sales in Latin America, Spain and Portugal

MODERN LAW OF CONTRACTS AND SALES IN LATIN AMERICA, SPAIN AND PORTUGAL

by

EDGARDO MUÑOZ

eleven
international publishing

Published, sold and distributed by Eleven International Publishing
P.O. Box 85576
2508 CG The Hague
The Netherlands
Tel.: +31 70 33 070 33
Fax: +31 70 33 070 30
Website: www.elevenpub.com

Eleven International Publishing is an imprint of Boom uitgevers Den Haag.

Cover design: Angema | Romijn Design, IJsselstein
Cover picture: sneska | iStockphoto.com
Layout: IM Publishing Services, Potts Point

ISBN 978-94-90947-03-3
NUR 828

Table of Contents

List of Abbreviations

A.C.	Actualidad Civil
AgRg	Agravo Regimental
AL	Arbitration Law
Am J Com L	American Journal of Comparative Law
Art.	Article
Arts.	Articles
AT	Audiencia Territorial
B2B	Business to Business
BGB	Bürgerliches Gesetzbuch (German Civil Code 1900 – today)
BIL	Bankruptcy and Insolvency Law
C2C	Consumer to Consumer
C y F	Cost and Freight
cass	Cassation
Cass civ	Civil Cassation
Cass pen	Criminal Cassation
Cass soc	Social Cassation
CC	Civil Code
CComP	Code of Commercial Procedure
cGMP	current Good Manufacturing Practice
Ch.	Chapter
CIDIP	Inter-American Specialized Conferences on Private International Law
CIF	cost insurance freight
CISG	Convention on the International Sale of Goods
CISG-AC	Advisory Council on the CISG
CLOUT	Case Law on UNCITRAL Texts
Com C	Code of Commerce
CPC	Code of Civil Procedure
CPCC	Code of Civil and Commercial Procedure
CPL	Consumers Protection Law
Ct Arb	Court of Arbitration
CRL	Copyrights Law
C.V.	Capital Variable
DSEC	Law on Documents, Signatures and Electronic Commerce
EBIT	earnings before interest and taxes
EC	European Community
EDI	Electronic Data Interchange
Ex.	Expiration
FAS	free alongside ship

FCA	Free Carrier
FOB	Free on Board
GAL	General Arbitration Law
GJ	Gaceta Judicial (Judicial Gazette)
GLSGC	Warrantees' Law for the Sale of Goods for Consumption
ICC	International Chamber of Commerce
Id Cendoj	Identification Number in Spain's Supreme Tribunal Database
INCOTERMS	International Commercial Terms
INDECOPI	National Institute for the Defence of the Competence and the Protection of the Intellectual Property (Peru)
IP	Intellectual Property
IPL	Intellectual Property Law
IPL (Venezuela)	International Private Law
JC	Judicial Code
JL	Judicial Law
JOL	Judicial Organic Law
JTR	Jurisprudencia de los Tribunales de la República
LC	Law of Companies
LCT	Law of Civil Trials
LDSEC	Law on Documents, Signatures and Electronic Commerce
LM	Law of Merchants
LRTS	Law on Retention of Title Sales
Ltda.	Limitada (Limited)
MAL	UNCITRAL Model Law on International Commercial Arbitration
MLEC	Model Law on Electronic Commerce
MLES	Model Law on Electronic Signatures
MOU	Memorandum of Understanding
MX$	Mexican Pesos
NJCL	Nordic Journal of Commercial Law
Nac.	Nacional
NCPI/BGSI	National Composite Policy Index
NOM	No Oral Modification Clause
OL	Organic Law
PICC	UNIDROIT Principles on International Commercial Contracts 2004
PIL	Private International Law
RC	Convention on the law applicable to contractual obligations (Rome Convention)
RDJ	Revista de Derecho y Jurisprudencia
REsp	Recurso Especial
RJC	Revista Juridica de Cataluna
S.A.	Sociedad Anónima
S.G.S.	Société Générale de Surveillance
SELIC	Sistema Especial de Liquidação e Custodia (Special System for Settlement and Custody)
SJF	Semanario Judicial de la Federacion
UCP	Uniform Customs and Practice for Documentary Credits
ULFIS	Uniform Law on the Formation of Contracts for the International Sale of Goods (1964)
ULIS	Convention relating to a Uniform Law on the International Sale of Goods (1964)

UNCITRAL	United Nations Commission for International Trade Law
UNECIC	United Nations Convention on the Use of Electronic Communications in International Contracts (2005)
UNIDROIT	International Institute for the Unification of Private Law
USD	Dollars of the United States of America
V.A.T	Value Added Tax
VJ	Vindobona Journal of International Commercial Law and Arbitration
WIPO	World International Property Organization

Acknowledgments

The author is extremely grateful to Prof. Dr. Ingeborg Schwenzer, LL.M. for her invaluable guidance and support while writing this book. The author would also like to thank his colleagues Claire Chabat, Pascal Hachem, Mohamed Hafez, Christopher Kee, Natia Lapiashvili, Alissa Palumbo, Jean Alain Penda Matipe and Sophia Yang, all members of the Global Sales Law Project of the University of Basel, for their support and many hours of their time to discuss and clarify the issues of this book.

The author would like to thank Dr. Florian Mohs LL.M. for his critical and helpful comments to the last draft of this work. The author would also like to thank those Global Sales Law Correspondents who provided some of the materials to develop this work: Lucía Mazzuca (Argentina), Luiz Felipe Calábria Lopes (Brazil), Luiz Gustavo Meira Moser (Brazil), Jorge Oviedo Albán (Colombia), Cristina López (El Salvador), Guillermo Coronado (Mexico), Ricardo Ampuero (Peru), Fernando Cantuarias (Peru), José Miguel Alarcão Júdice (Portugal) and Cristobal Reitze (Venezuela).

Also special thanks to Gabriela Vizcaino and Iulia Dolganova for their research assistance and thoughtful comments on the Argentinean and Brazilian jurisprudence, respectively.

Finally, the author owes particulars thanks to Miriam González Guillén, who did many big things to help him to get the work done, as well as many little things without which his work would have been impossible to accomplish. Thanks so much.

Initial Remark

In this work, the author aims to present the first and most comprehensive comparative study on modern law of contracts and sales in Latin America, Spain and Portugal (hereinafter the Ibero-American countries).[1] The sources consulted to build up this comparative study include the most recent scholarship published by Ibero-American authors. They also include a great number of court decisions and arbitral awards; which comprise the most up-to-date Ibero-American jurisprudence developed by the highest National Courts and ICC Arbitral Tribunals (most of them taken directly from the official source and integrated for the first time into a comparative study).

The work presents, from a comparative-functional approach, the solutions developed by the Ibero-American laws to give an answer to a specific event related to the sales contract. The English legal terms used to express such events are taken from the CISG English version, and for those issues that are not governed by the CISG, from the UNIDROIT PICC English version. The legal terms in Portuguese or Spanish were not literally translated into English, but rather the event that they express, or the function that they serve, have been converted into the uniform law (CISG or UNIDROIT PICC) English terms that express the same function or event.

This work aims to be a contribution to legal scholarship in the subject area of contract and sales law in Ibero-American countries. The approach taken should be useful for any law practitioner and researcher looking for a straightforward and well-supported legal answer to any of the topics covered by this work.

[1] This work covers the following countries that are historically considered as Ibero-American: Argentina, Bolivia, Brazil, Chile, Colombia, Costa Rica, Cuba, Dominican Republic, Ecuador, El Salvador, Guatemala, Honduras, Mexico, Nicaragua, Panama, Paraguay, Peru, Portugal, Spain, Uruguay and Venezuela. These same countries are part of the Organization of Ibero-American States with the addition of Andorra, Puerto Rico (commonwealth of the United States) and Equatorial Guinea, which are not considered in this work; *see* http://www.oei.es/.

Part 1

Sales Law – History and Applicable Rules

CHAPTER 1

ORIGINS OF SALES LAW

1. Introduction

The Ibero-American private law is irrefutably based in the Civil Law Tradition rather than in the Common Law Tradition. The Civil Law Tradition as it is generally understood today, made its appearance in the 12th century with the rediscovery of the *Corpus Juris Civilis* by the Glossators of the European Universities of Bologna and Paris.[1] The re-adoption of the Roman institutions principally in the areas of contracts and torts began to overlap with the local feudal traditions.[2] Then, the appearance of independent European nations in the 17th century started to permeate the idea of creating original national statutes that would unify the diffuse laws. The French Civil Code of 1804 was the first universally known example. One of the characteristics of this code was its generality and the interaction of its provisions covering a given set of facts.[3] For example, the general part relating to obligations would interact with a more specific part on ways of acquiring property when a breach of contract needed to be assessed. Such method would later become one of the characteristics of the whole Civil Law Tradition.

However, it would be an oversimplification to classify the whole group of Ibero-American legal systems as direct decedents of the French Civil Code of 1804. Some authors insist that when the Spanish and the Portuguese empires in Latin America lost their colonies in the 19th century, it was mainly the French civil law that the lawmakers of the new nations looked for inspiration.[4] These

1 Latin America: J. Barrera Graf, El Derecho Mercantil en la América Latina 22 (1963).

2 K.W. Dam, *Legal Institutions, Legal Origins, and Governance*, Olin Working Paper No. 303, at 5.

3 *Id.*, at 6.

4 R. La Porta *et al.*, *The Economic Consequences of Legal Origins*, 46(2) Journal of Economic Literature, American Economic Association 285, at 290 (2008).

sorts of statements have resulted in erroneous classifications, making Ibero-America to represent more than 40 percent of the French civil law countries in the world.[5]

The French Civil Code influenced some Ibero-American codes.[6] This can be attributed to its simplicity and the ideas of human democracy that were very present in the ideology of the new independent societies of Latin America. However, it is not accurate to state that Ibero-American private law is direct decedent of the French law. As further will be presented in detail, the law of contracts in the Spanish and the Portuguese empires during the colonial period, and in the first decades of independence, was Iberian original law based either in Roman law or in the local customs and commercial usages compiled in the form of Royal statutes.

Moreover, many authors, jurists, government agents and legislators have agreed on the fact that the civil and commercial codes produced in Ibero-America during the 19th and 20th centuries were influenced by more than one country's legal system.[7] Additionally, an exchange of legal principles, rules, systems and methods has occurred between the Ibero-American countries themselves;[8] resulting in a melting-pot of common legal institutions that have remained within the Ibero-American borders.

In this chapter, an overview on the origins of the sales law in the Ibero-American countries will be presented. Historical data will help us to support the idea that Ibero-American countries have formed a subsystem in the Civil Law Legal Family, which justifies the study of the modern practice of sales law in the region, separate from other Civil Law countries.

> Latin American former Spanish and Portuguese colonies ended up with codifications heavily influenced by the French legal tradition after gaining independence. Beyond the fact that Napoleon had invaded the Iberian Peninsula, the reasons were partly the new military leaders' admiration for Bonaparte, partly language, and partly Napoleonic influence on the Spanish and Portuguese codes

France: X. Blanc-Jouvan, Worldwide Influence of the French Civil Code of 1804, on the Occasion of its Bicentennial Celebration 1-6 (2004): believes that the influence of the French Code was absolute in Latin America specially in the Civil Law of Peru, Argentina and Brazil; M.L. Murillo, *The Evolution of Codification in the Civil Law Legal Systems: Towards Decodification and Recodification*, 11(1) Journal of Transnational Law & Policy 1, at 9 (2001): the French Civil Code served as the 'model' of several 19th century Latin American Civil Codes.

5 La Porta *et al.*, *supra* note 4, at 289 Fig. 1 The distribution of Legal Origin.

6 *See* the influence of the French Civil Code in more detail *infra* in 3.

7 *See for example* in 3.

8 *Id.*

2. Origins of Sales Law in the Spanish and the Portuguese Empires

During the Iberian colonisation period,[9] Latin American inhabitants saw their private activities regulated by the laws of the Kingdoms of Spain and Portugal. Before the Middle Ages, Spain had developed a codified body of laws called *Las Siete Partidas*; a compilation of common civil rules enacted in 1348 by King *Alfonso El Sabio* (The Wise).[10] The technique and the style of *Las Siete Partidas* were no different to any modern code. Neither was the ideology nor the content so different. *Las Siete Partidas* were Roman law in the version adapted by the glossators. They resemble a roman code on private law. This is one of the reasons why no other future law of the Spanish Empire could compete with them in the said area.[11] The *Quinta Partida* (the Fifth Part of *Las Siete Partidas*) is about the law of the obligations and the contracts. This codified body of rules did not distinguish between civil and commercial acts.[12] However, since trading activities started to be organised through consulates of commerce, more specialised series of ordinances came up. These ordinances were applied for the commercial activities taking place between the Colonies and the Empire.[13]

At the time of the discovery of America, the *Ley de Toro I* (Law of Bull I) had imposed to the royal tribunals the obligation to apply the different civil laws in force in the following order. First, the *Ordenanzas* (Ordinances) dictated by the Royal Court and by the King himself.[14] Second, the laws of the *Fueros* which consisted of a collection of Judgments coming from the Royal Tribunal *(Fuero Real)* or from the local judges of Castile *(Fuero Juzgo)*. Finally, *Las Siete Partidas*, which complemented the first two body of rules.[15] When the colonies started to develop, a special compilation of laws was produced for the new American territories. This was named *Recopilación de las Leyes de*

---

9 Portugal and Spain undertook a colonisation process in America that began in the 16th century and finished in the 19th century.

10 *See* Las Siete Partidas del Rey Alfonso El Sabio, Cotejadas con varios Códices Antiguos por la Real Academia de la Historia, Tomo III, Partida Cuarta, Quinta, Sexta y Séptima, Madrid en la Imprenta Real (1807).

11 Latin America: A. Guzmán Brito, Historia de la Codificación civil en Iberoamerica 40 (2006).

12 Latin America: Barrera Graf, *supra* note 1, at 17.

13 *Id*., at 17: First, *Las Ordenanzas de Burgo* y de *Sevilla* of 1494 and 1594, were provided with a *Casa de Contratacion para las Indias* (House of Commerce for the Indies) in 1503 and a *Tribunal Consular* (Consular Tribunal) in 1543. Second, the *Ordenanzas de Bilbao* were dictated in 1604.

14 Latin America: Guzmán Brito, *supra* note 11, at 34: these laws were found in the forms of compilations elaborated and completed during the years, such as *Nueva Recopilacion* of 1567, *Novisima Recopilacion* 1805.

15 Latin America: Guzmán Brito, *supra* note 11, at 34.

los Reynos de las Indias of 1680 (Compilation of Laws for the Kingdoms of the Indies). This compilation was composed of the above-mentioned Spanish Laws plus more specific administrative laws and merchants laws.[16]

An analogous phenomenon occurred in the Portuguese empire. The Portuguese law during the time of the colony, the set of rules at the time of the discovery of Brazil were the *Ordenaçoes Alfonsinas of 1446*, which are arguably the oldest code of the modern Europe.[17] Then in 1521 came the *Ordenaçoes Manuelinas*.[18] Finally, in 1603 *Felipe I* of Portugal[19] promulgated the *Ordenaçoes Philipinas*, which according to some authors remained the applicable civil law in Brazil until the enactment of the Brazilian Civil Code of 1917.[20] Similar to the Spanish ordinances the rules of the *Ordenaçoes Philipinas* had as their source the Visigoths codes, the first laws of the Portuguese Monarchy, *Las Siete Partidas*, the Justinian law and the annotated Roman codes at the Universities of Bologna and Paris.[21]

2.1. Spanish and Portuguese Empires Commercial Law

The institution of *Consulados* (merchants' guilds) is of great importance to understand the way in which trade was regulated and organised during the Spanish Empire. It is also important to show that since then special rules on commerce, including contracts, where independently created and applied in Spain and its colonies from the 16th to the 19th centuries.[22] A good example is *Ordenanzas de Bilbao*, which became in the 18th century the standard code for commercial law in Spain and its colonies. These ordinances would later play an important role in the development of the future Codes of Commerce of Spain, Portugal and Latin America.

The history of the *Consulados de Comercio* can be traced back to the Spanish merchant guilds originated in medieval times in response to the rapid rise of commerce in 13th century in Catalonia.[23] With the unification of the kingdoms of Castile and Aragon in the 15th century, the new Catholics Kings and it agents established more *Consulados*. They had a system of commercial justice based on verbal pleadings without attorneys, "in which precedent and

---

[16] *Id.*, at p. 34.

[17] Latin America: Barrera Graf, *supra* note 1, at 22.

[18] *Id.*, at 22.

[19] Felipe I of Portugal was also King of Spain known as Felipe II of Spain.

[20] Argentina: L. Moisset de Espanés, *El Método del Código Civil*, Academia Nacional de Derecho y Ciencias Sociales de Córdoba, http://www.acaderc.org.ar/doctrina/articulos/artelme todo delCódigocivil/?searchterm=explicativa, at 2.

[21] Latin America: Barrera Graf, *supra* note 1, at 22.

[22] This duality was inherited by most other Ibero-American legal systems; *see* Ch. 5.

[23] *See generally* R. Woodward, *The New Consulados de Comercio in the Spanish Empire 1778-1829*, Tulane University (1999), http://www.tulane.edu/~woodward/newcons.htm.

custom were important features, making Aragonese commercial law more similar to the system of English common law than to the Roman tradition."[24]

During 1792 and 1795, the Spanish King Charles IV authorised eight new *Real Consulados de Comercio* in the American colonies. Before that time, the merchants of Lima and Mexico had jealously guarded the exclusive consular privileges accorded to transatlantic merchants in the late 16th century.[25] The permits for the creation of new consulates were given to Caracas on 3 June 1793, Buenos Aires on 8 June 1793, Guatemala on 11 December 1793, Montevideo 30 January 1794, Havana 4 April 1794, Veracruz on 17 January 1795, Santiago de Chile on 26 February 1795, Guadalajara on 6 June 1795 and Cartagena on 15 June 1795.[26]

Different Ibero-American authors have reported on the activities of the consulates of commerce in the American Spanish colonies.[27] A detailed description on the organisation of consulates of South America is done by Olivera Garcia and Rippe.[28] The kind of issues submitted to the Consulate related to disputes between merchants, between merchants and their agents, sales, dealings, insurances, exchanges, transport of merchandise and companies' accounts.[29] The proceedings before the consulates were oral, of arbitral character, and dealt with swiftly. One interesting thing is that lawyers were not allowed to act in commercial matters. The Consulate Royal *Cedula* prohibited it, unless it was a very difficult matter, which needed the assistance of an expert.[30] In any case, proceedings were to be conducted "in plain manner, known truth and in good faith."[31]

2.2. *Las Siete Partidas* and *Ordenanzas de Bilbao*

Many authors agree on the fact that *Las Siete Partidas* and *Ordenanzas de Bilbao* were the main laws applying to civil and commercial matters in the Spanish Latin America from the 16th to the 19th century.[32] General descriptions

---

24 *Id.*

25 Mexican and Peruvian merchants were supported by the merchants of the *Casa de Contratacion para las Indias* (House of Commerce for the Indies) in Seville.

26 Woodward, *supra* note 23.

27 *See for example* Argentina: H. Camara, *Código de Comercio de la República Argentina*, *in* Instituto de Investigaciones Jurídicas (Ed.), Centenario del Código de comercio, at 110 (1991); Honduras: R. Ramírez, *Codificación Mercantil en la República de Honduras*, *in* Instituto de Investigaciones Jurídicas (Ed.), Centenario del Código de Comercio, at 432 (1991).

28 Uruguay: R. Olivera Garcia & S. Rippe, *Evolucion y Panorama del Derecho Mercantil Uruguayo*, *in* Instituto de Investigaciones Jurídicas (Ed.), Centenario del Código de Comercio, at 331 (1991).

29 *Id.*, at 314.

30 *Id.*

31 *Id.*

32 *See generally* Argentina: Camara, *supra* note 27; Chile: E. Cornejo Fuller, *El Código de*

relating to the areas they covered can be found in most of the works dealing with Ibero-American law history. However, no work examines the content of their provisions or the differences and similarities they shared with current Ibero-American laws. With the purpose of reporting in more detail, we now present a brief comparative analysis on the rules on sales contained in *Las Siete Partidas* and *Ordenanzas de Bilbao.*[33]

The definition of sale is found in *Las Siete Partidas, Partida V, Title V, Law I,* that is titled 'what is a sale'. *Las Siete Partidas* required mutual agreement on the price.[34] As a main obligation, in *Law XXVIII*, the seller must deliver the thing with all other things attached to it.[35] *Ordenanzas de Bilbao Chapter Eleven,* on the other hand, has no express definition of contract, but an implied definition can be inferred from the statement "[it] shall be made by two or more Merchants, and fulfilled according to qualities and circumstances of the deal."[36]

Legal capacity of the parties is one of the requirements for contact validity. *Las Siete Partidas* simply establishes in *Partida V, Title V, Law II* that those who can be obliged to each other can also sell. This approach was later followed on by the future Ibero-American commercial laws under which those individuals who cannot be bound by their own acts equally lack capacity to perform acts of commerce.[37] Faithful to its medieval style *Las Siete Partidas* give us an example: "*It is not possible then for a father to sell to his son things, and vice versa, given the fact that they are considered a unity.*"[38]

The forms to enter into a sale are multiple. In *Las Siete Partidas Partida V, Title V, Law VI* there are two main ways to conclude a sale: with letter (*con carta*) or without it. If done in writing the buyer shall inform the seller to do a letter as contract. The sale is not concluded until the letter is handed to the

Comercio Chileno y sus Principales Reformas, *in* Instituto de Investigaciones Jurídicas (Ed.), Centenario del Código de comercio (1991); Colombia: R. Bernal Gutierrez, *El Código de Comercio Colombiano (Historia y Proyecciones)*, *in* Instituto de Investigaciones Jurídicas (Ed.), Centenario del Código de comercio (1991); Latin America: Barrera Graf, *supra* note 1; Dam, *supra* note 2; Latin America: Guzmán Brito, *supra* note 11; Woodward, *supra* note 23; Honduras: Ramírez, *supra* note 27; Peru: C. Torres y Torres Lara, *La Codificación Comercial en el Peru de un Código 'Formal' a un Código 'Real'*, *in* Instituto de Investigaciones Jurídicas (Ed.), Centenario del Código de Comercio (1991); Spain: A. Rojo, *La Codificación Mercantil Española*, *in* Instituto de Investigaciones Jurídicas (Ed.), Centenario del Código de Comercio (1991); Uruguay: Olivera García & Rippe, *supra* note 28; Venezuela: A. Morales Hernandez, *Evolución Histórica y Tendencias de la Legislacion Mercantil Venezolana*, *in* Instituto de Investigaciones Jurídicas (Ed.), Centenario del Código de Comercio (1991).

33 Las Siete Partidas, *supra* note 10; Ordenanzas de la Ilustre Universidad y Casa de Contratación de la Villa de Bilbao, por el Rey Don Felipe Quinto (1737).

34 Las Siete Partidas, *supra* note 10, at 117.

35 *Id.*, at 189.

36 Ordenanzas de Bilbao, *supra* note 33, at 79.

37 *See infra* Ch. 21, 1.

38 Las Siete Partidas, *supra* note 10, at 117.

buyer by the seller, though a price was agreed, as there is the possibility open to both parties to change their minds. This rule is the predecessor of many Ibero-American provisions that establish the possibility to revoke the offer before the acceptance is received.[39] The letter must be signed by witnesses. If both parties agree on the thing(s) and the price, and none of them mention the letter the sale is concluded at that time.[40] This rule would later develop in the rule followed by all Ibero-American laws according to which the contract concluded between present persons, without reference to a fixed time for acceptance, must be immediately accepted.[41]

In addition, *Las Siete Partidas* and *Ordenanzas de Bilbao* granted full validity to contracts made by non-present persons. On the one hand, *Partida V, Title V, Law VIII* establishes that a sale can be passed through letters or messengers when agreeing upon it and on the price.[42] On the other hand, *Ordenanzas de Bilbao, Chapter Eleven, Num VII* reads that the deals made between non-presents shall be justified (proven) by the books' records, original letters received, and the copies made from them.[43] These means of proof would remain in future Ibero-American systems.[44] Remarkably, none of the statutes now presented had provisions on offer and acceptance as elements of contract formation. This is understandable given that Roman law did not expressly rule on this issue.[45]

Regarding the validity of contracts affected by mistake and duress, though *Las Siete Partidas* are brief on this issue, they cover the general principles established by modern and more detailed codes. On the one hand, *Partida V, Title V, Law III* establishes that nobody should be forced to sell his belongings.[46] On the other hand, *Partida V, Title V, Law LVI* establishes the consequences of such sales; they can be undone, as it can also be undone those sales made upon deceit for a price half of the real value.[47] The same effect would be later given to sales affected by mistake, fraud or duress.[48]

---

39 *See* generally *infra* Ch. 10, 1.3.1 & 1.3.2.

40 Las Siete Partidas, *supra* note 10, at 78.

41 *See infra* Ch. 10, 2.2.1.

42 Las Siete Partidas, *supra* note 10, at 180.

43 Ordenanzas de Bilbao, *supra* note 33, at 90.

44 *See infra* Ch. 15, 1.1.

45 Latin America: J.C. Moreira Alves, *Aspectos de la Formacion de los Contratos Obligatorios en las Fuentes Romanas y en algunos Paises Latinoamericanos*, *in* El Contrato en el Sistema Jurídico Latinoamericano, Vol. I, 121, at 126 (1998).

46 Although a similar principle would be only later expressly established by Guatemala Art. 681 CC ("nobody can be bound to contract but only when such refusal to contract constitutes an illegal act or an abuse of right"), the same is implied for all Ibero-American Laws; *see infra* Ch. 3 and Ch. 23.

47 Las Siete Partidas, *supra* note 10, at 203.

48 *See infra* Ch. 24, 2 & 3.

On the sort of things susceptible to be sold, *Las Siete Partidas* included rules that would mirror the modern Civil Codes.[49] *Las Siete Partidas Partida V, Title V, Law XV* prohibits the sale of things that in the modern civil law theory are things considered out of commerce.[50] Similarly, *Partida V, Title V, Law XVI* establishes a modern *Ordre Public* provision for things,[51] and *Partida V, Title V, Law XVII* is the modern restriction to contract on illegal goods.[52]

On the question of passing of risk *Las Siete Partidas Partida V, Title V, Law XXIII* establishes as a rule that the transfer of risk passes from the seller to the buyer at the same time of the meeting of the minds on the thing and the price. The same rule would later applied in some Ibero-American Civil Codes. However, under most commercial laws the risk passes from the seller to the buyer with the delivery of the goods.[53] Under *Las Siete Partidas*, when the contract is in writing the risk passes when the letter is handed to the buyer though it has not taken delivery of them.[54] The rule embodies the modern virtual delivery and the passing of risk from such a moment.[55]

Concerning the passing of property title, *Ordenanzas de Bilbao* requires the transferring of the thing (*Roman tradittio*) so that the passing of title take place. The same rule would later be adopted by a group of Ibero-American Laws.[56] An interesting situation is presented in the *Chapter Eleven Num XII* which states:

> [In] case that a merchant passes a contract or deal with another (first buyer) and before it was concluded by the delivery of the goods he passes a second sales contract with a different merchant (second buyer) to whom the goods were delivered this time; the first buyer may not have any right of claim against the second buyer, because the property of the goods was indeed transferred to the second buyer who took delivery.

The example embodies the requirement of *tradittio* of the goods. A solution later adopted by some Ibero-American laws.[57] However, the first buyer shall have the right of claim against the seller for damages and loss of profit.[58] In *Las Siete Partidas,* there is an express obligation to transfer the property of the thing sold.

Obligations of Seller and Buyer are covered in *Las Siete Partidas Law Partida V, Title V, XXVIII and XXXII* in a general way. The general obligation

---

49 *See generally infra* Ch. 6.
50 Las Siete Partidas, *supra* note 10, at 183.
51 *Id.*, at 184.
52 *Id.*
53 *See* Ch. 44, 3 & 1.
54 Las Siete Partidas, *supra* note 10, at 187.
55 *See* Ch. 44, 3 & 1.
56 *See infra* Ch. 45, 3.2.
57 *See infra* Ch. 45, 3.2 and Ch. 46.
58 Uruguay: Olivera García & Rippe, *supra* note 28, at 82. The remedy remained until now; *see infra* Ch. 46, 3.

for the seller is to deliver the goods with all other goods attached to them.[59] Also, free of encumbrances or third parties ownership rights.[60] This warranty to deliver goods property clean title would be further developed under modern Ibero-American sales laws.[61] The buyer's obligation was to pay the price.[62]

Ordenanzas de Bilbao contained more trade-developed rules on the area of conformity of the goods. According to *Chapter Eleven Num VIII* whenever a deal is negotiated based on thing's samples, the seller shall deliver the things in the agreed time, having the same quality as the samples. One sample will be held: by the seller; a second by the buyer; a third by the *Corredor Jurado* (if such was involved).[63] In case of conflicting views as to the quality of the goods, the conformity shall be established by comparing the three samples. A similar modality of sale would be later developed by all Ibero-American Commercial Laws.[64]

Moreover, *Chapter Eleven Num IX* states that when the deal is made without samples, in case of conflict on the time of delivery or the quality of the goods, the parties shall be bound by that stated in contract. If the buyer insists that the goods do not have the quality contracted, the parties shall be bound by the witness-expert declarations that will be designated by the parties.[65] In case of disagreement, the obligations and breaches of each party shall be assessed by the *Prior* or the *Consult*.[66]

Finally, *Ordenanzas de Bilbao* contained one of the most controversial rules for contract interpretation that would remain in future laws: the *Contra proferentem* principle that would apply to the seller.[67] Certainly, *Chapter Eleven, Num XII* establishes that, if in the instruments made because of a contract, there was any confusion, because of the obscurity in their clauses, the said clauses shall be interpreted at all times against the seller, who shall bear such fault for not having been able to explain himself in a proper way.[68]

As can be seen, *Las Siete Partidas* and *Ordenanzas de Bilbao* reflected some of the principles of traditional Roman law. These rules and principles would later be reflected in modern Ibero-American Civil Codes and Codes of Commerce.

---

59 The same obligation remains until now; *see infra* Ch. 35 and Ch. 36.
60 Las Siete Partidas, *supra* note 10, at 191.
61 *See infra* Ch. 38, 1.
62 Las Siete Partidas, *supra* note 10, at 89.
63 A *Corredor Jurado* was a modern commercial broker.
64 *See infra* Ch. 37, 3.3.
65 The same solution was adopted by future Codes of Commerce; *see infra* Ch. 37, 3.3.
66 Ordenanzas de Bilbao, *supra* note 33, at 81.
67 *See infra* Ch. 29, 7.
68 Ordenanzas de Bilbao, *supra* note 33, at 82.

3. Origins of Sales Law in Ibero-America's 19th and 20th Centuries

Once current Latin American countries achieved their independence from Spain and Portugal, the first years of legislation works were focused on the law for the organisation of their governments and the administration of the new territories, and not in the creation of private law statutes. Therefore, most of the private laws from the time of the colony remained in force until national codes were enacted; such was the case of *Las Siete Partidas*.[69] Similarly, the organisation through consulates remained for years after the respective declarations of independence, and *Ordenanzas de Bilbao* were given full validity for many years until the national Codes of Commerce were enacted.[70]

The civil codification in Latin America began after the independence process has finished. The idea was to avoid uncertainty of the applicable law, to stabilise the legal system, and to consolidate the new national regimes. According to Murillo, Civil Codes' sources in Latin America were: first, the 'Roman-Germanic family' or civil law tradition; second, the Spanish and the Portuguese laws enforced in Latin America before Civil Codes were drafted;[71] third, the French Civil Code of 1804; fourth, other Civil Codes of Germany, Spain, Switzerland, Sardinia, Austria and Prussia.[72]

In the following paragraphs, we present the sources and evolution of the main and most influential Ibero-American civil and commercial codes. These legislative works represent the origins of private law in the region. Ibero-American sales law principles and institutions could not be understood without considering its common history. Additionally, we will comment on the influence these codes had from both European and Latin American codes, both in their methods or on the content of their provisions.

---

[69] Latin America: Barrera Graf, *supra* note 1, at 23-25: stating that in Colombia a decree from 13 May 1825 established a hierarchy of laws placing in the top the few national new laws and just after all the Spanish statues in force during the colony, in Chile the same happened until in 1855 when the first the Chilean Civil Code drafted by Andres Bello came into force, in Paraguay *Las Siete Partidas* and the Leyes de Toro were applied until 1877; Argetina: Moisset De Espanés, *supra* note 20, at 2: stating that the *Ordenaçoes Philipinas* where valid until enactment of the Civil Code of 1917.

[70] Peru: Torres y Torres Lara, *supra* note 32, at 584; Latin America: Barrera Graf, *supra* note 1, at 25; Colombia: Bernal Gutiérrez, *supra* note 32, at 86; Honduras: Ramírez, *supra* note 27, at 427; Venezuela: Morales Hernández, *supra* note 32, at 274.

[71] Mainly Novísima Recopilación, Las Siete Partidas, and the Fuero Real.

[72] Murillo, *supra* note 4, at 2.

3.1. The Ibero-American Civil Codes Evolution

One of the most influential civil code of the region is Argentina's Civil Code of 1869. This was drafted by jurist Velez Sarsfield. Velez Sarsfield admitted the influence of the Brazilian jurist Teixeira de Freitas upon the method of the Argentinean Civil Code.[73] Sarsfield expressed: "... I have followed such a discussed method of the Brazilian great jurist (Teixeira de Freitas) in his wise and broad *Introduction to the Recompilation of the Laws of Brazil*."[74] Sarsfield also denied he had followed the French Civil Code method.[75] Velez Sarsfield produced an eclectic code that has at its source many European doctrines. However, he said that the majority of the articles had as its base the principles contained in *Las Siete Partidas*, the *Nueva Recopilacion*, and in the *Fuero Real*.[76] Argentina's Civil Code of 1869 had great influence in other Latin American Civil Codes. It was fully adopted by Paraguay in 1866,[77] Uruguay in 1869,[78] Panama in 1916 and Nicaragua in 1904.[79]

The Brazilian Civil Code of 1916 had a system that was taken from the Teixeira de Freitas *Consolidaçao e Esboço*.[80] Brazil was able to draw on the Portuguese and Italian codes, as well as those of Germany and Switzerland. The structure of the Code, particularly its 'General Part', is largely traceable to German influence.[81] This code remained in force until 2003 when the Civil Code of 2002 came into force. In 2002, Brazil enacted its latest Civil Code and the newest in Ibero-America. The works for this Code lasted for about 30 years. This Code follows the Brazilian tradition on the structure designed by Teixeira de Freitas. This new Code has unified the civil and commercial rules including those on contracts, as Teixeira de Freitas has proposed from the beginning.[82]

The Chilean Civil Code of 1855 was drafted by Andres Bello who believed that the Code should integrate the already known colonial laws. Following this idea, Andres Bello worked on *Las Siete Partidas* and for those issues not covered by them in the French Civil Code of 1804.[83] Andres Bello followed the system of the *Institutas* of the Roman law.[84] Concerning the substance of the Civil Code, Bello consulted *Las Siete Partidas* as he considered them one

---

73 Argentina: Moisset De Espanés, *supra* note 20, at 2.
74 Latin America: Guzmán Brito, *supra* note 11, at 271.
75 *Id.*
76 *Id.*, at 275.
77 *Id.*, at 333.
78 *Id.*, at 284.
79 Murillo, *supra* note 4, at 9.
80 Latin America: Guzmán Brito, *supra* note 11, at 311.
81 Murillo, *supra* note 4, at 10.
82 Latin America: Guzmán Brito, *supra* note 11, at 337.
83 *Id.*, at 204.
84 Dam, *supra* note 2, at 20.

of the statutes that best enclosed the roman jurisprudence.[85] The Chilean Civil Code influenced the Civil Code of Colombia of 1858,[86] Ecuador of 1858, El Salvador of 1860, Honduras 1880 (first Civil Code), Nicaragua 1867 (first Civil Code) and Venezuela of 1862 (first Civil Code).[87]

In Mexico, a Civil Code was enacted on 1828 in the Southeaster State of Oaxaca. This Code was influenced by the French Civil Code of Napoleon of 1804, and for this reason was not accepted in Mexico City.[88] It was until 1870 that the Civil Code for the Federal District and the Territory of Baja California was enacted. According to the code's commission, the 1871 Mexican Civil Code was based on, "principles of Roman law, our own Mexican complex legislation, the codes of France, Sardinia, Austria, and Portugal … in addition to past drafts completed in Mexico and Spain."[89] The Civil Code of 1928 was a copy of which Civil Code of 1884.

The Spanish Civil Code of 1889 was drafted following the project presented by jurist Garcia Goyena in 1885. But when enacted, Book III of Garcia Goyena's project was divided in Book III titled: Different modes of acquiring property and Book IV Obligations and Contracts; in order to respect the Spanish- Roman principle which considers that the acquisition of a thing must to have either a cause or an acquisition title,[90] and also a mode, *tradittio*,[91] and that legal acts as the sale or the donation are not modes for acquiring things but titles of property with obligatory consequences, consequently they must be in the Obligation and Contracts part and not in the Modes of Acquiring Property part.[92]

With this approach, the Spanish Civil Code departed from the European French tradition and came closer to the Latin American tradition of the Chilean Code.[93] The Codes considered by Garcia Goyena for the Production of the Spanish Code of 1889 were the traditional Spanish law, the Roman law and the French Civil Code of 1804. The commission in charge of the final draft also consulted the Codes of Italy 1865, Portugal 1857, Chile 1855 and Argentina 1869.[94] This Code had little influence on other Latin American Codes as it came at the end of the 19th century. It was in force in Puerto Rico and Cuba as Spanish colonies until these countries enacted their own national Civil Codes.[95]

---

85 Latin America: Guzmán Brito, *supra* note 11, at 208.
86 Future Colombia, but also included other territories of current Ecuador, Panama, Venezuela.
87 Latin America: Guzmán Brito, *supra* note 11, at 243.
88 *Id.*, at 154.
89 Dam, *supra* note 2, at 19.
90 *See* Ch. 9.
91 *See* Ch. 45.
92 Latin America: Guzmán Brito, *supra* note 11, at 295.
93 *See* Ch. 45.
94 Latin America: Guzmán Brito, *supra* note 11, at 295.
95 *Id.*, at 295.

3.2. The Ibero-American Codes of Commerce Evolution

Similarly, the Argentinean Code of Commerce of 1862 was a model for other Latin American Codes of Commerce. This was drafted by two prominent jurists Velez Sarsfield and Eduardo Acevedo. The quality of the Code of Commerce was such that it influenced other Commercial Codes such as the Uruguayan Code of Commerce of 1866 enacted with few small amendments.[96] Another example of this influence is the case of Paraguay. This country had first adopted the Spanish Code of Commerce of 1829 and later changed for the Argentinean Code of Commerce model in 1903.[97] The Code of Commerce from 1889 is in force up to today, but it has had many amendments and additions during its existence. However, the sales provisions have not changed since. Though there have been many attempts to unify the law of civil contracts and commercial contracts for the last century, it has never happened.[98]

The Chilean Commercial Code of 1867 has as its ancestors the French Code of Commerce of 1807 and the Spanish Code of Commerce of Spain 1829.[99] On the other hand, the Chilean Commercial Code of 1867 influenced the Codes of Commerce of Colombia,[100] Venezuela of 1873.[101]

The Codes of Commerce in Central America have a common history, since all Guatemala, Nicaragua, Costa Rica, Panama and El Salvador were a single nation between 1823 and 1840. The Codes of Commerce of Honduras 1880 and 1898 (an other Central American Countries) were influenced by *Ordenanzas de Bilbao*, the French Code of Commerce of 1807 and the Spanish Code of Commerce of 1829. It was influenced also by the Argentinean Code of Commerce, the Brazilian Civil Code and Code of Commerce and the Chilean Civil Code.[102]

In 1853, Peru adopted the Spanish Code of Commerce of 1829 with minor changes. Later in 1902, a similar adoption was made of the Spanish Code of Commerce of 1885 with some substantial changes, but none of them related to contracts.[103] In 1984, the Code of Commerce rules on sales, permute, deposit and securities were derogated and expressly unified with the provisions of the Civil Code.[104]

The influence of the French Code of Commerce of 1807 over the Spanish Code of Commerce of 1829 cannot be denied. The drafter Sainz de Andino had a strong French feeling. However, together with the French Law influences

---

96 Argentina: Camara, *supra* note 27, at 110.

97 *Id.*, at 117.

98 Argentina: Camara, *supra* note 27, at 127.

99 Chile: Cornejo Fuller, *supra* note 32, at 135.

100 Colombia: Bernal Gutiérrez, *supra* note 32, at 101.

101 Venezuela: Morales Hernández, *supra* note 32, at 280.

102 Honduras: Ramírez, *supra* note 27, at 425.

103 Peru: Torres y Torres Lara, *supra* note 32, at 588.

104 *Id.*, at 588.

converged the traditional Spanish, "*not just the merchants' law represented by Ordenazas de Bilbao, but also the Castilian law full of commercial obligations.*"[105] The Spanish Code of Commerce is characterised as a complex system of *renvois*. As the French code, starts by establishing that it applies to traders,[106] and subsequently defines traders as those who perform acts of commerce and those matriculated as traders.[107] It is worth noting that there are two exemptions to the subjective application of the code. First, the Spanish Code of Commerce would apply to sales contracts when there is a profit purpose of reselling the goods. The same approach would remain in the second Spanish Code of Commerce of 1885. This double condition is not found in the French Code 1804, which means that the Spanish Code of Commerce does not govern sales contracts when they have not the profit purpose of reselling the movables even though it is a regular act of commerce and it is passed by merchants.[108] The approach taken by the Spanish Code of Commerce is still followed by most of the Latin American Codes of Commerce.[109]

4. Conclusion

Between the 16th and 19th centuries, current Ibero-American territories and laws were divided in those created and administrated by the kingdom of Spain on one side, and on the other, by the kingdom of Portugal. Both Iberian Empires had early developed codified laws of common civil rules such as *Las Siete Partidas of 1348* and *Ordenaçoes Alfonsinas of 1446*, based in the Roman law and local customary laws. With the Empires' expansion in America, newer compilations of laws in the form of ordinances were produced and the administration of commerce, including the settlement of disputes between merchants, was given to the consulates.

Las Siete Partidas and *Ordenanzas de Bilbao* resembled traditional Roman compilations of laws, but at the same time, they were not far from the modern private law principles. The inclusion of legal rules defining what a sales contract was and governing the validity of contracts in general, the passing of property title and risk, the obligations of sellers and buyers, and the rules for contract interpretation, makes proof of the efficiency and of the influence they later would reflect in modern Ibero-American Civil Codes and Codes of Commerce.

The historic review on the Ibero-American Civil Codes has taught us that the French Civil Code influenced several 19th century Latin American Civil

[105] Spain: Rojo, *supra* note 32, at 484.
[106] France Art. 1, Com. C.
[107] Spain: Rojo, *supra* note 32, at 487.
[108] *Id.*, at 490.
[109] *See* Ch. 5. 1.1.

Codes, for example, the Civil Code of Oaxaca in México, the Bolivian Civil Code of 1831,[110] the Civil Code of Peru of 1852, and to some extent the Civil Code of Chile enacted in 1855. However, we also learned that many other countries played an important role in Ibero-American legislation, such as Germany, Spain, Switzerland, Sardinia, Austria and Prussia. In addition, that local Latin American Civil Codes were crucial in this task, such is the Civil Code of Chile, the Argentinean Civil Code and the Brazilian Civil Code. The same could be said about the Ibero-American Codes of Commerce where, even though European laws had a great influence, particularly the French Code of Commerce of 1807 and the Spanish Code of Commerce of 1829, also other notable commercial codes in Latin America were fundamental; namely the Chilean Code of Commerce of 1867 or the Argentinean Commercial Code of 1859.[111]

This inter-exchange of legal principles, rules, systems and methods occurring between Ibero-American countries has resulted in a melting pot of common legal institutions that have remained within the borders. This confirms our idea that Ibero-American countries have indeed formed a subsystem in the Civil Law Legal Family and justifies the study of the modern practice of sales law in the region separate from other Civil Law countries.

[110] On Bolivia's Civil Code History *see* Latin America: Guzmán Brito, *supra* note 11, at 161.

[111] For example, the Honduran 20th century Codes of Commerce (1940 and 1950) came from Europe; France, Germany, Italy, Spain, the Law of Obligations of Switzerland, but also from Mexico as the drafter of the Honduran Code of Commerce 1950 was Mexican jurist Joaquin Rodriguez Rodriguez, *see* Honduras: Ramírez, *supra* note 27, at 426. Also the Venezuelan Code of Commerce of 1862 had Spanish and French influence in it. A second Code of Commerce was enacted in 1873, as the last one, it had Spanish and French influences, but also was based on the Chilean Code of Commerce of 1865, *see* Venezuela: Morales Hernandez, *supra* note 32, at 280-288.

CHAPTER 2

UNIFORM LAWS AND PROJECTS

1. International Participation

Ibero-American countries' participation in international organisations has been active. Current country members of UNIDROIT are Argentina, Bolivia, Brazil, Chile, Colombia, Cuba, Mexico, Nicaragua, Paraguay, Portugal, Spain, Uruguay and Venezuela.[1] Nevertheless, none of the Ibero-American countries have signed or ratified the ULIS[2] or the ULFIS.[3] On the other hand, the 1983 UNIDROIT Convention on Agency has been signed by Chile and ratified by Mexico.[4]

In addition, the majority Ibero-American countries have membership at UNCITRAL.[5] Ibero-American countries participate in UNCITRAL instruments related to the Sales of Goods. For example, the Convention on the Limitation Period in the International Sale of Goods is in force in Argentina,

---

[1] Countries that are still not members of UNIDROIT are Costa Rica, Ecuador, El Salvador, Guatemala, Honduras, Panama and Peru; *see* UNIDROIT Membership in http://www.unidroit.org/english/members/main.htm (accessed on 23 February 2010).

[2] Convention relating to a Uniform Law on the International Sale of Goods (The Hague, 1 July 1964); *see* status in http://www.unidroit.org/english/implement/i-64ulis.pdf (accessed on 23 February 2010).

[3] Convention relating to a Uniform Law on the Formation of Contracts for the International Sale of Goods (The Hague, 1 July 1964); *see* status in http://www.unidroit.org/english/implement/i-64ulf.pdf (accessed on 23 February 2010).

[4] The 1983 UNIDROIT Convention on Agency is not in force until 10 ten countries ratify it. Up to now five countries have ratified it; *see* status in http://www.unidroit.org/english/implement/i-83.pdf (accessed on 23 February 2010).

[5] Bolivia Ex.2013, Chile Ex.2013, Colombia Ex.2010, Ecuador Ex.2010, El Salvador Ex.2013, Guatemala Ex.2010, Honduras Ex.2013, Mexico Ex.2013, Paraguay Ex.2010, Spain Ex.2010, and Venezuela Ex.2010. The rest have not currently membership: Argentina, Brazil, Costa Rica, Cuba, Nicaragua, Panama, Peru, Portugal and Uruguay; *see* http://www.uncitral.org/uncitral/en/about/origin.html (accessed on 23 February 2010).

Cuba, Mexico, Paraguay and Uruguay.[6] In addition, the UNECIC has been singed by Colombia, Honduras, Panama and Paraguay.[7] On the other hand, Mexico has adopted the MLES. Bolivia, Colombia, Dominican Republic, Ecuador, Guatemala, Mexico, Panama and Venezuela adopted or integrated into their national laws the MLEC.[8]

Participation of Ibero-American countries at the Hague Conference on Private International Law has been limited. Currently there are 12 Ibero-American members.[9] The 1955 Convention on the Law Applicable to International Sales of Goods was only accepted by Portugal.[10] The 1958 Convention on the Law Governing Transfer of Title in International Sales of Goods was not accepted at all for any of the Ibero-American countries. The 1971 Convention on the Recognition and Enforcement of Foreign Judgments in Civil and Commercial Matters is only in force in Portugal.[11] The 1978 Convention on the Law Applicable to Agency was signed by Argentina and Portugal.[12] The 1986 Convention on the Law Applicable to Contracts for the

---

[6] 1974 Convention on the Limitation Period in the International Sale of Goods as amended by the Protocol of 11 April 1980 (a); *see* Status in http://www.uncitral.org/uncitral/en/uncitral_texts/sale_goods/1974Convention_status.html (accessed on 23 February 2010).

[7] Colombia signature 27 September 2007; Honduras signature 16 January 2008; Panama signature 25 September 2007; Paraguay signature 26 March 2007; *see* STATUS of this Convention in http://www.uncitral.org/uncitral/en/uncitral_texts/electronic_commerce/2005Convention_status.html (accessed 23 February 2010).

[8] Colombia Law No. 527 governing the use of data messages, electronic commerce and digital signatures (Official Gazette No. 43.673, 21 August 1999); Dominican Republic Law No. 126-02 on Electronic Commerce promulgated on the 4 September 2002; Ecuador Law No. 67 on Electronic Commerce, Signatures and Data Messages of 17 April 2002 & Decree No. 3496 Rules for the Law on Electronic Commerce, Signatures and Data Messages of 31 December 2002; Guatemala Law Decree No. 47-2008 on the Recognition of Electronic Communications and Signature of 19 August 2008 and published on 23 September 2008 in the Official Gazette; Mexico adopted both the 1996 UNCITRAL Model Law on Electronic Commerce and the 2001 UNCITRAL Model Law on Electronic Signatures. This adoption was not made in single instruments but rather it was incorporated in different codes and statutes. Regarding the electronic communication in the area of private law, different provisions are contained in Mexico's Civil Code, Code of Commerce and Procedural Federal Civil Code; Panama Law No. 43 of 31 July 2001 on Electronic Commerce and Electronic Documents in General; Venezuela Law No. 37, 148 on Data Messages and Electronic Signatures published on 28 February 2001.

[9] Argentina since 28 April 1972; Brazil since 23 February 2001; Chile since 25 April 1986; Ecuador since 2 November 2007; Mexico since 18 March 1986; Panama since 29 May 2002; Paraguay since 28 June 2005; Peru since 29 January 2001; Portugal since 15 July 1955; Spain since 15 July 1955; Uruguay since 27 July 1983; Venezuela since 25 July 1979.

[10] Portugal on 12 April 1957.

[11] Portugal signed on 21 April 1983, ratified on 21 April 1983 and it entered into force in 20 August 1983.

[12] Argentina signed on 5 February 1992, ratified in 5 February 1992 and it entered into force in 1 May 1992; Portugal signed on 26 May 1978, ratified in 4 March 1982, and it entered into force in 1 May 1992.

International Sale of Goods was only signed and ratified by Argentina,[13] while 2005 The Convention on Choice of Court Agreements has only been ratified by Mexico.[14]

Participation of Ibero-American countries in uniform laws and projects has been bigger at a regional level.[15] All Latin American countries are member states of the Organisation of American States.[16] The 1975 Inter-American convention on the legal regime of powers of attorney to be used abroad is in force in all member states except for Colombia and Nicaragua.[17] On the other hand, the 1994 Inter-American Convention on the Law Applicable to International Contracts, also known as the Mexico City Convention, has been signed by Bolivia, Brazil and Uruguay, though it is only in force in Mexico and Venezuela.[18] Also all Latin American members of the Organisation, except for Cuba, have ratified the 1975 Inter-American Convention on International Commercial Arbitration, also known as Panama Convention.[19] Finally, the 1979 Inter-American Convention on the Extraterritorial Validity of Judgments and Arbitral Awards is in force in more than half of the Latin American countries.[20]

Portugal and Spain, are both member states of the European Community. The 1980 Convention on the Law Applicable to Contractual Obligations, also known as the Rome Convention, has direct application in both countries since 1994 and 1992 respectively.[21] The 2000 Council Regulation on jurisdiction and the recognition and enforcement of judgments in civil and commercial matters, also known as the Brussels Regulation, has direct application in these jurisdictions since 2000.[22]

Harmonisation and unification of private law in Latin America is characterised as having a traditional regionalist approach. As one commentator has noted, the Hague Conference on Private International Law has a reduced participation of Latin American countries because the political, social, and

---

13 Argentina in 4 October 1991.

14 Mexico in 26 September 2007.

15 Except for Spain and Portugal which are not part of the Organization of American States.

16 For the purposes of this report we cover the following Latin American states members at the OAS: Argentina, Bolivia, Brazil, Chile, Colombia, Costa Rica, Cuba, Dominican Republic, Ecuador, El Salvador, Guatemala, Honduras, Mexico, Nicaragua, Panama, Paraguay, Peru, Uruguay and Venezuela.

17 *See* Status in http://www.oas.org/juridico/english/Sigs/b-38.html (Accessed on 4 February 2010).

18 *See* Status in http://www.oas.org/juridico/english/Sigs/b-56.html (Accessed on 4 February 2010).

19 *See* Status in http://www.oas.org/juridico/english/Sigs/b-35.html (Accessed on 4 February 2010).

20 Except in Chile, Costa Rica, Salvador, Nicaragua, Honduras and Panama; *see* Status in http://www.oas.org/juridico/english/Sigs/b-41.html (Accessed on 4 February 2010).

21 EC Convention No. 80/934 of 19 June 1980.

22 EC Council Regulation No 44/2001 of 22 December 2000.

economic backgrounds of Latina America are sufficiently different from those of Western Europe to justify a distinctive legal approach towards unification of private law.[23] However, the Inter-American conventions follow so closely their Hague counterparts that one can conclude that Latin America's regionalist approach is based more in political reasons than in actual legal differences.[24]

2. CISG in the Ibero-American Countries

The CISG has been ratified by thirteen Ibero-American countries, including some major economies in the region such as Argentina, Chile, Mexico and Spain.[25] In addition, other important economies from the region like Brazil and Portugal are expected to join the CISG in the near future.[26]

The annual UNCITRAL conferences were prepared by Working Group II, which, from January 1970 onwards, prepared drafts for the plenary UNCITRAL sessions by analyzing ULIS and ULFIS.[27] Working Group II was established by the UNCITRAL at its second session in March 1969.[28] The purpose of the first meeting was to consider the comments and suggestions made by States

---

23 A.M. Garro, *Unification and Harmonization of Private Law in Latin America*, 40 American Journal of Comparative Law 587, at 597 (1992).

24 *Id.*

25 Argentina on 19 July 1983 with a reservation (a) and the Convention came into force on 1 January 1988; Chile signed the CISG on 11 April 1980 and ratified it on 7 February 1990, with a reservation under (a), and it entered into force on 1 March 1991; Colombia ratified the CISG on 10 July 2001 and it entered into force on 1 August 2002; Cuba did so on 2 November 1994 and the CISG entered into force on 1 December 1995; Dominican Republic ratified the CISG on 7 June 2010 and it entered into force on 1 July 2010; Ecuador also ratified the CISG on 27 January 1992 and it entered into force on 1 February 1993; El Salvador ratified the CISG on 27 November 2006 and it entered into force on 1 December 2007; Honduras ratified the CISG on 10 October 2002 and in came into force on 1 November 2003; Mexico did so on 29 December 1987 and the CISG entered into force on 1 January 1989; Paraguay ratified the CISG on 13 January 2006 and it entered into force in its territory on 1 February 2007; Peru ratified the CISG on 25 March 1999 and it entered into force on 1 April 2000; Spain ratified the CISG on 24 July 1990 and it came into force on 1 August 1991; Uruguay ratified the CISG on 25 January 1999 and it entered into force on 1 February 2000; Venezuela signed the CISG on 28 December 1981 but it is not in force as it has not ratified it; Bolivia, Brazil, Costa Rica, Guatemala, Nicaragua, Panama, and Portugal are not member states of the CISG; *see* Status in http://www.uncitral.org/uncitral/en/uncitral_texts/sale_goods/1980CISG_status.html (accessed on 23 February 2010).

26 Brazil: I. Dolganova & M. Boff, *A Case for Brazil's Adhesion to the 1980 UN Convention on Contracts for the International Sale of Goods*, 13(2) The Vindobona Journal of International Commercial Law and Arbitration 351, at 369, 353 n 10. (2009).

27 P. Schlechtriem, *Introduction*, *in* I. Schwenzer (Ed.), Schlechtriem & Schwenzer Commentary on the UN Convention on the International Sale of Goods 1, at 2 (2010).

28 Para. 1 of the UN document: A/CN.9/35 Report of the Working Group on the international sale of goods, first session.

> (…) in order to ascertain which modifications of the existing texts might render them capable of wider acceptance by countries of different legal, social and economic systems, or whether it will be necessary to elaborate a new text for the same purpose, or what other steps might be taken to further the harmonization or unification of the law of the international sale of goods.[29]

Only two Ibero-American countries, Brazil and Mexico, participated in Working Group II. Although, observers from Spain also attended the meeting. Both Brazil and Mexico played an active role in the analysis, the comments and the proposals undertaking by the Working Group II during the nine working sessions held. Special mention should be made to Professor Jorge Barrera-Graf, representative from Mexico, who was elected chairperson of the Working Group II from the first to the fifth session (1970-1974) and from the seventh to the ninth session (1976-1977).[30]

The adoption of the CISG final draft was done at the United Nations Conference on Contracts for the International Sale of Goods held in Vienna from 10 March to 11 April 1980.[31] Thirteen Ibero-American representatives out of sixty-two States participated in the Conference: Argentina, Bolivia, Brazil, Chile, Colombia, Costa Rica, Ecuador, Mexico, Panama, Peru, Portugal, Spain, and Uruguay.[32] Venezuela sent an observer to the Conference.[33]

29 *Id.*, at para. 3.
30 *See* UN document: A/CONF.97/19 Official Records (United Nations publication, Sales No. E.81.IV.3).
31 *See* UN document: A/CONF.97/18-Final Act.
32 *Id.*, at para. 3.
33 *Id.*, at para. 4.

Chapter 3

Contract and the Law

1. Freedom of Contract

In its most basic understanding the freedom of contract means different things. First, it infers that the parties are free to decide to enter into contracts or not to enter into contracts at all.[1] It also means to be free to choose with whom one may contract.[2] Such principle is expressly mentioned in Article 681 of Guatemala's Code of Commerce according to which nobody can be bound to contract but only when such refusal to contract constitutes an illegal act or an abuse of right.[3] Under this principle, State enterprises, private companies trading products of the basic shopping basket or monopolies are usually bound to contract unless there are legally or morally justified reasons to refuse.[4]

Additionally, and most importantly, the principle also means that the parties are free to shape the content of their contract – this includes the liberty to formulate a type of contract which is not necessarily described in statute or to mix and match from different and already recognised categories of contracts.[5] Most of the Ibero-American Civil Codes expressly[6] or impliedly[7] allow the agreement of the parties on mixed contracts.

---

1 Portugal: J. de M. Antunes Valera, Das Obrigações em Geral 232, 233 (2003).

2 *Id.*, at 232, 233.

3 Guatemala Art. 681 Com C.

4 Portugal: Antunes Valera, *supra* note 1, at 236, 239.

5 *Id.*, at 230, 231, 246.

6 Cuba Arts. 314, 315 CC; Mexico Art. 1858 CC; Honduras Art. 712 CC; Portugal Art. 405 CC.

7 Argentina Art. 1143 CC; Bolivia Art. 451 CC; Chile Art. 1438 CC; Costa Rica Art. 629 CC; Ecuador Art. 1481 CC; El Salvador Art. 1309 CC; Nicaragua Art. 1830 CC; Panama Arts. 1105, 1106 CC; Paraguay Art. 463 CC; Spain Arts. 1.254, 1.255 CC; Uruguay Art. 1260 CC; Venezuela Art. 1.140 CC.

Also freedom of contract means freedom from the requirement of form, including the freedom to include form requirements according to the particular desires of the parties,[8] and to decide on the method and form to alter or terminate their contract.[9]

In this chapter, we focus on two of the most appreciate meanings of the freedom of contract: first, the freedom to contractually defining the parties' obligations and, second, the freedom to choose the applicable law to the parties' contracts.

1.1. Contractually Defining Parties' Obligations

All Ibero-American countries expressly recognised the freedom of the parties to contractually define their contractual obligations.[10] Nevertheless, such freedom is not unlimited. Different limitations and requirements are established by domestic laws. Among these limitations we found the notion of the public order,[11] the moral,[12] the good customs,[13] the legal, social or public interest,[14] and the law.[15]

In multiple occasions the Ibero-American courts and tribunals have sustained the principle and define its limits.[16] Further examples on the limits

[8] *See* the freedom on the form of the sales contract as recognised by most Ibero-American jurisdictions, in Ch. 20, 1.

[9] *See* the freedom on the modification of concluded contracts as recognised by most Ibero-American jurisdictions, in Ch. 17.

[10] Argentina Art. 21 CC; Bolivia Art. 454 CC; Chile Art. 12 CC; Colombia Arts. 15, 16 CC; Costa Rica Art. 18 CC; Cuba Art. 5 CC; Ecuador Art. 11 CC; El Salvador Art. 12 CC; Guatemala Art. 19 JOL; Honduras Art. 11 CC & Art. 714 Com C; Mexico Art. 6 CC & Art. 372 Com C; Nicaragua Art. 2437 CC; Panama Art. 1106 CC; Peru Art. 1354 CC; Portugal Art. 398 CC; Spain Art. 1255 CC; Uruguay Art. 11 CC & Art. 209 Com C; Venezuela Art. 6 CC.

[11] *See* public order limitation in Argentina Art. 21 CC; Guatemala Art. 19 JOL; Honduras Art. 11 CC; Nicaragua Art. 2437 CC; Panama Art. 1106 CC; Uruguay Art. 11 CC; Venezuela Art. 6 CC.

[12] *See* moral limitation in Chile Art. 16 CC; Honduras Art. 11 CC; Nicaragua Art. 2437 CC; Panama Art. 1106 CC; Uruguay Art. 11 CC.

[13] *See* good customs limitation in Argentina Art. 21 CC.

[14] *See* legal, social or public interest limitation in Bolivia Art. 454 CC; Cuba Art. 5 CC; Guatemala Art. 19 JOL; Mexico Art. 6 CC; Peru Art. 1355 CC.

[15] Bolivia Art. 454 CC; Chile Art. 12 CC; Costa Rica Art. 19 CC; Ecuador Art. 11 CC; El Salvador Art. 12 CC; Guatemala Art. 19 JOL; Honduras Art. 11 CC & Art. 714 Com C; Nicaragua Art. 243 CC; Panama Art. 1106 CC; Peru Art. 1354 CC; Portugal Art. 398 CC; Uruguay Art. 209 Com C.

[16] ICC Final Award Case No. 11570 *Lex Contractus* Portuguese Law: the Sole Arbitrator explained that derived from the wording of Portugal Arts. 405, 406 CC the freedom to contract is granted to the parties of the same bargaining level; ICC Final Award Case No. 13542 *Lex Contractus* Spanish Law: explained that the *sui generis* mechanism to fixe the price was valid as it did not oppose Spain Art. 1449 CC, nor any law provision of direct application; Argentina Supreme Court, *Florencio, Madero y Cía. v. Lezama, Gregorio*, 1873, T. 14, at 102;

imposed by law to principle of freedom of contract may be found in the chapter of this work dealing with illegality and immorality of contracts.[17]

1.2. Freedom of Choice of Law Clauses

1.2.1. Freedom

The freedom of the parties to choose the applicable law to their contracts is expressly or impliedly recognised by many of the Ibero-American laws.[18] Nevertheless, the parties' possibility to choose a foreign law is, in many jurisdictions, reserved to international contracts.[19] Moreover, the Brazilian and the Uruguayan laws are among the few that do not allow choice of law clauses, since parties may not agree on the law that will govern the contract.[20] Also disputable is whether complete freedom of choice of law exists under the Colombian and the Paraguayan legal systems.[21]

Though currently only in force between Mexico and Venezuela,[22] the Mexican Convention confers the parties the right to choose the law applicable

upholding that the freedom of contract has its limits, and an agreement condemned by the law is always illicit and null, regardless of the form taken; Bolivia Supreme Court, *Sala Civil*, *Javier Hinojosa Huarachi v. Elsa Claros Soto y Luciano Rojas Pérez*: upholding that one of the limits imposed by the law is, for example, the sale of goods between spouses; El Salvador Supreme Court, *Cass civ*, *Alvarenga Bonilla v. Hsien Tang*, 1530 S.S., 30 September 2002; Peru Supreme Court, Resolution 002752-2006, 17 October 2006: establishing that the contract is the law for the parties provided it does not contradicts the national public order or other provisions of imperative character.

17 *See* Ch. 19.

18 Chile Art. 113 (2) Com C, Art. 1545 CC & Law Decree No. 2349 of 13 October 1978: freedom derived from parties' contractual autonomy as supported by Chile: A. Yrarrázaval & G. Ovalle, *Chile*, *in* D. Campbell (Ed.), Remedies for International Sellers of Goods, Vol. I, 297, 315 (2008); Costa Rica Art. 18 CC; Cuba Art. 7 CC; Guatemala Art. 31 JOL; Mexico Art. 13 (V) CC; Peru Arts. 2095, 2096 CC; Portugal Art. 3 RC; Spain Art. 3 RC; Venezuela Art. 29 PIL & Art. 116 Com C; *see also* supporting the freedom of choice of law in their respective laws Argentina: A. Boggiano, Derecho Internacional Privado Vol. II 173 (2006); Chile: M. Ramirez Necochea, Derecho Internacional Privado 193 (2005); Venezuela: O.M. Dos Santos, Contratos Internacionales en el Ordenamiento Jurídico Venezolano 73-75 (2000).

19 *See* Argentina: Boggiano, *supra* note 18, at 176; Though the laws of Mexico, Spain and Venezuela welcome choice of law clauses even in domestic contracts.

20 *See infra* in 3.

21 *Id.*

22 *See supra* Ch. 2, 1. According to the Mexico City Convention Art. 1, the Convention is applicable when the parties to a contract have their habitual residences or establishments in different State Parties or when the contract has objective ties with more than one State Party; ICC Final Award Case No. 11256 *Lex Contractus* Mexican Law: denying the application of the Convention since the scope of application conditions were not met since neither Canada nor the USA, where the buyers had their establishments, were a party to the Convention.

to their contract.[23] Such an election must be expressed either in a clause integrated into their contract or as a later agreement to the conclusion of the contract.[24] Absent an express choice of law, the election of the parties can be determined by the parties' behaviour and conduct.[25] For example, in a case with various foreign elements in which both parties based their pleadings exclusively on one law was found that the parties had made an implied choice of that law.[26]

Other factors contributing to find an implicit choice of law are the indirect reference to a law in the contract, the choice of a particular law in previous contracts, the language of the contract or the election of a particular court to settle the dispute.[27] However, under the Mexico City Convention the election of a certain court by the parties does not necessarily entail election of the applicable law.[28] A criterion which, on the contrary, has been admitted by the Argentinean Courts as an implied election of the Argentinean law.[29]

In addition, the Mexico City Convention permits the *dépeçage* in the choice of the applicable law. This is, to choose the application of a particular law to govern the whole of the contract, but also it is possible to subject separate aspects of the contractual relationship to different laws.[30]

Similarly, some scholars have sustained that if the parties have chosen one law to govern their contract, the judge may not infer that a single law regulates the whole contract.[31] The judge must again evaluate the intention of the parties and determine whether, by reasons of justice, a different law must govern a different part or area of the contract.[32]

1.2.2. Limits

Those Ibero-American laws which allow the parties to freely choose the applicable law also establish restrictions to the freedom of choice of law clauses. Some laws expressly state that they would not recognise the choice

---

23 *See* the Mexico City Convention Art. 7: the Mexico City Convention determines the law applicable to international contracts passed between parties that have their habitual residence or establishments in different States Parties or if the contract has objective ties with more than one State Party (Art. 1). But the law designated by the Convention shall be applied even if said law is that of a State that is not a party (Art. 2).

24 Mexico City Convention, Arts. 7, 8.

25 *Id.*, Art. 7.

26 Argentina: Boggiano, *supra* note 18, at 186, n 33.

27 Venezuela: Dos Santos, *supra* note 18, at 75-77.

28 Mexico City Convention, Art. 7.

29 Argentina: Boggiano, *supra* note 18, at 184-185.

30 Mexico City Convention, Art. 8; *see also* Venezuela: Dos Santos, *supra* note 18, at 75-77.

31 Venezuela: Dos Santos, *supra* note 18, at 77.

32 *Id.*

of a law in fraud.[33] The fraud to the law (*fraude à la loi*) is commonly defined by Ibero-American scholars as the intentional (malicious) alteration of the legal or factual situation, also known as connexion point, which is the basis of the conflict of laws rules to determine the applicable law.[34] Such alteration of the point of connection must result in the application of a (foreign) law other than the one that under normal circumstances should be applied.[35] The consequence is normally that the forum judge shall disregard the applicable law in fraud and apply the law derived from the conflict of law rules under normal circumstances.[36]

In addition, the exception of public order is present in most of the systems that recognised choice of law clauses in Ibero-America.[37] The public order exception functions as a protective barrier or reserve clause to the application of a foreign law susceptible to harm the fundamental values and principles of the forum law.[38] The economic, social and political values and principles founding the Ibero-American legal systems are usually contained in their respective National Constitutions and in the International Treaties to which they are members.[39] For example, the principles of due process, good faith interpretation and performance, the respect of human rights in general, *etc.*[40]

But the notion of the public order exception is not uniform. The application of the exception may change depending on the jurisdiction, the scholar or the judge that approaches the issue differently based on circumstances of time, place and form.[41] The consequences of the public order exception involves that the foreign applicable law, both by virtue of a choice of law or default

33 Mexico Art. 15 (I) CC; Spain Art. 12 (3) (4) CC; Peru: J. Basadre Ayulo, Derecho International Privado 2003 (2000).

34 Chile: Ramírez Necochea, *supra* note 18, at 127-128; Spain: A.P. Abarca Junco, Derecho Internacional Privado Vol. I 177 (2003); Portugal: A. Ferrer Correia, Lições de direito internacional privado 422 (2005).

35 Mexico: L. Pereznieto Castro, Derecho Internacional Privado, Parte General 207 (2005).

36 Spain: Abarca Junco, *supra* note 34, at 179; Portugal: Ferrer Correia, *supra* note 34, at 425.

37 Costa Rica Art. 18 CC; Guatemala Art. 31 JOL; Mexico Art. 15 (II) CC; Spain Art. 12 (3) CC; Venezuela Art. 8 PIL.

38 Argentina: Boggiano, *supra* note 18, at 181; Chile: Ramírez Necochea, *supra* note 34, at 123; Mexico: Pereznieto Castro, *supra* note 35, at 202-2003; Peru: C. Delgado Barreto *et al.*, Introducción al Derecho Internacional Privado, Vol. I, 334 (2002); Portugal: Ferrer Correia, *supra* note 34, at 406-407; Spain: Abarca Junco, *supra* note 34, at 209.

39 Argentina Art. 14 CC enumerates some norms considered of public order: the constitution, the criminal statutes, the administrative statutes, the fiscal statutes, the private law statutes considered essential for the protection of the individuals, the family and the property.

40 Peru: Delgado Barreto *et al.*, *supra* note 38, at 334.

41 Chile: Ramírez Necochea, *supra* note 34, at 123; Mexico: Pereznieto Castro, *supra* note 35, at 202-2003.

conflict rules, is disregarded by the forum judge who often will instead apply his own law.[42]

The *public order* exception differentiates from the *imperative norms*. The exception of public order only operates after the judge has made use of the conflict of law rules; so that on a case-by-case basis the judge determines whether the application of the foreign law, by virtue of a choice of law or default conflict rules, contradicts the general principles and values under which this law is based. The imperative norms, on the other hand, work prior to the use of the conflict of law rules since the imperative norms of the forum judge (and according to some also those of a third applicable law)[43] are always applied in priority to any foreign law.[44]

This distinction can be found in the Mexico City Convention which deals with the mentioned notions. On the one hand, it establishes that the law chosen by the parties shall be respected unless it is manifestly contrary to the public order of the forum.[45] While in a different provision it acknowledges that the provisions of the law of the forum shall be applied when they are mandatory.[46]

1.2.3. Disputable Freedom

In Brazil, as a matter of public policy, the judiciary system must follow the rules contained in the Civil Code Introductory Law.[47] The Introductory Law has a mandatory character and it does not allow the parties to freely choose the applicable law to their contracts.[48] Nevertheless, in isolated cases the Brazilian courts have welcomed the freedom of choice law granted by the Brazilian Arbitration Act. They have extended it to any international contract.[49]

---

42 Peru: Delgado Barreto *et al.*, *supra* note 38, at 334; Portugal: Ferrer Correia, *supra* note 34, at 418.

43 Argentina: Boggiano, *supra* note 18, at 190: upholding that Argentina Art. 1208 CC allows the Argentinean judge to apply a third country imperative provision that the parties expected to evade with a choice of law clause.

44 Mexico: Pereznieto Castro, *supra* note 35, at 202-2003; Peru: Delgado Barreto *et al.*, *supra* note 38, at 336; Spain: Abarca Junco, *supra* note 34, at 209.

45 Mexico City Convention, Art. 18.

46 *Id.*, Art. 11.

47 Brazil: D. Stringer, *Choice of Law and Choice of Forum in Brazilian International Commercial Contracts: Party Autonomy, International Jurisdiction, and the Emerging Third Way*, 44(33) Columbia Journal of Transnational Law 959, at 960.

48 Brazil Art. 8 Introductory Law; *see also* Peru: M. Albornoz, *El derecho aplicable a los contratos internacionales en el sistema interamericano*, Portal Jurídico Peruan (2008), http://www.ciberjure.com.pe/index.php?option=com_content&task=view&id=3531&Itemid=9: the author relies on the answers to 'Questionaire on International contracts' produced for the preparatory meeting (CIDIP V) for the Inter-American convention on the law applicable to international contracts. The 1942 Introductory Law was enacted for the Civil Code of 1916. Although a New Civil Code is in force since 2002, the 1942 Introductory Law reminded as the rule of interpretation and conflict of laws of the New Civil Code.

49 Brazil Appeal Tribunal of São Paulo, Registry 1.247.070-7, 18 December 2003: the Judge

In Uruguay, the Civil Code expressly establishes that the parties may not modify the rules that determine the applicable law and the competent jurisdiction.[50] The conflict of laws rules of Uruguay establish that issues regarding the existence, validity, nature and effects of contracts are governed by the law of the State where they shall be fulfilled.[51] Thus, in principle, the applicable law is the one established by the conflict of law rules and the freedom to choose a different law is not admitted.[52]

Under the Paraguayan and the Colombian laws, it is still disputable whether such freedom exists. The statutory laws do not expressly allow the parties to choose the applicable law to their contract neither clearly prohibit it.[53] The Civil Codes rules on conflict of laws establish that contracts to be fulfilled in the country's territory shall be (*exclusively*)[54] governed by the Colombian or the Paraguayan laws respectively.[55] This provision contains the *lex loci solutionis* or *lex loci executionis* principle of contracts' conflict of laws. The same is understood to eliminate the possibility to choose any law other than the law of the place where the contract will be fulfilled.[56]

In other words, any choice of foreign law clause would be considered invalid if the contract has to be fulfilled in Colombia or Paraguay. However, some authors consider that according to this rule the possibility of choosing a foreign law is open for every contract which is to be fulfilled abroad.[57]

On the other hand, some authors have defended the possibility to choose a foreign law or international instrument by relying upon the general freedom of the parties to contractually define their contractual obligations.[58] Also it is suggested that the fact that both States are members of international instruments which acknowledge the freedom to designate the applicable law to the contract, such as the New York Convention and the Panama

recognised the agreement of the parties to submit their contract to the laws of the United Kingdom.

50 Uruguay Art. 2403 CC (Appendix of the CC).

51 Uruguay Art. 2399 CC (Appendix of the CC).

52 Though some scholars have a different view, *see* Peru: Albornoz, *supra* note 48.

53 *See* Colombia: M.G. Monroy Cabra, *El Arbitraje Internacional en Colombia*, Sevilex, http://www.servilex.com.pe/arbitraje/congresopanama/b-07.php; Paraguay: B. Pisano, *La autonomía de la voluntad en el Derecho Internacional Privado Paraguayo*, Blog del CEDEP (2009), http://cedep.wordpress.com, at 10-11.

54 Adverb added in Paraguay Art. 297 CC.

55 Colombia Art. 20 (3) CC & Art. 869 Com C; Paraguay Art. 297 CC.

56 *See* Colombia: Monroy Cabra, *supra* note 53; Paraguay: Pisano, *supra* note 53, at 10-11.

57 *See* Colombia: Monroy Cabra, *supra* note 53; Paraguay: Pisano, *supra* note 53, at 10-11.

58 Colombia Arts. 20, 1602 CC: derived from the principle of parties' contractual freedom; Paraguay Art. 22 CC: supported by Paraguay: R. Moreno Ródriguez-Alcalá, *Paraguay*, *in* D. Campbell (Ed.), Remedies for International Sellers of Goods, Vol. III, 63, at 81 (2008).

Convention,[59] supports an affirmative view.[60] Finally, the possibility granted by the Paraguayan arbitration law to select any substantive law as the law applicable to substance adds a point, which makes the argument stronger.[61]

1.2.4. Freedom of Choice in Commercial Arbitration

Similarly, most countries' arbitrations laws recognise the principle of freedom of choice of law.[62] Including Brazil and Paraguay, where if the parties choose to exclude the judiciary system by choosing to solve the dispute by means of commercial arbitration they are free to agree on a set of rules that shall govern the contract,[63] including the CISG[64] (a possibility that, as mentioned, would be very disputable in cases settled by the forum judge).

As to the possibility to choose the law applicable to a contract under the Uruguayan and the Colombian arbitration laws, the freedom can be deduced from Article 3 of the Panama Convention, to which Uruguay is a member.[65] This establishes that absent an express agreement between the parties, the arbitration shall be conducted in accordance with the Rules of Procedure of the Inter American Commercial Arbitration Commission. These Rules expressly establish that the arbitral tribunal shall apply the law designated by the parties as applicable to the substance of the dispute.[66]

Those Ibero-American arbitration laws which are based on UNCITRAL Model Law clarify that any designation of the law or legal system of a given State shall be construed, unless otherwise expressed, as directly referring to the substantive law of that State and not to its conflict of laws rules.[67] The purpose of such rule is to avoid *renvois*, or the application of the conflict rules of one legal systems that would eventually lead to the application of the

59 *See* Ch. 2, 1.

60 *See* Paraguay: Pisano, *supra* note 53, at 12.

61 Paraguay Art. 32 AL.

62 Bolivia Art. 54 AL; Brazil Art. 2 AL; Chile Art. 28 AL; Costa Rica Art. 22 CC; El Salvador Art. 78 AL; Guatemala Art. 26 AL; Honduras Art. 88 AL; Mexico Art. 1445 Com C; Nicaragua Art. 54 AL; Panama Art. 43 AL; Paraguay Art. 32 AL; Peru Art. 117 AL; Spain Art. 34 AL.

63 Brazil Art. 2 AL; Paraguay Art. 32 AL.

64 Brazil Superior Tribunal of Justice, REsp 3.035/EX, Registry 2008/0044435-0, Minister Fernando Gonçalves, 20 May 2009: dismissing the challenge to the foreign award enforcement. In the Tribunal's consideration the choice of Swiss Law as the applicable substantive law to the contract and the Arbitral Tribunal's subsequent decision to apply the CISG as integral part of the Swiss National Law did not oppose the Brazilian Public Order; despite the fact that Brazil is not a CISG Member State (November 2009), regardless of whether the application of the CISG resulted from the application of the Conflict of Law rules or from the parties' direct choice, because the possibility is in line with Brazil Art. 2 AL.

65 *See* Ch. 2, 1.

66 Art. 33 Rules of Procedure of the Inter American Commercial Arbitration Commission.

67 *See* Chile Art. 28 AL; Guatemala Art. 26 AL; Mexico Art. 1445 Com C; Nicaragua Art. 54 AL; Paraguay Art. 32 AL; Peru Art. 117 AL; Spain Art. 34 AL.

substantive laws of a third system. On the contrary, the Costa Rican arbitration law establishes that if the parties did not make any specific reference to a substantive law the arbitral tribunal will apply the Costa Rican law, including the rules on conflict of laws.[68]

2. The Interplay Between Contract and the Default System

By expressly allowing the parties to freely define their obligations, the Ibero-American laws also recognise the primary position of parties' contractual will before the law.[69] As stated by the Costa Rican Supreme Court, the contract is the law for the parties, which are bound by the terms expressed in it.[70] Provided that the clauses in their contracts do not contradict the requirements and limitations already commented.[71]

This principle has been expressly recognised by some codes.[72] For example, Colombia's Code of Commerce establishes that the terms of a contract validly celebrated will be preferred to the supplementary legal norms and the mercantile usages.[73] In the same line, Peru's Civil Code dictates the legal provisions on contracts are supplementary to the will of the parties, unless they are imperative.[74]

Peruvian Supreme Court sustained that the contract was the law for the contractors and as such the contract had a primary position before the law.[75] The Court also explained that, derived from this primary position, the contractual terms could not be modified or overridden by subsequent (in time) statutory provisions or court decisions. However, the contract could be modified in case the new statutory provisions or court decisions are of public order or of imperative character.[76]

The issue concerning the interplay between contract and the default system is further reviewed in chapter 31 on the supplementation of the contract.

---

68 Costa Rica Art. 22 AL.

69 El Salvador Supreme Court, *Cass civ*, *Alvarenga Bonilla v. Hsien Tang*, 1530 S.S., 30 September 2002: the parties can give to their contract effects different to those established by law. The parties can modify their structure, extend, limit or suppress the usual obligations of a type of contract.

70 Costa Rica Supreme Court, Judgment 108, 18 July 1989.

71 *See* 1.

72 *See for example* Chile Art. 1545 CC; Colombia Art. 1062 CC & Art. 4 Com C; Ecuador Art. 1588 CC; El Salvador Art. 1416 CC; Peru Arts. 1353, 1356 CC; Portugal Art. 4 Com C.

73 Colombia Art. 4 Com C.

74 Peru Art. 1356 CC.

75 Peru Supreme Court, *Sala civil transitoria,* Resolution 002752-2006, 17 October 2006.

76 *Id.*

CHAPTER 4

CONFLICT OF LAWS RULES

1. Traditional Approach

Absent a choice of law, the applicable law to the contract will be determined by the relevant conflict of laws rules. Many Ibero-American conflict of laws rules make a *dépeçage* of the applicable law depending on whether the capacity of the parties, the form of the contract or the effects of the obligations have to be governed.[1]

Certainly, as to the capacity of the parties to enter into a contract, some Ibero-American Civil Codes refer to the law of the domicile[2] while others to the law of the individual's nationality.[3] Similarly, the capacity of legal entities

[1] Chile: M. Ramirez Necochea, Derecho Internacional Privado 187-188 (2005); ICC Final Award Case No. 13751 *Lex Contractus* German Law and Mexican Law to the agency relationship: reasoning that the parties submitted their agreement to the substantive laws of the Federal Republic of Germany. The submission as regards the merits of the matter is valid and binds the Tribunal. That does not imply, however, that the sufficiency of the Power of Attorney is to be solved under German Law.

[2] Argentina Arts. 6, 7 CC; Brazil Introductory Law Art. 7 CC; Colombia Art. 19(1) CC; Mexico Art. 13 (II) CC; Peru Art. 2070 CC: however a contract cannot be rescinded on the grounds of lack of legal capacity if such was concluded in Peru and the parties have legal capacity under Peruvian law (Art. 2070, sentence 3); Uruguay Art. 2393 CC; Venezuela Art. 16 PIL.

[3] Portugal Arts. 25 and 31(1) CC: however, the contract concluded in Portugal by a person considered incapable under the applicable law, cannot be rescinded on those grounds if the Portuguese law would considered that person as capable. This exception does not apply when the other party ought to be aware of such incapacity (Art. 28(1)(2) CC); Spain Art. 9(1) CC: however, the contracts concluded by an incapable foreigner under the law of his nationality will be valid in Spain if the cause of his incapacity is not recognised in the Spanish law; *see also* applicable in Portugal and Spain Art. 11 RC: In a contract concluded between persons who are in the same country, a natural person who would have capacity under the law of that country may invoke his incapacity resulting from another law only if the other party to the contract was

is governed by the law of their main place of business[4] or by the law of the place where they were constituted.[5] The latter is particularly true for commercial companies since all Latin American states are members to the Inter-American convention on conflicts of laws concerning commercial companies.[6]

With regards to the form of the contracts, many conflict of laws rules designate the law of the place of contract conclusion.[7] In Costa Rica, the law of the place of conclusion does not govern the form of the contract but only the matters concerning the interpretation or deficiencies of the contract.[8]

Regarding the validity, fulfilment, effects and extinction of the contracted obligations, many conflict rules point to the law of the place where the main obligations of the contract are to be fulfilled.[9] In sales contracts, the delivery of the goods is the main obligation, hence, the law at the place of delivery of the goods has been many times established as the applicable law.[10] The

aware of this incapacity at the time of the conclusion of the contract or was not aware thereof as a result of negligence; *see* Spain: J.C. Fernández Rozas & S. Sánchez Lorenzo, Curso de Derecho Internacional Privado 446 (1996).

4 Portugal Art. 33 CC.

5 Brazil Art. 11 Introductory Law CC; Peru Art. 2073 CC; Uruguay Art. 2394 CC; Venezuela Art. 20 PIL. In Spain Art. 9 (11) CC, the law applicable is that of the company's nationality (incorporation). However, companies domiciled in Spain (for example when they have in Spain their main place of business) are considered of Spanish nationality.

6 *See* Art. 2 of Inter-American convention on conflicts of laws concerning commercial companies http://www.oas.org/DIL/CIDIP-II-conflictscommercialcompanies.htm. Ratification status http://www.oas.org/juridico/english/sigs/b-40.html.

7 Chile Art. 17 CC; Brazil Introductory Law Art. 9 CC; Ecuador Art. 16 CC; El Salvador Art. 17 CC; Guatemala Arts. 28, 29 JOL; Mexico Art. 13 (IV) CC; Peru Art. 2094 CC; Portugal Art. 36 CC: unless the law of the substance imposes a different form for the validity of the contract; Spain Art. 11 (1) CC; Venezuela Art. 37 (1) PIL: but also the form can be valid if adjusted to the substantive law or the common domicile of the parties; *see also* Venezuela: O.M. Dos Santos, Contratos Internacionales en el Ordenamiento Jurídico Venezolano 71 (2000).

8 Costa Rica Art. 27 CC.

9 Argentina Arts. 1209, 1210 CC; Chile Art. 16 (3) CC; Costa Rica Art. 23 CC: only concerning the obligations and effects of contracts; Ecuador Art. 15 (2) CC; El Salvador Art. 16 (3) CC; Guatemala Art. 30 JOL: regarding fulfilment of obligations; Mexico Art. 13 (V) CC: regarding the effects of the contracts; Peru Art. 2095 CC: regarding the obligations; ICC Final Award Case No. 13518 *Lex Contractus* Argentinean Law by operation of the Conflict of Laws Rules in Argentina's Civil Code.

10 Argentina National Commercial Court of Appeals, *Mayer Alejandro v. Onda Hofferle GmbH & Co.*, 24 April 2000: upholding that in international sales, the main obligation of the contract is the delivery of the goods; the seller's obligation does not involve the payment of money. "[t]he contracting parties have included the clause FOB Buenos Aires, it is clear that the fundamental part of the contract was performed with the delivery of the goods on board the ship in the agreed port (in the same line 'Esposito e Hijos, R.L.C. Jocqueviel de Vieu', 10.10.85, and doctrine cited within, LL, 1986-D-46), which leads to the application of Argentinean law"; Argentina National Commercial Court of Appeals, *Cervecería y Maltería Paysandú S.A. v. Cervecería Argentina S.A.*, 21 July 2002 in CLOUT Abstract No. 636: the Court considered that in an international sale of goods the "most characteristic performance" is the delivery of the

solution is not always the best. The law of the place of delivery may not be the most appropriate law when none of the parties are connected to such a place. In response to this, modern national laws and conventions have close-connected the place of contract fulfilment to one of the parties residences or places of business.[11]

Alternatively, in Argentina and Peru, if the contract does not indicate a place to fulfil the main obligations, and a place cannot be deduced from the contract, the applicable law shall be the place of contract conclusion.[12] Moreover, under Argentina's conflict rules if the contract was passed by non-present persons in more than one place through the exchange of correspondence or mails, the effects of the obligations contracted by each of the parties shall be governed by the law of their respective domiciles.[13] Under the Peruvian conflict of laws, if the obligations have to be fulfilled in different countries, the contract shall be governed by the law of the place where the principal obligation must be performed, and in such cases cannot be determined, by the law of contract conclusion.[14]

In Brazil, the qualification and regulation of obligations are governed by the law of the country where they were agreed.[15]

2. Modern Approach

The Venezuelan Private International Law Statute and the Mexico City Convention follow a more modern approach based on the closest connection test. Accordingly, the contract shall be governed by the law with which it has the closest ties,[16] or is most directly linked.[17] The Court shall consider all the objective and subjective elements arising from the contract in order to determine the applicable law. It shall also take into account the general principles of commercial law accepted by international organisations.[18]

Some commentators consider that the objective elements or the circumstances to be considered, in order to determine the close connection required, are *inter alia*: the nationality, the habitual residence or domicile of

---

goods rather than the payment of the purchase price. Therefore, since the goods were delivered in Argentina, Argentinean law was applicable.

11 *See infra* 2.

12 Argentina Art. 1212 CC: if such is the debtor's domicile at the time of conclusion; Peru Art. 2095 CC.

13 Argentina Art. 1214 CC.

14 Peru Art. 2095 (2) CC.

15 Brazil Introductory Law Art. 9 CC; ICC Final Award Case No. 13870 *Lex Contractus* Brazil by operation of the Conflict of Laws Rules in Brazil Introductory Law CC.

16 Mexico City Convention Art. 9.

17 Venezuela Art. 30 PIL.

18 Mexico City Convention Art. 9; Venezuela Art. 30 PIL.

the parties, the place of contract conclusion, the place of the goods, the seat of the chosen court or arbitral tribunal, the place where the obligations are to be fulfilled, etc.[19] Nevertheless, other places post-formation may also become objectively relevant and closely connected with a certain jurisdiction.[20]

The Rome Convention on the law applicable to contractual obligations, which has direct application in Portugal and Spain refers to the principle of the proper law, or the law with most significant relationships or relevant contact.[21] But contrary to the above mentioned instruments, the Rome Convention clarifies that the "*contract is most closely connected with the country where the party who is to effect the performance which is characteristic of the contract has, at the time of conclusion of the contract, his habitual residence ...*"[22] The '*characteristic*' performance is that which constitutes the centre of gravity of the contract. Basically, the party providing the characteristic performance is the person to whom the payment is due, *i.e.* the seller who delivers the goods. The rule avoids the possibility to designate a law that may be unconnected to the parties.[23]

Yet again, both set of rules allow *dépeçage* of applicable laws. Following the text of the Mexico City Convention, "if a part of the contract were separable from the rest and if it had a closer tie with another State, the law of that State could, exceptionally, apply to that part of the contract."[24] The Venezuelan statute adds that the application of different laws to different aspects of a juridical relationship, shall be made harmoniously, with the aim of reaching the goals sought by each of those laws. Possible difficulties resulting from their simultaneous application shall be solved by considering the requirements imposed by equity in the specific case.[25]

---

19 Mexico: L. Pereznieto Castro, *Introducción a la Convención Interamericana sobre Derecho Aplicable a los Contratos Internacionales*, 13-14-15 Revista de Derecho Privado 137, at 145 (1994); *also* Peru: M.M. Albornoz, *El derecho aplicable a los contratos internacionales en el sistema interamericano*, Portal Jurídico Peruan (2008), http://www.ciberjure.com.pe/index.php?option=com_content&task=view&id=3531&Itemid=9.

20 Venezuela: J.A. Giral Pimentel, *La teoría de las vinculaciones*, Publicaciones Juridicas Venezolanas (1999), http://www.zur2.com/fcjp/117/giral.htm.

21 *See* Art. 4 RC.

22 *See* Art. 4.1 (2) RC.

23 P. Lagarde & M. Giuliano, *Report on the Convention on the law applicable to contractual obligations*, Journal Official n° C 282 du 31 October 1980, Art. 4, para. 3: "The submission of the contract, in the absence of a choice by the parties, to the law appropriate to the characteristic performance defines the connecting factor of the contract from the inside, and not from the outside by elements unrelated to the essence of the obligation such as the nationality of the contracting parties or the place where the contract was concluded. [...] The concept of characteristic performance essentially links the contract to the social and economic environment of which it will form a part [...] Which usually constitutes the centre of gravity and the socio-economic function of the contractual transaction."

24 Mexico City Convention, Art. 9 last para.

25 Venezuela Art. 7 PIL.

Part 2

Ambit of Sales Law

Chapter 5

General Remarks on the Ambit of Sales Law

1. General Approach Concerning B2B and C2C Contracts

Most of the Ibero-American countries still have two different sets of rules governing what is known under English contract law as Business to Business (hereinafter B2B) and Consumer to Consumer (hereinafter C2C) sales. These are the Civil Codes and the Codes of Commerce;[1] except for countries like Brazil, Peru and Paraguay which do not distinguish between B2B and C2C sales but instead have a unique body of rules governing every B2B and C2C sale.[2]

This work covers the C2C and B2B sales or what is categorised under the Ibero-American contract tradition as civil sales or commercial sales, respectively. Consequently, it is necessary to make clear at this point why and when a B2B transaction is primarily governed by the rules of the Codes of Commerce (and only supplemented by the Civil Code provisions) and also why and when a C2C transaction in the Ibero-American system is affected by the unique application of the Civil Code rules.

1 *See for example* ICC Final Award Case No. 13435 *Lex Contractus* Spanish Law, with implied exclusion of the CISG: "Under Spanish law a determination of the rules governing contracts for sale will depend on the nature of the sale. The legal system in fact distinguishes between three classes of sale: civil, governed by the Civil Code (…), commercial, governed by the Commercial Code (…), and international sales, a type which, whether civil or commercial, is governed by the United Nations Vienna Convention of 11 April 1980."

2 The Brazilian Civil Code of 2002, the Peruvian Civil Code Reform of 1984 and the Paraguayan Civil Code of 1987 have uniformed the rules of civil and commercial obligations and contracts in those respective jurisdictions; *see* Latin America: A. Guzman Brito, Historia de la Codificación civil en Iberoamerica 337 (2006); Peru: C. Torres y Torres Lara, *La Codificación Comercial en el Peru de un Código 'Formal' a un Código 'Real'*, *in* Instituto de Investigaciones Jurídicas (Ed.), Centenario del Código de Comercio, at 588 (1991).

On the other hand, the sale of goods categorised as Business to Consumer (hereinafter B2C) is excluded from this work.[3] With the intention of explaining what a consumer sale is, part 2 of this chapter presents a brief analysis of the scope of application of consumer protection laws in the Ibero-American systems.

1.1. B2B Sales

Generally, a sale is categorised as B2B, when as such it constitutes an act of commerce, within the definition established by the same Codes of Commerce, irrespective of the persons who perform those acts.[4] Generally, an act of commerce pursues a goal of economic speculation or a profit purpose,[5] which does not need to be expressed in the contract but which is rather assessed on a case by case basis.[6] The goal of economic speculation or a profit purpose has a subjective character that can only be subtracted from the mind of the contractor.[7]

In practice, most transactions passed between traders or companies are B2B and hence primarily governed by the provisions of the Codes of Commerce.[8]

[3] Unless when the respective countries' laws consider that the Consumer Protection Law is applicable to areas of the B2B or C2C sales, *e.g.* Ch. 13, 1 & 2.

[4] Costa Rica Art. 1 Com C; Ecuador Art. 1 Com C; El Salvador Art. 1 Com C; Honduras Art. 1 Com C; Mexico Art. 1 Com C; Nicaragua Art. 1 Com C; Portugal Art. 1 Com C; Spain Art. 2 Com C; Venezuela Art. 1 Com C.

[5] Argentina Art. 451 Com C: only the sale of movable goods is commercial. Immovables are excluded from the application of the code; Chile Art. 3 (1) Com C: only the sale of movable goods is commercial; Colombia Art. 20 (2) Com C: only the sale of movable goods is commercial; Costa Rica Ar. 438 (a) Com C: includes immovables acquired with reselling purposes; Ecuador Art. 3 (1) CC; El Salvador Art. 1013 Com C; Honduras Art. 763 (1) Com C; Mexico Arts. 75 (I, II, II), 371 Com C: includes immovables acquired with reselling purposes; Portugal Arts. 2, 463 (1-5) Com C: includes immovables acquired with reselling purposes; Spain Art. 325 Com C; Uruguay Art. 515 Com C: only the sale of movable goods is commercial; Venezuela Art. 2 (1-3) Com C; Spain Supreme Tribunal, 9 July 2008, *Id Cendoj:* 28079110012008100731; Spain Supreme Tribunal, 21 December 1981, *Id Cendoj:* 28079110011981100141; Spain Supreme Tribunal, 20 November 1984, *Id Cendoj:* 28079110011984100596.

[6] *See for example* Mexico Collegiate Tribunals, *Novena Época,* Registry 174'773, SJF XXIV, July 2006, at 1169.

[7] Spain Supreme Tribunal, 21 December 1981, *Id Cendoj:* 28079110011981100141; Spain Supreme Tribunal, 20 November 1984, *Id Cendoj:* 28079110011984100596; Mexico: O. Vásquez del Mercado, Contratos Mercantiles 195 (2008): because even if the profit sought is not achieved through the contract, the subjective profit purpose to sell and/or purchase is enough.

[8] Argentina Arts. 1-4 Com C; Chile Art. 1 Com C; Colombia Art. 1 Com C; Costa Rica Art. 1 Com C; Ecuador Art. 1 Com C; El Salvador Art. 1 Com C; Honduras Art. 1 Com C; Spain Art. 1 Com C; Mexico Collegiate Tribunals, *Novena Época,* Registry 186'332, SJF XVI, August 2002, at 1256; ICC Partial Award Case No. 12296 *Lex Contractus* Mexican Law: the Arbitral Tribunal noted that the applicability of the Code of Commerce was reinforced by Arts. 1 and 14

Ordinarily, traders are defined as persons and commercial companies that habitually trade.[9] But even though sales passed between traders are presumed to be B2B, a trader may be able to demonstrate that he did not pursue a goal of economic speculation or intend a profit purpose for a particular transaction, so that the transaction can be characterised as C2C or B2C.[10] Remember that a transaction only becomes B2B when such constitutes an act of commerce irrespective of the person who performs it: Business, Private person or Consumer.

For example, a contract passed between a trader whose common profitable business is the sale of fabrics and a buyer who acquires fabrics for resale purposes is automatically characterised as B2B sale. Similarly, a sale passed between a seller of cereals and a buyer who acquires the cereals in order to feed pigs purported to be sold to the public is characterised as B2B.[11]

However, if the sale is passed between a shoes' trader and a telecommunications company who occasionally acquire a number of shoes to be distributed between its employees for its personal use, such sale is rather likely to be considered a B2C transaction,[12] which involves the primary application of the consumer protection law on the buyer's benefit, supplemented by the sales rules contained in the Civil Codes.

1.1.1. Complementation

As many issues affecting the B2B contract of sale are not covered by the Codes of Commerce, the Civil Codes become the primary supplementary body of law to govern such issues.[13] Commercial codes' lacunas often concern

of the Com C, since respondent is a foreign merchant and claimant is a corporation organised under the General Corporations Law of Mexico.

9 Argentina Arts. 1, 2 Com C; Chile Art. 7 Com C; Colombia Art. 11 Com C; Costa Rica Art. 5(a) Com C; Ecuador Art. 2 Com C; El Salvador Art. 2 Com C; Honduras Art. 2 Com C; Mexico Art. 3(I) Com C; Nicaragua Art. 6 Com C; Portugal Art. 13 Com C; Spain Art. 1 Com C; Venezuela Art. 10 Com C.

10 *See* Argentina Art. 452(2) Com C; Costa Rica Art. 439 Com C; Nicaragua Art. 1 Com C; Uruguay Art. 516(1) Com C; Mexico: Vásquez del Mercado, *supra* note 7, at 194; El Salvador Supreme Court, *Cass civ, Instituto de Previsión Social de la Fuerza Armada v. Cooperativa de la Fuerza Armada, Limitada, o COOPEFA*, Ca.29-C-2004, 14 March 2005: although respondent was a trader, the transaction was not concluded with profit purposes but outside the range of commercial activities that respondent usually undertake in mass. The Court considered the transaction as a C2C one.

11 Spain Supreme Tribunal, 23 January 2009; *Id Cendoj:* 28079110012009100016.

12 *See* expressly Chile Art. 2(a) CPL; Mexico Art. 76 Com C; Spain Art. 326 (1). Com C. El Salvador Supreme Court, *Cass civ, Aseguradora Salvadoreña, Compañía de Seguros v. American International Group, Inc*, 1466 S.S., 31 March 2003.

13 *See* expressly Argentina Preliminary Title I & Art. 207 Com C; Bolivia Art. 866 Com C; Chile Arts. 2, 96 Com C; Colombia Arts. 2, 822 Com C; Costa Rica Arts. 2, 416 Com C; Ecuador Art. 5 Com C; El Salvador Arts. 1, 945 Com C; Honduras Art. 1 Com C; Guatemala Art. 694 Com C; Mexico Art. 2 Com C; Nicaragua Art. 2 Com C; Portugal Art. 3 Com C; Spain

the validity, formation, interpretation, avoidance and termination of the sales contract, as well as may issues relating to the rights and obligations of the parties.[14]

Equally, when the Codes of Commerce and the Civil Codes contain provisions dealing with the same aspects of the sale, a common question is how the provisions of both codes work for B2B. In all countries the Codes of Commerce provisions will prevail over those of the Civil Codes for those issues expressly governed by the first.[15] For example, if the Code of Commerce establishes a particular mechanism to terminate or avoid a contract, this shall be considered alone with no interference from the Civil Code provisions.[16] This principle is rooted in the old statutory Spanish law and commercial ordinances.[17]

1.1.2. *Lex Specialis*

The idea that experienced merchants expect laws to facilitate transactions and preferably to be in line with commercial practices and usages distinguishes the Codes of Commerce special provisions on B2B sales contracts.

Hence, for example, many Ibero-American legal systems establish special rules for B2B sales which distinguish them from those applicable to C2C sales, particularly, in matters regarding the remedies available for the

Art. 2 Com C; Venezuela Art. 8 Com C; El Salvador Supreme Court, *Cass civ, Alberto Zelaya y Zaldivar Gallardo v. Montenevado Comercial, S.A. De C.V.,* 1198-2001, 30 January 2001; ICC Final Award Case No. 12035 *Lex Contractus* Mexican Law: "When the Commercial Code is silent, the Mexican Civil Code is applicable."

14 *See* expressly stated Colombia Art. 822 Com C; Costa Rica Art. 416 Com C; Mexico Art. 81 Com C; Spain Art. 50 Com C; Uruguay Art. 191 Com C; El Salvador Supreme Court, *Cass civ, Aseguradora Salvadoreña, Compañía de Seguros v. American International Group, Inc,* 1466 S.S., 31 March 2003: stating that aspects relating to the validity and termination of commercial obligations are governed by the Civil Code provisions; ICC Final Award Case No. 13435 *Lex Contractus* Spanish Law with implied exclusion of the CISG: "The Contract is governed by the Spanish Commercial Code and, according to Article 2 of this Code, by commercial usage and, in default, by civil rules. (…) the requirements, modifications, exceptions, interpretation, termination and capacity of the parties in commercial contracts are governed by the general rules of the civil law (…) in all matters not expressly established in this Code [of Commerce] or in special laws."

15 *See* Bolivia Art. 866 Com C; Chile Arts. 2, 96 Com C; Colombia Art. 822 Com C; Costa Rica Art. 14 CC & Arts. 2, 416 Com C; Cuba Art. 8 CC; El Salvador Art. 4 CC & Art. 945 Com C; Guatemala Art. 13 JOL & Art. 1 Com C; Honduras Art. 4 CC & Art. 715 Com C; Mexico Art. 2 Com C; Portugal Art. 3 Com C; Spain Art. 2 Com C; Uruguay Art. 191 Com C; Venezuela Art. 14 CC & Art. 8 Com C.

16 El Salvador Supreme Court, Cass civ, Alberto Zelaya y Zaldivar Gallardo v. Montenevado Comercial, S.A. De C.V., 1198-2001, 30 January 2001.

17 *See* Ch. 1, 2.2; showing the interplay between *Las Siete Partidas* and *Ordenanzas de Bilbao*.

sale of livestock,[18] the time for and the effect of the acceptance,[19] the means and standards of proof,[20] the duty to deliver the goods' invoice and title documents,[21] the obligation to examine and give notice of any defects found on the goods,[22] the time of the passing of risk from the seller to the buyer,[23] *etc.*

1.2. C2C Sales

C2C sales, are all those not classified as B2B nor as B2C. Most of the time, the C2C will only be governed by the rules of the Civil Codes. The number of C2C sales is very small in international trade; though Internet websites such as E-bay have recently augmented the number of these sales. C2C sales are entered into by sellers who do not ordinarily enter into the transaction with a profitable purpose and who cannot be considered as suppliers under consumer protection laws. The buyer may usually buy the goods for his personal use but never with an intention of profitable resell, at least at the moment of conclusion.

The C2C sales are much more common in the domestic market. These commonly include sales of land or real state,[24] the sale of automobiles between individuals, the sale of materials or goods between peers which cannot fit into either the scope of application of the B2B or B2C sales.

This means that the Civil Code rules are very rarely applied alone to a single transaction. Nevertheless, the Civil Codes' rules on contracts and obligations still have an important role in the practice of sales of goods as they complement and provide the majority of the solutions to B2B.

18 *See* Ch. 6, 3.1.
19 *See* Ch. 10, 2.1.1.
20 *See* Ch. 15, 1.1.
21 *See* Ch. 36, 3.
22 *See* Ch. 40, 2 & 3.
23 *See* Ch. 44, 3 & 1.
24 The sale of land and real state is outside the scope of this work. However, reference is made to case law and provisions when the same principles are also applicable to sale of goods.

2. General Approach Concerning B2C Contracts

2.1. Preliminary Remarks

Most of the Ibero-American Political Constitutions expressly[25] or impliedly,[26] recognise the need for special treatment, protection and/or defence of consumers. In addition, most of the Ibero-American countries have enacted special laws for consumer protection and the establishment of equitable rules for consumers transactions.[27] However, there are still a few countries that apply the general provisions of the Civil Code to the supply of products and services without distinction between civil sales and consumers sales. This is the case in Bolivia and Cuba where no modern law for consumers transactions exists, though the Civil Code establishes special treatment for certain B2C contracts.[28]

[25] Art. 42 Argentinean Constitution; Art. 5 Brazilian Constitution; Art. 78 Colombian Constitution; Art. 46 Costa Rican Constitution; Art. 92 Ecuadorian Constitution; Art. 101 El Salvador Constitution; Art. 130 Guatemalan Constitution; Art. 347 Honduran Constitution; Art. 28 Mexican Constitution; Art. 51 Spanish Constitution; Art. 117 Venezuelan Constitution.

[26] Arts. 7, 132 Bolivian Constitution; Arts. 9, 63 Cuban Constitution; Art. 105 Nicaraguan Constitution; Art. 279 Panamanian Constitution; Arts. 27, 38, 72 Paraguayan Constitution; Art. 65 Peruvian Constitution.

[27] *See* all the following laws hereinafter referred as CPL: Argentina Law No. 24.240 Consumer Protection Law of 22 September 1993; Brazil Law No. 8,078, of 11 September 1990; Chile Law No. 19.496 Law for the Protection of Consumers Rights; Colombia Decree No. 3466 of 1982; Costa Rica Law No. 7472 Law for the Promotion of Competition and the Defence of Consumers; Ecuador Organic Law for the Defence of Consumers and Rules No. 116 of 10 July 2000 on the Organic Law for the Defence of Consumers; El Salvador Law Decree No. 776 of 2005 Consumer Protection and Decree No. 52 of May 2006 Rules for the Law of Consumer Protection; Guatemala Decree No. 006-2003 of 18 February, 2003 on the Law for Consumers and Users Protection; Honduras Decree No. 41-89 Law for Consumer Protection and the Agreement No. 264-8925 from 1989 established the Rules on the Law for Consumer Protection; The Mexican Federal Law for the Protection of the Consumer of 24 December 1992; Nicaragua Law No. 182 for Consumer Protection and the Decree no. 2187 of 3 September 1999 containing the Rules of the Law for Consumer Protection in Nicaragua; Panama Law No. 45 of 31 October 2007 for the Consumer Protection and Defence of the Competition; Paraguay Consumer Protection Law No. 1334 of 1998; Peru Law for Consumer Protection Decree No. 716 of 9 November 1991; Portugal Law 24/96 Consumers Law; Spain General Law for Consumer Protection and the Law 23/2003 of 10 July 2003 Guarantees in the Sale of Consumer Goods; Uruguay Law No. 17.250 for Consumer Defence; and Venezuela Law No. 4.898 for Consumer Protection, Official Gazette of 13 December 1995.

[28] In Cuba, the Civil Code to a certain extent deals with consumers' rights as it takes into account legal figures related to these. For example, the provisions of Title IV state that the goods that are sold in retail establishments of Commerce must have the measurement, weight, amount and quality, according to the legal regulations. In addition, the Law 62 of 1988, Criminal Code, in chapter VIII, Title V book II regulates the crime of deceit or damage to the consumers with sanction of prison from one to three years or fines.

2.2. Scope of Application

The Ibero-American Consumer Protection Laws apply to the supply of services and products passed between Suppliers and Consumers, and hence to B2C sales. Most of these laws uniformly define *suppliers* as natural and legal persons who develop all sort of commercial activities in a professional way or occasionally for the consumer's benefit, either for free and/or for a price.[29] However, not all the Ibero-American laws share the same definition of consumer. This causes the scope of the application of consumer protection laws to vary depending on the established legal definition of consumers.
The narrowest definition, and thus scope, is found in the Portuguese consumer protection law: consumers as those who are supplied with goods destined *not for professional use*.[30] The Portuguese law is close to the type of sales excluded by the CISG. CISG provisions do not apply to sales of goods bought for personal, family or household use, unless the seller, at any time before or at the conclusion of the contract, neither knew nor ought to have known that the goods were bought for any such use.[31]

On the other hand, many consumer protection laws have defined consumers as the natural or legal *ultimate persons*[32] who acquire goods, for free or for a price, for its own benefit or for his family or social group.[33] A few others integrate the same key element of *ultimate persons* but expressly adds that the person who without constituting the final beneficiary, acquires, stores, uses or consumes products with the purpose of integrating them in production, transformation or commercialisation process cannot be considered a consumer.[34]

Some other consumer protection laws do not even require the consumer to be the *ultimate person* who acquires goods.[35] This implies that all legal or natural persons, including businesses and professionals, who acquired products from suppliers are consumers. However, it should be understood that the sales falling under the scope of B2B sales are automatically excluded from the application of the consumer law provisions. Being, all the goods acquired by the buyer having in mind a goal of economic speculation or a profit purpose

29 Argentina Art. 2 CPL; Brazil Art. 3 CPL; Chile Art. 1 (2) CPL; Colombia Art. 1 CPL; Costa Rica Art. 2 CPL; Ecuador Art. 3 CPL; El Salvador Art. 6 (b) CPL; Mexico Art. 2 CPL; Nicaragua Art. 4 CPL; Panama Art. 33 CPL; Paraguay Art. 4 CPL; Peru Art. 33 CPL; Uruguay Art. 3 CPL; Venezuela Art. 3 CPL.

30 Portugal Art. 2 CPL.

31 Art. 2 (a) CISG.

32 The Spanish words used are *destinatario final*.

33 Argentina Art. 1 CPL; Brazil Art. 2 CPL; Chile Art. 1 CPL; Ecuador Art. 2 CPL; Nicaragua Art. 4 CPL; Paraguay Art. 4 CPL; Uruguay Art. 2 CPL.

34 Uruguay Art. 2 CPL; Venezuela Art. 2 CPL; Spain Art. 1 (2) CPL.

35 Salvador Art. 2 CPL; Guatemala Art. 3 CPL; Honduras Art. 2 CPL.

cannot fall into the B2C scope. Nor do sales in which the buyer acquires goods for his personal use, but in which the seller does not have the characteristics of a supplier, fall into the B2C scope. These sales are C2C sales.

Some countries have broadened the scope included in the definition of consumers to include, those artisans and small companies who acquire products or services to integrate them into a production process, for the supply of products or services to third parties.[36]

2.3. Special Provisions

Consumer protection laws in Ibero-America are often categorised as mandatory rules,[37] which means that many provisions cannot be waived by the parties' agreement.[38]

The special provisions incorporated into the Consumer protection laws, which deviate from the traditional civil or commercial codes provisions, relate to the formation of the contract, the obligations of the supplier [seller], the rights of the consumer [buyer],[39] the invalidity of what is considered abusive contract clauses in B2C relations, the liability for damages caused by the goods,[40] and more favourable guarantees of conformity to the consumer.

For example, offers to the public must contain the characteristics, conditions, content, utility and purpose of the products, so that the offer does not induce the consumer to mistake.[41] Namely, such information cannot be omitted if the omission can result in harm or danger on the consumer's health or security.[42]

2.3.1. Abusive Clauses

In addition, certain types of clauses are often considered abusive and invalid when inserted into B2C contracts of adhesion. These are: clauses that restrict

---

[36] Costa Rica Art. 2 CPL; Mexico Arts. 2, 99, 117 CPL: In Mexico, the scope is open up to claims not exceeding MX$ 319,447.46; Peru INDECOPI Tribunal, Resolution No. 422-2003/TDC-INDECOPI; reviewing the definition of *ultimate person* in Peru Art. 3 CPL: based on the information and knowledge asymmetry which exists between the supplier and the consumer, in cases in which the consumer is a micro or small company.

[37] Argentina Art. 65 CPL; Brazil Art. 1 CPL; Costa Rica Art. 12 CPL & Art. 20 CC; Ecuador Art. 1 CPL; Guatemala Art. 1 CPL; Mexico Art. 1 CPL Nicaragua Art. 2 CPL; Uruguay Art. 1 CPL.

[38] Chile Art. 4 CPL; Paraguay Art. 1 CPL; Venezuela Art. 8 CPL.

[39] For example the right to unilaterally avoid the contract under certain circumstances (e-commerce) and within a limited period of time; *see* Chile Art. 3*bis* CPL.

[40] *See* Ch. 55, 3.

[41] Costa Rica Art. 37 CPL; Mexico Art. 32 CPL; Peru Arts. 15, 20 CPL.

[42] Costa Rica Art. 37 CPL.

the rights of the consumer,[43] that are unclear or in a language other than Spanish,[44] that limit or extinguish the main obligation of the supplier,[45] that favour, in an excessive and disproportionate way, the position of the supplier, or that exonerate or limit the liability of the supplier for corporal damages, defective performance or delay.[46]

Similarly, clauses that enable the supplier to avoid the contract unilaterally, to modify its conditions,[47] to suspend his performance, or to limit or revoke the rights of the consumers when no breach of the latter has occurred are invalid.[48] Other clauses considered abusive and thus invalid are those which establish compensations, penalty clauses or monetary interest in favour of the supplier but that are disproportionate considering the damages that a consumer can recover under the same contract.[49]

Also invalid are those clauses that set out terms shorter than the statute of limitations or that bind the consumer to waive the protection of the law,[50] or subject the consumer to the jurisdiction of foreign courts.[51] However, under the Spanish law the consumer at his choice may agree to submit to the jurisdiction of an arbitral tribunal other than the one established by the same law.[52]

2.3.2. Special Remedies and Warranties

Consumer protection law generally contains remedies which are absent from the Civil and Commercial Codes, such as the substitution of the goods, the repair of the goods and the reimbursement of the price.[53] The consumer may choose to request the substitution of the goods, to rescind the contract or a reduction in the price and, in any case, a refund or compensation, when the goods are not in conformity, or do not offer the safety that, due to its nature, one expects from such goods in their reasonable use.[54]

Finally, consumer protection laws generally establish default warranties in relation to the conformity of the goods that sometimes go beyond those

---

43 Costa Rica Art. 42(a) CPL; Argentina Art. 37 (a) CPL.

44 Costa Rica Art. 42(h)(i) CPL; Mexico Art. 85 CPL; Peru Art. 16 CPL.

45 Costa Rica Art. 42(b) CPL; Mexico Art. 90 (II) CPL.

46 Costa Rica Art. 42(c)(d) CPL; Spain Art. 10*bis* CPL (general sense); Chile Art. 16(e)(g) CPL.

47 Peru Art. 13(a) CPL.

48 Costa Rica Art. 42(e) CPL; Mexico Art. 90(I)(III) CPL; Chile Art. 16(a) CPL.

49 Costa Rica Art. 42(e) CPL.

50 Argentina Art. 37(b) CPL.

51 Mexico Art. 90(IV)(VI) CPL.

52 Spain Art. 10(4) CPL.

53 *See* Ch. 49, 2.

54 Argentina Art. 10*bis* CPL; Mexico Art. 82 CPL; Peru Arts. 30, 31 CPL; Spain Arts. 3, 7 GLSGC; Chile Arts. 19, 20 CPL.

established by the Civil or Commercial Codes.[55] Goods are to comply with the quality and technical standards established by the government agencies in order to insure the health of the consumers, the protection of the environment, the social security, *etc.*[56] Also the implied conformity guarantee regarding the quality of goods must indicate, at least, the extension of coverage, the durations, the claim conditions, and the persons or entities who issue it and are responsible for them.[57]

3. General Approach concerning International and Domestic Sales

The CISG not distinguish between B2B and C2C sales. Thus, the CISG applies to sales of goods[58] between parties whose places of business are in different Contracting States, from the date of entry into force in those States.[59] Likewise, the CISG governs any international sale of goods having its applicable law as any of the substantive laws of the Ibero-American CISG Contracting States.[60] This means that as of the date of entry into force, the CISG is currently part of each of thirteen Ibero-American laws.[61] Hence, any of these individual national laws, when applicable, consists of the CISG itself as of the date of its incorporation into the country's law.[62]

---

[55] *See* Ch. 37.

[56] *See for example* Costa Rica Art. 43 CPL; Spain Art. 3 GLSGC.

[57] Argentina Art. 14 CPL; Costa Rica Art. 43 CPL; Mexico Art. 78 CPL; Spain Art. 11(2) CPL & Art. 11 GLSGC.

[58] However the CISG does not apply to the type of sales and goods that fall within Article 2 CISG: goods bought for personal, family or household use, unless the seller, at any time before or at the conclusion of the contract, neither knew nor ought to have known that the goods were bought for any such use; by auction; on execution or otherwise by authority of law; of stocks, shares, investment securities, negotiable instruments or money; ships, vessels, hovercraft or aircraft; electricity.

[59] Art. 1(1)(a) CISG; ICC Final Award Case No. 11826 *Lex Contractus* CISG and Mexican Law as suppletive law; Argentina National Commercial Court of Appeals, *Bravo Barros, Carlos Manuel Del Corazón De Jesús v. Martínez Gares, Salvador S*, 31 May 2007.

[60] Art. 1(1)(b) CISG: the CISG applies when the rules of private international law lead to the application of the law of a Contracting State.

[61] Argentinean law 1 January 1988; Chilean law 1 March 1991; Colombian law 1 August 2002; Cuban law 1 December 1995; Ecuadoran law 1 February 1993; Salvadoran law 1 December 2007; Honduran law 1 November 2003; Mexican law 1 January 1989; Paraguayan law 1 February 2007; Peruvian law 1 April 2000; Spanish law 1 August 1991; and Uruguayan law 1 February 2000; *see* Status in http://www.uncitral.org/uncitral/en/uncitral_texts/sale_goods/1980CISG_status.html (accessed on 10 February 2010).

[62] ICC Arbitral Award No.7565 in CLOUT Abstract No. 300; *see also* ICC Arbitral Award Case No. 6653 in CLOUT Abstract No. 103

This also means that, for example, an express reference to 'Spanish Laws' in an international sale of goods is thus subject to the CISG pursuant to Article 1(1) (b) of the CISG. In other words, the provisions of the Spanish Civil Code and Code of Commerce are automatically replaced by the CISG which therefore are applicable to the said contract in all issues covered by the CISG.[63] The express designation of a domestic law (in this case any of the CISG Ibero-American Member Sates laws) cannot be construed as an express reference to the provisions of the law that would apply at the national level.[64] Consequently, if the contractual parties want any of the national domestic codes to apply exclusively to their international sale, instead of the CISG, they must refer to the concerned '*Código Civil o Código de Comercio*' in their choice of law clause,[65] or must expressly or impliedly exclude the application of the CISG to the whole contract.[66]

Moreover, absent an agreement as to the applicable law, whenever the application of the conflict of laws provisions of the forum judge leads to the application of any of the CISG Contracting States laws, the CISG would apply in accordance with Article 1 (1) (b). Since according to this rule it is immaterial whether one of the parties' place of business is located in a non-Contracting State at the time of contract conclusion,[67] the CISG has often been

---

[63] ICC Final Award Case No. 11818 *Lex Contractus* CIG and Spanish Law as supplementary law.

[64] I. Schwenzer, & P. Hachem, *in* Ingeborg Schwenzer (Ed.), Schlechtriem & Schwenzer Commentary on the UN Convention on the International Sale of Goods, Art. 6, para. 14, at 108, 109 (2010); Brazil Superior Tribunal of Justice, REsp 3.035/EX, Registry 2008/0044435-0, Minister Fernando Gonçalves, published 20 May 2009: in the Superior Tribunal's view the choice of Swiss Law as the applicable substantive law to the contract and the Arbitral Tribunal subsequent decision to apply the CISG as integral part of the Swiss National Law did not oppose the Brazilian Public Order; despite the fact that Brazil is not a CISG Member State (May 2009), regardless of whether the application of the CISG resulted from the application of the Conflict of Law rules or the from the parties' direct choice, because the possibility is in line with Brazil Art. 2 AL.

[65] US Court of Appeals for the Fifth Circuit, 11 June 2003 - No. 02-20166 in CLOUT Abstract No. 575; ICC Final Award Case No. 13741 *Lex Contractus* CISG and Italian and Colombian Laws.

[66] Chile Supreme Court, *Sala* 1, *Rol* 1782-2007, 22 September 2008: upholding that the parties had impliedly excluded the application of the CISG as both parties based their pleadings exclusively on the Chilean Civil Code and the Code of Commerce provisions.

[67] Argentina National Commercial Court of Appeals, *Mayer Alejandro v. Onda Hofferle GmbH & Co.*, 21 April 2000 in CLOUT Abstract No. 701: the Court noted that, according to Argentine private international law, the contract is governed by the law of the place where the main obligation, *i.e.* the delivery of the charcoal, has to be performed. Given that the parties had agreed on 'FOB Buenos Aires', the main obligation had to be performed in Argentina, leading to the application of Argentine law. Hence, the Court concluded that the CISG was applicable pursuant to Article 1(1)(b); Argentina National Commercial Court of Appeals, *Cervecería y Maltería Paysandú S.A. v. Cervecería Argentina S.A.*, 21 July 2002 in CLOUT Abstract No. 636: the Court upheld that the CISG applied to the case by virtue of its Article 1 (1) (b), since

applied to, for example, Brazilian parties whose counter-parties are very often CISG Contracting States.[68]

the Argentinean rules of private international law pointed to the application of the law of Argentina, a contracting state of the CISG and regardless Uruguay, the seller place of business, was not yet a Contracting State to the Convention at the time the contract was concluded.

68 I. Dolganov, & M. Boff, *A Case for Brazil's Adhesion to the 1980 UN Convention on Contracts for the International Sale of Goods*, 13(2) The Vindobona Journal of International Commercial Law and Arbitration 351, at 355, 356 (2009).

Chapter 6

Goods

1. General Notions of Goods

1.1. Notion

The goods constitute the content of the main obligation of the seller,[1] and consequently, the Ibero-American laws establish the requirements and limits for the sale of certain goods. The literal translation of the word 'goods' in Spanish is '*los bienes*' but this is rarely used in the context of the Civil Code. Instead, the Ibero-American laws use the equivalent to the word 'things', this is '*las cosas*'. In the context of the CISG and under many Ibero-American Codes of Commerce, the term '*las mercaderías*' is used as the equivalent to the English term 'the goods'.

The above being said, the general principle in all the Ibero-American laws is that all types of goods can be sold; provided such is not prohibited by the law.[2] This means that, any prohibition to sell a specific type of goods must be expressly referenced in the law, because absent a prohibition, all goods can be sold.[3] Express prohibition to sell certain types of goods may be found in special laws.

Generally speaking, all tangible or intangible items susceptible to have value, or susceptible to be the object of individual rights, are things.[4] Some

---

1 *See* Ch. 34.

2 Argentina Art. 1327 CC; Bolivia Art. 593 CC; Chile Art. 1810 CC; Colombia Art. 1866 CC; Ecuador Art. 1776 CC; El Salvador Art. 1614 CC; Guatemala Art. 443 CC; Mexico Art. 747 CC; Peru Art. 882 CC; Spain Art. 1.271 CC; Uruguay Art. 1668 CC.

3 *See* Argentina: R. Compagnucci de Caso, Contrato de Compraventa 89 (2007); Peru: M. Castillo Freyre, El bien materia del contrato de compraventa: algunas consideraciones preliminares sobre el contrato de compraventa y estudio del capitulo segundo de dicho contrato en el código civil 124-125 (1995).

4 Argentina Art. 2312 CC; Bolivia Art. 74 CC; Costa Rica Art. 258 CC; El Salvador Art. 560

Ibero-American codes define tangible things as those which can be perceived by the senses, like a house, a book, and intangible as those consisting of mere rights, like the credits.[5]

In Argentina, scholars have agreed on the fact that only the material (tangible) things which are susceptible to having an economic value can be sold.[6] This notion is taken from a provision on the Civil Codes' general rules on goods[7] and the correlation that exists between these and the specific rules on sales. In this sense, in Argentina, the goods must be tangible, because intangible goods such as rights may be assigned but not sold.[8]

Although in both the sale of goods and the assignment of rights or credits the object of the contract is to transfer the property of the tangible or intangible item respectively, the distinction has practical implications since most Civil Codes contain specific rules for the assignment of rights and credits that may exclude or modify the application of the rules on sales.[9] However, the rules of assignment of intangibles often refer back to the rules on sales.[10] For example, in order to establish who can assign and who cannot.[11] This creates interplay between the rules of sales and assignments, which may not be always easy to keep on track.

However, in most other jurisdictions the solution is different. Many Civil Codes expressly establish that all tangible and intangible goods can be sold.[12] Thus, goods that can be sold may also include rights, inventions, credits, inheritances, *etc.*[13]

CC; Honduras Art. 599 CC; Panama Art. 324 CC; Paraguay Arts. 1872, 1873 CC; Portugal Art. 202 CC; Uruguay Art. 460 CC; Venezuela Art. 525 CC.

5 Chile Art. 566 CC; Colombia Art. 653 CC; Costa Rica Art. 258 CC; Ecuador Art. 602 CC; Honduras Art. 599 CC; Uruguay Art. 471 CC.

6 Argentina Art. 2311 CC; *see also* Argentina: Compagnucci de Caso, *supra* note 3, at 89.

7 Argentina Art. 2311 CC.

8 Though, in Argentina for example, the energy and the natural forces susceptible of appropriation can be sold Argentina Art. 2311 CC.

9 *See for example* Argentina Art. 1434 *et seq.* CC; Chile Art. 1901 *et seq.* CC; Costa Rica Art. 1101 *et seq.* CC.

10 *See for example* Costa Rica Art. 1103 CC: declaring that the assignment performed by means of a price determined in money, is governed by the same principles of the sale of tangible goods.

11 *See for example* Argentina Arts. 1439, 1441 CC.

12 Chile Art. 1810 CC; Colombia Art. 1866 CC; Ecuador Art. 1776 CC; El Salvador Art. 1614 CC; Paraguay Art. 142 CC; Spain Arts. 1.464, 462 CC; Uruguay Art. 460 CC; Venezuela Art. 1.490 CC; the following Civil Codes establish that, within the definition of sales, rights can also be transferred: Bolivia Art. 584 CC; Mexico Art. 2248 CC; Portugal Art. 874 CC; ICC Final Award Case No. 11570 *Lex Contractus* Portuguese Law: the Sole Arbitrator agreed that by virtue of the sales contract the shares or rights are transferred to the buyer in accordance to the transferring effect of the sales contract under Art. 874 of the Portuguese Civil Code.

13 Bolivia: W. Kaune Arteaga, Curso de Derecho Civil, Contratos, Vol. 2, 33 (1996); Mexico: R. De Pina, Elementos de Derecho Civil Mexicano, Contratos en Particular, Vol. IV, 25 (2007): noting that under Mexican Federal District Civil Code both goods and rights can be sold.

1.2. Goods Characteristics

1.2.1. Classification

1.2.1.1. Movables and Immovable

By their nature goods are movable or immovable.[14] Movable things are those that can be transported from a place to another, by moving themselves, like animals or by an external force, like all the inanimate things,[15] the copyrights,[16] etc. Immovable goods could be, for example, real estate, the Earth and everything naturally or artificially adhered to it, the hydrocarbon mines, deposits, the lakes, the springs, and the water reservoirs.[17] Immovable goods are out of the scope of the CISG and also of this work. However, reference to statutory law and case law regarding the sale of immovable will be made whenever the same legal principle applies to movables, *i.e.* to goods.

1.2.1.2. Fungible and Non-fungibles

Movable goods are also fungible or non-fungible.[18] Fungible goods are those in which all individuals of the species are equivalent to other individuals of the same species, and thus, can be replaced by another of the same quality and in equal amount.[19] The non-fungible cannot be replaced by others of the same qualities.[20] In a subjective approach the Honduran Civil Code establishes that things are presumed fungible when the contractors consider them like equivalents.[21] Non-fungible goods are those that do not have the attributes or condition of equivalence expressed for fungibles.[22]

---

[14] Argentina Art. 2313 CC; Bolivia Art. 75 CC; Chile Art. 566 CC; Colombia Art. 654 CC; Costa Rica Art. 253 CC; Cuba Art. 46 (1) CC; Ecuador Art. 603 CC; El Salvador Art. 560 CC; El Salvador Art. 566 CC; Guatemala Art. 442 CC; Honduras Art. 600 CC; Mexico Art. 752 CC; Paraguay Arts. 1874, 1880 CC; Portugal Art. 203 CC; Spain Art. 333 CC; Uruguay Art. 461 CC; Venezuela Art. 525 CC.

[15] Chile Art. 567 CC; Colombia Art. 655 CC; Ecuador Art. 604 CC.

[16] Mexico Art. 758 CC.

[17] Bolivia Art. 75 CC: the natural energies controlled by the man are included among the movables; Cuba Art. 46 (1) CC.

[18] Argentina Art. 2324 CC; Bolivia Art. 78 CC; Chile Art. 575 CC; Colombia Art. 663 CC; Costa Rica Art. 257 CC; Mexico Art. 763 CC; Portugal Art. 203 CC; Spain Art. 337 CC.

[19] Argentina Art. 2324 CC; Guatemala Art. 454 CC; Mexico Art. 763 CC; Paraguay Art. 1884 CC.

[20] Guatemala Art. 454 CC; Mexico Art. 763 CC.

[21] Honduras Art. 600 CC.

[22] Honduras Art. 600 CC.

1.2.2. Legal Requirements

The goods must fulfil some additional characteristics so that the contract of sale is valid. Some codes expressly enumerate the three main characteristics: first, goods must be of licit trade;[23] second, they must be determined or determinable; third, goods must exist or must be susceptible to exist in future.[24] These requirements will be reviewed in more detail in the next paragraphs. As to the sale of goods which are not the property of the seller, this question has different solutions in the Ibero-American laws. The issue does not only concern the obligation of the seller to transfer goods free of third party rights, but also the problem of the transfer of title by non-owners. The answer is not easy since the laws gather in different groups based on different historical approaches, which this work further reviews.[25]

1.2.2.1. Goods of Commerce

The goods in the commerce are those whose transfer is not expressly prohibited or subject to a public authorisation.[26] In order to know which goods can be traded, one would normally need to go back to the general principles on the object of obligations and contracts of the Civil Codes.[27] Such is the method of most of the Ibero-American Civil Codes.[28] One can generally include, for example: 1) goods that are out of the trade because they belong to the State or the Society;[29] 2) goods that are part of inheritances with express prohibition of transfer, and;[30] 3) goods owned in conjunct ownership and/or with express prohibition of transfer, *etc.*[31]

---

[23] *See for example* provisions declaring that the sale of goods which are out-of-trade is illegal and causes the absolute invalidity of the contract; Chile Arts. 1464 (1), 1682 CC; Colombia Arts. 1521 (1), 1741 CC; Ecuador Arts. 1507, 1725 CC; El Salvador Arts. 1335 (1), 1552 CC; *see also* Ch. 19, 2.

[24] Chile Art. 1461 CC; Colombia Art. 1518 CC; Ecuador Art. 1504 CC; El Salvador Art. 1332 CC; Mexico Art. 1825 CC; Panama Art. 1122 CC; Peru Art. 1532 CC; Venezuela Arts. 1.155, 1.156 CC; *see also* Bolivia: Kaune Arteaga, *supra* note 13, at 33; El Salvador: A.O. Miranda, De la Compraventa 122-124 (1996); Mexico: B. Perez Fernandez del Castillo, Contratos Civiles 92 (2008); Spain: M. Medina de Lemus, Derecho Civil: Obligaciones y Contratos II, Contratos en Particular, Vol. 2 39 (2004); Venezuela: J. L. Aguilar Gorrondona, Contratos y Garantias: Derecho Civil IV 202 (2008).

[25] *See* Ch. 46.

[26] Argentina Art. 2336 CC; Guatemala Art. 444 CC; Mexico Arts. 748, 749 CC; Paraguay Art. 1896 CC; Portugal Art. 202 (II) CC; *see also* El Salvador: Miranda, *supra* note 24, at 122.

[27] *See for example* Paraguay Art. 742 CC establishes a list of goods that cannot sold.

[28] *See for example* Argentina Arts. 953, 1167-1179 CC.

[29] *See* Argentina Arts. 2339-2341 CC; Ecuador Art. 623 CC; El Salvador Art. 571 CC; *see also* Venezuela: Aguilar Gorrondona, *supra* note 24, at 204.

[30] *See for example* Argentina Art. 2613 CC; Bolivia Art. 1005 CC.

[31] *See* Argentina Arts. 2693, 1364 CC; Bolivia Arts. 170, 1006 CC; Chile Art. 1812 CC;

In addition, many special laws, for example, domestic laws which control the sale of cultural goods[32] or arms,[33] and that are commonly based on the protection of the social interest, may establish further prohibitions.

1.2.2.2. Ascertained or Ascertainable Goods

Goods must be ascertained or ascertainable.[34] Some codes establish that goods must be ascertained as far as their species, although not in amount, provided that such can be ascertained.[35] As noted by some scholars, determination of the goods is always necessary, although a definitive determination can be established after the conclusion of the contract.[36] For example, the parties can agree on the sale of USD 1 million Guatemalan Coffee, and although the specific amount of coffee has not been established, there are means to determine the amount *i.e.* due consideration of the kilogram price that coffee with such characteristics has in the national or international market.

But the lack of definitive determination cannot extend beyond the date of performance or delivery of the goods. Yet again, some codes establish the intervention of third parties in order to ascertain the goods.[37] The period during which the goods lack definitive determination has an impact on the rules on the passing of property, since the property does not pass to the buyer until the goods are ascertained and identified in the contract, provided that the buyer is aware of such.[38] It also influences the default rules on the passing of risk since the risk of unascertained goods does not pass to the buyer until they have been measured, weighted or counted, or identified in some way to the contract.[39]

1.2.2.3. Existing Goods

As the sale of goods is by definition a commutative contract, the content of the main obligation of the seller must exist, either at the time of the conclusion of

Colombia Art. 1868 CC; Ecuador Art. 1778 CC; El Salvador Art. 1616 CC; *see also* Bolivia: Kaune Arteaga, *supra* note 13, at 34.

32 *See for example* Peru General Law for the Protection of the Cultural Patrimony, Art. 14.

33 *See* Peru Law No. 25054 of 19 June 1989 on the Fabrication, Commerce and Use of Arms; *see also* Venezuela: Aguilar Gorrondona, *supra* note 24, at 205.

34 Argentina Arts. 1170, 1333 CC; Chile Art. 1461 CC; Colombia Art. 1518 CC; Ecuador Art. 1504 CC; El Salvador Art. 1332 CC; Panama Art. 1124 CC; Paraguay Art. 746 CC; Peru Art. 1532 CC; Spain Art. 1.445 CC; Uruguay Art. 1283 CC; Venezuela Art. 1.155 CC.

35 Argentina Arts. 1170, 1333 CC; Chile Art. 1461 para. 2 CC; Colombia Art. 1518 para. 2 CC; Ecuador Art. 1504 para. 2 CC; El Salvador Art. 1332 para. 2 CC; Spain Art. 1.273 CC; Uruguay Art. 1283 CC; *see also* Mexico: Pérez Fernández del Castillo, *supra* note 24, at 92.

36 Argentina: Compagnucci de Caso, *supra* note 3, at 92; Mexico: De Pina, *supra* note 13, at 25; *see* different authors *in* Peru: Castillo Freyre, *supra* note 3, at 122-123.

37 Argentina Art. 1171 CC.

38 *See* Ch. 45, 3.1.2.

39 *See* Ch. 44, 2.

the contract or in future.[40] Thus, some Ibero-American laws expressly establish that if the goods agreed upon cease to exist, never exist, or are not susceptible to exist at the time of delivery, the sale has no effect.[41] If only part of the goods have perished at the risk of the seller, the buyer is entitled to choose between desisting[42] the contract or claiming the delivery of the remaining goods at a reduced price.[43]

On this point, the doctrine agrees that the part of the goods which perished must be relevant and important, and not simply irrelevant for the interest of the buyer or with no economic impact.[44] Indeed, Colombia's Code of Commerce uses the phrase "if a considerable part of the thing is missing at the time of the contract conclusion…".[45] Otherwise, the buyer may not be entitled to desist from the contract. As in the case of contract avoidance,[46] the judge may determine, on a case by case basis, whether the partial lost of the goods is relevant enough to allow the buyer to desist from the contract.[47]

1.3. Future Goods

On the other hand, the sale of future goods is permitted by the Ibero-American laws.[48] The possibility to sell future goods requires that the parties are aware that the goods do not exist at the time of the conclusion of the contract but that they are susceptible to exist in future.[49] Otherwise there would be a case in

---

40 Argentina Art. 1328 CC; Chile Art. 1461 CC; Colombia Art. 1518 CC; Ecuador Art. 1504 CC; El Salvador Art. 1332 CC; Mexico Art. 1826 CC; Peru Art. 1532 CC; Uruguay Art. 1283 CC; Venezuela Art. 1.485 CC.

41 Argentina Art. 1328 CC; Chile Art. 138 Com C; Colombia Art. 918 Com C; Ecuador Art. 182 Com C; Spain Art. 1.460 CC; Uruguay Art. 1672 CC; Venezuela Art. 1.485 CC; *see also* Peru: Castillo Freyre, *supra* note 3, at 121; Spain: Medina de Lemus, *supra* note 24, at 39.

42 El Salvador: Miranda, *supra* note 24, at 131: noting that the avoidance of the contract is not needed since the conclusion of the contract has been interrupted or in suspense.

43 Argentina Art. 1328 CC; Chile Art. 1814 para. 2 CC; Colombia Art. 1870 para. 2 CC & Art. 918 Com C; Ecuador Art. 1780 para. 2 CC; El Salvador Art. 1618 para. 2 CC; Peru Art. 1533 CC; Spain Art. 1.460 para. 2 CC; Uruguay Art. 1672 para. 2 CC.

44 Argentina: Compagnucci de Caso, *supra* note 3, at 95; El Salvador: Miranda, *supra* note 24, at 131.

45 Colombia Art. 918 Com C.

46 *See* Ch. 53, 1.

47 El Salvador: Miranda, *supra* note 24, at 131.

48 Argentina Arts. 1327, 1168, 1173 CC; Bolivia Art. 594 CC; Chile Art. 1813 CC; Colombia Art. 1869 CC & Art. 917 Com C; Costa Rica Art. 441 Com C; Ecuador Art. 1779 CC; El Salvador Art. 1617 CC; Peru Art. 1409 CC; Portugal Art. 880 CC; Spain Art. 1.271 CC; Venezuela Art. 1.156 CC.

49 El Salvador: Miranda, *supra* note 24, at 123; Peru: Castillo Freyre, *supra* note 3, at 120.

which goods were believed to exist at the time of conclusion but they did not exist in reality, and such a case leaves the sale with no effects.[50]

The laws automatically insert the sales of future goods in one of the two modalities under which such a sale may be entered. On the one hand, the sale of future goods has in principle the characteristics of a commutative contract with a suspensive condition.[51] In a contract for future goods, the contract does not come into force, *i.e.* the property does not pass to the buyer, until the goods exist. In the case of non-fulfilment of a suspensive condition, *i.e.* the future definitive existence of the goods, the contract does not produce effects.[52]

This situation forces the seller to reimburse any payment of the price already performed by the buyer, together with the interest generated.[53] In case of refusal by the seller, the buyer may consider claiming back the money paid through an unjustified enrichment action.[54] Relevant examples include the sale of future crops or vintages that never came into existence. Also common in practice, is the purchase of a complete future production of goods from a manufacturer.

The second type of sale of future goods falls into the modality of aleatory contracts.[55] Most of the Ibero-American laws permit this type of contract. But the sale of future goods can only be classified as an aleatory contract when the parties have so agreed, since this modality is subsidiary to the suspensive condition default rule. In other words, the sale of future goods is in principle conditioned by the existence of the goods, unless the buyer bears the risk of the goods that never come into existence or, that exist defectively or in less quantity.[56]

[50] Chile Art. 1814 CC; Colombia Art. 1870 CC & Art. 918 Com C; Ecuador Art. 1780 CC; El Salvador 1618 CC.

[51] *See* Bolivia Art. 594 CC; Chile Art. 1813 CC; Colombia Art. 1869 CC & Art. 917 Com C; Costa Rica Art. 1059 CC; El Salvador Art. 1617 CC; Peru Art. 1534 CC; Uruguay Art. 1671 CC; *see also* El Salvador: Miranda, *supra* note 24, at 129; Venezuela: Aguilar Gorrondona, *supra* note 24, at 204; *see also* Spain Supreme Tribunal, 31 December 1999 (ar. 9386).

[52] El Salvador: Miranda, *supra* note 24, at 129: Nevertheless, under some laws the sale of future goods is a contract containing an avoidance condition. Under Costa Rica Art. 441 CC the contract on future goods exists from the parties' agreement but if the goods never get to exist the contract is automatically avoided with all the effects of the avoidance; For the effect of the avoidance *see* Ch. 57.

[53] El Salvador: Miranda, *supra* note 24, at 132; For details on interest *see* Ch. 52.

[54] *Id.*; For details on unjustified enrichment *see* Ch. 58.

[55] Spain Supreme Tribunal, 31 December 1999 (ar. 9386).

[56] Argentina Arts. 1332, 1404 CC; Bolivia Art. 594 CC; Chile Art. 1813 CC; Colombia Art. 1869 CC & Art. 917 Com C; Ecuador Art. 1779 CC; El Salvador Art. 1617 CC; Peru Arts. 1535, 1536 CC; Portugal Art. 880 CC; Uruguay Art. 1671 CC.

2. Intangibles

2.1. Companies' Shares and Stock

Companies' shares and stock, although in nature are considered rights, they are also trade objects governed by the rules on commercial contracts[57] and, supplemented by the Civil Code rules.[58] Additionally, in most Ibero-American countries special provisions for the sale of companies, shares and stock are also found in their respective Laws of Companies,[59] and laws of stock market.[60] These laws, together with the Articles of Incorporation,[61] and the legal type of each company, may also have an impact on the general rules on sales contained in both the civil and commercial laws;[62] since they are considered *lex specialis*, and thus, they are applied in priority.

2.2. IP and CR Rights

The transfer of authorship or intellectual rights, such as software copyrights, is specially governed by the Ibero-American intellectual property laws[63] or

[57] Provided they are acquired with the intention make profits: Argentina Art. 451 Com C; Bolivia Art. 6 (3-5) Com C; Chile Art. 3 (2) (12) Com C; Colombia Art. 20 (4) Com C; Costa Rica Arts. 1, 120-139, 148-151 Com C; Ecuador Art. 3 Com C; El Salvador Art. 5 (I) (III) Com C; Guatemala Art. 4 Com C (2); Honduras Art. 4 (I) (II) Com C; Mexico Art. 75 (III) Com C; Portugal Art. 2 Com C; Uruguay Arts. 7 (1), 515 Com C; Venezuela Art. 2 (3) Com C; Mexico: O. Vásquez del Mercado, Contratos Mercantiles 195 (2008); Argentina Supreme Court, *Inversiones y Servicios S.A. v. Estado Nacional Argentino*, 19 August 1999; Spain Supreme Tribunal, 26 November 1987; *Id Cendoj:* 28079110011987101175; Spain Supreme Tribunal, 15 March 1994, *Id Cendoj:* 28079110011994101643; ICC Final Award Case No. 11570 *Lex Contractus* Portuguese Law.

[58] Except in countries like Brazil, Paraguay and Peru where a unified set of rules (Civil Codes) applies to any sale regardless of their civil or commercial character, *see* Ch. 5, 1. For example *see* Paraguay Arts. 1062-1070 CC.

[59] All hereinafter referred as LC: Argentina Law No. 19.550 Companies; Chile Law No. 18.046 Companies; Ecuador Law No. 000. RO/312 of 5 November 1999 Companies; Mexico General Law of Companies of 4 August 1934; Panama Law No. 32 Corporations of 26 February 1927; Peru General Law of Companies No. 26887.

[60] Spain Supreme Tribunal, 26 November 1987; *Id Cendoj:* 28079110011987101175; Spain Supreme Tribunal, 15 March 1994, *Id Cendoj:* 28079110011994101643.

[61] *See for example*, expressly stated in Paraguay Art. 1070 CC; also in Panama Law No. 32 Corporations of 26 February 1927: the issue is addressed in Chapter III Stock whereby the transfer of shares can be freely done by the company (Art. 68) or its members within the limits established in the by-laws or articles of incorporations (Arts. 20-39).

[62] *See* Ch. 21, 3.

[63] All hereinafter cited as IPL: Argentina Intellectual Property Law No. 11.723 of 28 September 1933 (updated) (as amended by Decree-Laws Nos. 12.063/57 and 1.224/58, and Laws Nos. 20.098, 23.741, 24.249, 24.286, 24.870 and 25.036); Ecuador Intellectual Property

copyrights laws.[64] Most of these laws expressly state that the transfer of IP rights or Copyrights is made through assignment.[65] Yet again, this creates an interplay between different provisions; in the first place, between the IP law and the assignments' rules of the Civil Codes; second, between these two and the rules on sales, either civil or commercial, since the rules on assignment often refer back to the rules on sales.[66]

Other IP Laws, expressly call for the use of sales contracts for the exploitation of an author's works.[67] Of course, most copyright laws expressly establish that the rights recognised to the author are independent of the property of the tangible object that contains the work.[68]

3. Special Items

3.1. Livestock

The sale of livestock receives special treatment.[69] For example, in some jurisdictions, the sale of livestock by farmers shall always be governed by

Law No. 83. of 08 May 1998 (Arts. 44-49); El Salvador Law for the Protection of Intellectual Property, Decree No. 604, of 15 July 1993; Spain Law on Intellectual Property, (approved by Royal Legislative Decree 1/1996 of 12 April 1996, and amended by Law 5/1998 of 6 March 1998, incorporating Directive 96/9/EC of the European Parliament and of the Council of 11 March 1996 on the Legal Protection of Databases).

64 All laws hereinafter cited as CRL: Bolivia Copyrights Law Decree No. 24.582 of 25 April 1997; Chile Copyrights Law No. 17.336 (No. 19.166) 28 August 1970 (17 September 1992); Colombia Copyrights Law No. 2 of 28 January 1982; Guatemala Copyrights Law Decree No. 33 (No. 56) of 19 May 1998; Panama Copyrights Law No. 15 of 8 August 1994; Paraguay Law No. 1328/98 on Copyright and Related Rights; Peru Copyrights Law Legislative Decree No. 822; Portugal Code of Copyrights and Related Rights No. 45/85 of 17 September 1985; Uruguay Law No. 9.739 on Copyrights of 17 December 1937; Venezuela Law on Copyrights of 14 August 1993.

65 Argentina Art. 51 IPL; Chile Art. 58 CRL; Colombia Arts. 182-186 CRL (the transfer must be recorded in notary public deed); Costa Rica Art. 89 CRL (declaring that the assignment shall be evidenced by a public or private deed executed before two witnesses); El Salvador Art. 8 IPL; Guatemala Art. 72 CRL (assignment must be in writing); Panama Art. 62 CRL (in writing requirement); Paraguay Art. 9 CRL; Peru Art. 9 CRL; Spain Art. 43 (1) IPL; Venezuela Art. 50 CRL.

66 *See for example* Argentina Arts. 1439, 1441 CC.

67 Ecuador Arts. 44-49 IPL; Mexico Art. 38 CRL & Art. 758 CC; Mexico: Vásquez del Mercado, *supra* note 57, at 191, 192.

68 Bolivia's Art. 3 CRL; Mexico Art. 38 CRL; Panama Art. 1 CRL; Paraguay Art. 3 CRL; Peru Art. 3 CRL Portugal Art. 9 CRL; Spain Art. 2 IPL.

69 For example, in Paraguay the special treatment is recognised in Art. 2070 CC that establishes that the passing of property of cattle will be credited in the form established by the special legislation (Paraguay Rural Code); Peru Art. 1521 CC establishes that the remedies for hidden defects in cattle will be governed by the special laws or by the usages, and absent such by the

the Civil Code's rules. That is, even if farmers perform them with an aim of making a resale profit, they are not granted a B2B character and, hence, the rules of the Code of Commerce would not apply to such transactions.[70] However, if such sales are passed by commercial entities with an aim of profits, such shall be categorised as a B2B sale.[71]

The distinction may have an impact at different levels of the contract, as the Civil Codes usually have specific provisions for the sale of cattle. At the stage of validity some laws establish limitations as to the persons who are permitted to sell cattle.[72] Also, for example, some Civil Codes declare that cattle cannot be traded if they suffer from contagious diseases, as the contrary would cause the invalidity of the contract.[73] The same happens if the animal turns out to be useless to perform the service or use to which they were intended to.[74]

At the performance phase, the standard of conformity of the goods may also vary. If two or more animals are sold jointly, the redhibitory action[75] will progress only for the one affected by defects; unless it appears that the buyer would not have bought the group without all being in conformity.[76] On the other hand, the remedy of contract avoidance does not exist for the sale of cattle passed in fairs or through public auctions.[77]

The sale of livestock also has an impact on the rules on risk and the limitation periods for actions.[78] On the one hand, the risk on the goods may be extended beyond the time of delivery.[79] For example, some codes establish that if cattle dies within the first three days of delivery, the seller will be liable, whenever the disease that caused the death existed before the contract.[80] On the other hand, redhibitory actions based on hidden defects have shorter limitation periods if the goods consist of cattle. For example, some laws establish a forty

rules of the Civil Code; Uruguay Art. 1727 CC refers to the Rural Code No. 10.024 in order to determine the limitation periods in the sale of cattle.

70 Argentina Art. 452 (3) Com C; Bolivia 8 (1) Com C; Colombia Art. 23 (4) Com C; Ecuador 3 (1) Com C; El Salvador Art. 1013 (II) Com C.

71 *See* Ch. 5, 1.

72 Argentina Arts. 298, 443 CC.

73 Guatemala Art. 1568 CC; Honduras Art. 1653 CC; Panama Art. 1265 CC; Spain Art. 1.494 CC.

74 Guatemala Art. 1568 CC; Honduras Art. 1653 CC; Panama Art. 1265 CC; Spain Art. 1.494 CC.

75 For details about the redhibitory remedies *see* Ch. 47, 1.

76 Honduras Art. 1650 CC; México Art. 2150 CC; Panama Art. 1262 CC; Spain Art. 1.491 CC.

77 Guatemala Art. 1569 CC; Honduras Art. 1652 CC; Panama Art. 1264 CC; Peru Art. 1522 CC; Spain Art. 1.493 CC.

78 *See* the general rules for other types of goods in Ch. 60.

79 *See* the general rules on risk for other types of goods in Ch. 44.

80 Honduras Art. 1656 CC; Mexico Art. 2153 CC; Panama Art. 1268 CC; Spain Art. 1.497 CC.

day limitation period to claim any redhibitory right, starting from the date of its delivery to the buyer.[81] The Mexican code is stricter with only twenty days from the date of contract conclusion.[82]

3.2. Ships and Vessels

In some Ibero-American countries, the sales of vessels and aircrafts are subject to the provisions of the Codes of Commerce;[83] irrespective of whether they are entered for profit purposes, personal use or are passed by a merchant under the definition of the codes.[84] Also under many laws the sale of vessels is subject to special formalities, for example, writing and registration requirements.[85]

On the other hand, the Bolivian law characterises ships, vessels and aircraft as movable goods in the Civil Code and the Code of Commerce.[86] The application of either of these sets of rules may depend on whether they are acquired for profit purposes (reselling) or personal use.[87] In Mexico, ships and vessels of all sorts are considered movable goods by the Civil Code.[88] Thus, they are susceptible to be sold under its rules.

Additional requirements may be established by the Navigation and Maritime Laws.[89]

---

81 Honduras Art. 1655 CC; Panama Art. 1267 CC clarifying that the time could be further reduced or extended according to the local usage; Spain Art. 1.496 CC clarifying that the time could be further reduced or extended according to the local usage; Venezuela Art. 1.525 CC.

82 Mexico Art. 2155 CC.

83 Argentina Art. 8 (7) Com C; Costa Rica Art. 438 (c) Com C; Ecuador Art. 3 (12) Com C; Honduras Art. 4 (III) Com C; Venezuela Art. 2 (18) Com C.

84 *See* Ch. 5.

85 Colombia Art. 97 Com C: declaring that the sale of aircraft and vessels must be registered before the Administrative Department of National Statistics; Guatemala Art. 1125 CC: the property titles of ships have to be registered in the Property Registry; Venezuela Art. 614 Com C: sales of vessels are passed by public deed.

86 Bolivia Art. 1396 CC & Art. 898 Com C.

87 *See* Ch. 5, 1.

88 Mexico Art. 756 CC.

89 For example Mexico's Navigation and Maritime Commerce Law of April 2006.

Chapter 7

Identifying the Boundaries of a Sales Contract

1. General Remarks

Generally, most of the Ibero-American Civil Codes share the basic definition of sale contained in Article 1582 of the French Civil Code of 1804: "A sale is an agreement by which one person binds himself to deliver a thing, and another to pay for it."[1] And even if different elements have been added to the definition of sale in many Ibero-American laws,[2] in essence the contract of sale remains the same. It is comprised of the agreement on the two main obligations of the parties: the delivery of goods and the payment of a price.[3]

1 Argentina Art. 1323 CC & Art. 450 Com C; Bolivia Art. 584 CC; Brazil Art. 481 CC; Chile Art. 1793 CC; Colombia Art. 1849 CC & Art. 905 Com C; Costa Rica Art. 1049 CC; Cuba Art. 334 CC; Ecuador Art. 1759 CC; El Salvador Art. 1597 CC; Guatemala Art. 1790 CC; Honduras Art. 1605 CC; Mexico Art. 2248 CC; Nicaragua Art. 2530 CC; Panama Art. 1215 CC; Paraguay Art. 737 CC; Peru Art. 1529 CC; Portugal Art. 874 CC; Spain Art. 1.445 CC; Uruguay Art. 1661 CC & Art. 513 Com C; Venezuela Art. 1474 CC.

2 For example, most civil or commercial codes establish that the price most be paid in money; *see* Argentina Art. 1323 CC; Bolivia Art. 584 CC; Brazil Art. 481 CC; Chile Art. 1793 CC; Colombia Art. 1849 CC & Art. 905 Com C; Cuba Art. 334 CC; Ecuador Art. 1759 CC; El Salvador Art. 1597 CC; Guatemala Art. 1790 CC; Mexico Art. 2248 CC; Paraguay Art. 737 CC; Peru Art. 1529 CC; Uruguay Art. 1661 CC. The laws that do not specify that payment of the price is in money are: Costa Rica Art. 1049 CC; Nicaragua Art. 2530 CC; Portugal Art. 874 CC; Venezuela Art. 1474 Com C. While some state that the price can be paid in money or other sign (signo): Honduras Art. 1605 CC; Panama Art. 1215 CC; Spain Art. 1.445 CC. And also some laws have established that the object of the sale is the delivery or transfer of goods: Colombia Art. 905 Com C; but many others establish that rights can also transferred by the contract of sale: Bolivia Art. 584 CC; Mexico Art. 2248 CC; Portugal Art. 874 CC; ICC Final Award Case No. 11570 *Lex Contractus* Portuguese Law.

3 *See* Ch. 34 and Ch. 41.

However, some intended sale agreements may go beyond the definition of the contract of sale. The parties may have, intentionally or unintentionally, added some elements which make the contract difficult to be exclusively categorised as a sale. Complex describable boundaries may have an impact in the exclusive application of sales rules. The fine line dividing contracts of sale and barter is the most well-known example of this. But it is also difficult to discern between contracts of sale and of goods to be manufactured. Similar difficulties arise in contracts for supply of goods and services, where the rules on sales may interplay with the rules on services contracts. Finally, the principles of sales contracts may also subsidiary apply to turnkey contracts. In this chapter, the boundaries that separate the application of the Ibero-American rules on sales from similar or often integrated contracts will be examined.

2. Barter and Sale

The Ibero-American laws take five different approaches to determine the rules applicable to transactions that involve the payment of the merchandise in part with goods and in part with money. In other words, five different solutions regarding the applicable rules for barter-sale mixed contracts are provided.

Within the first group there are those Civil Codes which consider that when the price consists partially of money and partially of another good, the contract will be considered to be one of barter if the goods are worth more than the money; and of sale when the money is equal or greater than the value of the good. Thus, the rules on barter shall apply in priority to such mixed contracts when the goods are worth more than the money; and the rules on sales shall apply when the money is equal or greater than the value of the goods.[4]

In the second group one may find a single country. Paraguay's Civil Code establishes that if the price consists partially of money and partially of the another good, the contract will be considered of barter, if the value of the good is equal or greater than the value in money, and of sale in the opposite case.[5] The difference between this and the first group approach is small. The rules of barter shall prevail over the sales rules when the value of the goods is equal or greater than the value in money. Whilst in the first group the equal value of the goods is not enough to trigger the application of the barter rules.

The third group of Civil Codes has established that the mixed contracts where the price of the sale consists partly of money and partly of another thing,

---

[4] Argentina Art. 1356 CC; Chile Art. 1794 CC; Colombia Art. 1850 CC & Art. 905 para. 2 Com C; Ecuador Art. 1760 CC; El Salvador Art. 1598 CC; Guatemala Art. 1853 CC; Mexico Art. 2250 CC; *see also* Mexico Supreme Court, *Séptima Época, Tercera Sala,* Registry No. 241287, SJF 87 Part 4, at 17. *See also* Bolivia: V. Camargo Marín, Derecho Comercial Boliviano 404 (2007).

[5] Paraguay Art. 756 CC.

shall be categorised according to the manifest intention of the parties.[6] In this sense, it does not matter what is the amount of the price partially paid with the goods exchanged or the value of the money paid in consideration. However, in cases of absence of manifest intention, the solution provided by this group of Civil Codes is equal to that proposed by the first group mentioned above.[7]

The Civil Code of Peru itself is a subgroup, which contains the same default principle as the third group.[8] But, contrary to the other Civil Codes belonging to the third group, the Peruvian Civil Code states that in cases where the intention of the parties is not clearly manifested the solution given by the second group[9] shall be considered.[10]

As a fourth group, we find those Ibero-American Civil Codes that because of a lack of elaborate rules relating to the contract of barter, the rules on sales apply to mixed contracts of barter-sale and also to the contract of barter alone.[11] Under this approach each party will be considered as seller of the thing that he delivers, and the price of the goods exchanged on the date of the contract will be the price that each party paid as consideration.[12]

Finally, the fifth group of codes is composed by those that do not expressly provide a solution for such mixed contracts. Also there is neither a provision establishing where these sorts of contracts should be categorised nor which specific rules shall apply. These codes are characterised by having a complete set of rules for the contract of barter. In their barter rules they indirectly refer to the application of the contract of sale rules as a complement, provided they are pertinent or compatible with the barter provisions.[13]

3. Contracts for Goods to be Manufactured

None of the Ibero-American Civil Codes or Codes of Commerce contain provisions regarding the contracts of sale of goods to be manufactured within the contract of sales provisions. However, different solutions are given to

6 Honduras Art. 1606 CC; Nicaragua Art. 2536 CC; Panama Art. 1216 CC; Spain Art. 1446 CC.

7 Honduras Art. 1606 CC; Nicaragua Art. 2536 CC; Panama Art. 1216 CC.

8 Peru Art. 1536 CC.

9 The second group is form by Paraguay Art. 756 CC.

10 Peru Art. 1536 CC.

11 Brazil Art. 533 CC; Costa Rica Art. 1100 CC; Mexico Art. 388 Com C: provides that the provisions regarding the contract of sale are applicable to the B2B barter, except when such contradicts the nature of the barter.

12 Expressly stated in Costa Rica Art. 1100 CC.

13 Cuba Art. 370 CC; Bolivia Art. 654 CC; Venezuela Art. 1.563 CC.

govern such contracts. Most of the Ibero-American Civil Codes expressly[14] or impliedly[15] allow the agreement of the parties on mixed contracts.

Additionally, some laws expressly give an answer as to the applicable rules to mixed contracts. For example, Mexico's Civil Code states that contracts that are not specifically regulated by the law will be governed by the general rules of contracts; by the stipulations of the parties, and by the provisions of the type of contract with which they have a closest analogy.[16] On this issue, a Mexican Collegiate Tribunal has sustained that when an agreement focuses in the work carried out by one party, based on models or designs provided by the other party, we are in front of a contract called *obra a precio alzado*;[17] the main purpose of which is to execute a work, and not before a contract of sale-whose purpose is the transfer of the property of the goods in consideration of a price in monetary terms.[18]

A complex integration and partition of rules is proposed by the Cuban Civil Code. This provides that the integrated contractual relations, totally or partially, by elements regarding diverse particular contracts, are governed by the provisions of these contracts, provided they do not contradict the specific character of each contract and the joint aim of the mixed contract.[19]

A second solution is proposed by those laws whose related contract provisions, such as those in the Contract of Work or the Leasing of Work and Services, re-*envoi* to the application of the sales or services rules. Under these countries if the main material is provided by the person who has ordered the work (buyer), providing the creator the rest (seller), the contract is of lease or work; in the opposite case, the contract is of sale of goods.[20] In this last case, the presumed sale is not concluded, and the risk on the goods does not pass, except by the approval of the party who ordered the work (buyer), unless he has been delayed in declaring whether he approves it or not.[21]

---

[14] Cuba Arts. 314, 315 CC; Mexico Art. 1858 CC; Honduras Art. 712 CC; Portugal Art. 405 CC.

[15] Argentina Art. 1143 CC; Bolivia Art. 451 CC; Chile Art. 1438 CC; Costa Rica Art. 629 CC; Ecuador Art. 1481 CC; El Salvador Art. 1309 CC; Nicaragua Art. 1830 CC; Panama Arts. 1105, 1106 CC; Paraguay Art. 463 CC; Spain Arts. 1.254, 1.255 CC; Uruguay Art. 1260 CC; Venezuela Art. 1.140 CC.

[16] Mexico Art. 1858 CC.

[17] Meaning contract of work for a fixed price.

[18] Mexico Collegiate Tribunals, *Novena Época,* Registry 195'508, SJF VIII, September 1998, at 1154: consequently, if the parties agreed that one of them will manufacture publicity banners with material of the other party's property, it should be concluded that the contract is one of work for a fixed price, and not a sale of goods.

[19] Cuba Art. 315 CC.

[20] Chile Art. 1996 CC; Ecuador Art. 1481 CC; El Salvador Art. 1784 CC; Honduras Art. 1762 CC; Nicaragua Art. 3044 CC.

[21] Chile Art. 1996 CC; Ecuador Art. 1481 CC; El Salvador Art. 1784 CC; Honduras Art. 1762 CC; Nicaragua Art. 3044 CC.

Under CISG Article 3, contracts for the supply of goods to be manufactured or produced are to be considered sales, provided that the party who orders the goods undertakes to supply a substantial part of the materials necessary for such manufacture or production. According to the CISG Advisory Council, the words 'substantial part' should not be quantified *a priori* in percentages based on the economic value of such part.[22] A case-by-case analysis is preferable and thus it should be determined on the basis of an overall assessment.[23]

In an interesting case submitted before an ICC Arbitral Tribunal, the buyer was required to supply the components listed in Schedule A of the Agreement. Therefore, the question before the Tribunal was whether the components were considered to be "a substantial part of the materials necessary for such manufacture or production". The Arbitral Tribunal's point of view was that, the fact that the object of the agreement was the assembly of the vehicles and, the definition of the 'Vehicles' corresponded to the description in Schedule B and the latter included the main elements of Schedule A, hence, the components to be provided by the buyer should be considered as 'substantial' because they were necessary for the product to be considered as a 'vehicle' under the agreement.[24]

4. Contracts for Supply and Services

Most Ibero-American countries have established definitions on contracts of services within the provisions of their respective Civil Codes.[25] Most Ibero-American Civil Codes considered the contract of services within the category of lease contracts.[26] In many Civil Codes, a lease is a contract in which the two parties are obliged reciprocally, one to grant the enjoyment of goods, or to execute a work or to render a service, and the other to pay a price for it.[27]

---

[22] CISG-AC, Opinion No. 4, Contracts for the Sale of Goods to Be Manufactured or Produced and Mixed Contracts (Art. 3 CISG), 24 October 2004. Rapporteur: Professor Pilar Perales Viscasillas, Comment 2.9.

[23] *Id.*

[24] ICC Final Award Case No. 11256 *Lex Contractus* Mexican Law: therefore, the Arbitral Tribunal was of the view that the agreement was out of the scope of application of the CISG and instead should be governed by the laws of Mexico as agreed in the agreement.

[25] Argentina Art. 1623 CC; Brazil Art. 594 CC; Chile Art. 1915 CC; Colombia Art. 1973 CC; Cuba Art. 320 CC; Ecuador Art. 1833 CC; El Salvador Art. 1703 CC; Honduras Art. 1681 CC; Nicaragua Art. 2810 CC; Panama Art. 1296 CC; Paraguay Art. 846 CC; Peru Art. 1764 CC; Portugal Art. 1154 CC; Spain Art. 1544 CC; Uruguay Art. 1776 CC; Venezuela Art. 1630 CC.

[26] Chile Art. 1915 CC; Colombia Art. 1973 CC; Cuba Art. 320 CC; Ecuador Art. 1833 CC; El Salvador Art. 1703 CC; Honduras Art. 1681 CC; Nicaragua Art. 2810 CC; Panama Art. 1296 CC; Peru Art. 1764 CC; Spain Art. 1544 CC; Uruguay Art. 1776 CC.

[27] Chile Art. 1915 CC; Colombia Art. 1973 CC; Ecuador Art. 1833 CC; El Salvador Art. 1703 CC; Honduras Art. 1681 CC; Nicaragua Art. 2810 CC; Panama Art. 1294 CC; Peru Art. 1764 CC Spain Art. 1544 CC; Uruguay Art. 1776 CC.

The Ibero-American laws provide different solutions to contracts for the sale of goods that include the rendering of a service or work over the goods. First, Nicaragua's Civil Code expressly states that the rules on sales regarding the agreement of the parties, the price, consent and other essential requirements shall apply to the lease of services.[28] At least on that part of the contract, the rules are uniform, thus, no contradiction or difficulty on the applicable provisions is faced.

A second solution is provided by those codes which establish that whenever the sale of goods involves a service, no matter to what extent, such transaction will be covered by the rules of services.[29]

A third solution is found in those already mentioned countries whose rules on Contracts of Work provide for the application of sales or service provisions in some circumstances.[30] If the service indeed constitutes a work, a recurrent provision establishes that whenever the creator provides the material for the preparation of a material work, the contract is of sale; but such contract is not concluded, except by the approval of the party who ordered the work.[31]

Fourth, the Peruvian law proposes a similar solution as the one contained in the CISG. A provision in the Civil Code establishes that the rules on the supply of services shall be applied when the supplier of services provides the materials, provided these do not constitute the predominant part.[32] On the contrary, such agreement shall be governed by the provisions on sales.

The last solution is found in the Ibero-American countries' laws which expressly or impliedly allow mixed contracts.[33] As mentioned before, some jurisdictions will propose to apply the provisions of the type of contract with which they have a closest analogy.[34]

A comparable conclusion was reached by an ICC Arbitral Tribunal.[35] The Tribunal referred to a rule developed by the Brazilian doctrine and case law under which the assessment of the preponderant elements over the rest of the contract's elements permits one to distinguish the true nature of the contract. In the case at stake, the seller was under the obligation to supply three turbo-compressors plus services consisting of the supervision of the turbo

---

28 Nicaragua Art. 2811 CC.

29 Argentina Art. 1623 CC; Bolivia Art. 736 CC; Cuba Art. 323.1 CC: Cuba's Civil Code contains special provisions for the contracts of services that required the delivery of a thing, thus, the rules on sales contracts are placed in a subsidiary position behind this *lex specialis*.

30 *See supra* 3.

31 Chile Art. 1996 CC; Ecuador Art. 1481 CC; El Salvador Art. 1784 CC; Honduras Art. 1762 CC; Nicaragua Art. 3044 CC.

32 Peru Arts. 1770, 1764-1769 CC: title applicable norms when the supplier of services provides materials.

33 Cuba Arts. 314, 315 CC; Mexico Art. 1858 CC; Honduras Art. 712 CC; Portugal Art. 405 CC.

34 Mexico Art. 1858 CC; Spain Supreme Tribunal, 7 December 2006, *Id Cendoj:* 28079110012006101236.

35 ICC Final Award Case No. 13458 *Lex Contractus* Brazilian Law and INCOTERMS 2000.

compressors' installation in a designated oil-platform. The Arbitral Tribunal noted that even though the parties agreed to a 'lump sum' price which included the whole group of obligations, the contract showed that the price was "*based on delivery CIF Quebec*," that the parties named their contract 'supply of compressors' and called themselves supplier and purchaser respectively. After due consideration of such elements the Tribunal found it evident that the supply of the turbo-compressors was the principal obligation, while the obligation to supervise the installation of these and their respective warranty was accessory; thus the nature of the contract was a sale of goods contract to which the rules on sales of the Brazilian law should apply.[36]

Article 3 of the CISG does not apply to contracts in which the preponderant part of the obligations of the party who furnishes the goods consists in the supply of labour or other services. According to the opinion of the CISG Advisory Council,[37] the word 'preponderant' should not be quantified by predetermined percentages of values, but on the basis of an overall assessment.

5. Turnkey Contracts

In all the Ibero-American Civil Codes special provisions are established for contracts where the supply of labour mixes with the delivery of goods. In the Ibero-American jurisdictions these contracts have been named in many different ways.[38] These types of contract are basically the equivalent of turnkey contracts.[39] All these contracts share a basic principle: the obligation of contractor to provide its work, knowledge or skills in an activity that may involve goods or materials.[40] However, the basic obligations of contractor and client differ in some jurisdictions. The boundaries between these types of contracts and those reviewed above are not always clear. In the following paragraphs, we present the distinctive characteristics of each approach.

On the one hand, in some Ibero-American countries, unless otherwise agreed, the default rule imposes upon the contractor the obligation to provide

36 ICC Final Award Case No. 13458 *Lex Contractus* Brazilian Law and INCOTERMS 2000.

37 CISG-AC Opinion 4, *supra* note 22, Comment 3.4.

38 For example in Argentina, Chile, Colombia, Ecuador, El Salvador, Honduras, Nicaragua such are *Contrato de Locacion de Obra a Precio Alzado*; in Bolivia *Contrato de Obra*; in Brazil *Contratos de empreitada*; in Costa Rica *Contrato de Obra por Ajuste o Precio Alzado*.

39 Spanish name for turnkey contracts is called *contrato mano en llave*.

40 Argentina Art. 1629 CC; Bolivia Art. 732 CC; Brazil Art. 610 CC; Chile Art. 2003 CC; Colombia Art. 2053 CC; Costa Rica Art. 1183 CC; Cuba Art. 323.1 CC; Ecuador Art. 1964 CC; El Salvador Art. 1791 CC; Guatemala Art. 2000 CC; Honduras Art. 1769 CC; Mexico Art. 2616 CC; Nicaragua Art. 3034 CC; Panama Art. 1340 CC; Paraguay Art. 852 CC; Peru Art. 1773 CC; Portugal Art. 1210 CC; Spain Art. 1588 CC; Uruguay Art. 1840 CC; Venezuela Art. 1630 CC.

the material.[41] On the other hand, some codes establish that, unless otherwise agreed, by default the client always provides the materials.[42]

In many Civil Codes though, there is no fixed default rules as to which of the parties must provide the material for the work. Their provisions limit themselves to recognising that the parties can freely agree to extend the obligations of the contractor and the client. A recurrent provision in these laws states that the execution of a work can be contracted by agreeing that the one who executes it (being the contractor) provides only its work or its industry, or that also provides the materials.[43]

In Paraguay, once the delivery of the work takes place, the rules on sales contracts shall apply.[44] Also interesting is that the agreed obligation of the contractor to provide the materials has an impact on the rules of the passing of title. The transfer of property will be verified by the reception of the finished work and not by the mere agreement of the parties of the contract.[45]

[41] Brazil Art. 610 CC; Mexico Art. 2616 CC; Portugal Art. 1210 CC.

[42] Bolivia Art. 736 CC except for different usages during that time; Cuba Art. 323 1 CC; Paraguay Art. 852 CC; Peru Art. 1173 CC.

[43] Argentina Art. 1629 CC; Panama Art. 1340 CC; Spain Art. 1518 CC; Uruguay Art. 1840 CC; Venezuela Art. 1630 CC.

[44] Paraguay Art. 853 CC.

[45] Paraguay Art. 853 CC; *see* the general rules on the transfer of property in Ch. 45, 3.1.

Chapter 8

Sales on Execution by Auction and Sales by Liquidators

Certain types of sales are expressly excluded from the scope of application of the CISG. Such is the case of sales by auction and sales on execution or by liquidators.[1] The sales by auctions are frequently governed by specific provisions. These types of sales has certain particularities for example, the formation of contract. For such a reason, the drafters of the CISG decided to exclude this category of sales from the scope of application of the CISG; all the more since sales by auction have a minor importance in international trade.

Similarly, the sales on execution are excluded from the CISG due to the existence of special rules which govern the form and effect of such sales in the place they are passed. Particularly, this kind of sale is characterised by the absence of negotiations between the parties involved. As will be further described with regards to the Ibero-American laws, the sales on execution are integrated into the procedural public law which varies depending of the legal system. These rules are of public order and aim to limit the faculties of the judicial or public bodies in charge of the execution, as well as to seek the best interest of the State, rather than to establish equitable rules between the contractors. The sales in execution are not sales in the sense of the Civil Codes and the rules on sales are only applied by analogy.[2]

Both sales by auction and on execution are also excluded from the ambit of this work. Nevertheless, in order to guide the reader through the specificities that can be encountered by the private buyer under this modality of sales, the following paragraphs provide a few examples of how sales concluded in execution through auction or by liquidators are special.

---

1 Art. 2(b)(c) CISG.

2 Venezuela: J.L. Aguilar Gorrondona, Contratos y Garantias: Derecho Civil IV 174 (2008).

1. Sales on Execution by Auction

The sales on execution are governed and affected by special provisions of the civil procedural[3] or commercial procedural codes[4] of the Ibero-American legal systems. The legal provisions on contracts and the legal provisions on sales in specific, which are contained in the civil and commercial laws, are only applied in a subsidiary way to the sale of goods in judicial execution.[5] In addition, these sales in execution are most of the time passed by judicial auction, which make them even more specific.

Special rules relate to the date and time when the auction has to be performed,[6] the publicity of the auction, the deposit for participation,[7] and the means of payment.[8] Other provisions establish a particular way to orally offer the goods and a way to close offers and acceptances, and the way of delivery of the auctioned goods.[9] Besides, the judge must adjudicate the goods to the best buyer.[10]

Under some laws, compensation derived from hidden defects on the movable goods may not be awarded in sales passed through public auctions.[11] The use of the public force may be available to the judge against the buyer in an auction which does not comply with his obligations.[12] The adjudication of the goods may be subject to certain form requirements, *e.g.* a notary public deed.[13]

---

3 Argentina Arts. 563-593 CPCC; Bolivia Art. 523-549 CPC; Brazil Art. 686 *et seq.* CPC; Chile Arts. 892-894 CPC; Colombia Art. 527 *et seq.* CPC; Costa Rica Art. 650 *et seq.* CPC; Ecuador Art. 475 *et seq.* CPC; El Salvador Art. 593 *et seq.* CPC; Guatemala Art. 224 *et seq.* CPCC; Mexico Art. 469 *et seq.* CPC; Panama 1700 *et seq.* JC; Peru Art. 725 *et seq.* CPC; Portugal Art. 886 *et seq.* CPC; Spain Art. 634 *et seq.* JL; Uruguay Art. 387 *et seq.* CPC; Venezuela Arts. 563-584 CPC.

4 El Salvador Art. 68 *et seq.* CComP.

5 *See for example* expressly stated Paraguay Art. 738 CC.

6 Chile Art. 489 CPC; Costa Rica Art. 653 CPC.

7 Costa Rica Art. 650 CPC.

8 Bolivia Arts. 523-549 CPC; Chile Art. 491 CPC; Mexico Art. 2325 CC (cash payment); Panama JL Art. 1722 (cash payment)

9 Colombia Arts. 527, 531 CPC.

10 Ecuador Art. 475 CPC; Peru Art. 1389 CC: the obligatory nature of each position stops when a better one is formulated; Uruguay Art. 387.1 CPC: the contract is concluded when the auctioneer adjudges the goods to the best biter. The sale must be granted to the best offeroror must be sold for a price of at least ¾ of the calculated value of the goods; Venezuela Art. 565 CPC: the judge must sell the goods to the best offerorafter having reviewed all the offers and the buyer should pay immediately.

11 Cuba Art. 351 CC.

12 El Salvador Art. 643 CPC.

13 Guatemala Art. 324 CPC.

2. Sales by Liquidators

Depending on the jurisdiction, sales by liquidators could be covered either by the Code of Commerce,[14] the bankruptcy or insolvency laws (hereinafter BIL)[15] or the laws of companies.[16] Special provisions affect the contract of sales of companies undergoing bankruptcy or insolvency proceedings. These are mostly addressed to the liquidating company, creditors and possible buyers. So, while some laws require the liquidator to sell the assets of the company by auction,[17] other laws allow the liquidator to undertake direct sales subject to the special rules imposed by law.[18]

On this point, Chile's commercial code establishes that the tangible goods of a company in bankruptcy will be sold by auction and the values that have been quoted on the stock-exchange will sold in that place, unless the creditors agree otherwise.[19] Under Peru's Law on Bankruptcy Proceedings, if after three attempts it is not possible to sell the goods of the company by judicial auction, the liquidator can sell such goods through direct sales.[20] Under the Portuguese BIL the administrator (liquidator) of the insolvency chooses the modality for the sales of the goods, being able to select any of the executive proceedings admitted or any other he finds more convenient.[21]

[14] Bolivia Art. 1614 Com C; Chile Art. 112 Com C; Costa Rica Art. 209 Com C; El Salvador Art. 326 Com C; Guatemala Art. 244 Com C; Honduras Art. 1318 Com C; Uruguay Book IV, Title IV Com C; Venezuela Arts. 347-352 Com C.

[15] *See* Argentina Art. 205 217 BIL; Bolivia Law No. 2495; Brazil Arts. 24, 50, 86, 129 BIL; Mexico Art. 146 *et seq.* BIL; Peru Art. 84 *et seq.* BIL; Portugal Art. 158 *et seq.* BIL.

[16] Ecuador Art. 398 *et seq.* LC.

[17] Chile Art. 112 Com C; Ecuador Art. 398 LC; Peru Art. 84 BIL.

[18] Argentina Art. 208 BIL; Chile Art. 112 Com C; Ecuador Art. 398 LC; Peru Art. 84 BIL.

[19] Chile Art. 112 Com C.

[20] Peru Art. 84.2 BIL.

[21] Portugal Art. 164 BIL.

PART 3

FORMATION OF THE CONTRACT

CHAPTER 9

THE CAUSE

1. Preliminary Remarks

Most of the Ibero-American laws make reference to the term cause either as an element of the existence or the validity of obligations[1] or contracts.[2] However, the study of the cause in the Ibero-American laws must focus on which type of cause constitutes an indispensable element for the existence, or for the validity of contracts, and on which type of cause has no impact on either the existence or the validity of contracts. In the following paragraphs, we will establish which cause, and to what extent, the cause is one of the elements for the formation of sales contracts under the Ibero-American laws.

The theory, the jurisprudence and the doctrine distinguish between three different classes of cause: first, the final cause; second, the impulsive cause; third, the efficient cause.[3] These three categories have often been mixed up by the doctrine and the jurisprudence, causing great debates and difficulties in establishing the relevance of the concept in the formation of the contract.[4]

---

1 Argentina Art. 499 CC; Chile Arts. 1445, 1467 CC; Colombia Arts. 1502, 1524 CC; Costa Rica Art. 527 CC (validity); Ecuador Art. 1510 CC; El Salvador Arts. 1316, 1338 CC.

2 Bolivia Art. 452 CC; Brazil Art. 166 CC; Cuba Art. 23 CC; Guatemala Art. 1251 CC (object as cause); Honduras Art. 1552 CC; Panama Art. 1112 CC; Peru Art. 140 CC; Spain Art. 1.261 CC; Uruguay Art. 1621 CC; Venezuela Art. 1.141 CC.

3 *See* Chile: R. Díez Duarte, La Compraventa en el Código Civil Chileno 259 (1993); Ecuador: C. Valdivieso Bermeo, Tratado de las Obligaciones y Contratos 37-38 (2005); Honduras: H. Carcamo Tercero, Eficacia e Ineficacia de los Contratos en Materia Civil 53 (2001).

4 *See generally* Latin America: A. Gambaro, *Causa y Contrato*, *in* El Contrato en el Sistema Jurídico Latinoamericano, Vol. I, 159 (1998); Chile: Díez Duarte, *supra* note 3, at 256: noting how in Chile the theory of the cause is not uniform as the Chilean Courts have expressed dissimilar views based on the three types.

1.1. The Final Cause

Only the final cause constitutes an element for the existence or the validity of contracts.[5] That is, absence of, or illegality in, the final cause could render the contract inexistent or invalid respectively. The final cause is the final goal in an abstract sense, which is the same for every category of contracts.[6] It cannot be modified by the parties' subjective expectations.[7] The final cause constitutes an intrinsic element which depends upon the nature of the contract, *i.e.* whether the contract is unilateral, bilateral, onerous, commutative, *etc.* The abstract goal of every contract is fixed by the law.[8] It cannot be arbitrarily changed by the parties. For example, in bilateral contracts the cause of the first party obligation is always represented by the other party's obligation.[9] The cause of the seller's obligation to deliver the goods or to transfer their property is constituted by the buyer's obligation to pay the price of the goods.

1.2. The Impulsive Cause

The impulsive cause, also known as the decisive reason of the agreement, is, on the contrary, an extrinsic element of the contract. It consists of the personal or individual goal or expectation that each of the parties have in that contract.[10] Thus, the decisive reason varies in every contract and depends on the parties.[11] This type of cause cannot be the same for every contract, even those with the same nature, because in a sale one buyer can purchase to satisfy a personal need, but another can do it with the aim of reselling and making economic profits.

According to the doctrine, the impulsive cause does not constitute an element or requirement for the formation of the contract.[12] The impulsive

---

5 Bolivia: R. Carrillo Aruquipa, Lecciones de Derecho Civil, Obligaciones 393 (2008); Ecuador: Valdivieso Bermeo, *supra* note 3, at 38; Honduras: Carcamo Tercero, *supra* note 3, at 53.

6 Argentina: R.L. Lorenzetti, Tratado de los Contratos Parte General 404 (2004): this author calls the final cause with the name objective final cause; Bolivia: Carrillo Aruquipa, *supra* note 5, at 396.

7 Bolivia: Carrillo Aruquipa, *supra* note 5, at 396.

8 *Id.*

9 Uruguay: V. Moldes Ruibal *et al.*, Contratos civiles y comerciales: técnica y práctica, Vol. 1 16 (2006); Bolivia: Carrillo Aruquipa, *supra* note 5, at 396-397; Bolivia Supreme Court, *Antonio Ivar Perales Guerrero v. Deysi Alvarez vda. de Perales*; Chile Supreme Court, RDJ, Vol. 24, Sec. 1, p 678 *cited in* Chile: Díez Duarte, *supra* note 3, at 256, n. 688.

10 Ecuador: Valdivieso Bermeo, *supra* note 3, at 38; Honduras: Carcamo Tercero, *supra* note 3, at 53.

11 Argentina: Lorenzetti, *supra* note 6, at 404: this author calls the impulsive cause with the name subjective final cause.

12 *Id.*; Ecuador: Valdivieso Bermeo, *supra* note 3, at 38; Honduras: Carcamo Tercero, *supra*

cause is so changeable and alterable that it would be unfair to rely on the accomplishment of internal ambitions or expectations to recognise the existence or validity of a contract.

1.3. The Efficient Cause

The efficient cause has nothing to do with the other two types of causes already mentioned. Indeed, the use of this term is not related with the cause of the contract but with the source of the obligations.[13] But as in many occasions the Ibero-American doctrine and the law has mixed up terms when trying to identify the cause of the obligation, in the sense of the source of the obligations, this has mislead many persons.[14] The Ibero-American laws recognise three main efficient causes (in the sense of sources) of the obligations, already present in roman law: the contract, the tort[15] and the unjustified enrichment.[16] But as mentioned, the term cause in such a case is not at all related to the existence or validity of contracts.

2. The Final Cause

2.1. General Remarks

Most of the Ibero-American laws recognise that only the final cause may be relevant for the existence and validity of the contract.[17] A group of Ibero-American Civil Codes share the following definition of cause:

> [...] The cause is understood as the [immediate][18] reason that induces to contract the obligation [...].[19]

note 3, at 53.

[13] *See* Ecuador: Valdivieso Bermeo, *supra* note 3, at 37; Honduras: Carcamo Tercero, *supra* note 3, at 53.

[14] *See for example* a misleading provision in Costa Rica Art. 632 CC stating that the originating causes of obligations, are: the contracts, the quasi-contracts, the crimes, the quasi-crime and the law.

[15] Regarding tort under the Ibero-American law *see* Ch. 57.

[16] Argentina: Lorenzetti, *supra* note 6, at 403. Regarding unjustified enrichment under the Ibero-American law *see* Ch. 58.

[17] Supporting the statement in their respective countries Argentina: Lorenzetti, *supra* note 6, at 404; Ecuador: Valdivieso Bermeo, *supra* note 3, at 38; Honduras: Carcamo Tercero, *supra* note 3, at 53.

[18] This word has been added in El Salvador's Civil Code in a legislative reform passed on 21 June 1907.

[19] *See* Chile Art. 1467 CC; Colombia Art. 1524 CC; Ecuador Art. 1510 CC; El Salvador Art. 1338 CC.

The statement makes reference to the intrinsic (immediate) motivation of the nature of the contract, and not to the personal extrinsic motivation of the parties. The same should be understood of other definitions of cause in the Ibero-American Civil Codes. For example:

> Bolivia: "[…] the reason that determines the will of both contractors […]";[20] Brazil: "[…] the determinant common reason to both parties […]";[21] Mexico: "[…] the aim or determining reason for the agreement of the parties […]";[22]

Accordingly, in a contract of sale, the obligation to deliver the goods is the final cause of the obligation contracted by the buyer to pay the price[23] and vice versa;[24] in the unilateral contracts, the obligation unilaterally contracted by one party has his cause in the benefits received by the other party. Such is expressly recognised in those countries whose definition of cause is expressed in the following way:

> […] in contracts involving a price (onerous) the cause is the benefit or promise of a thing or service on the other party; in the remunerative contracts the cause is the service or benefit that is remunerated, and in those of pure charity (beneficence) the cause is the mere freedom of the benefactor […].[25]

The same understanding of cause shall prevail even in those countries that do not expressly define the term cause but whose absence or illegality can have an impact on the existence or validity of contracts.[26] A fair and uniform treatment will only be achieved by recognising the abstract and unchangeable nature of the final cause, as the only relevant cause susceptible to affect the existence or validity of contracts.

---

20 Bolivia Arts. 490, 452 (3) CC.

21 Bolivia Art. 166 CC.

22 Mexico Art. 1831 CC.

23 Chile Supreme Court, RDJ, Vol. 21 Sec. 1, at 973 *cited in* Chile: Díez Duarte, *supra* note 3, at 256, n. 692: noting that the reason that induces the seller to deliver the goods it not other but to get the price from the buyer.

24 Bolivia Supreme Court, *Felipe Orozco Cabrera v. Hugo Aguirre Calderón y María Paz Villalba de Aguirre*: noting that the fact that a price never agreed and never paid was fixed in the contract is a falseness, hence, an illicit cause, being impossible to transfer the title of property because of lack of counter performance and the court considered the contract to be invalid; Chile Supreme Court, RDJ Vol. 78 Sec. 2, at 1 *cited in* Chile: Díez Duarte, *supra* note 3, at 257, n. 694: noting that the buyer agrees on the payment of the price with the intention to acquire the pacific and useful possession of the goods.

25 Honduras Art. 1569 CC; Panama Art. 1125 CC; Spain Art. 1.274 CC; Uruguay Art. 1287 CC.

26 Without definition of cause but non-existence or defect of cause affects the existence or validity of contracts: Argentina Arts. 499-502 CC; Costa Rica Art. 627 CC; Nicaragua Arts. 1872-1874 CC; Peru Art. 140 CC; Venezuela Arts. 1141, 1157, 1158 CC.

2.2. Existence of the Final Cause

The final cause must exist.[27] The absence of cause provokes the non-existence of the contract.[28] As provided by many Civil Codes, it is not necessary to express the cause in the contract.[29] As mentioned, the final clause is intrinsic to the nature of the contract, so that if the parties have agreed on a commutative contract, such as the sale of goods, it is implied that the cause of the obligation to deliver goods is, automatically, the counter obligation to pay the price.

2.3. True Cause

In addition to exist, the cause shall be real, as a false cause will give rise to the invalidity of the contract.[30] Nevertheless, some codes establish that the obligation will remain valid, although the cause expressed is false, if it is based on another true cause.[31] For example, if the parties have expressed that the cause of their contract was the gratuitous donation of materials for the construction of a warehouse, but this expressed unilateral contract cause is false, because the true reality was the delivery of the materials against the payment of a price in money, the contract shall survive the false cause of a donation and exist under the true cause of a sale of goods with full effect; unless such simulation has been made to evade obligations established by contract or law which may render the cause unlawful, as is further explained.

---

[27] Ecuador: Valdivieso Bermeo, *supra* note 3, at 39.

[28] As element for the existence of obligations: Argentina Art. 499 CC; Chile Arts. 1445, 1467 CC; Colombia Arts. 1502, 1524 CC; Costa Rica Art. 527 CC (validity); Ecuador Art. 1510 CC; El Salvador Arts. 1316, 1338 CC; as element for existence of contract: Bolivia Art. 452 CC; Brazil Art. 166 CC; Cuba Art. 23 CC; Guatemala Art. 1251 CC (object as cause); Honduras Art. 1552 CC; Panama Art. 1112 CC; Peru Art. 140 CC; Spain Art. 1.261 CC; Uruguay Art. 1621 CC; Venezuela Art. 1.141 CC; *see also* Argentina: Lorenzetti, *supra* note 6, at 414-415.

[29] Argentina Art. 500 CC; Chile Art. 1467 CC; Colombia Art. 1524 CC; Ecuador Art. 1510 CC; El Salvador Art. 1338 CC; Honduras Art. 1572 CC; Nicaragua Art. 1872 CC; Panama Art. 1128 CC; Spain Art. 1.277 CC; Uruguay Art. 1290 CC; Venezuela Art. 1.158 CC.

[30] *See* express reference in Honduras Art. 1571 CC; Panama Art. 1127 CC; Spain Art. 1275 CC; *see also* Argentina: Lorenzetti, *supra* note 6, at 416.

[31] Argentina Art. 501 CC; Nicaragua Art. 1873 CC; Spain Art. 1276 CC; Uruguay Art. 1289 CC.

3. The Illicit Cause

3.1. General Remarks

While absence of final cause provokes the non-existence of the contract, the illicit cause renders the contract invalid.[32] Thus, the cause must exist lawfully, not as a requirement for the existence but as an element for the validity of the contract.[33] This premise is expressed in group of Civil Codes providing that

> the promise to give something in payment for a debt that does not exist, lacks of cause; and the promise to give something in reward of a crime or an immoral act, has an illicit cause.[34]

In addition, many other Ibero-American laws expressly establish that the obligations based on an illicit cause are invalid and such will not have effects.[35]

The cause is generally considered to be unlawful when it is opposite to the public order, the law, the moral convention, or when it is used as a means to elude obligations.[36] To give exclusive examples of contracts rendered invalid because of immoral or prohibited causes is difficult because the issue of the unlawful cause mixes with the concept of the unlawful object of contracts.

3.2. Cause and Object

When the laws refer to the illicit cause, it is not clear whether they mean the object of the contract rather than the cause of the contract. These two are different concepts, but in practice they are usually confounded.[37] On the one hand, the term 'object' has been used indistinctly in almost every Civil Code

---

[32] *See* Latin America: F. Hionestrosa, *Validez e Invalidez del Contrato en el Derecho Latinoamericano*, *in* El Contrato en el Sistema Jurídico Latinoamericano, Vol. I, 199, at 212, 213 (1998); Bolivia Supreme Court, *Felipe Orozco Cabrera v. Hugo Aguirre Calderón y María Paz Villalba de Aguirre:* noting that the fact that a price never agreed and never paid was fixed in the contract is a falseness, hence, an illicit cause, being impossible to transfer the title of property because of lack of counter performance. The court considered the contract to be invalid.

[33] Argentina: Lorenzetti, *supra* note 6, at 415; on the grounds for invalidity of a contract for immorality or illegality as reviewed in Ch. 19.

[34] *See* Chile Art. 1467 CC; Colombia Art. 1524 CC; Ecuador Art. 1510 CC; El Salvador Art. 1338 CC.

[35] Argentina Art. 502 CC; Nicaragua Art. 1874 CC; Brazil Art. 166 (III) CC; Guatemala Art. 1301 CC (object as cause); Honduras Art. 1570 CC; Panama Art. 1126 CC; Spain Art. 1.275 CC; Uruguay Art. 1288 CC.

[36] Argentina Art. 502 CC; Bolivia Art. 849 CC; Chile Art. 1467 CC; Colombia Art. 1524 CC; Ecuador Art. 1510 CC; El Salvador Art. 1338 CC; Guatemala Art. 1301 CC (object as cause); Honduras Art. 1570 CC; Mexico Art. 1831 CC; Panama Art. 1126 CC; Spain Art. 1.275 CC.

[37] Honduras: Carcamo Tercero, *supra* note 3, at 51

to mean two different things:[38] the direct and indirect object, as called by the doctrine.[39] The direct object is the obligation which generates the agreement,[40] while the indirect object is the items or the act, positive or negative, that interests the parties.[41] For example, the direct object in a contract of sales is the obligations of doing what the buyer and seller shall perform.[42] The indirect object is the goods and the money in payment.[43]

On the other hand, the cause is the final goal in an abstract sense that depends of the nature of the contract. But when one talks about the final illicit cause, the concept of cause approaches that of the illicit direct object, constituted by the obligation which generates the agreement. Thus, it is not unusual that some codes, authors and judges view the direct object as assimilated to the cause and vice versa.[44]

For that reason, we have consolidated the study of grounds for invalidity of contracts, which materialise when its object or cause are affected by immorality or illegality, later in chapter 19. In that Section, examples of situations that can endanger the validity of contract on the basis of illegality and immorality are provided irrespective of whether the affected element is the cause or the object.

---

38 The reading of Chile Art. 1460 CC; Colombia Art. 1517 CC; El Salvador Art. 1331 CC; Ecuador Art. 1503 CC shows how the term object is indistinctly used and some times can difficultly be distinguished. Except for the Civil Code of Peru and Bolivia. In Peru the reading of Arts. 1402, 1409 CC specifically distinguishes between the Object consisting in creating, modification or terminating obligations and the things Object to the contract. In Bolivia Art. 965 CC specifically refers to the obligation against the good customs while Art. 485 CC refers to the material object of a contract; *see also* Venezuela Supreme Tribunal, Judgment 81, *Cass civ,* file 99312 of 30 March 2000.

39 Argentina: A.A. Alterini, Contratos civiles, comerciales, de consumo 216 (1998): classifies it with the names of immediate object and mediate object, respectively; Honduras: Carcamo Tercero, *supra* note 3, at 46; Mexico: S. León Tovar, Los Contratos Mercantiles 72 (2004); Spain: M. Medina de Lemus, Derecho Civil: Obligaciones y Contratos II, Teoria General Vol. 1 303 (2004); Uruguay: Moldes Ruibal *et al.*, *supra* note 9, at 15: understands that the contract has a proximate object which are the obligations and performances and a remote object which are the things, services and works.

40 Argentina: Alterini, *supra* note 39, at 216; Mexico: León Tovar, *supra* note 39, at 72: talks about the conduct of the parties manifested in the obligations of doing or giving; Spain: Medina de Lemus, *supra* note 39, at 303; Uruguay: Moldes Ruibal *et al.*, *supra* note 9, at 15; *see also* Peru Art. 1402 CC.

41 Argentina: Alterini, *supra* note 39, at 216; Mexico: León Tovar, *supra* note 39, at 72; Spain: Medina de Lemus, *supra* note 39, at p 303; Uruguay: Moldes Ruibal *et al.*, *supra* note 9, at 15; *see also* Peru Art. 1409 CC.

42 Argentina: Alterini, *supra* note 39, at 216.

43 *Id.*

44 Latin America: Hionestrosa, *supra* note 32, 213.

4. Conclusion

In brief, all the elements of the relevant causes converge in one provision of the Civil Codes of Chile, Colombia, Ecuador and El Salvador.[45] The relevant type of cause for the existence of the contract is the final cause, as an abstract and unchangeable goal which depends upon the nature of the contract. The final cause must exist and be real, in opposition to the false cause; and the cause must also be lawful, in opposition to the unlawful cause, which renders the contract void.

[45] Chile Art. 1467 CC; Colombia Art. 1524 CC; Ecuador Art. 1510 CC; El Salvador Art. 1338 CC: "[…] there is no obligation without a real and licit cause; but it is not required to express the cause. The mere freedom or benefit is sufficient cause. […] The cause is understood as the [immediate] reason that induces to contract the obligation; and by illicit cause the prohibited one by law, or opposite to moral convention or the public order […]."

Chapter 10

Offer and Acceptance

The Ibero-American laws and the CISG rely on the notion of manifest intention of the parties to conclude a contract as the primary element of the existence of contracts.[1] Intention to conclude a sales contract is manifested by the offer of one of the parties, and the acceptance of such offer by the other party.[2] Nevertheless, different requirements and rules can affect the existence and validity of both offers and acceptances. In the following paragraphs, these requirements and rules will be compared among the Ibero-American legal systems.

[1] Chile Supreme Court, RDJ, Vol. 7, Sec. 1, at 529 *cited in* Chile: R. Díez Duarte, La Compraventa en el Código Civil Chileno 331, n. 921 (1993): upholding that there cannot exist a contract without the manifest agreement of the parties. Manifest agreement is an essential element for the existence of the sales contract; Mexico Collegiate Tribunals, *Novena Época,* Registry 182'396, SJF XIX, January 2004, at 1535: confirming that absence of intent or object provokes the non-existence of the contract. Under CISG Art. 14 a proposal for concluding a contract constitutes a definitive offer if it indicates the goods and expressly or implicitly fixes or makes provisions for determining the quantity of the goods or the price. Hence, the vague proposals sent to the domicile of potential buyers or to their (e-)mail boxes, the offers made public through different means of advertisements, such as news paper or internet pages are not sufficiently definitive to constitute a binding offer.

[2] *See* Bolivia: W. Kaune Arteaga, Curso de Derecho Civil, Contratos, Vol. 1, 64-65 (1996); Costa Rica: A. Brenes Cordoba, G. Trejos & M. Ramírez, Tratado de los Contratos 57 (1998); El Salvador: A.O. Miranda, De la Compraventa 28-29 (1996); Mexico: O. Vásquez del Mercado, Contratos Mercantiles 157 (2008).

1. Offer

1.1. Definitiveness of Offer

Among the Ibero-American countries, statutory laws, courts and doctrine establish as a general rule for all contracts, that a valid offer must have all the constituent elements of the contract.[3] The two basic elements in a sales contract are the goods and the price. These elements are taken from the definition of the sale: the agreement by which one party binds himself to deliver goods, and the other party to pay a price for them.[4] But also, many other Ibero-American laws provide that a valid offer must, at least, contain the goods and the price,[5] or the way to determine both.[6]

[3] Argentina Art. 1148 CC; Bolivia Art. 826 Com C; Brazil Art. 429 CC; Colombia Art. 845 Com C; Guatemala Art. 1522 CC; *see also* Bolivia: V. Camargo Marín, Derecho Comercial Boliviano 408 (2007); Brazil: O. Gomes, Contratos 73 (2008); Ecuador: V. Cevallos Vásquez, Contratos Civiles y Mercantiles Vol. I, 234 (2005); El Salvador: A.O. Miranda, Guía Para el Estudio del Derecho Civil III, Obligaciones 31; Mexico: Vásquez del Mercado, *supra* note 2, at 157; Peru: A. Sierralta Ríos, La Compraventa Internacional y El Derecho Peruano 55 (1997); Spain: J. Llobet I Aguado, El Deber de Información en la Formación de los Contratos 21 (1996); Chile Supreme Court, RDJ, Vol. 36, Sec. 1, at 362 *cited in* Chile: Díez Duarte, *supra* note 1, at 123, n 351: noting that if the parties failed to agree on a price, there is no contract of sale, and thus the available remedy is the invalidity (rescission) of the contract and not the avoidance for ordinary breach as established in Chile Arts. 1489, 1873 CC; Colombia Supreme Court, *Cass civ*, 16 October 1980 and Colombia Supreme Court, *Cass civ*, 8 March 1995 *cited in* Colombia: J. Oviedo Alban, La Formación de Contrato: tratos preliminares, oferta, aceptación 37, n. 6 (2008); Mexico Collegiate Tribunals, *Novena Época,* Registry 177'335, SJF XXII, September 2005, at 1436; Portugal Supreme Tribunal of Justice, 4 October 2001; Portugal Supreme Tribunal of Justice, 12 March 2002.

[4] Argentina Art. 1323 CC; Bolivia Art. 584 CC; Brazil Art. 481 CC; Chile Art. 1793 CC; Colombia Art. 1849 CC; Costa Rica Art. 1049 CC; Cuba Art. 334 CC; Ecuador Art. 1759 CC; El Salvador Art. 1597 CC; Guatemala Art. 1790 CC; Honduras Art. 1605 CC; Mexico Art. 2248 CC; Nicaragua Art. 2530 CC; Panama Art. 1215 CC; Paraguay Art. 737 CC; Peru Art. 1529 CC; Portugal Art. 874 CC; Spain Art. 1.445 CC; Uruguay Art. 1661 CC; Venezuela Art. 1474 CC; *see also* Argentina National Civil Chamber, *Sala* D, *Adyco S.A. v. Mizrahi Aldo R.*, 4 August 1986, JA 1987-II-535.

[5] *See for example* implied references to these two elements: Bolivia Arts. 584, 611 CC; Brazil Art. 482 CC; Chile Art. 139 Com C; Cuba Art. 335 CC; Guatemala Art. 1791 CC; Honduras Art. 1610 CC; Mexico Art. 2249 CC; Nicaragua Art. 2540 CC; Panama Art. 1220 CC; Spain Art. 1450 CC; Uruguay Art. 1664 CC.

[6] Brazil Art. 483 CC; *see also* Colombia: Oviedo Alban, *supra* note 3, at 37: noting that the doctrine distinguishes between objective determination of the offer and subjective determination of the offer. The required objective determination regards all the constituent elements of the contract: namely-goods and price. The required subjective determination regards the specific person(s) to which the offer is addressed; *see generally* Spain: J. Fajardo Fernandez, La Compraventa con Precio Determinable (2001); *also* Argentina National Commercial Chamber, *Sala* D, *Castelar S.A. v. Maralc SRL,* 11 April 1990, JA 1990-IV-165; Mexico Collegiate Tribunals, *Novena Época*, Registry 177'052, SJF XXII, October 2005, p 2318.

1.1.1. Goods Determination

As to the determination of the goods in the offer, the Ibero-American sales laws closely follow the CISG. They require goods to be determined or determinable.[7] The goods agreed upon during the process of offer and acceptance must be determined as far as their species, although not in amount, provided that such can be determined.[8] For example, an Argentinean buyer can offer to buy USD 2 million Brazilian Gray Cement, and although the specific amount of cement has not been established, there are means to be determined *i.e.* by considering the ton's price that cement with such characteristics has in the international market. Hence, the goods can remain undetermined at the offer and acceptance phase, but this cannot continue after the date of delivery.[9] Moreover, as held by an Argentinean court, the determination of the goods shall not be confused with the existence of such goods, the fact that the goods have not yet been produced does not affect its determination.[10]

1.1.2. Price Determination

The price must also be established through the process of contract formation, since this constitutes one of the basic elements of the sale.[11] Generally, the Ibero-American laws allow the parties to freely determine the price of the goods in a B2B transaction, except when the special laws limit it or regulate it for public policy reasons, common in B2C.[12] Cuba is the only country that imposes, by default, an official price for local sales. Under its Civil Code the

---

7 *See* Ch. 6, 1.2.2.

8 *Id.*

9 Argentina: R. Compagnucci de Caso, Contrato de Compraventa 92 (2007); Mexico: R. De Pina, Elementos de Derecho Civil Mexicano, Contratos en Particular, Vol. IV, 25 (2007); *see* different authors *in* Peru: M. Castillo Freyre (Ed.), El bien materia del contrato de compraventa: algunas consideraciones preliminares sobre el contrato de compraventa y estudio del capitulo segundo de dicho contrato en el código civil 122-123 (1995).

10 Argentina National Commercial Chamber, *Sala* C, *Pandemonium v. Thinkercorp S.A.*, 13 November 1985.

11 Chile: O. Saldias Collao, El Contrato de Compraventa Internacional en el Comercio Chile-Union Europea 118 (2006); Argentina National Commercial Chamber, *Sala* D, *Castelar S.A. v. Maralc SRL,* 11 April 1990, JA 1990-IV-165: stating that "If the price is not determined or determinable, the sales agreement is invalid"; Chile Supreme Court, RDJ, Vol. 36, Sec. 1, at 362: noting that the price is an essential element of the contract of sale without which the contract is non-existent; Chile Supreme Court, RDJ, Vol. 44, Sec. 1, at 397: noting that the price of the sales contract shall be established in money; Spain Supreme Tribunal, 22 December 2000, *Id Cendoj:* 28079110002000100573: upholding that lack of determination of the price or of method to determine the price renders the contract non-existent.

12 *See* expressly Bolivia Art. 611 CC; Portugal Art. 883 CC.

price of the sale shall be that established in the official regulations, and only when these do not establish one, the price will be that agreed by the parties.[13]

1.1.2.1. Currency

The parties are indeed free to agree on the price of the goods to be made in a currency other than the official national currency at the place of payment or under the applicable law.[14] If the price agreed is in a foreign currency it does not make the contract invalid. The buyer may chose to pay the price in the agreed foreign currency or, alternatively, in its national currency equivalent according to the exchange rate established by the National indicators at the date of payment.[15]

1.1.2.2. Presumption

In principle, determination of the price is required. The sale passed without a determined price is still valid, provided there is a way to determine it.[16] Such determination becomes relevant regarding certain legal effects; e.g. the existence of the contract, the damages recovered for delay in payment,[17] the accessibility of a remedy based on gross disparity,[18] or hardship,[19] *etc.*

13 Cuba Art. 336 CC.

14 *See for example* Argentina Arts. 617, 619 CC; Bolivia Art. 795 Com C; Chile Art. 114 para. 2 Com C; Costa Rica Art. 771 CC; Ecuador Arts. 157, 158 Com C; Peru Arts. 1234, 1235 CC; *see also* Argentina: Compagnucci de Caso, *supra* note 9, at 116; Bolivia: Camargo Marín, *supra* note 3, at 400; Mexico: S. León Tovar, Los Contratos Mercantiles 54 (2004).

15 Bolivia: Camargo Marín, *supra* note 3, at 400; Costa Rica Supreme Court, Judgment 167, *Segunda Sala Civil,* 26 May 1995; Peru Supreme Court, *Sala civil permanente,* Resolution 000045-2001, 24 July 2001: acknowledged the value-based-theory of Peru Art. 135 CC, according to which parties are free to agree on the payment of obligations based on indexes of automatic adjustment fixed by the Central Bank of Reserves or based on other currencies, with the aim of preserving an constant value of the obligation contracted; Peru Supreme Court, *Sala civil transitoria,* Resolution 000028-2001, 23 August 2001: confirming the obligation to pay the price of the fishing boat either in dollars as agreed or in its national equivalent.

16 *See for example* Brazil Art. 488 CC; Colombia Art. 920 Com C; Portugal Art. 466 Com C; Venezuela Art. 134 Com C; *see also* Costa Rica: D. Baudrit Carrillo, Los Contratos Traslativos del Derecho Privado – Principios de Jurisprudencia 35 (2000); Spain: Fajardo Fernandez, *supra* note 6, at 46-47; Brazil Tribunal of Justice of the State of São Paulo, Appeal with Revision 1104540009, published 19 November 2007: the Court applied the Art. 488 of the Brazilian Civil Code, stating that the absence of express determination of the price does not make the contract inexistent if it is possible to determine it considering the circumstances of the negotiation; Colombia Arbitral Award, *Ignacio Moreno Restrepo v. Rodrigo Ospina Hernández*, Bogota, 15 March 1999 *cited in* Colombia: Oviedo Alban, *supra* note 3, at 40, n. 17 (2008).

17 *See* Ch. 52.

18 *See* Ch. 25.

19 *See* Ch. 51, 2.

The Ibero-American laws gather in various groups to show different ways to deduce a determination of the price. Under some laws, for example, the price shall be considered determined when the parties make reference to the price of the market or the stock market, national or foreign, on a fixed date,[20] or on the date of contract conclusion.[21] Also, many Ibero-American laws expressly establish that the price can be determined by means of indicators or parameters; for example, fungible goods regularly sold at the seller's domicile shall have the price of that market on the day of the delivery, unless otherwise agreed.[22]

An issue in which the price was determined by means of indicators was presented to ICC Arbitral Tribunal applying the Venezuelan law. The Tribunal faced the question of whether the seller had breached the agreement to sell at the price agreed under the contract.[23] The case concerned the sales of a type of oil used to produce asphalt known under the name of *Boscan* crude oil which is produced only in Venezuela. *Boscan* is always priced by reference to the posted price of a Mexican crude oil known as *Maya*. *Boscan*'s price is always lower than *Maya*'s price mainly because *Maya* is a lighter crude oil than *Boscan* and thus produces a larger percentage of light-ends. As is common in crude oil supply contracts, the parties agreed to determine the price on a periodic basis, in this case quarterly. For the first two quarters, the parties agreed to set the price at *Maya* less USD 5.00 a barrel (often expressed in the industry as 'Maya -5'). The price negotiations for the third quarter failed because the seller demanded a price of Maya + 1. In consideration of the method to determine the price established by the sales agreement, the Arbitral Tribunal found that the counter-offer to price Boscan at Maya plus a premium for the third quarter constituted a fundamental breach of the agreement.[24]

Under some laws, if the parties did not agree on the price and the goods have already been delivered, it will be presumed that the parties have accepted the current price the goods have on the day and in the place, in which the

---

[20] Brazil Art. 486 CC; El Salvador Art. 1014 Com C; Guatemala Art. 1797 CC; Mexico Art. 2251 CC; Peru Art. 1545 CC; In the following countries only in the sale of values, grains, liquids and other fungible goods: Honduras Art. 1608 CC; Nicaragua Art. 2538 CC; Panama Art. 1218 CC; Spain Art. 1448 CC; Argentina National Commercial Chamber, *Sala* D, *Castelar S.A. v. Maralc SRL,* 11 April 1990, JA 1990-IV-165: stating that "in accordance with Art. 1349 CC, the price shall be 'determined' when: the parties refer to the price of another determined good in the market; Brazil Tribunal of Justice of the State of São Paulo, Appeal with Revision 1057296004, published 26 December 2007: the Court considered admissible the parties stipulation that the harvest orange prices were based on the prices of the stock markets.

[21] Colombia Art. 921 Com C; Costa Rica Art. 446 Com C; Venezuela Art. 134 para. 2 Com C.

[22] Brazil Art. 487 CC; Chile Art. 1808 CC; Colombia Art. 1864 CC; Ecuador Art. 1774 CC; El Salvador Art. 1612 CC; Uruguay Art. 1666 CC.

[23] ICC Final Award Case No. 13478 *Lex Contractus* Venezuelan Law.

[24] *Id.*

contract was concluded,[25] or in which the goods were delivered.[26] In the case of different prices in the same day and place, the buyer will have to pay the average price.[27] This last rule also applies to the case in which the parties refer to the price of the day and place of contract conclusion.[28]

Other Ibero-American laws dictate that when the parties have not determined the price or a way to determine it, if the contract regards goods that the seller sells regularly, it is presumed that those have been agreed for sale upon the average price usually charged by the seller.[29] Alternatively, under some of these laws, when the sale regards goods with prices in the stock market or in the local market, the price will be that of the market or stock market at the place of delivery,[30] or the price at commercial establishments on the day of the conclusion of the contract.[31]

1.1.2.3. Determination by a Third Party, Arbitrators or Courts

In addition to the aforementioned methods for determining the price, most countries' laws establish that the parties can agree to leave such determination to a third party.[32] Only if the third party is not able or does not want to determine the price the sale shall be ineffective.[33] In Chile and Ecuador B2B

[25] Chile Art. 139 Com C; Ecuador Art. 184 Com C; Guatemala Art. 1796 CC.

[26] Argentina Art. 458 Com C; Colombia Art. 920 Com C; Uruguay Art. 523 Com C.

[27] Argentina Art. 458 Com C; Chile Art. 139 Com C; Ecuador Art. 184 Com C; Guatemala Art. 1796 CC; Uruguay Art. 523 Com C.

[28] Chile Art. 139 Com C; Ecuador Art. 184 Com C; Guatemala Art. 1796 CC.

[29] Bolivia Art. 613 CC; Brazil Art. 488 CC; Costa Rica Art. 446 part 2 Com C; El Salvador Art. 1014 part 2 Com C; Peru Art. 1547 part 1 CC; Portugal Art. 883 part 1 CC; ICC Final Award Case No. 13967 *Lex Contractus* Bolivian Law and INCOTERMS 2000: charging the average price of the goods during the term of the supply contract to certain goods whose price was not susceptible to be determined according to the method established by the same contract.

[30] Bolivia Art. 613 part 2 CC; Brazil Art. 486 CC; El Salvador 1014 *in fine* Com C; Peru Art. 1547 CC.

[31] Costa Rica Art. 446 *in fine* Com C; Portugal Art. 883 CC; Venezuela Art. 134 para. 3 Com C.

[32] Argentina Art. 459 Com C; Bolivia Art. 612 CC; Brazil Art. 485 CC; Chile Art. 1809 CC; Colombia Art. 1865 CC; Costa Rica Art. 1057 CC; Ecuador Art. 1775 CC; El Salvador Art. 1613 CC; Guatemala Art. 1796 CC; Honduras Art. 1607 CC; Mexico Art. 2251 CC; Nicaragua Art. 2537 CC; Panama Art. 1217 CC; Peru Art. 1544 CC; Portugal Art. 466 Com C; Spain Art. 1447 CC; Uruguay Art. 1667 CC & Art. 524 Com C; Venezuela Art. 1.479 CC; Argentina National Commercial Chamber, *Sala* D, *Castelar S.A. v. Maralc SRL,* 11 April 1990, JA 1990-IV-165: stating that "in accordance with Art. 1349 CC., the price shall be 'determined' when … the parties leave its determination to a third party (Art. 459 Com C)."

[33] Argentina Art. 459 Com C; Bolivia Art. 612 CC; Brazil Art. 485 CC; Chile Art. 1809 CC; Colombia Art. 1865 CC; Costa Rica Art. 1057 CC; Ecuador Art. 1775 CC; El Salvador Art. 1613 CC; Guatemala Art. 1796 CC; Honduras Art. 1607 CC; Mexico Art. 2251 CC; Nicaragua Art. 2537 CC; Panama Art. 1217 CC; Peru Art. 1544 CC; Portugal Art. 466 sole para. Com C; Spain Art. 1447 CC; Uruguay Art. 1667 CC; Venezuela Art. 1.479 CC.

sales, refusal or inability of the third party does not invalidate the sale. Rather the price becomes the current price the goods have on the day and in the place of contract conclusion.[34]

Likewise in a few countries, impossibility to determine the price would allow a national tribunal to intervene in order to fix the price himself in equity,[35] or to designate a third party to do it.[36] In Uruguay B2B sales the price shall be decided by arbitrators.[37]

1.1.2.4. Determination by One of the Parties

Finally, most Ibero-American laws provide that determination of the price cannot be left to the exclusive will of one of the parties, under penalty of rendering the contract of sale nonexistent.[38]

In an ICC Arbitration, the question arose as to whether a clause establishing that the price of the shares purchased was to be calculated based on the company's EBI, in which the buyer took a majority shareholder position following the purchase, caused that the price determination was left to the buyer's exclusive will.[39] The Arbitral Tribunal found that this was not the case because; first, the contract provided for the participation of an external audit expert in the determination of the price. The expert was not only expected to determine the price based on the documents approved by the board of directors but also had the duty to undertake independent verifications and adjustments based on factual data. Second, although the buyer, in his new position of majority shareholder, could indirectly influence the financial results of the company to cause fewer revenues in order to manipulate the price of the still unpaid shares to the seller, such influence was softened and limited by a series of legal duties aiming to preclude any abuse and bad faith conduct. For

[34] Chile Art. 140 Com C; Ecuador Art. 185 Com C.

[35] Portugal Art. 883 CC.

[36] Venezuela Art. 134 para. 4 Com C.

[37] Uruguay Art. 524 Com C.

[38] Argentina Art. 1355 CC; Brazil Art. 489 CC; Chile Art. 1809 CC; Colombia Art. 1865 CC; Ecuador Art. 1775 CC; El Salvador Art. 1013 CC; Honduras Art. 1609 CC; Mexico Art. 2254 CC; Nicaragua Art. 2539 CC; Panama Art. 1219 CC; Peru Art. 1543 CC; Spain Art. 1449 CC; Uruguay Art. 1666 CC; *see* Argentina National Commercial Chamber, *Sala* D, *Castelar S.A. v. Maralc SRL,* 11 April 1990, JA 1990-IV-165: stating that "(…) it seems not believable that the buyer concluded a sales contract without knowing the price of the acquired goods, deferring the possibility of fixing it to the seller-hypothesis of not only dubious credibility but also of notorious nullity as stated in Art. 1355 CC. Moreover, it has been said – Munoz 'Derecho Comercial, Contratos' t.2, if the buyer leaves to the will of the seller the subsequent fixing of the price, the contract will be 'valid' if such price is later accepted by the buyer. It is my understanding that such contract would not be exactly 'valid' but instead 'post-validated' by the acceptance-ratification-of the buyer."

[39] ICC Final Award Case No. 13542 *Lex Contractus* Spanish Law.

example, the company's directors statutory duty to act with diligence, probity and on the interest of the society or the buyer's statutory duty to act in good faith.[40]

1.2. Intention to be Bound

1.2.1. Manifestation

Similarly to the CISG, in the Ibero-America laws, the intent to be bound exists when there is a serious and definitive intent to enter into the contract.[41] Absent such intention, the proposal is just an invitation to offer.[42] As mentioned, intent to conclude a contract is manifested by offers and acceptances.[43] The individual intent of the offeror can be express or implied.[44] Intent is generally understood to be express when manifested verbally, in writing or by unequivocal signs.[45] Implied consent results from facts or presumed conduct.[46]

It is important to bear in mind that the offer shall be interpreted in the way a normal receiver in the position of the actual receiver would understand it, unless the receiver is aware of the actual intention of the other party.[47]

40 *Id.*

41 Brazil: Gomes, *supra* note 3, at 73; Colombia: Oviedo Alban, *supra* note 3, at 51; Ecuador: Cevallos Vásquez, *supra* note 3, at 235; El Salvador: Miranda, *supra* note 3, at 32; El Salvador: Miranda, *supra* note 2, at 29; Bolivia: Kaune Arteaga, *supra* note 2, at 66. Under Art. 14(1) CISG the proposal is required to indicate the intention of the offerorto be bound in case of acceptance. Also the proposal must be addressed to one or more specific persons in order to become an offer. Otherwise the proposal shall be considered merely an invitation to make offers, unless the contrary is clearly indicated by the person making the proposal.

42 Peru: Sierralta Ríos, *supra* note 3, at 55; Spain: Llobet I Aguado, *supra* note 3, at 22; Peru Supreme Court, *Sala civil permanente*, Resolution 005211-2007, 27 March 2008.

43 Argentina Art. 1144 CC; Cuba Art. 311 CC; Panama Art. 1113 CC; Paraguay Art. 674 CC; Uruguay Art. 1262 CC.

44 Argentina Art. 1145 CC; Bolivia Art. 453 CC; Chile Art. 1449 CC & Art. 103 Com C; Colombia Art. 1506 CC; Costa Rica Art. 1008 CC; Ecuador Art. 1492 CC; El Salvador Art. 1320 CC; Guatemala Art. 1252 CC; Honduras Art. 1551 CC; Mexico Art. 1803 CC; Nicaragua Art. 2448 CC; Paraguay Art. 674 CC; Peru Art. 141 CC; Venezuela Art. 1.138 CC; Peru Supreme Court, *Sala civil permanente,* Resolution 005211-2007, 27 March 2008.

45 Argentina Art. 1145 CC; Bolivia Art. 453 CC; Costa Rica Art. 1008 CC; Mexico Art. 1803 CC; Nicaragua Art. 2448 CC; Peru Art. 141 CC.

46 Argentina Art. 1145 CC; Bolivia Art. 453 CC; Chile Art. 1449 CC; Colombia Art. 1506 CC; Costa Rica Art. 1008 CC; Ecuador Art. 1492 CC; Honduras Art. 1551 CC; Mexico Art. 1803 CC; Nicaragua Art. 2448 CC; Paraguay Art. 674 CC; Peru Art. 141 CC.

47 El Salvador: Miranda, *supra* note 2, at 29; Portugal Supreme Tribunal of Justice, 22 May 2008; Portugal Supreme Tribunal of Justice, 19 February 2008, Portugal Supreme Tribunal of Justice, 27 November 2007, Portugal Supreme Tribunal of Justice, 21 June 2006: if the receiver knows the real intention of the declarer, that interpretation will prevail. If not, the interpretation of a normal receiver in that position.

The intention to be bound by written agreement requires a minimum correspondence in the document. An exception exists if the real intention of the parties is demonstrated differently.[48]

1.2.2. Offers Distinguished from Invitations to Offer

Some Ibero-American laws take a similar approach with regard to the person to whom the offer is directed. The undetermined offers as to the persons to whom they are addressed do not bind the offeror.[49] Certainly, although some laws expressly establish that any offer obliges the offeror unless the opposite results from the terms of the offer, the circumstances or nature of the business,[50] the common criteria is that an offer, to be valid, must be addressed to a determined person on a special contract, with all the constituent elements of that contract.[51]

For example, in Peru offers addressed to the public are considered an invitation to offer; where those who received the invitation become offerors and the person who invites the public becomes an offeree. Only if the offer to the public clearly indicates that it has the obligatory character of an offer, will the offer bind the offeror.[52] Under other laws, the undetermined offers contained in circulars, catalogues, notes of current prices, brochures, or in any other kind of printed announcements, are not obligatory for the offeror.[53] Even when the announcements are directed to determined people, they are always considered to have an implicit condition, that at the time of the acceptance the goods have not been already sold or that the price has not changed or that they still exist at the domicile of the offeror.[54] In Paraguay the dispatch of tariffs or lists of prices does not constitute an offer.[55]

---

[48] *See* Ch. 29, 1 & 2.

[49] *See* Bolivia: Kaune Arteaga, *supra* note 2, at 67; Brazil: Gomes, *supra* note 3, at 74; Colombia: Oviedo Alban, *supra* note 3, at 37: noting that subjective determination as to the specific person(s) to which the offer is addressed is generally required by the doctrine; Ecuador: Cevallos Vasquez, *supra* note 3, at 235; Portugal: L. de Lima Pinheiro, Dereito Comercial Internacional 269 (2005): noting that the offer to the general public does not bind the offeror unless the offeror has expressly manifested his intention to be bound by such an offer. The offeror intention can be understood from the particular circumstances: *e.g.* exhibition of the goods with prices.

[50] Brazil Art. 427 CC; Colombia Arts. 847, 848 Com C; Cuba Art. 318 CC; Guatemala Arts. 1521, 1629 CC; Mexico Art. 1084 CC; Paraguay Arts. 685 (Express reserve), 677 CC; Peru Art. 1382 CC.

[51] *See* expressly Argentina Art. 1148 CC & Art. 454 Com C; Chile Art. 105 Com C; Colombia Arts. 845, 847 Com C; Ecuador Art. 148 Com C; Paraguay Art. 685 CC; Peru Art. 1388 CC; Uruguay Art. 519 Com C.

[52] Peru Art. 1388 CC; *see also* Peru: Sierralta Ríos, *supra* note 3, at 56.

[53] Chile Art. 105 Com C; Ecuador Art. 148 Com C; Colombia Art. 847 Com C.

[54] Chile Art. 105 *in fine* Com C; Ecuador Art. 148 *in fine* Com C.

[55] Paraguay Art. 685 CC.

Nevertheless, under certain circumstances offers made to the general public may become binding on the offeror. For example, under the Costa Rican commercial law, the public advertisements in the form of notices, circular, or by other means undertaken by the merchants, do not oblige them with determined persons, but only with who first accepts them.[56] Under other laws, an offer made to the general public becomes binding when it contains the essential requirements for a conclusion of a contract.[57] Similarly, other laws expressly provide that the exhibition of merchandise to the public, with indication of the price, is considered as a binding offer,[58] and the offers to the public for a determined price, obliges the offeror.[59]

1.3. Binding Effect of Offers

1.3.1. General

Although such is not expressly established in the Ibero-American statutory laws, the offer becomes effective when it reaches the offeree, or more precisely when the offeree knows about it. This rule has been confirmed by a Mexican Collegiate Tribunal which upheld that the offer is perfect when it is known by the offeree.[60] Such can also be inferred from the principle that in contracts between present persons the parties are required to immediately make their will known after they know the will of the other party.[61]

Only few Civil Codes expressly establish the possibility to withdraw the offer while it has not yet reached the offeree.[62] The withdrawal of the offer before or at the same time it reaches the offeree, renders the offer ineffective.[63]

[56] Costa Rica Art. 445 Com C; Costa Rica: Brenes Cordoba, Trejos & Ramírez, *supra* note 2, at 58 (1998).
[57] Brazil Art. 429 CC; Bolivia Art. 827 Com C; Bolivia: Camargo Marín, *supra* note 3, at 408.
[58] Bolivia Art. 827 Com C; Colombia 848 part 1 Com C; Paraguay Art. 685 CC; Bolivia: Camargo Marín, *supra* note 3, at 408.
[59] Bolivia Art. 827 Com C; Colombia Art. 848 part 2 Com C; Guatemala Art. 1629 CC; Honduras Art. 720 Com C; Confirming the rule Costa Rica: Brenes Córdoba, Trejos & Ramírez, *supra* note 2, at 58.
[60] Mexico Collegiate Tribunals, *Novena Época,* Registry 177'335, SJF XXII, September 2005, p 1436.
[61] *See for example*, Brazil Art. 428 (I) CC; Paraguay Art. 675 CC.
[62] Bolivia Art. 826 Com C (offer communicated); Brazil Art. 428 CC; Colombia Art. 846 Com C; Mexico Art. 1808 CC; Portugal Art. 230 CC; Argentina National Civil Chamber, *Sala* A, *Municipalidad de Buenos Aires v. Consorcio Colombres,* 1175/77, 10 August 1988: stating that "(...) the offer may be revoked or withdrawn until its acceptance [...] before such offer reached the offeree." *See also* Bolivia: Camargo Marín, *supra* note 3, at 408: confirming the rule.
[63] *See* expressly Brazil Art. 428 (III) CC; Portugal Art. 230 CC; *see also* Mexico: Vásquez del Mercado, *supra* note 2, at 158; Portugal: J. de M. Antunes Valera, Das Obrigações em Geral 233 (2003)Portugal: De Lima Pinheiro, *supra* note 49, at 271.

Nevertheless, the same possibility exists in the rest of the Ibero-American provisions which allow the revocation of already known, and some times already accepted, irrevocable and revocable offers.[64]

The solution follows closely the CISG approach under which an offer becomes effective when it reaches the offeree. But an offer, even if it is irrevocable, may be withdrawn if the withdrawal reaches the offeree before or at the same time as the offer.[65]

1.3.2. Revocation of Offers

The general principle under the Ibero-American laws is that the offer can be revoked by the offeror while it has not been factually accepted by the offeree.[66] In other words, the revocation lacks effect if the offeree has already accepted the offer.[67] The Civil Code of Paraguay clarifies that the dispatch of the acceptance by the offeree is the relevant act that leaves the revocation without effect.[68] This solution concurs with Paraguay's rule under which the contract is deemed concluded at the time of dispatch of the acceptance.[69] Under Bolivia and Venezuela's Civil Codes, the offeror's knowledge of the acceptance is the relevant moment to leave the revocation without effect.[70] This solution also concurs with the Bolivian and Venezuelan Civil Codes information rule according to which, the contract is concluded when the acceptance is known by the offeror.[71]

64 *See infra* 1.3.2.
65 Art. 15 CISG.
66 Argentina Art. 1150 CC; Brazil Art. 428 (IV) CC; Chile Art. 99 Com C; Colombia Art. 846 Com C (noting that once communicated to the offeree, the offeror will not be able to revoke); Costa Rica Art. 1010 CC; Cuba Art. 318 CC; Ecuador Art. 143 CC; El Salvador Art. 969 CC; Guatemala Art. 1521 CC; Honduras Art. 718 Com C; Nicaragua Art. 2450 CC; Peru Art. 1384 CC (noting that the offeror must inform the offeree of his ability to revoke the offer at any time before acceptance); Uruguay Art. 1265 CC & Art. 204 Com C; Venezuela Art. 113 Com C (if the offeree had not began performance); *see also* Mexico: Vásquez del Mercado, *supra* note 2, at 158; Spain: E. Guardiola Sacarrera, La compraventa internacional: importaciones y exportaciones 56, n. 38 (2001): noting that from the finalist interpretation of Spain Arts. 1.261, 1.262 CC the offer can be revoked at any time before the offeror knows the acceptance of the offeree; Mexico Collegiate Tribunals, *Novena Época,* Registry 177'335, SJF XXII, September 2005, at 1436.
67 Cuba Art. 318 CC; El Salvador Art. 969 Com C; Paraguay Art. 680 CC; Portugal Art. 230 (2) CC; *see also* Portugal: De Lima Pinheiro, *supra* note 49, at 271.
68 Paraguay Art. 680 CC.
69 *See infra* 2.2.1.
70 Bolivia Art. 458 CC; Venezuela Art. 1.137 CC; Spain: Guardiola Sacarrera, *supra* note 66, at 56, n. 38: noting that from the finalist interpretation of Spain Arts. 1.261, 1.262 CC the offer can be revoked at any time before the offeror knows the acceptance of the offeree; *see* confirming the approach Bolivia: Kaune Arteaga, *supra* note 2, at 67.
71 *See infra* 2.2.1.

The problem may arise under the Spanish law, where some scholars consider that from the interpretation of Articles 1261 and 1262 of the Spanish Civil Code, an offer can be revoked at any time before the offeror knows the acceptance, while other rules provide that the contract will be concluded from the dispatch of the acceptance.[72] This means that the offeror may be able to revoke his offer if he effectively ignores the dispatch of the acceptance although the contract is already deemed to be concluded since such dispatch.

On the contrary, under some laws the offer will be effective if the offeree purely accepts it before knowing the offer had already been revoked by the offeror.[73] Under the Argentinean and the Colombian laws this means that if the offeree dispatches his acceptance ignoring the revocation by the offeror, the revocation has no effect.[74] While under the Costa Rican law, if the offeree gets to know of the revocation of the offer before his acceptance reaches the offeror, the revocation will be valid. Hence, under these laws (as it should be also the case under other laws which do not expressly establish a moment or event) the revocation should be left with no effect at the time of acceptance according to the rules on the time of contract conclusion.[75]

In addition, most of the Ibero-American laws dictate that an offer cannot be revoked, even before acceptance, if the offeror has renounced his right to revoke the offer,[76] either because he has obliged himself to uphold the offer until a certain time[77] or because the offer established a fixed time for

[72] Spain: Guardiola Sacarrera, *supra* note 66, at 56, n. 38 and Spain Art. 1.262 CC: the provision indeed follows the information theory of contract conclusion, however, the same establishes that the contract may be concluded since the offeree dispatches the acceptance and the offeror cannot, in good faith, ignore that fact. And also the Spanish Art. 54 Com C adopting the dispatch rule of contract conclusion.

[73] Argentina Art. 1156 CC; Costa Rica Art. 1010 CC; Nicaragua Art. 2450 CC; Colombia Art. 846 Com C.

[74] *See infra* 2.2.1.

[75] *See infra* 2.2.1.

[76] Argentina Art. 1550 CC; Chile Art. 99 Com C; Cuba Art. 317.1 CC; Ecuador Art. 143 CC; Peru Art. 1384 CC: noting that the offeror must inform the offeree of his ability to revoke the offer at any time before acceptance; the offer becomes irrevocable if the offeror fails to do so; Uruguay Art. 1265 CC & Art. 204 Com C; Venezuela Art. 1.137 para. 5 CC.

[77] Argentina Art. 1150 CC; Chile Art. 99 Com C; Cuba Art. 317.1 CC; Costa Rica Art. 443 (a) Com C; Ecuador Art. 143 CC; El Salvador Art. 969 CC; Honduras Art. 718 Com C; Uruguay Art. 1265 CC & Art. 204 Com C; Venezuela Art. 1.137 para. 5 CC; *see* Argentina National Civil Chamber, *Sala* A, *Municipalidad de Buenos Aires v. Consorcio Colombres,* 1175/77, 10 August 1988: stating that "(…) the offer may be revoked or withdraw until its acceptance, except if the right to revoke has been renounced or if an obligation to keep the offer in force for a certain term has been created (Art. 1150 CC) and (…) [if] the offeror has stated a term in which the offeree could accept or reject the offer, this commitment is equivalent to keeping the offer in force during such term. In such circumstances, the proposal is binding, and not even its revocation shall impede the perfection of the contract when the acceptance of the offer has been made during the term fixed; (…) except if the revocation had occurred before such offer reached the offeree"; Spain: P. Perales Vizcasillas, in D. Morán Bovio

acceptance,[78] or because the law establishes a default time to uphold the offer.[79]

Although the offers above-described are in principle irrevocable, the question arises as to the consequences of the 'revocation' of an 'irrevocable' offer. On the one hand, if the 'irrevocable' offer is accepted before being revoked, the principle says that the contract is deemed to be concluded and thus any refusal by the offeror to perform the concluded contract may give rise to contractual damages on the positive interest.[80] If the 'irrevocable' offer is, however, abruptly revoked before acceptance, this is, before the contract is factually concluded, the offeror may be liable for breach of pre-contractual duties, which will allow the offeree to recover damages on the negative interests.[81]

1.4. Termination of Offer

1.4.1. Rejection

An offer is ineffective when it is rejected by the offeree, or because of the caducity of the period for its acceptance.[82] Yet again, the refusal to accept the terms of the offer can be manifested expressly or impliedly.[83] The implied

(Ed.), Comentario a los Principios de Unidroit para los Contratos del Comercio Internacional Art. 2.4, 2.a, at 122 (2003): commenting on and comparing to the domestic Spanish law.

[78] Cuba Art. 317.1 CC; Guatemala Art. 1521 CC; Mexico Art. 1084 CC; Uruguay Art. 204 Com C; Venezuela Art. 1.137 para. 5 CC; Mexico Collegiate Tribunals, *Novena Época,* Registry 177'335, SJF XXII, September 2005, p 1436. Confirming Bolivia: Kaune Arteaga, *supra* note 2, 69; Brazil: Gomes, *supra* note 3, at 79, para. 47; Mexico: Vásquez del Mercado, *supra* note 2, at 158; Spain: Perales Vizcasillas, *supra* note 77, Art. 2.4, 2.a, at 122: commenting on and comparing to the domestic Spanish law.

[79] Costa Rica Art. 443 (b) Com C: duty to withhold the offer during 5 days if the parties are in the same place, 10 days in another place within the country and 1 month if in different countries.

[80] *See* Chile Art. 100 Com C; Colombia Art. 846 CC; Ecuador Art. 144 Com C; Venezuela Art. 113 Com C: compensation of damages is only due if the offeree had begun performance; Colombia: Oviedo Albán, *supra* note 3, at 76; Ecuador: Cevallos Vásquez, *supra* note 3, at 236; Spain: Llobet I Aguado, *supra* note 3, at 30; Colombia Supreme Court, *Cass civ,* 4 April 2001, *cited in* Colombia: Oviedo Alban, *supra* note 3, at 78, n. 105. For details on the damages on positive interest, also called expectation interest *see* Ch. 28, 2.2 and Ch. 50, 2.2.

[81] *See* expressly Colombia: Oviedo Albán, *supra* note 3, at 76; Spain: Llobet I Aguado, *supra* note 3, at 30; impliedly in Argentina Art. 1156 CC; Bolivia Art. 826 Com C; Chile Art. 100 Com C; Colombia Art. 846 CC; Ecuador Art. 144 Com C. For details on the damages on negative interest, also called reliance interest *see* Ch. 28, 2.3 and Ch. 50, 2.3.

[82] Art. 17 CISG; Colombia: Oviedo Alban, *supra* note 3, at 83.

[83] Art. 8 CISG.

refusal can be understood from facts indicating that the offeree does not accept the offer, for example, accepting a concurrent offer from a third offeror.[84] However, a rejection must have reached the offeror.[85]

1.4.2. Lapse of Time

Under the Ibero-American laws, offers to a present person, without reference to a fixed time for acceptance, terminate unless immediately accepted.[86] Acceptance must come as soon as the offeree knows of the offer. Often, offers are considered to take place between present persons when they are made verbally;[87] or by telephone or other equivalent means of immediate communication.[88] Thus, in absence of an immediate acceptance the offeror is released of everything he had offered.

As to the termination of offers in non-present-persons cases, under most laws offers terminate if there is no acceptance within the fixed period established by the offeror.[89] In some countries, the *reception*[90] or the *knowledge*[91] of the

---

84 Colombia: Oviedo Alban, *supra* note 3, at 83.

85 U.G. Schroeter, *in* I. Schwenzer (Ed.), Schlechtriem & Schwenzer Commentary on the UN Convention on the International Sale of Goods Art. 17, para. 2, at 312 (2010).

86 Argentina Art. 1151 CC; Brazil Art. 428 (I) CC; Chile Art. 97 Com C; Colombia Art. 850 Com C; Costa Rica Art. 1011 CC (unless otherwise agreed by the parties) & Art. 442 Com C; Cuba Art. 317.1. CC *contrario sensu*; Ecuador Art. 141 Com C; Guatemala Art. 1521 CC; Honduras Art. 718 Com C; Mexico Art. 1805 CC; Nicaragua Art. 2451 CC; Paraguay Art. 675 CC; Peru Art. 1385 (1) CC; Uruguay Art. 1263 CC & Art. 200 Com C; Venezuela Art. 110 Com C.

87 Argentina Art. 1151 CC; Colombia Art. 850 Com C; Costa Rica Art. 442 Com C; Ecuador Art. 141 Com C; Paraguay Art. 675 CC; Uruguay Art. 1263 CC & Art. 200 Com C.

88 Brazil Art. 428 (I) CC; Colombia Art. 850 Com C; Costa Rica Art. 442 Com C; Paraguay Art. 675 CC; Peru Art. 1385 (1) CC.

89 Bolivia Art. 455 CC & Art. 827 Com C (offer made to the public); Brazil Art. 428 (II) CC; Colombia Art. 453 Com C; Costa Rica Art. 1012 CC & Art. 443 Com C; Cuba Art. 317.1 CC; El Salvador Art. 969 Com C; Guatemala Art. 1521 CC; Honduras Art. 718 Com C; Mexico Art. 1806 CC; Nicaragua Art. 2452 CC; Paraguay Art. 679 CC; Peru Art. 1385 (1) CC; Uruguay Art. 1266 CC; Venezuela Art. 1.137 CC; Mexico Collegiate Tribunals, *Novena Época,* Registry 177'335, SJF XXII, September 2005, at 1436; Mexico Collegiate Tribunals, *Novena Época,* Registry 177'052, SJF XXII, October 2005, at 2318.

90 Bolivia Art. 815 Com C; Costa Rica Art. 444 Com C; El Salvador Art. 966 Com C; Guatemala Art. 1523 CC: But if the offer has not a fixed time for acceptance the offeror will be bound during the sufficient time necessary so that he knows of the acceptance; Mexico Art. 1807 CC & Art. 80 Com C; Peru Arts. 1373, 1374 CC; Uruguay Art. 1265 CC; Bolivia Art. 455 CC (*see* how the rule is different for sales covered by the Code of Commerce which follows the reception rule Art. 815 Com C); Chile Arts. 97, 105 Com C (broad interpretation); Cuba Art. 317.1 CC (*see* how the rule is different for sales covered by the Code of Commerce which follows the dispatch rule Art. 54 Com C); Honduras Art. 1553 CC; Panama Art. 1113 CC.

91 Bolivia Art. 455 CC (note how the rule is different for sales covered by the Code of Commerce which follows the reception rule Art. 815 Com C); Chile Arts. 97, 105 Com C (broad interpretation); Cuba Art. 317.1 CC (note how the rule is different for sales covered by

acceptance by the offeror is the relevant moment, while in other laws the *dispatch* of the acceptance by the offeree is the relevant act that keeps the offer existing and binding.[92]

Absent a fixed time for acceptance in the offer, the Ibero-American laws provide different solutions as to the caducity of the offer. Under some laws, offers terminate if they are not accepted within a reasonable,[93] sufficient,[94] or providential time;[95] or in accordance with the usages or the nature of the business.[96]

In other countries the rules differ depending on where the offeror and offeree are located. In these countries, offers terminate if they are not accepted or rejected within a default time established by the law if the person to whom the offer is addressed resides in the same place as the offeror.[97] When the parties are not domiciled in the same place, some laws establish that due consideration must be given to the time that the mail service normally takes to go and return.[98]

Similarly, Costa Rica and Nicaragua's laws distinguish three different caducity terms depending on the residence of the offeror and the offeree.[99] The offer will be considered terminated, if the offeree does not reply within

the Code of Commerce which follows the dispatch rule Art. 54 Com C); Honduras Art. 1553 CC; Panama Art. 1113 CC.

92 Brazil Art. 428 CC; Paraguay Art. 679 CC.

93 Brazil Arts. 466, 428 (II) CC: talks about sufficient and reasonable time.

94 Guatemala Art. 1523 CC: refers to sufficient time so that the offeror knows about the acceptance; Paraguay Art. 678 CC: if sufficient time passes so that its acceptance is known by the offeror, in normal circumstances, but he does not receive it; Peru Art. 1385 (2) CC: when sufficient time has passed for the acceptance to arrive at knowledge of the offeror, by the same means of communication used by this one.

95 Cuba Art. 317.1 CC.

96 Bolivia Art. 455 CC; Venezuela Art. 112 Com C: if the acceptance does not arrive at knowledge of the offeror within the necessary time for the exchange of the offer and the acceptance, according to the nature of the contract and the usages of the commerce.

97 Chile Art. 98 Com C (within 24 hours); Colombia 851 Com C (within 6 days); Ecuador Art. 142 Com C (within 24 hours); Uruguay Art. 1266 CC (within 24 hours); Venezuela Art. 111 Com C (within 24 hours).

98 Chile Art. 98 Com C; Colombia Art. 851 Com C (noting that if the offeree resides in different place, the time of the distance shall be added); Ecuador Art. 142 Com C (within the time that the first mail, which leaves after the twenty-four hours from receipt of the offer, takes); Mexico Art. 1806 CC (within three days, besides the necessary time it regularly takes to the public mail to go and return, or the time that it is judged enough, being no public mail, according to the distances and the means of the communications); Uruguay Art. 1266 CC (when the offeree lives elsewhere, the offer terminates if acceptance does not occur within 30 days since the necessary time has passed so that the two communications reach their destiny).

99 *See generally* Costa Rica: Brenes Córdoba, Trejos & Ramírez, *supra* note 2, at 57-58.

three days when he is in the same province; within ten, when not in the same province, but in the Republic; and within sixty days, when one is abroad from the Republic.[100]

Elapsing the time period mentioned in the preceding paragraphs, the offer will be considered as never made.

1.4.3. Judge Intervention

A few Ibero-American laws give the judge the final word on the time of caducity of the offer, absent an express reference in the offer itself.[101]

1.4.4. Death and Incapacity

In this regard, the solutions are not completely uniform in the Ibero-American laws. On the one hand, some laws expressly dictate that the offer terminates with the death or the loss of capacity of the offeror before he had received,[102] or known of,[103] the acceptance of the offeree. On the other hand, some laws expressly establish that the offer remains effective even though the offeror dies or loses his legal capacity between the time of dispatch of the offer and the acceptance by the offeree, unless the nature of the offer or the conduct of the offeror suggests otherwise.[104] However, under some laws, the offeree must be *unaware* of the death or loss of legal capacity occurred at the time of acceptance so that the offeror's heirs or legal representatives are bound to uphold the contract.[105]

Regarding unanticipated circumstances affecting the offeree, some laws state that the offer terminates with the death or loss of capacity of the offeree.[106]

---

[100] Costa Rica Art. 1012 CC (but *see also* distinction in commercial sales Costa Rica 443 Com C 5 days in the same province; 10 days within the Republic; and 1 month in different countries); Nicaragua Art. 2452 CC.

[101] El Salvador 969 Com C; Honduras 719 Com C.

[102] Guatemala Art. 1528 CC.

[103] Bolivia Art. 459 CC; Chile Art. 101 Com C; Ecuador Art. 145 Com C; Uruguay Art. 1268 CC.

[104] Colombia Art. 486 Com C; El Salvador 969 Com C; Honduras Art. 718 Com C; Peru Art. 1383 CC. Regarding the Brazilian legislation, the heirs of the offeror are responsible for the legal consequences of the offer, *see* Brazil: C.R. Gonçalves, Dereito Civil Brasileiro, Vol. III, Contratos e Atos Unilateralais 52-53 (2004).

[105] Costa Rica Art. 1014 CC; Mexico Art. 1809 CC; Nicaragua Art. 2454 CC.

[106] Bolivia Art. 459 CC; Peru Art. 1387 CC; Uruguay Art. 1268 CC.

1.4.5. Express or Implied Conditions

Some laws expressly recognise that offers addressed to the general public terminate when the merchandise offered becomes unavailable.[107] In the same way, an offeror can subject the effectiveness of his offer to an express or implied condition.

2. Acceptance

2.1. Declaration of Acceptance

Similarly, to the CISG approach, in the Ibero-American laws the offeree's declaration of acceptance is the complement of the offeror's intention to be bound by his offer.[108] In this way, the acceptance of the contract can also be express or implied.[109] Consent is generally understood to be express when it is manifested verbally, in writing or by unequivocal signs.[110] The implied consent results from facts or conduct.[111] With regard to this issue, a Spanish court has upheld that the reception of the goods by the buyer and their subsequent non-rejection constituted conduct of implied acceptance of the seller's offer, which binds the buyer to pay the price.[112]

Likewise, some Ibero-American laws expressly dictate that silence does not constitute a manifestation of assent. There are exceptions, however, in cases in which one of the parties has the obligation to explain itself, because

[107] Bolivia Art. 827 CC; Chile Art. 105 Com C; Colombia Art. 849 Com C; Ecuador Art. 148 Com C.

[108] Brazil Art. 432 CC; Colombia: Oviedo Alban, *supra* note 3, at 89. Under the CISG Art. 18 (1) acceptance is the statement or conduct of the offeree indicating assent to an offer.

[109] Argentina Art. 1145 CC; Bolivia Art. 453 CC; Brazil Art. 432 CC; Chile Art. 1449 CC & Art. 103 Com C; Colombia Art. 1506 CC; Costa Rica Art. 1008 CC; Ecuador Art. 1492 CC; El Salvador Art. 1320 CC; Guatemala Art. 1252 CC; Honduras Art. 1551 CC; Mexico Art. 1803 CC; Nicaragua Art. 2448 CC; Paraguay Art. 674 CC; Peru Art. 141 CC; Portugal Art. 217 CC; Venezuela Art. 1.138 CC; *see also* Brazil: Gomes, *supra* note 3, at 76; El Salvador: Miranda, *supra* note 3, at 33; Peru Supreme Court, *Sala civil permanente,* Resolution 005211-2007, 27 March 2008.

[110] Argentina Art. 1145 CC; Bolivia Art. 453 CC; Costa Rica Art. 1008 CC; Mexico Art. 1803 CC; Nicaragua Art. 2448 CC; Peru Art. 141 CC; Portugal Art. 217 CC.

[111] Argentina Art. 1145 CC; Bolivia Art. 453 CC; Chile Art. 1449 CC; Colombia Art. 1506 CC; Costa Rica Art. 1008 CC; Ecuador Art. 1492 CC; Honduras Art. 1551 CC; Mexico Art. 1803 CC; Nicaragua Art. 2448 CC; Paraguay Art. 674 CC; Peru Art. 141 CC; Portugal Art. 217 CC.

[112] Spain Audiencia Provincial de Lérida, 16 January 1991.

of its current silence and the previous statements create such obligation.[113] The Battles of Forms provide examples of this duty to speak and the consequences of silence under the circumstances.[114]

Under other countries' laws, silence constitutes a manifestation of assent when the usages or the circumstances authorise such meaning and an express declaration is not required, unless the contract or the law states otherwise.[115] For example, under the Bolivian B2B sales, the purchase order is considered accepted if the seller does not reject it within 10 days after its reception.[116] Under other laws, if the business is one of those in which an express acceptance is not a usage, or when the offer so establishes, the contract is concluded if the offer is not rapidly rejected.[117] The offeror bears the burden proof of the usage and of the invitation to offer.[118]

Closely following the CISG, the Bolivian, the Peruvian and the Venezuelan Civil Codes establish that if according to the usages, nature of the transaction or request of the offeror, the performance can be done without previous express acceptance, in this case, the contract forms at the moment and place in which the performance has begun. The offeree is obliged to immediately inform the offeror that the performance has begun.[119]

2.2. Time for and Effect of an Acceptance

The question as to when the acceptance becomes effective has a significant impact on several things, including, the binding character of the acceptance

113 Argentina Art. 919 CC; Cuba Art. 49.1 CC; Guatemala Art. 1253 CC; Peru Arts. 142, 1381 CC; *see* Argentina Supreme Court, *Roco, Juan C. y otra v. Provincia de Santa Fe*, 9 November 1989, *Fallos* 312:2152: stating that "[A]s long as there is not a legal obligation to inform, silence does not constitute an express or implied manifestation of assent."

114 *See* Ch. 13, 3.

115 Bolivia Art. 460 CC; Brazil Art. 111 CC; Portugal Art. 217 CC; *see also* Colombia: Oviedo Alban, *supra* note 3, at 90: noting that under the Colombian Law in order to mean acceptance, silence must be accompanied by unequivocal acts directed to the performance of the contract; El Salvador: Miranda, *supra* note 2, at 35; Portugal Supreme Tribunal of Justice, 13 March 2008: silence cannot be considered an acceptance to modifications of contract, if such is not agreed between parties.

116 Bolivia Art. 830 Com C.

117 Guatemala Art. 1526 CC; Peru Art. 1381 CC; Venezuela Art. 112 Com C.

118 Peru Art. 1381 CC.

119 Bolivia Art. 457 CC; Peru Art. 1381 CC; Venezuela Art. 1.138 CC; *see* explaining the rule Peru: M. Castillo Freyre, Tratado de la Teoria General de los Contratos Vol. I, 36 (2002). Under CISG Art. 18(2)(3) silence or inactivity does not in itself constitute an acceptance. However, the offeree may indicate assent by performing an act, such as one relating to the dispatch of the goods or payment of the price, without notice to the offeror. This type of acceptance is only possible if the offer so indicates or if such results from the practices which the parties have established between themselves or from a usage, provided that the act-acceptance is performed in due time.

for the offeree, the impossibility to revoke the offer, the time of the contract conclusion, the place of contract conclusion, and the applicable law.[120] The solution varies among legal systems, including the Ibero-American ones; since different rules have developed to answer this question.

2.2.1. Time of Contract Conclusion

As under the CISG,[121] in the Ibero-American laws, the offers made to a present person, without reference to a fixed time for acceptance, must be immediately accepted;[122] acceptance must come as soon as the offeree knows the offer.[123] Offers are considered to take place between present persons when they are made verbally.[124] Some countries' laws consider that contract negotiation by telephone or other equivalent means of immediate (electronic) communication are understood to take place between present persons,[125] while others laws categorise such negotiations as taking place between non-present persons.[126]

---

[120] *See* Bolivia: Kaune Arteaga, *supra* note 2, at 75-77; Colombia: Oviedo Alban, *supra* note 3, at 98; Peru: Castillo Freyre, *supra* note 119, at 33.

[121] Art. 18 (2) CISG.

[122] Argentina Art. 1151 CC; Brazil Art. 428 CC; Chile Art. 97 Com C; Colombia Art. 850 Com C; Costa Rica Art. 1011 CC & Art. 442 Com C; Cuba Art. 317.1. CC *contrario sensu*; Ecuador Art. 141 Com C; Guatemala Art. 1521 CC; Honduras 718 Com C; Mexico Art. 1805 CC; Nicaragua Art. 2451 CC; Paraguay Art. 675 CC; Peru Art. 1385 (1) CC; Uruguay Art. 1263 CC & Art. 200 Com C; Venezuela Art. 110 Com C; Mexico Collegiate Tribunals, *Novena Época,* Registry 205'193, SJF I, May 1995, p 349: confirming the rule; *see also* doctrinal references Ecuador: Cevallos Vásquez, *supra* note 3, at 234: confirming the rule; El Salvador: Miranda, *supra* note 3, at 34; El Salvador: Miranda, *supra* note 2, at 32; Mexico: León Tovar, *supra* note 14, at 68; Mexico: B. Perez Fernandez del Castillo, Contratos Civiles 23 (2008); Portugal: De Lima Pinheiro, *supra* note 49, at 271: confirming the rule.

[123] Peru: Castillo Freyre, *supra* note 119, at 27-29.

[124] Argentina Art. 1151 CC; Colombia Art. 850 Com C; Costa Rica Art. 442 Com C; Ecuador Art. 141 Com C: but if the offer was made in writing to a present person the acceptance shall be performed within 24 hours, *see* Art. 142 Com C; Paraguay Art. 675 CC; Uruguay Art. 1263 CC & Art. 200 Com C.

[125] Brazil Art. 428 CC; Chile Art. 97 Com C; Colombia Art. 850 Com C; Costa Rica Art. 442 Com C; Honduras Art. 716 Com C; Mexico Art. 1805 CC; Paraguay Art. 675 CC; Peru Art. 1385 (1) CC; Confirming Argentina: J.M. Farina, Contratos Comerciales Modernos 109-110 (1999): noting that communication through computers is instantaneously, thus such electronic contracts must be considered as passed between present persons, therefore such contract shall be considered concluded by immediate acceptance (Art. 1150 CC); Brazil: Gomes, *supra* note 3, at 80: noting that the rules on contracts conclusion between present persons will apply to contracts passed through electronic communications when the persons are considered to communicate instantaneously, BUT the rules for contracts between non-presents will apply to contracts passed through electronic communications when the persons are considered to communicate by correspondence; Mexico: León Tovar, *supra* note 14, at 68; Mexico: E. Elías Azar, La Contratacion por Medios Electronicos 222 (2005).

[126] Costa Rica Art. 442 Com C; *see also* Costa Rica: J.J. Obando Peralta, *Los Contratos Electrónicos y Digitales*, 39 AR: Revista de Derecho Informático (2001), http://www.alfa-

CISG contracts between non-present persons are concluded at the moment when an acceptance of an offer becomes effective.[127] Acceptance becomes effective at the moment the indication of assent reaches the offeror.[128] In this regard, the CISG follows the reception rule of contract conclusion. The contract is concluded when the acceptance of the offeree *reaches* the offeror, unless the acceptance is expressed by performing an act,[129] in which case the contract is concluded when performance begins.

In the Ibero-American laws, there is no uniform solution as to the time when the contract is concluded by non-present persons. Some countries rely on the reception rule of contract formation while others have either opted for the declaration rule, the information rule, the dispatch rule or even for a combination of two rules.[130]

Certainly, some systems follow the same reception rule. The contract is concluded when the acceptance reaches the offeror.[131] On the other hand, some countries' laws recognise the information rule as the precise moment of contract conclusion. That is, the contract is concluded when the offeror knows about the acceptance of its offer.[132] Other Ibero-American laws follow

redi.org/rdi-articulo.shtml?x=819: noting that the rules contained in Costa Rica's Civil Code and Code of Commerce shall be applied to the formation of e-commerce sales. This author considers that depending on whether the communication of the parties is instantaneous or not the rules on contract formation between present parties or those for non-present parties should apply respectively; El Salvador Art. 968 Com C; Guatemala Art. 1524 CC; confirming the rule El Salvador: Miranda, *supra* note 3, at 37.

[127] Art. 23 CISG.

[128] Art. 18 (2) CISG.

[129] Art. 18 (2) CISG.

[130] For a brief review of these rules and their advantages and disadvantages according to the Ibero-American doctrine *see* Bolivia: Kaune Arteaga, *supra* note 2, at 79-81; Peru: Castillo Freyre, *supra* note 119, at 28-32; El Salvador: Miranda, *supra* note 2, at 32-33; Mexico: Elías Azar, *supra* note 125, at 223.

[131] Bolivia Art. 815 Com C & Art. 29 LDSEC; Costa Rica Art. 444 Com C; El Salvador Art. 966 Com C; Guatemala Art. 1523 CC; Mexico Art. 1807 CC & Art. 80 Com C; Uruguay Art. 1265 CC; *see* confirming the rule in the respective law Costa Rica: M. Ramírez Altamirano, Derecho Civil IV, Vol. II, Los Contratos Traslativos de Dominio 48 (1991); El Salvador: Miranda, *supra* note 3, at 34; El Salvador: Miranda, *supra* note 2, at 34; Perez Fernandez, *supra* note 122, at 24; Mexico: León Tovar, *supra* note 14, at 68: noting that the reforms on electronic communications introduce to the Civil Code also acknowledge the reception rule; Mexico Collegiate Tribunals, *Novena Época,* Registry 205'193, SJF I, May 1995, p 349: confirming the rule.

[132] Bolivia Art. 455 CC (*see* how the rule is different for sales covered by Art. 815 Com C or whenever electronic communications are used: the reception rule); Cuba Art. 317.1 CC (*see* how the rule is different for sales covered by the Code of Commerce which follows the dispatch rule Art. 54 Com C); Honduras Art. 1553 CC; Panama Art. 1113 CC; Peru Art. 1373 CC (besides Peru Art. 1374 CC establishes that the offer is meant to be known by the receiver when it arrives at his address); *see* Peru: Sierralta Rios, *supra* note 3, at 57: noting that in Peru the system follows the information rule and Art. 1374 is only an additional presumption of knowledge of the offer established to give certainty to the offeree; Spain Art. 1.262 CC (or since

the dispatch theory of contract conclusion. Accordingly, contracts are deemed to be concluded when the offeree dispatches his acceptance to the offeror.[133] Finally, Chile and Ecuador laws seem to follow a declaration rule, that the contract has full effect, from the moment the offeree declares his acceptance.[134]

Some countries' laws have established double theories of contract conclusion: receipt-information and dispatch-information. Under the Portuguese law a contract is formed when the acceptance is received or acknowledged by the offeror.[135] Thus, the acceptance may be effective when even if not yet received, the offeror has knowledge of it.[136] Also Venezuela's Civil Code explains that the contract is concluded as soon as the offeror has knowledge of the acceptance by the offeree.[137] The acceptance however is presumed to be known by the offeror from the moment it arrives at his address, unless he proves that, with no fault, he was not able to know about the acceptance, even though it had arrived at his address.[138] Also interesting is a provision in the Argentinean Code of Commerce which establishes that when one party's intent to contract is communicated to an agent or emissary, such party is bound by his statement; even before it has been transmitted to the principal or the sender of the emissary.[139]

2.2.2. Time Limits to Accept

Similarly to the CISG approach,[140] under most of the Ibero-American laws offers shall be accepted before the offer expires according to the offer itself, the usages, or the law.[141]

---

the offeree dispatches the acceptance and the offeror cannot ignore that fact in good faith; *see also* that the Spanish Art. 54 Com C adopts the dispatch rule).

[133] Argentina Art. 1154 CC; Brazil Art. 434 CC; Colombia 864 Com C; Cuba Art. 54 Com C; Paraguay Art. 688 CC; Spain Art. 54 Com C (more precisely when the offeree replies to the offer or counter offer); Brazil Superior Tribunal of Justice, RO 39/MG, Minister Jorge Scartezzini, published 6 March 2006: the parties are bound by the contracts concluded *inter praesentes* at the moment when the offeree accepts the offer and *inter absentes* when the acceptance is dispatched.

[134] Chile Art. 101 Com C; Ecuador Art. 145 Com C.

[135] Portugal Art. 224 CC.

[136] Portugal: De Lima Pinheiro, *supra* note 49, at 270.

[137] Venezuela Art. 1.137 CC & Art. 115 Com C.

[138] Venezuela Art. 1.137 (5) CC.

[139] Argentina Art. 215 Com C.

[140] Art. 18 (2) CISG: an acceptance is not effective if the indication of assent does not reach the offeror within the time he has fixed, or if no time is fixed, within a reasonable time, in light of the circumstances of the transaction, including the rapidity of the means of communication employed by the offeror.

[141] *See supra* 1.4.

2.2.3. Duty to Communicate the Late Acceptance

Some Ibero-American laws expressly establish a duty to communicate late acceptance. Certainly, if the acceptance, under any circumstance, is delayed, this must be communicated to the offeree immediately; otherwise the offeror shall compensate the offeree for the damages and loss of profits that may occur to the offeree.[142]

2.2.4. Place of Contract Conclusion

While the CISG does not deal with the question of the place of contract conclusion, some Ibero-American laws expressly do. With present persons, the contract is logically concluded in the place they are at that time.[143] However, with non-present persons the solutions vary. On the one hand, some laws establish that contract conclusion occurs in the place of residence of the party who accepts the original offer or the counter-offer: the domicile of the offeree.[144] On the other hand, some laws consider the site where the offer or counter-offer was made as the place of contract conclusion: place of offer.[145] The Civil Codes of Peru and Uruguay establish that the contract is concluded at the place where the acceptance was known[146] or received[147] by the offeror: place of acceptance. In Argentina, the dispatch of the acceptance is the place where the contract is concluded.[148] The place of contract conclusion may be relevant to determine the applicable law to the form of the contract.[149]

2.2.5. Acceptance Withdrawal

According to CISG Article 22 an acceptance may be withdrawn if the withdrawal reaches the offeror before or at the same time as the acceptance would have become effective. Similarly, some Ibero-American laws expressly establish that acceptance can be withdrawn before or at the same time the

[142] Brazil Art. 430 CC; Chile Art. 98 Com C; Ecuador Art. 142 Com C; Guatemala Art. 1525 CC; Paraguay Art. 684 CC.
[143] *See* expressly Bolivia Art. 461 CC; *see also* Brazil: Gomes, *supra* note 3, at 82.
[144] Chile Art. 104 Com C; Ecuador Art. 147 CC.
[145] Bolivia Art. 462 CC (place of the offer's dispatch) & Art. 29 LDSEC; Brazil Art. 435 CC; Guatemala Art. 1524 CC; Honduras Art. 1553 CC; Panama Art. 1113 CC; Paraguay Art. 687 CC; Spain Art. 1.265 CC; Venezuela Art. 115 Com C.
[146] Peru Art. 1373 CC.
[147] Uruguay Art. 1265 CC.
[148] Argentina: Farina, *supra* note 124, at 109-110.
[149] *See* Ch. 4, 1.

offeror knows about it,[150] while others, dictate that the acceptance can be withdrawn if the withdrawal reaches the offeror before, or at the same time of the acceptance.[151]

2.3. Alterations between Offer and Acceptance

The acceptance must have certain characteristics to give legal effect to the offeror's intention to be bound by his offer. The pure acceptance constitutes the agreement of the offeree on all the terms of the offer. Though in practice, this ideal acceptance does not always happen. Some approaches have been developed in different legal systems in order to soften the requirement of a pure and full acceptance. The CISG is a good example of such approach.[152] Regrettably, the same cannot be said of the Ibero-American laws.

The Ibero-American laws do not distinguish between material and immaterial alterations of the offer in the acceptance. The primary and only rule is that any modification or addition to the offer renders the acceptance a new offer or counter-offer,[153] although the discrepancy is secondary.[154] This means that in order to have a valid contract, the counter-offer must be accepted by the other party with an acceptance mirroring all the terms of the counter-offer.[155]

---

[150] Argentina Art. 1149 CC; Bolivia Art. 458 CC; Guatemala Art. 1527 CC; Peru Art. 1386 CC.

[151] Brazil Art. 433 CC; Mexico Art. 1808 CC; Uruguay Art. 1265 CC.

[152] CISG Art. 19 distinguishes between an acceptance that is materially different from the terms of the offer and an acceptance which is immaterially different. Terms that alter the offer materially are additional or different terms relating to, among other things, the price, payment, quality and quantity of the goods, place and time of delivery, the extent of one party's liability, or the settlement of disputes. These examples of terms cannot be considered immaterial, thus any alteration made to them in the acceptance renders it a counter-offer. Other differences that materially alter the offer are to be considered by the court or the arbitral tribunal in a case by case basis, giving due consideration to the circumstances of the case and the importance of the alterations to the offer.

[153] Argentina Art. 1152 CC; Bolivia Art. 456 CC & Art. 815 Com C; Brazil Art. 431 CC; Chile Arts. 101, 102 Com C; Colombia Art. 855 Com C; Costa Rica Art. 1010 CC & Art. 444 Com C; Cuba Art. 54 Com C; Ecuador Arts. 145, 146 Com C; El Salvador Art. 966 Com C; Mexico Art. 1810 CC; Nicaragua Art. 2450 CC; Paraguay Art. 681 CC; Peru Arts. 1359, 1376 CC; Portugal Art. 233 CC; Spain Art. 1.261 CC & Art. 54 Com C; Uruguay Art. 1267 CC; Venezuela Art. 1.137 CC & Art. 114 Com C; *see also* Mexico Supreme Court, *Séptima Epoca, Tercera Sala,* SJF, Vol. 6, Part 4, at 18; Spain Supreme Tribunal, 26 March 1993; Spain Supreme Tribunal, 30 May 1996; Spain Supreme Tribunal, 5 December 1996.

[154] *See* doctrine Bolivia: Kaune Arteaga, *supra* note 2, at 71; Brazil: Gomes, *supra* note 3, at 73; Saldias Callao, *supra* note 11, at 96; Colombia: Oviedo Alban, *supra* note 3, at 103; Costa Rica: Baudrit Carrillo, *supra* note 16, at 28-31; El Salvador: Miranda, *supra* note 3, at 33; El Salvador: Miranda, *supra* note 2, at 30; Mexico: Vásquez del Mercado, *supra* note 2, at 157, 158; Peru: Sierralta Ríos, *supra* note 3, at 64; Portugal: De Lima Pinheiro, *supra* note 49, at 273; Spain: Guardiola Sacarrera, *supra* note 66, at 58.

[155] Costa Rica: Baudrit Carrillo, *supra* note 16, at 31; Mexico Collegiate Tribunals, *Novena*

The principle is known as the mirror image rule.[156] The same principle works when offers are emitted with alternative or divisible parts. So, for example, the Civil Codes of Argentina, Paraguay and Peru state that if the offer is alternative or includes separable parts, the acceptance of anyone of them will give rise to a valid contract. But if the offer cannot be divided, it will be considered a new offer (counter-offer) to contract.[157]

3. Language Problems

Under the Guatemalan law, contracts to be concluded and having effect in the Guatemalan territory shall be passed in the Spanish language.[158] The rest of the Ibero-American laws do not limit the parties to the use of the official languages of the legal system for the conclusion of contracts. Some laws expressly uphold the freedom of the parties to conclude their contracts in the language they consider advantageous.[159] As far as the parties' intent is not affected by communication gaps or misunderstandings, the contract shall remain valid,[160] and the parties shall be bound in the way and under the terms it appears they wanted to be bound.[161] Furthermore, foreign language misunderstandings and gaps may not be alleged if the parties have failed to undertake diligent and reasonable measures to overcome such misunderstandings.[162]

Although contracts in foreign languages are recognised, in legal proceedings all documents presented in a foreign language must be accompanied by a translation into Portuguese or Spanish.[163]

Época, Registry 205'193, SJF I, May 1995, p 349: confirming the rule; Peru Supreme Court, *Sala civil transitoria,* Resolution 001860-2002, 19 July 2002.

156 On the criticisms and disadvantages of this rigid rule *see* Colombia: Oviedo Alban, *supra* note 3, at 103.

157 Argentina Art. 1153 CC; Paraguay Art. 682 CC; Peru Art. 1377 CC.

158 Guatemala Art. 671 Com C.

159 Costa Rica Art. 411 Com C; Cuba Art. 51 CC; Paraguay Art. 399 CC.

160 Brazil Superior Tribunal of Justice REsp 151079/SP, Minister Barros Monteiro, published 29 November 2004.

161 Costa Rica Art. 411 Com C; Colombia Art. 823 Com C: but foreign language will be understood in the meaning that it has in Spanish; same statement *in* Bolivia: Camargo Marín, *supra* note 3, at 398.

162 Argentina National Commercial Court of Appeals, *Quilmes Combustibles, S.A. c.Vigan, S.A,* 15 March 1991: the mere fact that the standard terms were written in French language does not amount to mistake as a party would be expected to diligently take any reasonable measure to understand their meaning by means of translation.

163 *See for example* Chile Art. 347 CPC; Costa Rica Art. 395 CPC; Mexico Art. 271 CPC.

CHAPTER 11

MODERN FORMS OF CONTRACT CONCLUSION

1. Point by Point Negotiation

The Ibero-American trade practice shows that the sales contract can be passed through the traditional offer and acceptance relatively immediate process of contract conclusion or, alternatively, in the form of a continuous course of negotiations.[1] This second way of contract conclusion, used in modern times and often characterised by a slower and longer process of point by point negotiations, is more complex. Important questions arise, for example, as to the set of rules covering the pre-contractual phase and on the binding character of many forms of communications that the parties undertake prior to the conclusion of the contract.

For example, during the course of negotiations the parties often make use of different pre-contractual instruments designed to keep a record of their discussions and in order to arrange the potential final deal.[2] Usually the parties start by gathering and discussing their respective ideas about the future contract (*pourparlers*). At this stage, none of the parties have normally expressed his intention to be bound by any understood offer and most of the constituents of the contract remain unknown. However, soon after the parties may move ahead to more solid ground, recording their respective expectations or duties over the future sales contract, either in the form of letters of intent or memorandums of understandings.[3]

---

[1] Confirming the modern tendency Mexico Collegiate Tribunals, *Novena Época*, Registry 177'335, SJF XXII, September 2005, at 1436; *see also* Spain: J. Llobet I Aguado, El Deber de Información en la Formación de los Contratos 16 (1996).

[2] Mexico Collegiate Tribunals, *Novena Época*, Registry 177'335, SJF XXII, September 2005, p. 1436.

[3] *See generally* Spain: E. Guardiola Sacarrera, La compraventa internacional: importaciones y exportaciones 49-51 (2001); ICC Final Award Case No. 11404 *Lex Contractus* Argentinean Law: in the case at hand, the Arbitral Tribunal upheld that the MOU entered into by the parties

At the objective stage of negotiations, when no agreement has been reached, the parties are not bound to any of the expressions or communications undertaken.[4] Nor are the parties bound to reach the expected agreement, unless otherwise agreed.[5] Nevertheless, the parties may be liable for breach of pre-contractual obligations as recognised by the Ibero-America laws.[6] Such liability directly or indirectly derives from the breach of the good faith principle and related principles during negotiations.[7] On this issue, most Ibero-American authors and the jurisprudence consider that the most important role of the pre-contractual law provisions is to determine if one party's conduct is in accordance to the good faith principle having regard of the level of the parties' expectations.[8]

2. Letters of Intent

Letters of intent include many forms of expression made in writing by the parties during the course of negotiations.[9] Some letters of intent expressly establish their non-binding character.[10] Nevertheless, this sort of letter can have an evidentiary value upon the negotiation process, often useful at a later

---

was a binding agreement, inasmuch as it contains provisions that are clearly intended to impose rights and obligations on the parties.

4 Spain: Guardiola Sacarrera, *supra* note 3, at 50.

5 Mexico Collegiate Tribunals, *Novena Época*, Registry 177'335, SJF XXII, September 2005, at 1436.

6 *See* Ch. 27 and Ch. 28.

7 This good faith principle in contracts include duties of mutual collaboration, protection, information, secrecy, communication, *etc.*, *see* Chile: I.M. Zuloaga Rios, Teoría de la responsabilidad precontractual: aplicaciones en la formación del consentimiento de los contratos 89 (2007).

8 Brazil: C.R. Gonçalves, Dereito Civil Brasileiro, Vol. III, Contratos e Atos Unilateralais 49-50 (2004); Colombia: J. Oviedo Alban, La Formación de Contrato: tratos preliminares, oferta, aceptación 10 (2008); Guatemala: V. Aguilar Guerra, El Negocio Jurídico 279 (2004); R. Stiglitz, Tratativas Precontractuales, en Contratos, Teoria General, at 91 and H. Rosende Alvaréz, Responsabilidad Precontractual ..., *cited by* Chile: Zuloaga Rios, *supra* note 7, at 88, n. 115, and 91, n. 164, respectively; Spain: Guardiola Sacarrera, *supra* note 3, at 53; Spain: Llobet I Aguado, *supra* note 1, at 16, 17; ICC Final Award Case No. 11404 *Lex Contractus* Argentinean Law: stating that during negotiations the parties were under the obligation to abide by the rules of good faith. This is the general rule in all pre-contractual legal relations; Argentina National Commercial Court of Appeals, *Sala* A, *Pelisch, Juan y otro v. Imago Producciones, S.R.L. y/u otro*, 11 June 1974; Brazil Tribunal of Justice of Rio Grande do Sul, Civil Appeal 70012118220, Justice Marilene Bonzanini Bernardi, published 9 September 2005; Mexico Collegiate Tribunals, *Novena Época*, Registry 177'335, SJF XXII, September 2005, at 1436.

9 Argentina: A.A. Alterini, Contratos civiles, comerciales, de consumo 326 (1998).

10 Mexico Collegiate Tribunals, *Novena Época*, Registry 177'335, SJF XXII, September 2005, at 1436.

stage of interpretation.[11] Other letters simply inform about the willingness of one of the parties to start negotiations. Similarly, these letters have no contractual character and are only affected by the pre-contractual duties already mentioned.[12]

Some letters of intent, though, reach the character of the binding offer, and may constitute a partial agreement, whenever the intention to be bound has been expressly established by the issuer.[13] The given name of the letter of intent does not prevent the judge from interpreting the real character of the letter as the expression of a binding offer.[14]

3. Memorandum of Understandings

Modern practice also shows that prior to the formation of the contract, the parties can gradually attain some partial agreements. Often under the form of memorandums of understandings, these documents contain valuable information that may be reconsidered at a further stage as an element of interpretation.[15] The question then arises as to the binding legal character of these records. The Ibero-American codes does not expressly address the issue, but as noted by a recognised scholar, the modern reality requires these documents to have a legally binding effect; particularly in point by point negotiations where the parties have reached an agreement on certain points and must advance to deal with other pending points.[16]

An ICC Arbitral Tribunal upheld that a MOU which contains wording indicating the parties' intent to be bound by its provisions is a legally binding agreement. Such intent was indicated by provisions which, for example, restrained the participation of one of the parties in any other transaction without the prior written consent of the other party; which imposed confidentiality intended to survive the termination of the MOU; which

---

[11] ICC Final Award Case No. 13678 *Lex Contractus* Spanish Law: upholding that a "merger clause", under which any previous negotiations will be deemed superseded by the final writing, does not impede the arbitrator to take into account all relevant circumstances since the arbitrator's obligation to do so is established by the rules of interpretation of Spanish Law.

[12] Argentina: Alterini, *supra* note 9, at 327; Brazil: O. Gomes, Contratos 72 (2008).

[13] Argentina: Alterini, *supra* note 9, at 327.

[14] Spain: Guardiola Sacarrera, *supra* note 3, at 51.

[15] ICC Final Award Case No. 13278 *Lex Contractus* Spanish Law: the question arose as to whether the parties had agreed on a one-season contract with an option of renewal for a second season or whether the parties had entered into a one-season contract with automatic and compulsory renewal with slightly different terms for the second season. The Sole Arbitrator decided for the second option as it was consistent with the negotiations between the parties prior to signing the agreement. In particular with the MOU, which was signed a month before the agreement and expressly stipulated a period of two seasons.

[16] Argentina: Alterini, *supra* note 9, at 327.

governed the termination of the MOU in case of breach by one of the parties of its obligations; or which provided that no modification or amendment to the MOU may be made unless agreed in writing by both parties.[17]

[17] ICC Final Award Case No. 11404 *Lex Contractus* Argentinean Law.

Chapter 12

Electronic Communications

1. General Remarks

The majority of the Ibero-American civil and commercial codes were enacted during the nineteenth century.[1] For the formation of contracts between non present persons, these codes only considered the means of communications available in those years, namely: the mail letter and the telegraph.[2] Later, in the twentieth century, the telephone, the telex, the facsimile and the computer were invented. All these communication improvements redefined the concept of contracts celebrated between non-present persons, as communications were able to take place almost instantaneously.

However, many of the issues concerning the time and place of contract formation remained the same. With the aim of giving certainty and validity to the numerous transactions passed by means of electronic communications, many of the Ibero-American countries enacted legislative statutes containing new rules on contract formation. Bolivia,[3] Colombia, Dominican Republic, Ecuador, Guatemala, Mexico, Panama and Venezuela adopted or integrated into their national laws the MLEC.[4]

---

1 *See* Ch. 1, 3.

2 *See* Argentina: A.A. Alterini, Contratos civiles, comerciales, de consumo 297-298 (1998).

3 Bolivia Arts. 12-15 Law No. 080/2007 on Documents, Signatures and Electronic Commerce of 21 August 2008 follows very close the MLEC. Actually, one could easily conclude that although the status of adoptions provided by the UNCITRAL does not contemplate the country of Bolivia, Bolivian law seems to be an adoption of the MLEC.

4 Colombia Law No. 527 governing the use of data messages, electronic commerce and digital signatures, Official Gazette No. 43.673 of 21 August 1999; Dominican Republic Law No. 126-02 on Electronic Commerce, promulgated 4 September 2002; Ecuador Law No. 67 on Electronic Commerce, Signatures and Data Messages of 17 April 2002 and Decree No. 3496 Rules for the Law on Electronic Commerce, Signatures and Data Messages of 31 December 2002; Guatemala Law Decree No. 47-2008 on the Recognition of Electronic Communications

The new statutes expressly embrace many of the driving principles of the UNCITRAL. For example, the Colombian law requires that in the interpretation of such law, regard is to be given to its international origin and to the need to promote uniformity in its application and the observance of good faith.[5] In the same line, the Ecuadorian law acknowledges the principles of legal recognition, evidence force, functional equivalence, technological neutrality and the autonomy of the parties.[6] Finally, the Venezuelan Law grants and recognises the effectiveness and legal value of electronic signatures, the data messages and all intelligible information in electronic format, irrespective of its material support.[7]

Many other Latin American countries also enacted their own "original" rules for the use of electronic communications, electronic documents or digital signatures.[8] Spain and Portugal incorporated into their national statutes the EC Directives on Electronic Commerce and Digital Signatures.[9] The principles embraced by these statutes are also in accordance with the internationally agreed necessity of recognising the legal equivalency of electronics communications.[10]

Other Ibero-American countries have signed the 2005 – United Nations Convention on the Use of Electronic Communications in International Contracts. However, this Convention is not in force in any of these countries, principally because none of them have ratified it.[11]

---

and Signature of 19 August 2008 published 23 September 2008 in the Official Gazette; Mexico adopted both the 1996 MLEC and the 2001 MLES. This adoption was not made in a single instrument but rather it was incorporated in different codes and statutes. Regarding the electronic communication in the area of private law, different provisions are contained in Mexico's Civil Code, Code of Commerce and Procedural Federal Civil Code; Panama Law No. 43 of 31 July 2001 on Electronic Commerce and Electronic Documents in General; Venezuela Law No. 37,148 on Data Messages and Electronic Signatures published on 28 February 2001.

5 Colombia Art. 3 Law No. 527.

6 Ecuador Art. 6 Law No. 67.

7 Venezuela Art. 1 Law No. 37,148.

8 Argentina Law on Digital Signatures of December 2001; Bolivia Law No. 080/2007 on Documents, Signatures and Electronic Commerce of 21 August 2008; Chile Law No. 19.799 on the Electronic Documents, Digital Signatures and Services of Digital Signature's Certification of 12 April 2002; Costa Rica Law No. 8454 on Certificates, Digital Signatures and Electronic documents of 30 August 2005; Peru Law No. 27269 on Electronic Signatures and Certificates of May 2006; Uruguay Law Decree No. 382/003 on Digital Signatures of 17 September 2003.

9 Portugal Decree Law No. 7/2004 on Electronic Commerce of 7 January 2004 (adoption of the EU Directive No. 2000/31/CE) & Decree Law No. 290-D/99 on Electronic Documents and Digital Signatures; Spain Law No. 3472002 on the Information Society Services and E-commerce (adoption of the EU Directive No. 2000/31/CE) & Law No. 59/2003 on Electronic Signatures.

10 *See* Chile Art. 1 Law No. 19.799; Costa Rica Arts. 3, 5 Law No. 8454.

11 Colombia signature 27 September 2007; Honduras signature 16 January 2008; Panama signature 25 September 2007; Paraguay signature 26 March 2007; *see* Status of this Convention UNCITRAL.

2. Electronic Communications and Traditional Contract Formation Rules

Online or off-line, the conclusion of the contract occurs upon the meeting of the minds according to the traditional rules of contract formation.[12] The meeting of the minds constitutes an essential element for the existence of the sales contract. In both contexts, this is manifested by the offer of one of the parties, and the acceptance of such offer by the other party. But in current online contracts, the time and the place in which intents manifest, as well as the technology features required to ensure the authenticity of the manifest intent, have become an unsettled issue.[13] In the following paragraphs, some of the new legal provisions aiming to support the conclusion of contracts through electronic communications are presented.

The Ibero-American laws adopting or incorporating the MLEC are now furnished with complementary rules for the formation of contracts by means of electronic communications.[14] Among others issues, these rules are of great assistance in one of the most controversial issues of contract formation: the time and place of the dispatch or the reception of the data containing the intents of the parties to enter into, modify or terminate a contract.[15]

According to the majority of these laws, but contrary to the model rule established by the MELC, unless otherwise agreed between the originator[16] and the addressee,[17] it is presumed that the time of dispatch of data messages[18] takes place when they enter an information system[19] outside the control of the originator, or of the person who sent the data message on behalf of the originator.[20] Guatemala and Venezuela have stuck to the solution suggested by the MLEC, identifying the time of dispatch as the moment when the data

---

12 *See* Ch. 10.

13 Mexico: E. Elías Azar, La Contratacion por Medios Electronicos 220 (2005).

14 *See* Arts. 12-15 MLEC.

15 Art. 15 MLEC.

16 'Originator' of a data message means a person by whom, or on whose behalf, the data message purports to have been sent or generated prior to storage, if any, but it does not include a person acting as an intermediary with respect to that data message, *see* Art. 2 (c) MLEC.

17 'Addressee' of a data message means a person who is intended by the originator to receive the data message, but does not include a person acting as an intermediary with respect to that data message, *see* Art. 2(d) MLEC.

18 'Data message' means information generated, sent, received or stored by electronic, optical or similar means including, but not limited to, electronic data interchange (EDI), electronic mail, telegram, telex or telecopy, *see* Art. 2(a) MLEC.

19 'Information system' means a system for generating, sending, receiving, storing or otherwise processing data messages, *see* Art. 2(f) MLEC.

20 Colombia Arts. 23 Law No. 527; Ecuador Art. 11 Law No. 67; Mexico Arts. 91*bis* Com C; Pamana Arts. 22-25 Law No. 43.

message leaves an information system under the control of the originator, or of the party who sent it on behalf of the originator.[21]

To integrate this rule into the dispatch theory of contract conclusion followed by Colombia[22] would mean that the contract is concluded when the offeree's acceptance enters an information system outside of his control or of the person who sent the data message on behalf of him.[23]

On the other hand, the time of receipt of data messages occurs at the time when the data message enters the addressee's designated information system for the purpose of receiving data messages.[24] But if the addressee has not designated an information system, receipt occurs when the data message enters an information system of the addressee. In any case, if the data message is sent to an information system of the addressee that is not the designated information system, receipt of data messages occurs at the time when the data message is retrieved by the addressee.[25]

Incorporating this rule into the reception theory of contract conclusion contained in Bolivia, Guatemala, Mexico and Venezuela's laws,[26] means that the contract is concluded when the acceptance enters the offeror's designated information system for that purpose, or when the acceptance of the offeree enters an information system of the offeror, in case, the latter has not previously designated one. Alternatively, the contract is concluded at the time when the acceptance is retrieved by the offeror.[27]

Under the Spanish Law on the Information Society Services and E-commerce the acceptance concluding the contract is understood to be received when the offeror can have proof of it.[28] It is presumed that the offeror can have this

[21] Guatemala Art. 24 Law Decree No. 47-2008; Venezuela Art. 10 Law No. 37,148.

[22] Colombia Art. 864 Com C; *see also* other Ibero-American laws having the dispatch rule in Ch. 10, 2.2.1.

[23] Colombia Art. 23 Law No. 527.

[24] Colombia Arts. 23, 24 Law No. 527; Ecuador Art. 11 Law No. 67; Guatemala Art. 24 Law Decree No. 47-2008; Mexico Arts. 91, 91*bis*, 94 Com C; Panama Arts. 22-25 Law No. 43; Venezuela Art. 11 Law No. 37,148.

[25] Colombia Arts. 23, 24 Law No. 527; Ecuador Art. 11 Law No. 67; Guatemala Art. 24 Law Decree No. 47-2008; Mexico Arts. 91, 91*bis*, 94 Com C; Panama Arts. 22-25 Law No. 43; Venezuela Art. 11 Law No. 37, 148.

[26] Guatemala Art. 1523 CC; Mexico Art. 1807 CC & Art. 80 Com C; Venezuela Art. 1.137 (5) CC: the contract is concluded as soon as the offeror has knowledge of the acceptance by the offeree. The acceptance, however, is presumed to be known by the offeror from the moment it arrives at his address, unless he proves that, with no fault, he was not able to know about the acceptance, although the same has arrived at his address; Mexico Collegiate Tribunals, *Novena Época,* Registry 205'193, SJF I, May 1995, p 349: confirming the rule.

[27] Guatemala Art. 24 (b) Law Decree No. 47-2008; Mexico Art. 91 Com C.

[28] Spain Law No. 34/2002; *see also* Spain: C. Barriuso Ruiz, La Contratacion Electronica 197 (2006).

proof from the moment in which the acceptance has been stored in his e-mail server or in the storage space used for the reception of communications.[29]

In some other countries, the general scholarly opinion, as to the applicable rules to govern the formation of contracts passed by means of electronic communications is that, depending on whether the electronic means used by the parties allow them to communicate instantaneously or not, the traditional rules on contract formation for present parties or, those for non-present parties shall apply respectively.[30] Courts have often acted accordingly. A Brazilian Tribunal sustained that an offer made online may be changed anytime by the offeror prior to the acceptance by the offeree, since it is considered to be an *invitation ad offerendum* and, therefore, not binding.[31]

Then, for example, according to the *declaration* theory, followed by some countries that have no special provisions on the formation of contracts through electronic communications,[32] the acceptance concluding the contract will have full effect from the moment the offeree's acceptance is captured in a data message. For those Ibero-American laws that use the *dispatch* theory,[33] the contract would be deemed to be concluded when the electronic acceptance goes out from the information system of the offeree. Under the *reception* theory,[34] the contract would be concluded when the data message supporting the acceptance enters the information system used by the offeror. Finally, under the laws relying on *information* theory,[35] it would not be enough that the electronic offer enters a designated or non-designated system of the offeror, as the rule requires that the offeror opens his e-mail account or similar messages storage in order to know of the acceptance.

[29] Spain Art. 28 (2) Law No. 34/2002.

[30] *See* Argentina: J.M. Farina, Contratos Comerciales Modernos 109-110 (1999); Brazil: O. Gomes, Contratos 80 (2008); Costa Rica: J.J. Obando Peralta, *Los Contratos Electrónicos y Digitales*, 39 AR: Revista de Derecho Informático (2001), http://www.alfa-redi.org/rdi-articulo.shtml?x=819; Cuba: L. Hernandez Fernandez, *La oferta y la aceptación. Especial referencia a los contratos celebrados por medios electrónicos*, 2004 (23-24) Revista Cubana de Derecho 78; Mexico: Elías Azar, *supra* note 13, at 223.

[31] Brazil Tribunal of Justice of the State of São Paulo, Civil Recourse 71001411644, Justice Eduardo Kraemer, published 23 October 2007.

[32] Chile Art. 101 Com C; Ecuador Art. 145 Com C.

[33] *See for example* Argentina Art. 1154 CC; Brazil Art. 434 CC; Cuba Art. 54 Com C; Paraguay Art. 688 CC.

[34] *See for example* Costa Rica Art. 444 Com C; El Salvador Art. 966 Com C; Peru Art. 1373 CC (it actually follows the information theory but Art. 1374 CC establishes that the offer is meant to be known by the receiver when it arrives at his address); Portugal Art. 224 CC; Venezuela Art. 1.137 (5) CC (it actually follows the information theory but Art. 1.137(5) establishes that the offer is meant to be known by the receiver when it arrives at his address).

[35] *See for example* Cuba Art. 317.1 CC (*see* how the rule is different for sales covered by the Code of Commerce which follows the dispatch rule Art. 54 Com C); Honduras Art. 1553 CC; Panama Art. 1113 CC; Spain Art. 1.262 CC (or since the offeree dispatches the acceptance and the offeror cannot ignore that fact in good faith; *see* that the Spanish Art. 54 Com C adopts the dispatch rule).

It is worth noting that all the above mentioned rules are not only reserved for the issue of acceptance but may also be applied to the whole process of contract formation including the effects, withdrawal or revocation of the offer. Similarly, these provisions may be integrated into different stages of the performance of the contract. For example, the buyer's duty to timely inform the seller of any non-conformity of the goods[36] or, into any other information duty which requires the parties to opportunely send any sort of notice by means of data, in order to obey the principle of good faith.[37]

---

[36] *See* Ch. 40, 3.

[37] *See* Ch. 32.

Chapter 13

Standard Form Clauses

1. General Remarks

The provisions on contract formation of the nineteenth century Ibero-American civil and commercial codes were inspired by the intellectual enlightenment of the eighteenth century.[1] Accordingly, they were based upon the supposed equality of the parties' bargaining power.[2] The freedom of the parties was the driving principle of contract formation.[3] If one of the parties offered the sale of goods unilaterally, and the other party voluntarily accepted them, the binding character of all the terms of the agreement was unquestionable, unless they contradict the moral or the public order.[4]

The principle of social justice developed during the twentieth century changed the views on the unlimited freedom of contract in unbalanced situations. In response to such concern, special provisions for contracts passed through standard form clauses have been incorporated into the Ibero-American legal systems.[5] The Explanatory Memorandum of the Brazilian Civil Code of 2002 explained that due to the 'social function of the contract' the new code included norms on adhesion contracts, aimed at guaranteeing some protection to the adherent party *vis à vis* the offeror, endowed with advantages derived

---

1 *See* Ch. 1, 1. & 3.

2 *See* K.H. Neumayer, C. Ming & F. Dessemontet (Eds.), Convention de Vienne sur les contrats de vente internationale de marchandises: commentaire, at 8, para. 9 (1993).

3 *See* Ch. 3 and Ch. 20.

4 *See* Ch. 3.

5 *See for example* Brazil Arts. 423-424 CC; El Salvador Art. 976 Com C; Guatemala Art. 1600 *et seq.* CC & Arts. 672, 673 Com C; Honduras Arts. 724-730 Com C; Paraguay Art. 691 *et seq.* CC; Peru Arts. 1392-1400 CC; Portugal Law No. 446/85 on General Contractual Terms of October 1985; Spain Law No. 7/1998 on the General Conditions on Contracts, incorporation of the Council Directive 93/13/EEC of 5 April 1993 on Unfair Terms in Consumer Contracts.

from his higher position.[6] A Brazilian scholar comments that the standard form clauses are used in all the spheres despite being usually associated with contracts of adhesion in consumer relations.[7]

On this, Lorenzetti points out that, contrary to the tradition of free conclusion of contracts negotiated through offers and acceptance, a protective public order is deployed for B2B and C2C standard form clauses or adhesion contracts but at a lower level than for B2C situations.[8] However, many laws still associate standard form clauses with consumer protection rules. In Argentina, the Civil Code does not include provisions on standard form contracts or adhesion contracts. Authors have, nevertheless, suggested that the rules on Consumers Protection would apply to B2B.[9] In Mexico, the consumer protection law also contains rules applicable to adhesion contracts in B2B transactions.[10] In Spain the law on the General Conditions on Contracts applies in favour of consumers in the ordinary sense, but also to professionals adhering to the standard terms and conditions of a third party.[11]

1.1. Interpretation Principles

In the interpretation of standard form and adhesion contracts the principle of *contra proferentem* shall apply. Ambiguous clauses established unilaterally by one of the contractors are interpreted in the other party's favour or against the drafter of the clause.[12]

This rule of interpretation has gained recognition through the case law of the Ibero-American courts.[13] For example, the Argentinean Supreme Court has upheld that, in contracts with pre-established clauses which are ambiguous or

6 Point 22, letter g) of the Explanatory Memorandum of the Brazilian Civil Code of 2002 (*Exposição de Motivos do novo Código Civil de* 2002).

7 *See* Brazil: C.R. Gonçalves, Dereito Civil Brasileiro, Vol. III, 77 (2004).

8 Argentina: R.L. Lorenzetti, Tratado de los Contratos Parte General 680 (2004).

9 Argentina: A.A. Alterini, Contratos civiles, comerciales, de consumo 130 (1998).

10 Mexico Arts. 2, 99, 117 CPL: the definition of consumers includes those artisans and small companies who acquire products or services to integrate them into a production process, for the supply of products in all claims not exceeding MX$ 319,447.46.

11 *See* Spain Art. 2 Law No. 7/1998.

12 *See* this principle in Bolivia Art. 518 CC; Brazil Art. 423 CC; Chile Art. 1566 para. 2 CC; Colombia Art. 1624 para. 2 CC; Ecuador Art. 1609 para. 2 CC; El Salvador 1437 para. 2 CC; Guatemala Art. 1600 CC; Spain Art. 1288 CC; Paraguay Art. 713 CC; Uruguay Art. 1304 para. 2 CC.

13 Argentina Supreme Court, *P de M. I., J. M. v. Asociacion Civil Hospital Aleman cited in* Argentina: Lorenzetti, *supra* note 8, at 683, n. 11; Brazil Superior Tribunal of Justice, REsp 222148/SP, Minister Cesar Asfor Rocha, published 30 June 2003: dictating that an ambiguous clause on a health insurance contract must be interpreted in the most favourable way to the adhering party to cover the party's disease; Spain Supreme Tribunal, 5 September 1991, *cited in* X. O'Callaghan (Ed.), Código Civil Comentado Art. 1.288, at 1277 (2004).

which render it difficult to assess the precise scope of the obligation contracted by adhesion, in case of doubt the prevailing interpretation should favour the party who adhered to the clauses, and against the party who drafted them.[14]

Also applicable, to both standard form contracts and adhesion contracts, is the rule that the terms specifically agreed to, must prevail over the pre-established general conditions adhered to in mass,[15] unless the general terms are more beneficial for the adherent party.[16] This rule is supported by the principle of good faith recognised by most of the Ibero-American laws.[17] This principle does not only impose on the parties the duty to contract in good faith, but it also requires the judge to subject the interpretation of the parties' conduct and statements to the good faith principle.[18]

1.2. Abusive Clauses

The interpretation rules are completed with other provisions aiming to control the abusive clauses of standard contracts. The clauses that affect the essence of the contractual relationship, the freedom of contract, the balance of the performance of the contract, good faith, and that produce an abuse of right may be considered invalid.[19] More specific examples are provided in the following paragraphs.

---

[14] Argentina Supreme Court, *P de M. I., J. M. v. Asociacion Civil Hospital Aleman*, *cited in* Argentina: Lorenzetti, *supra* note 8, at 683, n. 11.

[15] *See* expressly established in El Salvador Art. 976 Com C; Guatemala Art. 672 (3) Com C; Honduras Art. 728 Com C; Peru Art. 1400 CC: dictating that the clauses added to the standard contract prevail over the original when they are incompatible, although the original ones had not lapsed; Portugal Art. 7 Law No. 446/85: dictating that terms which are specifically agreed prevail over any general contractual terms, even when set out in forms signed by the parties; Spain Art. 6 (1) Law No. 7/1998; Argentina Supreme Court of Justice of Buenos Aires, *Petriga de Portela v. Prov. de Buenos Aires*, *cited in* Argentina: Lorenzetti, *supra* note 8, at 685, n. 18; *see also* Argentina: Alterini, *supra* note 9, at 131: noting that the Argentinean Project for a Unique Code of 1987 Art. 1197 (3) had foreseen the validity of the special clauses over the general clauses, though the latter had not been cancelled, and of the incorporated clauses over the pre-existent clauses.

[16] Spain Art. 6 (1) Law No. 7/1998.

[17] Argentina Art. 1198 CC; Bolivia Art. 465 CC & Art. 803 Com C; Brazil Art. 422 CC; Chile Art. 1546 CC; Colombia Art. 1603 CC & Art. 863 Com C; Cuba Art. 6 CC; Ecuador Art. 1589 CC; El Salvador Art. 1417 CC; Guatemala Art. 17 JOL; Mexico Art. 1796 CC; Paraguay Art. 689 CC; Peru Art. 1362 CC; Portugal Art. 227 CC; Spain Art. 1258 CC & Art. 57 Com C; *see also* Chile: J. Lopez Santa Maria, Los Contratos: Parte General, Vol. 2, n. 595*bis* (2005).

[18] Argentina Supreme Court of Justice of Buenos Aires, *Petriga de Portela v. Prov. de Buenos Aires*, *cited in* Argentina: Lorenzetti, *supra* note 8, at 685, n. 18.

[19] Mexico Art. 85 CPL; *see also* Argentina: Lorenzetti, *supra* note 8, at 684; Mexico: J. Arce Gargollo, Contratos Mercantiles Atípicos 80-81 (2007); Spain: C. Barriuso Ruiz, La Contratacion Electronica 235, 236 (2006).

Generally, under many laws, clauses that exclude or reduce the responsibility of the party who drafted them are considered invalid.[20] Also invalid are the clauses that grant an exclusive right to the drafter to terminate the contract or to change their conditions, or that in anyway deprive the adherent party of some right without just cause.[21] Also are invalid those clauses that impede the adherent party to sue the other party, or that limit the adherent freedom to contract with third parties, or that impose to the adherent, the anticipated renounce of any right that could be found on the contract.[22]

For example, in a case submitted to the Argentinean National Chamber of Appeals on Administrative matters, a clause was found invalid that established that the transport of the goods to the factory or premises where they should be repaired, in case of non-conformity, should be borne by the buyer. The Appeal Chamber considered that such a provision was against the law as the seller was responsible for granting all necessary and related guarantees as provided by the applicable law in imbalanced deals.[23]

Those clauses that authorise the other party to act in the name of the adherent party, or that impose on the adherent party certain means of proof, or the burden of proof have the same illegal effect.[24] Also invalid are those clauses that impose a term or condition upon the right of the adherent to legal action, or that limits the right to raise exceptions, or the use of judicial procedures of which the adherent could resort to.

Similarly, clauses are invalid that allow the unilateral election of the competent judge to settle a dispute between the parties.[25] On this issue, the Ibero-American courts have upheld that a choice of forum clause in an B2B adhesion contract may only be voidable when there exists an evident imbalance in the parties' bargaining power.[26]

Finally, under the Mexican law the Ministry of Government may subject adhesion contracts to a prior registration in order to revise the terms incorporated in such contracts.[27] Under the Peruvian law, the same administrative authorisation is required for contracts of adhesion and standard

---

[20] Honduras Art. 727 Com C; Mexico Art. 90 CPL; Paraguay Art. 691 CC; Peru Art. 1398 CC.

[21] Honduras Art. 727 Com C; Mexico Art. 90 CPL; Paraguay Art. 691 CC; Peru Art. 1398 CC.

[22] Brazil Art. 424 CC; Honduras Art. 727 Com C; Mexico Art. 90 CPL; Paraguay Art. 691 CC; Peru Art. 1398 CC.

[23] Argentina National Chamber of Appeals in Federal Administrative Matters, *Sala* IV, *Wal Mart Argentina S.A. v. Dirección Nac. de Comercio Interior*, 13 April 2004.

[24] Honduras Art. 727 Com C; Mexico Art. 90 CPL; Paraguay Art. 691 CC; Peru Art. 1398 CC.

[25] Honduras Art. 727 Com C; Mexico Art. 90 CPL; Paraguay Art. 691 CC; Peru Art. 1398 CC.

[26] *See* Argentina National Commercial Court of Appeals, *Quilmes Combustibles, S.A. c. Vigan, S.A,* 15 March 1991; Brazil Superior Tribunal of Justice, AgRg no Ag 637639/RS, Minister Aldir Passarinho Junior, published 9 May 2005.

[27] Mexico Art. 90 CPL; Mexico: Arce Gargollo, *supra* note 19, at 80-81. *Also* Peru Art. 1394 CC: dictating that the Executive authority will indicate the goods and services that shall be contracted in accordance with general clauses of contract approved by the administrative authority.

form contracts.[28] Once such authorisation is granted, it is understood that all the abusive and advantageous clauses have been eliminated by the administrative authority, so that no adhering party can rely upon the special provisions on contracts of adhesion and standard form contracts.[29]

2. Requirements

2.1. Incorporation

In principle, it is irrelevant whether the standard terms form a separate annex to, or are incorporated into the document by reference.[30] Under some laws incorporation into a particular contract occurs once the general terms are known by the adhering party or when that party would have been able to know them acting with ordinary diligence.[31] In Peru, it is presumed that the other party knows the general clauses when they have been given to the public by suitable means of advertising.[32] Such suitable means of advertising may include links to publicly accessible websites.

However, the incorporation of standard form clauses should be done in a way favourable to the adhering party,[33] so that using ordinary care such party can acquire complete and effective knowledge of them. For example, general contractual terms must be communicated entirely[34] at an early stage, or at least in advance or simultaneously to the main document,[35] since terms supplied subsequently may not be validly incorporated and may not bind the adhering party.[36]

---

28 Peru Art. 1398 CC.

29 Peru Supreme Court, *Sala civil permanente,* Resolution 004913-2008, 29 April 2008.

30 *See for example* Spain Arts. 5, 7 Law No. 7/1998: terms must form part of the contract (*i.e.* by reference and by supplying a copy). Also Argentina National Commercial Court of Appeals, *Quilmes Combustibles, S.A. c.Vigan, S.A,* 15 March 1991.

31 Peru Art. 1397 CC; Honduras Art. 726 Com C; Portugal Art. 5 (1) (2) Law No. 446/85.

32 Peru Art. 1397 CC (declaring that they have to be approved by the administrative authority).

33 Argentina Art. 10 CPL; Honduras Art. 726 Com C; Peru Art. 1397 CC; Portugal Art. 5 (1) Law No. 446/85; Spain Arts. 5, 7 Law No. 7/1998.

34 Argentina Art. 10 CPL; Portugal Art. 5 (1) (2) Law No. 446/85; Spain Arts. 5, 7 Law No. 7/1998.

35 Argentina Art. 10 CPL; Spain Arts. 5, 7 Law No. 7/1998; Portugal Art. 5 (1) (2) Law No. 446/85: taking into consideration the importance of the contract and the length and complexity of the terms.

36 Spain Arts. 5, 7 Law No. 7/1998.

2.2. Transparency

2.2.1. General Remarks

The contracts with pre-established clauses must be drafted in a transparent, clear, concise, complete and easily reading way.[37] A Mexican Collegiate Tribunal has sustained that the drafter of an adhesion contract has the duty to use understandable and transparent statements that permit a party to comprehend the nature and scope of the obligations contracted.[38]

The legibility requirement may include the drafter's obligation to alert the adherent party of any important stipulation contained in the standard contract and which, because of different circumstances may not be easily perceived by the adherent party. Such alert or remark may be made using special font characters or other signs or methods that help the relevant clause to distinguish it from the rest of the contract. For example, the Guatemalan commercial law dictates that any relinquishment of a right will only be valid if it appears emphasised or in characters greater or different than those from the rest of the contract.[39]

As a consequence, terms which have not been effectively communicated shall be considered to be excluded from individual contracts. Also terms which have been communicated but where the duty to inform has been violated, so that effective knowledge of them is not attained, shall be disregarded.[40]

2.2.2. Language

The legibility requirement may include the obligation to use the national language, unless other legal provisions allow a foreign language.[41] In Mexico, the consumers protection law establishes that any adhesion contract executed within the national territory shall be drafted in Spanish, and characters shall be clearly readable in order to be valid.[42]

On the contrary, the Argentinean Commercial Court of Appeals explained that the mere fact that standard terms were drafted in French does not constitute

---

[37] Portugal Art. 8 Law No. 446/85; Spain Arts. 5, 7 Law No. 7/1998; *see also* Argentina: Alterini, *supra* note 9, at 131: noting that this principle is embodied in Argentina Art. 10 CPL, The Project for a Unique Code of 1987 Art. 1157, also in the Project of the Chamber of Deputies of 1993 Art. 1157 and the Project of the Executive Project of 1993, Art. 870; Peru: M. De la Puente y Lavalle, El contrato en general: comentarios a la sección primera del libro VII del Código civil, Vol. I, 723 (2001).

[38] Mexico Collegiate Tribunals, Registry 182'003, SJF XIX, March 2004, p 1533; *see also* Argentina: Lorenzetti, *supra* note 8, at 62.

[39] Guatemala Art. 672 (2) Com C.

[40] Portugal Art. 8 Law No. 446/85.

[41] *See* Ch. 10, 4.

[42] Mexico Art. 85 CPL.

a serious ground to invalidate the clause at stake. An opposite view would not give much certainty to parties' contracts. Furthermore, mistake cannot be alleged when the false understanding of the issue derives from the own party's negligent conduct. All the more since the clause at issue had been drafted in a language of which the translation was easily accessible.[43]

2.2.3. Surprising Clauses

Standard term contracts shall be free of surprising terms. This requirement is reflected in the PICC which establish that no term contained in standard terms, that is of such a character that the other party could not reasonably have expected it, is effective unless it has been expressly accepted by that party.[44]

Also the Portuguese law invalidates terms which, by the context in which they arise, by the heading which precedes them, or by the form in which they are presented graphically, go unnoticed by a party in the position of a normal contracting party.[45]

3. Battle of the Forms

3.1. General Remarks on the Battle of the Forms

It is common in sales contracts that the offeror when issuing his offer refers to his own general terms for sale, and that the offeree when accepting the offer refers to his own general terms for purchase. This leads to a battle of forms. In practice, parties would refer to their standard terms "more or less automatically, for example by exchanging printed and acknowledgement of order forms with the respective terms on the reverse side",[46] without even being aware of the conflict between their respective standard terms. This phenomena raises two questions with regards to the formation of the contract: First, whether the conduct of one of the parties operates as an acceptance of the other party's terms; or alternatively, whether and to what extent the concurrent or opposing standard terms create a binding agreement under certain points.

---

43 Argentina National Commercial Court of Appeals, *Quilmes Combustibles, S.A. c.Vigan, S.A,* 15 March 1991.

44 Art. 2.1.20 PICC.

45 Portugal Art. 8 Law No. 446/85.

46 *See* M.J. Bonell, The Unidroit Principles in Practice: Caselaw and Bibliography on the Unidroit Principles of International Commercial Contracts, Art. 2.1.22, Comment 3, at 156 (2006).

3.2. Last Shot Doctrine

The last shot doctrine means that

> if two parties have started to perform without objecting each other's standard terms, a contract would be considered to have been concluded on the basis of those terms which were the last to be sent or to be referred to.[47]

The Ibero-American laws do not have specific provisions on the battle of forms. Consequently, the traditional rules on contract formation contained in the civil and commercial codes apply to the exchange of forms.[48] The last shot doctrine takes place when a counter-offer is impliedly accepted by means of events or conduct performed by the one of the parties. Certainly, the acceptance of the sales contract can be express or implied.[49] The implied consent results from events or presumed conduct. Moreover, silence may constitute a manifestation of assent when the usages or the circumstances authorise such meaning, and the law or the contract do not require an express declaration. Similarly, if according to the usages, or the nature of the contract, performance can be done without previous express acceptance, the contract may be concluded at the moment and place in which the performance has begun.[50]

Hence, for example, when the seller's acceptance (seller's standard terms) contains modifications or additions to those in the original offer to purchase (buyer's standard terms) the seller's acceptance becomes a counter-offer whose terms could prevail over the original offer (buyer's standard terms) if the buyer's conduct, such as the payment of the price or the reception of the goods under the terms established in the counter-offer, implies acceptance.

Additionally, some of the Ibero-American commercial laws contain among their provisions on standard forms a mechanism of implied acceptance of forms that also reflects the last shot doctrine. Under El Salvador, Guatemala and Honduras' laws, in contracts made by means of forms or documents unilaterally issued by one party, if the standard terms of the document are different to those originally agreed, the other party can desist the contract or ask for its rectification within the fifteen days following the reception of the standard form document. Otherwise, silence would be understood as acceptance of the standard terms departing from the original agreement.[51] The Guatemalan law adds that, if within the fifteen following days, the party who dispatches the standard form does NOT declare that the rectification cannot be done, the rectification in all terms will be considered accepted.[52]

---

[47] *See Id.*, Art. 2.1.22, Comment 2, at 156.

[48] *See* Ch. 10.

[49] *See* Ch. 10, 2.1.

[50] *See* Ch. 10, 2.1.

[51] El Salvador 977 Com C; Guatemala Art. 673 Com C; Honduras Art. 729 Com C.

[52] Guatemala Art. 673 Com C.

3.3. Knockout Doctrine

According to the knockout doctrine, when the parties exchange or refer to their standard terms and they conflict in some points, a contract is concluded on the basis of the concurrent terms and of any standard terms which are common in substance,[53] while the diverging terms are automatically disregarded. Such is the solution adopted by the UNIDROIT PICC:

> where both parties use standard terms and reach agreement except on those terms, a contract is concluded on the basis of the agreed terms and of any standard terms which are common in substance unless one party clearly indicates in advance, or later and without undue delay informs the other party, that it does not intend to be bound by such a contract.[54]

[53] *See* Bonell, *supra* note 46, Art. 2.1.22, Comment 3, at 157.

[54] Art. 2.1.22 PICC.

Chapter 14

Sales Conditioned upon Events or Acts

In some instances, even though the parties have reached an agreement through any of the different means of contract formation, the existence of the contract may be suspended until the occurrence of certain events. The parties' agreement, the usage or the law may condition the existence of the sales contract to the occurrence of certain event or conduct. In the next paragraphs, we examine these special types of agreements.

1. Goods That is a Usage to Degust or to Try

Under the Ibero-American laws, when according to the usages[1] the goods must be tried or tasted by the buyer, the existence of the sale is conditioned to trial or degustation and approval.[2] This modality is commonly known as sales *ad gustum*. The rule only works on goods that due to their intrinsic characteristics or nature it has become a usage to try or to taste before buying. For example, the French Civil Code refers to wine, oil and other goods that is a usage to degust before purchasing.[3] Generally, one could speak of certain food products, animals, commodities, etc. Because of the type of goods, these sorts of sales would normally be passed between merchants having an aim to profit, and thus categorised as B2B sales.[4]

---

1 Usages of the place where the goods are; *see* Argentina: R. Compagnucci de Caso, Contrato de Compraventa 408 (2007).

2 Argentina Art. 1336 CC; Chile Art. 132 Com C; Colombia Art. 911 Com C; Costa Rica Art. 453 Com C; Ecuador Art. 172 Com C; El Salvador Art. 1022 Com C; Honduras Art. 1612 CC; Guatemala Art. 1799 CC; Mexico Art. 2257 CC: including goods that is a usage to weight and to measure; Nicaragua Art. 2542 CC; Panama Art. 1223 CC; Paraguay Art. 768 CC; Spain Art. 1.453 CC; Venezuela Art. 1.477 CC.

3 France Art. 1587 CC.

4 On the distinction between B2B and C2C *see* Ch. 5, 1.

The existence of the sale depends on the buyer's approval of the goods. As long as the buyer does not manifest its satisfaction of the goods, the whole transaction can be seen as a seller's unilateral and irrevocable offer to sell. Everything relies on the buyer's subjective appreciation of the goods. The buyer reserves his right to try and refuse. As pointed out by some, the buyer's decision cannot be revised under allegations of abuse of rights.[5] The degustation has a subjective character regardless of the objective quality of the goods.[6]

The only restriction imposed by the law relates to the time within which the buyer shall try or degust the goods and make his decision to refuse or to validate the transaction. In the Argentinean law, the time to perform the degustation or testing shall be that agreed to by the parties. In absence of agreement of the issue the seller may apply to the competent court asking to fix a time period.[7] In Chile and Ecuador, the buyer may perform degustation or testing within three days after the seller has required him to do so.[8]

In Colombia and Guatemala, a three day period for degustation and testing starts running from the moment the seller places the goods at the buyer's disposal or from the time of real delivery of the goods.[9] In Costa Rica, degustation and testing of the goods at the seller's possession shall be performed within the time referred in the contract, or according to the usages, and in absence of both, when the seller requires so,[10] but if the goods have already been delivered to the buyer, he shall degust or test them within 24 hours after delivery.[11] In El Salvador and Venezuela degustation and testing of the goods shall be performed within the time referred to in the contract, or according to the usages, and in absence of both when the seller requires, regardless of whether the goods are at the seller's possession or have been already delivered to the buyer.[12] In Paraguay, ninety days from the agreement are granted to the buyer in order degust and accept the goods.[13]

The consequences for the buyer's failure to try or degust, and thus accept the goods within the agreed or default time are different depending on the

---

5 Argentina: Compagnucci de Caso, *supra* note 1, at 412.

6 Though it seems that in Spain an objective standard has been given to the rule; *see id.*, at 412; Spain: M. Medina de Lemus, Derecho Civil: Obligaciones y Contratos II, Contratos en Particular, Vol. 2, 72 (2004).

7 Argentina: Compagnucci de Caso, *supra* note 1, at 413.

8 *See* Chile Art. 131 Com C: by analogous application of the rule applying to goods subject to test or trial; Ecuador Arts. 172, 171 Com C.

9 Colombia Art. 912 Com C: delivery must be performed within 24 hours from the conclusion of the contract unless a different period results from the agreement of the parties, the usages or practices established or the nature of the goods; *see* Colombia Art. 912 (3) Com C; Guatemala Art. 1799 CC.

10 Costa Rica Art. 453 (1) Com C.

11 Costa Rica Art. 453 (2) Com C.

12 El Salvador Art. 1022 Com C; Venezuela Art. 1.477 CC.

13 Paraguay Art. 768 *in fine* CC.

law. In Argentina, El Salvador and Paraguay the buyer's failure to manifest refusal or acceptance within the established time amounts to acceptance of the contract.[14] Under the Chilean, the Ecuadorian, the Guatemalan and the Venezuelan laws, failure to perform and manifest leaves the contract non-existent.[15] In Colombia and Costa Rica the consequences depend on whether the goods were at the seller's possession or already delivered to the buyer. In the first case, the contract is considered non-existent and the seller can freely disposed of the goods.[16] In the second case, the contract is understood to be concluded.[17]

2. Sales of Goods Conditioned to Satisfaction

By agreement, the parties can also condition the existence of the sale to the mere buyer's satisfaction of the goods.[18] Portugal Civil Code offers a second option to avoid the existing contract in the case of the buyer's dissatisfaction.[19] This type of agreement is not common in practice, since similar to the *ad gustum* modality, it leaves to the buyer's complete subjective discretion the last word regarding the conclusion or frustration of the contract; depending on whether the goods please him or not.[20] The only difference lies in the fact that in the sale *ad gustum* the contract is about goods that, due to their intrinsic characteristics or nature, it has become a usage to try or degust, regardless of any agreement on this issue. While in the case where the goods are subject to the buyer's satisfaction, the rule is based on the agreement of the parties.

Yet again, within a certain period after the delivery of the goods,[21] the buyer shall manifest his satisfaction or dissatisfaction regarding the goods and thus make his decision to refuse or validate the transaction. Under Argentina's law the time to manifest satisfaction shall be agreed to by the parties, and in absence of such, the seller may apply to the competent court to fix a period.[22] Similarly, in the Brazilian law, the time to manifest satisfaction shall be agreed to by the parties and absent an agreement, the seller may unilaterally fix the time by means of judicial or private notice.[23] In Colombia, the three-day

[14] Argentina Art. 1337 CC; El Salvador Art. 1022 Com C; Paraguay Art. 768 *in fine* CC.

[15] Chile Art. 131 Com C: by analogous application of the rule applying to goods subject to test or trial; Ecuador 172, 171 Com C; Guatemala Art. 1799 CC; Venezuela Art. 1.477 CC.

[16] Colombia Art. 912 (1) Com C; Costa Rica Art. 453 (1) Com C.

[17] Colombia Art. 912 (3) Com C; Costa Rica Art. 453 (2) Com C.

[18] Argentina Art. 1365 CC; Brazil Arts. 509, 511 CC; Colombia Art. 911 Com C: after degustation or trial; Paraguay Art. 768 CC; Peru Art. 1571 CC; Portugal Art. 923 CC.

[19] Portugal Art. 924 CC.

[20] Argentina: Compagnucci de Caso, *supra* note 1, at 405.

[21] *See for example* Brazil Art. 509 CC; Colombia Art. 912 Com C; Portugal Art. 923 CC.

[22] Argentina Art. 1379 CC.

[23] Brazil Art. 512 CC.

period for manifesting satisfaction starts running from the moment the seller places the goods at the buyer's disposal or from the time of real delivery of the goods.[24] In Paraguay, ninety days from the agreement is granted to the buyer in order to manifest his satisfaction on the goods.[25] In Peru, manifestation of satisfaction shall be express or implied within the time referred in the contract, or according to the usages, and in absence of both, within the time fixed by the seller.[26]

Regarding the consequences of the buyer's failure to manifest in time whether the goods satisfied him or not, the laws are not uniform. According to Argentina, Paraguay and Peru's Civil Codes the lack of manifestation during the established period confirms the conclusion of the contract.[27] In Brazil, failure to manifest satisfaction leaves the contract nonexistent.[28] In Colombia, the consequences depend on whether the goods were at the seller's possession or already delivered to the buyer. In the first case, the contract is considered non-existent and the seller can freely dispose of the goods.[29] In the second case, the contract is understood to be concluded.[30]

3. Sales Subject to Test or Trial

In addition, parties can agree that their sale would be conditioned to trial or test of the goods.[31] The existence of the contract is suspended until the goods are tried or tested. Although, under other laws the test or trial condition does not determine the existence of the sale but instead its potential avoidance.[32] Similar to the goods subject to the buyer's satisfaction, the rule derives from the agreement of the parties. However, according to the doctrine[33] and the

---

24 Colombia Art. 912 Com C: delivery must be performed within 24 hours from the conclusion of the contract unless a different period results from the agreement of the parties, the usages or practices established or the nature of the goods, *see* Colombia Art. 912 (3) Com C; Guatemala Art. 1799 CC.

25 Paraguay Art. 768 CC.

26 Peru Art. 1571 CC.

27 Argentina Art. 1378 CC; Paraguay Art. 768 CC; Peru Art. 1571 CC: understood from the logic of the section and the reading of Art. 1572 *in fine* CC.

28 Brazil Arts. 509-512 CC: harmonic reading.

29 Colombia Art. 912 (1) Com C.

30 Colombia Art. 912 (3) Com C.

31 Argentina Art. 1336 CC & Art. 455 Com C; Bolivia Art. 835 Com C; Brazil Arts. 510, 511 CC; Chile Art. 131 Com C; Colombia Art. 911 Com C; Costa Rica Art. 454 Com C; Ecuador Art. 171 Com C; El Salvador Art. 1023 Com C; Guatemala Art. 1799 CC; Paraguay Art. 768 CC; Peru Art. 1572 CC; Portugal Art. 925 CC; Spain Art. 1.453 CC & Art. 328 Com C; Uruguay Art. 520 Com C; Venezuela Art. 1.478 CC.

32 Argentina Art. 455 Com C; Spain Art. 328 last para. Com C; Uruguay Art. 520 Com C.

33 Argentina: Compagnucci de Caso, *supra* note 1, at 408; Spain: Medina de Lemus, *supra* note 6, at 72.

jurisprudence[34] it differs from the latter and the sales *ad gustum* in an important point. The buyer, in this case, does not have the discretional faculty to reject the goods that do not please him.[35] Instead, the buyer is bound to accept the goods that, after test or trial, fulfil the quality, quantity and characteristics expressly or impliedly agreed.[36] Absent an agreement, the buyer shall still accept the goods that after test or trial meet the characteristics required for the goods of the same type.[37]

The Spanish Supreme Tribunal has explained that such provision does not grant to the buyer the right to reject the goods based on subjective reasons. The proof has an objective standard. Hence, there is no ground of breach without real proof that objectively demonstrates the deficient quality of the goods and without opportunity for the seller to verify the results of the test that the buyer says to have practiced.[38]

Again, the laws impose to the buyer a limitation period to try or test the goods. Under Argentina and Uruguay's commercial laws, the buyer must try the goods within three days after the seller requires him to do so.[39] In the Brazilian law, the time to test and manifest conformity shall be agreed to by the parties, but in absence of such, the seller may unilaterally fix the time by means of judicial or regular notice.[40] In Chile and Ecuador, the buyer shall test the goods within three days after the seller has required him to do so.[41] In Colombia and Guatemala, a three-day period for testing starts running from the moment the seller places the goods at the buyer's disposal or from the time of real delivery of the goods.[42] In Costa Rica, El Salvador, Peru and Portugal the testing shall be made in the form and time agreed, and in absence of such, according to the usages.[43] In Paraguay, a ninety-day period from the agreement is granted to the buyer in order to try the goods.[44]

Accordingly, under the Paraguayan, the Peruvian, the Portuguese and the Spanish laws, the buyer's failure to undertake the test within the established

---

34 Spain Supreme Tribunal, 25 June 1999, *Id Cendoj:* 28079110001999100407.

35 *Id.*

36 *See for example* Portugal Art. 925 (1) CC; *see also* Argentina: Compagnucci de Caso, *supra* note 1, at 413.

37 Argentina: Compagnucci de Caso, *supra* note 1, at 413.

38 Spain Supreme Tribunal, 25 June 1999, *Id Cendoj:* 28079110001999100407.

39 Argentina Art. 455 Com C; Uruguay Art. 520 Com C.

40 Brazil Art. 512 CC.

41 *See* Chile Art. 131 Com C; Ecuador Arts. 172, 171 Com C.

42 Colombia Art. 912 Com C: delivery must be performed within 24 hours from the conclusion of the contract unless a different period results from the agreement of the parties, the usages or practices established or the nature of the goods, *see* Colombia Art. 912 (3) Com C; Guatemala Art. 1799 CC.

43 Costa Rica Art. 454 Com C; El Salvador Art. 1023 Com C; Peru Art. 1572 CC; Portugal Art. 925 (2) CC: but in absence of such the seller may unilaterally fix the time.

44 Paraguay Art. 768 *in fine* CC.

time for trial amounts to acceptance of the contract.[45] On the other hand, in a very dysfunctional approach the laws of Argentina, Brazil, Chile, Ecuador, Guatemala and Uruguay establish that if the buyer fails to try or test the goods during the established period of time the sale is considered with no effect.[46] In Colombia, the consequences again depend on whether the goods were at the seller's possession or already delivered to the buyer. In the first case, the contract is considered non-existent and the seller can freely dispose of the goods.[47] In the second case, the contract is understood to be concluded.[48] The rest of the laws analysed remained silent as to the consequences.

4. Sales of Goods that are not Displayed to the Buyer

Many Ibero-American Codes of Commerce contain a rule stating that in cases where the buyer had not seen the goods, and these cannot be classified with a specific quality which is known in the trade concerned, it is understood that the sale does not exist until the buyer inspects the goods and accepts them without reservation.[49] The case seems to be unusual in practice, since objectively most of the goods traded are already part of some sort of classified commerce which distinguishes between different levels of quality.

In Chile and Ecuador B2B sales, the existence of the sales contract of goods seen by the buyer at the time of contract conclusion is conditional upon the fitness of the delivered goods as agreed on the contract.[50] Experts are engaged to asses the fitness of the goods.[51]

---

[45] Paraguay Art. 768 *in fine* CC; Peru Art. 1572 CC; Portugal Art. 925 (2) CC; Spain Supreme Tribunal, 25 June 1999, *Id Cendoj:* 28079110001999100407.

[46] Argentina Art. 455 Com C; Brazil Arts. 509-512 CC (harmonic reading); Chile Art. 131 Com C; Ecuador Art. 171 Com C; Guatemala Art. 1799 CC; Uruguay Art. 520 Com C.

[47] Colombia Art. 912 (1) Com C; Costa Rica Art. 453 (1) Com C.

[48] Colombia Art. 912 (3) Com C.

[49] Bolivia Art. 836 Com C; Chile Art. 130 Com C; Colombia Art. 911 Com C; Ecuador Art. 170 Com C; Mexico Art. 374 Com C; Portugal Art. 470 Com C; Spain Art. 328 Com C.

[50] Chile Art. 133 Com C; Ecuador Art. 173 Com C; a similar provision in Colombia Art. 915 Com C.

[51] Chile Arts. 133, 134 Com C; Ecuador Arts. 173, 174 Com C; a similar provision in Colombia Art. 916 Com C.

Chapter 15

Burden and Standard of Proof

1. Traditional Contract Formation

The Ibero-American civil and commercial codes present some rules on the proof of contracts.[1] These are supplemented by the procedural codes which also contain provisions applied generally to the legal acts or facts.[2] However, the first may often override the application of the latter.[3] The following paragraphs describe what seems to be a uniform approach regarding the means of evidence, their standard and the allocation of the burden of proof in the contract of sale.

1.1. Means of Proof and Their Evidentiary Value

Generally, the sale of goods can be proven by any kind of means available to the parties: e.g. public documents such as notary deeds, documents signed under private signature, by accepted invoices, correspondence, a company's

---

1 *See* Argentina Arts. 1190-1194 CC; Brazil Art. 219 *et seq.* CC; Chile Art. 1699 CC; Colombia Art. 1757 *et seq.* CC; Ecuador Art. 1742 *et seq.* CC; El Salvador Art. 1569 *et seq.* CC; Honduras Art. 1495 *et seq.* CC; Paraguay Art. 699 *et seq.* CC; Peru Arts. 1374, 1381 CC; Portugal Art. 341 *et seq.* CC; Spain Art. 1.216 *et seq.* CC; Uruguay Art. 1573 *et seq.* CC; Venezuela Arts. 1.137, 1.354 *et seq.* CC.

2 Argentina Art. 377 *et seq.* CPCC; Bolivia Art. 373 *et seq.* CPC; Chile Arts. 341-409 CPC; Costa Rica Arts. 317 *et seq.* CPC; Ecuador Art. 117 *et seq.* CPC; El Salvador Art. 237 *et seq.* CPC; Mexico Art. 79 *et seq.* CPC; Panama Art. 780 *et seq.* CPC; Paraguay Art. 246 *et seq.* CPC; Peru Art. 192 *et seq.* CPC; Spain Art. 217 (1) (2) LCT.

3 *See* expressly established in Bolivia Art. 786 Com C: stating that the principles and norms on contracts and obligations, as well as the standard of proof stated in the Civil Code and Code of Civil Procedure are applicable to the commercial transactions; Paraguay Art. 703 CC: noting that the contracts shall be proven in accordance to the Civil Procedural Code (CPC) only in absence of express provisions in the Civil Code; Spain Art. 217 (5) LCT.

registries, but also by the declaration of witnesses,[4] confession,[5] *etc.*[6] The fact that the sale of goods is categorised by the laws as a consensual agreement,[7] means that any obligation is effective from the time of the parties' meeting of the minds, without any legal pre-established requirement on the form.[8] The parties can enter into a sales contract in writing, orally or in any other possible way that indicates intent and agreement.[9] Thus, any means of proof are available provided they do not affect the moral or the personal freedom of the litigants or third parties, and provided they are not specifically prohibited by law.[10] For example, under some jurisdictions the *in writing* form is considered as the only valid means of proof for certain sales contracts.[11]

In an interesting case, a Peruvian Appeal Court dismissed a claim for specific performance of a sale of goods on the grounds that from the invoices and waybills, no evidence of the existence of a contract could be established.[12] The Supreme Court reversed this decision upholding that the sale of goods does not need to be materialised in any document, and when a document is presented the same should be evaluated as proof, but when no paper document exists the judge should consider all the evidentiary means available in order to solve the internal-subjective conflict of interests.[13]

In addition, all the Ibero-American laws grant different levels of evidentiary value depending on the characterisation of documents.[14] The so called public

---

4 *See* expressly Chile Art. 128 Com C; Ecuador Art. 168 Com C; Uruguay Art. 192 (6) Com C; Venezuela Art. 128 Com C.

5 Venezuela Supreme Tribunal, Judgment 72, *Cass civ*, file 99-973 of 5 February 2002: confirming the evidentiary value of out of court confessions made by one party to the other.

6 *See for example* arts. numerating the means of proof in Argentina Art. 208 Com C; Chile Art. 1699 para. 2 CC; Colombia Art. 1757 para. 2 CC; Ecuador Art. 1742 para. 2 CC; El Salvador Art. 1569 para. 2 CC; Honduras Art. 1496 CC; Mexico Art. 79 CC; Panama Art. 780 CPC; Peru Art. 192 CPC; Uruguay Art. 192 Com C; Venezuela Art. 124 Com C.

7 Bolivia: W. Kaune Arteaga, Curso de Derecho Civil, Contratos, Vol. 2, 58 (1996); Argentina: G.A. Borda, Manual de Contratos 100 (2004); Venezuela: J.L. Aguilar Gorrondona, Contratos y Garantias: Derecho Civil IV 176 (2008); Portugal: L. De Lima Pinheiro, Dereito Comercial Internacional 276 (2005).

8 *See* Chile Art. 1801 CC; Colombia Art. 1857 CC; Ecuador Art. 1767 CC; El Salvador Art. 1605 CC; Venezuela Art. 1.161 CC; Colombia Art. 864 Com C; Peru Art. 1352 CC; *also* S. Mexico: León Tovar, Los Contratos Mercantiles 74 (2004); Spain: M. Medina de Lemus, Derecho Civil: Obligaciones y Contratos II, Contratos en Particular, Vol. 2, 44 (2004): for the sale of goods the parties are not required to enter into a contract in a specific form.

9 *See* Ch. 20, 1.

10 *See for example* Argentina Art. 378 CPCC; Brazil Art. 225 CC: declaring the photographic, cinematographic reproductions, registers and, in general, any other mechanical or electronic reproductions of facts or things make full proof, if the party, against who these are presented, does not allege their inaccuracy; Panama Art. 780 CPC; Paraguay Art. 246 CPC.

11 For more details *see* Ch. 20, 1.1.2.

12 Peru Supreme Court, *Sala civil transitoria,* Resolution 001010-2003, 26 August 2003.

13 *Id.*

14 *See* Chile: R. Jijena Leiva, Comercio Electronico, Firma Digital y Derecho 166-168 (2005):

documents are vested with authentic and binding (full) evidentiary value.[15] This character is expressly granted to documents passed by government agents, judges, certified commercial brokers and public notaries within the scope of their authority and in the form legally prescribed.[16] For example, a contract of sale concluded by the parties under the seal and in the presence of a certified public notary or commercial broker is vested with authenticity. The public deed issued by a notary does not need further elements to be *prima facie* recognised as authentic with regards to its content and identity of the parties who manifested their intents.[17]

Contracts can also be evidenced by private documents.[18] Generally, the *private document* is integrated by the document, the writing and the signature. Papers, photographs, records, electronic means or related forms are documents that support the manifest intent.[19] The signature gives authorship or ownership to the document which supports the manifest intention. A signature can be any symbol or method deployed with the intention to be connected with or used to authenticate the source of the document.[20] Examples of signatures range from the fingerprint, the personal seal, the traditional handwriting signature, the arithmetic password, to the modern and sophisticate digital signature.[21]

In the private documents the authorship is an essential element to acquire complete proof value.[22] The legal presumption is that the party who signed a document is indeed the issuer, and the signature proves his express intent in

explaining the classification of documents, their notion and proof value according to Chile's evidentiary rules.

15 Chile Arts. 1699, 1700, 1706 CC; Costa Rica Art. 370 CPC; Ecuador Arts. 1743, 1744 CC; El Salvador Arts. 1570, 1571, 1577 CC; Honduras Arts. 1497, 1499 CC; Spain Art. 1.218 CC; Uruguay Art. 1574 CC.

16 *See for example* Argentina Art. 980 CC: noting that the notary public must act within the scope of powers and in the territorial jurisdiction; Argentina Art. 986 CC: requiring the form established by law; Chile Art. 1701 para. 2 CC & Arts. 342-345 CPC; Costa Rica Art. 369 CPC; Ecuador Art. 1743 CC; El Salvador Art. 1570 CC; Honduras Art. 1497 CC; Spain Art. 1.216 CC; Uruguay Art. 1574 CC; Venezuela Art. 1.357 CC.

17 *See for example* Argentina Arts. 994, 995 CC; Chile Art. 1700 CC; Costa Rica Arts. 370, 371 CPC; Ecuador Arts. 1743, 1744 CC; El Salvador Arts. 1570, 1571 CC; Spain Arts. 1.218, 1.218 CC; Uruguay Art. 1576 CC; Venezuela Art. 1.360 CC; Chile: Jijena Leiva, *supra* note 14, at 170.

18 Argentina Art. 208 (3) Com C; Brazil Art. 219 CC; Chile Art. 1702 CC & Art. 346 CPC; Costa Rica Art. 379 CPC; Ecuador Art. 1746 CC; El Salvador Arts. 1573, 1577 CC; Honduras Art. 1507 CC; Spain Art. 1.225 CC; Uruguay Art. 1581 CC & Art. 192 (3) Com C.

19 *See* Costa Rica Art. 368 CPC.

20 El Salvador Supreme Court, *Cass civ, Pineda Solis v. Hernández Landa Verde*, 1593 S.S., 11 May de 2004.

21 *See infra* 2.

22 *See* Brazil Art. 222 CC: dictating that when the authenticity of a telegram is contested the original one signed will constitute full proof; Chile Arts. 1702, 1704 CC; Costa Rica Art. 372 CPC; Ecuador Art. 1749 CC; El Salvador Arts. 1574, 1575 CC; Peru Art. 193 CPC; Uruguay Art. 1581 CC; Venezuela Arts. 1.368, 1.374 CC.

the document.[23] The presumed signatory party cannot repudiate the document unless he proves that the signature has been forged, or that the original data was modified.[24] The private documents recognised by the parties, either expressly or in absence of proof, on the contrary, have the same evidentiary value that the public documents.[25]

The non-signed documents, such as the mail letter, telegraphs, e-mails, and other similar documents, supported by any means of communications issued by the parties, also have evidentiary value.[26] The value of these documents is measured by the judge giving due consideration to the circumstances of the case, the conduct of the parties, the general usages and the practices established between the parties.[27]

Thus, for example, Courts have held that if an offer was issued or accepted through fax, it is unsustainable to contest the proof value of a means of communication which has been used to express the party's will.[28] Similarly, a Mexican Collegiate Tribunal explained that even if a regular e-mail raises the problem of its authenticity and integrity, which may prevent it from

---

[23] *See* Brazil Art. 219 CC: stating that the declarations on signed documents are presumed true in relation to the signatories; Chile Art. 1702 CC; Costa Rica Arts. 372, 379 CPC; Honduras Art. 1508 CC.

[24] *See for example* Argentina Art. 1028 CC; Honduras Art. 1508 CC; Uruguay Art. 1583 CC; Venezuela Arts. 1.364, 1.365 CC; Bolivia Supreme Court, *Sala Civil*, *Rosalina Rodríguez Vega de Villarroel v. Félix Tapia Villarroel y otros*: the expert witness test proved that the signature was forged and thus no intent for the sale of real estate existed. The sale was declared not to exist; El Salvador Supreme Court, *Cass civ, Pineda Solis v. Hernandez Landa Verde*, 1593 S.S., 11 May de 2004.

[25] Argentina Art. 1026 CC; Bolivia Art. 1297 CC: Brazil Art. 219 CC; Chile Art. 1702 CC; Ecuador Art. 1746 CC; El Salvador Art. 1573 CC; El Salvador Art. 1575 CC; Honduras Art. 1507 CC; Spain Art. 1.225 CC; Uruguay Art. 1581 CC; Venezuela Art. 1.363 CC; Bolivia Supreme Court, *Sala Civil*, 11 March 2003, *Carla Cecilia Chacón de Pino v. Luis Iriondo Angola*: declaring that the photocopies of a sales contract presented by the claimant and recognised by the respondent acquired full evidentiary value.

[26] Argentina Art. 208 (4) Com C; Brazil Arts. 222, 223, 225 CC; Chile Art. 1698 CC; Colombia Art. 175 CPC; Costa Rica Arts. 388, 391 CPC; Ecuador Arts. 1748, 1577 CC; El Salvador Art. 999 (III) (IV) Com C; Honduras Art. 1510 CC; Panama Arts. 780 part 2, 781 CPC; Paraguay Arts. 411, 412 CC; Peru Art. 193 CPC; Uruguay Art. 1588 CC & Art. 192 (4) Com C; Venezuela Arts. 1.374, 1.374 CC; *see also infra* 2.

[27] *See* Colombia Arts. 187, 189, 190 CPC; Ecuador Art. 119 CPC; Peru Arts. 193, 194 CPC; Paraguay Art. 412 CC; Mexico Collegiate Tribunals, Registry 186'287, SJF XVI, August 2002, p. 1279: information found in the Internet that cannot be categorised as public or private signed documents is considered simple documents that may help the judge to create a clear conviction of the case. *See also* Argentina: R.L. Lorenzetti, Tratado de los Contratos Parte General 438 (2004).

[28] Argentina National Commercial Chamber, *Sala* D, *Chiarini, Roberto L. v. Leoco Industrieanlagen GmbH & Cia. KG*; Mexico Collegiate Tribunals, *Novena Época,* Registry 199'602, SJF V, January 1997, p. 442: upholding the validity of a sale of goods agreement passed by telefax communications as the law does not impose any restriction.

attaining full evidentiary value, when an e-mail incorporates an advance electronic signature, such e-mail can constitute evidence, provided it is not duly challenged by the other party.[29]

The commercial documents also have probative value. Regarding specifically the contract of sale, most of the Ibero-American commercial laws require sole-traders and companies to keep records of their transactions in the so called *books of commerce*.[30] These accounting records have an evidentiary value between traders.[31] The commercial books are usually subject to certain formalities which may affect their proof value.[32]

Likewise companies and traders are required to store copies of any business correspondence dispatched and received, in such a way that the content can be

---

[29] Mexico Collegiate Tribunals, Registry 181'356, SJF XIX, June 2004, p 1425.

[30] *See for example* Argentina Arts. 43, 44, 47 Com C; Bolivia Arts. 25 (6), 36 Com C; Chile Art. 25 Com C; Colombia Art. 48 Com C; Costa Rica Art. 382 CPC; Ecuador Arts. 37, 39 Com C; El Salvador Art. 435 Com C; Guatemala Art. 368 Com C; Mexico Art. 33 Com C; Paraguay Arts. 11 (c), 74 Com C; Portugal Art. 31 Com C; Spain Art. 27 Com C; Venezuela Art. 32 Com C; The Codes of Commerce would generally rely on the General Principles on Accountancy by requiring that the book of financial statements contain: I. The ordinary balance sheets; II. The extraordinary balance sheets due to the liquidation of the business, the suspension of payments or bankruptcy resulting from legal statutes or the decision of the merchant; III. A summary of the inventories contained in each balance sheet; IV. A summary of the accounts that are grouped to form the line items in the balance sheet; V. A statement of profits and losses for each balance sheet; VI. A statement of the composition of the equity; VII. Any other statements that may be necessary to reflect the economic and financial situation of the merchant; VIII. The form in which the distribution of profits or application of losses has been verified; *see for example* Bolivia Art. 37 Com C; Chile Art. 25 Com C; Ecuador Art. 39 Com C; El Salvador Art. 435 (para. 3) Com C; Paraguay Art. 75 Com C; Portugal Art. 31 Com C; Venezuela Art. 32 Com C.

[31] *See for example* Chile Arts. 34-36 Com C: noting that the judge can compare the books of two traders involved in a sales dispute in order to collect evidence of the transaction; Chile Art. 39 Com C: noting that the records have full proof value against the issuer; Ecuador Arts. 47, 48, 50 Com C: noting that the judge can compare the books of two traders involved in a sales dispute in order to collect evidence of the transaction; Ecuador Art. 51 Com C: noting that the records have full proof value against the issuer; Mexico Art. 44 Com C: exhibition is limited to cases in which the issuer of the records has an interest on it or liability is presumed in trial; Paraguay Arts. 96, 97 Com C: exhibition is forced in trials but only when the books are of direct relevance to a point of the case at hand; Portugal Arts. 43, 44 Com C: exhibition is forced in trials but only when the books are of direct relevance to a point of the case at hand; Spain Arts. 31, 32 (3) Com C: exhibition is limited to cases in which the issuer of the records has an interest on it or liability is presumed in trial; Venezuela Arts. 38, 39, 42 Com C.

[32] *For example* Bolivia Art. 40 Com C: stating that the books of commerce must be sealed and authorised by notary public; Colombia Arts. 19 (2), 28 (7) Com C: stating that books of commerce must be registered in the Public Registry; Guatemala Art. 372 Com C: books shall be authorised by the Registry of Commerce; Paraguay Art. 78 Com C; Bolivia Supreme Court, *Sala Civil,* 6 March 2002, *Guillermo Farwig Guillén v. Sociedad Bol-Art S.A.*: upheld a decision of lower instance courts that rendered their judgments based on the expert witness report in preference to the book of commerce records that did not fulfil the legal requirements to constitute full proof between merchants.

kept during a certain time.[33] Business correspondence has evidentiary value.[34] The judge can require the disclosure of such records in order to integrate them or compare them with the evidence presented by the parties.[35]

The commercial invoice issued by the seller also constitutes evidence. Many Ibero-American commercial laws establish the duty of the seller to deliver the invoice.[36] The invoice proves the existence and the essential elements of the sales contract, *i.e.* the goods and the price.[37] In order to constitute evidence against the buyer, he must, expressly or impliedly, accept the invoice.[38] In this regard, the Bolivian Code of Commerce establishes that once the invoice has been accepted by the buyer, the sale is considered to have been duly performed in the way established by the invoice, which binds the buyer to pay the agreed price.[39] The elements of the invoice must also match the records contained in the books of commerce.

In the same way that the invoice constitutes a means of evidence of the existence of sales, the same is true of import documents, bills of lading, letters of credit and other related documents of the international sale of goods.[40]

---

[33] Bolivia Art. 51 Com C (during 5 years Art. 52 CC); Chile Art. 45 Com C; Colombia Art. 54 Com C; Ecuador Art. 58 Com C; El Salvador Arts. 435 para. 2, 454 Com C; Guatemala Art. 382 Com C (during 5 years); Mexico Arts. 47, 48, 49 Com C (during 10 years); Portugal Art. 40 Com C (during 10 years); Spain Art. 30 Com C (during 6 years); Venezuela Art. 44 Com C (during 10 years).

[34] *See for example* Costa Rica Art. 431 (e) Com C; El Salvador Art. 999 (III) (IV) Com C; Nicaragua Art. 111 (e) Com C.

[35] *See for example* Chile Art. 47 Com C; Portugal Art. 43 Com C.

[36] *See* Argentina Art. 474 Com C; Bolivia Art. 834 Com C; Chile Art. 160 Com C; Colombia Art. 944 Com C; Costa Rica Art. 448 Com C; Ecuador Art. 201 Com C; Nicaragua Art. 362 Com C; Portugal Art. 476 Com C; Uruguay Art. 557 Com C; Venezuela Art. 147 Com C.

[37] Mexico Collegiate Tribunals, *Novena Época,* Registry 197'122, SJF VII, January 1998, at 1097: confirming the evidentiary value of the invoice issued by the seller and in possession of the buyer, since under Mexican commercial usages the original invoice is only delivered to the buyer once he has made payment.

[38] Bolivia Art. 718 Com C; Chile Art. 160 Com C; Costa Rica Arts. 431(c), 460 Com C; Ecuador Art. 164 Com C; El Salvador Art. 999(II) Com C; Guatemala Arts. 591, 593 Com C; Mexico Art. 1391(VII) Com C; Nicaragua Art. 111(d) Com C; Venezuela Art. 124 para. 6 Com C.

[39] Bolivia Art. 718 Com C; *see also* Costa Rica Art. 460 Com C; Guatemala Art. 593 Com C; Bolivia: V. Camargo Marín, Derecho Comercial Boliviano 259 (2007).

[40] *See* expressly mentioned in Chile Art. 149 Com C; ICC Final Award Case No. 13967 *Lex Contractus* Bolivian Law and INCOTERMS 2000: the Arbitral Tribunal considered that even if the goods were not invoiced, the bills of lading had proven the delivery of the goods and, hence, the obligation to pay their price.

1.2. Standard of Proof

As sustained by the Paraguayan Supreme Court, the system of proofs assessment is based on the principle of sound judgment and constructive criticism.[41] This means that the judge or the arbitrator constructs his own free conviction based on the influence that the facts discussed and the proofs submitted have produced on him. The judge is actually allowed to move away or disregard those proofs that he finds irrelevant for the judgement.[42]

1.3. Burden of Proof

1.3.1. Traditional Rules

The question of who bears the burden of proving the existence or breach of contractual obligations is very important. The parties to a contract are almost never allowed to decide between them who will bear the burden of proof.[43] Even when the possibility to do so is understood to reduce the uncertainty on this issue.[44]

Under the Ibero-American laws, the traditional rule is that the burden of proof as to the constituent events which give rise to a right of claim is borne by the claimant, and the existence of an event that impedes, modifies or extinguishes the right of the claimant must be proven by the respondent.[45] Hence, in the contract of sale, the claimant must prove the existence (formation)

---

41 Paraguay Supreme Court, Judgment 1345, 5 October 2004, *Angel Aníbal Núñez Ortiz v. La República Compañía Paraguaya De Seguros Generales S.A.*

42 El Salvador Supreme Court, *Cass civ, Pineda Solis v. Hernández Landa Verde*, 1593 S.S., 11 May de 2004.

43 *See for example* Bolivia Art. 1284 CC: it is void the agreement that shifts the burden of proof unless the law expressly allows it; Mexico Art. 85 CPC: expressly stating that the right to prove and the means of proof can no be renounced; Portugal Art. 345 CC: noting that is void the agreement that shifts the burden of proof when such affects a non-disposable right or when such a reallocation renders the exercise of one of the parties rights excessively difficult. Also it is void the agreement that excludes a means of proof.

44 Argentina: Lorenzetti, *supra* note 27, at 450.

45 Argentina Art. 377 CPCC; Bolivia Art. 183 CC & Art. 375 CPC; Chile Art. 1698 CC; Colombia Art. 1757 CC & Art. 177 CPC; Costa Rica Art. 317 CPC; Ecuador Art. 1742 CC & Arts. 117-118 CPC; El Salvador Art. 1569 CC & Arts. 237, 238 CPC; Honduras Art. 1495 CC Mexico Arts. 81, 82, 84 CPC; Panama Art. 784 CPC; Paraguay Art. 249 CPC; Portugal Art. 342 CC; Spain Art. 217 (1) (2) LCT; Uruguay Art. 1573 CC; Venezuela Art. 1.354 CC; El Salvador Supreme Court, *Cass civ, Estadios Deportivos de El Salvador, S.A.de C.V. v. Asociación de Clubes de Liga Mayor,* CCS1041.96; ICC Final Award Case No. 13663 *Lex Contractus* Spanish Law: confirming the rule established by Spain Art. 217(1)(2) LCT. The claimant succeeded in proving the he had performed his obligations under the contract and that the respondent had not performed his obligations. The respondent failed to prove that he was exempted from performing.

of its credit *vis à vis* the defendant, who, on the other hand, must prove any exemption which releases him from the obligations created, or must prove that he has already performed the obligation.[46]

In this respect, the Peruvian Supreme Court has sustained (reversing the decisions of the first and appeal instances which had allocated all the burden on the claimant) that, with regards to the process of avoidance of a sales contract, based on the lack of payment of the price, the claimant [seller] has the burden to prove the existence of the contract, Whilst, the buyer [respondent] has the burden to prove that he has paid the price which constitutes one of his obligations and that he affirms to have performed.[47]

1.3.2. Modern Approach

Ibero-American scholars have proposed additional rules aiming to establish a more efficient and fair proof allocation system. Lorenzetti considers one parties' greater technical background shall influence the dynamic allocation of the proof.[48] Thus, the burden of proving technical or complex events shall be allocated to the party who is better positioned to prove them.[49]

But technical background is not the only factor that shall influence the dynamics of the burden of proof. Peyrano proposes a more flexible evidentiary system based on the circumstances surrounding the case at hand. The party bearing the burden of proof shall be the one who is better placed to do it.[50] In other words, the judge shall consider which party poses the most efficient means to do so. Either, because he already has the information needed, or because the allocation to that party would render the process cheaper or quicker.

In principle, from the traditional rule on the burden of proof, one could establish, for example, that the offeror interested in the enforcement of a supposedly existing sale would need to prove: 1) that his offer has all required

---

46 ICC Final Award Case No. 11367 *Lex Contractus* Portuguese Law: upholding that he burden of proof rests on each party in order to prove its own allegations: the seller shall prove that the invoices were due and remain outstanding, and the buyer that the seller defaulted from its obligations under the contract; ICC Final Award Case No. 13743 *Lex Contractus* Spanish Law: "The Spanish Supreme Tribunal held in 2001 that the creditor has to prove the constituent elements of its claim (the existence of the obligation), whilst the debtor has to prove the extinction of the obligation, i.e. the fulfilment or payment, which includes, according to Art. 1157 of the Spanish Civil Code, the delivery (*dare* obligation) and the performance of the promised act (*facere* obligation) (*see* Tribunal Supremo, Civil Chamber, decision No. 973/2001 of 24 October 2001)."

47 Peru Supreme Court, *Sala civil transitoria,* Resolution 001656-2003, 25 November 2003.

48 Argentina: Lorenzetti, *supra* note 27, at 452.

49 *Id.*, at 452.

50 *See generally* J. Peyrano, El Derecho probatorio posible y su realización judicial, en PEIRANO/CHIAPPINI, Tácticas en el proceso civil, Rubinzal-Culzoni, Santa Fe, 1990, t. III, p. 39 *cited in* Argentina: Lorenzetti, *supra* note 27, at 454, n. 35.

elements; 2) that the offer was accepted by the offeree in due time and; 3) that such acceptance mirrored his offer. The offeree, on the other hand, could negate all the claims of the offeror leaving to the latter the burden to prove any and all of his claims. Alternatively, the offeree could raise some of the impediments for the existence of the contract as the offeror wants it. For example, the offeree could prove that his acceptance was not pure but contains modifications to the offer that were never accepted by the other party.

But the issue is not always that simple. The duty of proving certain events of the process of contract formation renders the allocation of the burden crucial.[51] Some of these events are so difficult to prove, that both parties try their best to be released from any duty to prove them. For example, one such event is the time when the acceptance was known (information theory) by the offeror and which constitutes, under many laws, the relevant event for the conclusion of the contract.[52] In principle, the offeree interested in the existence of the contract would be required to prove that the offeror had knowledge of the acceptance, but such a thing may not always be easy to achieve.

In this regard, some Civil Codes have correctly shifted the burden of proof. The acceptance is presumed to be known by the offeror from the moment it arrives at his address, unless he proves that he was not able to know about it, although the same has arrived at his address;[53] or unless he proves that it was impossible to know the offer had arrived.[54]

It is perhaps in these cases that the dynamics of burden allocation should be made flexible to the judge or the arbitrator. So that the party who is better placed to bear the proof is called to provide the evidence. For example, even if, in principle, the traditional approach would require the offeror to prove that he timely revoked the offer before acceptance,[55] the burden of proof might be reallocated to the offeree so that he proves that he did not have knowledge of the revocation made by the offeror before accepting the offer. The offeree may be better placed to prove that, although the offeror has dispatched his revocation or the revocation has reached the offeree, he ignored the revocation.

2. Electronic Communications

As mentioned in the previous chapter, the majority of the Ibero-American civil and commercial laws were enacted during the nineteenth century, when

[51] Bolivia Supreme Court, *Julio Ramiro Saniz Balderrama v. Galindo S.A.*: denying the voidability of the contract based on the buyer's claim that he was induced by fraud to enter into the sale. The Court sustained that fraud cannot be presumed but has to be proven by the affected party.

[52] *See* Ch. 10, 2.2.1.

[53] Venezuela Art. 1.137(5) CC.

[54] Peru Art. 1374 CC.

[55] Costa Rica Art. 1010 CC; Nicaragua Art. 2450 CC; *see also* Argentina Art. 1156 CC.

the means of communications for contract conclusion between non-present persons were limited to mailed letters and the telegraph. As the century came to its end and the twentieth century went by, new inventions such as the telephone, the telex, the facsimile and the computer redefined the manner to enter into transactions.

However, many of the issues concerning the evidentiary value of the records accessible to the parties remained the same. Broadcast voices or images raised the same or greater evidentiary problems in civil and commercial trials than those posed by the contracts celebrated verbally. Although, in practice, the first would have the advantage to keep the record of the communication, most procedural laws were not designed (nor was the spirit of jurists) until recently, to recognise such means of proof.[56]

In recent years, some Ibero-American countries enacted legislative statutes containing new rules on the evidentiary value of electronic communications. Bolivia,[57] Colombia, Dominican Republic, Ecuador, Mexico, Panama and Venezuela adopted or integrated into their national laws the MLEC and/or the MLES with intention of strengthening the evidentiary value of electronic data.[58] On the other hand, many other Ibero-American countries have enacted their own "original" rules on the evidentiary value of electronic communications and digital signatures,[59] while others have limited themselves to digital signatures.[60]

Some of these laws expressly acknowledge that information in the form of data messages[61] shall be given due evidential value; as it cannot be denied the admissibility of data messages in evidence on the sole ground that it is

[56] *See* Chile: Jijena Leiva, *supra* note 14, at 166-168: explaining how in Chile even after the enactment of the Law No. 19.799 the mentality of the average jurist represented an obstacle to the recognition of the evidential value of e-mails, faxes, etc.

[57] Bolivia Arts. 12-15 Law No. 080/2007. Actually, one could easily conclude that although the status of adoptions provided by the UNCITRAL does not contemplate the country of Bolivia, Bolivian law seems to be and adoption of the MLEC.

[58] Colombia Law No. 527; Dominican Republic Law No. 126-02; Ecuador Law No. 67 & Decree No. 3496; Guatemala Law Decree No. 47-2008; Mexico adopted both the 1996 MLEC and the MLES. This adoption was not made in single instruments but rather they were incorporated in different codes and statutes. Regarding the electronic communication in the area of private law, different provisions are contained in Mexico's Civil Code, Code of Commerce and Procedural Federal Civil Code; Panama Law No. 43; Venezuela Law No. 37,148.

[59] Chile Law No.19.799; Costa Rica Law No. 8454; Portugal Decree Law No. 7/2004 & Decree Law No. 290-D/99; Spain Law No. 34/2002 & Law No. 59/2003; *see also* Mexico: E. Elías Azar, La Contratacion por Medios Electronicos 276-277 (2005): acknowledging the similarity of the principles of the MLEC and the EC Directive on Electronic Signature.

[60] Argentina Law No. 25.506; Peru Law No. 27269; Uruguay Law Decree No. 382/003.

[61] 'Data message' means information generated, sent, received or stored by electronic, optical or similar means including, but not limited to, electronic data interchange (EDI), electronic mail, telegram, telex or telecopy, *see* Art. 2(a) MLEC.

presented in such a form.[62] Moreover, in assessing the evidential value of data messages, many laws require the judge to take into consideration, among other relevant factors, the reliability of the manner in which the data message was generated, stored or communicated, the manner in which the integrity of the information was maintained and in which its originator was identified.[63]

On this issue, a Mexican Collegiate Tribunal upheld that among the means of electronic communications was the 'Internet', which constitutes a worldwide dissemination system of information in different areas, which also allows determining the official or unofficial character of the information accessed. In the Tribunal's view the Internet constitutes an advance of science, hence, due evidentiary value should be given to the information found on it.[64] In a different decision, a Collegiate Tribunal explained that the judge does not need to be an expert to carry out an Internet discovery (*Inspección*) consisting of verifying the existence of a particular information on a webpage which can be done by a common person, since, contrary to the expert-witness, the discovery does not require the person (the judge) to have technical knowledge in the field.[65]

Similarly, many of the new statutes recognise that in the context of contract conclusion, unless otherwise agreed by the parties, an offer and its acceptance may be expressed by means of data messages, and the contract shall not be denied validity or enforceability on the sole ground that data messages were used for that purpose.[66] Indeed, the recognition of legal validity or enforcement of data messages is not limited to the context of offers and acceptance. Any declaration of intent or other statement made between the parties in the context of their contractual relation shall be given full evidentiary value, irrespective of whether it is in the form of electronic data.[67]

[62] Bolivia Art. 7(II)(III) Law No. 080/2007; Chile Art. 3 Law No. 19.799 (with not advanced signature according to Art. 2(f); Costa Rica Art. 3 Law No. 8454; Colombia Art. 10 Law No. 527; Dominican Republic Arts. 4, 9 Law No. 126-02; Ecuador Arts. 2, 52 Law No. 67; Mexico Art. 89*bis* Com C; Panama Arts. 5, 10 Law No. 43; Portugal Art. 3(1) & 4 Decree Law No. 290-D/99; Spain Art. 3(7)(8)(9) Law No. 59/2003; Venezuela Art. 4 Law No. 37,148.

[63] Bolivia Art. 33 Law No. 080/2007; Colombia Art. 10 Law No. 527; Dominican Republic Art. 10 Law No. 126-02; Ecuador Art. 55 Law No. 67; Mexico Art. 210-A CPC; Panama Art. 11 Law No. 43; Mexico: Elías Azar, *supra* note 59, at 283.

[64] Mexico Collegiate Tribunals, *Novena Época,* Registry 186'243, SJF XVI, August 2002, at 1306: relying on Arts. 188 and 210-A of Mexico Federal Civil Code of Procedures.

[65] Mexico Collegiate Tribunals, Registry 177'198, SJF XXII, September 2005, p 1532.

[66] Bolivia Arts. 27, 28 Law No. 080/2007; Chile Art. 3 Law No. 19.799; Costa Rica Art. 5(a) Law No. 8454; Colombia Art. 14 Law No. 527; Dominican Republic Art. 13 Law No. 126-02; Ecuador Arts. 45, 46 Law No. 67; Mexico Art. 1803 CC; Panama Art. 11 Law No. 43; Portugal Art. 25(1) Decree Law No. 7/2004; Spain Arts. 23, 24 Law No. 34/2002; Venezuela Art. 14 Law No. 37,148.

[67] Bolivia Art. 22 Law No. 080/2007; Chile Art. 5 Law No.19.799; Colombia Art. 15 Law No. 527; Costa Rica Art. 5(a) Law No. 8454; Dominican Republic Art. 14 Law No. 126-02; Ecuador Arts. 45, 46 Law No. 67; Mexico Art. 89*bis* Com C; Panama Art. 11 Law No. 43;

As previously described, the Ibero-American laws grant different levels of evidentiary value depending on the characterisation of documents. On the one hand, we mentioned that public documents were given full value when passed under the signature or seal of government agents, judges, certified commercial brokers and public notaries within the scope of their authority and in the form legally prescribed.[68] On the other hand, private documents acquire complete evidential value, when signed by the parties, unless one of the parties proves that the signature has been forged, or that the original data was modified.[69]

In this context, the role of the new statutes on electronic communications and digital signatures is not only to recognise the equivalence of handwriting signatures and electronic signatures. Additionally, these statutes equal the evidentiary value that electronically signed public and private documents can have in court proceedings *vis à vis* traditionally paper signed documents.[70] For example, a recurring provision in some laws provide that a commonly called, advanced electronic signature shall have the value and effect of a handwriting signature. *Advanced electronic signatures* are generally understood to be under the exclusive control and unique use of one person, they are susceptible to verification and also able to alert when the information or the message to which they are linked is modified.[71]

Moreover, the commercial documents, such as books of commerce, business correspondence and commercial invoices, maintain their evidentiary value even though they are preserved or stored through electronic means. Certainly, some Ibero-American laws establish that when certain documents, records or information are required by law to be retained, the requirement is met if the electronic or digital information contained therein is accessible so as to be usable for subsequent reference.[72]

Portugal Art. 25 (1) Decree Law No. 7/2004; Spain Arts. 23, 24 Law No. 34/2002; Venezuela Art. 15 Law No. 37,148.

[68] *See supra* 1.1.

[69] *See supra* 1.1.

[70] *See* Argentina Arts. 3, 11 Law No. 25.506; Bolivia Arts. 7, 35 Law No. 080/2007; Chile Arts. 4, 5 Law No. 19.799; Colombia Art. 7 Law No. 527; Costa Rica Art. 9 Law No. 8454 & Art. 414 C Com C; Dominican Republic Art. 6 Law No. 126-02; Ecuador Arts. 14, 51 Law No. 67; Panama Art. 7 Law No. 43; Peru Arts. 1, 2 Law No. 27269; Portugal Art. 3(1)(2)(3), 7 Decree Law No. 290-D/99; Spain Art. 3(6)(7) Law No. 59/2003; Venezuela Art. 6 Law No. 37,148.

[71] *See* Bolivia Arts. 34, 35 Law No. 080/2007; Colombia Art. 28 Law No. 527; Dominican Republic Art. 31 Law No. 126-02; Ecuador Arts. 14, 51 Law No. 67; Chile Arts. 4, 5 Law No.19.799: means signed with advance digital signature according to Art. (2)(g); Costa Rica Art. 12 Law No. 8454; Mexico Art. 97 Com C; Panama Art. 25 Law No. 43; Portugal Art. 3(2)(3), 5, 7 Decree Law No. 290-D/99: means signed with advance digital signature according to Art. 2(c); Spain Art. 3(6)(7) Law No. 59/2003: means signed with advance digital signature according to Art. 3(2); Uruguay Arts. 3, 4 Law Decree No. 382/003; Venezuela Art. 6 Law No. 37,148.

[72] Argentina Art. 12 Law No. 25.506: but the documents shall be digitally signed; Bolivia

In addition, these laws require the electronic or digital information to be retained in the format in which it was generated, sent or received, or in a format which can be demonstrated to accurately represent the information generated, sent or received.[73] Also in many cases, the information preserved must allow the identification of the origin and destination of a data message, as well as the date and time when it was sent or received.[74] Consequently, digital invoices, electronic books of commerce, electronic business correspond, *etc.*, have equal evidentiary value as those contained in traditional paper records.[75]

Art. 11 Law No. 080/2007; Colombia Art. 12 Law No. 527; Costa Rica Art. 6 Law No. 8454; Dominican Republic Art. 11 Law No. 126-02; Ecuador Art. 8 Law No. 67; Mexico Arts. 48, 93*bis* Com C; Panama Art. 12 Law No. 43; Venezuela Art. 8 Law No. 37,148.

[73] Bolivia Art. 11 Law No. 080/2007; Colombia Art. 12 Law No. 527; Costa Rica Art. 6 Law No. 8454; Dominican Republic Art. 11 Law No. 126-02; Ecuador Art. 8 Law No. 67; Mexico Arts. 48, 93*bis* Com C; Panama Art. 12 Law No. 43; Venezuela Art. 8 Law No. 37,148.

[74] Bolivia Art. 11 Law No. 080/2007; Colombia Art. 12 Law No. 527; Costa Rica Art. 6 Law No. 8454; Dominican Republic Art. 11 Law No. 126-02; Ecuador Art. 8 Law No. 67; Mexico Arts. 48, 93*bis* Com C; Panama Art. 12 Law No. 43; Venezuela Art. 8 Law No. 37,148.

[75] *See* expressly recognised in Colombia Art. 12 last para. Law No. 527; Mexico Art. 48 Com C; Panama Art. 12 last para. Law No. 43.

CHAPTER 16

AGENCY

1. General Remarks on Agency

The Ibero-American Civil Codes distinguish between legal and voluntary representation.[1] This work focuses on the voluntary representation or also known as agency. According to this legal concept the principal[2] authorises the agent[3] to act on his behalf.[4] The contract under which the principal voluntary

[1] Legal representation results from the law, irrespective of the intent of the principal, for example, parents or tutors have legal representation over infants; *see* Argentina: A.A. Alterini, Contratos civiles, comerciales, de consumo 311 (1998).

[2] All Ibero-American codes use Spanish word *mandante* (or *representado* in the case of Peru Civil Code) to mean Principal; *see* Chile Art. 2116 CC for a code's definition.

[3] All Ibero-American codes use Spanish word *mandatario* (or *representante* in the case of Peru Civil Code) to mean Agent; *see* Chile Art. 2116 CC for a code's definition.

[4] Some codes distinguish between the agency with representation and without representation. For this work we analyse the rules on agency with representation characterised by the fact that the agent acts on behalf of the principal and not in his own name. For the express distinction *see* Guatemala Art. 1686 CC; Mexico Arts. 2560, 2561 CC; Peru Arts. 1806, 1809 CC; Peru Arts. 1178, 1180 CC; Spain Art. 1717 CC; Venezuela Art. 1.684 CC; ICC Final Award Case No. 9400 *Lex Contractus* Colombian Law: explaining that in order to determine whether the contractual relationships between the parties can be characterised as commercial agency, the Arbitral Tribunal should examine the actual situation. The Tribunal found that the licen*see* had sold the products and had acted on its own behalf and risk and not on behalf or at risk of the licensor. Thus, an essential element of Art. 1317 of Colombia's Code of Commerce relating to the commercial agent was missing; ICC Final Award Case No. 10818 *Lex Contractus* Portuguese Law: the Arbitral Tribunal considered that there was no express mandate agreement between seller and one of his subsidiaries, and no implied mandate could be derived from the circumstances, since there are no indications whatsoever that the seller's subsidiary was subordinated to seller. Nor were there any indications that allow a finding to the effect that there was a mandate between seller and seller's subsidiary, since "according to Article 1157 of the Portuguese Civil Code a mandate is a contract where one of the Parties undertakes to perform

grants the authorisation of representation to the agent is known as *mandato* both in Spanish and Portuguese.[5]

Additionally, most Ibero-American Codes of Commerce contain specific rules on the authorisation and representation duties of business managers and certain employees.[6] As their main duty is the administration of the business mandated by the company, the Codes of Commerce have assimilated such relationship with an agency relationship and have established specific rules to be applied in such situations. The managers and employees act on behalf of the principal, who may be the company or the owner of the business,[7] and such relationship is to be declared in every legal transaction they enter into.[8] The rules on mandato apply supplementary to the acts performed by the directors and employees on behalf of the company.[9]

The rule integrated in all the Ibero-American Civil Codes for the contract of agency (mandato) is that the legal acts committed or the obligations contracted by the agent within the scope of his powers, and on behalf of the principal, are considered to be performed by the principal himself.[10]

Under most of the Ibero-American laws, the principal may grant authorisation expressly or impliedly.[11] In the same way the acceptance by the agent can be manifested.[12] The authorisation could be granted in writing or

---

one or more juridical acts for the account of the other party." However, the seller's subsidiary performed most of the duties on its own account.

[5] Most Ibero-American codes categorised the mandate as a contract; *see for example*: Bolivia Art. 804 CC; Guatemala Art. 1686 CC; Peru Art. 1790 CC; Portugal Art. 1157 CC; Spain Art. 1709 CC; However, some Civil Codes also contain specific rules on representation of obligations directly applicable to agency; *see for example*: Colombia Arts. 1317-1331 CC; Peru Arts. 145-167 CC; Venezuela Art. 1.684 CC.

[6] *See* Argentina Art. 132 *et seq.* Com C; Bolivia Art. 73 *et seq.* Com C; Chile Arts. 232, 237, 325 *et seq.* Com C; Mexico Art. 309 *et seq.* Com C; Paraguay Arts. 53 LM; Spain Art. 283 *et seq.* Com C; Portugal Art. 248 *et seq.* Com C; Venezuela Art. 94 *et seq.*; *see also* Argentina: Alterini, *supra* note 1, at 314.

[7] To name some express provisions *see* Paraguay Art. 57 LM; Portugal Art. 250 Com C; Spain Art. 285 Com C. Though in the opinion of Argentina: Alterini, *supra* note 1, at 311: the companies directors do not act on behalf of the company but the company perform acts through its directors.

[8] Argentina Art. 136 Com C; Bolivia Art. 73 Com C; Chile Art. 325 Com C; Mexico Art. 311 Com C; Paraguay Art. 56 LM; Portugal Art. 250 Com C; Spain Art. 284 Com C; Venezuela Art. 96 Com C.

[9] *See* Argentina Art. 1870 paras 2, 3 CC; Brazil Art. 1.173 CC; Bolivia Art. 63 CC; Guatemala Arts. 1696, 1697 CC; Peru Art. 165 CC.

[10] Argentina Art. 1946 CC; Brazil Arts. 663, 675 CC; Bolivia Art. 805 CC; Chile Art. 2116 CC (the principle is taken from the definition though no express obligation is written); Mexico Art. 2546 CC; Paraguay Art. 880 CC; Spain Art. 1725 CC; Venezuela Art. 1.691 CC; Spain Supreme Tribunal, 27 January 2000, A.C. 462/2000.

[11] Brazil Art. 656 CC; Chile Art. 2123 CC; Mexico Art. 2547 CC; Paraguay Art. 880 CC; Spain Art. 1710 CC; Venezuela Art. 1.685 CC.

[12] Chile Art. 2124 CC; Paraguay Art. 880 CC; Spain Art. 1710 CC; Venezuela Art. 1.685 CC.

orally.[13] The authorisation and the acceptance are understood to be impliedly granted when they result from conduct that give certitude to the intent of one of the parties;[14] for example, in cases of spontaneous execution of the agency agreement by the agent.[15] In some countries, authorisation shall be granted in public deed[16] or shall be signed by both parties with the attendance of two witnesses and, in order to be valid, their signatures shall be ratified by a notary public.[17]

Mexico is the only Ibero-American country which is part of the still unforced 1983 Geneva Convention on Agency in the International Sale of Goods (hereinafter the Agency Convention).[18] According to Article 12 of the Agency Convention whenever an agent acts on behalf of a principal within the scope of his authority, and the third party knew or ought to have known that the agent was acting as an agent, the acts of the agent shall directly bind the principal and the third party to each other.

1.1. Applicable Law

For some Ibero-American countries, the applicable law that governs the power of representation is that of the place where the authorisation was granted.[19] Though, some laws state that for matters requiring special authorisation such shall be granted in the form established by the lex fori.[20] Besides, some other laws and courts sustain that the voluntary representation is regulated by the law of the State where the authorisation is performed.[21]

---

[13] Argentina Art. 917 CC; Mexico Art. 2550 CC (in Mexico the oral mandate shall be ratified in writing before the business finishes according to Mexico Art. 2552 CC).

[14] Argentina Art. 918 CC; Brazil 659 CC; Chile 2124 CC; Paraguay Art. 881 CC.

[15] Mexico Art. 2547 CC; Paraguay Art. 881 CC; Venezuela Art. 1.685 CC.

[16] In Guatemala Art. 1687 CC (authorisation in public deed shall be granted for business exceeding one thousand *quetzales*); Mexico Art. 2555 CC; Peru Art. 156 CC (the authorisation shall be granted in public deed for agency involving the transfer of goods' property of the principal).

[17] Mexico Art. 2555 CC.

[18] Mexico ratified the Agency Convention the 22 of December of 1987; Chile signed the Convention in 17 of February 1983 but has not ratified the instrument.

[19] Guatemala Art. 1700 CC; Paraguay Art. 23 CC (supported by dissenting opinion of Ministry Sosa Elizeche who considered that the validity and the form of the authorisation is subject to the law of the place where the power was granted, in Paraguay Supreme Court, Judgment 224, 18 May 2001, *Diego Pizziolo v. Nereo Tiso Y Otros*.

[20] Guatemala Art. 1700 CC.

[21] Portugal Art. 39 CC; Spain Art. 21 CC; Paraguay Supreme Court, Judgment 224, 18 May 2001, *Diego Pizziolo v. Nereo Tiso Y Otros*: upholding that matters regarding the validity, effects and scope of the power of representation granted abroad are governed by the place of performance of the authorisation. Nevertheless, in dissenting opinion Ministry Sosa Elizeche considered that the validity and the form of the authorisation is subject to the law of the place where the power was granted.

In addition, a regional conflict of laws instrument points to the place where the authorisation was granted. The 1975 Inter-American convention on the legal regime of powers of attorney to be used abroad is in force in all Latin American jurisdictions except for Colombia and Nicaragua.[22] The main purpose of this Convention is to provide an instrument by which powers of attorney validly issued by one Party to the Convention will be valid in any another State Party, provided they comply with the provisions thereof.[23]

This Convention establishes that the law of the place in which the power of attorney was issued governs the formalities concerning extraterritorial use of the power of attorney.[24] However, the Convention allows the party issuing the power of attorney to submit to the law of the State in which the power of attorney is to be enforced.[25] The Convention also establishes that if the law of the State in which a power of attorney is to be enforced requires formalities which are essential to its validity in that State, such law will govern the power.[26]

2. Authority of Agents

2.1. Establishment and Scope

For some of the Ibero-American Civil Codes, specific authorisation[27] for the sale goods is required,[28] while in other Civil Codes general authorisation for

[22] The Convention is in force in the following countries: Argentina, Chile, Colombia, Costa Rica, Dominican Republic, Ecuador, El Salvador, Guatemala, Honduras, Mexico, Panama, Paraguay, Peru, Uruguay and Venezuela; *see* Status in http://www.oas.org/juridico/english/Sigs/b-38.html (Accessed on 5 March 2010).

[23] Art. 1, Convention on the Powers of Attorneys.

[24] Art. 2, Convention on the Powers of Attorneys.

[25] *Id.*

[26] *Id.*

[27] The Argentinean Civil Code, as most other Civil Codes, uses the word special power of representation but in the opinion of Argentina: Alterini, *supra* note 1, at 312 the correct expression is 'express authorisation'. Spain Art. 1713 CC and Venezuela Art. 1.688 C use the term '*mandato expreso*', however, X. O'Callaghan, Xavier (Ed.), Código Civil Comentado, Art. 1713, at 1732 (2004), considers that the term 'expressed' is misunderstood with the 'express' way of granting or accepting the authorisation.

[28] Bolivia Art. 810 CC and Brazil Art. 661 CC: both require specific mandate for the transfer of property of goods; Guatemala Art. 1693 CC: states that general authorisation with special clause is needed for the agent to transfer the property of the principal or to negotiate and to conclude contracts; Mexico Art. 2554 CC: requires that the principal grants a general power for acts of transmission of property so that the agent can transfer the principal's goods; Peru Art. 167 CC; Spain Art. 1713 CC; Venezuela Art. 1.688 CC.

managerial acts would suffice to sell or purchase goods.[29] Despite the fact that the agent can only act in accordance with the specific authorisation granted by the principal, the agent should also be able to perform other related tasks necessary to achieve his mandate.[30]

Also interesting is that some Civil Codes require the agent to have a special power to enter into arbitration agreements.[31] Under the Mexican law the question arose whether Article 2587 of the Civil Code requires the express authorisation of the agent to pass an arbitration agreement.[32] An ICC Arbitral Tribunal has successfully addressed the question with a thorough interpretation of the Mexican law provisions on the contract of mandate. The Tribunal upheld that the provision only applies to an attorney with a judicial mandate who is in the course of court litigation and wants to withdraw from the proceedings to move the matter to arbitration; so according to the law an attorney is unable "to submit to arbitration the dispute which he is defending in court, except if his power of attorney specifically includes a reference to such authority."[33]

Regarding the acts or contracts passed by business managers[34] and employees[35] some Ibero-American Codes of Commerce establish that the

---

29 Argentina Art. 1881 CC; Chile Art. 2132 CC: it suffice general authorisation for managerial purposes to purchase goods necessary for industry developed; Paraguay Arts. 883, 884 CC.

30 Bolivia Art. 811 CC; Chile Art. 2134 CC; Peru Art. 1792 CC; ICC Final Award Case No. 13751 *Lex Contractus* German Law and Mexican Law to the agency relationship: if an attorney is authorised to perform all types of acts which fall within the 'general authorisation to administer assets' or the 'authorisation to exercise ownership acts', the attorney has the same powers as if he was the owner of the assets. "Third parties who interact with attorneys who hold a general mandate are thus protected: the principal cannot invoke that the scope of the power is insufficient and that the agreement is consequently null and void."

31 Paraguay Art. 884 (c) CC; Spain Art. 1713 CC; Venezuela Art. 1.689 CC.

32 Mexico Art. 2.587 CC states that "a court representative (litigation lawyer) does not require a special power or a special clause [in the power of attorney], except in the following cases: (i) to withdraw (the litigation), (ii) to settle, (iii) to submit to arbitration, (iv) to depose (on behalf of the principal), (v) to assign assets [in lieu of payment], (vi) to challenge [judges], (vii) to receive payments."

33 ICC Final Award Case No. 13751 *Lex Contractus* German Law and Mexican Law to the agency relationship.

34 Most Ibero-American Codes of Commerce refer to the Spanish term *factores* or *administradores*, or the Portuguese term *gerente de comercio*, which is understood as the person to whom the trader, company or the owner of a business entrusts the administration of his businesses; *see* Argentina Art. 132 Com C; Bolivia Art. 72 Com C; Brazil Art. 1.172 CC; Chile Art. 325 Com C; Mexico Art. 309 Com C; Paraguay Art. 53 LM; Portugal Art. 248 Com C; Spain Art. 283 Com C; Venezuela Art. 94 Com C.

35 Most Ibero-American Codes of Commerce refer to the term *dependientes* (or *mancebos* Spain Art. 295 Com C): which is understood as the person to whom the owner of the business has granted the authority to execute certain activities of the business; *see* Bolivia Art. 90 Com C; Mexico Art. 309 Com C; Paraguay Art. 63 LM; Venezuela Art. 94 Com C. The main difference between managers and employees is that the manager has general administration powers and duties while the employee is only authorised to participate on behalf of the business

managers will be considered having the special authorisation of the principal to manage his business.[36] The lack of formal requirements in the authorisation will only affect the relationship established between the company or the owner (principal) and the manger or employee (agent), and not the validity of the contracts by the agent with third parties.[37] An exception exists when third parties knew of the lack of authorisation at the conclusion of the contract.[38]

In an ICC Arbitration governed by the Portuguese law, the buyer argued that Mr. X had no authority to sign the certificate test approval of the delivered and installed equipment on the buyer's behalf. The Sole Arbitrator rejected the argument since the buyer's CEO in Portugal, acknowledged in his deposition that Mr. X had been hired by the buyer to verify certain aspects of the plant. As a result, the logical consequence of this statement was that Mr X, as buyer's employee, was authorised to sign certificates on behalf of his employer. Should Mr. X have lacked such powers, good faith would have required the buyer to immediately inform the seller that the certificate was null and void due to the lack of authority of the signatory. The buyer never did so, and never challenged Mr. X's authority before the filing of this arbitration.[39]

In the case of managers and employees of a business, general authorisation will be understood to grant authority to perform all acts related to the administration of the business.[40] Whenever the owner or principal intends to reduce the scope of the authorisation he must express the limitation to which the agent shall be subject.[41] In some jurisdictions the authorisation and its limitations must be stated in writing,[42] in notary public deed,[43] and must be registered before the Registry of Commerce.[44]

---

in certain activities; *see for example* Mexico Art. 321 Com C; Venezuela Art. 94 Com C; Chile Art. 343 Com C; Paraguay Art. 63 LM; Venezuela Art. 99 Com C: "the employees cannot bind the principal except if the principal expressly grants authorisation for certain operations related to the business."

[36] Argentina Art. 133 Com C; Portugal Art. 249 Com C.

[37] Argentina Art. 134 Com C; Portugal Art. 249 Com C.

[38] Portugal Art. 249 Com C.

[39] ICC Final Award Case No. 11367 *Lex Contractus* Portuguese Law.

[40] Argentina Art. 135 Com C; Bolivia Art. 73 Com C; Brazil Art. 1.173 CC; Chile Art. 340 Com C; Paraguay Art. 55 LM; Portugal Art. 249 Com C; Venezuela Art. 95 Com C.

[41] Argentina Art. 135 Com C; Bolivia Art. 73 Com C; Chile Art. 340 Com C; Paraguay Art. 55 LM; Venezuela Art. 95 Com C.

[42] Mexico Art. 310 Com C.

[43] Bolivia Art. 90 Com C; Venezuela Art. 100 Com C.

[44] Bolivia Art. 73 Com C; Brazil Art. 1.174 CC (registration before the Registry of Commercial Companies); Chile Arts. 339, 344 Com C (the authorisation shall be registered and published); Paraguay Art. 54 LM; Venezuela Art. 95 Com C (in addition to be registered the authorisation will be exposed in the tribunal's facilities); El Salvador Supreme Court, *Cass civ, Daglio y Compañía S.A. C.V. v. Sociedad Regional de Inversiones S.A. de C.V.,* 1294-2001, 19 August 2001: the obligation to register the authorisation may only be relevant when the manager or employee has been given authorisation to perform trade activities.

In this sense, the principals cannot be exonerated from the acts performed by their managers or employees, even when the principal alleges that the agent abused the faculties conferred, or that they performed acts that were not ordered, if there was a previous authorisation.[45]

Also most Codes of Commerce state that the dispatch or the taking of delivery of merchandise by the managers or employees will be considered executed by the principal.[46]

The authorisations granted by a company acting as principal to the managers and representatives must be within the scope of the company's activities or in conformity with the document of incorporation and statutes.[47]

Some laws expressly prohibit the agent to perform acts that would conflict with the interest of the principal.[48] For example, the agent shall not personally buy the goods that the principal has asked him to sell, nor shall he sell to the principal his own goods, unless such a thing has been expressly approved by the principal,[49] or the law,[50] or unless the circumstances of the transaction eliminate the possibility of a conflict of interest.[51] Further, agents cannot negotiate in their own names or get involved in business of the same nature as those mandated by the principal,[52] unless expressly authorised by the principal.[53]

2.2. Lack of Authority

The rule in the Ibero-American laws and the Agency Convention is that the principal is bound by the obligations contracted by the agent within the scope of the powers granted.[54] Consequently, the principal can only be released if the

[45] Argentina Art. 142 Com C; Bolivia Art. 75 Com C; Chile Art. 327 Com C.

[46] Argentina Art. 153 Com C; Bolivia Art. 94 Com C; Costa Rica Art. 472 Com C; Mexico Art. 324 Com C; Paraguay Art. 69 LM; Spain Art. 295 Com C.

[47] Argentina Art. 58 LC; Brazil Art. 47 CC; Guatemala Art. 1697 CC; Uruguay Arts. 25, 79 LC; Ecuador: C. Valdivieso Bermeo, Tratado de las Obligaciones y Contratos 30 (2005); ICC Final Award Case No. 13750 *Lex Contractus* Venezuelan Law: the Tribunal also rejected buyer's contention that Mr. X's signature of the Agreement bound the seller to the Agreement since, according to seller's by-laws, the only representative authorised to sign contracts on seller's behalf was its Managing Director (Mr. Y) and there is nothing in the file showing that Mr. Y delegated his powers to Mr. X.

[48] Paraguay Art. 60 (a) LM.

[49] Chile Art. 2144 CC; Peru Art. 166 CC.

[50] Peru Art. 166 CC.

[51] *Id.*

[52] Argentina Art. 141 Com C; Chile Art. 331 Com C; Mexico Art. 312 Com C; Portugal Art. 253 Com C; Spain Art. 288 Com C; Venezuela Art. 98 Com C.

[53] *Id.*

[54] Peru Art. 160 CC; Spain Art. 1714 CC; *also* Spain Supreme Tribunal, 27 January 2000, AC. 462/2000; ICC Final Award Case No. 13751 *Lex Contractus* German Law and Mexican Law to the agency relationship: the Arbitral Tribunal came to the conclusion that, in accordance with

agent has acted outside its authority,[55] unless the principal timely ratifies the obligations contracted.[56] For some countries such ratification must be made according to the same formal requirements of the agency agreement.[57] For other countries the ratification must be express or result from unequivocal facts or conduct.[58]

Under the Agency Convention if the third party neither knew nor ought to have known of the lack of authority of the agent, he may be released from the deal if he gives notice of his refusal to become bound by ratification.[59] However, if the third party knew or ought to have known, he may not refuse to become bound by ratification.[60]

In a case submitted before an ICC Arbitral Tribunal, the authorisation of the buyer's agent contained two limitations, namely that the purchase transaction had to be 'de riguroso contado', which means in cash, and without generating a 'pasivo con cargo al patrimonio' of respondent, this is, a deficit in the respondent's patrimony balance sheet. The respondent alleged that the Aircraft Purchase Agreements violated both limitations. Since the Aircraft Purchase Agreements provided for full payment of the purchase price at the latest on the date of delivery of the asset, the Arbitral Tribunal concluded that in accordance with the Mexican law, the authorisation granted to the agent was sufficient to execute the Aircraft Purchase Agreements on behalf of the respondent.[61] Moreover, the Tribunal upheld that even if one assumes

---

Mexican Law, the agency agreement was sufficient for the agent to execute the agreements on behalf of respondent and that, in doing so, the agent did not violate any limitation contained in the agency agreement.

55 Art. 15 Agency Convention; Bolivia Art. 821 CC; Brazil Art. 662 CC; Chile Art. 2160 CC; El Salvador Art. 1920 CC; Guatemala Art. 1703 CC; Mexico Arts. 1802, 2583 CC; Peru Art. 161 CC; Spain Art. 1717 CC; Venezuela Art. 1.698 CC.

56 Art. 15 Agency Convention; Bolivia Art. 821 CC; Brazil Art. 662 CC; Chile Art. 2160 CC; El Salvador Art. 1920 CC; Guatemala Art. 1712 CC; Mexico Arts. 1802, 2583 CC; Peru Art. 162 CC; Venezuela Art. 1.698 CC; El Salvador Supreme Court, *Cass civ, Trujillo Lopez v. De Paz Ayala,* 1219-2001, 9 February 2001; Peru Supreme Court, *Sala civil transitoria, cass,* Resolution 002670-2001; Spain Supreme Tribunal, 21 February 1990, A.C. 515/1990; Spain Supreme Tribunal, 13 December 1994, A.C. 341/1995.

57 Mexico Art. 1802 CC; Peru Art. 162 CC.

58 Brazil Art. 662 CC; Guatemala Art. 1712 CC; Mexico Arts. 1802, 2234 CC; Venezuela Art. 1.698 CC; Peru Supreme Court, *Sala civil transitoria, cass,* Resolution 002670-2001: sustaining that a sales contract could not be declared null as the seller (the principal) had ratified the sale of real property by non-authorised agent with the delivery of the property to the buyer and subsequent authorisation to the agent; ICC Final Award Case 13751 *Lex Contractus* German Law and Mexican Law to the agency relationship: In accordance with Arts. 1802 and 2234 of Mexico's Civil Code, a buyer can tacitly ratify a sale and purchase agreement passed by the agent lacking authority by voluntarily complying with any of the obligations assumed in a contract *e.g.* by either accepting the possession of the asset.

59 Art. 15 para. 2 Agency Convention.

60 *Id.*

61 ICC Final Award Case No. 13751 *Lex Contractus* German Law and Mexican Law to the

ad arguendum that the agency agreement was insufficient to validly authorise the agent to execute the Aircraft Purchase Agreements, the respondent had, at a later stage, ratified the execution - and a subsequent ratification prevents the nullity of the Agreements. In the case at hand, the respondent's behaviour at the relevant time, clearly shows that he was considering himself the owner of the Aircraft, since it was a proven fact that after the conclusion of the purchase agreement, the respondent executed a letter of intent with a third company undertaking to sell the Aircraft to that third company.[62]

The sale passing by an agent lacking authority or acting beyond the scope of his capacity is invalid. The question arises as to the kind of invalidity which will affect the sale. Whether such is absolute (invalidity), on the grounds that there was no intent of the principal to enter into the sale, or whether such is relative (voidability), as the sale passed by the non-authorised agent is susceptible of confirmation or ratification by the principal.[63] The Mexican and the El Salvadorian Supreme Courts have upheld the last approach.[64]

2.3. Apparent Authority

The second paragraph of Article 14 the Convention on Agency establishes that where the conduct of the principal causes the third party reasonably and in good faith to believe that the agent has authority to act on behalf of the principal, and that the agent is acting within the scope of that authority, the principal may not invoke against the third party the lack of authority of the agent.

In an ICC Arbitral Tribunal's view, the preceding rule is a widely accepted principle of international commerce.[65] In the case at hand, the respondent alleged that the purchase agreement violated two limitations imposed on the authority granted to the respondent's agent. The Tribunal upheld that even if such was found to be the case, the respondent had created an impression that agent was duly authorised because: first, the agent was not a stranger, who came into contact with the claimant without introduction by the principal; second, it was also a proven fact that the agent had an office at the premises of

agency relationship: the Arbitral Tribunal, relying on the Mexican jurisprudence, decided that the expression in Art. 2255 of Mexico Civil Code the buyer shall pay *al contado* means before or at the time of delivery. Then, the Tribunal considered that the prohibition to create *pasivos* reinforced the idea that the transaction must be *al contado*, and not on deferred payment terms.

[62] ICC Final Award Case 13751 *Lex Contractus* German Law and Mexican Law to the agency relationship.

[63] For more details on absolute invalidity and voidability *see* Ch. 24.

[64] Mexico Supreme Court, *Novena Época,* Registry 172'566, SJF XXV, May 2007, at 251; El Salvador Supreme Court, *Cass civ, Trujillo Lopez v. De Paz Ayala,* 1219-2001, 9 February 2001.

[65] ICC Final Award Case 13751 *Lex Contractus* German Law and Mexican Law to the agency relationship.

the respondent, increasing the appearance that he formed part of respondent's organisation. Third, in the notarisation of the agreements, the Notary Public, chosen and paid by respondent, did not raise any issue regarding the insufficiency of the agency authorisation, but rather declared that the agent had the legal capacity needed to pass the transaction.[66]

The same principle is accepted under the Ibero-American laws. The contracts passed by managers or employees will be understood to be passed by the owner of the business, when it can be legally presumed, by positive acts, that the agent followed the orders of the owner.[67] Also if the principal has given reason to believe, with positive acts or serious omissions, that the agent acted as his representative, he will not be able to invoke the lack of representation with respect to third parties.[68]

Further, the agency agreement does not terminate in the eyes of the third party until they knew or ought to have known that the agency agreement was effectively terminated by the principal,[69] and, hence, the principal will be bound by the obligations contracted.[70]

2.4. Sub-agency

For some Ibero-American laws, the agent can delegate his authorisation when the agency agreement allows it,[71] or when it is not expressly prohibited.[72] However, when the substitution of the agent has not been granted by the principal, the acts of the sub-agent shall not bind the principal,[73] and the agent will be liable for the acts committed by the sub-agent.[74] The agent will be also liable in case the principal had authorised the substitution and the agent

---

66 *Id.*

67 Argentina Art. 138 Com C; Bolivia Art. 75 Com C; Mexico Art. 316 Com C; Paraguay Art. 58 LM; Spain Art. 286 Com C; Venezuela Art. 97 (2) Com C.

68 Bolivia Art. 87 Com C; Guatemala Art. 670 Com C; El Salvador Art. 979 Com C.

69 Argentina Art. 1964 CC; Paraguay Art. 910 CC.

70 Argentina Art. 1967 CC; Paraguay Art. 910 CC.

71 Argentina Art. 1942 CC; Bolivia Art. 818 CC (if the nature of the agreement allows it); Guatemala Arts. 1702, 1707 CC; Mexico Art. 2574 CC; Peru Art. 157 CC; Portugal Art. 1165 CC; ICC Final Award Case No. 11556 *Lex Contractus* Mexican Law: respondent alleged that the agency agreement is *intuitu personae*, and could not be assigned. The Arbitral Tribunal upheld that according to Arts. 2574, 2575 and 2576 of the Mexican Federal Civil Code, the agent can assign its rights and obligations if it is expressly authorised. The Tribunal found that the assignment was consistent with the terms of Management Agreement itself, which allows the assignment to an affiliate without respondent's consent provided that notice is given to respondent.

72 Bolivia Art. 818 CC; Chile Art. 2135 CC; Spain Art. 1721 CC; Venezuela Art. 1.695 CC.

73 Argentina Art. 1942 CC; Chile Art. 2136 CC; Paraguay Art. 907 CC: so that the principal is released from his obligations *vis à vis* third parties these must be aware of the circumstances; Spain Art. 1721 CC; Venezuela Art. 1.695 CC.

74 Bolivia Art. 818 CC; Chile Art. 2135 CC; Paraguay Art. 904 CC.

chooses an inappropriate sub-agent,[75] or someone with notorious insolvency or incapacity.[76] In addition, the agent is not authorised to grant the sub-agent powers which are not included in the authorisation or that are broader than those he was originally granted.[77]

The managers or the employees cannot delegate their duties to others unless given express authorisation from the principal.[78] If a manager or employee delegates his authorisation, he will be liable for the acts of the delegate.[79]

3. Disclosed and Undisclosed Agency

The principal shall only be liable for the acts performed by the agent within the scope of his authorisation. The agent who has exceeded his authorisation is liable to third parties when he has not disclosed the scope of his authorisation.[80] But whenever a third party is aware of the fact that the agent is acting outside his authorisation, the third party will not have any right against the agent.[81]

On the other hand, the contracts celebrated by managers or employees of a business that appears to belong to the business or company shall also be understood to be celebrated by the owner of the business, even though the agent does not declare so at the time of their conclusion, whenever such contracts are related to the business activities.[82]

On this issue, Article 13 of the Agency Convention states that where the agent acts on behalf of a principal within the scope of his authority, his acts shall only bind the agent and the third party if the third party neither knew nor ought to have known that the agent was acting as an agent, or if it follows from the circumstances of the case, for example by a reference to a contract of commission, that the agent undertakes to bind himself only.

In an interesting case, the Spanish Supreme Tribunal drew the same rule based on the principle of good faith. The Tribunal prevented two persons who feign to buy in their own names from relying on the corporate principle that

75 Peru Art. 158 CC.

76 Mexico Art. 2575 CC; Paraguay Art. 904 CC; Spain Art. 1721 CC.

77 Guatemala Art. 1702 CC; Paraguay Art. 904 CC.

78 Paraguay Art. 60 (b) LM; Spain Art. 296 Com C. In writing: Argentina Art. 161 Com C; Chile Art. 330 Com C; Mexico Art. 325 Com C.

79 Argentina Art. 161 Com C; Spain Art. 296 Com C.

80 Chile Art. 2154 CC; El Salvador Supreme Court, *Cass civ, Trujillo Lopez v. De Paz Ayala,* 1219-2001, 9 February 2001.

81 Mexico Art. 2584 CC; El Salvador Supreme Court, *Cass civ, Trujillo Lopez v. De Paz Ayala,* 1219-2001, 9 February 2001.

82 Argentina Art. 138 Com C; Bolivia Art. 75 Com C; Brazil Arts. 1.175, 1.176 CC; Chile Art. 328 Com C; Mexico Art. 315 Com C; Paraguay Art. 58 LM; Spain Art. 286 Com C; Venezuela Art. 97 (1) Com C.

a company is a legal entity different from its members. The two persons were found liable to pay the price of the goods as they maliciously concealed to the seller the fact that they were trading on behalf of a company.[83]

4. Liability of Agents

Different Ibero-American laws and in the Agency Convention use the same principle. The agent acting outside or without authority is thus liable before the principal for those acts performed outside the scope its authority.[84] The agent is also liable before third parties who have acted in good faith, when the agent has not provided them with enough information about his authority and for those acts performed in his own name.[85] This rule includes managers and employees.[86] However, the agent shall not be liable if the third party knew or ought to have known that the agent had no authority or was acting outside the scope of his authority.

When the agent has not attained the legal age required to have full legal capacity, in such cases the acts committed by the agent will bind the principal and the third parties. However, the principal or the third parties do not have a claim against the agent.[87]

The agent is liable to the principal for the minor lack of diligence,[88] or care and skill,[89] particularly when the agent is remunerated which is usually the case in international trade. Also managers and employees have a duty to act with care and skill. They are liable for negligence and for not following the instructions and orders of the employer.[90]

---

83 Spain Supreme Tribunal, 12 March 1993.

84 Art. 16 Agency Convention; Bolivia Art. 816 CC; Brazil Art. 665 CC; Mexico Art. 1980 CC; Spain Art. 1725 CC; El Salvador Supreme Court, *Cass civ, Trujillo Lopez v. De Paz Ayala,* 1219-2001, 9 February 2001.

85 Art. 16 Agency Convention; Brazil Art. 663 CC; Chile Arts. 2151, 2154 para. 2 CC; Paraguay Art. 897 CC; Spain Art. 1725 CC; Venezuela Art. 1.691 CC; El Salvador Supreme Court, *Cass civ, Trujillo Lopez v. De Paz Ayala,* 1219-2001, 9 February 2001.

86 Argentina Art. 139 Com C; Chile Art. 328 Com C; Mexico Art. 313 Com C; Paraguay Art. 59 LM; Portugal Art. 252 Com C; Spain Art. 287 Com C.

87 Chile Art. 2128 CC; Paraguay Art. 882 CC; Venezuela Art. 1.690 CC.

88 Guatemala Art. 1705 CC; Venezuela Art. 1.692 CC: imposes the obligation to act as a *bonus pater familias.*

89 Chile Art. 2129 CC.

90 Mexico Art. 327 Com C; Paraguay Art. 68 LM; Spain Art. 297 Com C.

Chapter 17

Modification of a Concluded Contract

1. General Remarks on the Modification of a Concluded Contract

The general principle in the Ibero-American private laws, as well as in the CISG, is that the parties can modify or terminate their sales contract by mutual agreement.[1] This principle derives from the consensual nature of the sales contract.[2] The freedom of contract is not limited to the creation of obligations but extends to their modification or termination.

Unilateral modification is not possible for sales of goods' contracts.[3] In the same way the conclusion of a valid contract requires the common agreement of the parties, its modification or termination also requires the intent of all parties involved. Following this rule, any modification must integrate the elements of validity for every obligation or contract such as, the mutual consent, the legal capacity of the parties, the licit object, and the cause, *etc.*[4] The Peruvian Supreme Court has acknowledged such freedom stating that once the parties have concluded their contract, the same can be modified during performance or even after, in which case the agreement of the parties is again required.[5]

---

1 Art. 29(1) CISG; Argentina Art. 1363 CC; Bolivia Art. 450 CC; Dominican Republic Art. 1134 CC; Mexico Art. 172 CC; Peru Art. 1351 CC; Portugal Art. 406 CC; Venezuela Art. 1.133 CC; Peru Supreme Court, *Sala civil permanente,* Resolution 005211-2007, 27 March 2008.

2 Argentina: G.A. Borda, Manual de Contratos 100 (2004); Bolivia: W. Kaune Arteaga, Curso de Derecho Civil, Contratos, Vol. 2, 58 (1996).

3 Paraguay: A. Sierralta Ríos, La Compraventa Internacional de Mercaderias y el Derecho Paraguayo 94 (2000).

4 Bolivia Art. 452 CC; Chile Art. 1445 CC; Colombia Art. 1502 CC; Costa Rica Art. 627 CC; Cuba Art. 23 CC; Ecuador Art. 1488 CC; El Salvador Art. 1316 CC; Guatemala Art. 1251 CC; Honduras Art. 1552 CC; Nicaragua Art. 1832 CC; Panama Art. 1112 CC; Paraguay Art. 673 CC; Peru Art. 140 CC; Spain Art. 1.261 CC; Venezuela Art. 1.141 CC.

5 Peru Supreme Court, *Sala civil permanente,* Resolution 005211-2007, 27 March 2008.

Article 29(2) of the CISG states that a contract in writing requiring any modification or termination by agreement shall be in writing, shall not otherwise be modified or terminated. Similarly, under the Ibero-American laws, the form of modification can result from the law or the agreement of the parties.[6] The law has categorised the sale of goods as a consensual agreement.[7] This means that, in principle, the contract is validly concluded at the time of the parties' meeting of the minds, without any legal pre-established requirement on the form.[8] Consequently, the parties can modify or terminate a sales contract in writing, orally or in any other possible way that indicates intent,[9] including the implied intent by conduct.[10]

In an ICC Arbitration, the question arose as to whether the buyer had the obligation to acquire a minimum volume of goods as established in a clause of the written contract. From a combined assessment of the evidence taken as a whole, the Arbitral Tribunal concluded that

> both parties coincided in their intention to annul this contract clause and its obligational content by mutual waiver, a ground for extinction which did not extend to the whole of the Contract but only to that part of its contents which ceased to be of interest to the contracting parties.[11]

Nevertheless, there may be some exceptions to the consensual principle and certain *ad probation* requirements established by some Ibero-American laws, which, will be further reviewed in this work.[12]

Additionally, even when the law does not require any pre-established form for the sale of goods, nothing impedes the parties to agree on a certain form for modification of their contract, including agreement on certain solemnities.[13]

---

6 *See generally* Ch. 20.

7 Argentina: Borda, *supra* note 2, at 100; Bolivia: Kaune Arteaga, *supra* note 2, at 58.

8 *See* Ch. 20.

9 *See* Ch. 10. *Also* ICC Partial Award Case No. 12296 *Lex Contractus* Mexican Law: referring to 78 and 79 of Mexico Com C the Tribunal explained that an agreement is concluded by the 'mere consent' of the parties, unless the law expressly requires that it be in writing or meet other formalities. In the case at hand, the issue was whether the modification of a franchise agreement was purported to be in writing. The Tribunal upheld that although Art. 136 of Mexico's Intellectual Property Law establishes that the licensing of a trademark should be registered at the Mexican Industrial Property Institute in order to produce effects against third parties, the said requirement has no application whatsoever to questions concerning the existence or validity of the agreements themselves or of the obligations that they create as between the parties.

10 ICC Final Award Case No. 12755 *Lex Contractus* Argentinean Law: upholding the implied acceptance of a modified payment schedule by means of the seller's non rejection of a payment made by the buyer according to his proposed payment schedule.

11 ICC Final Award Case No. 13435 *Lex Contractus* Spanish Law with implied exclusion of the CISG.

12 *See* Ch. 20, 1.2.

13 *See* Ch. 20, 2.

On the other hand, the question arises on whether in cases of lack of agreement the parties are bound to respect a specific form of contract modification. Under the Portuguese law, when the 'in writing form' for contract conclusion is not required by law, but the parties agree on adopting such, the oral stipulations made after the conclusion of the contract are still valid.[14]

To the contrary, under the Peruvian law, absent an agreement, any modification or termination shall mirror the original form under which the contract was passed.[15] The effect of this rule is that any oral modification will have no effect in sales contracts concluded in writing. Nevertheless, the Peruvian Supreme Court has already disregarded the literal meaning of the rule, upholding that the parties' modification of their contract is to take place in the form that better suits them, (orally, in writing, *etc.*) provided the parties had not already agreed on a specific form for any modification of the contract.[16]

2. Entire Contract or Merger Clauses

The Ibero-American laws allow modification or termination of contracts partially or entirely.[17] Parties may also agree to supersede any previous agreement reached during negotiations by expressly agreeing so through a called merger clause. A merger clause generally limits the evidentiary value of previous statements or agreements. It aims to avoid contradictions between the agreements reached during the length of the contractual relationship. However, the question arises on whether such a clause also limits or modifies the principles of interpretation established by law.

In this regard, it has been considered that a merger clause does not impede the arbitrator from considering all other relevant circumstances in the interpretation of the contract; since the rules of interpretation of the Spanish law establish the adjudicator's duty to do so.[18]

3. No Oral Modification Clauses

The CISG allows the parties to derogate a non oral modification clause in an implied way. The second sentence of Article 29(2) reads: "a party may be

[14] Portugal Art. 222 (2) CC.

[15] *See* Peru Art. 1413 CC; Peru: A. Sierralta Ríos, La Compraventa Internacional y El Derecho Peruano 79 (1997).

[16] Peru Supreme Court, *Sala civil permanente,* Resolution 005211-2007, 27 March 2008.

[17] ICC Final Award Case No. 13435 *Lex Contractus* Spanish Law with implied exclusion of the CISG.

[18] ICC Final Award Case No. 13678 *Lex Contractus* Spanish Law.

precluded by his conduct from asserting such provision to the extent that the other party has relied on that conduct."

Such permission is not expressly granted by any of the Ibero-American legal statutes. Indeed, some authors from the region consider the same as excessive.[19] However, one could not deny that similar situations may require a flexible solution that could indeed be found in the Ibero-American laws.

For example, the Roman law principle of *venire contra factum proprium*, recognised in the Ibero-American jurisprudence and doctrine, may provide a similar solution.[20] Relying on this doctrine, an ICC Tribunal has found that a NOM clause has no effect against a *de facto* oral modification when one of the parties' conduct has encouraged or tolerated such oral modification, to the extent that the other party has relied on that conduct.[21]

A Mexican Collegiate Tribunal sustained that contracts can be impliedly modified (orally) by the parties based on the principle of party autonomy, provided the public order, the moral conventions or the good customs are not affected, and despite the fact that the parties had agreed on an 'in writing' modification clause.[22]

An ICC Arbitral Tribunal also acknowledged that one cannot rule out the possibility of an amendment other than in writing even in the presence of NOM clause. However, in the Tribunal's opinion the existence of such a NOM clause requires a very strong showing of the parties' contrary intent.[23]

---

19 Paraguay: Sierralta Ríos, *supra* note 3, at 94.

20 *See* Ch. 33, 1.

21 ICC Final Award Case No. 13435 *Lex Contractus* Spanish Law with implied exclusion of the CISG: noting that the modification did not need to be recorded in writing since the Contract did not so require; "nevertheless, even if it had been required, the conduct of the [seller] would in any event prevail, expressed by unequivocal own acts in its own interests, which would prevent it from invoking the need for written form of the termination agreement since the other party has relied on that conduct."

22 Mexico Collegiate Tribunals, *Novena Época,* Registry 172234, SJF XXV, June 2007, at 1048.

23 ICC Final Award Case No. 11404 *Lex Contractus* Argentinean Law.

Part 4

Validity

Chapter 18

General Remarks on the Validity of Contracts

1. General Remarks

The rules on the validity of contracts interfere with the parties' freedom where, at the time of contract conclusion, primary principles protected by the law are considered to be at risk. Examples of such principles are: the legal certainty of the transaction, the free and informed will to contract, and the bargaining balance of the deal.

So, as to protect the interests of society, the Ibero-American laws may deny validity to agreements which do not conform to the law nor conform to the ethical principles on which the positive law is based.[1] Furthermore Ibero-American laws may impose certain formal requirements to the contract in order to achieve an expected legal certainty as to the effects and meaning of agreement reached by the parties[2] – although not usually in sales contracts.

Additionally, the Ibero-American laws establish mechanisms to redress or rescind the contract where one party's, or both parties', free and informed will to enter into the contract is found to have been affected by relevant conduct or circumstances, *i.e.* mistake, fraud or duress.[3] Indeed, even another different mechanism, known as gross disparity, is used to safeguard the legal order against the pernicious social effects of unfair dealings.[4]

---

1 *See* Ch. 19.

2 *See* Ch. 20.

3 *See* Ch. 22 and Ch. 23.

4 *See* Ch. 25.

2. CISG

Article 4(a) CISG expressly excludes some questions of validity from the scope of application of the Convention.[5] It is generally agreed, that the CISG does not determine whether agreements are to be considered illegal or immoral under domestic or international law. Nor does the CISG govern questions concerning the legal capacity of the parties, the authority of agents to enter into the contract of sale, or the voidability of contract, on the grounds of mistake, fraud, duress or gross disparity.[6] These questions are thus governed by the applicable domestic law in accordance with the conflict of law rules of the *forum.*[7]

[5] Art. 4(a) CISG. Except for the form of the international sale of goods contract, since Art. 11 provides that these contracts are free from requirements as to the form, except if a State has made a reservation under Art. 96.

[6] ICC Final Award Case 13184 *Lex Contractus* CISG and Mexican Law as supplementary law.

[7] ICC Final Award Case 13184 *Lex Contractus* CISG and Mexican Law as supplementary law. For details as to the Applicable Law *see* Ch. 4.

Chapter 19

Illegality, Immorality and Impossibility of the Contract

1. General Remarks

Illicit contracts can be classified depending on the kind of legal infringement.[1] The prohibited contract is one which goes against the public order. The immoral contract is the one contrary to the good customs. The illegal contract is that which opposes the rule of law.[2] In this chapter, the illegal and immoral contracts, as well as the generic impossibility of the contract are examined.

In every Ibero-American legal system the contract that offends the law is invalid.[3] The contract that offends the moral conventions and the good customs, *i.e.* morality, is also invalid.[4] Since every legal order is dominated by the idea of morality, it is common that contracts which do not conform with

[1] Brazil: O. Gomes, Contratos 182-183 (2008).

[2] *Id.*, at 183.

[3] Argentina Arts. 953, 1167CC; Bolivia Art. 489 CC; Brazil Art. 166 (II) (III) CC; Ecuador Art. 1511 CC; Chile Art. 1468 CC; Colombia Art. 1518 CC; El Salvador Art. 1332 CC; Honduras Art. 1564 CC; Mexico Art. 8 CC & Art. 77 Com C; Peru Prelim. Provision V & Art. 1403 CC; Portugal Arts. 280 (1), 281 CC; Spain Arts. 6.3, 1271 (3), 1275 CC; Uruguay Arts. 1283, 1284 CC; Venezuela Arts. 1155, 1157 CC; *see* Argentina: G.A. Borda, Manual de Contratos 91 (2004); Mexico: S. León Tovar, Los Contratos Mercantiles 72-73 (2004).

[4] Argentina Art. 953 CC; Bolivia Arts. 489, 490, 965 CC; Ecuador Art. 1504 CC; Chile Art. 1461 CC; Colombia Art. 1525 CC; El Salvador Art. 1339 CC; Mexico Art. 1830 CC; Peru Prelim. Provision Art. V CC; Portugal Arts. 280 (2), 281 CC; Spain Art. 1275 CC; Uruguay Arts. 1283, 1284 CC; Venezuela Art. 1157 CC; *see* Argentina: Borda, *supra* note 3, at 91: according to this author the morality requirement goes together with the legality requirement since mostly every immoral act has been covered already by the law; Mexico: León Tovar, *supra* note 3, at 72-73; Spain: M. Medina de Lemus, Derecho Civil: Obligaciones y Contratos II, Teoria General Vol. 1, 304 (2004): Spain Art. 1271 (3) CC mentions the term object as a thing but it should be read as any obligation that is contrary to law and the good customs.

the law will also not conform with the ethical principles on which the positive law is based, and *vice versa*. This is expressed in many national civil codes as,

> if the object of a contract is to perform, performance is required to be fiscally and morally possible [...] it is morally impossible the performance that is prohibited by law or contrary to the good customs.[5]

In the Ibero-American laws, the grounds for invalidity of a contract materialise when its object or cause are affected by immorality or illegality.[6] The object and the cause are two terms which can confound.[7] For current purposes, the focus is on the requirement of legality and morality of contracts irrespective, of whether it concerns the direct object or the cause.[8]

2. Grounds for Illegality

Under several Ibero-American Civil Codes the sale of goods which are *res extra commercium* (outside of commerce) are considered an illicit[9] *e.g.* the sale of narcotics in certain amounts and between unauthorised persons,[10] the sale of rights or privileges which cannot be transferred to another person, and goods subject to a judicial order.[11] Similarly illicit are the sales of books of which publishing has been prohibited by a competent authority, obscene posters, pictures, sculptures, and printings that abuses the freedom of expression.[12]

Other examples of illegal contracts include those which are contrary to the rules of fair market competition. For example, the Spanish Supreme Tribunal has declared the invalidity of contractual clauses that, against the EC Law, impose the exclusive purchase of products, impede the fair competition and the entrance of products coming from other EC members to the Spanish market.[13] Furthermore, the Argentinean Supreme Court has stated that the general right

---

[5] Chile Art. 1461 CC; Colombia Art. 1518 CC; Ecuador Art. 1504 CC; El Salvador Art. 1332 CC; Honduras Art. 1564 CC; Uruguay Art. 1824 CC.

[6] El Salvador Supreme Court, *Cass civ, Sociedad Antonio Comandari Hijos Y Compañía v. BENDECK, et al.*, 93-C-2006, 14 March 2007.

[7] For details *see* Ch. 9, 3.2.

[8] The indirect object, *i.e.* the thing (including the goods), has previously been revised in Ch. 6.

[9] *See for example* Spain Art. 1271 CC; Uruguay Art. 1282 CC.

[10] Uruguay: V. Moldes Ruibal *et al.*, Contratos civiles y comerciales: técnica y práctica, Vol. 1, 16 (2006).

[11] *See* Ecuador: C. Valdivieso Bermeo, Tratado de las Obligaciones y Contratos 3 (2005); Honduras: H. Carcamo Tercero, Eficacia e Ineficacia de los Contratos en Materia Civil 47-49 (2001); *see also* Chile Art. 1464 CC; Colombia Art. 1521 CC; Ecuador Art. 1507 CC; El Salvador Art. 1335 CC; Honduras Art. 1517 CC.

[12] *See* Ecuador: Valdivieso Bermeo, *supra* note 11, at 37; Honduras: Carcamo Tercero, *supra* note 11, at 47-49; *see also* Chile Art. 1466 CC; Ecuador Art. 1509 CC; El Salvador Art. 1337 CC.

[13] Spain Supreme Tribunal, 20 November 2008, *Id Cendoj:* 28079110012008101099.

of freedom of contract does not overcome any illegality arising when there is a contravention of a rule protecting free market competition.[14]

On other occasions, arbitral tribunals have, for example, denied the validity of agreed monetary interest at a rate contrary to the public policy rules, at the place of enforcement, even though the agreed rate was in accordance with the selected applicable law.[15]

3. Grounds for Immorality

Commentators from different Ibero-American jurisdictions define moral standards differently, albeit also similarly. Borda, suggests the general opinion is that the Argentinean Civil Code contemplates the average moral of a community in a determined time.[16] Similarly, Gomes defines *os bons costumes* as the group of principles that in a determined place and time constitute the guidelines for social behaviour within the framework of the minimal rules of average morality.[17] For Ripert the average moral is given by the Christian moral.[18] While for Salerno, the good customs are correlated with the suitable social behaviour of mankind according to the natural law.[19] The driving idea is, thus, that it is never good to harm somebody or to affect the virtues that must be practiced for the general welfare of society. Clearly, the concept is amorphous. Consequently, the judge and the arbitrator are compelled to appreciate the issue with the eyes of a prudent and honourable person.

Although in most cases the immoral concurs with the illicit, there are still cases in which courts have invalidated contracts considered immoral, despite no legal provision establishing their illegality. Examples of immoral contracts may include, the sale obtained thanks to the traffic of political influences, the contract for the sale of natural unrecoverable resources, the sale of human

---

[14] Argentina Supreme Court, *Autolatina Argentina S.A. v. Resolución No. 54/90 Subsecretaría de Transportes Marítimos y Fluviales*, 19 December 1991.

[15] ICC Final Award Case No. 11317 *Lex Contractus* Spanish Law: the respondent challenged the application of this rate of interest monthly compounded on the grounds that it was contrary to the Brazilian law on usury which is public policy. The claimants alleged that the said rules do not apply to contracts with foreign companies and that, in particular, they do not apply to the terms of the contract which were not governed by the Brazilian law, but by Spanish law, which has no similar provisions to those of the Brazilian Law on Usury. The Arbitral Tribunal found that the prohibition contained in Brazil's Law on Usury did apply, on the basis that it was a public policy rule which could not be derogated from by those who operate in Brazil, including foreign parties.

[16] Argentina: Borda, *supra* note 3, at 92.

[17] Brazil: Gomes, *supra* note 1, at 185.

[18] Quoted by Argentina: Borda, *supra* note 3, at 42.

[19] Argentina: M.U. Salermo, Contratos Civiles y Comerciales 129 (2007).

organs, the payment of monetary interest considered usury, the sale having any kind of relation to immoral activities, for example, the purchase of equipment for bordello-houses, *etc.*[20]

The fact that a clause or the whole contract offends the morals and the good customs is enough to invalidate the contract totally or partially.[21]

4. Impossibility of the Obligation

If the obligation is already impossible before the contract formation, such *ab initio* impossibility renders the contract invalid.[22] The rule was applied by an ICC Arbitral Tribunal when considering the Brazilian law. In that case, the seller was to first register the product with the Brazilian Authorities. After registration was granted it would then authorise the buyer to retail the product. At the time of the conclusion of the contract this arrangement appeared to be possible. However, it took 4 years for the seller to finally obtain the registration of its product. By that time it was no longer legally permissible for the holder of the registration of a medicinal product to grant to another company the right to market the product in question. The Tribunal concluded that the contract was nullified as stipulated in Art. 166 of the Brazilian Civil Code. Although not initially impossible, but as the result of a supervening event, the performance of the object of the legal transaction entered into by the parties was ultimately impossible.[23] The Tribunal reasoned that the distinction between initial and subsequent impossibility was irrelevant, as the consequences would be the same: the invalidity of the legal transaction. The Tribunal supported this view by means of references to Brazilian scholars upholding that the invalidity whereby the action or transaction is affected, may be original or contemporaneous and successive (or subsequent) to the contract.[24]

[20] *See* Argentina: Borda, *supra* note 3, at 93; Salerno, *supra* note 19, at 130.

[21] Spain: F. Infante Ruiz & F. Oliva Blázquez, *Los Contratos Ilegales en el Derecho Europeo*, 3 InDret 1, at 26 (2009).

[22] *See* express reference in Brazil Art. 166 (II) CC; Portugal Art. 401 (1) CC; Spain Arts. 1272, 1261 (2) CC; *see also* Argentina: R.L. Lorenzetti, Tratado de los Contratos Parte General 598 (2004); Portugal: J. De M. Antunes Valera, Das Obrigações em Geral 404 (2003); Spain Supreme Tribunal, 14 May 2009, *Id Cendoj:* 28079110012009100320.

[23] ICC Final Award Case No. 13530 *Lex Contractus* Brazilian Law.

[24] *Id.*

CHAPTER 20

FORMAL REQUIREMENTS

1. Legal Requirements

1.1. Direct Requirements

In the Ibero-American legal systems, the particular form a contract takes can result from the law or the agreement of the parties. The Civil Codes and Codes of Commerce normally enumerate the types of contracts which must be in writing or/and by public deed under penalty of invalidity.[1] Free form is presumed,[2] unless a particular contract is listed or absent the list itself in the referred statutes.[3] Sale of goods contracts are not typically listed; nevertheless, some movables may be affected by formal requirements.[4]

---

[1] Argentina Arts. 1184 (1), 1185 CC; Bolivia Arts. 491, 492 CC & Art. 787 Com C; Brazil Art. 107 CC; Chile Art. 1801 CC; Colombia Art. 1857 CC; Ecuador Art. 1767 CC; El Salvador Art. 1605 CC; Mexico Art. 79 Com C; Portugal Art. 220 CC; Spain Arts. 1280 CC & 51, 52 Com C; *see also infra* Ch. 24.

[2] *For example* ICC Partial Award Case No. 12296 *Lex Contractus* Mexican Law: referring to Arts. 78 and 79 of Mexico's Code of Commerce the Tribunal explained that an agreement is concluded by the 'mere consent' of the parties, unless the law expressly requires that it be in writing or meet other formalities.

[3] This is the case of Portugal Art. 219 CC; Peru Art. 1352 CC; *see* Bolivia: V. Camargo Marín, Derecho Comercial Boliviano 397 (2007); Mexico: O. Vásquez del Mercado, Contratos Mercantiles 159 (2008); Peru: A. Sierralta Ríos, La Compraventa Internacional y El Derecho Peruano 50-51 (1997).

[4] Automobiles are often required to be entered into public deed; *see* Bolivia Supreme Court, *Sala Civil, Rosalina Rodríguez Vega de Villarroel v. Félix Tapia Villarroel y otros*: quoting Bolivia Arts. 1395 (3), 1318 (1) CC sustained that lack of legal formality presumes the nullity of the contract until the contrary is proven by the affected party; Paraguay Supreme Court, Judgment 878, 19 November 2001, *Martín Ma. Del Puerto J. Y Osvaldo López v. Cirila Rojas Vda. De Aguirre*: quoting Paraguay Arts. 2071, 357 (c), 361 CC, sustained that the sale of a truck passed by private instrument does not fulfil the public deed requirement and thus,

In addition, many Codes of Commerce expressly dictate that, unless otherwise established, the validity of B2B contracts is not subjected to any special form. Parties are bound in the manner and under the terms in which it appears they intended to be bound regardless of the form and the language used for the conclusion of the contract.[5]

Moreover, the laws classify the sale of goods as a consensual agreement.[6] This means that the contract is validly concluded from the time of the parties' meeting of the minds on the main elements of the contract, without any pre-established legal requirement of form.[7] As a consequence the parties can enter into a sales contract in writing, orally or in any other possible way that indicates intent.[8]

shall be declared invalid; Vessels are also subject to special formalities under may laws, for example, writing requirements and their register in different registries: Colombia Art. 97 Com C: declaring that the sale of aircraft and vessels must register before the Administrative Department of National Statistics; Guatemala Art. 1125 CC: the property titles of ships have to be registered in the Property Registry; Venezuela Art. 614 Com C: the sale of vessels must be passed by public deed. Out of the scope of this work, land and real state are subject to different formal requirements such as the in writing contract that would normally be passed before a Notary Public and the requirement to register the deed in the Registry of Property. In this regard, Argentina: G.A. Borda, Manual de Contratos 100 (2004); Spain: M. Medina de Lemus, Derecho Civil: Obligaciones y Contratos II, Teoria General Vol. 1, 307 (2004).

5 Costa Rica Art. 411 Com C; Guatemala Art. 671 Com C; Mexico Arts. 78, 79 Com C.

6 Argentina: Borda, *supra* note 4, at 100; Bolivia: W. Kaune Arteaga, Curso de Derecho Civil, Contratos, Vol. 2, 58 (1996); Portugal: L. De Lima Pinheiro, Dereito Comercial Internacional 276 (2005); Venezuela: J.L. Aguilar Gorrondona, Contratos y Garantias: Derecho Civil IV, 176 (2008).

7 *See also* Chile Art. 1801 CC; Colombia Art. 1857 CC & Art. 864 Com C; Ecuador Art. 1767 CC; El Salvador Art. 1605 CC; Peru Art. 1352 CC; Venezuela Art. 1.161 CC; Uruguay Art. 514 Com C; El Salvador Supreme Court, *Cass civ*, *Aseguradora Salvadoreña, Compañia de Seguros v. American International Group, Inc,* 1466 S.S., 31 March 2003: according to law the conclusion of commercial contract does not require any special form; Mexico Collegiate Tribunals, *Novena Época*, Registry 199'602, SJF V, January 1997, at 442: upholding the validity of a sale of goods agreement passed by telefax communications as the law does not imposes any restriction; Peru Supreme Court, *Sala civil transitoria*, Resolution 001010-2003, 26 August 2003: upholding that the sale of goods do not need to be materialised in any document; ICC Partial Award Case No. 12296 *Lex Contractus* Mexican Law; *see also* Mexico: S. León Tovar, Los Contratos Mercantiles 74 (2004): the contract of sale of goods does not require any special form for its validity; Spain: M. Medina de Lemus, Derecho Civil: Obligaciones y Contratos II, Contratos en Particular, Vol. 2, 44 (2004): for the sale of goods the parties are not required to enter into a contract in an specific form.

8 Venezuela Supreme Tribunal, Judgment 319, *Cass civ*, file 99-044 of 17 July 2002; *see also* Ch. 10, 2.2, regarding the express and implied way to accept an offer to contract.

1.2. Indirect Requirements

Some jurisdictions consider the *in writing* form as the only valid means of proof for some sale of goods contracts.[9] The Civil Codes of Argentina, Chile, Ecuador, El Salvador and Paraguay contain a rule establishing that contracts beyond a certain amount cannot be proven by witnesses.[10]

The same rule applies for B2B contracts including sale of goods under the Argentinean, Spanish and the Uruguayan law.[11] In Argentina and Uruguay contracts of an amount higher than 200 pesos can be only proven by witnesses if there is a previous written proof, which is generally understood, as any document issued by the party who seeks to negate the existence of the contract.[12]

Under the above mentioned cases, the conclusion of the contract in writing is an *ab probationem*[13] rather than an *ad sustantiam*[14] requirement for the existence of the contract. This means that the form is imposed with a view to strengthening the proof. Its omission does not affect the contract itself.[15] However, the effect could be devastating since even though the contract exists the limited means of proof could render the rights acquired ineffective.[16]

The rest of Ibero-American laws share a liberal approach regarding the means of proof admitted. The sale of goods can be proven by different means, *e.g.*, public documents such as notary deeds, documents signed under private

---

[9] For an explanation on the form required for certain sales by the Argentinean Civil Code *see* Argentina: Borda, *supra* note 4, at 99, 110.

[10] Argentina Art. 1193 CC: the contracts beyond ten thousand pesos (increased by the law 17.711 as before it was one thousand *see* Argentina: Borda, *supra* note 4, at 110) shall be made in writing and cannot be proven by witnesses; Chile Art. 1709 CC: the contacts that involve the delivery of a thing that is worth more that two tax units shall be in writing, and according to Chile Art. 1708 CC an obligation that by law was to be passed in writing but was not will not be admitted as proof; Ecuador Art. 1753 CC and El Salvador Art. 1580 CC mirror the rule of Chile Art. 1709 CC; *see* Peru: Sierralta Rios, *supra* note 3, at p 51; Chile Supreme Court, *Sala* 1, *Rol* 4989-02, *cass*, 10 June 2004; Chile Supreme Court, *Sala* 1, *Rol* 239-04, *cass*, 18 May 2006.

[11] Argentina Art. 209 Com C; Spain Art. 51 Com C; Uruguay Art. 193 Com C.

[12] Argentina Art. 209 Com C; Uruguay Art. 193 Com C.

[13] *See contrario sensu* Bolivia Supreme Court, *Sala Civil*, *NOVA S.R.L. v. Consorcio Minero S.A.*; Mexico: León Tovar, *supra* note 7, at 74; Venezuela: Aguilar Gorrondona, *supra* note 6, at 177: the sale of vessels is required to be passed by public deed (Venezuelan Art. 594 Com C) but the requirement is just *ad probationem* and not *ab sustantiam*.

[14] For the distinction *see* Spain: Medina de Lemus, *supra* note 4, at 306; Venezuela Supreme Tribunal, Judgment 323, *Cass civ*, File 00-254 of 6 October 2000.

[15] Argentina: Borda, *supra* note 4, at 99; Venezuela Supreme Tribunal, Judgment 323, *Cass civ*, File 00-254 of 6 October 2000.

[16] Argentina Art. 975 CC & Art. 210 Com C; Chile Art. 1708 CC; Ecuador Art. 1752 CC; El Salvador Art. 1579 CC; Paraguay Art. 701 CC; Uruguay Art. 192 Com C; Chile Supreme Court, *Sala* 1, *Rol* 1120-04, *cass*, 26 January 2006.

signature, by accepted invoices, correspondence, company registries and also by the declaration of witnesses.[17]

The CISG's principle of parties' autonomy includes the freedom of choice on the form of the contract.[18] According to Article 11 of the CISG, a sales contract is not subject to any requirement as to form; parties can manifest their intention to enter into a contract in writing or in any other form. Freedom of form ranges from the conclusion of the contract throughout its modification or termination.[19] However, three Ibero-American countries having the *ab probationem* requirement for domestic sales made the CISG Article 96 declaration.[20] These States declared that any provision of Article 11, Article 29 or Part II of the CISG that allowed a contract of sale or its modification or termination by agreement or any offer, acceptance or other indication of intention to be made in any form other than in writing, would not apply where any party had his place of business in its territory.[21]

2. Form Stipulations by Parties

Although generally the law does not require any pre-established form for the sale of goods, nothing prevents the parties from agreeing on the form for the conclusion of their contract, including agreement on certain solemnities.[22] Courts and arbitral tribunals have upheld that the form of the contract agreed to by the parties shall be respected.[23] This is yet another example of freedom of contract, found in all the Ibero-American laws, and applying not just to

---

[17] *See* Ch. 15, 1.1.

[18] K.H. Neumayer, C. Ming & F. Dessemontet (Eds.), Convention de Vienne sur les contrats de vente internationale de marchandises: commentaire, Art. 11, at 127 (1993); Portugal: De Lima Pinheiro, *supra* note 6, at 276.

[19] Neumayer, *supra* note 18, Art. 11, p 127. *See* Ch. 17.

[20] Argentina, Chile and Paraguay. On the other hand, Ecuador and El Salvador did not make the reservation though Ecuador Art. 1753 CC and El Salvador Art. 1580 CC mirror the rule in Art. 1709 of Chile's Civil Code.

[21] *See* Status, Declarations and Reservations in UNCITRAL website.

[22] Argentina Art. 1186 CC; Bolivia Art. 493 CC; Chile Art. 1802 CC; Colombia Art. 1858 CC; Ecuador Art. 1768 CC; El Salvador Art. 1606 CC; Paraguay Art. 701 CC; Portugal Art. 223 CC; Peru Art. 1411 CC; Spain Arts. 1278, 1279 CC. *Also* Argentina: Borda, *supra* note 4, at 100.

[23] Bolivia Supreme Court, *Sala Civil*, 6 February 2007, *Empresas Agrícolas Ganaderas San Jorge y Rincón Chuchío v. CITIBANK N.A. Sucursal Bolivia*; Peru Supreme Court, *cass*, Resolution 001211-2005, 22 July 2005; ICC Final Award Case No. 13750 *Lex Contractus* Venezuelan Law: the Arbitral Tribunal recognised that under Venezuelan law it is not necessary to have a signed document to have a binding agreement. However, such was irrelevant at the case at hand as the parties agreed on having a formal and written document, authorised by their representatives after all the required approvals had been obtained, in order to have a binding agreement.

the freedom of choice of law clauses,[24] or the freedom to contractually define substantive obligations,[25] but also to the form under which the contract is concluded, or modified,[26] or terminated.

A failure to comply with an agreed form would be considered a lack of an *ad sustantiam* requirement leading to the invalidity of the contract:[27] in contrast to an *ab probationem* requirement as discussed above in the context of default rules.

Under many laws parties can withdraw from the sales agreement if the form previously agreed is not fulfilled, provided the goods have not yet been delivered.[28] That is, withdrawal from the contract is possible whenever the form agreed is not met, unless the parties have acted in an inconsistent manner.[29]

---

24 *See* Ch. 3.

25 *Id.*

26 *See* Ch. 17, 1.

27 *See* expressly stated Bolivia Art. 493 CC; Peru Art. 1411 CC; Bolivia Supreme Court, *Sala Civil*, 6 February 2007, *Empresas Agrícolas Ganaderas San Jorge y Rincón Chuchío v. CITIBANK N.A. Sucursal Bolivia*; Peru Supreme Court, *cass*, Resolution 001211-2005, 22 July 2005. Both Courts establishing that if the parties have agreed to adopt a determined form for the conclusion of their contract, that form is required for its validity; ICC Final Award Case No. 13750 *Lex Contractus* Venezuelan Law: the Arbitral Tribunal further dismisses buyer's contention that the sole purpose of the written agreement was to record and document an agreement already concluded, taking into account the circumstances surrounding the renewal itself, the history of dealings between the parties and industry practice. Instead, the Arbitral Tribunal found that these formalities were conditions precedent for the agreement to come into existence; *see also* Bolivia: R. Carrillo Aruquipa, Lecciones de Derecho Civil, Obligaciones 424 (2008).

28 Chile Art. 1802 CC; Colombia Art. 1858 CC; Ecuador Art. 1768 CC; El Salvador Art. 1606 CC.

29 *Contrario sensu see* ICC Final Award Case No. 13750 *Lex Contractus* Venezuelan Law: the Arbitral Tribunal found that the two deliveries of 'orimulsion' did not amount to tacit consent or ratification of the agreement, but rather were made on a spot basis, while waiting for the required approvals of the agreement from seller's authorities.

CHAPTER 21

LEGAL CAPACITY

1. General Remarks on Legal Capacity

Legal capacity is generally understood as the ability to enter into a legal relation or to acquire rights and obligations.[1] The general principle is that any person who has not been declared incapable by law has legal capacity to contract.[2] The law distinguishes between two types of legal incapacities: *de iure* and *de facto*.[3] Lack of capacity *de iure* is also known as lack of legitimacy.[4] This sort of incapacity tries to prevent one party from taking advantage of its position to enter into a contract. For example, a company's directors and managers are restrained from contracting with the company that they represent unless previous authorisation is granted by the stockholders.[5] Another example is the lack of capacity of a company to buy its own shares.[6] On the other side, the

[1] Brazil Art. 1 CC; Argentina: A.A. Alterini, Contratos civiles, comerciales, de consumo 204 (1998); Brazil: O. Gomes, Contratos 53 (2008); Ecuador: C. Valdivieso Bermeo, Tratado de las Obligaciones y Contratos 26 (2005); Ecuador: V. Cevallos Vásquez, Contratos Civiles y Mercantiles Vol. I, 160 (2005); Mexico: S. León Tovar, Los Contratos Mercantiles 76 (2004); Venezuela: J. Mélich-Orsini, Doctrina General del Contrato, para. 64 (2006); Spain: M. Medina de Lemus, Derecho Civil: Obligaciones y Contratos II, Teoria General Vol. 1, 286 (2004).

[2] Chile Art. 1446 CC; Colombia Art. 1503 CC; Ecuador Art. 1489 CC; El Salvador Art. 1317 CC; Honduras Art. 1555 CC; Uruguay Art. 1278 CC; Mexico Art. 1798 CC; Venezuela Art. 1.143 CC; X. O'Callaghan, (Ed.), Código Civil Comentado Arts. 199, 1263, at 291, 1223 (2004).

[3] The Spanish words used are *incapacidad de derecho* and *incapacidad de hecho*. Ecuador's doctrine makes reference to *capacidad legal* (*de iure*) and *capacidad jurídica* (*de facto*) *see* Ecuador: Valdivieso Bermeo, *supra* note 1, at 26. In Portuguese the term used are *incapacidad juridica* and *incapacidad natural*; O'Callaghan, *supra* note 2, Arts. 1263, 1264, at 1223, 1230.

[4] Argentina: Alterini, *supra* note 1, at 204; Venezuela: Melich-Orsini, *supra* note 1, para. 82.

[5] Argentina Arts. 158, 271, 273 LC; Argentina: M.U. Salermo, Contratos Civiles y Comerciales 121 (2007).

[6] Venezuela Art. 263 Com C; Venezuela: Melich-Orsini, *supra* note 1, para. 82.

lack of legal capacity *de facto* has been established by the law to people with deficiencies; those who do not have sufficient maturity, suffer from mental illnesses or are affected by circumstances that do not allow them to exercise their rights.[7] For example, the infant, the bankrupt trader, the demented, the prisoner. The present focus is on the comparative analysis of both types of capacities to enter into sale of goods' contracts.

Under all the Ibero-American commercial laws, natural and legal persons must first have legal capacity under the Civil Codes in order to perform trade activities.[8] The requirement is logical. The activities of trade involve the formation of legal relations. Traders celebrate contracts and acquire obligations on a daily basis. Persons who cannot be bound by their own regular conduct equally lack capacity to perform commercial transactions.[9] Consequently, the provisions on legal capacity contained in the Civil Codes are applicable to the commercial contracts subject to modifications and restrictions imposed the Codes of Commerce.[10]

2. Capacity of Natural Persons

As previously mentioned, the general principle is that any person has legal capacity to contract unless they are declared legally incapable by law. All the Ibero-American laws distinguish between two levels of legal incapacity: absolute lack of legal capacity and relative lack of legal capacity.[11] The distinction has an effect on the degree of validity of contracts.

2.1. Absolute Lack of Capacity

On the one hand, the persons affected by absolute lack of legal capacity are normally infants, those that are mentally ill,[12] deaf, and those who cannot express themselves by any means.[13] For some countries the infants are those

[7] Argentina: Alterini, *supra* note 1, at 205; Brazil: Gomes, *supra* note 1, at 53.

[8] Argentina Art. 1 Com C; Brazil Art. 972 CC; Chile Art. 7 Com C; Colombia Art. 12 Com C; Ecuador Art. 8 Com C; El Salvador Art. 7 Com C; Honduras Art. 6 Com C; Mexico Art. 81 Com C; Uruguay Art. 1 Com C.

[9] Argentina Art. 9 Com C; Mexico Art. 5 Com C; Uruguay Art. 8 Com C; Mexico: León Tovar, *supra* note 1, at 77.

[10] *See* Ch. 5, 1.

[11] *See for example*, Argentina Arts. 54, 55 CC; Brazil Arts. 3, 4 CC; Ecuador: Valdivieso Bermeo, *supra* note 1, at 27; Ecuador: Cevallos Vásquez, *supra* note 1, at 161; Peru: M. Castillo Freyre, Tratado de la Teoria General de los Contratos Vol. I, 42, 47 (2002); Venezuela: Melich-Orsini, *supra* note 1, para. 65.

[12] Spain Art. 200 CC; Venezuela Art. 393 CC.

[13] Argentina Arts. 54, 55 CC; Brazil Art. 3 CC; Ecuador Art. 1490 CC; Chile Art. 1447 CC;

men younger than 14 years and the women younger than 12 years[14] while for some other countries are those persons younger than 14[15] or 16 years.[16] The contracts purportedly entered into by absolutely legally incapable persons are absolutely invalid.[17] The absolute invalidity is declared by the judge. It cannot be corrected by ratification of the parties nor by the course of time.[18]

2.2. Relative Lack of Capacity

Persons affected by relative lack of legal capacity are young adults who have not attained the legal age,[19] consuetudinary drunks and drugs addicts,[20] bankrupts[21] and convicts.[22] Peru's Civil Code includes mentally affected persons.[23] The contracts passed by relatively incapable persons are voidable.[24] This means that they can be corrected by the course of the time or by ratification of the parties, after judicial declaration at the request of a party.[25]

Colombia Art. 1504 CC; El Salvador Art. 1318 CC; Honduras Art. 1555 CC; Peru Art. 43 CC; Spain Art. 200 CC; Uruguay Art. 1279 CC.

14 Argentina Art. 127 CC; Chile Art. 26 CC; Ecuador Art. 21 CC; El Salvador Art. 26 CC; Uruguay Art. 91 CC.

15 Colombia Art. 34 CC.

16 *See* Brazil Art. 3 (I) CC; Peru Art. 43 CC.

17 *See* Ecuador: Valdivieso Bermeo, *supra* note 1, at 28; Peru: Castillo Freyre, *supra* note 11, at 42; Ecuador Art. 1490 CC; Chile Art. 1447 CC; Colombia Art. 1504 CC; El Salvador Art. 1318 CC; Honduras Art. 1555 CC; Peru Art. 219 (2) CC; Uruguay Arts. 1560, 1279 CC.

18 *See* Ch. 24.

19 Argentina Arts. 54, 55 CC; Brazil Art. 4 (I) CC: young adults are persons between the ages of 14 to 17; Chile Art. 26 CC; Colombia Art. 34 CC; Ecuador Art. 21 CC: women from 12 to 17 and men from 14 to 17; El Salvador Art. 26 CC; Peru Art. 44 CC: persons older than 16 and younger than 18; Uruguay Art. 1280 CC; Ecuador: Valdivieso Bermeo, *supra* note 1, at 27. In most Ibero-American systems the legal age is 18 years: Brazil Art. 5 CC; Ecuador Art. 21 CC; Chile Art. 26 CC; El Salvador Art. 26 CC; Mexico Art. 646 CC; Uruguay Art. 280 (2) CC; Venezuela Art. 18 CC; though in some countries it is 21 years: Argentina Art. 127 CC.

20 Brazil Art. 4 (II) CC; Peru Art. 44 (6) (7) CC.

21 Argentina Art. 1160 CC & Art. 107 Law 24.522; Ecuador Art. 7 Com C; El Salvador Art. 11 (3) Com C; Honduras Art. 9 (2) Com C; Mexico Art. 12 Com C: the trader in bankruptcy has legal capacity but is forbidden to perform commercial activities; Uruguay Art. 29 Com C; Venezuela Art. 939 Com C; Ecuador: Valdivieso Bermeo, *supra* note 1, at 28 according to this author the Ecuadorian law categorises them with the name of *interdictos*.

22 El Salvador 11 (2) Com C; Honduras Art. 9 (1) Com C; Peru Art. 44 (8) CC; Venezuela Arts. 408, 1145 CC.

23 Peru Art. 44 (2) (3) (4) CC.

24 Ecuador Art. 1490 CC; Chile Art. 1447 (3) CC; Colombia Art. 1504 (3) CC; El Salvador Art. 1318 (3) CC; Honduras Art. 1555 (3) CC; Peru Art. 221 (1) CC; Uruguay Art. 1560 para. 3 CC.

25 *See* Ch. 24.

2.3. Liability of the Incapable

Under some laws, the legally incapable person will nevertheless be bound by the obligations contracted.[26] Other jurisdictions weigh the apparentness of incapacity. B2B contracts are void for all the parties whenever the lack of legal capacity is apparent. If the lack of legal capacity is not apparent, the solution depends on the conduct adopted by the parties.[27] The party which hides its lack of capacity binds itself but does not acquire any rights to force the other party to perform the contracted obligations.[28]

In Argentina, once the invalidity or voidability of the contract has been declared the capable party cannot require the incapable (absolute or relative) to return the goods or the price.[29] Unless, it is proven that the goods exist and/or unjustified enrichment took place.[30] The idea behind the rule is to protect the legally incapable party from the exploitation of the other party, since it is usual that the incapable has already disposed of the goods or the money at the time of the invalidity or voidability declaration.[31]

3. Capacity of Legal Persons

Despite the fact that companies' legal capacity comes from different sources, they have the same rights to acquire and transfer goods through most of the ways established by law, just as the natural persons do.[32] Companies are also traders.[33] Companies generally acquire legal personality from the moment their members enter into the contract of company[34] or at the time of incorporation and registry.[35]

[26] *See for example* Brazil Art. 973 CC.

[27] *See for example* Uruguay Art. 30 Com C.

[28] *See for example* Uruguay Art. 30 Com C.

[29] Argentina Art. 1165 CC.

[30] Argentina Art. 1165 CC; *see also* Ch. 58.

[31] Argentina: Alterini, *supra* note 1, at 210.

[32] Argentina Art. 41 CC: Brazil Art. 52 CC; Honduras Art. 59 CC; *see also* Bolivia: J. Ovando Ovando, Sociedades Comerciales, Doctrina y Legislación Nacional 45 (2008).

[33] *See for example* Brazil Art. 982 CC; Uruguay Art. 1 Com C; Salerno, *supra* note 5, at 113.

[34] Mexico Art. 2 LC; Uruguay Art. 2 LC; ICC Final Award Case No. 11556 *Lex Contractus* Mexican Law: respondent alleged that at the time of the assignment Claimant was not yet registered in the Public Registry of Commerce in Mexico City and thus it had no authority to execute the assignment. The Tribunal noted that Claimant was constituted with the signature of the company's agreement proven by public deed on 22 January 2001. Although this act of establishment was only registered on 8 March 2001, Claimant had been established on 22 January 2001, and had the legal capacity to enter into the agreement of 23 January 2001 by which the original party in the agreement assigned to Claimant the agreement. Consequently, the Tribunal considers that the company's contract registration has had retrospective and ratifying effect.

However, for most Ibero-American jurisdictions the legal capacity of a company does not depend on the fulfilment of the incorporation requirements.[36] The company in the process of formation has legal capacity.[37] Nevertheless, the members, directors and agents may be personally liable for the transactions made during the process of formation.[38]

The company *de facto* and the defective company also have legal personality. In this case, members, directors and agents are conjointly liable with the company for the acts performed.[39] In addition, the declaration of invalidity of a company has no retroactive effect, which means that only future acts are invalid but not the previous ones,[40] unless invalidated on other grounds.[41]

A companies' legal capacity is limited by law[42] and its incorporation documents.[43] For example, a limitation to the company's legal capacity derives from the company's objects itself.[44] In this sense, company representatives can only bind the company to those acts which are within its objects,[45] and according to the scope of authorisation given by the documents of incorporation or by-laws.[46] The law also imposes limits on the activities of certain types of companies. As a basic example, Civil Associations may not be allowed to have as their main activity the trade of merchandise for a profit purpose, as under some laws contracts which oppose the type adopted are voidable.[47]

---

35 Bolivia Art. 133 Com C; Brazil Arts. 45, 985 CC; Bolivia: Ovando Ovando, *supra* note 32, at 47.

36 The validity of contract of company is subject to formal requirement (in writing public deed) and registry (Registry of Commerce or Companies), *see for example* Bolivia: Ovando Ovando, *supra* note 32, at 84; Uruguay Arts. 6, 7 LC.

37 *See for example* Uruguay Art. 19 LC.

38 *See* Uruguay Art. 21 LC.

39 Bolivia Art. 135 Com C; Uruguay Art. 39 LC; *see also* Bolivia: Ovando Ovando, *supra* note 32, at 84-85.

40 *See* Uruguay Art. 29 LC.

41 Uruguay Art. 30 LC. On the issue of the illicit cause and object *see* Ch. 9 and Ch. 19.

42 Argentina Art. 2 LC; Uruguay Art. 2 LC.

43 *See* ICC Final Award Case No. 13524 *Lex Contractus* Mexican Law; The name normally given in Spanish Language to the documents of incorporation is *Acta Constitutiva, Estatutos Sociales, Clausulas del Estatuto see* Brazil Art. 985 CC; El Salvador Art. 1318 CC; Salerno, *supra* note 5, at 113.

44 Argentina Art. 35 CC & Art. 11 (3) LC; Colombia Art. 99 Com C; El Salvador 354 Com C; Salerno, *supra* note 5, at 113.

45 *See* Argentina Art. 58 LC; Guatemala Art. 1697 CC; Uruguay Art. 79 LC.

46 Brazil Art. 47 CC; Ecuador Valdivieso Bermeo, *supra* note 1, at 30; ICC Final Award Case No. 13750 *Lex Contractus* Venezuelan Law: the Tribunal also rejected buyer's contention that Mr. X's signature of the Agreement bound the seller to the Agreement since, according to seller's by-laws, the only representative authorised to sign contracts on seller's behalf was its Managing Director (Mr. Y) and there is nothing in the file showing that Mr. Y delegated his powers to Mr. X.

47 Uruguay Art. 25 LC.

Chapter 22

Mistake

1. General Remarks on Mistake

Mistake is generally understood as a party's false or inexact understanding about certain issues relating to an act or contract,[1] at the time of the entering into the contract.[2] The Civil Codes distinguish four main types of mistakes: error of law, mistake of facts, mistake in the motivations and mistake of expression.[3] Due to the principle of *ignorantia legis non excusat*[4] in most countries, except in Brazil,[5] error of law does not affect the validity of the

[1] For the concept of mistake in Ibero-American modern doctrine *see* Bolivia: R. Carrillo Aruquipa, Lecciones de Derecho Civil, Obligaciones 408 (2008); Costa Rica: A. Brenes Cordoba, G. Trejos & M. Ramírez, Tratado de los Contratos 67 (1998); Honduras: H. Carcamo Tercero, Eficacia e Ineficacia de los Contratos en Materia Civil 38 (2001); Nicaragua: J.J. Herrera Espinoza *et al.*, Contratos Civiles y Mercantiles 10.12 (2006); Peru: M. Castillo Freyre, Tratado de la Teoria General de los Contratos Vol. I, 48 (2002); Venezuela: J. Mélich-Orsini, Doctrina General del Contrato para. 137 (2006).

[2] Mexico Collegiate Tribunals, *Novena Época*, Registry 191'033, SJF XII, October 2000, at 1279.

[3] Countries like Chile, Honduras, Ecuador and El Salvador only distinguish between two types: error of law and error of fact, *see* Ecuador: C. Valdivieso Bermeo, Tratado de las Obligaciones y Contratos 32 (2005); Civil Codes like that of Mexico only refers to the error on the motivations. For a conceptual understanding of the different kinds of error *see* Bolivia: W. Kaune Arteaga, Curso de Derecho Civil, Contratos, Vol. 1, 92 (1996); Nicaragua: Herrera Espinoza *et al.*, *supra* note 1, at 10.13-10.17.

[4] Peru Supreme Court, Resolution 000070-2001, *Sala civil transitoria*, 25 April 2002: upholding that it is a general principle of law that no person can allege in its favour the ignorance of the law, thus, the defendant cannot based his defence on the mere fact that he is domiciled in Germany, hence unfamiliar with the legal provision of Peruvian law on contract, specially if the defendant had agreed to submit to jurisdiction of Peru's Tribunals in case of dispute derived from the sales contract.

[5] Brazil Art. 139 (III) CC.

contract.[6] In this chapter we focus on the mistake of facts,[7] the mistake on the motivations and the mistake of expression.

As a principle, parties' intent must be manifested free of mistake,[8] since such is a requirement for the validity of contracts in all systems.[9] However, not every mistake affects a contract's validity. For most Ibero-American jurisdictions, a minor misunderstanding regarding the contract does not amount to a relevant mistake which would cause the voidability of the contract.[10] If the mistaken party had known the true state of the matter and would have still entered into the contract, then, mistaken intent cannot be alleged.[11] Only objectively recognised circumstances can render a mistake legally significant or relevant,[12] and must be proven by the party who alleges its existence.[13] Thus, the question of whether a mistake is relevant or irrelevant is at the core of the law of mistake.

---

6 Argentina Art. 923 CC; Chile Art. 1452 CC; Colombia Art. 1509 CC; Ecuador Arts. 13, 1495 CC; El Salvador Art. 1323 CC; Honduras Art. 6 CC; Paraguay Art. 285 CC; Venezuela Art. 1147 CC; Nicaragua Art. 2462 CC. *Contrario sensu* the error of law can only result in contract's rescission when it was the principal or unique cause; supported by Venezuela Supreme Tribunal, Judgment 363, *Cass soc*, file 01-474 of 19 December 2001; supported by doctrine Ecuador: Valdivieso Bermeo, *supra* note 3, at 32: the rule responds to the principle of *lex imperious* under which a party cannot alleged to ignore the law; Costa Rica: Brenes Cordoba, Trejos & Ramírez, *supra* note 1, at 71; Honduras: Carcamo Tercero, *supra* note 1, at 38.

7 This sort of error would normally cover mistakes as to the contract's obligations, the characteristics of the thing and the parties identity.

8 The Ibero-American Civil Codes identify three main intent's vices: mistake (*error*), fraud (*dolo*) and duress (*violencia* or *amenaza*); *see* Argentina Art. 922 CC; Bolivia Art. 473 CC; Cuba Art. 69 CC; Chile Art. 1451 CC; Colombia Art. 1508 CC; Ecuador Art. 1494 CC; El Salvador Art. 1322 CC; Honduras Art. 1556 CC; Mexico Art. 1812 CC; Spain Art. 1265 CC; Venezuela Art. 1146 CC.

9 Bolivia Art. 549 (4) CC; Cuba Art. 69 CC; Chile Art. 1445 CC; Ecuador Art. 1488 CC; El Salvador Art. 1316 CC; Mexico Art. 1795 CC; Venezuela Arts. 1141, 1142 CC; Ecuador: V. Cevallos Vásquez, Contratos Civiles y Mercantiles Vol. I, 159 (2005); Costa Rica: Brenes Cordoba, Trejos & Ramírez, *supra* note 1, at 64.

10 On this *see* Ecuador: Valdivieso Bermeo, *supra* note 3, at 32; Mexico Collegiate Tribunals, *Octava Época*, SJF IX, February 1992, p 137: upholding that a mistake in the number of the house in a lease contract does not amount to significant mistake.

11 Costa Rica: Brenes Cordoba, Trejos & Ramírez, *supra* note 1, at 67.

12 Bolivia: Kaune Arteaga, *supra* note 3, at 93: a relevant mistake should be determinant, essential and objectively recognised.

13 Brazil Arts. 138-139 CC; Peru Art. 201 CC; Peru: Castillo Freyre, *supra* note 1, at 51; Bolivia Supreme Court, *Sala Civil* 22 April 2003, *Bárbara Tapia vda. de Casas v. Petrona Cazas vda. de Mayta*: a party basing his claim on an essential error on the nature of the contract did not prove that he had entered into a contract different to the sales contract or that the object of the contract was different to the one understood at the conclusion. The party failed to prove *error in negotio* or *error in corpore*; Brazil Tribunal Justice of the State of Rio Grande do Sul, Civil Appeal 70021924683, published 4 December 2007: according to the Court's decision, in

2. Relevant Mistakes

Some Ibero-American laws have taken a subjective approach to assess the relevance of contractual mistakes. Under these laws a mistake in motivation must, in some way, have an effect on the principal reason moving one or both parties to contract in order to be considered as relevant.[14] Here the standard is on the subjective motivations of the parties and the subjective effect produced for each of them.[15]

Other legal systems also adopt a subjective approach with a distinctive element. In Portugal and Peru the mistake in motivation only vitiates the contract if the decisive reason is expressly manifested and accepted by the other party.[16] In this case, the other party's understanding on this issue establishes a certain objectivity.[17]

For most other laws, a casuistic method establishes a non-exhaustive list of cases of objectively relevant mistakes.[18] Accordingly, a mistake may have a vitiating effect on the parties' consent when it bears on the nature of the act performed or on the specific thing or matter of the contract.[19] In this case, both parties normally have a different understanding of the same transaction, thus both parties have the right to claim the rescission of the contract.[20]

---

order to be able to rescind the contract, the mistake needs to be substantial and proved by the party who invokes it.

[14] Cuba Art. 73 CC; Honduras Art. 1557 CC; Mexico Art. 1813 CC*: t*he decisive ground for the intention of any of the parties; Spain Art. 1.266 CC; Costa Rica: Brenes Cordoba, Trejos & Ramírez, *supra* note 1, at 67; Mexico Collegiate Tribunals, *Séptima Época*, Registry 249211, SJF VI, p 139: on the consequences of vices affecting the decisive ground for the intention of any of the parties; ICC Final Award Case No. 13184 *Lex Contractus* CISG and Mexican Law as supplementary law: agreeing with respondents' view that pursuant to Art. 1813 of the Mexico's Civil Code a contract could only be invalidate where the mistake relates to the Claimant's determinative purpose of entering into the contract as proved by its declarations at the time of execution or the circumstances of the execution.

[15] Mexico Collegiate Tribunals, *Novena Época*. SJF XXV, June 2007, at 1170: held that the fact that the seller did not disclose the fact that he was not in possession of the property titled amounted to mistake on the buyer's eyes since the buyer needed the property title in order to get a bank loan necessary to pay the goods.

[16] Portugal Art. 252 CC; Peru Art. 205 CC; Peru: Castillo Freyre, *supra* note 1, at 51.

[17] E.A. Kramer & T. Probst, *Defects in the Contracting Process*, *in* A.T. von Mehren (Ed.), International Encyclopedia of Comparative Law, Vol. VII Contracts, Ch. 11, 8 (1999).

[18] For the implications of this casuistic method *see Id.*, at 9.

[19] Chile Art. 1453 CC; Colombia Art. 1510 CC; Ecuador Art. 1496 CC; El Salvador Art. 1324 CC: in all the preceding codes: "when one of the parties had understood loan and the other party donation," or "when in a sales contract one party has understood to sell one thing and the other party to buy something different"; Argentina Arts. 924, 926, 927 CC; Bolivia Art. 474 CC; Brazil Art. 139 (I) CC; Paraguay Art. 286 (a) (c) (d) CC; Costa Rica: Brenes Cordoba, Trejos & Ramírez, *supra* note 1, at 68; Nicaragua: Herrera Espinoza *et al.*, *supra* note 1, at 10.14; Bolivia: Kaune Arteaga, *supra* note 3, at 97, 98.

[20] Venezuela: Melich-Orsini, *supra* note 1, para. 140.

In the same group of countries, there is also significant mistake when the substance of the object contracted is different from what is believed.[21] From an objective perspective this kind of mistake takes place when one party mistakes the materials from which the goods are made, irrespective of his subjective understanding of the materials.[22] Error as to the thing's quality does not amount to a significant mistake. Except in some jurisdictions and in cases where the goods represent the principal reason for motivating one of the parties to contract and the other party was aware of this.[23]

A few Ibero-American legal systems attempt to distinguish between objectively relevant and irrelevant mistakes on the basis of abstract conceptual criteria,[24] such as the concept of the *diligent person*. For example, in Brazil and Peru the objective standard requires the mistake to be noticed by the other party in the position of an average diligent person taking into consideration the circumstances of the deal.[25]

In addition, courts and tribunals has sustained that a mistake cannot be alleged when the false understanding of the issue derives from the own party's negligent conduct.[26] In an interesting ICC arbitration, the seller alleged that it had given to the buyer a right to terminate the contract, as the result of a mistake induced by the buyer.[27] In the case at hand, a clause originally proposed by the seller allowed him to terminate in case there was a change of control in the buyer's company. A new draft was submitted by the buyer to the seller giving the same right to the buyer. The arbitral tribunal accepted that

---

[21] Chile Art. 1454 CC; Colombia Art. 1511 CC; Ecuador Art. 1497 CC; El Salvador Art. 1325 CC: in all the preceding codes "like if for example one of the parties assumes the thing is a bar of silver, but in reality the object is a mass of a similar metal"; Argentina Arts. 924, 926, 927 CC; Bolivia Art. 475 (1) CC; Brazil Art. 139 (I) CC; Nicaragua Art. 2455 (2) CC; Guatemala Art. 1258 CC; Paraguay Art. 286 (a) (c) (d) CC; Spain Art. 1266 CC; Costa Rica: Brenes Cordoba, Trejos & Ramírez, *supra* note 1, at 68; Nicaragua: Herrera Espinoza *et al.*, *supra* note 1, at 10.15; Brazil Tribunal of Justice of the State of Rio Grande do Sul, Civil Appeal 70019324029, published 23 August 2007: a discrepancy between the real year of the fabrication of a farm machine (1989) and the year contained on the contract (1991) configured a substantial mistake about the quality of the object.

[22] Venezuela: Melich-Orsini, *supra* note 1, para. 144.

[23] Chile Art. 1454 CC; Colombia Art. 1511 CC; Ecuador Art. 1497 CC; El Salvador Art. 1325 CC; Nicaragua Art. 2455 (2) CC. In Argentina Art. 928 CC is actually the opposite since a mistake on the quality does not invalids the contract even if the quality of the thing is the essential reason acknowledged by the parties.

[24] For further background on the conceptual approach *see* Kramer & Probst, *supra* note 17, at 11.

[25] Brazil Art. 138 CC; Peru Arts. 201, 203 CC: stating that the error only invalidates the act when according to the circumstances of the case a normal diligent person could have noticed the mistake; Peru: Castillo Freyre, *supra* note 1, at 51.

[26] Argentina National Commercial Court of Appeals, *Quilmes Combustibles, S.A. c. Vigan, S.A*, 15 March 1991: the mere fact that the standard terms were written in French language does not amount to mistake as a party would be expected to diligently take any reasonable measure to understand their meaning by means of translation.

[27] ICC Final Award Case 11256 Lex Contractus Mexican Law.

the buyer's covering letter did not refer to this change. However, the arbitral tribunal did not accept the seller's suggestion that it did not carefully review the buyer's new draft further to the covering letter. The control of the buyer was important for the seller, such was the reason why it took the initiative to introduce the clause. Thus, the arbitral tribunal could not believe that the seller did not check whether the counterproposal presented by the other party met its expectations.[28]

A mistake about the identity of the other party does not amount to a significant mistake unless it is the principal motivation for the contract.[29] For some scholars, this sort of mistake can hardly affect the intent of the parties to a sales contract.[30] When a party purchases goods, he cares about the goods' characteristics rather than about the seller's identity. For this reason, a mistake on the identity of the seller or the buyer cannot invalidate the transaction since it is not made *intuitus personae*.[31]

A small group of Ibero-American Civil Codes refers to the mistake of expression. The Portuguese Civil Code states that when the will declared does not correspond to the real will of the party, the declaration is voidable from the moment the other party knew or could not have ignored the relevance, for the first party, of the element mistaken.[32] This sort of mistake does not vitiate the will itself since there is no false or erroneous representation or, understanding of the reality but instead, there is simply an expression of intent which is different from the real interior individual will.[33] Under the Brazilian law, the mistake of expression while indicating a person or a thing does not vitiate the contract when it is possible to discover the intended person or thing by analysing the context and the circumstances.[34] In these cases, the affected party only has the possibility to ask for the rectification.[35]

---

[28] ICC Final Award Case 11256 *Lex Contractus* Mexican Law.

[29] Argentina Arts. 924, 925, 926, 927 CC; Bolivia Art. 475(2) CC; Brazil Art. 139(I)(II) CC; Chile Art. 1455 CC; Colombia Art. 1512 CC; Ecuador Art. 1498 CC; El Salvador Art. 1326 CC; Nicaragua Art. 2467 CC; Guatemala Art. 1259 CC; Spain Art. 1266 CC; Paraguay Art. 286(a)(c)(d) CC. *See also* Costa Rica: Brenes Cordoba, Trejos & Ramírez, *supra* note 1, at 68; El Salvador Supreme Court, *Cass civ, Inversiones J. R., S.A. de C.V. vrs. Industrial de Alimentos S.A. de C.V.*, CCS1118.98.

[30] Guatemala: V. Aguilar Guerra, El Negocio Jurídico 226 (2004).

[31] *Intuitius Personae* is for example the contract of agency, donation or lease, *see* Costa Rica: Brenes Cordoba, Trejos & Ramírez, *supra* note 1, at 70; Honduras: Carcamo Tercero, *supra* note 1, at 39; Nicaragua: Herrera Espinoza *et al.*, *supra* note 1, at 10.17; Venezuela: Melich-Orsini, *supra* note 1, para. 145; Bolivia: Kaune Arteaga, *supra* note 3, at 99.

[32] Portugal Art. 247 CC; *see also* Peru Arts. 208, 209 CC; Peru: Castillo Freyre, *supra* note 1, at 52.

[33] Venezuela: Melich-Orsini, *supra* note 1, para. 138.

[34] Brazil Art. 142 CC.

[35] Nicaragua: Herrera Espinoza *et al.*, *supra* note 1, at 10.16; Mexico Collegiate Tribunals, *Octava Época*. SJF IX, February 1992, p 137: a mistake in the number of the house in a lease contract does not amount to significant mistake.

The same would be the case for the mistake of calculation which, only gives grounds to its rectification.[36] For example, the seller by mistake quotes the price because of the use of a dollar $ sign rather than the pounds £ sign. Or the same seller by mistake makes a wrong currency conversion transmitting a lower price than the real one. The seller receives from the buyer an unfair price and has as his only remedy its correction.

[36] Bolivia Art. 476 CC; Brazil Art. 143 CC; Guatemala Art. 1260 CC; Honduras Art. 1557 CC; Mexico Art. 1814 CC; Nicaragua Art. 2456 CC; Peru Art. 204 CC; Portugal Art. 285 CC; Spain Art. 1.266 CC; Bolivia: Kaune Arteaga, *supra* note 3, at 101; Peru: Castillo Freyre, *supra* note 1, at 51.

Chapter 23

Fraud and Duress

1. General Remarks on Fraud and Duress

Fraud and duress lead to defective consent in all the Ibero-American legal systems.[1] Generally, intent is affected by fraud when one of the contracting parties intentionally provokes by fraudulent behaviour, a mistake in the mind of the other party who, there upon, enters into a contract that otherwise, would have not concluded.[2]

[1] The Ibero-American Civil Codes identify three main consent's defects: mistake (*error*), fraud (*dolo*) and duress (*violencia* or *amenaza*); *see* Argentina Art. 922 CC; Bolivia Art. 473 CC; Cuba Art. 69 CC; Chile Arts. 1445, 1451 CC; Colombia Art. 1508 CC; Costa Rica Art. 1020 CC; Ecuador Arts. 1488, 1494 CC; El Salvador Arts. 1316, 1322 CC; Honduras Art. 1556 CC; Guatemala Art. 1257 CC; Mexico Arts. 1795, 1812 CC; Nicaragua Arts. 2455-2470 CC; Spain Art. 1265 CC; Venezuela Arts. 1141, 1142, 1146 CC; *see also* Costa Rica: A. Brenes Cordoba, G. Trejos & M. Ramírez, Tratado de los Contratos 64 (1998); Ecuador: V. Cevallos Vásquez, Contratos Civiles y Mercantiles Vol. I, 159 (2005); Ecuador: C. Valdivieso Bermeo, Tratado de las Obligaciones y Contratos 30 (2005); Guatemala: V. Aguilar Guerra, El Negocio Jurídico 250-253 (2004); Mexico: S. León Tovar, Los Contratos Mercantiles 79 (2004).

[2] Argentina Art. 931 CC; Argentina: A.A. Alterini, Contratos civiles, comerciales, de consumo 365 (1998); Bolivia: R. Carrillo Aruquipa, Lecciones de Derecho Civil, Obligaciones 407 (2008); Mexico: León Tovar, *supra* note 1, at 81; Guatemala: Aguilar Guerra, *supra* note 1, at 262; Ecuador: Valdivieso Bermeo, *supra* note 1, at 35; Costa Rica: Brenes Cordoba, Trejos & Ramírez, *supra* note 1, at 78; Nicaragua: J.J. Herrera Espinoza *et al.*, Contratos Civiles y Mercantiles 10.8 (2006); Peru: M. Castillo Freyre, Tratado de la Teoria General de los Contratos Vol. I, 53 (2002); E.A. Kramer & T. Probst, Defects in the Contracting Process, *in* A.T. von Mehren (Ed.), International Encyclopedia of Comparative Law, Vol. VII Contracts, Ch. 11, 74, para. 158 (1999); Bolivia Supreme Court, *Sala Civil* 1, 29 September 2004, *Marcial Xavier Pérez y otra v. Teddy Mercado Mendoza*: considering that the seller would have shown good faith if the contract has manifested the real state of the vehicle, fact that would have fundamentally influenced the decision of the buyers to acquire it.

Nevertheless, the fraudulent conduct may not always cause a mistake in the other party's mind.[3] Although some laws limit the scope of fraud to cases of mistaken parties,[4] many others do not limit the scope with a definition of fraud,[5] or their provisions are constructed with words which are broad enough to include cases where intent is vitiated by artifices but no mistake is provoked.[6] The text of the Civil Codes of Honduras, Nicaragua and Spain do not require the deceived party to have entered into a contract due to a mistake. For these codes there is fraud when one party induces, through insidious words or connivances, the other party to enter into a contract that he would not, otherwise, have concluded.[7]

The intention to cause damage or prejudice to the other party is not required for the existence of fraud.[8]

Duress occurs when a contracting party (or a third party) intentionally forces the other party, by physical or moral pressure, to conclude a contract, which the victim would have never entered into but for such pressure.[9] In this sense, duress is constituted by three requirements. First, there must be an effect on one of the parties' intent through fear,[10] caused by violence,[11] intimidation,[12]

---

3 Costa Rica: Brenes Cordoba, Trejos & Ramírez, *supra* note 1, at 79.

4 Bolivia Art. 482 CC; Cuba Art. 71 CC; Guatemala Art. 1261 CC; Mexico Art. 1815 CC; Peru Art. 210 CC; Portugal Art. 253 CC; Mexico: León Tovar, *supra* note 1, at 81; Guatemala: Aguilar Guerra, *supra* note 1, at 263; Bolivia Supreme Court, *Sala Civil* 1, 29 September 2004, *Marcial Xavier Pérez y otra v. Teddy Mercado Mendoza:* the basis of fraud as a vice of the intent is in the deceit, which, in the case at hand, supposes the intention to produce in the buyer a false knowledge, a mistaken or an erroneous mental representation about the qualities of the vehicle … [that] leads to the mistake.

5 Brazil Art. 145 CC; Chile Art. 1458 CC; Colombia Art. 1515 CC; Ecuador Art. 1501 CC; El Salvador Art. 1329 CC.

6 Argentina Art. 931 CC; Paraguay Art. 290 CC; Honduras Art. 1560 CC; Nicaragua Art. 2469 CC; Spain Art. 1.269 CC.

7 Argentina Art. 931 CC; Honduras Art. 1560 CC; Nicaragua Art. 2469 CC; Paraguay Art. 290 CC; Spain Art. 1.269 CC; Nicaragua: Herrera Espinoza *et al.*, *supra* note 2, at 10.7.

8 Bolivia Supreme Court, Sala Civil 1, 29 September 2004, *Marcial Xavier Pérez y otra v. Teddy Mercado Mendoza.*

9 Kramer & Probst, *supra* note 2, at 187, para. 354; Argentina: Alterini, *supra* note 2, at 367; Bolivia: Carrillo Aruquipa, *supra* note 2, at 408-409; Mexico: León Tovar, *supra* note 1, at 81; Guatemala: Aguilar Guerra, *supra* note 1, at 267, 268; Nicaragua: Herrera Espinoza *et al.*, *supra* note 2, at 10.18.

10 The Spanish word used is *temor see* the Title of Paraguay Art. 293 CC; Cuba Art. 72 CC.

11 Bolivia Art. 477 CC; Dominican Republic Art. 1111 CC; Honduras Art. 1558 CC; Guatemala Art. 1264 CC; Mexico Art. 1819 CC; Nicaragua Art. 2468 CC; Peru Art. 214 CC; Panama Art. 1118 CC; Spain Art. 1.267 CC; Venezuela Art. 1150 CC.

12 Argentina Art. 937 CC; Guatemala Art. 1264 CC; Honduras Art. 1558 CC; Nicaragua Art. 2468 CC; Panama Art. 1118 CC; Peru Art. 214 CC; Spain Art. 1258 CC.

coercion,[13] force[14] or threat.[15] All these terms in their original Spanish and Portuguese versions indicate some kind of pressure exercised over one of the parties inducing fear or using physical violence in the contracting process.[16] Second, the fear alleged by one of the parties must be due to the other party's improper behaviour.[17] This establishes a standard since not every kind of pressure avoids the contract. Finally, there must be a causative link between coercive behaviour and the conclusion of the contract. These requirements will be explained below in more detail.

2. Fraud

The essence of fraud consists in a party's fraudulent behaviour affecting the intent of the other contracting party.[18] Nevertheless, fraudulent behaviour is subject to certain standards. Not every behaviour affecting intent will amount to fraud. A certain degree of looseness with the truth is allowed in special circumstances.[19] For example, in trade puffery and exaggerations may be used to present a product to potential buyers.[20] Accordingly, usual suggestions or artifices do not constitute illicit deceit, when they are considered justified according to the perception of commerce.[21]

Fraud should be grave.[22] Fraud is grave whenever it has influenced the conclusion of the contract, hence, it does not therefore correspond to the

13 Brazil Art. 151 CC; Portugal Art. 255 CC.

14 Argentina Art. 936 CC; Colombia Art. 1513 CC; Chile Art. 1456 CC; Ecuador Art. 1499 CC; El Salvador Art. 1327 CC; Paraguay Art. 293 CC.

15 Cuba Art. 72 CC; Mexico Art. 1819 CC.

16 Some Ibero-American countries have adopted the dualistic Roman distinction between *vis* (violence) and *metus* (fear or intimidation) for example Argentina, Mexico, Panama, Paraguay, Spain, Peru. Some others adopted the unitary approach of the French Civil Code under the heading of *violence*. In practice the distinction is relevant regarding the standards required so that fear can render the contract voidable; *see for example* Argentina Arts. 936, 937 CC; Argentina: Alterini, *supra* note 2, at 367.

17 Kramer & Probst, *supra* note 2, at 173, para. 361.

18 *Id.*, at 77, para. 162; Argentina: Alterini, *supra* note 2, at 366; Mexico: León Tovar, *supra* note 1, at 8; Ecuador: Valdivieso Bermeo, *supra* note 1, at 35; Costa Rica: Brenes Cordoba, Trejos & Ramírez, *supra* note 1, at 79; Nicaragua: Herrera Espinoza *et al.*, *supra* note 2, at 10.8.

19 Kramer & Probst, *supra* note 2, at 86, para. 178; Guatemala: Aguilar Guerra, *supra* note 1, at 264, 265; Costa Rica: Brenes Cordoba, Trejos & Ramírez, *supra* note 1, at 84; Nicaragua: Herrera Espinoza *et al.*, *supra* note 2, at 10.9.

20 Bolivia: Carrillo Aruquipa, *supra* note 2, at 408; Spain: J. Llobet I Aguado, El Deber de Información en la Formación de los Contratos 131 (1996).

21 *See for example* Portugal Art. 253 (2) CC; Spai: Llobet I Aguado, *supra* note 20, at 131.

22 Argentina Art. 932 CC four requirements are impose: 1.-To be grave, 2.-To be the determining cause of the action, 3.-To cause a substantial damage, 4.-There must not be fraud from both parties; Mexico Arts. 1816, 1817 CC; Portugal Art. 253 (2) CC; Spain Art. 1270 CC.

standard of *dolus bonus*.[23] Incidental fraud as opposed to grave fraud does not normally affect the validity of the contract: Nevertheless, the deceiving party may be compensated for any damage caused.[24] Incidental fraud is when the deception has not affected the decisive reason for entering into the contract (although without such the contract would have been concluded under different terms).[25] Finally, there must be a casual link between the one party's deceiving conduct and the other party's determining reason to contract.[26]

In a case submitted before an ICC Arbitral Tribunal a dispute arose between a respondent who was a Mexican beer producer and the claimant who was one of the respondents' two only distributors in the United States. The Tribunal found that the respondent's conduct satisfied the definition of both misrepresentation (fraud) and bad faith in Article 1815 of the Mexican Civil Code. Nevertheless, the Tribunal considered that the legal effect of misrepresentation or bad faith under the Mexican law depends upon its importance to the formation of the contract. In the case at hand, the concealed facts had not been a determinative cause of the contract within the meaning of Article 1816 of Mexico's Civil Code. The determinative cause of the agreement resided in its commercial terms. The respondents' deception relating to the duration in particular, the rights of renewal, and the termination clause was of lesser significance. Consequently, there were no sufficient grounds to cancel the contract because of the alleged misrepresentation.[27]

There are different ways to commit or to suffer from fraud. Fraud can be performed by positive or negative acts.[28] Active inducement of a mistake is the main form of fraud.[29] Some Ibero-American Civil Code have expressly mentioned that such positive inducement consist in the representation of

---

[23] Kramer & Probst, *supra* note 2, at 88, para. 180; Mexico: León Tovar, *supra* note 1, at 81; Spain: Llobet I Aguado, *supra* note 20, at 136.

[24] *See* Argentina Art. 934 CC; Brazil Art. 146 CC; Chile Art. 1458 para. 2 CC; Colombia Art. 1515 para. 2 CC; Ecuador Art. 1501 para. 2 CC; El Salvador Art. 1329 para. 2 CC; Honduras Art. 1561 CC; Nicaragua Art. 2470 para. 2 CC; Paraguay Art. 291 para. 2 CC; Peru Art. 211 CC; Spain Art. 1270 para. 2 CC; Argentina: Alterini, *supra* note 2, at 366; Guatemala: Aguilar Guerra, *supra* note 1, at 267; Costa Rica: Brenes Cordoba, Trejos & Ramírez, *supra* note 1, at 83; Nicaragua: Herrera Espinoza *et al.*, *supra* note 2, at 10.9; Spain: Llobet I Aguado, *supra* note 20, at 136.

[25] *See for example* the definition under Peru Art. 211 CC; Spain: Llobet I Aguado, *supra* note 20, at 136.

[26] *See for example* Argentina Art. 932 CC; Guatemala Art. 1262 CC; Mexico Arts. 1816, 1817 CC; Portugal Art. 253 (1) CC; Spain Art. 1270 CC; Guatemala: Aguilar Guerra, *supra* note 1, at 266.

[27] ICC Final Award Case 13184 *Lex Contractus* CISG and Mexican Law as supplementary law.

[28] Argentina: Alterini, *supra* note 2, at 366; Argentina Arts. 931, 933 CC refer to positive fraud and negative fraud respectively; Costa Rica: Brenes Cordoba, Trejos & Ramírez, *supra* note 1, at 81; Nicaragua: Herrera Espinoza *et al.*, *supra* note 2, at 10.9.

[29] Argentina: Alterini, *supra* note 2, at 366.

untruth facts as true or in hiding the truth.[30] However, most of the Civil Codes simply refer to fraud without referring to fraudulent means[31] or merely mention them in general terms.[32] Such general terms seem to share the view that any active behaviour includes insidious words, artifices, ingenuity or intrigues deployed to induce the other party to enter into a contract.[33]

Fraud may also occur through inaction as expressly stated in many Ibero-American Civil Codes.[34] This fraudulent behaviour usually 'materialised' in the form of silence or in the failure to disclose relevant information.[35] On this issue, a Mexican Collegiate Tribunal[36] explained that there exists reticence (*conclusive silence*) when one of the parties do not communicate to the other party facts which are unknown by the latter but that were known by the previous, who, knowing them, would have not concluded the contract under the terms agreed. Such reticence causes the rescission of the contract if the same induces to mistake.[37] In the case at hand, the seller omitted to inform the buyer that he did not possess the property title of the immovable goods. For the Tribunal, it is obvious that the seller induced the buyer to mistake, since the seller knew that the buyer intended to acquire the goods through a loan, and in order to get a loan the buyer needed the property title of the immovable goods. Equally, if the buyer had known that the seller did not have the document representing the goods he would have not entered into the transaction.[38]

In this regard, one may distinguish between *conclusive silence* and *mere silence*.[39] The type of silence usually called *conclusive* communicates a meaning

---

30 Argentina Art. 931 CC; Paraguay Art. 290 CC.

31 Bolivia Art. 482 CC; Brazil Art. 145 CC; Cuba Art. 71 CC; Chile Art. 1458 CC; Colombia Art. 1515 CC; Ecuador Art. 1501 CC; El Salvador Art. 1329 CC; Mexico Art. 1816 CC; Peru Art. 210 CC.

32 Dominican Republic Art. 1116 CC; Guatemala Art. 1261 CC; Honduras Art. 1560 CC; Nicaragua Art. 2469 CC; Panama Art. 1120 CC; Portugal Art. 253 CC; Spain Art. 1.269 CC; Venezuela Art. 1154 CC.

33 Costa Rica: Brenes Cordoba, Trejos & Ramírez, *supra* note 1, at 82.

34 Argentina Art. 933 CC; Brazil Art. 147 CC; Honduras Art. 2469 para. 2 CC; Paraguay Art. 290 CC; Peru Art. 212 CC; Portugal Art. 253 (1) CC *contrario sensu*.

35 Bolivia Supreme Court, *Sala Civil* 1, 29 September 2004, *Marcial Xavier Pérez y otra v. Teddy Mercado Mendoza:* considering that the seller would have shown good faith if the contract has manifested the real state of the vehicle, fact that would have fundamentally influenced the decision of the buyers to acquire it.

36 Referring to a provision of the Civil Code of the State of Jalisco (one of the 31 Federated States of Mexico).

37 Mexico Collegiate Tribunals, *Novena Época*, Registry 172'151, SJF XXV, June 2007, at 1170.

38 *Id.*

39 Spain: A. Martínez Cañellas, *El incumplimiento esencial del contrato de compraventa internacional de mercaderías*, Doctoral thesis, Universitat de les Illes Balears, Facultat de Dret. Àrea de Dret mercantil Palma de Mallorca 179 (2001), http://www.tdx.cat/TDX-0308105-

while the *mere silence* simply denotes the lack of any communications.[40] An example of *conclusive silence* may take place during the negotiations for the sale of goods affected by intellectual property rights when the buyer requests the seller to confirm that such goods are free from any right or claim of a third party and the seller remains silent. After the conclusion of the contract, the buyer realises that he is not able resell the merchandise without an expensive licence granted by a third party holding the patent's rights. The distinction has practical implications since the *conclusive silence* may constitute fraud irrespective of any duty to disclose, while mere silence, (*e.g.* the buyer did not mentioned anything), may only violate the duty to disclose information.[41]

Finally, one party's fraudulent conduct cannot be presumed, but it has to be proven by the induced party.[42]

3. Duress

There are different ways in which improper pressure can be exercised by one party over the other.[43] Violence as means of pressure can take the form of physic or moral force.[44] Some Civil Codes expressly recognised two modalities of pressure by distinguishing between *violence* as physical force and *threats* as moral force.[45] Hence, threats to cause serious harm is also recognised as

095856.; Spain: Llobet I Aguado, *supra* note 20, at 142; Kramer & Probst, *supra* note 2, at 94, para. 194.

[40] Kramer & Probst, *supra* note 2, at 94, para. 194.

[41] *See* Spain: Martínez Cañellas, *supra* note 39, at 179; Spain Supreme Tribunal, 24 April 2009, *Id Cendoj:* 28079110012009100358; *see also* Ch. 27, 3.

[42] Brazil Art. 147 CC; Chile Art. 1459 CC; Colombia Art. 1516 CC; Ecuador Art. 1502 CC; El Salvador Art. 1330 CC; Spain Art. 1214 CC; Spain: Llobet I Aguado, *supra* note 20, at 187.

[43] Many Ibero-American legal systems have related the concept of duress with notions of violence or force. Violence: Bolivia Art. 477 CC; Dominican Republic Art. 1111 CC; Guatemala Art. 1264 CC; Honduras Art. 1558 CC; Mexico Art. 1819 CC; Nicaragua Art. 2468 CC; Panama Art. 1118 CC; Peru Art. 214 CC Spain Art. 1.267 CC; Venezuela Art. 1150 CC. Force: Argentina Art. 936 CC; Colombia Art. 1513 CC; Chile Art. 1456 CC; Ecuador Art. 1499 CC; El Salvador Art. 1327 CC; Paraguay Art. 293 CC.

[44] Not to be equate to *fuerza irresistible* (irresistible force) which amount to *vis absoluta*. It refers to less coercive physical violence that vitiates a contracting party's consent but does not impede it; *see* Argentina: Alterini, *supra* note 2, at 369; Bolivia: Carrillo Aruquipa, *supra* note 2, at 408-409; Guatemala: Aguilar Guerra, *supra* note 1, at 270; Costa Rica: Brenes Cordoba, Trejos & Ramírez, *supra* note 1, at 74; Peru: Castillo Freyre, *supra* note 2, at 58.

[45] Argentina Art. 937 CC; Guatemala Art. 1264 CC; Honduras Art. 1558 CC; Mexico Art. 1819 CC; Nicaragua Art. 2468 CC; Peru Art. 214 CC; Panama Art. 1118 CC; Spain Art. 1258 CC; Argentina: Alterini, *supra* note 2, at 367; Guatemala: Aguilar Guerra, *supra* note 1, at 267, 268; Nicaragua: Herrera Espinoza *et al.*, *supra* note 2, at 10.19.

conduct that vitiates one party's intent.[46] But threats should not be mistaken for a mere warning that does not have any influence on the future harm.[47]

Not every minor pressure exercised over a party will amount to duress and entail the voidability of the contract. Thus, some minimal standards have been introduced by the Ibero-American laws in order to preserve the security of legal transactions.[48] An objective approach is taken by the Mexican Civil code which does not focus on the subjective fear found in the party but on whether the threat entails a danger to his life, honour, freedom, health or patrimony.[49]

Some Ibero-American laws have established objective standards mitigated by subjective casuistic considerations. One group of countries first evaluate whether a party entered into a contract due to some reasonable and well-founded fear, justified by the nature and the gravity of evil.[50] The circumstances surrounding the case and the personal characteristics of the party should be considered in the evaluation of the existence of reasonable and founded fear.[51] Under other countries' laws, the duress must be of a nature susceptible to impress a *reasonable person*, who *fears* to get exposed or to expose his belongings before such present and *significant evil*.[52]

The exploitation of a contracting party's necessity does not constitute duress. In the Ibero-American laws, duress must arise from human behaviour in contrast to circumstantial pressure that arises from a natural state of necessity.[53] A group of countries lead by the Chilean Civil Code have clearly expressed that pressure may be performed by any person.[54] While in a second group including Portugal and Mexico the human element is implied from

---

46 Bolivia Art. 841 CC; Cuba Art. 72 CC; Mexico Art. 1819 CC; Mexico: Leon Tovar, *supra* note 1, at 81-82; Bolivia Supreme Court, *Sala Civil, Erwin Antelo Justiniano v. Luis Fernando Antelo López*: the respondent, a buyer who had acquired the property using threats that gave to him unfair advantages was forced to give the property back and to paid the damages caused to the seller.

47 Kramer & Probst, *supra* note 2, at 191, para. 395.

48 Regarding the standards imposed by different codes and the doctrinal comments *see* Argentina: Alterini, *supra* note 1, at 968; Guatemala: Aguilar Guerra, *supra* note 1, at 268-270; Costa Rica: Brenes Cordoba, Trejos & Ramírez, *supra* note 1, at 75; Nicaragua: Herrera Espinoza *et al.*, *supra* note 2, at 10.19.

49 Mexico Art. 1819 CC; Mexico: León Tovar, *supra* note 1, at 81.

50 Argentina Arts. 937, 937 CC; Brazil Arts. 151, 152 CC; Panama Art. 1118 CC; Paraguay Art. 293 CC; Peru Arts. 215, 216 CC; Honduras Art. 1558 CC; Nicaragua Art. 2468 CC; Spain Art. 1267 CC.

51 Argentina: Alterini, *supra* note 2, at 968; Costa Rica: Brenes Cordoba, Trejos & Ramírez, *supra* note 1, at 75; Nicaragua: Herrera Espinoza *et al.*, *supra* note 2, at 10.19.

52 Bolivia Art. 478 CC; Chile Art. 1456 CC; Colombia Art. 1513 CC; Dominican Republic Art. 1112 CC; Ecuador Art. 1499 CC; El Salvador Art. 1327 CC; Guatemala Art. 1265 CC; Venezuela Art. 1151 CC (*persona sensate*).

53 Argentina: Alterini, *supra* note 2, at 368; Nicaragua: Herrera Espinoza *et al.*, *supra* note 2, at 10.19.

54 Chile Art. 1457 CC; Colombia Art. 1514 CC; Ecuador Art. 1500 CC; El Salvador Art. 1328 CC.

terms such physic force or *threats*.[55] They confirm that the pressure necessarily relates to a person's behaviour. However, some scholars consider that violence can come from external circumstances such as force majeure: facts that create a situation affecting one party's will. The party who exploits the other party's necessity can exercise pressure in a decisive moment.[56]

In summary, for duress to exist, there must be a casual link between the coercive behaviour exercised by one party and the coerced intent of the other party to enter into a contract. Nevertheless, a first link must be established between the improper behaviour and the fear caused to the victim, while the second link required is between the victim's fear of imminent evil and his decision to conclude the contract.[57]

---

55 Bolivia Art. 479 CC; Cuba Art. 72 CC; Mexico Art. 1819 CC; Paraguay Art. 293 CC; Portugal Arts. 255 (1), 256 CC.

56 Costa Rica: Brenes Cordoba, Trejos & Ramírez, *supra* note 1, at 71.

57 Kramer & Probst, *supra* note 2, at 219, para. 443.

Chapter 24

Consequences Invalidity and Voidability

1. Invalidity

The contract whose cause or object is affected by illegality or immorality is invalid. When accessory clauses are affected, the contract will remain valid and the illegal or immoral clauses will be invalid.[1] For example, an illicit and thus a wholly invalid contract would be the one under which the parties agree on the sale and purchase of human organs or culturally protected pieces, whereas an exorbitant penalty clause would be invalidated while the rest of the contract remains valid.[2]

The invalidity affecting the illegal or immoral transactions is absolute.[3] This means that the invalidity can be raised by any person, whether or not a party to the contract (including the State),[4] who holds a legitimate interest in it, either because the contract injures it or because the invalidity of the same would profit from it.[5] Judges or arbitrators may also find an agreement

1 *See* expressly Bolivia Art. 550 CC; Mexico Art. 2238 CC; Paraguay Art. 365 CC; Peru Art. 224 CC; Argentina: G.A. Borda, Manual de Contratos 92 (2004).

2 *See* Ch. 50, 5.1.1.7.

3 Argentina Art. 1044 CC; Bolivia Art. 549 (3) CC; Chile Art. 1682 CC; Colombia Art. 1741 CC; Costa Rica Art. 835(1) CC; Ecuador Art. 1725 CC; Mexico Art. 2225 CC; Peru Art. 219 (3)(4)(5) CC; Paraguay Art. 357 (b) CC; Uruguay Art. 1560 CC; *see* Bolivia: R. Carrillo Aruquipa, Lecciones de Derecho Civil, Obligaciones 424, 42 (2008); Latin America: F. Hionestrosa, Validez e Invalidez del Contrato en el Derecho Latinoamericano, *in* El Contrato en el Sistema Jurídico Latinoamericano, Vol. I, 199, at 214 (1998); Spain: F. Infante Ruiz & F. Oliva Blázquez, *Los Contratos Ilegales en el Derecho Europeo*, 3 InDret 1, at 23 (2009).

4 The term in Spanish is *Ministerio Público*.

5 Argentina Art. 1047 CC; Bolivia Art. 551 CC; Brazil Art. 168 CC; Chile Art. 1683 CC; Colombia Art. 1742 CC; Costa Rica Art. 837 CC; Ecuador Art. 1726 CC; El Salvador Art. 1553 CC; Mexico Art. 2226 CC Peru Art. 220 CC; Paraguay Art. 359 CC; Uruguay Art. 1561 CC; El Salvador Supreme Court, *Cass civ, Sociedad Antonio Comandari Hijos Y Compañía v. BENDECK, et al.*, 93-C-2006, 14 March 2007: noting that the non-related persons to the

illegal or immoral *ex officio*, *i.e.* without it being pleaded by a party.[6] Absolute invalidity means that the illegal and immoral transaction is not limited by a time period in which to bring the claim before a competent court, and that parties to the transaction are unable to cure the invalidity by endorsement or substantiation of the transaction.[7] Parties who entered into a contract aware of its invalidity may be prevented from raising the invalidity of the transaction as a defence.[8] Furthermore, a clause or agreement under which any of the parties purportedly waive a right to seek the invalidity of the illegal or immoral transaction is itself considered illegal.[9]

2. Voidability

In the Ibero-American legal systems a legally relevant mistake, the substantial fraud or duress affecting one party's intent results in the voidability of the contract.[10] Voidability, in this sense, means that the contract is effective and valid but is later rescinded.[11] In this basis, a contract can only be rescinded with a legal action brought by the aggrieved party followed by the declaration of rescission by the competent judge.[12] Consequently, neither the other party

contract which are affected by the *vice absoluta* can claim the rescission of the contract if they hold a legitimate interest.

6 Argentina Art. 1047 CC; Bolivia Art. 551 CC; Chile Art. 1683 CC; Colombia Art. 1742 CC; Costa Rica Art. 837 CC; Ecuador Art. 1726 CC; Peru Art. 220 CC; Paraguay Art. 359 CC; Uruguay Art. 1561 CC.

7 Argentina Art. 1047 CC; Bolivia Arts. 552, 553 CC; Chile Art. 1683 CC (only after 10 years); Colombia Art. 1742 CC (only after 10 years); Costa Rica Art. 837 CC; Ecuador Art. 1726 CC (only after 15 years); Peru Art. 220 CC; Uruguay Art. 1561 CC (only after 30 years).

8 Argentina Art. 1047 CC; Chile Art. 1683 CC; Colombia Art. 1742 CC; Ecuador Art. 1726 CC; Peru Art. 222 CC; Uruguay Art. 1561 CC.

9 *See* expressly Chile Art. 1469 CC; Ecuador Art. 1512 CC.

10 The Spanish terms contained by the Ibero-American Civil Codes to denote voidability are *anulidad* or *nulidad relativa*; *see* Argentina Art. 1045 CC; Bolivia Art. 554 (4, 5) CC; Brazil Art. 171 (2) CC; Chile Art. 1682 para. 3 CC; Colombia Art. 1741 para. 2 CC; Ecuador Art. 1725 para. 3 CC; El Salvador Art. 1552 para. 2 CC; Guatemala Art. 1303 CC; Honduras Art. 1587 CC; Mexico Art. 2228 CC; Nicaragua Art. 2202 para. 1 CC; Paraguay Art. 357 (c) CC; Peru Art. 221 para. 2 CC; Portugal Arts. 254, 287 CC; Spain Art. 1.300 CC; Venezuela Art. 1146 CC; Mexico Collegiate Tribunals, *Novena Época*, Registry 182'396, SJF XIX, January 2004, at 1535: confirming that vices in intent affect the contract with *vice* relative.

11 Argentina Art. 1046 CC; Cuba Art. 74 CC; Chile Art. 1687 CC; Paraguay Art. 356 para. 2 CC.

12 Argentina Art. 1048 CC; Brazil Art. 177 CC; Chile Art. 1684 CC; Colombia Art. 1743 para. 1 CC; Ecuador Art. 1727 CC; El Salvador Art. 1554 CC; Guatemala Arts. 1309, 1310 CC; Mexico Art. 2230 CC; Peru Art. 222 CC; Venezuela Art. 1.146 CC; Spain Art. 1.302 CC; *see* E. A Kramer & T. Probst, *Defects in the Contracting Process*, *in* A.T. von Mehren (Ed.), International Encyclopedia of Comparative Law, Vol. VII Contracts, Ch. 11, 136, para. 281

nor third parties can seek the declaration of rescission.[13] This is contrary to the remedy of invalidity that may be invoked by non-related persons to the contract as it aims to protect the general interest of society.[14]

On the other hand, the party whose intent is defective is not obliged to proceed actively against the other party. It may be the case that the affected party prefers to exercise his right passively, as a defence.[15] For example, when one party claims the performance of obligations under the sales of goods contract, the affected party could simply invoke his right of voidability in order to be released from his contractual obligations.

In addition, some Ibero-American legal systems expressly grant the possibility of partial rescission which can lead to judicial modification of the contractual terms to fit the circumstances.[16] This is based on the assumption that parties to the contract would still want to maintain the rest of the contract provided it is feasible and fair under the circumstances.[17]

2.1. Rectification and Confirmation

There is also the possibility of subsequent rectification of the mistake, as well as the possibility of confirmation of the vitiated contract by fraud or duress.[18] The right of the affected party to confirm or validate the contract comes from the same right to claim the rescission.[19] Unlike the requirement of a court judgment in cases of rescission, confirmation of a vitiated contract is made by unilateral declaration.[20] It is made either expressly or tacitly,[21] *e.g.* conclusive

(1999): the judge cannot raise the issue of voidability *propio mutuo* because it is not the judge's job to avoid the contract if such is not requested by the affected party.

13 Bolivia Supreme Court, *Sala Civil*, *Rosalina Rodríguez Vega de Villarroel v. Félix Tapia Villarroel y otros*: upholding that the law grants the remedy to persons with legitimate interest such as the party in a contract who seeks its nullity.

14 *See supra* 1.

15 Argentina Art. 1058 bis CC; Bolivia Art. 557 CC; Panama Art. 1153 CC; Portugal Art. 287 para. 2 CC; Venezuela Art. 1.346 para. 3 CC.

16 Brazil Art. 184 CC; Guatemala Art. 1308 CC; Mexico Art. 2238 CC Peru Art. 224 para. 1 CC; Portugal Art. 292 CC.

17 Kramer & Probst, *supra* note 12, at 136, para. 281.

18 *See for example* Brazil Art. 169 CC; Guatemala Art. 1301 CC; Mexico Collegiate Tribunals, *Novena Época*, Registry 182'396, SJF XIX, January 2004, at 1535: confirming that the transactions affected by *vice relativa* are susceptible to be rectified or confirmed by the affected party. This possibility does not exist for contracts affected by invalidity, *see supra* 1.

19 Bolivia Art. 558 para. 1 CC; Brazil Art. 172 CC; Chile Art. 1684 CC; Colombia Art. 1743 para. 1 CC; Ecuador Art. 1727 CC; El Salvador Art. 1554 CC; Mexico Art. 2233 CC; Panama Art. 1146 CC; Paraguay Art. 366 CC; Peru Art. 230 CC; Portugal Art. 288 CC; Spain Art. 1311 CC; Venezuela Art. 1.351 CC.

20 Argentina Art. 1054 CC; Panama Art. 1147 CC; Paraguay Art. 370 CC; Spain Art. 1312 CC; Venezuela Art. 1.351 para. 1 CC.

21 Brazil Arts. 173, 174 CC; Chile Art. 1693 CC; Colombia Art. 1752 CC; Ecuador Art. 1737

confirmative acts performed by the affected party while being conscious of the vitiated contract.[22]

In this regard, some Ibero-American Civil Codes have established formal requirements such as, an in writing confirmation[23] or the requirement to follow the formalities established for the conclusion of the contract.[24] The confirmation makes the contract effective retroactively and thus binding on both parties from the time of its conclusion.[25]

2.2. Time Limits

Rescission for defects in consent must be invoked within a certain period. The period may begin to run from the time the mistake was discovered, or discoverable, or from the conclusion of the contract, despite the fact the mistaken party was or was not aware of the mistake.[26] Regarding fraud, some laws fix the starting point in conjunction with a future event such as the time of discovery of the deception, while others refer to a past event such as the conclusion of the contract irrespective of any future contingency. The length of the limitation period also varies from country to country.[27] With regard to duress, all codes establish a relative limitation period, which runs from the moment the duress ceases.[28]

CC; El Salvador Art. 1564 CC; Guatemala Art. 1304 CC; Peru Arts. 230, 231 CC; Spain Art. 1.311 CC; Kramer & Probst, *supra* note 12, at 1143, para. 295.

22 Chile Art. 1695 CC; Colombia Art. 1754 CC; Ecuador Art. 1739 CC; El Salvador Art. 1566 CC; Guatemala Art. 1304 CC; Mexico Art. 2234 CC; Venezuela Art. 1.351 para. 2 CC; Mexico Collegiate Tribunals, *Novena Época*, Registry 187'474, SJF XV, March 2002, p. 1395: confirming that the mistake induced by fraud is also susceptible to be expressly or impliedly confirmed; ICC Final Award Case No. 13184 *Lex Contractus* CISG and Mexican Law as supplementary law: the Tribunal considered that the conduct of the innocent party when learning of the deception of the other party was important pursuant to Art. 1823 of Mexico's Civil Code. The Claimant learnt of the deception regarding the terms of the clause at dispute at the middle of the ten-year distribution agreement, and instead of raising any objection the claimant's immediate response was to seek to preserve the contractual relationship.

23 Argentina Art. 1061 CC: writing requirement for express confirmation; Peru Arts. 230, 232 CC; Venezuela Art. 1.351 para. 1 CC.

24 Chile Art. 1694 CC; Colombia Art. 1753 CC; Ecuador Art. 1738 CC; El Salvador Art. 1565 CC; Guatemala Art. 1305 CC; Paraguay Art. 368 CC; Peru Art. 232 CC; Venezuela Art. 1.351 para. 1 CC.

25 Argentina Art. 1065 CC; Bolivia Art. 558 para. 3 CC; Guatemala Art. 1307 CC; Mexico Art. 2235 CC; Panama Art. 1148 CC; Paraguay Art. 371 CC; Portugal 288 para. 4 CC; Spain Art. 1313 CC.

26 *See* Ch. 60, 2.

27 *Id.*

28 *Id.*

3. Effects of Rescission

3.1. Invalidity

The more common approach is that the invalidity does not deprive the contract of effects until such time as it is declared invalid by a judge.[29] In the context of the illegal and immoral sales contract, this means that the property of the goods passes from seller to the buyer at the time of contract conclusion, but is later considered to have never passed if the invalidity is declared. Under the Paraguayan law, however, the invalid contracts have no effect even when the invalidity has yet to be declared by the judge.[30]

The effects of the invalidity declaration place the parties in the situation they were, as if the contract was never concluded.[31] Hence, for example, the property of the goods automatically falls back to the seller. The parties are ordered to give back their respective performances together with the fruits and interest, provided both parties are unaware of the illegality of the transaction, otherwise only the party unaware of such a situation can get back his performance.[32]

3.2. Voidability

Rescission on the grounds of voidability for mistake, fraud or duress also has a retroactive effect. The parties must be restored to the position they were before the conclusion of the contract. Thus, the parties must return their respective

---

[29] Bolivia Art. 547 CC; Mexico Art. 2226 CC; Peru Art. 222 CC; Spain Art. 1303 C; Bolivia: Carrillo Aruquipa, *supra* note 3, at 425; Mexico: S. León Tovar, Los Contratos Mercantiles 78 (2004); Spain: Infante Ruiz & Oliva Blázquez, *supra* note 3, at 26.

[30] Paraguay Art. 356 CC.

[31] Bolivia: Carrillo Aruquipa, *supra* note 3, at 425; Latin America: Hionestrosa, *supra* note 3, at 218; Mexico: León Tovar, *supra* note 29, at 78; Spain: Infante Ruiz & Oliva Blázquez, *supra* note 3, at 27.

[32] Bolivia Art. 965 CC; Chile Arts. 1468, 1687; Costa Rica Art. 844 CC; Ecuador Arts. 1511, 1731 CC; Uruguay Art. 1565 CC: all the codes previously mentioned expressly state such effect provided both parties are unaware of the illegality of the transaction, otherwise only the party unaware of such situation can get back his performance; Argentina Art. 1050 CC; Mexico Arts. 2226, 2239 CC; Peru Art. 222 CC; Paraguay Art. 361 CC; Spain Art. 1303 CC; Spain: Infante Ruiz & Oliva Blázquez, *supra* note 3, at 27.

performances,[33] whenever the contract was performed.[34] The Ibero-American jurisprudence indicates that where a sales contract has been declared rescinded the buyer is under the obligation to return the goods to the seller,[35] and the latter to reimburse the payment;[36] unless restitution is materially or legally impossible either because the goods have been completely lost or destroyed, or because they have become goods out of commerce by law.[37]

The parties must also return the benefits they had obtained from the rescinded contract. Thus, the seller not only has an obligation to reimburse the price he received,[38] but he must also pay the interest on the purchase price from the date of payment.[39] On the other hand, the buyer must not only make restitution of the goods but also of all benefits that he obtained from the goods. These benefits include the natural fruits *i.e.* the products derived from the goods themselves; or the indirect fruits of the goods, *e.g.* the money earned out of hiring or licensing the reproduction of the goods.[40] The seller is also entitled to compensation for the deterioration of the goods caused by the buyer from the time he received the goods, and the buyer may be reimbursed the improvements made to the goods.[41]

---

[33] Argentina Art. 1052 CC; Brazil Art. 182 CC; Cuba Art. 71 CC; Chile Art. 1687 CC; Colombia Art. 1746 para. 1 CC; Ecuador Art. 1737 CC; El Salvador Art. 1557 CC; Guatemala Art. 1314 CC; Mexico Art. 2239 CC; Panama Art. 1154 CC; Paraguay Art. 361 CC; Portugal Art. 289 para. 1 CC; Spain Art. 1303 CC; Bolivia Supreme Court, *Sala Civil*, *Erwin Antelo Justiniano v. Luis Fernando Antelo López*: the respondent, a buyer who had acquired the property using threats which gave to him unfair advantages was forced to give the property back and to paid the damages caused to the seller.

[34] If the contract is rescinded before any performance neither party is under the duty to perform; *see* Bolivia 547 para. 1 CC.

[35] Bolivia Supreme Court, *Sala Civil*, *Erwin Antelo Justiniano v. Luis Fernando Antelo López*: the respondent, a buyer who has acquired the property using threats that gave to him unfair advantages was forced to give the property back and to paid the damages caused to the seller; Peru Supreme Court, *Sala civil transitoria*, Resolution 000070-2001, 25 April 2002.

[36] Peru Supreme Court, *Sala civil transitoria*, Resolution 000070-2001, 25 April 2002.

[37] Mexico Collegiate Tribunals, *Novena Época*, Registry 184'840, SJF XVII, February 2003, p. 1103.

[38] Chile Supreme Court, RDJ, Vol. 42, Sec. 1, at 282 *cited in* Chile: R. Díez Duarte, La Compraventa en el Código Civil Chileno 123, n. 345 (1993).

[39] Chile Supreme Court, RDJ, Vol. 78, Sec. 2, at 1, *cited in* Chile: Díez Duarte, *supra* note 38, at 328, n. 911 & RDJ, Vol. 72, Sec. 1, at 65, *cited in* Chile: Díez Duarte, *supra* note 38, at 332, n. 927; Peru Supreme Court, Resolution 000070-2001, *Sala civil transitoria*, 25 April 2002; Spain Art. 1303 CC; Spain: Infante Ruiz & Oliva Blázquez, *supra* note 3, at 27.

[40] Argentina Art. 1053 CC; Chile Art. 1687 CC; Colombia Art. 1746 para. 1 CC; Ecuador Art. 1737 CC; El Salvador Art. 1557 CC; Guatemala Art. 1315 CC; Mexico Art. 2240 CC; Panama Art. 1154 CC; Paraguay Art. 361 CC; Portugal Art. 289 para. 1 CC; Spain Art. 1303 CC; Spain: Infante Ruiz & Oliva Blázquez, *supra* note 3, at 27.

[41] Chile Art. 1687 CC; Colombia Art. 1746 para. 1 CC; Ecuador Art. 1737 CC; El Salvador Art. 1557 CC; Guatemala Art. 1316 CC.

According to the Argentinean law, the restitution of price's interest must be calculated from the day in which the sum of money was paid, and the restitution of the fruits shall take place from the date the productive goods were delivered.[42] In Mexico, the same interest and fruits are not due until the date when the claim was submitted before a court or tribunal.[43]

It is important to point out that, in cases of reciprocal fraud, *i.e.* the case where each party is deceived by the other, the Ibero-American legal systems has taken the view that neither of the parties is entitled to claim the rescission of the contract.[44] Except for the Civil Code of Portugal, according to which each party is entitled to void the contract.[45]

4. Damages

The aggrieved party will normally suffer some loss and consequently will seek to obtain compensation for damages.[46] Following the doctrine of *culpa in contrahendo,* the Spanish doctrine and the jurisprudence have sustained that the damages for invalidity or voidability allow the aggrieved party (in good faith) to recover all the expenses he incurred in the conclusion of the contract and all the alternative business opportunities he gave up in reliance of the contract.[47]

However, it may also be possible that the aggrieved party chooses to confirm the contract but to keep his right to claim damages.[48] Though most of the Civil Codes do not expressly mention this option, the fact that these remedies are separated and independent from each other validates the view that the confirmation of the contract when such is possible, does not entail the

42 Argentina Art. 1054 CC.

43 Mexico Art. 2240 CC.

44 Expressly mentioned Mexico Art. 1817 CC; Peru Art. 213 CC; Spain Art. 1.270 CC; Impliedly mentioned by Chile Art. 1458 CC; Guatemala Art. 1262 CC.

45 Portugal Art. 254 para. 1 CC.

46 Chile Art. 1687 CC; Colombia Art. 1746 para. 1 CC; Ecuador Art. 1737 CC; El Salvador Art. 1557 CC; Portugal Art. 227 CC; Bolivia Supreme Court, *Sala Civil*, *Erwin Antelo Justiniano v. Luis Fernando Antelo López:* the respondent, a buyer who acquired the property using threats that gave to him unfair advantages was forced to give the property back and to paid the damages caused to the seller; Spain: J. Llobet I Aguado, El Deber de Información en la Formación de los Contratos 183 (1996).

47 Spain: Llobet I Aguado, *supra* note 46, at 184; Spain: Infante Ruiz & Oliva Blázquez, *supra* note 3, at 31: referring to scholars such as García Rubio and Asúa Gonzalez and to the decision of the Spanish Supreme Tribunal dated 2 June 2000. On the concept of *reliance interest see* Ch. 28, 2.1.

48 Expressly mentioned Brazil Art. 175 CC.

loss of the right to claim damages.[49] Some authors maintain that, in case of contract confirmation, damages may be available on the positive interest.[50]

[49] Spain: Llobet I Aguado, *supra* note 46, at 183; Kramer & Probst, *supra* note 12, at 166, para. 345.

[50] Spain: Llobet I Aguado, *supra* note 46, at 184. On the concept of *expectation interest see* Ch. 28, 2.2.

CHAPTER 25

GROSS DISPARITY

1. General Remarks on Gross Disparity

In many Ibero-American legal systems the remedy of rescission or voidability on the basis of gross disparity in a sale of goods' contract is not longer inaccessible.[1] A group of civil codes do permit rescission based on gross disparity only in two cases, namely in cases of contracts under guardianship and for absentees.[2] Others have expressly withdrawn the possibility to claim the rescission of sales of movable goods,[3] while in others rescission is inaccessible regardless of the type of goods.[4] Finally, some legal systems that under some circumstances may grant the remedy for C2C sales, expressly exclude the B2B contracts from such remedy.[5] In the end, the remedy of rescission or voidability of sales of goods on the basis of gross disparity is only available in Argentina, Bolivia (excluded B2B), Brazil, Honduras, Mexico (excluded B2B), Paraguay, Peru and Portugal.[6]

These Ibero-American laws address the issue of gross disparity under the doctrine of *lesión*. The latter has its origins in the Roman Law institution

[1] To *see* the linguistic difference between rescission and voidability in this context *see infra* 3.

[2] Cuba Art. 76 CC; Spain Art. 1.291 CC; Venezuela Art. 1.350 CC; Uruguay Art. 1277 CC only for testamentary partition.

[3] Chile Art. 1891 CC & Art. 126 Com C; Colombia Art. 1949 CC; Ecuador Art. 1858 CC & Art. 163 Com C.

[4] Nicaragua Art. 2562 CC; El Salvador Art. 1686 CC.

[5] Bolivia Art. 825 Com C; Mexico Art. 385 Com C; Spain Art. 344 Com C; Uruguay Art. 196 Com C; Bolivia: V. Camargo Marín, Derecho Comercial Boliviano 406 (2007); Mexico: S. León Tovar, Los Contratos Mercantiles 169 (2004); Mexico: O. Vásquez del Mercado, Contratos Mercantiles 208 (2008).

[6] Argentina Art. 954 CC; Bolivia Art. 561 CC; Brazil Art. 157 CC; Honduras Art. 753 CC; Mexico Art. 2228 CC; Paraguay Art. 671 CC; Peru Art. 1447 CC; Portugal Art. 282 CC.

of *leasio enormis* introduced by the Justinian's code.[7] Under this doctrine the strict Roman Law principle of freedom of contract was softened by allowing one party, who had sold land for less than half of its real price, could claim rescission of the sale on the grounds of *leasio enormis*.[8] The Roman jurisprudential practice soon after extended the remedy to other kinds of contracts; including the sale of movable goods.[9] The reason underlying this doctrine was that a contract could be rescinded whenever the reciprocal contractual obligations of the parties were grossly disproportionate.[10] This conception was inherited by the Ibero-American Civil Codes from *Las Siete Partidas* and the French Civil Code of 1804.[11]

In modern practice, gross disparity permits the rescission or modification of the contract when the expected equal relationship between the parties has been disrupted at the time of the conclusion of the contract. However, gross disparity is not directly related to any defect or vice in the parties' intent.[12] Its purpose is NOT to protect one of the contracting parties' free and informed will but rather to safeguard the legal order against the pernicious social effects of unfair dealings.[13]

In this regard, the Peruvian Supreme Court held that the institution of gross disparity represents a limitation to the principle of freedom of contracts, which aims to keep in line the common balance of every *onerous* and commutative contracts.[14]

2. Test Elements

The orthodox concept of gross disparity was based on the contract's substantive unfairness. A first model to ascertain the degree of fairness or unfairness of the contractual terms presupposes the existence of a reliable objective parameter

---

7 Spain: R. Álvarez Vigaray & R. De Aymerich, La Resición por Lesión en el Derecho Civil Español Común y Floral 1 (1989): explaining that although most scholarship studies trace the doctrine of *leasio enormis* back to *lex secunda* of the Justinian's code, the truth is that such doctrine was already applied in Roman law of the Classical Period; R. Zimmermann, The Law of Obligations – Roman Foundations of the Civilian Tradition 259 (1990).

8 Spain: Álvarez Vigaray & De Aymerich, *supra* note 7, at 16; Zimmermann, *supra* note 7, at 262.

9 Zimmermann, *supra* note 7, at 262.

10 *See* E.A. Kramer & T. Probst, *Defects in the Contracting Process*, *in* A.T. von Mehren (Ed.), International Encyclopedia of Comparative Law, Vol. VII Contracts, Ch. 11, 182, para. 376 (1999).

11 *See Partida V, Title V, Law LVI*; France Art. 118 CC: lesion vitiates the contract with respect to contracts with incapables and land.

12 Except for Mexico's Civil Code Art. 2230 which categorise lesion as one of the vices of consent; *see also* Mexico: León Tovar, *supra* note 5, at 169.

13 Kramer & Probst, *supra* note 10, at 184, para. 379.

14 Peru Supreme Court, *Sala civil permanente,* Resolution 001253-2004, 9 August 2005.

alone, namely the price. This model is still present in a group of the Ibero-American Civil Codes.[15] As mentioned, the remedy is not anymore available for the sale of goods under these codes. But as an example of an objective measurement of the disparity, under these laws a seller is granted the remedy whenever the price he receives is less than half the fair price of the property sold at the conclusion of the contract.[16] Reciprocally, a buyer is entitled to rescind the sale when the fair price of the property at the time of conclusion, is less than half the price he paid by the buyer.[17] The price received or given is considered on its own.

However, this objective measurement did not always produce the *best* or *fair* outcome, as it could be that a low price could bring some benefit to both parties. Considering this, some Ibero-American legal systems, which still make the remedy available, have added additional criteria to the price:[18] the inexperience or necessity of the aggrieved party.[19] The idea is that unless one of the parties is in a weak or disadvantageous position, the law should not interfere with the contract.

This approach also requires some abuse of the disadvantageous position of one of the parties, namely exploitation.[20] For example, Argentina and Bolivia's law establish that an imbalanced contract may be rescinded "[...] provided that the lesion results from the exploitation of urgent needs, carelessness or ignorance of the affected party."[21]

Also worthy to note is that in addition to the exploitation element and weak position of the aggrieved party, some of these laws have objectively established a presumption of gross disparity based on fixed percentages regarding the real value of the obligation,[22] while others only refer to apparent or manifest disproportion.[23]

In a case decided by the Bolivian Supreme Court it was first established that 50% of the market price of the goods paid by the buyer was indeed

---

15 Chile Art. 1888 CC; Colombia Art. 1946 CC; Ecuador Art. 1855 CC.

16 Chile Art. 1889 CC; Colombia Art. 1947 CC; Ecuador Art. 1856 CC.

17 Chile Art. 1889 CC; Colombia Art. 1947 CC; Ecuador Art. 1856 CC.

18 Kramer & Probst, *supra* note 10, at 182, para. 377.

19 Ibero-American Civil Codes normally would give to the weaker party, affected by necessity, lightness, inexperience, extreme need, or misery, the option to file a claim for rescission or modification; *see for example* Argentina Art. 954 CC; Bolivia Art. 565 (I)I CC; Portugal Art. 283 (I) CC; Peru Supreme Court, *Sala civil permanente,* Resolution 001253-2004, 9 August 2005.

20 Argentina Art. 954 CC; Bolivia Art. 561 CC; Brazil Art. 157 CC; Honduras Arts. 753, 754 CC; Paraguay Art. 671 CC; Peru Art. 1447 CC; Portugal Art. 339 CC.

21 Argentina Art. 954 CC; Bolivia Art. 561 para. I CC; Bolivia Supreme Court, *Sala Civil, Julia Fernández Aparicio v. Isidro Soruco Fernández.*

22 Bolivia Art. 563 para. II CC: 50% less of the real value of the obligation; Honduras Art. 754 CC: 50% less of the real value of the obligation; Peru Arts. 1447, 1448 CC: from 40% up to 60% less of the real value of the obligation for cases of urgent need.

23 Argentina Art. 954 CC; Bolivia 561 para. I CC; Paraguay Art. 671 CC.

disproportionate. Subsequently, the court confirmed that the conditions under which the seller had signed the contract, this is, taken out from hospital by his son (the buyer) before the end of medical treatment, affected the seller with urgency and ignorance of the terms of the contract.[24]

For either the value assessment, the modification or the readjustment of the parties' reciprocal obligations, the Ibero-American Civil Codes go back to the time of the conclusion of the contract.[25] The disproportion must also be present at the time of claim filed by the aggrieved party.[26]

At an international level, modern uniform instruments such as the UNIDROIT PICC have equally combined the requirement of gross disparity in parties' obligations with the abusive conduct of one party over the disadvantageous position of the other.[27]

3. Rescission or Voidability of the Contract

Under most of the Ibero-American legal systems gross disparity gives a right to rescind the contract. Some of the laws use the term *rescisión* to describe the remedy granted for cases of lesion.[28] Others use the term *voidability*.[29] Some laws normally make the linguistic distinction in Spanish or Portuguese because these remedies originate from different contractual situations. One is based on fraud, mistake or duress that originates from a defect in the contracting process while the other aims to remedy the monetary harm caused by the unfair dealing.[30] Nevertheless, in practice their effects are similar. Both have a retroactive effect, which means that whenever it is possible the parties must be restored to the position they were before the conclusion of the contract.[31] The parties must return their respective performances.[32]

---

[24] Bolivia Supreme Court, Sala Civil, *Julia Fernández Aparicio v. Isidro Soruco Fernández.*

[25] Argentina Art. 954 CC; Bolivia Art. 563(3) 565(I) CC; Brazil Art. 157 paras. 1, 2 CC; Honduras Arts. 754, 755 CC; Paraguay Art. 671 CC; Peru Art. 1449 CC. Under Peru Arts. 1450, 1451 CC the readjustment of the value can be spontaneously made by the defendant.

[26] Argentina Art. 954 CC; Paraguay Art. 671 CC.

[27] *See* Art. 3.10 PICC; Spain: L. Alvarado Herrera, *in* D. Morán Bovio (Ed.), Comentario a los Principios de Unidroit para los Contratos del Comercio Internacional, Art. 310, 1, at 203 (2003).

[28] Bolivia, Honduras and Peru, in Spanish *rescisión*. For an etymological reference of the term rescission *see* Argentina: M.U. Salermo, Contratos Civiles y Comerciales 241 (2007).

[29] Argentina, Mexico and Paraguay, in Spanish *anulidad*. Brazil and Portugal in Portuguese *anulação*; El Salvador Supreme Court, *Cass civ, Contreras Castro v. Garza Heredia,* 247-C-2004, 5 May 2005: explaining that 'rescission' and 'voidability' are both terms used to describe the so called relative invalidity.

[30] Kramer & Probst, *supra* note 10, at 184, para. 379.

[31] *See* Ch. 24. *See also* Argentina: Salermo, *supra* note 28, at 243.

[32] Argentina Art. 1052 CC; Brazil Art. 182 CC; Cuba Art. 71 CC; Chile Art. 1647 CC; Colombia Art. 1746 para. 1 CC; Ecuador Art. 1737 CC; El Salvador Art. 1557 CC; Guatemala

The limitation period to claim the remedy varies from country to country, ranging from six months to two years.[33]

Art. 1314 CC; Mexico Art. 2239 CC; Panama Art. 1154 CC; Paraguay Art. 361 CC; Portugal Art. 289 para. 1 CC; Spain Art. 1303 CC.

[33] Bolivia Art. 564 CC (2 years); Honduras Art. 756 CC (1 year); Peru Art. 1454 CC (6 months): Peru Supreme Court, *Sala civil permanente*, Resolution 001253-2004, 9 August 2005: upholding that under Peruvian Law there are two different limitation periods: 1) Six month limitation period for cases in which the infringing party has performed his obligation starting to count from the time of performance or; 2) Two years limitation period for cases in which the infringing party has NOT performed his obligation, in which case the period starts running from the time of contract conclusion.

Chapter 26

Dispute Resolution Clauses

1. Admissibility

1.1. Choice of Court Clauses

Most Ibero-American legal systems expressly allow the contracting parties to agree on a forum selection clause in order to determine where to settle their present or future contractual disputes.[1] An exception is Uruguay, where parties may not modify the rules that determine the competent jurisdiction.[2] The Uruguayan rules on competent jurisdiction establish that the competent courts to settle disputes arising from international matters shall be those of the place to which the rules on the applicable law point to or, at the claimant's option, the courts at the respondent's domicile.[3] As mentioned, the Uruguayan law does not allow the parties to choose the applicable law to their contractual relations.[4] Consequently, the competent courts for matters concerning the existence, validity, nature and effects of contracts shall be those of the place where they are to be performed, as pointed out by the conflict rules.[5]

---

1 Argentina Art. 1 CPCC; Brazil Art. 12 Introductory Law CC & Arts. 88, 111 CPC; Mexico Art. 23 CPCC; Peru Art. 25 CPC & Art. 2060 CC; Portugal Art. 65 (A) CPC; Spain Art. 22 (2) OL; Venezuela Art. 47 IPL; Argentina National Commercial Court of Appeals, *Quilmes Combustibles, S.A. c.Vigan, S.A,* 15 March 1991: only in international transactions.

2 Uruguay Art. 2403 CC (Appendix of the Civil Code).

3 Uruguay Art. 2401 CC (Appendix of the Civil Code).

4 *See* Ch. 3, 1.2.

5 Uruguay Art. 2399 CC (Appendix of the CC).

1.2. Arbitration Agreements

In the area of international commercial arbitration the freedom of choice of the mechanism of arbitration is provided and acknowledged by domestic laws,[6] and international instruments such as New York Convention[7] and the Panama Convention,[8] both of which all the Ibero-American countries have adopted.[9]

On this issue, an ICC Arbitral Tribunal dismissed the respondent's allegation as to the lack of arbitration agreement among the parties, based on the fact the parties had failed to execute an agreement that is subsequent to the arbitration agreement and is mandatory under Argentine arbitration law (*compromiso*). The Tribunal held that pursuant to the New York Convention, which has been ratified by Argentina, the agreement to submit future disputes to arbitration must be enforced without the requirement of passing a subsequent arbitration agreement or *compromiso*.[10]

The forum or place of arbitration elected could be connected or unconnected to the dispute or the defendant. The parties may consider important to choose a truly neutral forum for disputes arising out of their contractual relationship. They may also wish to take advantage of the special expertise of judges in a particular court or of the arbitration law in the seat. Then, whether or not a nexus exists between the dispute or the defendant and the forum chosen, the Ibero-American legal systems recognises the validity of forum selection clause or arbitration agreement in the area of contracts.[11]

1.3. Unenforcement

The reason used by the Ibero-American courts for refusing to enforce an exclusive choice of court or arbitration agreements would usually be based on public policy. This may be done either at the jurisdictional stage or at the recognition and enforcement stage. At the jurisdictional stage, the court may

---

6 Argentina Art. 736 CPCC; Brazil Art. 3 AL; Mexico Art. 1416 Com C; Peru Art. 2064 CC & Art. 1 AL; Portugal Art. 1 AL; Spain Art. 2 (1) AL; Venezuela Art. 3 AL; Venezuela Supreme Tribunal, Judgment 82, *Cass*, file 00-423 of 8 February 2002.

7 Art. II NY Convention.

8 Art. 1 Panama Convention.

9 All Ibero-American countries are member States of the NY Convention; *see* http://www.uncitral.org/uncitral/en/uncitral_texts/arbitration/NYConvention_status.html All the Latin American countries have adopted the Panama Convention; *see* http://www.oas.org/juridico/english/sigs/b-35.html.

10 ICC Final Award Case No. 11949 *Lex Contractus* Argentinean Law, Seat of Arbitration Buenos Aires, Argentina.

11 El Salvador Supreme Court, Civil Appeal, *Cuéllar Vásquez v. Estado de El Salvador, como sucesor de ANTEL*, 46-AP-2005, 5 December 2006; Peru Supreme Court, *Sala civil transitoria,* Resolution 005192-2006, 21 July 2008: acknowledging the Constitutional freedom to agree on arbitration as the mechanism to settle any dispute arising from a contractual relationship.

decide that the forum selection clause which points to another forum is invalid for public policy reasons.[12] Under the same basis, the validity of the arbitration agreement could be challenged before the arbitral tribunal or the competent court at the place of arbitration.

In a case subjected to an ICC Arbitral Tribunal, the respondent sustained that the subject matter of the dispute (applicability of the Argentinean Emergency Legislation) was a public order issue and therefore could not be submitted to arbitration. The Tribunal dismissed such allegation considering that an arbitral tribunal cannot be automatically deprived from its jurisdiction because of the public order nature of a statute which it needs to analyze or apply.[13]

At the recognition and enforcement stage, the competent court may hold that no execution of the foreign judgment or award is possible because such is contrary to the principles of public policy of the country.[14] Frequently the public policy reasons for invalidating choice of court clauses are related to a concern over unequal bargaining power.[15]

2. Special Form Requirements

2.1. Choice of Court Clauses

While some Ibero-American laws require the forum selection clauses to be in writing,[16] others have recognised the possibility to impliedly agree on the jurisdiction of a court. This is simply done by voluntary submission of the defendant or appearance of the plaintiff before a court; by means of filing a claim or responding to one without any objection as to the jurisdiction of the court.[17]

---

[12] *See for example* Peru Art. 2060 CC.

[13] ICC Final Award Case No. 11949 *Lex Contractus* Argentinean Law, Seat of Arbitration Buenos Aires, Argentina.

[14] Brazil Superior Tribunal of Justice, REsp 3.035/EX, Registry 2008/0044435-0, Minister Fernando Gonçalves, 20 May 2009: dismissing the challenge to the foreign award enforcement. In the Superior Tribunal's view the choice of Swiss Law as the applicable substantive law to the contract and the Arbitral Tribunal subsequent decision to apply the CISG as integral part of the Swiss National Law did not oppose the Brazilian Public Order; despite the fact that Brazil is not a CISG Member State (November 2009), regardless of whether the application of the CISG resulted from the application of the Conflict of Law rules or the from the parties' direct choice, because the possibility is in line with Brazil Art. 2 AL.

[15] *See* Argentina National Commercial Court of Appeals, *Quilmes Combustibles, S.A. c. Vigan, S.A,* 15 March 1991; Brazil Superior Tribunal of Justice, AgRg no Ag 637639/RS, Minister Aldir Passarinho Junior, published 9 May 2005.

[16] Brazil Art. 111 CPC; Venezuela Art 44 PIL.

[17] Mexico Art. 23(I)(II)(III) CPC; Argentina Art. 2 CPCC; Peru Art. 26 CPC; Spain Art. 22(2) CC; Venezuela Arts. 44, 45 IPL.

2.2. Arbitration Agreements

Regarding international commercial arbitration, both the New York Convention and the Panama Convention establish some formal requirements for the validity of arbitration agreements. Under Article 1 of the Panama Convention the agreement shall be set forth in an instrument signed by the parties, or in the form of an exchange of letters, telegrams, or telex communications. The same requirement is provided in Article II (2) of the New York Convention only with the historical omission of telex communications.

Similarly, those Ibero-American countries who have adopted the MAL require the agreement to be in writing.[18] For these laws the requirement is met when such is contained in a document signed by the parties or in an exchange of letters, telex, telegrams or other means of telecommunication providing a record of the agreement, or in an exchange of statements of claim and defence in which the existence of an agreement is alleged by one party and not denied by another.[19]

To date, only Peru has incorporated into his arbitration law the amendments made to the MAL in 2006.[20] One of the changes included concerns the special formal requirement of the arbitration agreement. The *in writing* requirement has been completely extended, so that, although there is no previous agreement, if one of the parties submits a dispute to one or more arbitrators who accepts it and the other party afterwards also accepts to submit it, there is a valid arbitration agreement.[21]

The Argentinean domestic arbitration law imposes further special form requirements.[22] Agreements must be formalised in public or private deeds containing the date, name and domicile of the contracting parties; also the name and domicile of arbitrator unless a third party is nominated to appoint them;[23] the issues submitted and their circumstances; and the penalty to be paid by the party who refuses to comply with the agreement.[24]

On this issue, an ICC Arbitral Tribunal, in partial award on its jurisdiction, acknowledged that the Argentinean law indicates that any arbitration agreement or arbitration clause shall be in writing. However, the ratification of the New York Convention and the Panama Convention by Argentina gives

---

18 Mexico Art. 1423 Com C; Spain Art. 9 AL; Venezuela Arts. 5, 6 AL.

19 ICC Final Award Case No. 13184 *Lex Contractus* CISG and Mexican Law as supplementary law; seat of arbitration Mexico: the Arbitral Tribunal noted that, although respondent raised jurisdictional objections at the outset of the proceedings, respondent later waived those objections when executing the Terms of Reference.

20 *See* the MAL with amendments at http://www.uncitral.org/pdf/english/texts/arbitration/ml-arb/07-86998_Ebook.pdf.

21 Peru Art. 10 AL.

22 *See* Argentina Art. 740 CPCC.

23 Argentina Art. 743 CPCC.

24 *Id.*

more flexibility to international arbitration than to domestic arbitration. In international commercial arbitration the 'in writing' requirement is met when such is contained in a document signed by the parties, or in the form of an exchange of letters, telegrams, or telex communications. Accordingly, the Tribunal upheld that the exchange of communications between the parties by others means of telecommunication providing a record of the arbitration agreement is in accordance with both Conventions and creates a valid arbitration agreement.[25]

[25] ICC Preliminary Award on the Jurisdiction of the Arbitral Tribunal Case No. 12231 *Lex Contractus* Argentinean Law, Seat of Arbitration Buenos Aires, Argentina.

Part 5

Pre-Contractual Liability

Chapter 27

Pre-Contractual Duties

1. General Remarks on Pre-Contractual Duties

All the Ibero-American laws recognise the freedom of the parties to enter into negotiations, to decide on the terms to negotiate and for how long to continue with their efforts to reach an agreement.[1] This is in consonance with the principle of freedom of contract.[2] However, the parties' freedom is limited. At a pre-contractual stage, parties have to comply with fundamental principles of fair dealing and good faith.[3]

2. Good Faith in Negotiations

It is a common principle in all the Ibero-American laws to require contracts to be concluded in good faith.[4] This has been broadly interpreted to mean that at a pre-contractual stage parties shall conduct themselves in accordance to the principle of good faith.[5] Portugal's Civil Code expressly dictates such

[1] Argentina: G. Sozzo, Antes del contrato: los cambios en la regulación jurídica del período precontractual 108 (2005); Mexico Collegiate Tribunals, Registry 177335, SJF XXII, September 2005, at 1436.

[2] *See generally* Ch. 3.

[3] Chile: J. Lopez Santa Maria, Los Contratos: Parte General, Vol. 2, n. 600 (2005); Colombia: J. Oviedo Alban, La Formación de Contrato: tratos preliminares, oferta, aceptación 10 (2008); Spain: J. Llobet I Aguado, El Deber de Información en la Formación de los Contratos 14 (1996).

[4] Argentina Art. 1198 CC; Bolivia Art. 465 CC & Art. 803 Com C; Brazil Art. 422 CC; Chile Art. 1546 CC; Colombia Art. 1603 CC & Art. 863 Com C; Cuba Art. 6 CC; Ecuador Art. 1589 CC; El Salvador Art. 1417 CC; Guatemala Art. 17 JOL; Mexico Art. 1796 CC; Paraguay Art. 689 CC; Peru Art. 1362 CC; Portugal Art. 227 CC; Spain Art. 1258 CC & Art. 57 Com C; *see also* Chile: Lopez Santa Maria, *supra* note 3, at n. 595*bis*.

[5] *See* ICC Final Award Case No. 11404 *Lex Contractus* Argentinean Law: stating that during

obligation.[6] A breach to the duty during negotiations and at the time of contract formation engenders liability on the breaching party.[7]

Nevertheless, what does the good faith obligation specifically require? While for some scholars the duty only requires the parties to negotiate with clear and trusty voices,[8] others sustain that it also imposes the obligation to not abandon negotiations unexpectedly or arbitrary.[9] This last sub-duty is not expressly contained in the Ibero-American laws;[10] however, academic works[11] and the jurisprudence[12] have often defended its existence and application.

The UNIDROIT PICC acknowledge both requirements in international commercial contracts. Under their provisions, "[...] a party who negotiates or breaks off negotiations in bad faith is liable for the losses caused to the other party."[13] Bad faith conduct also includes to enter into negotiations and to continue with them without a real intention of concluding a contract with the other party.[14] However, the duty not to abandon negotiations arbitrarily would always depend on the circumstances of the case. In particular, the extent to which the other party, because of the breaching party, has reasons to rely on the positive outcome of the negotiations and on the number of points over which an agreement had already been reached.[15]

For some, the abuse of the reasonable reliance, generally, supposes that the parties have been negotiating for sufficient time so that some trust is already built among them.[16] Thus, the duty of good faith cannot be said to be contravened

---

negotiations the parties were under the obligation to abide by the rules of good faith. This is the general rule in all pre-contractual legal relations; Argentina National Commercial Court of Appeals, *Sala* A, *Pelisch, Juan y otro v. Imago Producciones, S.R.L. y/u otro,* 11 June 1974.

6 Portugal Art. 227 CC.

7 *See generally* Ch. 28.

8 Argentina: F. López de Zavalia, Teoria de los Contratos, Vol. 1, 295 (2003); Chile: Lopez Santa María, *supra* note 3, at n. 598.

9 Argentina: A.A. Alterini, Contratos civiles, comerciales, de consumo 330 (1998); Argentina: Sozzo, *supra* note 1, at 108; Spain: Llobet I Aguado, *supra* note 3, at 18.

10 Argentina: Sozzo, *supra* note 1, at 110; Spain: Llobet I Aguado, *supra* note 3, at 18.

11 Colombia: Oviedo Albán, *supra* note 3, at 24; Guatemala: V. Aguilar Guerra, El Negocio Jurídico 288 (2004); Spain: Llobet I Aguado, *supra* note 3, at 18, 19.

12 *See* Argentina National Chamber of Civil Appeals, *Sala A*, 3 August 1960, *cited in* Chile: I.M. Zuloaga Rios, Teoría de la responsabilidad precontractual: aplicaciones en la formación del consentimiento de los contratos 185 (2007); Chile Court of Appeals of Concepción, 6 June 1996, *cited in* Zuloaga Rios, *id.*, at 188; Mexico Collegiate Tribunals, Registry 177335, SJF XXII, September 2005, p 1436; Portugal Supreme Tribunal of Justice, 2 May 1981.

13 Art 2.1.15 (2) PICC.

14 Art 2.1.15 (3) PICC.

15 M.J. Bonell, The Unidroit Principles in Practice: Caselaw and Bibliography on the Unidroit Principles of International Commercial Contracts, Art. 2.1.15, at 140 (2006); *see also* Ch. 11.

16 Argentina: Sozzo, *supra* note 1 at 110; Spain: Llobet I Aguado, *supra* note 3, at 20; Spain: P. Perales Vizcasillas, *in* D. Morán Bovio (Ed.), Comentario a los Principios de Unidroit para los Contratos del Comercio Internacional Art. 2.15, 2.a, at 150 (2003): commenting on and comparing to the domestic Spanish law; Chile Court of Appeals of Concepción, 6 June 1996,

at an early stage, when the contacts just began. The duty can only be breached at an advanced stage of negotiations that is characterised for its permanence and also for the considerable amount of contacts or approaches already made between the parties.[17] On the other hand, an advanced stage of negotiations may not be required for certain types of contracts. Namely, contracts where the breaching party approaches the offended party aggressively; *e.g.* consumer and adhesions contracts.[18] This standard also seems adequate for B2B negotiations where a considerable amount of assets are needed before closing the deal.

In addition, it is required to identify the cause of the break off in negotiations. A distinction should be made between situations where the interruption is due to voluntary acts and those derived from objective circumstances that may affect the future contract.[19] In the first case, one would need to evaluate how justified or unjustified it was for the reticent party to abruptly stop negotiating; *e.g.* production shortcuts, financial situation, *etc.* In the second case, one must identify whether objective events reasonably prevent the reticent party to continue negotiating; *e.g.* special laws just enacted, court orders, *etc.*[20] In brief, these assessments are directed to ensure that the disruption is not arbitrary.

In this respect, an ICC Arbitral Tribunal sustained that the termination of negotiations due to impossibility to reach a common understanding on the future agreement is not *per se* an indication of bad faith.[21] In the case at hand, both parties submitted that an agreement on the future contract was reached during X meetings on Y dates. After these meetings, both parties prepared their own draft of the agreement and claimed that it corresponded to the agreement reached on the said meetings. However, the drafts prepared by the parties were very different to each other. The Arbitral Tribunal could not find evidence that the respondent's conduct was the cause of such difference and that such conduct constitutes a violation of good faith.[22]

cited in Chile: Zuloaga Rios, *supra* note 12, at 188; Mexico Collegiate Tribunals, Registry 177335, SJF XXII, September 2005, at 1436.

17 Spain: Ma.P. Garciá Rubio, La Responsabilidad precontractual en el Derecho Español 121 (1991).

18 Argentina: Sozzo, *supra* note 1, at 111.

19 Asúa González, *La Culpa …*, *cited by* Argentina: Sozzo, *supra* note 1, at 116, n. 24; Spain: Llobet I Aguado, *supra* note 3, at 38.

20 Asúa González, *La Culpa …*, *cited by* Argentina: Sozzo, *supra* note 1 at 116, n. 24.

21 ICC Final Award Case No. 11404 *Lex Contractus* Argentinean Law.

22 *Id.*

3. Information Duties

The duty to act in good faith comes together with the duty to inform and other related obligations.[23] The good faith principle includes every sort of values embraced by justice and which shall be protected by the parties to a contract.[24] For the Ibero-American jurist the term good faith evokes the idea of loyalty, rectitude, and correctness.[25]

The information duty consists in upholding always the truth and in the disclosure of certain facts susceptible to affect the other's party decision.[26] In particular, a party who is not in the position to conclude a contract must immediately stop the negotiations and inform the other party of the circumstances relevant to the case.[27] This, for example, could include, information about the parties' solvency to enter into the sales contract.[28]

The Ibero-American courts have upheld the principle in a number of occasions.[29] Worthy to mention is the Colombian Supreme Court decision upholding that among the duties of loyalty and correctness in negotiations there are those that require the parties to inform and declare in relation to the object, circumstances and peculiarities of the deal they want to reach and which are of great importance to achieve an agreement free of misunderstandings.[30]

Also a good example of this duty is found in the Paraguayan Civil Code, under which the party who knew, or ought to have known, the existence of an element that may cause the termination of the contract, and does not give notice of such to the other party, shall compensate for the damages caused.[31]

---

[23] Argentina: Alterini, *supra* note 9, at 330; Chile: Lopez Santa María, *supra* note 3, at n. 598; Colombia: Oviedo Albán, *supra* note 3, at 17.

[24] A duty inferred from Argentina Art. 1056 CC according to Argentina: Lopez de Zavalia, *supra* note 8, at 299.

[25] Chile: Lopez Santa María, *supra* note 3, at n. 579*bis*; Colombia: Oviedo Albán, *supra* note 3, at 12; Portugal: J. De M. Antunes Valera, Das Obrigações em Geral 268 (2003).

[26] Argentina: Alterini, *supra* note 9, at 330; Spain: Llobet I Aguado, *supra* note 3, at 42.

[27] Argentina: Lopez de Zavalia, *supra* note 8, at 299; Chile: Lopez Santa María, *supra* note 3, at n. 600.

[28] Chile: Lopez Santa María, *supra* note 3, at n. 598.

[29] *See* Spain Supreme Tribunal, 24 April 2009, *Id Cendoj:* 28079110012009100358.

[30] Colombia Supreme Court, 4 April 2001, *Cass civ*, Ministry Jorge Antonio Rugeles, *cited in* Colombia: Oviedo Albán, *supra* note 3, at 18-19.

[31] Paraguay Art. 690 CC.

However, the duty does not impose a conduct to disclose information that the other party can know by himself[32] or that it is too personal or irrelevant for the case.[33]

At a glance, the above-mentioned examples could be mistaken with cases of fraud. It has been said that fraudulent behaviour can materialise in the form of silence or in the failure to disclose relevant information.[34] However, there is a distinction between fraud made by means of *conclusive silence* and the breach of the information duty.[35] The type of silence usually called *conclusive* communicates a meaning while the *mere silence* simply denotes the lack of any communications.[36] The distinction has practical implications since the *conclusive silence* may constitute fraud irrespective of any duty to disclosed, while a *mere silence*, (*e.g.* the seller requested nothing), will only breach a duty of information.[37]

4. Confidentiality Duties

In the same way a breach of the duty to disclose results in liability, the breach of confidentially during negotiations can constitute a tort conduct.[38] Common standards would require a trusted secret to be kept confidential.[39] An opposite conduct would give rights for a tort action against the breaching party irrespective of the continuance of negotiations.[40] But also the liability could

[32] ICC Final Award Case No. 11520 *Lex Contractus* Argentinean Law: the claimant alleged that the delay in performance was attributable to the respondent's negligence in providing accurate information at the time of contract conclusion. The Tribunal declared that for any experienced contractor the elements which arguably caused the delay in performance were foreseeable and indeed respondent's duty to provide with accurate or complete information was fulfilled.

[33] Argentina: Lopez de Zavalia, *supra* note 8, at 300.

[34] *See* Ch. 23, 2.

[35] Spain: A. Martínez Cañellas, *El incumplimiento esencial del contrato de compraventa internacional de mercaderías*, Doctoral thesis, Universitat de les Illes Balears, Facultat de Dret. Àrea de Dret mercantil Palma de Mallorca 179 (2001), http://www.tdx.cat/TDX-0308105-095856; E.A. Kramer & T. Probst, *Defects in the Contracting Process*, *in* A.T. von Mehren (Ed.), International Encyclopedia of Comparative Law, Vol. VII Contracts, Ch. 11, 94, para. 194 (1999).

[36] Spain: Martínez Cañellas, *supra* note 35, at 179; Kramer & Probst, *supra* note 35, at 94, para. 194.

[37] *See* Ch. 23, 2.

[38] Argentina: Lopez de Zavalia, *supra* note 8, at 300; Chile: Lopez Santa María, *supra* note 3, at n. 600.

[39] Colombia: Oviedo Albán, *supra* note 3, at 21.

[40] The remedy can derive from *tort liability* but also from an express violation of legal provisions since many Intellectual Property and Competition Laws impose a duty of confidentiality; *see* Colombia: Oviedo Albán, *supra* note 3, at 22.

arise from contractual duties since there may be binding effects regarding some implied agreements,[41] such as the subsidiary pre-contractual conditions of confidentiality under which each party may be liable for non-performance.[42]

Though the standard of confidentiality is difficult to define, the general opinion is that it only concerns information expressly declared as confidential.[43] The UNIDROIT PICC embrace the same duty in Article 2.1.16. According to Bonell's comment, information that a party may either disclose to third persons irrespective of the conclusion of the contract cannot be considered confidential.[44] For example, information that a seller gives to his clients many times, with the intention of building some interest on the transaction, could include, technical details of production and marketing.[45] The buyer could then use such information with different sellers to induce more favourable purchase conditions.

Finally, the Brazilian Civil Code expressly refers to the parties' duty to respect, until the conclusion of the contract, as in its execution, the principle of probity.[46] Such constitutes a complementary principle of good faith, besides the principles of trust, information and loyalty. It could be said that there is no good faith without probity.[47] Parties must show to have complete and confirmed integrity and strong moral principles. Probity imposes a high standard of correct moral behaviour during negotiations.

[41] Portugal Supreme Tribunal of Justice, 23 January 2001.
[42] *See for example* Ch. 11, 3. For the importance of determining the nature of the liability arising from pre-contractual duties and its practical implications *see* Ch. 28.
[43] M.J. Bonell, The Unidroit Principles in Practice: Caselaw and Bibliography on the Unidroit Principles of International Commercial Contracts Art. 2.1.16, at 141 (2006).
[44] *Id.*
[45] *Id.*
[46] Brazil Art. 422 CC.
[47] Argentina: Sozzo, *supra* note 1 at 326.

Chapter 28

Liability for *Culpa in Contrahendo*

1. Basis for Pre-Contractual Liability

Most Ibero-American legal systems offer general pre-contractual liability provisions (*in contrahendo* liability).[1] Such liability directly or indirectly derives from the breach of good faith and related principles during negotiations.[2] Most Ibero-American authors consider that the most important role of the pre-contractual provisions is to determine if one party's conduct is in accordance to the good faith principle having regard to the level of the parties' expectations.[3]

In addition, Ibero-American scholars and courts have also submitted the thesis of *in contrahendo* in relation to the damages caused because of the conclusion of a voidable contract. For instance, in favour of the party induced to enter into the contract under fraud or duress.[4]

---

1 Argentina Arts. 934, 1056 CC; Bolivia Art. 465 CC; Brazil Art. 465 CC; Chile Art. 1558 CC; Colombia Art. 863 Com C; Ecuador Art. 1601 CC; El Salvador Art. 1429 CC; Guatemala 18 JOL & Art. 1645 CC; Mexico Art. 1796 CC; Peru Art. 1418 CC; Spain Art. 7 CC; Portugal Art. 227 CC; Paraguay Art. 690 CC.

2 Chile: I.M. Zuloaga Rios, Teoría de la responsabilidad precontractual: aplicaciones en la formación del consentimiento de los contratos 89 (2007): this good faith principle in contracts include duties of mutual collaboration, protection, information, secrecy, communication, *etc.*; Portugal: J. De M. Antunes Valera, Das Obrigações em Geral 268 (2003); *see generally* Ch. 27.

3 Colombia: J. Oviedo Alban, La Formación de Contrato: tratos preliminares, oferta, aceptación 10 (2008); Guatemala: V Aguilar Guerra, El Negocio Jurídico 279 (2004); R. Stiglitz, Tratativas Precontractuales, en Contratos, Teoria General, p 91 and Chile H. Rosende Álvarez, Responsabilidad Precontractual …, *cited by* Zuloaga Ríos, *supra* note 2, at 88, n. 115, and 91, n. 164, respectively; Portugal: Antunes Valera, *supra* note 2, at 270.

4 *See* Portugal: Antunes Valera, *supra* note 2, at 269, 270; Spain Supreme Tribunal, 24 April 2009, *Id Cendoj:* 28079110012009100358; Spain: J. Llobet I Aguado, El Deber de Información en la Formación de los Contratos 184 (1996); Spain: P. Perales Vizcasillas, *in* D. Morán Bovio (Ed.), Comentario a los Principios de Unidroit para los Contratos del Comercio Internacional

Nevertheless, there is some disagreement as to the nature of the liability; the doctrine is divided between contractual liability and tortious liability, and other types of liabilities.[5] The disagreement continues at the time of writing. The majority of the Ibero-American scholars refer to the first studies on the topic coming from European jurists, such as Ihering,[6] Fagella[7] and Saeilles[8] or from the Argentinean Brebbia,[9] to explain the different approaches of the theory.[10] The Ibero-American jurisprudence is rather uniform. Most courts support the tortious nature of the pre-contractual liability[11] and few defend the contractual nature of any *culpa in contrahendo*.[12]

Art. 2.15, 2.a, at 151 (2003): commenting on and comparing to the domestic Spanish law; Spain: F. Infante Ruiz & F. Oliva Blázquez, *Los Contratos Ilegales en el Derecho Europeo*, 3 InDret 1, at 31 (2009): referring to scholars such as M.P. García Rubio, *Responsabilidad por ruptura injustificada de negociaciones: A propósito de la Setencia (Sala 1ª) de 16 de mayo de 1988*, 4 La Ley 1112 (1989), and C.I. Asúa Gonzalez, La culpa in contrahendo: tratamiento en el derecho alemán y presencia en otros ordenamientos (1989) and to the decision of the Spanish Supreme Tribunal dated 2 June 2000; Paraguay Art. 690 CC: expressly covering information that one party ought to have known (since the party who knew, or ought to have known, the existence of an element that may cause the termination of the contract, and does not give notice of such to the other party, is liable for the damage caused).

5 Colombia: Oviedo Albán, *supra* note 3, at 26; Spain: M.P. García Rubio, La Responsabilidad precontractual en el Derecho Español 59 (1991); Guatemala: Aguilar Guerra, *supra* note 3, at 288.

6 *Ihering,* Das Schuldmoment im römischen Privatrecht, (1879). Though his theory was developed for liable conducts occurred once the offer had been received but before the contract, is interesting to *see* that the *culpa in contrahendo* for Ihering had a contractual nature.

7 *Fagella,* Dei periodi precontrattuali e della loro vera ed esatta construzione scientifica. Fagella extended the period to the negotiations stage before the emission of the offer.

8 His doctrine and as that of Ihering states that the pre-contractual liability has a contractual nature.

9 R. Brebbia, Culpa "in contrahendo". Brebbia states that the duty of diligence must exist also before the conclusion of the contract, *see* Chile: Zuloaga Rios, *supra* note 2, at 21.

10 *See for example* Argentina: G. Sozzo, Antes del contrato: los cambios en la regulación jurídica del período precontractual 17-45 (2005); Chile: Zuloaga Rios, *supra* note 2, at 19-24; Colombia: Oviedo Albán, *supra* note 3, at 25; Portugal: Antunes Valera, *supra* note 2, at 268; Spain: García Rubio, *supra* note 5, at 60-71; Guatemala: Aguilar Guerra, *supra* note 3, at 284.

11 Chile Court of Appeals of Concepción, 6 June 1996 *cited in* Chile: Zuloaga Rios, *supra* note 2, at 188; Colombia Supreme Court 11 May 1970; 28 June 1989; 27 June 1990; 12 August 2002, all *cited in* Colombia: Oviedo Albán, *supra* note 3, at 28, n. 60; Mexico Collegiate Tribunals, Registry 177335, SJF XXII, September 2005, at 1436; Paraguay Supreme Court, Judgment 45, *Bartolome Sánchez v. El Estado Paraguayo*; Portugal Supreme Tribunal of Justice, 4 April 2006; Portugal Supreme Tribunal of Justice, 13 March 2007; Spain Supreme Tribunal, *Sala* 6, 2 May 1984, RJA 1984, No. 2.950.

12 Portugal Supreme Tribunal of Justice, 23 January 2001.

1.1. Contract Approach

Under this approach, the party who negotiates in bad faith is responsible based on contractual liability. Though no contract exists at this stage, the approach is based on the assumption that either expressly or impliedly the parties have agreed to carry out negotiations with the best views to enter into a contract.[13] The abrupt break off in negotiations from one of the parties without allowing a natural end constitutes an infringement of that agreed, and thus, the rules applied are those of contractual liability.[14]

Indeed, this was the conception that Ihering had in mind.[15] He considered that any offer constitutes an implicit agreement that the contract would be concluded in normal conditions and that the duty of diligence would prevail before, and at that time. If the contract is not concluded, or it is with defects of intent., the presumption is that the duty of diligence was breached and thus the responsible party shall provide compensation for the damages caused because of his negligence.[16]

1.2. Tort Approach

In most Ibero-American legal systems, the pre-contractual liability arises from tort conducts.[17] Consequently, bad faith conduct during negotiations gives a right of compensation for damages that such conduct may cause. This approach is based on one party's wrong behaviour affecting the other party's patrimony.[18] It has nothing to do with a contractual relationship because, it has occurred before any contract has been concluded. Such responsibility simply derives from the principle of good faith that obliges any individual to act with probity and correctly, preventing them to cause damage to others.

In this regard, the Paraguayan Supreme Court has sustained that while dealing with pre-contractual relationships, it must be understood that the principles of tort liability are applied, since the current statutory legislation

---

13 Argentina: F. López de Zavalia, Teoria de los Contratos, Vol. 1, 286 (2003) referring to Fagella's theory.

14 J. Ballesteros, Instituciones de la Responsabilidad Civil, 69 *cited in* Colombia: Oviedo Albán, *supra* note 3, at 29, n. 62.

15 Ihering is himself the first defendant of this approach, *see Chile:* Zuloaga Rios, *supra* note 2, at 22.

16 *Id.*

17 *See* expressly Argentina Art. 1056 CC; Argentina: Lopez de Zavalia, *supra* note 13, at 289; Spain: Perales Vizcasillas, *supra* note 4, Art. 2.15, 2.a, at 150: commenting on and comparing to the domestic Spanish law.

18 Argentina: Lopez de Zavalia, *supra* note 13, at 289; Spain: Perales Vizcasillas, *supra* note 4, Art. 2.15, 2.a, at 150: commenting on and comparing to Spain Art. 1902 CC; Mexico Collegiate Tribunals, Registry 177335, SJF XXII, September 2005, p 1436; *see also* Ch. 55, 2.

does not contain any specific provision on the nature of pre-contractual liability.[19] This is, indeed, the current state of the majority of the Ibero-American systems.

Of course, the nature of liability may depend on whether there was a specific agreement on the way to negotiate or not. If the parties had fixed the rules of negotiations, any breach of such would amount to contractual liability.[20] If by contrast, negotiations were held spontaneously, compensation, is due based on tort liability.[21]

The distinction has practical implications concerning the extent of liability. If the nature of the liability arises from a breach of contractual obligations, the extension of compensation would include positive damages. While a tort conduct would only give grounds for compensation of negative damages.[22] A more detail description on the extent of liability is provided below in this chapter.

1.3. Legal Obligation Approach

The nature of the pre-contractual liability can also derive from an express legal obligation. This approach is taken in legal systems, which expressly or impliedly address the issue by means of legal provisions.[23] In Portugal, for example, Article 227 of the Civil Code expressly states that the parties in negotiation shall proceed, at the preliminary stage, in accordance with the rules of good faith under penalty of compensating the other party for the damages caused. The same express provision is found in Article 863 of Colombia's Code of Commerce.

2. Extent of Liability

The question of whether the Ibero-American laws grant only negative damages or also positive damages has no straightforward answer. While for the majority of scholars compensation is only granted for negative damages,[24]

[19] Paraguay Supreme Court, Judgment 45, *Bartolome Sánchez v. El Estado Paraguayo*.

[20] *See for example* Ch. 11, 3.

[21] Chile: J.A. Orrego Acuña, De la Responsabilidad Precontractual 16, http://www.juanandresorrego.cl/trabajos_publicados/pfd/articul_entheos_de_la_responsabilidad_precontractual.pdf.

[22] Colombia: Oviedo Albán, *supra* note 3, at 31.

[23] Argentina: Lopez de Zavalia, *supra* note 13, at 289, 290.

[24] Argentina: G. Sozzo, Antes del contrato: los cambios en la regulación jurídica del período precontractual 220 (2005); Chile: Orrego Acuña, *supra* note 21, at 5; Guatemala: Aguilar Guerra, *supra* note 3, at 289; Chile: Zuloaga Ríos, *supra* note 2, at 166-168: presents a list of Ibero-American authors sharing the opinion; Colombia: Oviedo Albán, *supra* note 3, at 31;

a minority consider that positive damages could also be claimed.[25] In addition, the Ibero-American jurisprudence on the topic is not consistent. Though in most courts the trend is to consider only negative damages.[26] A judgment from the Portuguese Supreme Tribunal of Justice extended the liability to positive damages.[27]

The distinction came early in time when Ihering identified two different aspects of the contract that had failed: the positive interest, which relies on the validity of the contract, and the negative interest, which relies on the invalidity, or voidability of the same.[28] On the one hand, if the contract was valid but some damages were caused what corresponds is the compensation for the damages based on the positive interest, also known as the *expectation loss* or interest; which aims to put the affected party in the position he would have been if the contract was performed. This means that compensation derives from the breach of the contract.[29] On the other hand, if the contract is invalid and damage was caused what corresponds is compensation for the damage based on the negative interest, also know as the *reliance interest*.[30]

2.1. Reliance Interest

In the Ibero-American contemporary doctrine, the position is that the affected party may only have a right to claim negative damages.[31] As mentioned, negative damages intend to place the party in the situation it was before the harmful act occurred.[32] In the context of pre-contractual liability, the affected party who had already incurred some expenses upon reliance of the negotiations

Portugal: Antunes Valera, *supra* note 2, at 271; Spain: Perales Vizcasillas, *supra* note 4, Art. 2.15, 2.a, at 151: commenting on and comparing to the domestic Spanish law.

25 *See* J.M. Aparicio, Contratos, 1 1997, *cited in* Colombia: Oviedo Albán, *supra* note 3, at 32; Spain: García Rubio, *supra* note 5, at 113.

26 Argentina National Commercial Court of Appeals, *Sala* A, *Pelisch, Juan y otro v. Imago Producciones, S.R.L. y/u otro,* 11 June 1974; Argentina National Commercial Court of Appeals, *Sala E*, *Farley, Omar D. v. LR1-Radio El Mundo*, 5 June 1996; Colombia Supreme Court, *Cass*, 23 November 1989 *cited in* Colombia: Oviedo Albán, *supra* note 3, at 33, n. 16; Mexico Collegiate Tribunals, Registry 177335, SJF XXII, September 2005, at 1436; Portugal Supreme Tribunal of Justice, decisions of 5 May 2006, 11 November 2004, 28 February 2002, 21 December 2005 and 11 September 2007; Spain Supreme Tribunal, *Sala* 6, 2 May 1984, RJA 1984, No. 2.950.

27 Portugal Supreme Tribunal of Justice, 2 May 1981.

28 Chile: Zuloaga Rios, *supra* note 2, at 25.

29 For more details *see* Ch. 50, 2.

30 Chile: Zuloaga Rios, *supra* note 2, at 25. For more details *see* Ch. 24, 4.

31 Argentina: Sozzo, *supra* note 24, at 220; Chile: Orrego Acuña, *supra* note 21, at 5; Colombia: Oviedo Albán, *supra* note 3, at 31; Guatemala: Aguilar Guerra, *supra* note 3, at 289; Portugal: Antunes Valera, *supra* note 2, at 271; Spain: Perales Vizcasillas, *supra* note 4, Art. 2.15, 2.a, at 151: commenting on and comparing to the domestic Spanish law.

32 Argentina: Sozzo, *supra* note 24, at 217.

and with the view of reaching an agreement shall be compensated the amount of money representing such expenses, and also for the loss derived from other business opportunities missed in reliance of the expected contract.[33]

These two constitutive elements of negative damages have been identified in the Ibero-American doctrine by the legal terms of *the emerging damage* and the *prevented chance* respectively.[34] Following this conceptualisation, the Ibero-American courts have granted compensation for the expenses incurred during the negotiations and for the lost business opportunities of the claimant.[35]

Hence, among the emerging damage should be calculated *e.g.* the cost for the trips, meetings, legal advice, telephone calls, and documentation produced with views of reaching an agreement.[36]

A more difficult task is to determine the prevented chance or lost opportunity. This must be only confined to the loss of other opportunities to contract with a third party. It requires then to show real evidence of parallel business chances and the real loss incurred.[37]

2.2. Expectation Loss

As before mentioned, the positive damages intend to place the party in the situation it should have been if the contract was executed.[38] It consists in repairing all the damages produced as if the contract was in execution. Such

---

[33] ICC Final Award Case No. 11404 *Lex Contractus* Argentinean Law; Argentian: Lopez de Zavalia, *supra* note 13, at 302; Argentina: Sozzo, *supra* note 24, at 217; Spain: Perales Vizcasillas, *supra* note 4, Art. 2.15, 2.a, at 151: commenting on and comparing to the domestic Spanish law.

[34] The Spanish terms are *daño emergente* and *perdida de oportunidad*. Nevertheless, there is still not uniform agreement in the doctrine to include the prevented chance within negative damages. Zuloaga Ríos presents a list of Ibero-American authors and their diverging opinions with regards to the elements constituting the negative damages in Chile: Zuloaga Rios, *supra* note 2, at 166-168. Also the following authors do not consider that the prevented chance can be claimed in pre-contractual stages: J. Mosset Iturraspe, Contratos ... at 427 *cited by* Argentina: Sozzo, *supra* note 24, at 221; Guatemala: Aguilar Guerra, *supra* note 3, at 279.

[35] Argentina National Commercial Court of Appeals, *Sala B, Muraro, Heriberto v. Eudeba, S.E.M.*, 7 February 1989; Colombia Supreme Court, *Cass*, 23 November 1989 *cited in* Colombia: Oviedo Albán, *supra* note 3, at 32, 33, n. 76; Mexico Collegiate Tribunals, Registry 177335, SJF XXII, September 2005, at 1436; Paraguay Supreme Court, Judgment 45, Bartolome *Sánchez v. El Estado Paraguayo*: though in the present case the claimant failed to prove the *emerging damage* and the *prevented chance*; Spain Supreme Tribunal, *Sala* 6, 2 May 1984, RJA 1984, No. 2.950.

[36] ICC Final Award Case No. 11404 *Lex Contractus* Argentinean Law.

[37] Spain: García Rubio, *supra* note 5, at 233; ICC Final Award Case No. 11404 *Lex Contractus* Argentinean Law: decided not to award damages for loss of chance as there was absolutely no indication on the record that such other chances existed for claimant.

[38] Argentina: Sozzo, *supra* note 24, at 217; Chile: Orrego Acuña, *supra* note 21, at 5; For more details *see* Ch. 50, 2.

remedy gives the creditor what he was counting on as if the other party had fulfilled the agreement. So far, not many Ibero-American authors,[39] and also only few cases,[40] consider that pre-contractual liability should be extended to positive damages. On the other hand, courts have been reluctant to compensate with positive damages, namely by means of loss of profits since they correspond to the idea of positive interest.[41]

39 Spain: García Rubio, *supra* note 5, at 113.

40 Portugal Supreme Tribunal of Justice, 2 May 1981.

41 Argentina National Commercial Court of Appeals, *Sala* A, *Pelisch, Juan y otro v. Imago Producciones, S.R.L. y/u otro,* 11 June 1974; Argentina National Commercial Court of Appeals, *Sala E*, *Farley, Omar D. v. LR1-Radio El Mundo*, 5 June 1996.

Part 6

Interpretation and Supplementation of the Contract

CHAPTER 29

INTERPRETATION

1. General Remarks

Under the Peruvian and the Portuguese laws, it is presumed that the declarations expressed in a contract correspond to the common will of the parties; the party who denies such concurrence must prove it.[1] Indeed, such is the approach generally taken by the Ibero-American laws. A contract reciprocally, legally and objectively performed by both of the parties does not need legal interpretation. In such cases, the intention of the parties is *prima face* correctly understood by each of them without misunderstandings or without further proof of diverging intents.

Regrettably, this is not always the case, since often the parties do not fulfil their agreements due to diverging considerations, poor drafting skills, bad counsel and all other elements causing discrepancy in parties' intentions, aspirations, ideas, etc. In such cases, adjudicatory intervention takes place in order to interpret the contract based on the intention of the parties, and other criteria.[2] The parties' right to have their contract interpreted simultaneously imposes a duty to the adjudicator.[3]

---

1 Peru Art. 1361 CC supported by Peru Supreme Court, *Sala civil permanente,* Resolution 002671-2001, 12 August 2002; Portugal Arts. 236, 238 CC supported by ICC Final Award Case No. 11570 *Lex Contractus* Portuguese Law.

2 Argentina: F. López de Zavalia, Teoria de los Contratos, Vol. 1, 422, 423 (2003).

3 Venezuela: J. Mélich-Orsini, Doctrina General del Contrato 377 (2006); ICC Final Award Case No. 13678 Lex Contractus Spanish Law: a merger clause does not impede the arbitrator from considering all other relevant circumstances in the interpretation of the contract; since the rules of interpretation of the Spanish law establish the adjudicator's duty to do so.

The Ibero-American jurisprudence[4] and the doctrine[5] have often sustained that the interpretation of a contract shall be performed only when the contract is obscure, ambiguous, or unclear, but never when the terms are clear or unequivocal.[6] From this perspective, interpretation means to discover the true meaning and effect of the unclear, obscure and ambiguous agreement.[7]

This perception has been criticised by some scholars[8] and reversed by some courts and tribunals which consider that interpretation as a mental exercise always takes place regardless of the degree of perfection of the contractual clauses; since there is always effort, knowledge and skills applied by the person before the contract.[9] El Salvador's Supreme Court has established that despite the clarity of the clauses, interpretation takes place when, for instance, the same are opposite to the contract's nature or to the manifest intent of the parties.[10] Hence, interpreting rather, means to determine under which conditions the parties entered into the contract and as well as its consequences.[11]

---

[4] Bolivia Supreme Court, *Sala Civil,* 6 February 2007, *Empresas Agrícolas Ganaderas San Jorge y Rincón Chuchío v. CITIBANK N.A. Sucursal Bolivia*; Chile Supreme Court, 10 June 1929, RDJ, Vol. 27, Sec. 1, at 365; Spain Supreme Tribunal, 2 April 1994, *Id Cendoj:* 28079110011994103098; ICC Final Award Case 11256 *Lex Contractus* Mexican Law; ICC Final Award Case 11722 *Lex Contractus* Mexican Law: "only when the words of a contract appear to contradict the evident intent of the parties will their intentions prevail"; ICC Final Award Case No. 11570 *Lex Contractus* Portuguese Law; ICC Final Award Case No. 13678 *Lex Contractus* Spanish Law: applying the rule established by Spain Art. 1281(2) CC.

[5] Argentina: R.L. Lorenzetti, Tratado de los Contratos Parte General 458 (2004); Bolivia: W. Kaune Arteaga, Curso de Derecho Civil, Contratos, Vol. 1 178-179 (1996); For a panorama of the 19th century scholars who sustained this view Chile: J. López Santa Maria, Los Contratos: Parte General, Vol. 2, nn. 640-652 (2005).

[6] The principle is known with the Latin expression *in claris non fit interpretation* embraced in Mexico Art. 1851 CC; Spain Art. 1281 (2) CC; *see* Venezuela Supreme Tribunal, Judgment 202, *Cass civ*, file 99-458 of 14 June 2000; Venezuela: Mélich-Orsini, *supra* note 3, at 409.

[7] Brazil: O. Gomes, Contratos 238 (2008); Chile Supreme Court, RLJC Vol. IV, *Código Civil*, 1 ed., 1954, at 246, No. 29 *cited in* Chile: López Santa María, *supra* note 5, at n. 655: decided that a contract with precise and clear terms cannot be subjected to the rules of interpretation contained in the Civil Code.

[8] Argentina: López de Zavalía, *supra* note 2, at 421; For an insight in the doctrine favourable to this perception *see* Chile: López Santa Maria, *supra* note 5, at n. 657; X. O'Callaghan (Ed.), Código Civil Comentado Art. 1.281, at 1264 (2004)..

[9] Chile Court of Appeals, RDJ, Vol. 44, 1947 Sec. 9, at 88, *cited in* Chile: López Santa María, *supra* note 5, n. 658; ICC Final Award Case No. 11256 *Lex Contractus* Mexican Law: explaining that the '*in claris non fit interpretation*' principle may be true *in abstracto*, "but in most of the cases where there is a dispute as to the practical effect of the application of contractual provisions to a factual situation not expressly addressed by the parties in the contract, the terms used by the parties do not offer a clear and unambiguous solution to that dispute."

[10] El Salvador Supreme Court, *Cass civ, Barahona de Renderos v. Paredes Medrano*, 80-C-2005, 18 October 2005.

[11] Bolivia: Kaune Arteaga, *supra* note 5, at 164; Brazil: Gomes, *supra* note 7, at 239; Mexico: R. Sánchez Medal, De los contratos civiles: teoría general del contrato, contratos en especial, registro público de la propiedad 75 (2002); O'Callaghan, *supra* note 8, Art. 1.281, at 1264

The different individual rules of interpretation established by the Ibero-American laws have not the same nature, nor the same function or hierarchy.[12] According to some scholars, the subjective rules of interpretation apply in preference to the rules of objective interpretation.[13] Among the subjective rules, we find those that aim to establish the concrete, effective and real intention of the parties.[14] The objective rules of interpretation, on the other hand, seek to reconstruct an ideal or abstract will of the contractors.[15] Indeed, the objective rules work also in a hierarchical order. As will be further explained, *ultima ratio* principles such as the *Contra Proferentem* and *Favor Debitoris*, operate in a subsidiary basis.

2. Intention of the Parties

Under this approach, the judge and the arbitrator are required to discover the real intention of the parties beyond the mere literal meaning of the words declared by the parties.[16] It looks to construct the internal will of the party as the original source of intent. For some scholars such involves a psychological examination of the parties' state of mind; a need to deeply penetrate into the contractor's psyche in order to discover their intentions at the time of contract conclusion.[17]

This subjective approach has rules of systematic interpretation designed to help in the interpretative task. The systematic interpretation as postulated by the Ibero-American laws is based on the need of coherence between the clauses integrating the whole agreement.[18] Every single term provides a bit

---

12 Hierarchy does not mean that some of the rules worth more than the others, but it rather means that some shall be temporarily applied first and the rest subsequently. When the adjudicator realises that certain rule is useless in the task, he should pass to the second group; *see* Uruguay: J. Rodriguez Russo, La Interpretacion del Contrato 163 (2006); *see also* the Spanish Case Law in this regard *in* O'Callaghan, *supra* note 8, Art. 1.281, at 1266, 1267.

13 Uruguay: Rodríguez Russo, *supra* note 13, at 163, n. 55; *see* 2.

14 *Id.*; Guatemala: V. Aguilar Guerra, El Negocio Jurídico 358 (2004).

15 *See* 3 & 6.

16 Argentina Art. 218 (1) Com C; Bolivia Art. 510 (1) CC; Brazil Art. 112 CC; Chile Art. 1560 CC; Colombia Art. 1618 CC; Ecuador Art. 1603 CC; El Salvador Art. 1431 CC; Guatemala Art. 1593 CC; Mexico Art. 1851 CC; Paraguay Art. 708 CC; Portugal Art. 239 CC; Uruguay Art. 1298 CC & Art. 296 (1) Com C; Bolivia Supreme Court, 28 July 2005, *Empresa DICA S.R.L. v. José Fernando Cadima Camacho*: confirming the principle with statutory and doctrinal referents; ICC Final Award Case No. 11404 *Lex Contractus* Argentinean Law: the literal wording of the MOU at stake created ambiguity with regards to its scope of application. The Tribunal made use of the rule of interpretation in Art. (1)(4) Com C; Brazil: Gomes, *supra* note 7, at 241.

17 Chile: López Santa María, *supra* note 5, at n. 625.

18 *See* Bolivia Supreme Court, *Estudio Jurídico Moreno Baldiviezo v. Prefectura de Tarija*: confirming that in the interpretation of contracts it should be considered the totality of their

of significance to the others,[19] and isolated clauses would not always reflect its authentic meaning.[20] In this regard, many Ibero-American laws call for interpreting the contract's clauses conjunctively, giving to the unclear clauses the significance resulting from the contract taken as a whole,[21] or giving to the terms the meaning that better suits the overall contract.[22]

In an ICC Arbitration governed by the Spanish law, the question arose as to whether the parties had agreed on a one-season contract with an option of renewal for a second season or whether the parties had entered into a one season contract with automatic and compulsory renewal with slightly different terms for the second season. Referring to Article 1285 of the Spanish Civil Code, the Sole Arbitrator noted that different contractual provisions advanced an interpretation in favour of the two seasons' term. Specifically, the last part of the disputed term clause in the contract established a pre-emption right given to the claimant to extend the contract for a third season. Further, two other clauses in the contract, read in conjunction, foresaw the possibility of renewal for a third season, which would make no sense if there were no automatic renewal from the first to the second season. Finally, the Sole Arbitrator considered that the two seasons' term was consistent with the negotiations between the parties prior to signing the agreement. In particular with the MOU, which was signed a month before the agreement and expressly stipulated a period of two seasons.[23]

In addition, some Civil Codes give the judge or the arbitrators certain guidelines as to the extent of interpretation they can practice. On the one hand, the judge or arbitrator shall not go further into the matters that were not included and that do not correspond to business contracted, even though

---

clauses, seeking to unveil the meaning that results from the transaction as a whole; Peru Supreme Court, *Sala civil transitoria,* Resolution 002380-2007, 12 December 2007: preventing the avoidance of the contract through a systematic interpretation of the contract which showed that no time of payment was established in the contract, hence, avoidance on the grounds of delay of payment could not work before establishing an agreed or judicially decided date of payment; Spain Supreme Tribunal, 28 July 1990, A.C. 977/1997 *cited in* O'Callaghan, *supra* note 8, Art. 1.285, at 1275.

19 Venezuela: Mélich-Orsini, *supra* note 3, at 410.

20 Uruguay: Rodríguez Russo, *supra* note 12, at 191.

21 Argentina Art. 218 (2) Com C; Bolivia Art. 514 CC; Guatemala Art. 1598 CC; Paraguay Art. 709 CC; Peru Art. 169 CC; Spain Art. 1.285 CC; Uruguay Art. 1299 CC & Art. 296 (2) Com C; ICC Final Award Case No. 13685 *Lex Contractus* Paraguayan Law: in order to unveil the meaning of an unclear clause, the Arbitral Tribunal considered a subsequent clause inserted in the same contract; basing his interpretation on Paraguay Art. 709 CC.

22 Argentina Art. 218 (2) Com C; Chile Art. 1564 para. 1 CC; Colombia Art. 1622 para. 1 CC; Ecuador Art. 1607 para. 1 CC; El Salvador Art. 1435 para. 1 CC; Uruguay Art. 1299 CC & Art. 296 (2) Com C; El Salvador Supreme Court, *Cass civ*, *Cuenca Rodríguez v. Banco Ciscatlan, S.A.*, 1732 S.S., 19 June 2004.

23 ICC Final Award Case No. 13278 *Lex Contractus* Spanish Law.

the parties used general terms to describe their obligations.[24] For example, a contract of sale where the delivery of the goods is agreed to take place at the buyer's premises cannot be interpreted as to impose to the seller the obligation to hire insurance for the merchandise up to that place.

On the other hand, in contracts providing examples with the aim of explaining certain obligations, it cannot be presumed that the parties intended to leave out situations which are not expressed within it and that naturally derive from the transaction.[25] For example, a clause in contract of sales of goods requiring the merchandise to be delivered free of encumbrances such as, for example, third parties' intellectual property rights do not release the seller from its obligation to deliver the merchandise free of any other sort of encumbrances.

3. The Reasonable Person Standard

None of the Ibero-American laws makes preference to such objective rule of interpretation. Nevertheless, Arbitral Tribunals have already applied similar principles in the interpretation of the parties' understanding of the contractual relation. For example, in one case the dispute regarded the actual agreement of what was in the Sole Arbitrator's view a non-recourse provision limiting the seller's available remedy to the recovery of goods in case the buyer failed to pay the price. The Sole Arbitrator noted that the recommendation made by the seller's lawyers not to accept the non-recourse provision must have been seriously taken into account, as it was reasonable to expect that:

> as a matter of diligent business conduct, a company entering into an important deal will view the advice of its lawyers as a serious matter. The decision, at the end, belongs to the company, yet it is reasonable to assume that the lawyers' recommendation has been given due consideration.[26]

Thus, the non-recourse provision that the seller accepted was clear and fully known to such party.

A similar standard is contained in the Argentinean and the Uruguayan laws.[27] As a principle of contract interpretation the terms in a contract shall be understood in the sense that the *general usage* gives to them despite the

[24] Bolivia Art. 515 CC; Chile Art. 1561 CC; Colombia Art. 1619 CC; Ecuador Art. 1608 CC; El Salvador Art. 1436 CC; Guatemala Art. 1594 CC; Mexico Art. 1852 CC; Paraguay Art. 710 CC; Spain Art. 1283 CC; Uruguay Art. 1305 CC; This rule is not found in the Argentinean Civil Code *see* in this regard Paraguay: M.A. Pangrazio (Ed.), Código Civil Paraguayo Comentado Art. 710, at 493 (1990).

[25] Bolivia Art. 516 CC; Chile Art. 1565 CC; Colombia Art. 1623 CC; Ecuador Art. 1604 CC; El Salvador Art. 1432 CC; Guatemala Art. 1601 CC; Paraguay Art. 711 CC; Uruguay Art. 1307 CC.

[26] ICC Partial Award Case 12949 *Lex Contractus* Mexican Law.

[27] Argentina Art. 217 Com C; Uruguay Art. 1297 CC; *see* Argentina Art. 16 CC: application

fact that one of the parties claims to have understood them differently. Only in cases of word's ambiguity, the judge or arbitrator can look at the common intention of the parties rather than to the literal sense of the terms.[28]

The 'general usage',[29] should be understood as the meaning a term has in the common language,[30] with the following exceptions: (1) when the contract or the law attributes a specific meaning; (2) when the usages and customs of the place of contract conclusion or the practices among the parties designate a particular meaning; (3) when it is about words relating to scientific, artistic or technical language which have a precise meaning.[31]

Although this objective rule triggers the section of contract interpretation in both the Argentinean Code of Commerce and the Uruguayan Civil Code, and despite the fact that Supreme Court of Uruguay has defended his priority,[32] many authors still consider that such does not constitute the first rule of interpretation. For most Uruguayan and the Argentinean scholars the first rule is still that the significance of the terms is given by the parties' subjective intention.[33]

4. Surrounding Circumstances and Subsequent Conduct

As an element of interpretation, many Ibero-American systems expressly require to take into account the parties' overall conduct and the circumstances of the contract in order to reveal the common intention of the contractors.[34] The judge and the arbitrator shall consider all the facts susceptible to make clearer the intention of the parties and the purpose of certain clauses.[35] This

of analogous principles in case of legal lacunas in the Civil Code; Argentina: López de Zavalía, *supra* note 2, at 442; Uruguay: Rodríguez Russo, *supra* note 12, at 179.

28 Argentina 218(1) Com C; Uruguay Art. 296(1) Com C; ICC Final Award Case No. 11404 *Lex Contractus* Argentinean Law: applying the rule of interpretation in Art. 218 (1)(4) Com C in order to determine the scope of application of the MOU.

29 The Spanish Word is *uso general*.

30 Argentina: A.A.Alterini, Contratos civiles, comerciales, de consumo 415 (1998).

31 Argentina: Alterini, *supra* note 30, at 415.

32 Uruguay Supreme Court, Judgment 92, 12 April 2004 *cited in* Uruguay: Rodríguez Russo, *supra* note 12, at 182, n. 48.

33 For an overview of different opinions on this issue *see* Uruguay: Rodríguez Russo, *supra* note 12, at 179-183. A rule that has a second place in the list and that seems to have a supplementary character, *see* Argentina Art. 218 (1) Com C; Uruguay Art. 1298 CC & Art. 296 (1) Com C.

34 Argentina Art. 218 (4) Com C; Bolivia Art. 510 (2) CC; Mexico Art. 1855 CC; Spain Art. 1282 CC; Uruguay Art. 1301 CC & Art. 296 (4) Com C.

35 Bolivia Supreme Court, 15 February 2005, *Alejandro Ramírez Mamani v. Guillermo Franco Gómez*: overturning the decision of the Appeal Court as the later has failed to interpret the contract due regard of the circumstances and conduct of the parties; ICC Final Award Case No. 11404 *Lex Contractus* Argentinean Law; ICC Final Award Case No. 11256 *Lex Contractus*

exercise also allows the adjudicator to define the extent of the obligations contracted.[36]

In this regard, Ibero-American scholars have recognised the difficulties in defining what should be understood as the 'circumstances'. A usual opinion calls for considering the general ambiance of the contract, the previous and concurrent facts and conduct of the parties,[37] *e.g.* talks, telephone conversations, reunions, private documents, messages, letters of intent, MOU, previous draft and negotiations, drafts, company's acts, *etc.*[38]

The latter may always be considered notwithstanding the fact that the contract may itself contain a so called 'merger clause', under which any previous negotiations in which the parties to the contract had considered different terms will be deemed superseded by the final writing.[39]

Some laws provide guidelines on the sort of facts and conduct surrounding the contractors' relationship that are to be considered in the interpretation process. For example, a contract can be interpreted based on the terms agreed to by the parties in *another* contract on the same subject.[40] In addition, the practical performance of the terms agreed which were explicitly or impliedly approved by the parties' constitute a relevant conduct in contract's interpretation.[41]

Mexican Law: the Tribunal considered the parties' negotiations, their expectations in so far as they were disclosed and the basic principle according to which any party is expected by the other to behave in good faith; ICC Final Award Case No. 13678 *Lex Contractus* Spanish Law.

36 Chile: López Santa María, *supra* note 5, at n. 632.

37 *Id.*

38 *See generally* Ch. 11; O'Callaghan, *supra* note 8, Art. 1.282, at 1272; ICC Final Award Case No. 11256 *Lex Contractus* Mexican Law: the disagreement arose on whether the contractual terms of a supply of goods contract imposed on the buyer the obligation to purchase minimum volumes of vehicles or merely provided that in case such volumes were not met, the buyer would loose its exclusivity right. The Arbitral Tribunal considered that nothing in the negotiations supported the first interpretation. On the contrary, the buyer had expressly rejected a draft according to which failure to meet the minimum volume would have been a cause for termination of the agreement for breach. Even if for a first period, termination of the agreement appeared as one of the remedies contemplated in case the buyer failed to order the minimum quantities, such remedy was deleted in the draft of a second agreement. The seller representative had received a copy of the marked draft, in which it appeared that such termination had been deleted. He also received on the same day a non-marked copy. The Tribunal considered that even if seller's representative had only received this non-marked copy such a removal could not pass unnoticed. Therefore, the seller could not argue that the parties had a different intent from the one which appears in the Agreement. Its initial intent was apparently different but the seller accepted the buyer's position that was eventually reflected in the agreement.

39 ICC Final Award Case No. 13678 *Lex Contractus* Spanish Law: upholding that such a clause does not impede the arbitrator to take into account all relevant circumstances since the arbitrator's obligation to do so is established by the rules of interpretation of Spanish Law.

40 Chile Art. 1564 para. 2 CC; Colombia Art. 1622 para. 2 CC; Ecuador 1607 para. 2 CC; El Salvador Art. 1435 para. 2 CC.

41 Chile Art. 1564 para. 3 CC; Colombia Art. 1622 para. 3 CC; Ecuador 1607 para. 3 CC;

On this issue, an ICC Sole Arbitrator considered that all the surrounding circumstances included accessory contracts signed by one of the contracting parties with third parties, having a direct relation with the implementation of the contract, as well as some press releases issued in relation to the contract.[42]

Regarding the point in time of parties' behaviours, the Spanish Civil Code expressly calls for paying attention to the parties' conduct simultaneously and subsequently to the conclusion of the contract.[43] Similarly, under the Paraguayan Civil Code, regard is to be had to their total behaviour, even after the contract conclusion.[44] In Argentina and Uruguay's law, only the subsequent conduct is to be considered.[45] Still, most scholars and the Supreme Court of Uruguay have sustained that previous and concurrent conduct influences the interpretation.[46]

In an ICC Arbitration governed by the Argentinean law, from the reading of the contract it was ambiguous which party had to bear X cost. The Tribunal decided the issue looking at the actual behaviour of the parties during the performance of the contract. The Tribunal noted that the Claimant paid the conflicting bills for more than two years without raising any objection. Further, the facts and the circumstances proved that there was never an indication of any agreement among the parties to make the respondent responsible for those charges.[47]

5. The Nature and the Type of Contract

Additionally, many Ibero-American laws call for interpreting the dubious words in a way that suits better the nature of the contract.[48] For example, in the

---

El Salvador Art. 1435 para. 3 CC; ICC Final Award Case No. 10299 *Lex Contractus* Chilean Law: applying Chile Art. 1564 CC, and from the parties' conducts, the Arbitral Tribunal was convinced that the parties were aware that the permit required by the sale/purchase agreement had not been obtained but that, as all necessary steps to obtain it had been taken, both parties were confident that the permit would be granted without a problem. Thus, the seller could not be found in breach.

42 ICC Final Award Case No. 13278 *Lex Contractus* Spanish Law: referring to Spain Art. 1282 CC.

43 Spain Art. 1282 CC. Though the Spanish Civil Code provision does not make reference to acts or conduct previous to the conclusion of the contract, these shall also be taken into account *see* O'Callaghan, *supra* note 8, Art. 1.282, at 1272.

44 Paraguay Art. 708 para. 2 CC; ICC Final Award Case No. 13685 *Lex Contractus* Paraguayan Law: basing his decision on Paraguay Art. 708 CC.

45 Argentina Art. 218 (4) Com C; Uruguay Art. 1301 CC & Art. 296 (4) Com C; ICC Final Award Case No. 11404 *Lex Contractus* Argentinean Law: applying Art. 218 (1) (4) Com C.

46 Uruguay Supreme Court, Judgment 258, 7 November 2001, *cited in* Uruguay: Rodríguez Russo, *supra* note 12, at 199, n. 118.

47 ICC Final Award Case No. 11520 *Lex Contractus* Argentinean Law.

48 Argentina Art. 218 (3) Com C; Bolivia Art. 510 (2) CC; Chile Art. 1563 (1) CC; Colombia

sale of commodity products an offered price per unit of USD 5,000.00 shall be interpreted as quoting the price of each ton rather than of each kilogram; not only because of general practice but also because of the quantitative volume of these transactions.

The type of contract shall also be considered in the interpretation process.[49] However, this does not mean that the correct interpretation of the contract shall respect the name or characterisation that the parties have given to it, since the proper name and characterisation emerges from the nature of the provisions and obligations agreed irrespective of the name assigned by the parties.[50]

An interesting case, submitted before an ICC Arbitral Tribunal applying the Brazilian law, gathered many of the elements above mentioned. In the case at hand, the parties entered into a long-term agreement (First Agreement) for the sale and purchase of iron ore FOBM (free on board at the mine) whereby the buyer was granted preferential rights to buy the surplus mine production of the seller. Four years after, following an offer to purchase the seller's surplus mine production made by a third buyer, the buyer decided to exercise its preferential rights and to buy such production from seller (Second Agreement). Before doing so the buyer requested the seller about the conditions under which the third buyer was acquiring the goods. The seller ignored the request and simply acknowledged reception of the buyer's offer to purchase and confirmed that the Second Agreement would mirror the terms of the offer available to the third buyer.[51] Although it was undisputed that the buyer was granted a preferential right on the seller's surplus production of iron ore, the dispute arose concerning the conditions of delivery of the minerals under the Second Agreement. The buyer considered that the delivery should be made, at its choice, either FOBT (free on board at the port) or FOBM (free on board at the mine), as stated in the third buyer's offer, while the seller insisted that the said delivery should be made FOBM – as stated in the First Agreement. The majority of the members of the Arbitral Tribunal decided that it was the FOBT that applies to the Second Agreement, on the grounds that (1) although the First Agreement, calling for the FOBM term, is a contract, it also allows the parties to subsequently alter its terms through subsequent agreements, (2) the buyer's right of preference under the First Agreement means, in itself, that the buyer should benefit from the same conditions of the offer as originally made to the third buyer, which included an option for the third buyer to select FOBT terms, (3) the Second Agreement is subsequent to the First Agreement

Art. 1621 para. 1 CC; Ecuador 1606 para. 1 CC; El Salvador Art. 1434 para. 1 CC; Guatemala Art. 1595 CC; Mexico Art. 1854 CC; Paraguay Art. 712 CC; Peru Art. 170 CC; Spain 1.286 CC; Uruguay Art. 1300 para. 2 CC & Art. 296 (3) Com C.

49 Bolivia Art. 510 (2) CC; Mexico Art. 1876 CC.

50 Mexico: Sánchez Medal, *supra* note 11, at 78; O'Callaghan, *supra* note 8, Art. 1.287, at 1264.

51 ICC Final Award Case No. 14375 *Lex Contractus* Brazilian Law.

and the seller could have chosen to establish the Second Agreement under a FOBM term when the buyer requested the conditions of the third buyer offer but instead leave the possibility of the FOBT terms.[52]

6. *Favor negotii*

Many Ibero-American laws recognise the principle of *favor negotii* in contract interpretation.[53] The principle is based in the historic idea of preservation of legal transactions. Such seems reasonable if one considers that parties enter into contracts with the intention of creating an effective legal relationship and not with the idea of concluding something with no effect.[54] It has been categorised as an objective rule of interpretation applied on a subsidiary basis after the subjective rules have been proved insufficient.[55]

On this basis, whenever a clause in a contract has a variety of meanings, the most favourable interpretation that produces effects shall be given.[56]

In an ICC Arbitration case governed by the Paraguayan law, the parties had opposing views as to whether a first clause in their agreement mentioning the obtaining of a bank loan by the respondent established a condition for the contract's entry into force, or whether the clause was instead an obligation imposed upon the respondent. The same contract had a second clause stating that the contract would enter into force immediately after the approval by certain government entities. Such authorisation had been proven to take place. The Tribunal reached the conclusion that interpreting the first clause as a condition for the entry into force of the contract would mean that the second clause was ineffective. Whereas interpreting the first clause as a mere

52 *Id.*

53 The principle is found in the Ibero-American doctrine with the Spanish term of "*principio de conservación del contrato*," *see for example* Guatemala: Aguilar Guerra, *supra* note 14, at 364; Mexico: Sánchez Medal, *supra* note 11, at 77; Uruguay: Rodríguez Russo, *supra* note 12, at 209; Venezuela: Mélich-Orsini, *supra* note 3, at 410.

54 Mexico: Sánchez Medal, *supra* note 11, at 77.

55 Uruguay: Rodríguez Russo, *supra* note 12, at 210; *see also* Spain Supreme Tribunal, 28 September 1997, A.C. 32/1997: establishing the same hierarchy, *cited in* O'Callaghan, *supra* note 8, Art. 1.284, at 1275.

56 Argentina 218 (3) para. 1 Com C; Bolivia Art. 511 CC; Chile Art. 1562 CC; Colombia Art. 1620 CC; Ecuador Art. 1605 CC; El Salvador 1433 CC; Guatemala Art. 1596 CC; Mexico Art. 1853 CC; Paraguay Art. 712 CC; Uruguay Art. 1300 CC & Art. 296 (3) Com C; ICC Partial Award Case No. 12949 *Lex Contractus* Mexican Law: dictating that in accordance with Mexico Art. 1853 CC "the inapplicability of the parties' covenants cannot be the preferred solution. Should a clause admit different interpretations, the interpreter has to presume that the appropriate one is that which produces an effect"; ICC Final Award Case No. 13524 *Lex Contractus* Mexican Law; Mexico Supreme Court, *Tercera Sala, Quinta Época,* SJF CXIX, at 775.

obligation upon the respondent would give full effect to both the first and the second clauses. The Tribunal decided accordingly.[57]

7. *Contra Proferentem*

The principle of *contra proferentem* is present in almost all the Ibero-American laws.[58] The ambiguous clauses established unilaterally by one of the contractors shall be interpreted in the other party's favour or against the drafter of the clause.[59] The ambiguity must be persistent and invincible, to the level that the adjudicator recognised himself incapable to penetrate the obscure contract and to unveil the true intention of the parties after he has made use of other rules of interpretation.[60]

This rule was born as an extension of the *favor debitoris* principle of interpretation. In Roman times normally the creditors imposed the terms of the contract.[61] In old Iberian law the principle was established to be applied against the seller.[62] Nowadays the rule has gained importance in the area of contract of adhesion.[63] Indeed, in Bolivia, Guatemala and Peru the *contra proferentem* rule is expressly designed to apply in cases of contracts imposing general terms by one of the parties.[64] However, the Bolivian Supreme Court has already applied the principle, by analogy, to other types of contracts.[65]

In an ICC Arbitration governed by the Portuguese law, the dispute among the parties was whether the Contract required the seller to deliver equipment which had to reach the capacity mentioned in one clause or whether the seller had to deliver equipment which had to meet the duty cycle contained in the Appendix. The buyer argued that the seller had assumed an obligation of result, *i.e.* to deliver equipment that meets the capacity. The seller argued that

[57] ICC Final Award Case No. 13685 *Lex Contractus* Paraguayan Law: using the rule set forth in Paraguay Art. 712 CC.

[58] Bolivia Art. 518 CC; Brazil Art. 423 CC; Chile Art. 1566 para. 2 CC; Colombia Art. 1624 para. 2 CC; Ecuador Art. 1609 para. 2 CC; El Salvador 1437 para. 2 CC; Guatemala Art. 1600 CC; Spain Art. 1288 CC; Paraguay Art. 713 CC; Uruguay Art. 1304 para. 2 CC.

[59] ICC Final Award Case No. 13685 *Lex Contractus* Paraguayan Law: basing decision on Paraguay Art. 713 CC.

[60] Paraguay: Pangrazio, *supra* note 24, Art. 713, at 494; O'Callaghan, *supra* note 8, Art. 1.288, at 1277: the *Contra Proferentem* is not a rule of interpretation but a solution for situations of impossible interpretation.

[61] Uruguay: Rodríguez Russo, *supra* note 12, at 231.

[62] *See* Ch. 1, 2.2.

[63] Spain Supreme Tribunal, 5 September 1991, A.C. 50/1992 & Spain Supreme Tribunal, 22 July 1992, A.C. 15/1993, both *cited in* O'Callaghan, *supra* note 8, Art. 1.288, at 1277; *see* Ch. 13.

[64] Bolivia Art. 518 CC; Guatemala Art. 1600 CC; Peru Art. 1401 CC.

[65] Bolivia Supreme Court, Sala Civil, 11 March 2002, *René Jorge Rojas y Sonia Veliz de Jorge v. Celia Veliz de Aranda*: applying the contra proferentem to monetary obligations.

the equipment actually met the duty cycle foreseen in the contract, that it never agreed to guarantee the capacity, and that if the capacity foreseen was not reached, this was due to the fact that the equipment was not correctly driven and that the complementary parts had not been correctly designed by buyer. The Sole Arbitrator acknowledged that the contract was unclear on this point. After due consideration, the Arbitrator found that the contract was to be construed in the way proposed by the seller, since the requirement was drafted by the buyer and even gave instructions to the seller on the calculation of the duty cycle. If the buyer had wanted the seller to guarantee a certain performance, it should have included a clause clearly setting out such an obligation, and the parameters and conditions under which the performance had to be reached; but the buyer had failed to do so.[66]

8. *Favor Debitoris*

This principle has inspired many of the Latin American laws and has become a common component of the system of contracts in the region.[67] After the *contra proferentem* principle the *favour debitoris* stands as an *ultima ratio* rule,[68] in case none of the subjective or objective rules of interpretation serve in the interpretation process, as expressly stated by the Spanish Code of Commerce.[69] According to this principle, the ambiguous clauses shall be interpreted in favour of the debtor[70] or at least in a less onerous manner to the debtor.[71]

The principle is based on the idea that in the adjudicator's dilemma between jeopardizing the interest of the creditor, by interpreting the debtor's obligation in a restrictive manner, and jeopardizing the interest of the debtor, by interpreting the creditor's rights extensively, the logic indicates that the adjudicator must choose to cause less harm by reducing the rights of the creditor and the obligations of the debtor.[72]

---

66 ICC Final Award Case No. 11367 *Lex Contractus* Portuguese Law.

67 Argentina: Lorenzetti, *supra* note 5, at 34.

68 In our opinion the logical hierarchy requires to apply first the *contra proferentem* rule and after the rule of *favor debitoris,* as such is the order established in Chile Art. 1566 1 CC; Colombia Art. 1624 CC; Ecuador Art. 1609 CC; El Salvador 1437 CC; *see also* on the hierarchy of the interpretation rules Uruguay: Rodríguez Russo, *supra* note 12, at 163, 222.

69 Spain Art. 59 Com C; Chile: López Santa María, *supra* note 5, at n. 701.

70 Argentina Art. 218 (7) Com C; Chile Art. 1566 para. 1 CC; Colombia Art. 1624 para. 1 CC; Ecuador Art. 1609 para. 1 CC; El Salvador 1437 para. 1 CC; Guatemala Art. 1602 CC; Spain Art. 59 Com C; Uruguay Art. 1304 para. 1 CC & Art. 296 (7) Com C.

71 Paraguay Art. 714 CC.

72 *A. Sacchi*, Interpretatione, 402 *cited in* Uruguay: Rodríguez Russo, *supra* note 12, at 224.

9. Equity

Also in case of doubt or uncertainty, some laws establish that onerous contracts[73] shall be interpreted in a sense in which the equity of the obligations prevails or the maximum reciprocity of interests is guaranteed.[74]

[73] Onerous contracts are those which involve payment in consideration such as the sale or the barter.

[74] Argentina Art. 218 (3) sentence 2 Com C; Bolivia Art. 517 CC; Mexico Art. 1857 CC; Paraguay Arts. 712, 714 CC; Spain Art. 1289 CC; Portugal Art. 237 CC; Uruguay Art. 296 (3) Com C; Bolivia Supreme Court, 28 July 2005, *Empresa DICA S.R.L. v. José Fernando Cadima Camacho*: confirming the principle with statutory and doctrinal references; ICC Final Award Case No. 11570 *Lex Contractus* Portuguese Law: referring to the principle contained in Portugal Art. 237 CC.

Chapter 30

Practices and Usages

1. General Remarks

In the Ibero-American legal systems, the general usages[1] and the practices between the parties work as supplementary source of law and as a tool for interpretation of contracts.[2] Usages are a supplementary source of legal obligations when their objective solutions are automatically incorporated in the contractual relationships. Contracts are often completed by supplementary mechanisms as it is uncommon that the parties have in mind all the consequences that the contract could entail.[3] In the case of usages, the process of supplementation consists in adding to the expressly agreed terms of the parties the solutions of the binding usages for the whole construction of the contract.[4]

---

1 Ibero-American laws use the terms usages and customs to mostly refer to what is known as *usage* in the meaning of the CISG, though for some cases they refer to usage between the parties, meaning practices between the parties in the sense given by the CISG; *see* Colombia: J. Oviedo Albán, Usos y Costumbres en el Derecho Privado Contemporáneo 3, http://www.derecho-comercial.com/Doctrina/oviedo01.pdf: noting that the doctrine has commonly differentiated between the terms custom and usage. According to Rocco the term usage in modern law, in a wide sense, would include from the individual habits to the true and proper legal customs. In this sense, customs are understood as the general conduct composed by the public events, uniform, reiterated and which are obligatory for certain community. Usages could be distinguished from customs by the publicity and uniformity of the latter. Usages are normally conducts followed by the parties that with the time become binding on them. But Ibero-American civil and commercial codes do not distinguish between the terms custom and usage.

2 Brazil: O. Gomes, Contratos 238 (2008); Guatemala: V. Aguilar Guerra, El Negocio Jurídico 367-369 (2004); Mexico: O. Vásquez del Mercado, Contratos Mercantiles 40 (2008); Uruguay: J. Rodriguez Russo, La Interpretacion del Contrato 202-203 (2006); Venezuela: J. Mélich-Orsini, Doctrina General del Contrato 420 (2006).

3 Guatemala: Aguilar Guerra, *supra* note 2, at 350.

4 Argentina: F. López de Zavalia, Teoria de los Contratos, Vol. 1, 431 (2003); Venezuela:

As a tool of interpretation of contracts, usages are the means to discover the true meaning and effect of limited, unclear, obscure and ambiguous clauses.

2. Trade Usages

2.1. Notion and Requirements

The Ibero-American doctrine has identified three main constituent elements so that usages acquire binding character. First, general behaviour or conduct becomes consuetudinary law when they are reproduced for certain time.[5] As noted by Argentina: Lorenzetti, a requirement to be reproduced during long or immemorial time would clash with the modern practice of trade characterised by fast changing techniques of negotiation and marketing.[6] Second, it should be a generalised opinion that such conduct is binding. On this, the judge or the arbitrator should decide whether the general opinion is notorious or whether its binding character must be proven by the interested party.[7] Third, the repeated conduct should be reasonable and moral. The immoral and unreasonable behaviours cannot attain the level of binding rules.[8]

In this line, some Ibero-American codes give a definition of usages and establish the necessary requirements so that usages benefit of binding character. Namely, trade usages replace the silence of the law when the constituent conduct is uniform, public, performed generally in the country or a certain locality and reiterated by a long space of time that will be carefully evaluated by the Courts of Commerce.[9]

However, not every usage containing the above-mentioned elements automatically becomes the applicable rule. As a supplementary rule, usages can take different positions within the interplay between the contract and the law. According to doctrinal and legislative distinctions, the place that usages have *vis à vis* the statutory law and the contract's provisions differ from country to country, from Civil Codes to Commercial Codes and, from general provisions to special provisions.

Mélich-Orsini, *supra* note 2, at 380.

[5] Mexico: Vásquez del Mercado, *supra* note 2, at 40; Most Ibero-American laws leave open the time required at the Judge's discretion, though under some laws as the Ecuador Art. 4 Com C the conduct must be reiterated by more than a fixed (ten years) time.

[6] Argentina: R.L. Lorenzetti, Tratado de los Contratos Parte General 57 (2004).

[7] *Id.*

[8] *Id.*, at 57; Mexico: Vásquez del Mercado, *supra* note 2, at 40.

[9] Chile Art. 4 Com C; Colombia Arts. 3, 7 Com C; Costa Rica Art. 3 CC & Art. 3 Com C; Ecuador Art. 4 Com C; Panama Art. 13 CC; Spain Art. 3 CC; Venezuela Art. 9 Com C.

2.2. Supplementary Source

2.2.1. *Praeter Legem*

The principle is that usages may be applied *praeter legem* or in cases not regulated by the law.[10] In this case, usages work as gap-fillers for the statutory law. Many Ibero-American laws give to usages the place of the rule of law in case of silence of the Civil Codes[11] or the Codes of Commerce.[12] For example, in the sale of animals under the Brazilian law, the stated periods of guarantee for defects will be those established by the special law, or, in absence of this, by the local usages.[13]

In a case submitted to an ICC Sole Arbitrator the question arose as to whether the seller was obligated to provide spare parts, service and technical support to the buyer. The Sole Arbitrator sustained that in accordance to trade usages whose observance is mandatory as set forth in Mexico's Article 1445 of the Code of Commerce and Article 1796 of the Civil Code, the seller should provide, within the limits of prevailing market conditions with respect to price, availability and quality, the buyer with spare parts, services and technical support in connection with the machines fully paid. In the Sole Arbitrator's opinion, the obligation was supported by an implicit understanding in any commercial sale of goods to be used in an industrial process, since it is a reasonable expectation for a buyer, at the time of the execution of a sales contract, that the seller (and manufacturer in this case) would have the capacity and willingness to do so as needed in the regular course of business.[14]

2.2.2. *Secundum Legem*

In addition, usages can also be applied *secundum legem*. The statutory law would expressly refer to the application of usages, generally in absence of express agreement of the parties.[15] Such is the solution sustained in many

[10] Bolivia Supreme Court, *Sala Civil*, 10 April 2003, *Juan Pablo Prudencio Borda v. Servicio Prefectural de Caminos Chuquisaca*: indicating that the parties are bound by their contract and by all that derives from the nature of the contract according to the provisions of law, and absent the latter, according to the usages.

[11] Argentina Art. 17 CC; Bolivia Art. 520 CC; Chile Art. 2 CC; Costa Rica Arts. 1, 3 CC; Cuba Art. 355.1 CC; Ecuador Art. 2 CC; El Salvador Art. 2 CC; Honduras Art. 2 CC; Mexico Art. 1796 CC; Panama Art. 13 CC; Spain Art. 3 CC.

[12] Chile Art. 4 Com C; Colombia Art. 7 Com C; Costa Rica Arts. 2, 3 Com C; Ecuador Art. 4 Com C; Venezuela Art. 9 Com C.

[13] Brazil Art. 455 para. 2 CC.

[14] ICC Partial Award Case No. 12949 *Lex Contractus* Mexican Law.

[15] *See* expressly Argentina Arts. 17, 219 Com C; Chile Art. 2 CC; Costa Rica Art. 436 Com C; Ecuador Art. 2 CC; El Salvador Art. 2 CC; Honduras Art. 2 CC; Portugal Art. 3 CC; Uruguay Art. 297 Com C; *see also* Argentina: A.A. Alterini, Contratos civiles, comerciales, de consumo 58 (1998); Argentina: Lorenzetti, *supra* note 6, at 205.

areas of the law that grant full validity to the usages. If the parties have omitted clauses of absolute necessity for the performance of the contract, it is presumed that the parties have voluntarily submitted to the solution given by the usages or customs of the place of contract performance.[16]

Bolivian law makes express reference to these usages in many instances.[17] For example, unless otherwise agreed to, the place of performance shall be that established by the usages.[18] Under other laws, in the sale on documents, the *tradittio* or delivery of the goods is substituted by the delivery of its representative title and other documents according to the usages.[19] Finally, Brazilian scholar Gonçalves considers that when a contract establishes the quantity of the goods, but it does not indicate their weight or measure, the practices and usages of the place of contract performance will fill in the gap.[20]

2.2.3. *Contra Legem*

Additionally, usages can be applied *contra legem*. Usages override the statutory law when the law expressly establishes so. There are multiples instances of usages applied *contra legem* in contracts in general and in sales in specific. In the following paragraphs, we provide a non-exhaustive list of examples.

Under the Brazilian law, for example, offers to the public are equivalent to a definitive offer when they contain the essential elements of a contract, unless the opposite results from the usages.[21] In Chile and Uruguay's laws, the default rule establishes that the risk on the goods normally passes from the seller to the buyer at the contract conclusion,[22] unless the usages give to the buyer the right to first try, test or taste the goods. In such a case, the risk will pass only once he does so and approves the goods.[23]

In the Bolivian law, when there has not been an agreed time for performance, the creditor can demand performance immediately unless otherwise established by the usages.[24] The Venezuelan Code of Commerce provides a similar rule.[25] Under some laws, if according to the usages the obligation can be performed without previous acceptance, the contract is entered into at the moment and

[16] Argentina Art. 219 Com C; Costa Rica Art. 436 Com C; Uruguay Art. 297 Com C.

[17] *See* examples in Bolivia Arts. 460, 588, 803, 830, 865 CC.

[18] Bolivia Art. 310 CC.

[19] Brazil Art. 529 CC; El Salvador Art. 1027 Com C; Peru Art. 1580 CC; Portugal Art. 937 CC.

[20] Brazil: C.R. Gonçalves, Dereito Civil Brasileiro, Vol. III, Contratos e Atos Unilateralais 202 (2004).

[21] Brazil Art. 429 CC.

[22] Chile Art. 142 Com C; Uruguay Art. 1335 CC.

[23] Chile Art. 143 (2) Com C; Uruguay Art. 1335 (3) CC.

[24] Bolivia Art. 311 CC.

[25] Venezuela Art. 112 Com C.

place in which the performance has begun,[26] or as soon as the behaviour of the other party's manifest intent to conclude the contract.[27]

Under other laws, when the business is one of those in which an express acceptance is not usual, the contract is concluded if the offer is not rapidly rejected.[28] The burden of proof of the usage and the invitation to offer is on the offeror.[29]

In Portugal, in the sale concluded based on models or samples, the seller guarantees equal qualities as those of the sample, unless according to the usages the sample only serves to indicate an approximate of the qualities of the goods.[30] Likewise, the performance of the obligation is fulfilled integrally, unless according to the usages performance could be carried out in instalments.[31] Regarding the price, this is paid at the moment and the place of the delivery, except if according to the usage the price is not paid at that time.[32]

Then again, other laws establish that in the sale goods which are usual to try or degust beforehand,[33] the existence of the sale is conditioned to trial or degustation and approval.[34]

2.3. Interpretative Rules

As mentioned, usages also work as rule of interpretation of the parties' agreement.[35] According to some laws, the usages that constitute a tool of the interpretation are those of the place of contract conclusion;[36] other laws refer

---

26 Bolivia Art. 457 CC; Peru Art. 1381 CC; Venezuela Art. 1.138 CC; *see* explaining the rule in Peru: M. Castillo Freyre, Tratado de la Teoria General de los Contratos Vol. I, 36 (2002).

27 Portugal Art. 234 CC; Portugal: J. De M. Antunes Valera, Das Obrigações em Geral 222-224 (2003): for example when a bookseller delivers to his habitual client the new editions of the usually requested books and the client does not reject them in a reasonable time.

28 Guatemala Art. 1526 CC; Peru Art. 1381 CC; Venezuela Art. 112 Com C.

29 Peru Art. 1381 CC.

30 Portugal Art. 919 CC.

31 Portugal Art. 763 (1) CC.

32 Portugal Art. 885 (1) (2) CC.

33 Usages of the place where the goods are; *see* Argentina: R. Compagnucci de Caso, Contrato de Compraventa 408 (2007).

34 Argentina Art. 1336 CC; Chile Art. 132 Com C; Colombia Art. 911 Com C; Costa Rica Art. 453 Com C; Ecuador Art. 172 Com C; El Salvador Art. 1022 Com C; Honduras Art. 1612 CC; Guatemala Art. 1799 CC; Mexico Art. 2257 CC: including goods that is a usage to weight and to measure; Nicaragua Art. 2542 CC; Panama Art. 1223 CC; Paraguay Art. 768 CC; Spain Art. 1.453 CC; Venezuela Art. 1.477 CC.

35 Guatemala: Aguilar Guerra, *supra* note 2, at 369; Interestingly the Civil Code of Costa Rica also considers the general usage as a rule of interpretation of the law: Costa Rica Art. 1 CC: dictating that the usages and the general principles of Law are non-written sources of the legal ordering and will serve to interpret and to integrate the written law.

36 Argentina Art. 218(6) Com C; Guatemala Art. 1599 CC; Uruguay Art. 1302 CC & Art. 296(6) Com C. As under these laws the relevant usages are those at the place of contract

to the usages at the place of the applicable substantive law,[37] while others speak generally of usages with no reference to any particular place.[38]

The usages have an interpretative function only when the clauses of the contract are ambiguous, so that *prima facie* it is not possible to discover the real intent of the parties according to the subjective rules of interpretation.[39] The meaning of this rule is that the terms of the contract that have more than one meaning shall be understood in the sense that the *usages* gives to them, unless the parties have expressly given these terms a different meaning.[40] So that, despite the fact that one of the parties claims to have understood it differently, the meaning given by the usage will prevail.[41]

As pointed out by Argentina: Lorenzetti, the usages are of different types and affect different areas of the contract.[42] There are usages regarding the value of the weight or the size of the goods. In addition, the technique or scientific words are affected by the meaning they have in certain industries. These usages bound the parties when they knew them or ought to have known them with average diligence, unless their application is unreasonable.[43]

In this regard, an interesting case was presented before the three jurisdictional levels of the Uruguayan judicial system. In three instances, it was sustained that in a parties' agreement on the existence of the contract that one of them understood as a loan and the other as a sale, one should categorise the contract as a loan of merchandise, since it was the usage between merchants on seeds to lend each other merchandise when one was short.[44]

Also in a case submitted to an ICC Arbitral Tribunal applying the Venezuelan law, the question arose as to whether some formal requirements constitute a condition for the existence of a renew supply of goods agreement. On the one hand, the seller argued that the agreement never received the necessary corporate and government approvals; it was never signed and hence never gained effect. In response to this allegation, the buyer argued that the sole purpose of the written agreement was to record the agreement

---

conclusion, it is advisable to know where the contract was concluded. To know about the solution adopted as to the place of contract conclusion *see* Ch. 10, 2.2.4.

[37] Honduras Art. 1582 CC; Mexico Art. 1856 CC; Nicaragua Art. 2502 CC; Panama Art. 1138 CC; Spain Art. 1.287 CC. As under these laws the relevant usages are those at the place of the applicable law to the substance, it is advisable to know what is the applicable law. To know about the solution adopted as to the applicable law to the substance *see* Ch. 3 and Ch. 4, 1.

[38] Chile Art. 6 Com C; Colombia Art. 5 Com C; Costa Rica Art. 4 Com C; Paraguay Art. 2 Com C.

[39] Guatemala: Aguilar Guerra, *supra* note 2, at 367; *see* Ch. 29, 1.

[40] Argentina: Lorenzetti, *supra* note 6, at 467.

[41] Argentina Art. 217 Com C; Uruguay Art. 295 Com C.

[42] Argentina: Lorenzetti, *supra* note 6, at 467.

[43] *Id.*

[44] *See* Uruguay Judgments of the first, the second and the third instances published in *La Justicia Uruguaya*, Vol. 37, 1958, case 3774, at 289-296, *cited in* Uruguay: Rodríguez Russo, *supra* note 2, at 204, n. 141.

already concluded. The Tribunal dismissed the buyer's allegations because the conclusion of contracts through a written document signed by the parties' representatives was consistent with the industry's practice, in light of the importance of transactions at stake and the nature of the industry.[45]

With regards to the interplay between the different rules of interpretation, one could conclude that the meaning of a term shall be the one it has in the common language, with the following exceptions: (1) when the contract or the law attributes a specific meaning; (2) when the usages or the practices among the parties designate a particular meaning; (3) when it is about words relating to scientific, artistic or technical language which have a precise meaning.[46]

3. International Usages and Usages in Arbitration

Under Article 9 CISG, the parties are bound by any usage to which they have agreed. The parties are considered to have impliedly made applicable to their contract a usage of which the parties knew or ought to have known and which in international trade is widely known to, and regularly observed by, parties to contracts of the type involved in the particular trade concerned.[47]

Likewise, the Mexico City Convention establishes that in addition to the provisions on the applicable law, the guidelines, customs, and principles of international commercial law as well as commercial usages and practices generally accepted shall apply in order to discharge the requirements of justice and equity in the particular case.[48]

Only few Ibero-American laws refer to the application or binding character of international usages; always giving them a second place after the local usages. On the one hand, Costa Rica's Code of Commerce distinguishes between local, national and international usages, and gives them an order of prevalence.[49] The provision reads: concerning the application of the usages, the national usages will prevail over the international; and the special ones over the generals.[50] On the other hand, Colombia's Code of Commerce establishes that the treaties or international conventions of commerce not ratified by Colombia and the international trade usages that fulfil the conditions of the national usages shall be applied to the trade issues that cannot be solved according to the substantive laws.[51]

Indeed, the approach expressly taken by the Colombian Code of Commerce and the Mexico City Convention must be the solution in the rest

45 ICC Final Award Case No. 13750 *Lex Contractus* Venezuelan Law.
46 Argentina: Alterini, *supra* note 15, at 415.
47 Art. 9(2) CISG.
48 Art. 10 the Mexico City Convention.
49 Same understanding Mexico: Vásquez del Mercado, *supra* note 2, at 44.
50 Costa Rica Art. 2 Com C.
51 Colombia Art. 7 Com C.

of the Ibero-American laws. The international trade usages shall apply, in second place after the law and the agreement of the parties, as long as they fulfil the characteristics required for usages in general, according to the civil and commercial laws. That is, if international usages are continuous, public, accepted by the international community, and are in accordance with the public order of the *lex fori*,[52] they should apply to international transactions.

In addition, the Panamanian arbitration law establishes the duty of the arbitral tribunal to consider the mercantile usages and practices and the principles on international commercial contracts of UNIDROIT.[53]

The arbitration laws also refer to the usages. The vast majority may reference to the 'relevant trade usages' applicable to the case and apply them as complementary rule of law.[54] Therefore, as exemplified by an ICC Arbitral Tribunal,

> [R]elevant trade usages, in a case like the present, which involves the sale of two Aircraft between a Mexican and a German party, must be deemed to imply trade usages generally accepted and applied by international merchants who engage in this type of trade. The concept of 'relevant trade usages' is wider than the narrow concept of 'custom of the country' adopted in other parts of the Mexican legal system.[55]

Brazilian arbitration law goes beyond as it expressly establishes that the international rules of commerce and general principles of law can be chosen as the applicable law to the dispute.[56]

4. Practices between the Parties

The practices established between the parties are also relevant to supplement and to define the content of the contract.[57] CISG Article 9 expressly dictates that the parties are bound by any practices they have established between themselves. Many Ibero-American codes expressly require taking into account the parties' overall conduct in order to reveal the common intention of the contractors.[58] This exercise also allows the adjudicator to define the extent

[52] *See supra* 2.

[53] Panama Art. 27 AL.

[54] Bolivia Art. 54 AL; Chile Art. 28(4) AL; Costa Rica Art. 22 AL; Mexico Art. 1445 Com C; Nicaragua Art. 54 AL; Panama Art. 26 AL; Paraguay Art. 32 AL; Spain 34 (3) AL; Venezuela Art. 8 AL.

[55] ICC Final Award Case No. 13751 *Lex Contractus* German Law and Mexican Law to the agency relationship.

[56] Brazil Art. 2 (2) AL.

[57] Argentina: Alterini, *supra* note 15, at 61; Mexico: Vásquez del Mercado, *supra* note 2, at 40: this author call them *usos convencionales* (conventional usages).

[58] Argentina Art. 218 (4) Com C; Bolivia Art. 510 (2) CC; Mexico Art. 1855 CC; Spain Art. 1282 CC; Uruguay Art. 1301 CC & Art. 296 (4) Com C.

of the obligations contracted.[59] Thus, for example, if a seller has repeatedly accepted the claims of a buyer regarding the quality and quantity of goods after one month from the delivery the parties have established a practice between themselves, which cannot be subsequently denied by the parties.

In an ICC case, the respondent argued that he did not pay some invoices because the claimant had failed to collect the price at the respondent's domicile as established by the default rule on the payment of obligations. The Arbitral Tribunal dismissed the respondent's allegations on the basis that, as a matter of fact, a practice regarding the time and place of payment had already been established between the parties according to which respondent would pay monthly the price agreed at the claimant's domicile.[60]

In a different ICC arbitration case, a dispute arose between a respondent, a Mexican beer producer (seller), and claimant, (distributor 1) which was one of the respondents' two only distributors in the United States. The claimant alleged that contrary to the established practice between the parties[61] the new distributorship agreement signed for the next 10 years was to have substantially the same terms as the agreement signed between the respondents and distributor 2 except for the territory's clause. However, the respondents had materially changed the duration and the termination provision of the agreement to be substantially less favourable than those included in the distributor 2 agreement. The claimant thus sought to have the duration, termination and renewal rights provisions of his agreement changed to be the same as those of the distributor 2 agreement. The Tribunal considered that as matter of fact, the previous distributor agreement passed between the respondent and the claimant and the respondent and distributor 2 had always had identical clauses relating to the duration, termination and renewal terms.[62] In addition, the Arbitral Tribunal acknowledged that the respondent's strategy of the two competitive distributors included the practice of simultaneous negotiation of the agreements beginning from a common draft.[63]

---

59 Chile: J. Lopez Santa Maria, Los Contratos: Parte General, Vol. 2, n. 632 (2005).

60 ICC Final Award Case No. 13524 *Lex Contractus* Mexican Law: the Tribunal referred to Mexican jurisprudence to reach this conclusion.

61 The claimant based this claimed on Mexico Art. 1145 Com C and Art. 9 (1) CISG; ICC Final Award Case No. 13184 *Lex Contractus* CISG and Mexican Law as supplementary law.

62 However, the Tribunal considered that such a fact "does not create a 'practice' to that effect within the meaning of Article 9(1) of the UN Convention, where the Claimant had not seen and did not know the term, termination and renewal provisions" of distributor 2 agreement, "and had never discussed the term, termination and renewal with the respondents prior," *see* ICC Final Award Case No. 13184 *Lex Contractus* CISG and Mexican Law as supplementary law.

63 But "there was no 'usage' that the term, termination and renewal would be identical within the meaning of Article 9(1) of the UN Convention, Article 1445 of the Mexican Code of Commerce or Article 17.2 of the ICC Rules", *see* ICC Final Award Case No. 13184 *Lex Contractus* CISG and Mexican Law as supplementary law.

> However, the practice also involved a final period of private negotiation between the respondents and each importer, and during this period the competitive rivalry was directed towards securing the most favourable terms possible for the respondents, knowing that any concessions achieved at this stage could remain confidential. While these private negotiations concentrated on commercial terms such as quotas, it was also the opportunity for the respondents to address contractual issues affecting an individual importer, and for the importers to negotiate individual advantages.[64]

Also in a case submitted to an ICC Arbitral Tribunal applying the Venezuelan law, the question arose as to whether some formal requirements constitute a condition for the existence of a renewed supply of goods agreement. On the one hand, the seller argued that the agreement never received the necessary corporate and government approvals, it was never signed and hence never entered into effect. In response to this, the buyer argued that the sole purpose of the written agreement was to record the agreement already concluded. The Tribunal dismissed the buyer's allegations on the grounds that (1) the text of the draft agreement as well as the prior agreement between the parties showed that the parties intended to renew their prior agreements through a written document, signed by the parties' duly authorised representatives, (2) the parties' conduct in executing contracts over their relationship also confirmed this practice.[65]

The practices between the parties are connected with the general usages automatically incorporated within the contract. But contrary to the general behaviour or conduct followed in a specific area of the trade, the established practices are limited to the parties' sphere which occasionally are different or contrary to the general usages. In the hierarchy of application, the special usages prevail over the general usages, while the practices established between the parties take first place before any kind of usage.[66]

---

64 ICC Final Award Case No. 13184 *Lex Contractus* CISG and Mexican Law as supplementary law.

65 ICC Final Award Case No. 13750 *Lex Contractus* Venezuelan Law.

66 Argentina: Alterini, *supra* note 15, at 61; Mexico: Vásquez del Mercado, *supra* note 2, at 42.

Chapter 31

Supplementation of the Contract

1. General Remarks on Supplementation of the Contract

In conjunction to the interpretation of a contract is the question of its supplementation.[1] Considering it is uncommon that the parties have in mind all the consequences and effects that the contract could entail, contracts are often completed by the supplementary mechanisms.[2] In this sense, the process of supplementation consists in adding to the express terms agreed to by the parties, other statutory rules, usages and practices which are necessary for the whole construction of the contract.[3]

The Ibero-American statutory laws have many times referred the supplementation mechanism. For example, some laws establish that clauses of common usage are presumed though are not expressed.[4] Most other laws also establish that besides the agreed terms, under the principle of good faith the parties are bound by all the consequences that, according to contract's nature, derive from the usage and the law.[5]

---

[1] The Ibero-American doctrine identifies the English term *supplementation* with the Spanish words of *integración*; *see for example*, Argentina: F. López de Zavalía, Teoria de los Contratos, Vol. 1, 430, 431 (2003); Guatemala: V. Aguilar Guerra, El Negocio Jurídico 344-356 (2004); Venezuela: J. Mélich-Orsini, Doctrina General del Contrato 418 (2006).

[2] Guatemala: Aguilar Guerra, *supra* note 1, at 350.

[3] Argentina: López de Zavalía, *supra* note 1, at 431; Brazil: O. Gomes, Contratos 241 (2008); Mexico: R. Sánchez Medal, De los contratos civiles: teoría general del contrato, contratos en especial, registro público de la propiedad 79 (2002); Venezuela: Mélich-Orsini, *supra* note 1, at 380; Mexico Collegiate Tribunals, *Novena Época,* Registry 204'714, SJF II, August 1995, p. 319.

[4] Bolivia Art. 513 CC; Chile Art. 1563 para. 2 CC; Colombia Art. 1621 para. 2 CC; Ecuador 1606 para. 2 CC; El Salvador Art. 1434 para. 2 CC; Guatemala Art. 1519 CC; Mexico Art. 1839.

[5] Argentina Art. 1198 CC; Bolivia Art. 803 Com C; Brazil Art. 422 CC; Chile Art. 1546 CC; Colombia Art. 1603 CC & Art. 863 Com C; Cuba Art. 6 CC; Ecuador Art. 1589 CC; El

2. Supplementing Omitted Terms

The supplementation task of omitted terms takes into account, first, the terms regarding the essential requirements of the contract and, second, the terms that directly derive from the nature of the obligations contracted. On the one hand, the essential terms in a contract cannot be renounced but at risk of disappearing or invalidating the contract in question.[6] For example, pretending to absolutely eliminate the obligation to deliver the goods, transferring the title of property in some countries, or of paying a price in a sales contract, is not permitted. On the other hand, the natural clauses are those which are the normal consequence of the contract, and which are understood to be included in the contract. For example, the obligation to inspect the merchandise, within a certain time established by law, after delivery.[7] In the last case, the parties may renounce to this natural obligation by agreeing a fix time for inspection.[8]

The Mexican Civil Code and the El Salvadorian Supreme Court have been clear in this regard. The parties can agree on the clauses that they believe to be the more convenient; but those referring to the essential elements of the contract or those which are a natural consequence of the contract will be considered as inserted though are not expressed, unless the law permits to renounce the latter and that the parties have expressly done so.[9]

It is important to note that there may be accidental terms which required an express or implied agreement to be binding and that does not have a supplementary function; for example, the duty to comply with all government regulations in the country where the merchandise is to be sold, to comply with any ethical values in the goods' production,[10] or the inclusion of a penalty clause.[11]

3. Deriving Terms to be Supplemented

The doctrine has distinguished between auto-supplementation and hetero-supplementation.[12] On the one hand, auto-supplementation operates *within*

Salvador Art. 1417 CC; Guatemala Art. 17 JOL; Mexico Art. 1796 CC; Paraguay Art. 715 CC; Peru Art. 1362 CC; Portugal Art. 762 CC; Spain Art. 1258 CC & Art. 57 Com C; Venezuela Art. 1160 CC.

[6] Mexico Collegiate Tribunals, *Novena Época,* Registry 204'714, SJF II, August 1995, p. 319.

[7] *See* Ch. 40.

[8] Mexico: Sánchez Medal, *supra* note 3, at 79.

[9] Mexico Art 1839 CC; El Salvador Supreme Court, *Cass civ*, *Alvarenga Bonilla v. Hsien Tang*, 1530 S.S., 30 September 2002.

[10] *See* Ch. 37, 2.3.

[11] El Salvador Supreme Court, *Cass civ*, *Alvarenga Bonilla v. Hsien Tang*, 1530 S.S., 30 September 2002.

[12] In this regard *see 'autointegración y heterointegración' in* Argentina: López de Zavalía,

the contract. When the terms of the contract do not cover all situations and an analogous one emerges, such situation shall be governed by analogy (*analogia legis*). When such analogy is not enough to govern the emerging situation, the solution is taken from the general principles inspiring the contract (*analogia iuris*).[13]

Conversely, hetero-supplementation operates *out* of the contract, adding solutions that cannot be obtained from the contract itself. Such solutions derive from the imperative law and the natural rules contained in the individual legal systems.[14] Indeed, the law integrates the contract with a good number of supplementary rules. On the one hand, the *imperative* rules automatically add clauses that cannot be missed and/or substitute clauses that contradict the public order.[15] This is what some scholars call the automatic harmonisation process of the contract with the imperative law.[16] For example, imperative rules on standard form clauses and adhesion contracts will automatically modify the rules on interpretation and validity of certain clauses.[17]

On the other hand, the law completes the contract with natural (non-imperative) provisions in cases in which the parties have not expressly or impliedly agreed upon.[18] When the non-conceived situation materialises, the law will intervene so that the adjudicator can fulfil the lacuna of the contract.[19] For example, if the parties to a sales contract did not agree on the time and place of passing of risk of the goods, the adjudicator, to complete the contract, will consult the relevant provisions contained in the applicable law.[20]

In addition, when the agreed clauses *within* a contract and the *essential* or *natural* supplementary terms established by the applicable law to the specific type of contract are not enough, the supplementation continues with the consequences deriving from the principle of good faith, the usages, the practices, the general principles of the law and the equity.[21]

---

supra note 1, at 431; Guatemala: Aguilar Guerra, *supra* note 1, at 351.

13 Argentina: López de Zavalía, *supra* note 1, at 431; Guatemala: Aguilar Guerra, *supra* note 1, at 351.

14 Argentina: López de Zavalía, *supra* note 1, at 431; Guatemala: Aguilar Guerra, *supra* note 1, at 351, 352.

15 Guatemala: Aguilar Guerra, *supra* note 1, at 352, n. 5008.

16 Venezuela: Mélich-Orsini, *supra* note 1, at 419.

17 *See generally* Ch. 13, 1.

18 Guatemala: Aguilar Guerra, *supra* note 1, at 352, n. 508.

19 Venezuela: Mélich-Orsini, *supra* note 1, at 419.

20 *See* Ch. 44, 3.

21 *See* Ch. 32, 3 and Ch. 30, 2.2 & 4.

Part 7

Good Faith and related Concepts

CHAPTER 32

GOOD FAITH

1. General Remarks

The principle of good faith is recognised in all the Ibero-American laws.[1] The notion of good faith has its origins in the Roman Law principle of *bona fides*.[2] As in Roman Law, the modern good faith principle is understood as proper contractual behaviour.[3] The principle introduces a moral rule of an abstract nature that often covers other duties such those of trusty conduct, probity, cooperation, information, honesty, loyalty, and antonyms such as bad faith, incidental fraud or negligence.[4]

The principle of good faith is often referred to as an objective standard that aims to control or supplement the content of the contract. However, the principle of good faith may also be used as an objective standard, regarding one party's state of mind or intention, that may limit the liability or the effects of the unwinding of the contract.

---

1 Argentina Art. 1198 CC; Bolivia Art. 465 CC & Art. 803 Com C; Brazil Art. 422 CC; Chile Art. 1546 CC; Colombia Art. 1603 CC & Art. 863 Com C; Cuba Art. 6 CC; Ecuador Art. 1589 CC; El Salvador Art. 1417 CC; Guatemala Art. 17 JOL; Mexico Art. 1796 CC; Paraguay Art. 689 CC; Peru Art. 1362 CC; Portugal Art. 227 CC; Spain Art. 1258 CC & Art. 57 Com C.

2 Argentina: R.L. Lorenzetti, Tratado de los Contratos Parte General 142 (2004); for the precise meaning and function in Roman Law *see* Mexico: S. Bialostosky de Chazán, *La buena fe de los contratos*, 1970(79 80) Revista de la Facultad de Derecho de México 1104.

3 Argentina: Lorenzetti, *supra* note 2, at 142; Brazil: C.R. Gonçalves, Dereito Civil Brasileiro, Vol. III, Contratos e Atos Unilateralais 33 (2004); Colombia: A. Solarte Rodríguez, *La buena fe contractual y los deberes secundarios de conducta*, 108 Vniversitas, at 288 (2004); Mexico: Bialostosky de Chazán, *supra* note 2, at 1116; Spain: J. Llobet I Aguado, El Deber de Información en la Formación de los Contratos 13 (1996).

4 Brazil: Gonçalves, *supra* note 3, at 33; Colombia: Solarte Rodríguez, *supra* note 3, at 303-310; Spain: Llobet I Aguado, *supra* note 3, at 38, 39.

2. Good Faith as a Control of Unfair Conduct and Clauses

Liability may arise for breach of the principle of good faith. This is, the party who knew, or ought to have known, the existence of an element that may cause the termination of the contract, and does not give notice of such to the other party, is liable for damages.[5] The liability may arise when the contract has not yet been concluded,[6] or when the contract has been concluded under fraud or incidental fraud.[7] It may also occur that the contract concluded is valid but is unfavourable in relation to particular terms for one of the parties that suffered the consequences of the other party's bad faith or negligent conduct. In this context, standard form clauses in adhesion contracts that affect good faith and that produce an abuse of rights are often considered invalid.[8] For example, the parties' freedom, to raise or to lower the standard of breach required for the avoidance of the contract, may encounter a limit in the duty to behave in good faith.[9]

3. Good Faith in the Supplementation of the Contract

The good faith principle also supplements the content of the contract.[10] Many default obligations aiming to prevent unfair results originate from the principle of good faith. For instance, the buyer's duty to timely inform the seller about any non-conformity of the goods,[11] the seller's duty to package the goods in

---

5 *See* Paraguay Art. 690 CC: expressly covering information that one party ought to have known.

6 *See* pre-contractual liability Sec. 28; Colombia: Solarte Rodríguez, *supra* note 3, at 311, 312; Portugal: J. De M. Antunes Valera, Das Obrigações em Geral 270 (2003); Spain: P. Perales Vizcasillas, *in* D. Morán Bovio (Ed.), Comentario a los Principios de Unidroit para. los Contratos del Comercio Internacional Art. 2.15, 2.a, at 151 (2003): commenting on and comparing to the domestic Spanish law.

7 Incidental fraud as opposed to grave fraud does not normally affect the validity of the contract: Nevertheless, the deceiving party may be compensated for any damage caused: Argentina Art. 934 CC; Brazil Art. 146 CC; Chile Art. 1458 para. 2 CC; Colombia Art. 1515 para. 2 CC; Ecuador Art. 1501 para. 2 CC; El Salvador Art. 1329 para. 2 CC; Honduras Art. 1561 CC; Nicaragua Art. 2470 para. 2 CC; Paraguay Art. 291 para. 2 CC; Peru Art. 211 CC; Spain Art. 1280 CC; Argentina: A.A. Alterini, Contratos civiles, comerciales, de consumo 366 (1998); Guatemala: V. Aguilar Guerra, El Negocio Jurídico 267 (2004); Costa Rica: A. Brenes Cordoba, G. Trejos & M. Ramírez, Tratado de los Contratos 83 (1998); Nicaragua: J.J. Herrera Espinoza *et al.*, Contratos Civiles y Mercantiles 10.9 (2006); Portugal: Antunes Valera, *supra* note 6, at 269; Of course, besides damages, the contract affected by grave fraud, as opposed to incidental fraud, may be rescinded on such grounds, *see* Ch. 23, 2 and Ch. 24, 4.

8 *See* Ch. 13, 1.2.

9 *See* Ch. 47, 2.

10 Colombia: Solarte Rodríguez, *supra* note 3, at 301; *see also* Ch. 31.

11 *See* Ch. 40, 1.

a manner adequate to preserve and protect them,[12] *etc.* On the other hand, the good faith principle gives the opportunity to remedy a defective performance in cases of early performance.[13] It also imposes on the aggrieved party the duty to mitigate the damages caused by the breaching party.[14] Finally, with the aim of balancing the liability of the parties in a breach of contract, the principle of good faith may preclude a party from seeking the remedies available for breach of contract when such a breach was, to some extent, caused by his own behaviour or conduct.[15]

4. Good Faith State of Mind or Intention

The principle of good faith may also be used as an objective standard, regarding one party's state of mind or intention, that limits the liability and the effects of the unwinding of the contract. For example, the debtor of the obligation in good faith is only liable for the damages and loss of profits that he foresaw or could have foreseen at the conclusion of the contract, while the debtor in bad faith is also liable for unforeseeable damages.[16] Likewise, only the buyer in good faith, *i.e.* who ignored that the goods were other people's goods, has the right to claim the remedies available under the sale by non-owners.[17] In addition, the avoidance of the contract does not entitle the seller to recover the goods or to claim any property right against third parties who in good faith had acquired the goods from the buyer in breach.[18] Finally, in the context of unjustified enrichment and undue payment, the party in good faith must only give back what remains from the performance unjustifiably received.[19]

5. Good Faith Exclusion or Limitation

Although only impliedly stated in few provisions of the Ibero-American laws, the duty to behave in good faith may not be excluded or limited.[20] The mandatory nature of the duty to act in good faith can be deducted, for instance, from the prohibition established by the public order of the *lex forum*.[21] As

12 *See* Ch. 37, 3.4.
13 *See* Ch. 36, 3.
14 *See* Ch. 50, 7.
15 *See* Ch. 51, 3.
16 *See* Ch. 50, 4.
17 *See* Ch. 46, 3.
18 *See* Ch. 57, 3.
19 *See* Ch. 58, 3.
20 *See for example* Mexico 1822 CC; Peru Art. 218 CC; both codes stating that is illegal to renounce to the right to rescind the contract on the grounds of fraud.
21 Costa Rica Art. 18 CC; Guatemala Art. 31 JOL; Mexico Art. 15 (II) CC; Spain Art. 12 (3)

mentioned, the public order exception limits the freedom of the parties to contractually define the content of their contract and the applicable law.[22] Among the concepts embraced by the notion of public order is the good faith principle of contract negotiation, interpretation and performance.[23]

CC; Venezuela Art. 8 PIL.

22 *See* Ch. 3, 1.2.2.

23 Peru: C. Delgado Barreto *et al.*, Introducción al Derecho Internacional Privado, Vol. I, 334 (2002).

CHAPTER 33

VENIRE CONTRA FACTUM PROPRIUM AND ABUSE OF RIGHTS

In addition to the principle of good faith, other related concepts are also important for the performance of the contract. For example, the principle of cooperation that requires the parties to cooperate in the fulfilment of any main and ancillary obligation. Likewise, the notion of abuse of rights, which, based on the principle of good faith, establishes an objective standard impeding a party's rights to be exercised in a way and under circumstances susceptible to be legally censured. Also the doctrine of *venire contra factum proprium* which, based on the general duty of good faith, imposes on the parties the duty of respect in any legal situation previously created by their own conduct, when such conduct has caused the reliance of the other party.

1. Venire Contra Factum Proprium

The Roman law principle of *venire contra factum proprium* is impliedly recognised by some statutory provisions of the Ibero-American laws.[1] The same is based on the idea that nobody can assert his right in contradiction with a previous conduct, when such conduct, objectively interpreted according to

[1] *See for example* Argentina Art. 468 Com C; Chile Art. 157 Com C; Colombia Art. 927 Com C; Ecuador Art. 200 Com C; Mexico Art. 371 Com C; Spain Art. 330 Com C; Uruguay Art. 537 Com C: all these provisions state that the buyer is not obliged to take delivery of goods in shorter quantity than that agreed in the contract, but if the buyer accept such partial delivery the sale would be understood to be concluded for the partial quantity delivered although the rest never comes. The buyer may, though, required the seller to perform the whole of the contract or to compensate for the damages incurred. Argentina Art. 470 Com C; Costa Rica Art. 469 Com C; Uruguay Art. 540 Com C; all these codes state that if the buyer returns the goods and the seller accepts them, it is presumed that seller has agreed in the avoidance of the contract.

the law, the usages and the good faith principle, justifies reliance that such right would not be asserted, or when subsequently exercised, it clashes with the law, the usages or the good faith.[2]

Courts consider that the doctrine of *venire contra factum proprium* is based on the general duty of good faith.[3] Since all the Ibero-American laws require contracts to be concluded in good faith,[4] the principle imposes upon the parties the duty of respect and submission to any legal situation previously created by their own conduct.[5]

1.1. Contradictory Conduct of One of the Parties

The first requirement deduced from the doctrine of *venire contra factum proprium* consists in the contradictory conduct of one of the parties. The Argentinean Supreme Court has considered that the contradictory conduct which shows disloyalty is contrary to the law.[6] In the same line, a Mexican Collegiate Tribunal sustained that the principle establishes a limit on the subjective legal rights, so that any party's claim which is contrary to the previous objective conduct of that party is inadmissible.[7]

Similarly, the Court of Appeals of Santiago in Chile considered that the legal claims of a party cannot flagrantly contradict his previous conduct since the legal situation previously created by such conduct must prevail in order to achieve legal certainty.[8]

---

[2] *See for example* ICC Final Award Case No. 13435 *Lex Contractus* Spanish Law with implied exclusion of the CISG: relying on the doctrine developed by Spanish case law the Tribunal found that "the own acts of the supplier expressed the free intent given to modification of the contractual price-fixing-provision. A duty is thus imposed of consistency and respect for reasonable expectations created on the other party or on third parties."

[3] El Salvador Supreme Court, *Cass civ, Ortíz de Hernández v. Campos Rivera*, 1346-2001, 24 July 2002; Spain Supreme Tribunal, 4 February 2009, *Id Cendoj*: 28079110012009100039; Supreme Tribunal, 18 October 2006, *Id Cendoj:* 28079110012006101032; Spain Supreme Tribunal, 6 April 2006, *Id Cendoj:* 28079110012006100366.

[4] Argentina Art. 1198 CC; Bolivia Art. 465 CC & Art. 803 Com C; Brazil Art. 422 CC; Chile Art. 1546 CC; Colombia Art. 1603 CC & Art. 863 Com C; Cuba Art. 6 CC; Ecuador Art. 1589 CC; El Salvador Art. 1417 CC; Guatemala Art. 17 JOL; Mexico Art. 1796 CC; Paraguay Art. 689 CC; Peru Art. 1362 CC; Portugal Art. 227 CC; Spain Art. 1258 CC & Art. 57 Com C; *see also* Chile: J. Lopez Santa Maria, Los Contratos: Parte General, Vol. 2, n. 595*bis* (2005).

[5] El Salvador Supreme Court, Civil Appeal, Edificadora. *Salvadoreña S.A. de C.V. v. Estado de El Salvador*, 1612 S.S, 7 July 2004; El Salvador Supreme Court, Civil Appeal, *Landaverde v. Estado y Gobierno de El Salvador, Agricultura y Ganadería*, 1507 S.S, 19 August 2002.

[6] Argentina Supreme Court, *Cía. Azucarera Tucumana SA. v. Estado Nacional*, 21 September 1989.

[7] Mexico Collegiate Tribunals, *Octava Época,* Registry 222109, SJF VIII, August 1991, at 165.

[8] *See* Chile Appeal Court of Santiago, *Décima Sala,* 13 September 2006.

1.2. Reliance of the other Party

The second requirement of the doctrine consists in one party's reliance on the situation created by the other party's opposite conduct. On this, Court of Appeals of Santiago de Chile explained that every person was bound by his own conduct and statements, to keep an adequate conduct *vis à vis* the trust and reliance created on the other party's mind; the reliance that the first party is going to accomplish his promise.[9]

Following this premise, The Supreme Court of Chile denied one party's right to move to arbitration proceedings since he had previously voluntarily submitted to the jurisdiction of the national courts for the settlement of issues arising from a contract containing an arbitration clause, without mentioning the existence of such clause or even objecting the jurisdiction of the national competent court.[10]

1.3. Standard of Conduct

In order to limit the application of the v*enire contra factum proprium* doctrine, the Spanish Supreme Tribunal explained that the rule is not applicable when the factual precedents or the precedent conduct invoked has an ambiguous or non-concrete character, or lack of the transparency required to produce a legal change. In any case, true declarations of intent are needed in order to create, modify or extinguish a legal relation.[11]

In the same line, an ICC Arbitral Tribunal, in application of the Argentinean law, upheld that the alleged conduct or behaviour shall be deliberated, full of meaning and transparency, and most importantly, the parties shall subsequently act in reliance of such conduct.[12]

2. Abuse of Rights

Generally speaking, in the Ibero-American systems the notion of abuse of rights regards to the exercise of one party's rights in a way and under

[9] *See* Chile Appeal Court of Santiago, *Décima Sala,* 13 September 2006.

[10] Chile Supreme Court,-*Rol* 228-03, 9 November 2004.

[11] Spain Supreme Tribunal, 18 October 2006, *Id Cendoj:* 28079110012006101032; Spain Supreme Tribunal, 6 April 2006, *Id Cendoj:* 28079110012006100366; ICC Final Award Case No. 13435 *Lex Contractus* Spanish Law with implied exclusion of the CISG: stating that according to the doctrine developed by Spanish case law for acts to be classified as own acts these must be "definitive, continuing and of unequivocal nature, in the sense of being an expression of a consent aimed at creating, defining, fixing, modifying, extinguishing or establishing a certain legal situation or relationship."

[12] ICC Final Award Case No. 12755 *Lex Contractus* Argentinean Law.

circumstances susceptible to be legally censured. The notion of abuse of right imposes certain limits to the freedom to assert personal rights recognised by the law.

Most Ibero-American systems have expressly embraced the notion.[13] In other systems, where no express reference is made in the statutory law, the jurisprudence acknowledges his consideration.[14] Nevertheless, depending upon the country's law and the jurisprudence different criteria has been established in order to determine under which circumstances the exercise of a right may become abusive.

2.1. Approaches

There are two main approaches taken in order to typify the abuse of rights. On the one hand, there are those legal systems that integrate a subjective element by having due regard to the misconduct and faulty intent of the party which holds his right. On the other hand, are those legal systems which include an objective element by taking into consideration the final goal of the legal rule and which considers that only when the said goal is exceeded or disrespected, an abuse of rights takes place. On many occasions, though, the laws have adopted dual or mixed approaches to characterise the abuse of rights.

2.1.1. Subjective

Within the legal systems categorised as subjective, some understand that the abuse of rights take place when there is intention or purpose to annoy or cause a prejudice to the other party.[15] The main deficiency of this approach consists in the difficulty to prove the deception (*dolo*) of the party making tort to the other party through his right.[16]

A second solution is proposed by those laws which only regard the conduct of the party who has caused harm to the other party, though such conduct is

[13] Argentina Art. 1071 CC; Bolivia Art. 107 CC; Brazil Art. 187 CC; Costa Rica Art. 22 CC; Guatemala Art. 1653 CC; Mexico Art. 1912 CC; Paraguay Art. 372 CC; Peru Preliminar Art. II CC; Portugal Art. 334 CC; Spain Art. 7 CC; Venezuela Art. 1.185 CC.

[14] Chile Supreme Court, *Rol* 228-03, 9 November 2004; El Salvador Supreme Court, *Cass civ, Ortíz de Hernández v. Campos Rivera*, 1346-2001, 24 July 2002.

[15] Bolivia Art. 107 CC: note that it has a mixed approach as it also follows the economic and social goal of the right solution further mentioned in this Chapter; Guatemala Art. 1653 CC; Mexico Art. 1912 CC; Paraguay Art. 372 CC: note that it has a mixed approach as it also follows the economic and social goal of the right solution further mentioned in this Chapter.

[16] Mexico Collegiate Tribunals, *Novena Época,* Registry 186700, SJF XVI, July 2002, p. 1231: sustained that the compensation granted by Art. 1912 of Mexico's Civil Code does not only require the causation of damage and the lack of utility for the party holding the right, but it also requires the subjective element consisting in the intention to cause the damage by the party holding the right.

absent of deception (*dolo*). Under this approach the burden of proving the intention to harm disappears, as the negligent conduct suffices; for example, when a party to a contract exercises his right of avoidance of the contract without obtaining any personal benefit from such an action. Such seems to be the approach taken by the Chilean Supreme Court, though mixed with the legitimate interest approach reviewed in the following paragraphs. The Court explained that the assertion of a right should have as a limit the satisfaction of a serious and legitimate interest that 'does not cause harm or prejudice to other persons'. Thus, an abuse of rights will take place if legal claims cause economical damage since if the latter does not occur one cannot talk about an abusive exercise of a right. The abuse is then characterised by the result and the liability that it creates.[17]

The Costa Rican and the Spanish Civil Code adopt conjunctively the two solutions mentioned above. The prejudice caused can be intentional or accidental.[18]

2.1.2. Objective

Objective approaches take into consideration the economic and social purposes that motivate the enactment or creation of the right in question.[19] The solution proposes to consider whether the right was asserted in accordance with the objectives pursued by the legislator.

In a similar objective approach, some laws consider that the exercise of a right is abusive when such goes against the moral and the good conventions. Hence, Argentina, Brazil, Portugal and Venezuela embrace a mixed solution as, not only the infringement of the economic and social goals of the law constitutes an abuse of rights but, also the breach of the limits of the god faith and, the moral or the good conventions.[20]

2.2. Parties' conduct

Finally, it may be worth remembering that, as explained by an ICC Arbitral Tribunal whilst applying the Portuguese law, even if 'abuse of right' is

[17] *See* Chile Supreme Court,-*Rol* 228-03, 9 November 2004.

[18] Costa Rica Art. 22 CC; Spain Art. 7 (1) (2) CC: "any act or omission in a contract, that because of the circumstances, its object or the intention of a party, surpasses the normal limits of the a right, with damages to the counter-party or a third person, will give rise to due compensation or to the adoption of the necessary measures to stop the abuse."

[19] Argentina Art. 1707 CC; Bolivia Art. 107 CC; Brazil Art. 187 CC; Paraguay Art. 372 CC; Portugal Art. 334 CC; Venezuela Art. 1.185 part 2 CC; ICC Final Award Case No. 10044 *Lex Contractus* Portuguese Law.

[20] Argentina Art. 1707 CC; Brazil Art. 187 CC; Portugal Art. 334 CC; Venezuela Art. 1.185 part 2 CC.

established under the provisions of the statutory laws, in a long-term contract the parties, must react within a reasonable time, in order to allege the violations of their contractual relationship. As "if they do not react, time heals the possible breaches and brings about the 'convalescence' of the contract which is, thus, tacitly modified."[21]

[21] ICC Final Award Case No. 10044 *Lex Contractus* Portuguese Law: supporting his view on Portugal Art. 340 CC.

Part 8

Obligations of the Seller

Chapter 34

General Remarks on the Obligations of the Seller

1. Contractual Terms and Default Obligations

The Ibero-American laws allow the contracting parties to freely establish the extent of their obligations and recognise the primary position of parties' free determination.[1] Although some limitations are established by the public order, the morality, the social interest and the imperative law.[2] The Peruvian Civil Code clearly presents the principle with the statement: "unless they are imperative, legal provisions on contracts are supplementary to the will of the parties."[3]

In this regard, many of the obligations imposed by the Ibero-American laws and the CISG are not imperative but supplementary. For example, although one of the main obligations of the seller is the delivery of the goods immediately or in a reasonable time after the contract's conclusion, the parties are free to agree on the time and place to do so.[4] In addition, parties can freely establish the time for the transfer of property.[5] The parties can agree, for example, that the delivery or the transfer of title occurs once the complete price for the goods is paid.[6]

1 *See generally* Ch. 3.
2 In this regard *see* Ch. 3, 1.2.2 & Ch. 19.
3 Peru Arts. 1353, 1356 CC.
4 *See* Ch. 35, 3.
5 *See* Ch. 45, 2.
6 *See* Ch. 42, 5.1.

2. Main Obligations

The Ibero-American laws impose three main obligations on the seller.[7] First, the delivery of the sold goods to the buyer;[8] second, the delivery of conforming goods or the warranty of material defects;[9] third, the transfer of title and possession or compensation for eviction.[10] As in the CISG, the Ibero-American laws associate the duty to deliver with the obligations of conformity of the goods and the transfer of title.[11] However, not all the Ibero-American laws require the seller to be the owner of the goods at the time of contract conclusion.[12]

3. Potential Ancillary Obligations

Multiple subsidiary obligations can arise from the contract itself or from the relevant national law.[13] On the one hand, the contract may call for the delivery of specific documents often essential in international transactions, such as bills of lading, receipts, certificates of origin and other related documents.[14] In addition, the contract may require proof of compliance with international standards, such as a S.G.S certificate, insurance of the goods, or the use of certain type of transport. In many instances, the degree of compliance or the failure to comply is a question that can only be answered by the contract, and not by the CISG or the Ibero-American laws.

---

7 *See* the Ibero-American doctrinal references on this issue in Argentina: R. Compagnucci de Caso, Contrato de Compraventa 40, 124 (2007); Bolivia: W. Kaune Arteaga, Curso de Derecho Civil, Contratos, Vol. 2, 123 (1996); Mexico: S. León Tovar, Los Contratos Mercantiles 151 (2004); Portugal: L. De Lima Pinheiro, Dereito Comercial Internacional 281 (2005); Spain: E. Guardiola Sacarrera, La compraventa internacional: importaciones y exportaciones 63 (2001); Venezuela: J.L. Aguilar Gorrondona, Contratos y Garantias: Derecho Civil IV, 213 (2008).

8 *See* Ch. 35.

9 *See* Ch. 37.

10 *See* Ch. 38.

11 Under the CISG, the main obligations of the seller are the delivery of the conforming goods, the transfer of their property and the related documents. These obligations must be performed so that the buyer can acquire the property and the use of conforming goods. This rule is in accordance with the Roman law principle of *tradere vacua possession* of the goods present in Ibero-American laws, *see* Arts. 30, 34, 35, 71 CISG; *see also* Mexico: O. Vásquez del Mercado, Contratos Mercantiles 204 (2008); Mexico: León Tovar, *supra* note 7, at 151; Portugal: De Lima Pinheiro, *supra* note 7, at 28; Venezuela: Aguilar Gorrondona, *supra* note 7, at 217.

12 *See* Ch. 46, 2.

13 Mexico Art. 372 Com C is clear on this with the statement "on sales contracts the parties are bound by any legal clause they agree upon."

14 *See* Ch. 36.

On the other hand, the laws may also impose subsidiary obligations to the seller. The seller's obligations may be extended by certain national standards from which the parties may not deviate. For example, domestic Ibero-American laws may require that certain products are produced with specific ingredients or may prohibit the use of others.[15] It can also happen that the domestic law requires products to be labelled with specific information and that they are transported in special packages. Although the parties can always agree otherwise, such ancillary obligations may become binding when the seller knew or ought to have known them and a particular purpose to be imported or sold in the concern market was expressly made known to him.[16]

---

15 *See* Ch. 37, 2.3.2.

16 Art. 35(2)(b) CISG. P. Schlechtriem, *The Seller's Obligations Under the United Nations Convention on Contracts for the International Sale of Goods*, *in* N.M. Galston & H. Smit (Eds.), International Sales: The United Nations Convention on Contracts for the International Sale of Goods, Matthew Bender, Ch. 6, 6-1 to 6-35, at 6-4, http://www.cisg.law.pace.edu/cisg/biblio/schlechtriem10.html.

CHAPTER 35

DELIVERY

1. General Remarks on Delivery

All the Ibero-American laws and the CISG concur that the delivery of the goods is the main obligation of the seller.[1] The obligation has effects on other issues such as the transfer of risk, property and the cost of transportation.[2] The delivery of the goods must be performed in the form agreed by the parties and, absent an agreement, according to the provisions of the substantive applicable law.[3]

The delivery of the goods can be executed materially, legally or virtually. The material delivery takes place with the physical reception of the goods.[4] The legal delivery occurs when the law establishes it. For example, when the

[1] Art. 30 CISG; Argentina Arts. 1323, 1409, 1414 CC; Bolivia Art. 614 CC; Brazil Arts. 481, 491, 502 CC; Chile Art. 1824 CC; Colombia Art. 1880 CC; Dominican Republic Art. 1604 CC; Ecuador Art. 1791 CC; El Salvador Art. 1627 CC; Honduras Art. 1620 CC; Nicaragua Art. 2582 CC; Mexico Art. 2283 CC; Paraguay Art. 759(b)(d) CC; Peru Art. 1549 CC; Portugal Arts. 879, 882, 406 CC; Spain Arts. 1.461, 1.474, 1.484 CC; Venezuela Arts. 1265, 1474, 1486 CC; *see also* Costa Rica: D. Baudrit Carrillo, Los Contratos Traslativos del Derecho Privado – Principios de Jurisprudencia 48-49 (2000); Spain: E. Guardiola Sacarrera, La compraventa internacional: importaciones y exportaciones 63 (2001); Bolivia Supreme Court, *Severo Vega Veizaga v. René Reyes Reyes y Rosa Rivas de Reyes,* 200003-*Sala Civil*-1-067: the seller failed to deliver the goods agreed and under the particular circumstances entitled the buyer to seek the avoidance of the contract; Peru Supreme Court, *Sala civil transitoria,* Resolution No. 002838-2001, 25 January 2002: the seller failed to deliver the goods agreed hence the breach entitled the buyer to seek the avoidance of the contract.

[2] *See generally* Ch. 45, Ch. 44, 3 & Ch. 36.

[3] *See infra* 2 & 3.

[4] Argentina Arts. 2377, 2378 CC & Art. 461 Com C; Colombia Art. 923 (3) Com C; Ecuador Art. 194 (1) Com C; Mexico Art. 2284 CC; Uruguay Art. 527 Com C; Venezuela Art. 1.489 CC sentence 1, Art. 149 (1) Com C; Mexico: O. Vásquez del Mercado, Contratos Mercantiles 203 (2008); Spain *Audiencia Provincial Zaragoza*, Sec. 4, 20 January 1999.

buyer fails to take delivery on time, the goods are considered as delivered.[5] The virtual delivery takes place when the merchandise is handed over to the buyer through, for example, the bill of lading, the invoice, the representative documents or any other means established by the contract, the law or the usages, even if the goods are not materially delivered.[6]

This last approach fits well with the modern practice of sales made through the exchange of documents. Under this type of sales, the seller fulfils his obligation to deliver when he hands over the goods to the buyer by delivering the required documents.[7] In countries like Spain, with no similar statutory provision, scholars and courts recognise that the delivery (and *tradittio*) also takes place as soon as the seller allows the buyer to dispose of the goods by handing over the property titles in the time and the place agreed.[8]

2. Place of Delivery

2.1. Contractual Agreement

The primary rule under both the Ibero-American sales laws and the CISG is that the place of delivery of the goods is the place mutually agreed to by the

---

5 *See* Argentina Art. 2386 CC & Art. 462 Com C; Uruguay Art. 528 Com C: Argentina and Uruguay's provisions stating that where no time or person was selected by the buyer to take delivery, the seller fulfil his obligation to deliver if he do so at the buyer's domicile; Colombia Art. 923 (4) Com C; Mexico Art. 2284 CC; Spain Art. 332 Com C: if the buyer refuses taking delivery or he is in delay, the seller is considered to have fulfilled his obligation to deliver if he performs a judicial deposit of the goods; Spain Supreme Tribunal, 10 January 2007 *Id Cendoj:* 28079110012007100999: the seller's judicial deposit of the goods would allow him to claim the specific performance of the buyer obligation or to prove he had fulfilled his obligation in case the buyer seek the declaration of avoidance.

6 Argentina Arts. 2385, 2388 CC & Arts. 461, 463(3)(4) Com C; Bolivia Arts. 850, 864 Com C; Brazil Art. 529-532 CC: the delivery of the documents is understood to be the delivery of the goods; Chile Art. 149(1) Com C; Colombia Art. 923(1) Com C; Ecuador Art. 194(2) Com C; Guatemala Art. 695 para. 1 Com C; Mexico Art. 2284 para. 3 CC & Art. 378 Com C; *see also* Costa Rica Art. 466(b)(c)(f) Com C; Nicaragua Art. 355 Com C; Uruguay Art. 529(3)(4) Com C; Venezuela Art. 1.489 CC & Art. 149(2)(3) Com C; *see also* Argentina Art. 463(2) Com C; Chile Art. 149(2) Com C; Ecuador Art. 194(3) Com C; Uruguay Art. 529(2) Com C: under Argentina, Chile, Ecuador and Uruguay's Com C when the buyer marks the goods with his mark with the consent of the seller; Spain Supreme Tribunal, 22 November 2006, *Id Cendoj:* 28079110012006101175: applying Spain Art. 339 Com C upheld that the buyer was bound to pay the price from the time the goods were at his disposal; Mexico: Vásquez del Mercado, *supra* note 4, at 203.

7 Mexico: S. León Tovar, Los Contratos Mercantiles 151, 153 (2004); Mexico: Vásquez del Mercado, *supra* note 4, at 208, 209; Venezuela: J.L. Aguilar Gorrondona, Contratos y Garantias: Derecho Civil IV, 219 (2008).

8 *See* Spain: Guardiola Sacarrera, *supra* note 1, at 64; Spain Supreme Tribunal, 22 December 2000, *Id Cendoj:* 28079110002000100627.

parties.[9] The rule corresponds to the principle of 'freedom of contract' since choosing the place of delivery is not an issue that disturbs the public order.[10]

Parties may commonly designate the place of delivery of the goods by inserting within their contracts a selected national or international term of commerce. For example, among the Ibero-American countries, Bolivia, Costa Rica, El Salvador and Guatemala have integrated into their laws some commercial terms known by the acronyms FOB, CIF, C y F and FAS.[11] On the other hand, the International Commercial Terms or INCOTERMS,[12] distinguish between four different categories of terms depending on the place where the goods have to be placed at the buyer's disposal. These groups could be summarised into two big categories depending on whether one deals with sales at departure (Groups E, F and C) or sales at arrival (Group D). Hence, the exact place of delivery could be as follows:

Under Ex works the seller delivers when he places the goods at the disposal of the buyer at the seller's premises or another named place *e.g.* works, factory, warehouse, *etc.*[13] The goods do not need to be loaded on any collective vehicle. If no specific places or points have been agreed and there are several available, the seller may choose the one he considers convenient.[14] The Bolivian law has a similar term of commerce called 'origin's point' or EX, according to which the goods are to be delivered at the place and in the date or within the period of time agreed.[15] Regrettably, the Bolivian law provides no further details.

Free Carrier delivery (FCA) is completed when the seller delivers the goods to the carrier or another person nominated by the buyer at the named place. If the named place is the seller's premises, when the goods are loaded on the means of transport, but if the place was any other when the goods are at the disposal of the carrier or another person nominated by the seller.[16]

---

9 Art. 31 CISG; Argentina Art. 1410 CC & Art. 460 Com C; Bolivia Art. 620 CC; Brazil Art. 493 CC; Chile Art. 1588 CC & Art. 144 para. 1 Com C; Costa Rica Art. 451 Com C; Colombia Arts. 754(4), 1646 CC & Art. 923(3) Com C; Ecuador Art. 1631 CC & Art. 189 para. 1 Com C; El Salvador Art. 1458 CC; Mexico Art. 2291 CC & Art. 86 Com C; Peru Art. 1553 CC; Paraguay Arts. 752 para. 1, 760 CC & Art. 923 Com C; Spain Art. 1171 CC; Venezuela Art. 1492 CC; Mexico: Vásquez del Mercado, *supra* note 4, at 204; Mexico Collegiate Tribunals, *Novena Época*, Registry 201'660, SJF IV, August 1996, p. 642.

10 Argentina: R. Compagnucci de Caso, Contrato de Compraventa 135 (2007); Colombia: A. Tamayo Lombana, Alberto, El Contrato de Compraventa su Régimen Civil y Comercial 127 (2004); Mexico: León Tovar, *supra* note 7, at 153.

11 Bolivia Art. 852 *et seq.* Com C; Costa Rica Art. 473 *et seq.* Com C; El Salvador 1030 *et seq.* Com C; Guatemala Art. 697 *et seq.* Com C.

12 ICC introduced the first version of Incoterms in 1936.

13 ICC, Incoterms 2000: ICC official rules for the interpretation of trade terms, at 155.

14 *Id.*, at 156.

15 Bolivia Art. 852 Com C.

16 ICC, *supra* note 13, at 162; ICC Final Award Case No. 13967 *Lex Contractus* Bolivian Law and INCOTERMS 2000: upholding that in FCA is the seller's obligation to arrange and pay

As to the term Free alongside ship (FAS), the seller must place the goods alongside the vessel nominated by the buyer at the loading place named by the buyer at the named port of shipment.[17] Under the national term of commerce 'FAS' the place of delivery is alongside the vehicle transporting the goods, with no restriction to maritime transport, *i.e.* vessels, but also includes any sort of transport.[18]

The Free on board (FOB), the Cost and freight (CFR) and the Cost, insurance and freight (CIF) terms impose the seller the obligation to deliver the goods at the named port of shipment and on board the vessel nominated by the buyer.[19] The same place of delivery is referred by the national terms of commerce FOB, C y F[20] and CIF with the difference that under these terms no limitation to maritime transport exists, but include any sort of transport.[21]

With regards to the terms Carriage paid to (CPT) and Carrier and Insurance paid to (CIP) the seller must deliver the goods to the carrier contracted or if there are subsequent carriers to the first carrier for transport to the agreed point at the named place.[22]

The called 'Delivery' terms require the seller to place the goods at the disposal of the buyer: on the arriving means of transport not unloaded at the named place of delivery at the frontier (DAF); on board of the vessel at the unloading point referred in the name port of destination (DES); on the named quay at the named port of destination (DEQ); or at that of any other person named by the buyer, on any arriving means of transport not unloaded at the named place of destination (DDU & DDP).[23]

2.2. Default System

Few solutions are provided by the Ibero-American sales laws. Under many laws, two situations are distinguished. Absent an agreement on the contrary, 1) the ascertained goods have to be delivered in the place they are at the time of contract conclusion; 2) in all other cases [of unascertained goods] the delivery shall take place in the seller's domicile.[24]

---

for the delivery at the named place, even if under certain circumstances the named place is the seller's main place of business and the goods need to be first transported to such place.

17 ICC, *supra* note 13, at 170.

18 Bolivia Art. 854 Com C; Guatemala Art. 698 Com C.

19 ICC, *supra* note 13, at 178, 186, 194.

20 C y F National Term is similar to CFR Incoterm.

21 Bolivia Arts. 857, 862 Com C; For Costa Rica, El Salvador and Guatemala the place of delivery in CIF and C y F terms is not express but the same place as FOB could be implied in an harmonic interpretation of their provisions; *see* Costa Rica Arts. 475, 473 Com C; El Salvador Arts. 1030, 1034, 1035 Com C; Guatemala Arts. 697, 702, 704 Com C.

22 ICC, *supra* note 13, at 202, 210.

23 ICC official rules for the interpretation of trade terms.

24 Argentina Arts. 1410, 747 part 2 CC & Art. 461 Com C; Bolivia Art. 620 CC; Brazil Art.

The Spanish law does not establish any default rule regarding the place of delivery. Some scholars propose to look at the general provisions on contracts and obligations.[25] These refer to the place where the contract had been concluded, or in absence of this, to the place where the goods are at the time of contract conclusion, and in any other case to the seller's domicile.[26] Nevertheless, the Supreme Tribunal has clarified that unless otherwise agreed, the goods are to be delivered at the seller's domicile.[27]

The solutions proposed by most of the Ibero-American laws are limited if we compare them with those proposed by the CISG. The complexity of current international trade demands further options. The CISG contemplates two additional situations.

The first, and often common situation, involves the carrying of the goods. Under CISG article 31 (a), the seller is released from his obligation to deliver when he delivers the goods to the first carrier for transmission to the buyer. The Costa Rican and the Paraguayan laws contain a similar provision stating that the seller is released of the obligation to deliver when he hands over the goods to the carrier or messenger, whenever the goods have to be transported.[28] The rule has further implications as it also determines the moment when the risk of the goods passes from the seller to the buyer.[29]

The second and subsidiary situation concerns the sale of unascertained goods to be produced or manufactured. The rule established by the CISG requires, as *sine qua non* condition, that the parties, at the time of the conclusion of the contract, knew the place where such goods were or where the same should be produced or manufactured.[30] The condition accomplished,

---

493 CC; Chile Art. 1588 CC & Art. 144 para. 3 Com C; Colombia Art. 1646 CC; Ecuador Art. 1631 CC & Art. 189 para. 3 Com C; El Salvador Art. 1458 CC: all these countries refer to the place for the payment of obligations in general but the doctrine agree that the rule applies to determine the place of delivery of the goods, Mexico Art. 2291 CC; Peru Art. 1553 CC & Arts. 344, 423 Com C; Paraguay Art. 752 para. 1 CC: unless the parties were unaware of the place where the goods are at that time, in any other case the goods shall be delivered at the seller's domicile at that time; Uruguay Art. 527 Com C; Venezuela Arts. 1492, 1296 CC; *see* doctrinal references in Argentina: Compagnucci de Caso, *supra* note 10, at 135-136; Bolivia: W. Kaune Arteaga, Curso de Derecho Civil, Contratos, Vol. 2, 131 (1996); Colombia: Tamayo Lombana, *supra* note 10, at 129; Mexico: Vásquez del Mercado, *supra* note 4, at 204; Peru: A. Sierralta Ríos, La Compraventa Internacional y El Derecho Peruano 82 (1997); Venezuela: Aguilar Gorrondona, *supra* note 7, at 220; Argentina National Chamber of Commerce, *Sala* D, *Castelar S.A. v. Maralc SRL,* 11 April 1990, JA 1990-IV-165: "As there was no agreement in relation to the place of delivery in the present case, Art. 461 Com C shall apply, stating the place where the goods were at the time of the sale as the place of delivery. (...)."

[25] Namely to Spain Art. 1171 CC.

[26] Spain: M. Medina de Lemus, Derecho Civil: Obligaciones y Contratos II, Contratos en Particular, Vol. 2, 56 (2004).

[27] *See* Spain Supreme Tribunal, 13 May 1993, *Id Cendoj:* 28079110011993101284.

[28] Costa Rica Art. 474 Com C; Paraguay 752 para. 2 CC.

[29] *See* Art. 67(1) CISG & Ch. 44, 3.

[30] Art. 31(b) CISG.

the CISG indicates that the seller is released from his obligation to deliver when he places the merchandise in that place.[31]

Besides, CISG Article 32 imposes on the seller obligations relating to goods handed over to a carrier. The seller must identify the goods as agreed in the contract or by making marks or with the shipping documents. If the goods are not duly identified the seller must give notice of consignment, specifying the goods to the seller.[32] If the seller is bound by the contract to arrange the carriage of the goods to an agreed place he must do so bearing in mind the appropriateness of means of transportation to the circumstances and the usual terms for such transportation.[33]

These detailed obligations, (CISG Article 31(a)(b) and 32(1)(2)(3)) have no parallel in the Ibero-American laws. All Ibero-American related provisions were drafted considering situations of direct delivery. The Ibero-American laws could, with some difficulty, be applied to situations where the goods are required to be left at the carrier disposal and not at the buyer's disposal.[34] Nevertheless, the Ibero-American laws are flexible enough to provide solutions to similar situations. In this regard, the rules of contract interpretation and supplementation, the usages and the good faith principle[35] play an important role in determining the subsidiary obligations derived from the delivery of the goods to a carrier, absent a specific agreement on this issue.[36]

3. Time of Delivery

3.1. Contractual Agreement

The principle in both the Ibero-American laws and the CISG is that the goods must be delivered at the time agreed by the parties.[37] Similar to the place

31 *Id.*

32 Art. 32(1) CISG.

33 Art. 32(2) CISG.

34 Guardiola Sacarrera, *supra* note 1, at 63.

35 *See* Ch. 29, Ch. 30 and Ch. 32, 3.

36 According to Compagnucci de Caso the principle of good faith in Argentina Art. 1198 CC imposes to the seller the delivery of documents, titles (antecedents), proofs of tax payments, all related documents to the goods, the duty to inform about the nature and manage of the goods, and all necessary acts to achieve the objective of the contract, *see* Argentina: Compagnucci de Caso, *supra* note 10, at 126.

37 Art. 33 (a) CISG; Argentina Art. 1409 CC & Art. 464 Com C; Bolivia Art. 621 CC & Art. 843 Com C; Chile Art. 1826 CC & Art. 144 para. 1 Com C; Colombia Art. 1882 CC & Art. 924 Com C; Costa Rica Art. 465 Com C; Ecuador Art. 1793 CC & Art. 189 para. 1 Com C; El Salvador Art. 1629 CC; Mexico Art. 379 Com C; Paraguay Art. 760 CC; Peru Art. 1552 CC; Portugal Art. 473 Com C; Spain Art. 337 Com C; Uruguay Art. 530 Com C; Venezuela Art. 1.493 CC; Mexico: Vásquez del Mercado, *supra* note 4, at 204; ICC Final Award Case No. 14083 *Lex Contractus* Brazilian Law.

of delivery, the parties are free to choose the time of performance of their obligations since this is not an issue that disturbs the public order.[38]

The CISG establishes, in addition, that where there is no fixed date but a period of time was specified, or can be determinable, for the delivery, the seller is released from his obligation if he delivers the goods at any time within that period, unless the circumstances indicate the buyer is to choose a date.[39]

3.2. Default System

The Ibero-American laws provide different solutions depending on the individual jurisdictions and on whether the sale is characterised as B2B or C2C.[40] Under many countries B2B sales, if no time was fixed for delivery, the seller shall place the goods at the buyer's disposal within twenty-four hours of the conclusion of the contract.[41] Similarly, Bolivia's Code of Commerce grants to the seller forty - eight hours to deliver the goods from the conclusion of the contract, unless additional time is needed giving due consideration to the nature of the transaction or the means of the delivery.[42]

On the other hand, under many countries' C2C sales, the default rule requires the seller to deliver the goods immediately after the conclusion of the contract.[43] In Argentina, Bolivia and Paraguay C2C sales, the date of the delivery will be chosen unilaterally by the buyer.[44]

Both approaches are unfit for international sales contracts. The immediate delivery or the delivery within twenty-four hours is unrealistic in international and even in domestic trade. Nor does the exclusive buyer's choice of the date give much certainty as to the time to perform or to other correlated issues such as the passing of risk.[45]

---

[38] Peru Supreme Court, *Sala civil transitoria,* Resolution No. 002838-2001, 25 January 2002: acknowledging that unless otherwise agreed by the parties, delivery has to be made immediately after the conclusion of the contract.

[39] Art. 33(b) CISG.

[40] For details on the distinction between B2B and C2C *see* Ch. 5, 1.

[41] Argentina Art. 464 Com C; Chile Art. 144 para. 2 Com C; Colombia Art. 924 Com C: unless the nature of the contract or the characteristics of the delivery require a longer time period; Costa Rica Art. 465; Ecuador Art. 189 para. 2 CC; Mexico Art. 379 Com C; Portugal Art. 473 Com C: only if the goods were seen by the buyer, if the goods have not been seen the buyer may require the competent court to fix the time of delivery; Portugal Art. 473 sole para. Com C; Spain Art. 337 Com C; Uruguay Art. 530 Com C.

[42] Bolivia Art. 843 Com C.

[43] Chile Art. 1826 CC; Colombia Art. 1882 CC; Ecuador Art. 1793 CC; El Salvador Art. 1629 CC; Peru Art. 1552 CC; Peru Supreme Court, *Sala civil transitoria*, Resolution No. 001584-2002, 2 July 2002; Peru Supreme Court, *Sala civil transitoria,* Resolution No. 002838-2001, 25 January 2002: acknowledging that unless otherwise agreed by the parties, delivery has to be made immediately alter the conclusion of the contract.

[44] Argentina Art. 1409 part 2 CC; Bolivia Art. 621 (II) CC; Paraguay Art. 760 CC.

[45] *See* how the passing of risk is linked with the place and time of delivery in Ch. 44.

On the other hand, the CISG provides, absent an agreement on the contrary, that the seller shall deliver the goods within a reasonable time after the conclusion of the contract.[46] In one of the earliest Ibero-American cases applying the CISG, the *Audiencia Provincial de Barcelona* held that the buyer had accomplished his obligation to deliver the goods within a reasonable time, although the goods were received by the buyer after their selling season.[47] The *Audiencia Provincial* recognised the importance of punctual delivery of seasonal merchandise in trade. However, it considered that as the parties have not agreed on a fixed date for delivery, the seller was required to deliver within a reasonable time after the conclusion of the contract as stated in Article 33(c) of the CISG, and the seller did so since the buyer had accepted their reception without raising any objection even if the trade season was already over.[48]

[46] Art. 33(c) CISG.

[47] Spain Audiencia Provincial Barcelona, 20 June 1997, published in RJC, 1997, 4, at 111-112.

[48] *Id.*

CHAPTER 36

COSTS, LICENCES AND DOCUMENTS

1. Transportation and Insurance Costs

1.1. Contractual Allocation

As in many related contractual duties, the obligation to cover the cost of the transportation and/or of the insurance for the goods can be freely allocated between the parties. Such is recognised in the Ibero-American laws and in the CISG; which yet again acknowledge the primacy of the principle of parties' freedom of contract.[1] The parties may commonly establish the part of the cost for transportation or insurance that each of them shall bear. They do so by inserting into their contract a national term of commerce[2] or an INCOTERM belonging to the category 'C' or 'D'.[3] Acronyms followed by the names of specific world places, *e.g.* cities, ports, *etc.*, are enough to trigger a series of obligations regarding the cost of transportation and the cost for insurance of the goods.[4]

---

1 Art. 32(2)(3) CISG; Argentina Art. 1415 CC & Art. 460 Com C; Bolivia 852 Art. *et seq.* Com C; Brazil Art. 531 CC; Costa Rica Art. 473 *et seq.* Com C; Guatemala Art. 697 *et seq.* Com C; Mexico Art. 2285 CC; Uruguay Art. 525 Com C.

2 Among the Ibero-American countries Bolivia, Costa Rica and Guatemala have integrated into their commercial laws the commercial terms known as FOB, CIF, C y F and FAS; *see* Bolivia Art. 852 *et seq.* Com C; Costa Rica Art. 473 *et seq.* Com C; El Salvador Art. 1030 *et seq.* Com C; Guatemala Art. 697 *et seq.* Com C.

3 The 'D' terms also require the seller to pay the cost of transportation to the place of destination *i.e.* DAF, DES, DEQ, DDU and DDP.

4 *See for example* ICC Final Award Case No. 13967 *Lex Contractus* Bolivian Law and INCOTERMS 2000: upholding that the seller has the obligation to arrange and pay for the delivery at the named place, even if under certain circumstances the named place is the seller's main place of business and the goods need to be first transported to such place.

Under the 2000 version of the INCOTERMS, the 'C' terms are those where the seller has to contract for the carriage but without assuming the risk of loss of or damage to the goods or additional cost due to events occurring after shipment or dispatch: *i.e. CFR, CIF, CPT* and *CIP*.[5] The national terms of commerce known under the acronyms CIF and C y F also contain the seller's obligation to hire and to bear the cost of transport of the goods to the indicated place.[6]

According to the CIF and CIP terms the seller must hire the insurance and bear the insurance cost. Such insurance must be obtained as agreed in the contract so that the buyer or any other person having a legitimate interest can claim directly to the insurer. The insurance must be contracted with underwriters or an insurance company of good reputation. The minimum insurance shall cover the price provided in the contract, plus ten percent, and shall be provided in the currency of the contract.[7]

Under the CIF national term of commerce, the seller shall contract an insurance covering all the risks or the usual risks to which the goods are exposed,[8] for the total price of the goods plus ten percent.[9] Additionally, the seller shall deliver the insurance policy in favour of the buyer or person designated by him.[10]

However, these obligations are normally considered subsidiary to the main obligations. Many contracts may not include terms of commerce allocating the cost of transportation or insurance. Absent an agreement on this issue, the CISG does not have default rules for the allocation of these obligations, but the Ibero-American laws do, at least in relation to the issue of the transportation of the goods to the place of delivery.

1.2. Default Rule

In most Ibero-American countries, unless otherwise agreed, the seller shall cover the necessary expenses, including transportation, to deliver materially[11] the goods to the place of delivery and the buyer shall bear all those expenses incurred after delivery.[12] For example, if the parties agree the delivery of the

5 *See generally* ICC, Incoterms 2000: ICC official rules for the interpretation of trade terms.

6 Bolivia Arts. 855, 856, 859(1) Com C; Costa Rica Art. 473 Com C; El Salvador Arts. 1030, 1031(1), 1034 Com C; Guatemala Arts. 699, 704 Com C.

7 ICC, *supra* note 5, at 194, 210.

8 El Salvador Art. 1031(II) Com C: no reference to the extra 10% of the total price of the goods.

9 Bolivia Arts. 858, 859(2) Com C; Costa Rica Art. 473 Com C.

10 Bolivia Arts. 858, 859(2) Com C; El Salvador Art. 1031(III) Com C.

11 Chile Supreme Court, RDJ Vol. 27, Sec. 1, at 190, *cited in* Chile: R. Díez Duarte, La Compraventa en el Código Civil Chileno 149, n. 393 (1993): specifying that Chile Art. 1825 CC refers to the material delivery of the goods and not to the virtual delivery.

12 Argentina Art. 1415 CC & Arts. 460, 461 Com C; Bolivia Art. 619 CC & Art. 844 Com

goods to take place in Cartagena, Colombia, the seller will bear the cost of the land or maritime transportation up to Cartagena. However, if in the same case the buyer taking delivery in Cartagena is planning to use some of the goods in Quito, Ecuador, he must pay for the transportation cost and related expenses after the delivery in Cartagena to Quito.

The Argentinean National Chamber of Commerce interpreting this rule held that, in a case where the parties had agreed the delivery of the goods in a different place other than the place of conclusion with no specification about the transportation, it should be understood that the seller should bear the cost of the carriage up to that place.[13] On the other hand, the Spanish Supreme Tribunal explained that when no place of delivery was agreed, and the seller fulfils his obligation by placing the goods at his own domicile, if the goods are later sent to the buyer's place of business or a different place, it should be understood, unless otherwise agreed, that the cost and risk of transportation was at the buyer's side.[14]

Regarding the cost of insurance not much has been stated in the Ibero-American laws. The Brazilian Civil Code may be one of the few that deals with the issue. According to its provisions, if among the documents delivered by the seller there is a insurance policy covering the risk of transportation, the cost of insurance shall be borne by the buyer, except if the seller knew of any loss or defect in the goods.[15]

C; Chile Art. 1825 CC; Colombia Art. 1881 CC & Art. 909 para. 2 Com C; El Salvador Art. 1628 CC; Ecuador Art. 1792 CC; Mexico Art. 2285 CC & Art. 382 (I) (II) Com C; Spain Art. 338 Com C; Uruguay Art. 525 Com C; Venezuela Art. 1491 CC; *see also* Bolivia: V. Camargo Marín, Derecho Comercial Boliviano 405 (2007); Mexico: O. Vásquez del Mercado, Contratos Mercantiles 204 (2008).

13 Argentina National Chamber of Commerce, *Sala* D, *Expreso los Angeles c. Fábrica de Muebles*, 3 March 1984; National Chamber of Commerce, *Sala* D, *Castelar S.A. v. Maralc SRL,* 11 April 1990, JA 1990-IV-165: "[in the case] the parties have not stated a place of delivery. The seller sent the goods to the office of the buyer and expected to charge for such service in addition to the agreed price. If the delivery was agreed to be done at the office of the seller, there would be no doubts that transportation to the office of the buyer should have been charged to the buyer. Similarly, if delivery was agreed to be done at the office of buyer, the seller should have been in charge of the costs of transpiration; such solution was reached in relation to '*Felipe Campagna* e *hijos SRL, LL 1984-D-683*' held by this court. As there was no agreement in relation to the place of delivery in the present case, Art. 461 Com C shall apply, stating the place where the goods were at the time of the sale as the place of delivery. (…) Hence, the transportation from the goods to the office of the buyer shall be in charge of the buyer (…)."

14 *See* Spain Supreme Tribunal, 13 May 1993, *Id Cendoj:* 28079110011993101284.

15 Brazil Art. 531 CC.

2. Licences

2.1. Necessity of State Approval

Absent an agreement on the contrary, the Ibero-American laws state that the seller shall cover the necessary expenses, and in consequence bear the necessary steps such as State approvals, to deliver the goods to the place of delivery; and the buyer shall do the same after delivery.[16]

2.2. Import Export Licences

The parties to a sales contract are also free to allocate the obligations in connection to the passing of the merchandise through the customs of the country of export or import. They normally do so by agreeing in a national term of commerce or in an INCOTERM.

The obligation imposed by the concerned INCOTERM does not only include the payment of the duty or other charges, but also the performance and payment of whatever administrative matters are connected with the passing of the goods through customs, and the information to the national authorities in this connection.

The general principle in the INCOTERMS is that the seller must procure an export licence and the buyer must procure an import licence.[17] But in cases where the buyer must simply collect the goods from the seller, as in the Ex Works INCOTERM, it is the buyer who must also obtain the export licence.[18]

The same approach is followed by some national terms. Under the Bolivian and the Guatemalan laws a FOB or a FAS term of commerce imposes to the seller the duty to pay any taxes, rights or expenses necessary to place the goods on board or along side (respectively), and to obtain the concerned documents in order to be delivered to the buyer.[19] As to the terms of commerce CIF and C y F, the laws expressly allocate to the seller the duty to pay any export tariff or rights needed for the export of the goods.[20]

Additionally, following the Ibero-American general default rule stating that the seller must cover the necessary expenses to the place of delivery, the

---

16 Argentina Art. 1415 CC & Art. 460 Com C; Bolivia Art. 619 CC & Art. 844 Com C; Chile Art. 1825 CC; Colombia Art. 1881 CC & Art. 909 para. 2 Com C; El Salvador Art. 1628 CC; Ecuador Art. 1792 CC; Mexico. Art. 2285 CC; Uruguay Art. 525 Com C; Venezuela Art. 1491 CC.

17 C. Widmer, *in* Ingeborg Schwenzer (Ed.), Schlechtriem & Schwenzer Commentary on the UN Convention on the International Sale of Goods Art. 31, para. 85, at 526 (2010).

18 Such is not the case for FCA or FAS Incoterms, *see* generally ICC, *supra* note 5.

19 Bolivia Arts. 853(2), 854 Com C; Guatemala Arts. 697, 698 Com C.

20 Bolivia Arts. 859(4), 856 Com C.

seller must also bear the necessary steps up to the place of delivery and the buyer shall bear all those necessary steps after delivery.[21]

3. Documents

3.1. Documents of Title

Most of the Ibero-American Codes of Commerce establish the duty of the seller to deliver the invoice representing the goods.[22] Despite this, the obligation to hand over the property documents has not been extensively covered in the Ibero-American statutory laws. This may be explained by the fact that in half of the Ibero-American countries the passing of title operates concurrently with the meeting of the minds on the goods and the price.[23] Accordingly, some authors consider that the transfer of the documents representing the title of ownership generally takes the character of an ancillary obligation.[24] However, as further presented, the Ibero-American jurisprudence has often taken an active role in imposing the duty to deliver the documents representing the goods.

The above being said, the obligation to deliver the documents is implicit in the Civil Codes of Brazil and Paraguay under the sale by documents.[25] On the other hand, the Bolivian, the Peruvian, the Portuguese and the Venezuelan Civil Codes may have the rule which is closest to the text in the CISG; as they do not only require the delivery of the goods but also the delivery of documents and titles related to the property or possession of the goods sold.[26]

In this regard, the Bolivian Supreme Court has sustained that if the seller fails to deliver the documents and titles relating to the property sold and which are needed to acquire full ownership or possession, the buyer is entitled to claim the specific performance of such statutory obligation,[27] or the avoidance

---

21 Argentina Art. 1415 CC & Art. 460 Com C; Bolivia Art. 619 CC & Art. 844 Com C; Chile Art. 1825 CC; Colombia Art. 1881 CC & Art. 909 para. 2 Com C; El Salvador Art. 1628 CC; Ecuador Art. 1792 CC; Mexico Art. 2285 CC; Uruguay Art. 525 Com C; Venezuela Art. 1491 CC.

22 *See* Argentina Art. 474 Com C; Bolivia Art. 834 Com C; Chile Art. 160 Com C; Colombia Art. 944 Com C; Costa Rica Art. 448 Com C; Ecuador Art. 201 Com C; Nicaragua Art. 362 Com C; Portugal Art. 476 Com C; Uruguay Art. 557 Com C; Venezuela Art. 147 Com C.

23 *See* Ch. 45, 3.1.

24 *See* in this regard Peru: A. Sierralta Ríos, La Compraventa Internacional y El Derecho Peruano 86 (1997).

25 Brazil Arts. 529-532 CC; Paraguay Art. 786 CC.

26 Bolivia Art. 617 CC; Peru Arts. 1549, 1551 CC; Portugal Art. 882 (3) CC; Venezuela Art. 1.495 CC.

27 Bolivia Supreme Court, Sala Civil, 10 June 2002, *Jaime Roger Lema Gonzáles v. Bo. Gunnar Byren Johansson.*

of the contract.[28] The Peruvian Supreme Court has also acknowledged the same effect in relation to the breach of the duty to deliver the documents and titles representing the property and right of use of the goods.[29]

Additionally, a Spanish Tribunal sustained that a seller had failed to fulfil his main obligation to deliver the goods since the physical delivery does not suffice. The Tribunal explained that the seller was bound to deliver the goods legally, by handing over the documents that would allow the buyer to freely use and exploit the goods.[30]

The CISG concedes to the seller the option to cure any omission or mistake in the documents.[31] The opportunity to remedy operates in cases of early reception of the documents. The Ibero-American laws do not expressly grant the same concession. However, such could be deduced from the principle of contract preservation *Favor negotti* and good faith.[32] These are sources of interpretation and supplementation in the Ibero-American contract law.[33]

3.2. Other Documents

Although only few Ibero-American laws expressly establish default rules on the obligation to hand over documents relating to the goods,[34] the rest may not always exempt the seller from complying with such. Similar obligations can derive from a systematic interpretation and supplementation of the contract, the usages or the good faith principle.[35] All of these sources play an important role in determining the subsidiary obligations derived from the delivery of the goods.[36]

Additionally, a contract may describe in detail the documents that the buyer needs in order to take possession of the goods. It may do so by reference to the INCOTERMS that impose several subsidiary duties to the

---

28 Bolivia Supreme Court, Sala Civil, *Francisco de Asis Perales v. Rolando Soliz Velásquez.*

29 Peru Supreme Court, *Sala civil transitoria*, Resolution No. 002534-2006, 2 April 2007.

30 Spain Audiencia Provincial Vitoria, 6 April 1985.

31 Art. 34 CISG.

32 Mexico: S. León Tovar, Los Contratos Mercantiles 151 (2004); Portugal: L. De Lima Pinheiro, Dereito Comercial Internacional 281 (2005); Venezuela: J.L. Aguilar Gorrondona, Contratos y Garantias: Derecho Civil IV, 217 (2008).

33 In this regard *see* Ch. 29 & Ch. 31.

34 Brazil Arts. 529-532 CC; Paraguay Art. 786 CC; Peru Arts. 1549, 1551 CC; Portugal Art. 882 (3) CC; Venezuela Art. 1.495 CC.

35 *See* Bolivia Supreme Court, *Sala Civil*, 10 June 2002, *Jaime Roger Lema Gonzáles v. Bo. Gunnar Byren Johansson. See also* generally Ch. 31.

36 According to Argentina: R. Compagnucci de Caso, Contrato de Compraventa 126 (2007), the principle of good faith in Argentina Art. 1198 CC imposes to the seller the delivery of documents, titles, proofs of tax payments, all related documents to the goods, the duty to inform about the nature and administration of the goods, and all necessary acts to achieve the purpose of the contract.

seller. These documents may include bills of lading, insurance certificates, invoices, clearance documents, certificates of origin, etc. On this issue, an ICC Sole Arbitrator decided that in the light of the sales agreement and of the INCOTERM DAF, the seller had a duty to provide an original certificate of origin to the buyer and therefore found that the seller was *prima facie* liable to compensate the buyer for the consequential losses incurred because of late delivery of the said document.[37]

Similarly, in a sales of goods subject to the CIF and C y F national terms of commerce, the seller shall provide the buyer with the invoice, the transportation documents, (*e.g.* negotiable bill of lading, a non negotiable sea-waybill or inland waterway document), the certificate of origin, the insurance policy, and any other document that the buyer may need to import the goods in the final destination.[38]

[37] ICC Final Award Case No. 14633 *Lex Contractus* Incoterms, CISG, UNIDROIT PICC.

[38] Bolivia Art. 859(5) Com C; El Salvador Art. 1031(III); Guatemala Art. 700(3) Com C.

Chapter 37

Conformity of the Goods

1. Subtle Distinctions: The Ibero-American Laws *v.* CISG

Under the Ibero-American laws, liability of the seller for the lack of conformity of the goods is primarily based on the breach of a statutory legal warranty.[1] Besides the obligation to deliver the goods, the seller has an independent obligation to guarantee that the goods do not contain defects that could make them improper for, or reduce, the function or the use they are usually given.[2]

Following this warranty, the Ibero-American laws distinguish between the delivery of goods containing the mentioned defects (*redhibitory vices*) and the delivery of the goods which are completely different to those agreed (*aliud pro alio*).[3] The liability for the defects is known under the name of warranty of *saneamiento*.[4] In contrast, the delivery of different goods or *aliud pro alio*

[1] Spain: A.M. Morales Moreno, *in* L. Díez Picazo y Ponce De León (Ed.), La Compraventa Internacional de Mecaderias- Comentario sobre la Convención de Viena Art. 35, IV, at 290-292 (1998).

[2] Argentina Art. 2164 CC; Brazil Art. 441 CC; Chile Art. 1858 (2) CC; Colombia Art. 1915 (2) CC; Ecuador Art. 1825 (2) CC; El Salvador Art. 1660 (2) CC; Guatemala Art. 1559 CC; Mexico Art. 2142 CC; Paraguay Art. 1789 CC; Portugal Art. 913 (2) CC; Spain Art. 1484 CC; Uruguay Art. 1718 CC; Venezuela Art. 1.518 CC. *See also* Argentina: R. Compagnucci de Caso, Contrato de Compraventa 207 (2007); Brazil: C.R. Gonçalves, Dereito Civil Brasileiro, Vol. III, Contratos e Atos Unilateralais 114 (2004); Venezuela: J.L. Aguilar Gorrondona, Contratos y Garantias: Derecho Civil IV, 255 (2008).

[3] *See* in this regard Spain: E. Guardiola Sacarrera, La compraventa internacional: importaciones y exportaciones 75 (2001); Spain Supreme Tribunal, 20 November 2008 *Id Cendoj:* 28079110012008101062.

[4] The different names given are *e.g.* in Argentina *saneamiento por vicios redhibitorios* (warranty for redhibitory defects) *see* Argentina Art. 1414 CC and Argentina: Compagnucci de Caso, *supra* note 2, at 205; In Brazil's Civil Code the opening section has the name of *Dos Vícios Redibitórios* in articles 441-446; *see also* the same express warranty in B2B sales Chile

constitutes in itself a breach of the obligation to deliver.[5] The distinction has an impact on the remedies available,[6] on the standards of non-conformity required by the law for the termination of the contract,[7] and on the different limitation periods to file law suits.[8]

The CISG evades any type of categorisation regarding the types of defects or non-conformity of the goods. The CISG limits itself to establishing default criteria, absent an express agreement, to determine the conformity of the goods under a single *suis generis* approach.[9] Hence, any type of discrepancy relating to the quantity or the quality, regardless of the type of defect – apparent or hidden – or the delivery of goods which are different to those agreed, is covered by the parameters of conformity established under Article 35.

The only Ibero-American system that takes a CISG approach is Portugal. In the Portuguese law, the sale of defective goods according to the contract or the law constitutes a breach of contract *per se* which does not need commencement of a particular or independent legal action.[10] In this way, the Portuguese law departs from the redhibitory vices approach taken by the rest of the Ibero-American laws.[11]

2. Contractual Requirements

The Ibero-American sales laws require the delivery of conforming goods according to the contract.[12] The contract is the first instrument establishing the

Art. 154 Com C; Colombia Art. 936 Com C; Costa Rica Art. 467 Com C; Ecuador Art. 191 Com C; Mexico Art. 384 Com C; Spain Art. 345 Com C; Uruguay Art. 549 Com C.

[5] *See* Brazil Tribunal of Justice of the State of São Paulo, Appeal with Revision 965123400, published 12 April 2006: the Tribunal differentiated between the delivery of goods containing hidden defects and delivery of different goods from the ones contractually established, avoiding a contract under which a label company produced a wrong label written 'language' instead of 'languages' for a school of languages; Spain Supreme Tribunal, 28 October 2008, *Id Cendoj:* 28079110012008100918.

[6] *See* Ch. 47, 1.

[7] *See* Ch. 53, 1.

[8] *See* Ch. 60, 2.

[9] Spain: Morales Moreno, *supra* note 1, Art. 35, IV, at 291.

[10] *See* Portugal's Civil Code section called *Venda de coisas defectuosas* in Arts. 913-922.

[11] ICC Final Award Case No. 11367 *Lex Contractus* Portuguese Law: "It is not disputed that since Roman times, the *actio quanti minoris* is one of the remedies available to a buyer." However, "[…] Defendant has not proven that such a remedy is available under general Portuguese law."

[12] *See* expressly Costa Rica Art. 421 Com C; Ecuador Art. 176 Com C; Venezuela Art. 135 Com C; Mexico: S. León Tovar, Los Contratos Mercantiles 155 (2004). Same approach as in Art. 35(1) CISG: the principle under the CISG is that the delivered goods shall be those described in the contract. Thus, the contract must specifically indicate the quality, the quantity and the description of goods that are the object of the transaction. The goods shall also be contained and packaged in the manner required by the contract.

standard of conformity of the goods. If the goods do not match with any of the points required by the contract the buyer is in breach. Yet again, the rules of contract interpretation in the Ibero-American laws are crucial in order to establish the meaning and effects of the terms agreed regarding the conformity of the goods.[13]

2.1. Description

Some Ibero-American laws expressly provide that the obligation to deliver encompasses the obligation to give to the buyer all that the contract describes.[14] Thus, a contract would normally set up the three essential components of the goods: the quantity, the quality and the description. The descriptive element of the goods is always somehow present in the contract.[15] Any difference between the description of the goods and those delivered, though obvious, represents a breach of contract.[16] In practice, the goods are normally described by establishing the type, gender, or the particular purposes they are intended to.

2.2. Quantity

Under the Ibero-American laws, if the seller delivers a quantity of goods which is smaller than that agreed, the buyer has the option to take delivery or to refuse the minor quantity. This has expressly been recognised in the rule

> if the buyer spontaneously takes delivery of only part of the quantity of the goods agreed, the contract is deemed to be concluded for the goods received, even if, the seller fails to deliver the rest of the goods, unless the buyer expressly requires specific performance of the rest.[17]

As under these laws the delivery of goods in a different quantity represents a breach of the obligation to deliver rather than an issue of non-conforming goods, the buyer who refuses to take delivery can make resort to any of the remedies provided for in the ordinary breach of contract.[18] This approach

---

[13] In this regard *see* Ch. 28 & Ch. 9.

[14] Panama Art. 1239; Spain Art. 1469 CC.

[15] Without description, for example, it is impossible to apply the first default interpretative criterion of CISG Art. 35(2)(a) … are fit for the purposes for which goods of the same description would ordinarily be used.

[16] I. Schwenzer, *in* I. Schwenzer (Ed.), Schlechtriem & Schwenzer Commentary on the UN Convention on the International Sale of Goods Art. 35, para. 10, at 573 (2010).

[17] Argentina Art. 468 Com C; Chile Art. 157 Com C; Colombia Art. 927 Com C; Ecuador Art. 200 Com C; Mexico Art. 374 Com C; Spain Art. 330 Com C; Uruguay Art. 537 Com C.

[18] Although the remedy of avoidance is hardly to be granted by a court due to the relatively high standard of breach required, the buyer could claim specific performance in the case of

differs to the CISG, that categorises the delivery of goods in a quantity that does not correspond to the contract as an issue of non-conformity rather than as an issue of non-delivery. The distinction has practical consequences in CISG sales. Under the rules of lack of conformity the buyer has the obligation to examine the goods within a short period and to give notice to the seller in a reasonable time.[19] If the buyer fails to do so, he looses his right to relay on a lack of conformity of the goods.[20] Lack of total delivery is not subject to such rules.[21]

2.3. Quality

The Ibero-American laws recognise a modality of sales called sale of goods of determined quality.[22] According to such modality, whenever a contract fixes the specific quality of the goods, the seller fulfils the obligation to deliver if they match the quality required.[23] Thus, if the contract required the delivery of, for example, one thousand bottles (75 cl.) of read wine, Argentinean-Cabernet 2006, and the seller so delivered, the buyer the cannot refuse to take delivery and must pay the price.[24] Under some laws, if the buyer refuses to take delivery on the grounds of non-conformity, experts will be appointed to decide on the conformity of the goods by comparing the goods sent by the seller with the quality called for in the contract.[25]

On the other hand, if the buyer takes delivery of the goods with no objection as to their quality within the time prescribed by law[26] or under the contract, and further manipulates the goods or even distributes them among his clients, such conduct may be considered as an implied acceptance of the quality;[27]

---

missing quantity, or compensation for storage and handling cost in case of delivery in a greater quantity; *see* Ch. 53, 1 and Ch. 49, 1.2.

19 Arts. 38, 39 CISG.

20 *See* Ch. 40, 4.

21 *See also* Spain: Morales Moreno, *supra* note 1, Art. 35, X, at 297.

22 *See for example* Argentina Art. 1338 CC; Ecuador Art. 176 Com C; Mexico Art. 373 Com C; Paraguay Art. 769 CC; Portugal Art. 469 Com C; Spain Art. 327 Com C.

23 Argentina: G.A. Borda, Manual de Contratos 267 (2004); Mexico: León Tovar, *supra* note 12, at 155; Portugal: L. De Lima Pinheiro, Dereito Comercial Internacional 286 (2005).

24 *See for example* Argentina Art. 1338 CC; Mexico Art. 373 Com C; Paraguay Art. 769 CC; Portugal Art. 469 Com C; Spain Art. 327 Com C.

25 Argentina Art. 456 Com C; Mexico Art. 373 Com C; Spain Art. 327 Com C; Uruguay Art. 521 Com C. In the case of Mexico's Civil Code by two experts nominated by each of the parties and a third expert nominated by the experts already nominated by the parties, *see* Mexico Art. 373 Com C.

26 This is without fulfilling his duty to inspect and to give notice about any defects in the goods, *see* Ch. 40, 4.

27 Spain AT Albacete, 11 July 1980.

which may bind him to pay the price of the goods and may prevent any intent to avoid the contract or claim damages.[28]

2.3.1. Ethical Values

An interesting debate has arisen on whether the seller must comply with so called 'ethical values' on the manufacture of the goods, and on whether the buyer has a CISG's remedy based on the delivery of 'ethically tainted' goods.[29] Among the ethically tainted goods in some societies are, for example, products manufactured by children, food grown and harvested by illegal immigrants, or employees under insane and unsafe conditions with grave health hazards or with pesticides, or even the production of livestock with hormones, genetically modified food and animal feed, *etc.*[30]

The matter seems to be in the centre of the north *v.* south debate. It has originated from demonstrations and campaigns mostly in the developed world. These campaigns demanded fair trade and the boycott of goods produced in circumstances violating the consumers' convictions and in some cases the national laws of those countries. Thus, the values affected are normally those of the buyer's jurisdiction, and not of the seller's domicile.

Merchants domiciled in Ibero-America, as those overseas, can easily get involved in a controversy of this kind. For example, Ibero-American parties participating in the UN Global Compact may be considered bound by the ethical values embraced by such a project, according to Article 9(1) CISG.[31] Similarly, when the contract expressly provides that the goods are to be produced or manufactured according to specific ethical standards and the seller fails to do so, a breach of contract occurs under Article 35(1).[32] Yet, in the absence of an express agreement to that respect, a breach of contract may occur under Article 35(2)(b), if the seller sells his products in 'fair trade' markets and the seller could not ignore that fact.[33]

---

[28] Spain Supreme Tribunal, 14 May 1992, *Id Cendoj:* 28079110011992103723.

[29] P. Schlechtriem, Non-Material Damages – Recovery Under the CISG?, 19 Pace International Law Review 89, at 98 (2007); I. Schwenzer & B. Leisinger, *Ethical Values and International Sales Contracts*, *in* R. Cranston, J. Ramberg & J. Ziegel (Eds.), Commercial Law Challenges in the 21st Century; Jan Hellner in memorium 249, at 261 (2007), http://www.cisg.law.pace.edu/cisg/biblio/schwenzer-leisinger.html.

[30] Schlechtriem, *supra* note 29, at 98; Schwenzer & Leisinger, *supra* note 29, at 260-261.

[31] Schwenzer & Leisinger, *supra* note 29, at 137; *see* the list of Ibero-American companies participating in the UN Global Compact at www.unglobalcompact.org/.

[32] Schwenzer & Leisinger, *supra* note 29, at 139.

[33] *Id.*, at 140.

2.3.2. cGMP

The quality of certain types of goods such as food products, pharmaceuticals, and medical devices is in many countries controlled by established Good Manufacturing Practice or GMP also referred to as current Good Manufacturing Practice (cGMP). These practices are recognised worldwide for the control and management of manufacturing and quality control testing of products.

Enterprises in the Ibero-American countries often trade goods subject to such practices. For many medical and pharmaceutical products standards of manufacture are directly required by the government agencies. Thus, specific obligations are imposed upon the buyer who knew or ought to have known of these official requirements at the import's country.

In Ibero-America for example, certain products imported or sold must comply with technical standards, permits, or sanitary certificates issued by the government agency concerned, describing their characteristics or specifications.[34] These standards are known in Mexico by the acronym NOMs.[35]

Normally these national standards need to be reviewed, and if necessary, modified by the concerned authority. This procedure of modification makes the official standards dynamic, and sellers and importers shall be aware of constant specifications changes.

In addition, foreign and domestic products must include, before its commercialisation, a label containing the standard specifications regarding general product labelling. Compliance of these standards are often verified by the government or authorised certifying entity. A product subject to compliance with standards shall usually bear the confirmation of compliance.

2.4. Packaging

According to the CISG, if the parties have agreed that the goods should be packaged or contained in a particular manner, the goods do not conform to the contract unless they comply with the terms agreed.[36] This reflects the primary position that the CISG gives to the obligation to package and contain the goods in a proper manner.

---

[34] For a more detailed review on the topic consult the handbooks designed by the Bomchil Group Doing Business in Latin America. http://www.bomchilgroup.org/doing_business_in_latin_america/index.html.

[35] A NOM is an acronym for *Norma Oficial Mexicana* which loosely translated means official Mexican standard. In addition to being official product standards, however, NOMs are also mandatory product standards which apply to products produced in Mexico as well as to products imported into Mexico. NOMs are developed by the Mexican Bureau of Standards (*Direccion General de Normas* or DGN) which reports to the Mexican Commerce Ministry.

[36] Schwenzer, *supra* note 16, Art. 35, para. 11, at 574.

In the Ibero-American laws, the obligation to package the goods in a manner adequate to preserve and protect them is by default an ancillary obligation.[37] But an express agreement on the manner or characteristics of the packaging and a subsequent failure to comply with such agreement may trigger many remedies in the buyer's favour. In a case submitted to the Spanish Supreme Tribunal, the buyer was allowed to recover damages derived from the seller's in bulk delivery of 1.800 Metric Tonnes of Calcic Ammonic nitrate 26.5% (NAC 26.5%), instead of packing the goods in raffia sacks as agreed in the contract.[38]

3. Default Requirements for Conformity

Absent an expressed agreement on the quality, quantity and description of the goods, the Ibero-American statutes and jurisprudence have established both subjective and objective default standards to determine the conformity of the goods sold.

3.1. Fitness for a Particular Purpose

In the Ibero-American statutory laws, the standard of conformity based on the particular purpose made known to the seller is uncommon. Except in countries like Peru and Portugal, where the goods must have the characteristics promised by the seller, the value given to them and further, made them appropriate for the purpose they were bought for.[39] In Colombia, the Code of Commerce expressly grants the buyer the remedy of avoidance for delivered goods containing defects which made them improper for the purpose expressed in the contract.[40]

On this issue, the Ibero-American scholars agree that some contracts may contain a contractual purpose or use that is given to the goods. When this happens, the seller shall guarantee the conformity of the goods, based on the particular purpose.[41] In the same line, the Argentinean National Civil Chamber, explained that the fact that Article 2174 of the Civil Code provides solely for two actions – the redhibitory and the *quantity minoris* – does not entail that the

---

[37] *See for example* Bolivia Arts. 862: stating that provided the packaging is not in an evident bad state the buyer may not refuse payment. On the contrary, the CISG gives a primary position to the obligation to package and contain the goods in a proper manner, *see* Art. 35 CISG.

[38] Spain Supreme Tribunal, 12 July 2007, *Id Cendoj:* 28079110012007100879.

[39] Peru Art. 1505 CC; Portugal Art. 913 (1) CC.

[40] Colombia Art. 934 Com C.

[41] *See* Colombia: A. Tamayo Lombana, El Contrato de Compraventa su Régimen Civil y Comercial 179 (2004): "in order to evaluate the conformity of goods bought for a particular use the same objective requirements for the goods intended for ordinary purposes shall apply."

buyer is unable to pursue the exact compliance of the obligation assumed by the seller when, once the goods were delivered, hidden defects appear which make the goods unfit for the intended purpose or reduce considerably the use expected by the buyer.[42]

The intended particular purpose may include, for example, the suitability of the goods traded in certain places. In a case submitted to a Brazilian State Supreme Tribunal, the seller was supposed to provide the buyer with organic orange juice destined to be sold and consumed in Europe. The juice delivered contained more sugar concentration than required under the contract, being therefore inadequate for the European market. Despite the seller's allegation that it was still possible to commercialise the juice, the Tribunal upheld that the seller did not fulfil the contractual purpose.[43]

The CISG also requires that the goods are fit for a particular purpose, when such purpose is impliedly or expressly made known to the seller at the time of the conclusion of the contract.[44] Except where the buyer did not rely on the seller's skills and judgement or where the circumstances show that it was unreasonable for the buyer to rely on it.[45]

3.2. Fitness for Ordinary Use

In the Ibero-American laws, unfitness for the ordinary use of the goods also results in non-conformity. The seller is liable for any defects of the goods which make them improper for, or reduce, the function they are ordinarily given.[46] In other words, when the goods do not serve for their ordinary use or only serve imperfectly, the buyer may have a right of avoidance of the contract or for proportionate reduction of the price.[47]

Under this objective requirement, the defects must be in the goods themselves and must impede them to accomplish, totally or partially, the

---

42 Argentina National Civil Chamber, *Sala* F, *González, Roberto v. Sáez, Federico C*, 7 November 2003, Lexis No. 1/1000184.

43 Brazil Tribunal of Justice of the State of Santa Catarina, Civil Appeal 2008.042773-6, 18 December 2008.

44 Art 35(2)(b) CISG.

45 *Id.*

46 Argentina Art. 2164 CC; Brazil Art. 441 CC; Guatemala Art. 1559 CC; Mexico Art. 2142 CC; Paraguay Art. 1789 CC; Portugal Art. 913º (2) CC; Spain Art. 1484 CC; Uruguay Art. 1718 CC; Venezuela Art. 1.518 CC; Costa Rica: D. Baudrit Carrillo, Los Contratos Traslativos del Derecho Privado – Principios de Jurisprudencia 51 (2000).

47 Chile Art. 1858 (2) CC; Colombia Art. 1915 (2) CC & Art. 934 Com C; Ecuador Art. 1825 (2) CC; El Salvador Art. 1660 (2) CC. Chile, Colombia, Ecuador and El Salvador Civil Codes use the verb *rescindir* which literary means to rescind. But such is a mistake of the drafters, since the appropriate verb was *resolver* which means to avoid, the remedy for breach of contract; this view is supported by El Salvador: A.O. Miranda, De la Compraventa 250 (1996).

purpose for which they were created. Consequently, the mere dissatisfaction of the buyer based on different personal expectations or hopes for something more or better are not enough to trigger a redhibitory or estimatory claim.[48] Nor a change in the use for which the goods were intended legitimates the buyer to claim the remedies available.[49]

Under some laws, when the quality of the goods is not determined or described with exactness in the contract, the buyer cannot request the best quality and the seller cannot deliver the worse quality, but rather the seller is only required to deliver goods of medium or regular quality.[50] Similarly, if the goods are only designated in the contract by their species, the seller must deliver goods of standard quality.[51] Experts may be engaged to asses the fitness of the goods.[52]

3.3. Sale by Sample / Model

In the Ibero-American laws, the sales by sample or model constitute one of the many modalities of sales. Sales by samples are recognised as an enforceable practice among traders that intend to give celerity and security to business transactions.[53] Under this type of sale, the conformity of the goods is no longer assessed based on a generic quality,[54] but rather by comparing the quality of the goods delivered with the quality of the goods held out as a sample.[55] The Brazilian law adds that the sample, prototype or model will prevail over the contract description of the goods.[56] This rule is derived from the seller's

---

48 *See* Ch. 53, 1.1.

49 *Id.*

50 Chile Art. 145 Com C; Colombia Art. 914 Com C; Costa Rica Art. 421 Com C; Ecuador Art. 190 Com C; Guatemala Art. 690 Com C; Mexico Art. 87 Com C.

51 Bolivia Art. 304 CC; Chile Art. 134 Com C (*see also* Chile Arts. 136, 137 Com C); Ecuador Art. 174 Com C; Bolivia: G. Castellanos Trigo & S. Auad La Fuente, Derecho de las Obligaciones en el Código Civil Boliviano 53 (2008).

52 Chile Arts. 133, 134 Com C; Ecuador Arts. 173, 174 Com C. Similar provision in Colombia Art. 916 Com C.

53 El Salvador: Miranda, *supra* note 47, at 519; Mexico Collegiate Tribunals, *Quinta Época*, Registry 385712, SJF CXIII, p 696.

54 As it occurs for the sales under the modality of determined quality; *see* above in this Sec., B, III.

55 Argentina Art. 456 Com C; Bolivia Art. 835 Com C; Brazil Art. 484 CC; Chile Art. 135 Com C; Colombia Art. 913 Com C; Costa Rica 455 Com C; Ecuador Art. 175 Com C; El Salvador Art. 1024 Com C; Guatemala Art. 1800 CC; Mexico Art. 2258 CC & Art. 373 Com C; Paraguay Art. 1793 (2) CC; Peru Art. 1573 CC; Portugal Art. 919 CC & Art. 469 Com C; Spain Art. 327 Com C; Uruguay Art. 521 Com C; Argentina: Borda, *supra* note 23, at 268; Mexico: León Tovar, *supra* note 12, at 155.

56 Brazil Art. 484 CC; Brazil: O. Gomes, Contratos 283 (2008).

obligation to provide the buyer with adequate information on the goods, related with the principle of good faith.[57]

Under most laws, if the goods delivered do not match the samples or models the sale is automatically avoided.[58] However, under Portugal's Code of Commerce the contract is estimated to never exist.[59] The buyer cannot refuse to receive the goods provided they conform to the samples.[60] In some countries, if the buyer refuses to take delivery based on an alleged lack of conformity, experts will be appointed to decide on the conformity of the goods by comparing the samples held out to the seller with the goods delivered.[61]

3.4. Usual Packaging

According to the CISG, the seller shall also warrant that the goods will be contained and packaged in a manner that is usual for such goods or in a manner adequate to preserve and protect the goods.[62] There is no similar provision in the Ibero-American laws. However, it should be understood that the same default obligation, to package the goods in a manner adequate to preserve and protect them, results from the principle of good faith.[63] The Ibero-American civil laws require obligations and contracts to be fulfilled in good faith.[64] Contracts are to be concluded in good faith and, thus, are binding on the parties' not only in what has been expressed in them but also in all that emanates form the nature of the obligation, the law, the equity or the usages.

Consequently, the seller is not only bound to deliver the goods but also to take all the necessary steps so that after the passing of risk the buyer can securely handle the goods. Such steps can include an adequate package to preserve and protect the goods for a reasonable time. The Argentinean code is

[57] Brazil: Gonçalves, *supra* note 2, at 223.

[58] Argentina Art. 456 Com C; Bolivia Art. 835 Com C; Chile Art. 135 Com C; Colombia Art. 913 Com C; Ecuador Art. 175 Com C; Guatemala Art. 1800 CC; Peru Art. 1573 CC; Spain Art. 327 Com C; Uruguay Art. 521 Com C para. 2.

[59] Portugal Art. 469 Com C, provided the buyer examines the goods within 8 days from delivery and informs the seller of the non-conformity, *see* Portugal Art. 471 Com C.

[60] Spain Supreme Tribunal, 1 July 1991, *Id Cendoj:* 28079110011991101272.

[61] Argentina Art. 456 Com C; Colombia Art. 913 Com C; Spain Art. 327 Com C; Uruguay Art. 521 Com C. In the case of Mexico by two experts nominated by each of the parties and a third expert nominated by the experts already nominated by the parties, Mexico Art. 2258 part 2 CC & Art. 373 part 2 Com C.

[62] Art 35(2)(d) CISG.

[63] The opinion is shared by Portugal: De Lima Pinheiro, *supra* note 23, at 286.

[64] Argentina Art. 1198 CC; Bolivia Art. 803 Com C; Brazil Art. 422 CC; Chile Art. 1546 CC; Colombia Art. 1603 CC & Art. 863 Com C; Cuba Art. 6 CC; Ecuador Art. 1589 CC; El Salvador Art. 1417 CC; Guatemala Art. 17 JOL; Mexico Art. 1796 CC; Paraguay Art. 715 CC; Peru Art. 1362 CC; Portugal Art. 762 CC; Spain Art. 1258 CC & Art. 57 Com C.

also exemplificative, dictating that the contracts must be performed in good faith acting with care and diligence.[65]

4. Knowledge of the Buyer of the Non-Conformity

Under the Ibero-American laws, due consideration should be given to the buyer's situation and conduct. If the buyer could not have been unaware of the defects by taking the necessary due diligence, or if he knew or ought to have known the defects because of his profession, expertise, business or activities, the buyer cannot blame the seller for the non-conformity of the goods delivered.[66] Hence, the defects must be hidden in a way that a person in the buyer's position is unable to notice them.[67]

5. Time of Non-Conformity

5.1. Contract Conclusion

While under CISG article 36 (1), the conformity of the goods must be assessed at the time of the transfer of risk, the Ibero-American laws follow a different solution. The goods must be affected by defects before or concurrently to the contract conclusion, so that the buyer can make effective his right for a

---

65 Argentina Art. 1198 CC.

66 Argentina Art. 2173 CC; Bolivia Art. 631 CC; Chile Art. 1858(3) CC; Colombia Art. 1915(3) CC; Ecuador Art. 1825 (3) CC; El Salvador Art. 1660(3) CC; Guatemala Art. 1560 CC; Mexico Art. 2143 CC; Paraguay Art. 1790(b)(c) CC; Peru Art. 1504 CC; Spain Arts. 1484, 1485 CC; Uruguay Art. 1718 CC; Venezuela Art. 1519 CC.

67 Argentina: Compagnucci de Caso, *supra* note 2, at 222-223; Bolivia: W. Kaune Arteaga, Curso de Derecho Civil, Contratos, Vol. 2, 149 (1996); Chile: R. Díez Duarte, La Compraventa en el Código Civil Chileno 167, 168 (1993); Colombia: Tamayo Lombana, *supra* note 41, at 179, 180; Mexico: León Tovar, *supra* note 12, at 15; Argentina National Chamber of Civil Appeals, *Sala* E, ED, 92-682, *cited in* Argentina: Compagnucci de Caso, *supra* note 2, at 222, n. 216; Argentina National Civil Chamber, *Sala* F *González, Roberto v. Sáez, Federico C*, 7 November 2003, Lexis No. 1/1000184: found that a buyer who has been assisted by professionals and experts cannot invoke the existence of hidden defects because the expertise of the buyer or her advisors was such that the defects could not go unnoticed; Brazil Tribunal of Justice of the São Paulo, Civil Recourse 71001123140, published 4 May 2007: decided that a buyer was aware of the defects of a truck because its price was much less than the regular market price; Venezuela Supreme Tribunal, Civil and Mercantile Chamber for the Federal District and the State of Miranda, 14 May 1956, JTR, Vol. VIII, Book II, p 752, *cited in* Venezuela: Aguilar Gorrondona, *supra* note 2, at 258, n. 5: the same was decided in a Venezuelan court which sustained that the defects on an automobile sold were not hidden since the buyer was an expert in the field.

redhibitory action.[68] Only the defects existing before or at the time of contract conclusion are considered as redhibitory defects. However, scholars agree that defects which exist in its germ or origin at the contract conclusion but that become apparent only after, fall also into the category.[69] For example, genetic or innate defects in animals or the composition of food products or pharmaceuticals products that only show up after the conclusion of the sale, but whose source was present before that time.

5.2. Guarantees

Under the Ibero-American laws, the seller may also be liable for any lack of conformity, even after the conclusion of the contract, due to the breach of any warranty he has made on the goods. For example, the seller may have represented that the goods would remain fit for the particular purpose made known to him or that the goods would retain certain characteristics for a certain period of time.[70] This is clearly expressed in the Portuguese rule under which the seller shall repair or substitute the goods when such substitution is required and possible, when he is bound, by the contract or the usages, to guarantee the fine performance of the goods.[71] Many other laws also sustain that where the seller has expressly guaranteed the conformity of the goods for a certain time the buyer may give notice to the seller of any non-conformity of the goods during that time.[72]

Besides, the default provisions on the time of non-conformity are neither imperative nor of public order, but supplementary to the will of the parties.[73] Hence, a seller would still be liable for any defect of the goods, even after the conclusion of the contract or the passing of the risk to the buyer, if the parties have expressly or impliedly agreed that the seller would guarantee their fitness

[68] Chile Art. 1858 (1) CC; Colombia Art. 1915 (1) CC; Ecuador Art. 1825 (1) CC; El Salvador Art. 1660 CC; Paraguay Art. 1789 CC; Argentina: Compagnucci de Caso, *supra* note 2, at 213; Bolivia: Kaune Arteaga, *supra* note 67, at 150; Chile: Díez Duarte, *supra* note 67, at 167.

[69] Bolivia: Kaune Arteaga, *supra* note 67, at 150; Colombia: Tamayo Lombana, *supra* note 41, at 177.

[70] Mexico: O. Vásquez del Mercado, Contratos Mercantiles 205, 206 (2008).

[71] Portugal Art. 921 CC.

[72] Bolivia Art. 838 Com C; Brazil Art. 446 CC; Colombia Art. 932 Com C; Costa Rica Art. 452 Com C; El Salvador Art. 1021 Com C Paraguay Art. 753 CC; Peru Art. 1523 CC Venezuela Art. 1.526 CC.

[73] Argentina: Compagnucci de Caso, *supra* note 2, at 219-220; Bolivia: Kaune Arteaga, *supra* note 67, at 153; Chile: Díez Duarte, *supra* note 67, at 170; Colombia: Tamayo Lombana, *supra* note 41, at 176, 177, 185-187; El Salvador: Miranda, *supra* note 47, at 262; Venezuela: Aguilar Gorrondona, *supra* note 2, at 262.

for a certain period.[74] The possibility is expressly supported by the statement "[T]he parties can agree to make redhibitory the defects that, by their nature, are not redhibitory."[75]

6. Burden of Proof

In the Ibero-American laws, the burden of the proof of the hidden defects falls on the buyer. The buyer shall prove that the defects existed before the sale took place. Absent proof to the contrary, it is assumed that the defects appeared after the conclusion of the contract.[76] However, it would correspond to the seller to prove that the defects were apparent or that the buyer knew or ought to have known them.[77]

---

[74] El Salvador: Miranda, *supra* note 47, at 256-257; Venezuela: Aguilar Gorrondona, *supra* note 2, at 263.

[75] *See for example*, Argentina Art. 2167 CC; Bolivia Arts. 624 (II), 628 CC; Chile Art. 1863 CC; Colombia Art. 1920 CC; Ecuador Art. 1830 CC; El Salvador Art. 1665 CC; Guatemala Art. 1544 CC; Paraguay Art. 1792 CC; Portugal Art. 921 CC; *see also* Chile: Díez Duarte, *supra* note 67, at 168; El Salvador: Miranda, *supra* note 47, at 256-257.

[76] Argentina Art. 2168 CC; Mexico Art. 2159 CC; Paraguay Art. 1791 CC; Uruguay Art. 1724 CC.

[77] Mexico: León Tovar, *supra* note 12, at 157.

CHAPTER 38

THIRD PARTY PROPERTY RIGHTS

1. General Remarks on Third Party Property Rights

Most of the Ibero-American laws declare that the two main obligations of the seller are the delivery of the goods and their warranty in case of redhibitory defects and/or eviction.[1] However, this does not necessarily mean that under all the Ibero-American laws the goods must be free from any right or claim from a third party at the time of contract conclusion in order to have a valid sale. As further developed, in the Ibero-American laws there is no uniform answer as to whether the seller must be the owner of the goods.[2]

What the Ibero-American laws grant to the buyer is a right of compensation against eviction. Eviction as rooted in the Roman law means to be defeated in a civil trial.[3] The Ibero-American laws generally define eviction as the buyer's loss or deprivation of his right of property, use or exploitation over the goods, established by a competent court as consequence of a third party's previous right over the goods.[4]

---

[1] Argentina Arts. 1323, 1409, 1414 CC; Bolivia Art. 614 CC; Brazil Arts. 481, 491, 502 CC; Chile Arts. 1824, 1837 CC; Colombia Art. 1880 CC; Dominican Republic Art. 1604 CC; Ecuador Art. 1791 CC; El Salvador Art. 1627 CC; Honduras Art. 1620 CC; Nicaragua Art. 2582 CC; Mexico Art. 2283 CC & Art. 384 Com C; Paraguay Art. 759(b)(d) CC; Peru Art. 1549 CC; Portugal Arts. 879, 882, 406 CC; Spain Arts. 1.461, 1.474, 1.484 CC; Venezuela Arts. 1265, 1474, 1486 CC; Bolivia: W. Kaune Arteaga, Curso de Derecho Civil, Contratos, Vol. 2, 139 (1996); Costa Rica: D. Baudrit Carrillo, Los Contratos Traslativos del Derecho Privado – Principios de Jurisprudencia 49-55 (2000); El Salvador: A.O. Miranda, De la Compraventa 208 (1996); Mexico: O. Vásquez del Mercado, Contratos Mercantiles 202 (2008).

[2] *See* Ch. 46, 1.

[3] *See* Argentina: R. Compagnucci de Caso, Contrato de Compraventa 153 (2007); Bolivia: Kaune Arteaga, *supra* note 1, at 139; Brazil: C.M. Da Silva Pereira, Instituçaoes de Dereito Civil, Vol. III, Contratos, Electrônica 90 (2003); Chile: R. Díez Duarte, La Compraventa en el Código Civil Chileno 155 (1993).

[4] Argentina Art. 2091 CC; Bolivia Arts. 625 (I), 626 CC; Chile Arts. 1838, 1839 CC;

The mere fact that in the CISG the transfer of property title constitutes a main obligation means it departs from the Ibero-American system of eviction in an important way. In the CISG system, there is no need for a third party's legal action and of a competent court final judgment to trigger the remedies available to the buyer.[5] The buyer has many remedies available against the seller for breach of his contractual duty to deliver the clean property, with no need to wait for a third party's legal action. In addition, many remedies are available for disturbances or third party claims even though they are unfounded, *i.e.*, even when third parties do not hold an apparent legitimate right over the goods.[6]

The above said, under the Ibero-American laws the remedies for ordinary breach of contract may be granted to the buyer if the seller's obligation to transfer clean property title can be deduced from the contract.[7]

2. Third Party Rights

Three main concurrent requirements are necessary to compensate the buyer for eviction in the sale of encumbered goods. First, there must be deprivation of the rights of property, use or exploitation of the goods acquired by the buyer. Second, such deprivation must come from a judicial order or a recognised right. Finally, the third party property right must be previous or contemporaneous to the contract of sales.[8] The two last conditions will be briefly reviewed and compared with the CISG system in parts 3 and 4 of this chapter. The first of them stands as follows.

Colombia Arts. 1894, 1895 CC; Ecuador Arts. 1805, 1806 CC; El Salvador Arts. 1640, 1641 CC; Mexico Art. 2119 CC; Paraguay Art. 1759 CC; Peru Art. 1491 CC; Spain Art. 1.475 CC; *see also* Argentina: Compagnucci de Caso, *supra* note 3, at 154; Chile: Díez Duarte, *supra* note 3, at 156; Mexico: S. León Tovar, Los Contratos Mercantiles 162 (2004); Venezuela: J.L. Aguilar Gorrondona, Contratos y Garantias: Derecho Civil IV, 237, 238 (2008).

5 Spain: J.M.M. Gonzalez, *in* L. Díez Picazo y Ponce De León (Ed.), La Compraventa Internacional de Mecaderias – Comentario sobre la Convención de Viena Art. 41, III, at 357 (1998).

6 *See infra* 3.

7 Particularly in B2B sales, *see* Spain Supreme Tribunal, 15 November 2006, *Id Cendoj*: 28079110012006101110: upholding that the seller failed to comply with an implied main obligation to deliver clear registry records as the buyer intended to get a loan mortgaging the goods.

8 Argentina Art. 2091 CC; Bolivia Arts. 596, 624(I) CC; Chile Arts. 1838, 1839 CC; Colombia Arts. 1894, 1895 CC; Ecuador Arts. 1805, 1806 CC; El Salvador Arts. 1640, 1641 CC; Mexico Art. 2119 CC; Peru Art. 1491 CC; Spain Art. 1475 CC; Venezuela Art. 1.504 CC; Bolivia Supreme Court, *Sala Civil*, *Gladys Pedriel Ribera v. Dora Barroso vda. de Rivero*: declaring the avoidance of the contract because the three requirements had been fulfilled; El Salvador Superior Tribunal, RJ 25, 1 December 1907, at 447-449, *cited in* El Salvador: Miranda, *supra* note 1, at 559.

The deprivation of the goods or the disturbance of the rights acquired by the buyer must exist.[9] Such can be total or partial.[10] The deprivation commonly has its origin in a revendication action filed by a third party.[11] A successful revendication action will eventually deprive the buyer of his rights over the goods. Disturbance, on the other hand, should not be mistaken with mere threats that do not encumber the goods.[12] Although, legitimate fear usually allows the buyer to take measures to protect himself from the possible eviction pending before a court, for example, by suspending the payment of the goods.[13]

Finally, the buyer cannot rely upon his right of compensation against eviction if he knew or ought to have known that the goods were affected by encumbrances or agreed to take at his own risk the goods subject to third party rights. This exemption to the seller's liability has been recognised in both the CISG[14] and in many Ibero-American laws.[15]

3. Third Party Claims

The Ibero-American laws require the deprivation of the goods to be real and effective.[16] In other words, for the eviction to take place a competent court must render a final judgment depriving the buyer of his rights over the goods.[17] Only

---

[9] *See* on this Brazil: Da Silva Pereira, *supra* note 3, at 90; Venezuela: Aguilar Gorrondona, *supra* note 4, at 240; Bolivia Supreme Court, *Sala Civil, Francisco de Asis Perales v. Rolando Soliz Velásquez*: denying the remedy of eviction and damages because the buyer did not prove that he had been partially or totally deprived from the goods acquired or that he had suffered some sort of disturbances.

[10] Argentina Art. 2093 CC; Bolivia Arts. 625, 626 CC; Brazil Arts. 450 sole para, 455 CC; Chile Art. 1838 CC; Colombia Art. 1894 CC; Ecuador Art. 1805 CC; El Salvador Art. 1640 CC; Mexico Art. 2119 CC; Peru Art. 1501 CC; Spain Art. 1475 CC.

[11] An action by which a man demands a thing of which he claims to be owner. It applies to immovable's as well as movables; to corporeal or incorporeal things. Source: Bouviers Law Dictionary 1856 Edition; *see also* Ch. 59.

[12] Argentina: Compagnucci de Caso, *supra* note 3, at 163; Bolivia: Kaune Arteaga, *supra* note 1, at 140; El Salvador: Miranda, *supra* note 1, at 214.

[13] *See* Argentina: Compagnucci de Caso, *supra* note 3, at 162; Venezuela: Aguilar Gorrondona, *supra* note 4, at 241; *see also* Ch. 48.

[14] Art. 41 CISG.

[15] Argentina Art. 2101(2)(3) CC; Brazil Art. 457 CC; Chile Art. 1839 CC; Colombia Art. 1895 CC; Ecuador Art. 1806 CC; El Salvador Art. 1641 CC; Mexico Art. 2121 CC & Art. 384 Com C; Paraguay Arts. 1759, 1767 CC; Peru Arts. 1500(4), 1539 CC; Spain Arts. 1.475, 1.477 CC; Uruguay Art. 551 Com C; Venezuela Arts. 1.505, 1.507 CC.

[16] Bolivia: Kaune Arteaga, *supra* note 1, at 140; El Salvador: Miranda, *supra* note 1, at 214; Venezuela: Aguilar Gorrondona, *supra* note 4, at 240-241; Bolivia Supreme Court, *Sala Civil, Francisco de Asis Perales v. Rolando Soliz Velásquez*: denying the remedy of eviction damages because the buyer did not prove that he had been partially or totally deprived from the goods acquired or that he had suffered some sort of disturbances.

[17] Argentina Art. 2091 CC; Bolivia Art. 625(II) CC; Chile Art. 1838 CC; Colombia Art. 1894

the closing of legal proceedings opens the possibility to claim compensation for the damages caused by the seller.[18] The mere threats or menaces of being deprived by third parties do not among to eviction. Contrary to the CISG, the Ibero-American laws are stricter in this point, since the third parties' unfounded pretensions do not trigger the buyer's right for compensation.[19]

4. Time of Third Party Rights and Claims

Under the Ibero-American laws, the third party's alleged rights over the goods must be prior to the sales' conclusion.[20] The condition is understandable, as in many Ibero-American systems, the property title passes to the buyer at the time of contract conclusion.[21] Under these systems, the buyer would effectively become the owner at the time of contract conclusion when the goods are effectively clean. However, the same may not be adequate for those systems under which the property passes until the *tradittio* of the goods.[22] Under those systems, the contract may be concluded but the property title may not yet pass to the buyer. Between the time of contract conclusion and the effective *tradittio* there is a period of time where the seller could affect the goods. In such circumstances, the remedy against eviction would remain inoperative.

CC; Ecuador Art. 1805 CC; El Salvador Art. 1640 CC; Mexico Art. 2119 CC; Peru Art. 1491 CC; Spain Art. 1475 CC; Uruguay Art. 1713 CC; *see also* Brazil: Da Silva Pereira, *supra* note 3, at 90-91; Chile: Díez Duarte, *supra* note 3, at 157; Mexico: León Tovar, *supra* note 4, at 163; Venezuela: Aguilar Gorrondona, *supra* note 4, at 241; El Salvador Superior Tribunal, RJ 25, 1 December 1907, at 447-449, *cited in* El Salvador: Miranda, *supra* note 1, at 559.

18 Argentina: Compagnucci de Caso, *supra* note 3, at 168; Mexico: León Tovar, *supra* note 4, at 163.

19 Spain: L.J. Gutierrez Jerez, *La obligacion de saneamiento por eviccion y la transmision del dominio en la compraventa*, *in* J. Aguirre Zamorano (Ed.), La Compraventa Ley de Garantías 13, at 48 (2006). Art. 41 CISG: the seller must guarantee the *undisturbed possession*. The goods must be free from any third party claim. These claims can be founded or unfounded. The obligation of the seller is to protect the buyer from any expenses, disturbances, or incertitude over the merchandise although they may not prosper in legal actions.

20 Argentina Art. 2091 CC; Bolivia Arts. 596, 625 (I) CC; Brazil Art. 447 CC; Chile Art. 1839 CC; Colombia Art. 1895 CC; Ecuador Art. 1806 CC; El Salvador Art. 1641 CC; Mexico Art. 2119 CC; Peru Art. 1491 CC; Spain Art. 1.475 CC; *see also* Brazil: Da Silva Pereira, *supra* note 3, at 91.

21 *See* Ch. 45, 3.1.

22 *See* Ch. 45, 3.2.

Chapter 39

Third Party Intellectual Property Rights

1. General Remarks on Third Party Intellectual Property Rights

The Ibero-American laws do not have an express provision dealing with the topic of goods affected by third parties' intellectual property rights and claims. However, that does not mean that the seller can be released in a similar case. The general duty to guarantee the undisturbed use and exploitation of the goods may make the remedy available to the buyer.

As mentioned in the previous chapter, the Ibero-American laws grant to the buyer a right of compensation against eviction. The warranty covers the loss or deprivation suffered by buyer, not only in his right of property over the goods, but also in his right of use or exploitation.[1] The existence of intellectual property rights held by a third party usually deprives the buyer to use or resale the goods. Thus, a buyer evicted in the use or commercialisation of the goods should, in principle, have a right to activate any remedies available for eviction cases.

Evidently, the CISG system offers more protection to the buyer. Under the CISG, subject to seller's territorial limitation of liability,[2] the buyer has

[1] Argentina Art. 2091 CC; Bolivia Arts. 625 (I), 626 CC; Chile Arts. 1838, 1839 CC; Colombia Arts. 1894, 1895 CC; Ecuador Arts. 1805, 1806 CC; El Salvador Arts. 1640, 1641 CC; Mexico Art. 2119 CC; Paraguay Art. 1759 CC; Peru Art. 1491 CC; Spain Art. 1.475 CC; *see also* Argentina: R. Compagnucci de Caso, Contrato de Compraventa 154 (2007); Chile: R. Díez Duarte, La Compraventa en el Código Civil Chileno 156 (1993); El Salvador: A.O. Miranda, De la Compraventa 208 (1996); Mexico: S. León Tovar, Los Contratos Mercantiles 162 (2004); Venezuela: J.L. Aguilar Gorrondona, Contratos y Garantias: Derecho Civil IV, 237, 238 (2008).

[2] Art 42(1)(a)(b) CISG: the seller obligation is limited to any third party's IP right in the State where the goods will be resold or used, if such was contemplated at the time of contract conclusion, or where the buyer has his place of business.

many remedies available against the seller for breach of his duty to deliver goods free of intellectual property rights and claims. Contrary to what happens in most eviction systems,[3] a CISG buyer does not need to wait for the commencement of a third party's legal action against him, and a competent court or government agency's final decision evicting the goods, to turn against the seller.[4]

On the other hand, the principle of good faith present in Ibero-American law may impose a similar duty to a seller.[5] The Spanish Supreme Tribunal has upheld that obligations such as the one requiring the seller to deliver goods with clean property or use registry records, can be deducted or implied from the obligation to act in good faith, which has a special importance between traders.[6]

Certainly, as a trader would acquire the goods for business purposes, the buyer should be able to use, manipulate and commercialise the goods. Hence, the seller may not only be bound to deliver the goods required by the contract, but also to guarantee that the goods will not be subject to third parties' intellectual property rights that may affect their use or their commercialisation in the intended place.

2. Scope of Intellectual Property Rights

The sort of rights and claims falling within the scope of the intellectual property can be subtracted from the international instruments that have attained global consensus.[7] Generally, such would include rights resulting from the industrial, scientific, literary, artistic fields.[8] Hence, the obligation to deliver goods free of third parties' property rights must be understood in the broadest sense. Intellectual property could include, for example, the rights of authorship on works, phonograms, and broadcasts, patents on inventions in all fields

---

[3] Except for Brazil Art. 502 CC and El Salvador: these establish an independent liability of the seller for all debts or rights that encumber the goods up to the time of delivery; *see* El Salvador: Miranda, *supra* note 1, at 209-210.

[4] *See* Ch. 38, 2.

[5] Argentina Art. 1198 CC; Bolivia Art. 803 Com C; Brazil Art. 422 CC; Chile Art. 1546 CC; Colombia Art. 1603 CC & Art. 863 Com C; Cuba Art. 6 CC; Ecuador Art. 1589 CC; El Salvador Art. 1417 CC; Guatemala Art. 17 JOL; Mexico Art. 1796 CC; Paraguay Art. 715 CC; Peru Art. 1362 CC; Portugal Art. 762 CC; Spain Art. 1258 CC & Art. 57 Com C; Venezuela Art. 1.160 CC.

[6] Particularly in B2B sales, *see* Spain Supreme Tribunal, 15 November 2006, *Id Cendoj:* 28079110012006101110: upholding that the seller failed to comply with an implied main obligation to deliver clear registry records prevented the buyer to freely dispose or use the goods.

[7] I. Schwenzer, *in* I. Schwenzer (Ed.), Schlechtriem & Schwenzer Commentary on the UN Convention on the International Sale of Goods Art. 42, para. 4, at 662 (2010).

[8] Art. 2(VIII) WIPO Convention, 14 July 1967 (28 September 1979).

of human endeavour, scientific discoveries, industrial designs, trademarks, service marks, and commercial names and designations, protection against unfair competition, *etc.*[9]

What is relevant is the substantive definition of intellectual property rights.[10] Issues as to the registrability and the categorisation of the rights are irrelevant. Nor is it important the nature that the relevant law gives to the legal responsibility. The liability of the breaching party can arise either from infringement of special domestic laws on intellectual property or tort rules, competition law, restitution law, *etc.*[11] The key question is whether the third party's intellectual property right is susceptible to hinder the undisturbed use of the goods.[12]

3. Territorial Restriction

The CISG requires the seller to deliver goods free of intellectual property rights or claims in the country where the goods were contemplated to be used[13] or in absence of a designated place, in the buyer's place of business.[14]

The use and resale should not be understood as alternatives but should be read cumulatively, since the buyer can try to resell the goods in one jurisdiction while his costumers may use them in another country.[15] No express designation of the place of use or resale is necessary. It is enough that the parties had contemplated where the goods were to be used or resold. This can be drawn from the circumstances of the contract, *e.g.* the place of delivery of the goods.[16]

4. Knowledge of the Seller

Under CISG Article 42(1) the seller will only be liable if at the time of the conclusion of the contract he knew or could have not been unaware of any right or claim over the goods based on intellectual property rights.[17] This departs from the approach taken in CISG Article 41 and the Ibero-American warranty of eviction, where the ignorance of any third party's right impeding

9 *Id.*

10 Schwenzer, *supra* note 7, Art. 42, para. 4, at 62.

11 *Id.*

12 P. Schlechtriem, *in* I. Schwenzer (Ed.), Schlechtriem & Schwenzer Commentary on the UN Convention on the International Sale of Goods Art. 42, para. 4, at 664 (2010).

13 Art. 42(1)(a) CISG.

14 Art. 42(1)(b) CISG.

15 Schwenzer, *supra* note 7, Art. 42, para. 10, at 666.

16 Schwenzer, *supra* note 7, Art. 42, para. 11, at 666.

17 Art. 42(1) CISG.

the normal exploitation or use of the goods does not release the seller from his liability. Certainly, under the Ibero-American laws the knowledge of the seller is almost irrelevant. The seller's unawareness may only release him from being liable for any increase on the price occurred between the contract conclusion and the eviction and/or the cost of any voluntary and unnecessary improvement made to the goods by the buyer.[18]

5. Knowledge of the Buyer

Similar to the CISG,[19] under the Ibero-American laws, the buyer cannot rely upon his right of compensation against eviction if he knew or ought to have known that the goods were affected by encumbrances, or if he had agreed to take at his own risk the goods subject to third party rights.[20]

---

[18] Argentina Art. 2123 CC; Bolivia Arts. 625, 596(III) CC; Chile Arts. 1849, 1850 CC; Colombia Arts. 1906, 1907 CC; Ecuador Arts. 1816, 1817 CC; El Salvador Arts. 1651, 1652 CC; Mexico Art. 2127 CC; Paraguay Art. 1774 CC; Peru Art. 1494(7) CC.

[19] Art. 42(2)(a) CISG: the seller is not liable for any third party right and claim based on intellectual property if, at the time of the contract conclusion, the buyer knew or could have not been unaware of them. Neither there is liability for intellectual property claims or rights if the goods were produced by the seller based in technical drawings, designs, formulae or specifications furnished by the buyer.

[20] Argentina Arts. 2101(2)(3), 2106 CC; Brazil Art. 457 CC; Chile Arts. 1839, 1852(3) CC; Colombia Arts. 1895, 1909(3) CC; Ecuador Arts. 1806, 1819(3) CC; El Salvador Arts. 1641, 1648(3)(4) CC; Mexico Art. 2121 CC & Art. 384 Com C; Paraguay Art. 1764 CC; Peru Art. 1500(4) CC; Spain Arts. 1.475, 1.477 CC; Uruguay Art. 551 Com C; Venezuela Arts. 1.505, 1.507 CC.

Chapter 40

Examination and Notice

1. General Remarks on the Examination of the Goods and Notice

While many Ibero-American Codes of Commerce impose on the buyer a duty to examine the goods (B2B sales), only few Civil Codes contained a similar express obligation (C2C).[1] The reason may well be that the sales rules under the Civil Codes were mostly designed for C2C transactions under which it was assumed that the buyer has already seen and knows the goods and there is no liability in case of apparent defects (or if by any circumstance the buyer knew them or ought to have known them).[2] As no explicit requirement for the buyer to examine the goods and notify the seller of defects is established, the buyer, in a C2C sale, has to bring a claim based on a redhibitory action within a fixed period of time.[3]

Notwithstanding the above mentioned, the duty to examine the goods and the burden to notify the seller of any lack of conformity can also be constructed on the basis of the principle of good faith.[4] It is a common principle in all Ibero-American Civil Codes to require contracts to be concluded and performed in good faith.[5] This can be broadly interpreted to indicate that the buyer is

---

[1] *See infra* 2 & 3.

[2] *See* Ch. 37, 4.

[3] *See* Ch. 60, 2.2.

[4] Spain: A.M. Morales Moreno, *in* L. Díez Picazo y Ponce De León (Ed.), La Compraventa Internacional de Mecaderias – Comentario sobre la Convención de Viena Art. 38, III, at 327 (1998); Spain Supreme Tribunal, 14 May 1992, *Id Cendoj:* 28079110011992103723: the Tribunal found that the buyers had acted in bad faith because even when the goods contained defects impeding his proper use they remained quiet during the whole time until the citation to proceedings and did not inform the seller about them.

[5] Argentina Art. 1198 CC; Bolivia Art. 803 Com C; Brazil Art. 422 CC; Chile Art. 1546 CC; Colombia Art. 1603 CC & Art. 863 Com C; Cuba Art. 6 CC; Ecuador Art. 1589 CC; El

under an expected duty to examine the goods within a reasonable time or as required by the usages, and also under a duty to inform the seller about any facts susceptible to affect the performance of contract.[6]

2. Examination

2.1. Obligation

The Ibero-American laws give to the seller the option to expressly require the buyer to immediately examine the quality and quantity of the goods delivered.[7] On the other hand, many Ibero-American commercial laws impliedly require the buyer to examine the goods.[8] The only law that clearly requires the buyer to examine the goods within a reduce time limit is the Portuguese law.[9]

Examination of the goods in the Ibero-American laws helps to mitigate the damages that non-conforming goods can bring to both parties. Prompt examination gives certainty as to the fulfilment of parties' performances. As explained by a Spanish Tribunal, the rule seeks to protect the seller of late or unexpected claims regarding the proper performance of the contract and possible defects of the goods.[10]

In a very early case, a third instance El Salvadorian Court sustained that the many coffee installments delivered and received by the buyer, who immediately weighed them, examined them, and later stored them, made proof of the correct fulfilment of the seller's delivery obligation, and prevented the buyer from subsequently refusing payment of the price alleging a supposed non-conformity of a portion of the first installments.[11]

Similarly, the Spanish Supreme Tribunal dismissed the buyer's right to refuse taking delivery of the second installment of goods, based on apparent

Salvador Art. 1417 CC; Guatemala Art. 17 JOL; Mexico Art. 1796 CC; Paraguay Art. 715 CC; Peru Art. 1362 CC; Portugal Art. 762 CC; Spain Art. 1258 CC & Art. 57 Com C.

6 *See* Ch. 32, 1-3.

7 Argentina Art. 472 Com C; Chile Art. 146 Com C; Colombia Art. 939 Com C; Spain Art. 336 last para. Com C; Uruguay Art. 547 Com C; Venezuela Art. 145 para. 3 Com C.

8 On the one hand, some Codes of Commerce dictate that with the goods' examination the buyer preserves his rights to file a legal claim: El Salvador Art. 1019 para. 3 Com C; Spain Art. 336 para. 3 Com C; On the other hand, many commercial laws implicitly require a fast examination of the goods; since they require the buyer to raise any non-conformity allegation within different time limits depending on whether the goods lack of apparent quality and quantity, or whether they are affected by internal defects: Chile Art. 159 Com C; El Salvador Art. 1019 para. 2 Com C; Spain Art. 336 (2) Com C; Spain Supreme Tribunal, 11 May 1999, *Id Cendoj:* 28079110001999100864.

9 Portugal Art. 916 CC & Art. 471 Com C.

10 Spain AT Toledo, Sec. 1, 18 October 1996.

11 El Salvador Supreme Court, Judgments 10-12, October 1933, at 118-125, *cited in* El Salvador: A.O. Miranda, De la Compraventa 439 (1996).

lack of conformity, because the buyer had already taken delivery of the first installment of exactly the same goods with no objection as to their quality, but rather informed the seller that he would pick up the remaining quantity as soon as space was available.[12]

2.2. Time for Examination

Only few Ibero-American laws expressly establish a time limit for the examination of goods. The El Salvadorian, the Portuguese and Spanish Codes of Commerce require the examination of the goods to take place at the time the buyer takes delivery unless such is impossible.[13] In the rest of the commercial laws, the time limits established relate to obligation to give notice.[14]

3. Notice Requirement

3.1. Details of Notice

Most Ibero-American laws are silent as to the characteristics or details that the notice should contain. The Codes of Commerce of Costa Rica and Mexico require the buyer to give notice *in writing* about any allegations related to the lack of quality or quantity of goods.[15] Under the CISG, the notice should specify the nature of the non-conformity.[16] The CISG does not establish the standard that such notice should respect. The buyer is free to choose the means to perform this duty, unless otherwise agreed.[17] However, it is not enough that the buyer manifest its existence in a vague or ambiguous way.[18] He must at least describe the type of non-conformity, *e.g. aliud*, defects of quantity or quality.[19] The amount of the information shall depend on the circumstances of the case. The breach of the buyer's duty to give notice is asserted on a case-by-case basis.

---

12 Spain Supreme Tribunal, 25 June 1999, *Id Cendoj:* 28079110001999100407.

13 El Salvador Art. 1019 para. 2 Com C; Portugal Art. 471 Com C; Spain Art. 336 part 2 Com C.

14 *See infra* 3.2.

15 Costa Rica Art. 450 Com C para. 2; Mexico Art. 383 Com C; Mexico: O. Vásquez del Mercado, Contratos Mercantiles 205 (2008).

16 Art. 39(1) CISG.

17 Art. 6 CISG.

18 Portugal: L. De Lima Pinheiro, Dereito Comercial Internacional 287 (2005).

19 Spain: Morales Moreno, *supra* note 4, Art. 39, VIII, at 339.

3.2. Time for Giving Notice

The Ibero-American laws provide time limits for complaints based on lack of conformity of the goods. Generally, all laws provide two different time limits depending on whether the goods lack apparent quality and quantity, or whether they are affected by internal defects. The distinction is based on the idea that the lack of apparent quality and quantity can be noticed relatively easy and in less time than the internal defects that normally take a longer time to be noticed.[20]

Regarding the apparent defects of the goods, generally understood to be discovered once the goods have been released from their package, the Spanish Code of Commerce requires the buyer to denounce any apparent defects of quality or quantity within 4 days after delivery.[21] In Argentina, Chile and Uruguay the buyer receiving goods under the same circumstances is only given 3 days to denounce any apparent defects.[22] In Costa Rica and Mexico, the buyer has 5 days,[23] while in Ecuador and El Salvador the buyer has 8 days.[24] In Guatemala, the buyer has up to 15 days from delivery.[25]

As to the non-apparent or internal defects the Spanish and the Mexican Codes of Commerce extend the time to complain to 30 thirty days, running from the delivery of the goods.[26] El Salvador extends the time to denounce the non-apparent defects to 15 days, but from the date the buyer discovered them or from the date the parties have agreed so.[27] The Costa Rican law only gives 10 days to, running from the delivery of the goods, unless otherwise agreed.[28] Uruguay's Code of Commerce fixes a 6-month period running from the date of delivery.[29] In Argentina, the Code of Commerce establishes that the time limit to denounce internal defects shall be fixed by Courts, but this period should not go beyond 6 months from the date of delivery.[30] In Colombia, any

[20] Mexico Supreme Court, *Quinta Época*, SJF XCVII, p 260; Mexico Supreme Court, *Quita Época*, SJF LXXIII, at 699 *cited in* Mexico: S. León Tovar, Los Contratos Mercantiles 158, 160 (2004).

[21] Spain Art. 336 (2) Com C; Spain Supreme Tribunal, 11 May 1999, *Id Cendoj:* 28079110001999100864.

[22] Argentina Art. 472 Com C; Chile Art. 159 Com C; Uruguay Art. 546 Com C.

[23] Costa Rica Art. 450 para. 2 Com C; Mexico Art. 383 Com C.

[24] Ecuador Art. 192 para. 2 Com C; El Salvador Art. 1019 para. 2 Com C.

[25] Guatemala Art. 705 Com C.

[26] Mexico Art. 383 Com C; Spain Art. 342 Com C; Mexico: Vásquez del Mercado, *supra* note 15, at 205; Spain Supreme Tribunal, 23 January 2009, *Id Cendoj:* 28079110012009100016; Spain Supreme Tribunal, 8 June 2006, *Id Cendoj:* 28079110012006100603.

[27] El Salvador Art. 1019 para. 4 Com C.

[28] Costa Rica Art. 450 para. 3 Com C.

[29] Uruguay Art. 548 Com C.

[30] Argentina Art. 473 Com C.

allegation as to the quality or quantity of the goods, regardless of the type of defects, *i.e.* hidden or apparent, must be made within 5 days after delivery.[31]

On this issue, the Spanish Supreme Tribunal has upheld that the requirement of notice must be flexibly interpreted. The legal rigidity of the period for notice and its briefness can be excessive in cases where the assessment of the defects encounters special difficulties, due to the nature or characteristics of the goods, which may require technical tests or operations.[32]

This flexible approach has been reflected in some statutory provisions. For example, the Bolivian law only grants 10 days to give notice to any sort of defect.[33] However, in sales involving the transport of goods, the Bolivian law grants a longer 90 day period running from the unloading of the goods at the place of arrival, and the period may be extended by the judge if under the circumstances, it is justified that the buyer was unable to inspect the goods before that time.[34] Similarly, in Venezuela, 2 days are granted from delivery, unless longer time is needed due to the particular conditions of the goods or of the personal situation of the buyer.[35]

In Brazil, the Civil Code establishes that the buyer has 30 days from the effective delivery of the goods to claim redhibitory actions or the reduction of price.[36] But if the buyer was already in possession of the goods the limitation period is reduced to 15 days.[37] However, if the defect, by its nature, could only be discovered later, the limitation period shall start running from the moment the buyer became aware of it.[38]

Under the Portuguese Civil Code, the notice of non-conformity shall be given within 30 days after the defects on the goods were known and, alternatively, within 6 months after the delivery of the goods.[39] As in the CISG system,[40] this second time limit is subsidiary to the first one. It only operates in cases in which the buyer never knew the defects on the goods. Moreover, in the cases involving the carriage of goods, the time limit just referred to shall start running from the time of effective reception of the goods by the buyer and not from the contractual date of delivery.[41]

In B2B sales in which the seller has expressly guaranteed the conformity of the goods for a specific time, some laws require the buyer to inform the seller within 30 days, from the time he became aware of any malfunctioning of the

31 Colombia Art. 931 para. 2 Com C.
32 Spain Supreme Tribunal, 14 May 1992, *Id Cendoj:* 28079110011992103723.
33 Bolivia Art. 848 Com C (10 days).
34 Bolivia Art. 863 Com C.
35 Venezuela Arts. 144, 145 para. 2 Com C.
36 Brazil Art. 445 CC.
37 *Id.*
38 Brazil Art. 445 (1) CC.
39 Portugal Art. 916 (2) CC.
40 *See* Art. 39 CISG.
41 Portugal Art. 922 CC.

goods.[42] Other laws require the buyer to inform the seller within 30 days, running from the time he became aware of any defects on the goods.[43] The Peruvian Civil Code only grants 7 days.[44]

The freedom of the parties to modify such fatal periods has been recognised by the Spanish Supreme Tribunal. The Tribunal upheld that these provisions are of a voluntary character and of facultative application, susceptible to be modified by the agreement of the parties.[45]

In order to give certainty to the computation of the time limits referred to by the law, some laws expressly establish that 'days' are understood as to be working days of 24 hours; the 'months' are according to the Gregorian calendar; and the 'year' is of 365 days.[46]

Finally, under many Civil Codes the buyer must inform the seller of the beginning of proceedings against him regarding third party property rights or encumbrances affecting the goods.[47] Such requirement comes from the duty to cooperate whenever third parties' judicial claims arise.[48] The seller has an obligation to appear before any court in the defence of the buyer's rights over the goods. In order to do so, and eventually compensate for the eviction, the buyer shall give notice to the seller before submission of the defence.[49]

4. Consequences of Failure to Notify

4.1. General Consequences

Under the Ibero-American laws, failure of a buyer to react, complain or give notice in due time about any lack of quality and quantity or defects in the goods, engenders the loss of any right and action to rely upon the lack of

42 Bolivia Art. 838 Com C; Colombia Art. 932 Com C; El Salvador Art. 1021 Com C.

43 Brazil Art. 446 CC; Costa Rica Art. 452 Com C; Paraguay Art. 753 CC; Venezuela Art. 1.526 CC.

44 Peru Art. 1523 CC.

45 Spain Supreme Tribunal, 29 March 1995 *in* Spain: S. Vázquez Barros, Contratos de compraventa y permuta: comentarios, formularios, jurisprudencia: legislación básica y bibliografía (2003). (Ref: FGV-614).

46 Costa Rica Art. 417 Com C; Mexico Art. 84 Com C; Spain Art. 60 Com C.

47 Bolivia Art. 627 (I) CC; Brazil Art. 456 CC; Chile Art. 1843 CC; Colombia Art. 1899 CC; Ecuador Art. 1810 CC; El Salvador Art. 1645 CC; Mexico Art. 2124 CC; Paraguay Art. 1770 (a) CC.

48 Chile: R. Díez Duarte, La Compraventa en el Código Civil Chileno 157, 158 (1993); El Salvador: Miranda, *supra* note 11, at 211, 212; Colombia Supreme Court, 24 March 1947, GJ LXII, p. 84; Colombia Supreme Court, 19 December 1952, GJ LXXIII, p. 751.

49 Chile Art. 584 CPC; Colombia. Art. 54 CPC; El Salvador Art. 225 CPC; Mexico Art. 2124 CC.

conformity;[50] such as the specific performance, the avoidance of the contract, the redhibitory remedies or the compensation for damages.[51]

In the sale made by samples, if the buyer, after delivery, has inspected the goods with no objection as to the quality, he shall be precluded from avoiding the contract on the grounds of difference between the goods delivered and the sample used during the negotiations.[52] In a case submitted to a El Salvadorian Court, a buyer filed a claim for the avoidance of the contract based on the supposed difference between the samples negotiated and the tobacco delivered. Experts were appointed by the Court. The experts' exam confirmed that the tobacco sold was of a lower quality than that currently exhibited at the seller's premises. However, the experts acknowledged that they could not confirm that the tobacco's samples examined were the same according to which the contract was concluded. The Court denied the avoidance of the contract upholding that even if the samples examined by the experts had corresponded to those negotiated, the buyer, in order to conserve his right for the avoidance, should have informed or at least complained in due time about any lack of conformity on the goods.[53] Thus, the buyer was precluded to avoid the contract since he should bear the consequences caused by his own omission.[54]

As previously mentioned, if the buyer fails to inform the seller about the beginning of proceedings against him, which are based on property title claims over the goods, and a final judgment of the court evicts the buyer, the seller cannot be held liable to compensate.[55]

---

50 Bolivia Art. 848 Com C; Brazil Art. 446 CC; Chile Art. 158 Com C; Colombia Arts. 931, 939 Com C; Costa Rica Arts. 450, 452 Com C; Ecuador Art. 192 Com C; El Salvador Art. 1019 para. 1 Com C; Mexico Art. 383 Com C; Paraguay Art. 753 CC; Peru Art. 1523 CC; Portugal Art. 917 CC; Spain Arts. 336 para. 1, 342 Com C; Uruguay Art. 545 Com C; Venezuela Art. 1.526 CC & Art. 144 Com C para. 2; Mexico Supreme Court, *Quinta Época*, SJF LXXIII. at 699 *cited in* Mexico: León Tovar, *supra* note 20, at 158, 160; ICC Final Award Case No. 11367 *Lex Contractus* Portuguese Law; Venezuela: L.A. Rodriguez, Comentarios sobre: Contratos 89 (2007).

51 Spain Supreme Tribunal, 23 January 2009, *Id Cendoj:* 28079110012009100016; ICC Final Award Case No. 13918 *Lex Contractus* Spanish Law: the Sole Arbitrator found that as the buyer had failed to follow the procedure established by the contract with regards to the time limits, the form and requirements of the notice to raise any claim on the financial situation of the company purchased, the buyer was precluded from compensation for damages as such was the consequence established by the same contract in case of failure to follow the mentioned procedure.

52 El Salvador: Miranda, *supra* note 11, at 519.

53 El Salvador Art. 1019 para. 1 Com C.

54 This was the case of an early decision from a second instance Court of El Salvador, Judgment RJ No. 19, 1 October 1901, at 475-478 *cited in* El Salvador: Miranda, *supra* note 11, at 519.

55 Bolivia Art. 627 (II) CC; Brazil Art. 456 sole para. CC; Chile Art. 1843 part 2 CC; Colombia Art. 1899 part 2 CC; Ecuador Art. 1810 part 2 CC; El Salvador Art. 1645 part 2 CC; Mexico Collegiate Tribunals, *Novena Época*, Registry 187'228, SJF XV, April 2002, at 1261.

4.2. Exceptions – Knowledge of the Seller

Under the CISG, the buyer's failure to give notice shall not cause the loss of his right to rely on the non-conformity if the seller knew or could not have been unaware of the facts related to the lack of conformity of the goods.[56]

The Ibero-American laws do not expressly address the issue. However, the principle of good faith imposes upon the parties a duty of information.[57] In particular, the duty to inform obliges the seller to disclose certain facts susceptible to affecting the buyer's decision to purchase the goods.[58] The breach of this duty can have many different consequences in Ibero-American law. Among them, the avoidance of the contract,[59] or the duty to compensate for the damages and lost profits caused.[60] For example, the Paraguayan Civil Code states that the party who knew, or ought to have known, the existence of an element that may cause the avoidance of the contract, and does not give notice of such to the other party shall compensate for the damages caused.[61]

---

56 Art. 40 CISG.

57 Spain: Morales Moreno, *supra* note 4, Art. 40, V, at 351; Mexico: León Tovar, *supra* note 20, at 156.

58 Argentina: A.A. Alterini, Contratos civiles, comerciales, de consumo 330 (1998); Colombia Supreme Court, 4 April 2001, *Sala de Casación Civil*, *cited in* Colombia J. Oviedo Alban, La Formación de Contrato: tratos preliminares, oferta, aceptación 18-19 (2008); *see also* Ch. 27, 3.

59 *See for example* Mexico Art. 2144 CC; Spain Arts. 1.269, 1.270 CC.

60 *See for example* Mexico Art. 2145 CC; Spain Art. 1.270 (2) CC; *see also* Ch. 50.

61 Paraguay Art. 690 CC.

Part 9

Obligations of the Buyer

CHAPTER 41

GENERAL REMARKS ON THE OBLIGATIONS OF THE BUYER

1. Contractual Terms and Default Obligations

The Ibero-American laws allow the parties to define their obligations and recognise the primary position of parties' free determination, within the limits established by the law.[1] Peru's Civil Code clearly presents the principle in the statement "the legal provisions on contracts are supplementary to the will of the parties, unless they are imperative."[2]

In this regard, many of the obligations imposed by the Ibero-American sales laws and the CISG are not imperative but supplementary.[3] For example, even if it is imperative for the buyer to make payment of the price,[4] the parties could always agree on the time for payment, regardless of the default rule on this issue.[5] The same flexibility applies regarding the place of payment; despite the fact that the default rule calls for payment at the seller's place of business, the parties can freely agree otherwise.[6]

2. Main Obligations

As one of the main obligations under the sales contract, all the Ibero-American laws require the buyer to pay the price of the goods sold.[7] Peru's Civil Code

1 In this regard *see* Ch. 3, 1.
2 Peru Arts. 1353, 1356 CC.
3 *See* Ch. 31.
4 *See* Ch. 42; Art. 53 CISG.
5 *See* Ch. 42, 3.
6 *See* Ch. 42, 2; Art. 57 (1) (a) CISG.
7 Argentina Art. 1424 CC; Bolivia Art. 636 CC; Brazil Arts. 481, 327 CC; Chile Arts. 1871,

may have the most comprehensive provision on this issue. It does not only require the buyer to pay the price at the place and at the time agreed, but also in the way contracted, *e.g.* cheque, credit card, letter of credit, *etc.*, and absent an agreement, the price shall be paid in cash.[8]

Some laws expressly oblige the buyer to receive the goods,[9] while others provide this obligation in a generic duty to cooperate in the fulfilment of the contract,[10] either by receiving the goods[11] or by performing any other intrinsic obligations.[12] In Spain and Venezuela, for example, there is no express obligation on this issue, however, the refusal or the non-appearance of the buyer to take delivery of the goods in due time would amount to avoidance of the contract in the seller's benefit.[13]

3. Potential Ancillary Obligations

Multiple subsidiary obligations can arise from the contract itself[14] or from the relevant national law. For example, the contract may call for the payment of the price through a documentary letter of credit. The potentially ancillary obligations to comply with such a request are multiple. The procedure and requirements can change depending on the type of letter of credit and the standards to which the parties have voluntarily submitted.[15]

1872 CC; Colombia Arts. 1928, 1929 CC; Ecuador Arts. 1838, 1839 CC; El Salvador Arts. 1673, 1674 CC; Guatemala Art. 1825 CC; Mexico Art. 2293 CC & Art. 380 Com C; Nicaragua Art. 2660 CC; Paraguay Art. 763 CC; Peru Art. 1558 CC; Portugal Art. 885 CC; Spain Art. 1.500 CC; Uruguay Art. 1728 CC; Venezuela Art. 1.527 CC; Chile Supreme Court, RDJ, Vol. 21, Sec. 1, at 219 *cited in* Chile: R. Díez Duarte, La Compraventa en el Código Civil Chileno 172, n. 458 (1993): stating that the obligation to pay the price persist even when the goods sold belong to third persons.

8 Peru Art. 1558 CC.

9 Argentina Art. 1427 CC; Bolivia Art. 846 Com C; Colombia Art. 943 Com C; Guatemala Art. 1830 CC; Paraguay Art. 764 CC; Peru Art. 1565 CC.

10 *See for example*, Spain: A. Cabanillas Sánchez, *in* L. Díez Picazo y Ponce De León, La Compraventa Internacional de Mecaderias – Comentario sobre la Convención de Viena Art. 53, II, at 462 (1998); Venezuela: J.L. Aguilar Gorrondona, Contratos y Garantias: Derecho Civil IV, 266 (2008).

11 Chile Art. 1827 CC & Art. 153 Com C; Colombia Art. 1883 CC; Ecuador Arts. 1794, 1532 CC; El Salvador Arts. 1630, 1360 CC; Spain Art. 1.505 CC; Venezuela Art. 1.531 CC & Art. 141 Com C.

12 Bolivia Art. 568 CC; Brazil Art. 422 CC; Portugal Art. 813 CC; Uruguay Art. 1431 CC; In Mexico scholars recognise the obligation of the buyer to take delivery and associate it with articles 377 and 387 of the Code of Commerce, *see* Mexico: S. León Tovar, Los Contratos Mercantiles 168 (2004).

13 Spain Art. 1.505 CC; Venezuela Art. 1.531 CC.

14 Mexico Art. 372 Com C is clear on this: on sales contracts the parties are bound by any legal clause they agree upon.

15 *See* Ch. 42, 4.

In addition, the buyer may need to comply with some extra obligations derived from the inclusion in the contract of a selected international term of commerce. As mentioned, the INCOTERMS distinguish between four different categories of terms depending on the place where the goods have to be placed at the buyer's disposal. For example, according to the ExWorks INCOTERM the buyer must obtain at his own risk and expense any import or export licence or any other official authorisation, and carry out all customs formalities for the export of the goods. In addition to this obligation, the second group known with the letter 'F', *i.e. FCA, FAS*, and *FOB*, requires the buyer to contract at his own expense for the carriage of the goods from the named place. Finally, under the third group or 'C' terms, *i.e. CFR, CIF, CPT* and *CIP*, and fourth group or 'D' terms, *i.e. DAF, DES, DEQ, DDU* and *DDP*, the buyer must obtain at his own risk and expense any import or any other official authorisation, and carry out all customs formalities for the import of the goods and for their transit through any country.[16]

Then again, the laws may also impose extra obligations to the buyer. The buyer's obligations may be extended by certain national provisions from which the parties may not deviate. For example, domestic Ibero-American laws may establish that payment of the price can only be made in domestic currency.[17]

---

16 *See generally* ICC official rules for the interpretation of trade terms.

17 *See* Ch. 42, 1.

CHAPTER 42

PAYMENT

1. Currency and Exchange Rates

Under the Ibero-American laws, the parties are free to agree on the price of the goods to be made in a currency other than the official national currency at the place of payment or under the applicable law.[1] In addition, the parties are also free to establish which party shall bear the cost resulting from the conversion of one currency into another.[2] Under Bolivian law, the debtor of the obligation bears the expenses resulting from the payment, unless otherwise agreed.[3]

According to CISG Article 54 the buyer's obligation to pay the price includes the duty to take the necessary steps and measures, as may be required under the contract or any laws and regulations, so that payment can be performed.[4] The burden is on the buyer since he is better placed than the seller to accomplish the obligation. The Ibero-American laws do not contain a similar provision as the one contained in CISG Article 54. However, the same duties can be subtracted from the principles of cooperation and good faith present in the Ibero-American contracts laws.[5] The parties to a sales contract are not only obliged to perform the main obligations but also to cooperate in the fulfilment of any other ancillary obligation attached to the main ones.

---

1 *See* Ch. 10, 1.1.2.

2 *See* ICC Final Award Case No. 10299 *Lex Contractus* Chilean Law: sellers agreed that they will in all cases bear any cost resulting from the conversation of USD into Chilean pesos, for payment of the purchase price, which exceeds of USD 5,000.

3 Bolivia Art. 319 CC; Bolivia: G. Castellanos Trigo & S. Auad La Fuente, Derecho de las Obligaciones en el Código Civil Boliviano 90 (2008).

4 *See* further comments as to the obligations comprised in Art. 54 CISG in F. Mohs, *in* I. Schwenzer (Ed.), Schlechtriem & Schwenzer Commentary on the UN Convention on the International Sale of Goods Art. 54, paras. 2-7, at 811-813 (2010).

5 Spain: A. Cabanillas Sánchez, *in* L. Díez Picazo y Ponce De León, La Compraventa

2. Place of Payment

In international sales of goods, determination of the place of payment is very important. On the one hand, the buyer will have an understandable interest to pay the price in his own country, where less manoeuvres are necessary to perform. On the other hand, the seller has an advantage in being paid in his country's domicile, as there he could freely and relatively soon dispose of the money paid in consideration for the goods. Such diverging interests sometimes respond to issues regarding the type of currency and the exchange controls in force in some countries.

All Ibero-American laws follow the CISG rule under which the buyer shall pay the price in the place agreed within the contract.[6] However, the default rules, absent an agreement, slightly vary among the countries. In the vast majority of the Ibero-American systems, except for Brazil,[7] the buyer shall pay the price in the place of delivery of the goods.[8] Thus, payment shall NOT be made at the buyer's domicile as would normally be the case in other type of contracts,[9] but at the place of delivery. Consequently, if a fixed place for delivery has already been agreed to by the parties, as the law allows them to

Internacional de Mecaderias – Comentario sobre la Convención de Viena Art. 54, II, at 465 (1998).

6 Art 57 (1) CISG; Argentina Art. 1424 CC; Brazil Art. 327 CC; Bolivia Art. 636 (I) CC; Chile Art. 1872 CC & Art. 155 para. 2 Com C; Colombia Art. 1929 CC; Costa Rica Art. 419 Com C; Ecuador Art. 1839 CC; El Salvador Art. 1674 CC; Guatemala Art. 1825 CC; Mexico Art. 2294 CC; Nicaragua Art. 2661 CC; Paraguay Art. 763 CC; Peru Art. 1558 CC; Portugal Art. 885 (2) CC; Spain Art. 1.500 CC; Uruguay Art. 1728 CC; Venezuela Art. 1.527 CC; Bolivia: V. Camargo Marín, Derecho Comercial Boliviano 400 (2007); Mexico: O. Vásquez del Mercado, Contratos Mercantiles 206 (2008).

7 Except for Brazil Art. 327 CC: the payment of the goods shall be made at the seller's domicile, unless the parties have agreed otherwise, or when a different thing is required by the law, the nature of the obligation or the circumstances of the case.

8 Argentina Art. 1424 CC; Bolivia Art. 636(II) CC & Art. 862 Com C; Chile Art. 1872 CC & Art. 155 para. 2 Com C; Colombia Art. 1929 CC; Ecuador Art. 1839 CC; El Salvador Art. 1674 CC; Guatemala Art. 1825 CC; Mexico Art. 2294 CC & Art. 380 Com C; Nicaragua Art. 2661 CC; Paraguay Art. 763 CC; Peru Art. 1558 CC; Portugal Art. 885(1) CC; Spain Art. 1.500 CC; Uruguay Art. 1728 CC; Venezuela Art. 1.527 CC.

9 That would be normally the case for other contracts since the General Obligations Part of these Civil Codes states that obligations including that of payment must be performed immediately and at the debtors domicile (in the case of sales would be the buyer's domicile), *see* Costa Rica Art. 419 C Com. However, this rule does not apply to sales contracts since the special rules on sales contracts override the General Obligations Rules; *see* on this Chile: R. Díez Duarte, La Compraventa en el Código Civil Chileno 173 (1993); El Salvador: A.O. Miranda, De la Compraventa 278 (1996); Mexico Collegiate Tribunals, *Novena Época*, Registry 183'410, SJF XVIII, August 2003, at 1831.

do,[10] the same agreement would be extended to the place of payment without need of special clause on this issue.[11]

As the place to pay the price depends upon the place of delivery of the goods, absent an agreement on the contrary on both, the determination of the place of payment would require asserting, initially, the expected place of delivery. In this issue, most of the above mentioned laws establish that unless otherwise agreed, ascertained and identified goods have to be delivered in the place where they were at the time of the conclusion of the contract, while in all other cases (of unascertained goods) the delivery shall take place in the seller's domicile.[12] This means that in absence of agreement as to the place of delivery and payment, the buyer shall pay the price at the place where the ascertained and identified goods were at the conclusion of the contract, and for unascertained goods at the seller's domicile.

The Civil Codes of Peru, Portugal and Venezuela contain an alternative default rule in absence of agreement as to the place of payment. In Peru and Venezuela, if payment cannot be performed at the place of delivery, the price will be paid at the buyer's domicile,[13] while in Portugal if payment at the place of delivery is impossible it will be executed at the seller's domicile.[14] Additionally, in countries like Argentina and Uruguay when the sale has been agreed to be by installments, or when the usages of the place concede some additional time after delivery to perform payment, the price shall be paid by the buyer at his own domicile.[15]

Conversely, in Brazil the payment of the goods shall be made at the seller's domicile, unless the parties have agreed otherwise, or when a different thing is required by the law, the nature of the obligation or the circumstances of the case.[16] In addition, whenever two places are designated, the buyer shall choose one at his own discretion.[17] The Brazilian Civil Code further establishes that to reiterate payment of the price in a different place supposes the relinquishment of the seller to what was the agreed in the contract or the provision of the law.[18]

Following the rules of virtual delivery or delivery through documents present in some Ibero-American laws, we can infer that payment of the price should be performed in the place of deliverance of the bill of lading, of the invoice, or of any other documents representing the goods.[19]

---

10 *See* Ch. 35, 2.1.

11 Chile: Díez Duarte, *supra* note 9, at 173; El Salvador: Miranda, *supra* note 9, at 278.

12 *See* Ch. 35, 2.2.

13 Peru Art. 1558 *in fine* CC; Venezuela Art. 1.527 *in fine* CC.

14 Portugal Art. 885 (2) CC.

15 Argentina Art. 1424 *in fine* CC; Uruguay Art. 1728 *in fine* CC.

16 Brazil Art. 327 CC.

17 *Id.*

18 Brazil Art. 330 CC.

19 For detailed rules on the virtual delivery *see* Ch. 35, 1; *see also* Mexico: S. León Tovar,

As mentioned, in every sale of goods, national or international, it is of great importance to determine the place where the price has to be paid. On the one hand, a buyer's failure to pay the price at the place of payment, according to the agreement of the parties or the default rules, may give to the seller a right for the avoidance of the contract.[20] On the other hand, a seller's failure to collect the price at the agreed or default place of payment may prevent him to seek the avoidance of the contract.[21]

3. Time of Payment

In the Ibero-American laws, as in the CISG, the primary rule is that the buyer shall pay the price at the time agreed by the parties in their contract.[22] However, according to the Chilean Supreme Court the time of payment must be sufficiently determined by the parties. The time of payment of the price may not be sufficiently determined when, for example, it is understood that the buyer is given the possibility to get some money first.[23]

Absent an agreement, the vast majority of the Ibero-American laws declare, as the CISG does, that the buyer shall pay the price at the time of delivery of the goods or their documents.[24] Thus, payment is not made immediately after

Los Contratos Mercantiles 151, 153 (2004); Venezuela: J.L. Aguilar Gorrondona, Contratos y Garantias: Derecho Civil IV, 219 (2008).

[20] *See* Ch. 53, 2.2.

[21] Mexico Collegiate Tribunals, *Novena Época*, Registry 201'660, SJF IV, August 1996, at 642.

[22] Arts. 58 (1), 59 CISG; on the CISG *see* the comments *in* Mohs, *supra* note 4, Art. 59, para. 1, at 858; Argentina Art. 1424 CC; Brazil Art. 331 CC; Bolivia Art. 636 (I) CC & Art. 860 Com C (agreed CIF National Term of Commerce buyer pays against the delivery of the documents concerned); Chile Art. 1872 CC & Art. 155 para. 2 Com C; Colombia Art. 1929 CC & Art. 947 Com C; Ecuador Art. 1839 CC; El Salvador Art. 1674 CC; Guatemala Art. 1825 CC & Art. 694 Com C; Mexico Art. 2294 CC; Nicaragua Art. 2661 CC; Paraguay Art. 763 CC; Peru Art. 1558 CC; Portugal Art. 885 (2) CC; Spain Art. 1.500 CC; Uruguay Art. 1728 CC & Art. 530 Com C; Venezuela Art. 1.527 CC; *see also* Bolivia: Camargo Marín, *supra* note 6, at 400; Mexico: Vásquez del Mercado, *supra* note 6, at 206.

[23] Chile Supreme Court, RDJ, Vol. 78, Sec. 2, at 1, *cited in* Chile: Díez Duarte, *supra* note 9, at 123, n. 336.

[24] Art. 58(1) CISG; Mohs, *supra* note 4, Art. 59, para. 4, at 859: for example, the buyer may only be required to pay upon receipt of the invoice; Argentina Arts. 1424, 464 CC & Art. 465 Com C; Bolivia Arts. 636(II), 850(3) CC on the sale by documents & Art. 860 Com C agreed CIF National Term of Commerce the buyer pays against the delivery of the documents concerned; Chile Art. 1872 CC & Art. 155 para. 2 Com C; Colombia Art. 1929 CC & Art. 947 Com C; Ecuador Art. 1839 CC; El Salvador Art. 1674 CC; Guatemala Art. 1825 CC & Art. 701 Com C agreed CIF National Term of Commerce the buyer pays against the delivery of the documents concerned; Mexico Art. 2294 CC & Art. 380 Com C; Nicaragua Art. 2661 CC; Paraguay Art. 763 CC; Peru Art. 1558 CC; Portugal Art. 885(1) CC; Spain Art. 1.500 CC & Art. 339 Com C; Uruguay Art. 1728 CC & Art. 530 para. 2 Com C; Venezuela Art. 1.527 CC;

the conclusion of the contract as would normally be the case in other type of agreements,[25] but until the time of the delivery of the goods.[26] Consequently, if a specific time for delivery has already been fixed by the parties, as the parties are allowed to do by law,[27] the same agreement would extend as to time of payment with no need for a special clause on this issue.[28]

Hence, the time of payment is to concur with the time of delivery of the goods. Absent an agreement to the contrary on both, the determination of the time of payment would require asserting, initially, the time of delivery. Among Ibero-American law we find small variations as to the time within which the seller shall deliver the goods. For example, according to some countries' laws the default rule requires that the seller deliver the goods immediately or twenty-four hours after the conclusion of the contract. This means that under such rule payment would also be required at that time. Under other laws, if no time was commonly agreed, the date of the delivery will be chosen unilaterally by the buyer. Hence, the time of payment is left at the buyer's election.[29]

Brazil is the only Ibero-American country which does not subordinate the time of payment to the time of delivery but instead has an independent provision on this issue. According to article 331 of Brazil's Civil Code, unless otherwise agreed, the seller can immediately ask payment to the buyer.

All the above-mentioned approaches are unfit for sales contracts. The immediate payment or the payment within twenty-four hours is unrealistic in international and even in national trade. Nor does exclusive election by the buyer of the date give much certainty as to the time to perform payment.

Mexico Art. 380 Com C establishes that the buyer shall pay the price 'in cash' (de contado), but the Supreme Court and ICC Tribunals have interpreted the term 'in cash' as meaning that the buyer shall pay the price before or at the time of the delivery of the goods, *see* Mexico Supreme Court, Registry 240'067, *Tercera Sala*, SJF IV, p. 14; ICC Final Award Case No. 13751 *Lex Contractus* German Law and Mexican Law to the agency relationship.

[25] That would be normally the case for other contracts since the General Obligations Part of these Civil Codes (but also some Commercial laws as Costa Rica Art. 418(a)(b) Com C) dictates that obligations including that of payment must be performed immediately and at the debtors domicile (in the case of sale would be the buyer's domicile). However, this rule does not apply since the special rules on sales override the General Obligations Rules; *see* on this Chile: Díez Duarte, *supra* note 9, at 173; El Salvador: Miranda, *supra* note 9, at 278.

[26] Spain Supreme Tribunal, 22 November 2006, *Id Cendoj:* 28079110012006101175: applying Spain Art. 339 Com C upheld that the buyer was bound to pay the price from the time the seller placed the goods at his disposal.

[27] *See* Ch. 35, 3.1.

[28] Chile: Díez Duarte, *supra* note 9, at 173; El Salvador: Miranda, *supra* note 9, at 278; *see* Argentina National Commercial Chamber, *Sala* D, *Castelar S.A. v. Maralc SRL*, 11 April 1990, JA 1990-IV-165: "(…) as the goods were received by the claimant, notwithstanding that invoices have not been submitted, the delay in payment was produced (…)."

[29] For more details on the time of delivery of the goods *see* Ch. 35, 3.2.

Concerning the time of payment in the sales made by documents, the buyer shall pay the price when the seller hands over the required documents.[30] Following the rules of virtual delivery present in some Ibero-American laws, payment of the price should take place when the goods are placed at the buyer's disposal through the deliverance of the bill of lading, the invoice, or by any other means authorised by the trade usage.[31]

4. Modes of Payment

According to CISG article 58 (2), if the contract involves the transport of the goods, the seller can dispatch the goods on the terms whereby the goods or the representative documents will not be handed to the buyer except against payment of the price.

One of the ways to implement this condition is through a documentary letter of credit. The parties are free to agree to have the price paid through a documentary letter of credit. For example, a buyer wants to purchase $2,000,000 worth of goods from the seller. The seller agrees to sell the goods and gives the buyer 50 days to pay for them, on the condition that they are provided with a 50 days' letter of credit for the full amount. The potentially ancillary obligations to comply with such request are multiple: To start with, the buyer shall go to his bank, hereinafter B-BANK, and requests a $2,000,000 letter of credit, with the seller as the beneficiary. Subsequently, B-Bank sends a copy of the letter of credit to the seller's bank, hereinafter S-BANK, which notifies the seller that the payment is available and that he can ship the goods that the buyer has ordered, with the full assurance of payment upon presentation of the stipulated documents in the letter of credit and compliance with the terms and conditions of the letter of credit. After verification of the documents, the terms and conditions, B-BANK can transfer the $2,000,000 to the S-BANK which then deposits the amount at the seller's account with S-BANK.[32]

The above mentioned is only an example. The procedure and requirements can change depending on the type of letter of credit and the standards to which the parties have voluntarily submitted. A letter of credit clause in a sales contract could for example state, "payable against [list of documents - state original or copy, state acceptable issuers of documents]" or "Subject

---

[30] *See* expressly Bolivia Art. 850 (3) Com C; Guatemala Art. 695 para. 2; Mexico: León Tovar, *supra* note 19, at 151, 153; Mexico: Vásquez del Mercado, *supra* note 6, at 209; Venezuela: Aguilar Gorrondona, *supra* note 19, at 219.

[31] For more details on the virtual delivery *see* Ch. 35, 1.

[32] In an ICC case, the Sole Arbitrator upheld that as the buyer refused to amend the Letter of Credit in order to make it 'fully workable', pursuant to the sales contract and in light of his duty of good faith, the buyer breached the sales contract and the seller therefore validly terminated the contract, *see* ICC Final Award Case No. 14633 *Lex Contractus* Incoterms, CISG, UNIDROIT PICC, Trade Practices.

to UCP 600". The UCP is an acronym of Uniform Customs and Practice for Documentary Credits: a set of rules on the issuance and use of letters of credit.[33]

The UCP 600 are applied to any documentary credit when the text of the letter of credit clause expressly indicates that it is subject to these rules. They are binding on all parties to the letter of credit, usually the parties to the sales contract and their banks, unless expressly modified or excluded by them.[34] In this case, the degree of compliance or the failure to comply with the obligation to pay the price is a question that is answered by the terms agreed in the contract, and not only by the CISG or the Ibero-American laws.

5. Means of Securing Payment

5.1. Retention of Title

In the Ibero-American laws, a mechanism to secure payment can be established if the parties enter into a sales contract subject to *pactum reservati dominii.*[35] Under these types of sales the parties agree that the seller remains the owner of the goods even after their delivery.[36] In other words, the seller retains the title of ownership until the buyer completely meets the condition imposed, *e.g.* the payment of the price, that a period of time elapses or that any other fact occurs.[37]

This modality of sales is very important and common in the practice. The insertion of clauses of title retention is commonly made in the sale of goods by instalments as a means of securing payment.[38] Such is purported to be less

---

33 *See generally*, ICC, UCP 600 Drafting Group, International Chamber of Commerce & ICC Banking Commission, 2007, Commentary on UCP 600: Article-by-article analysis. Paris, France: International Chamber of Commerce.

34 *Id.*

35 Bolivia Arts. 585, 839 CC: requirement to register the non fungible goods; Brazil Art. 521 CC; Colombia Art. 750 CC & Art. 952 Com C; Chile Arts. 680, 1874 CC; Ecuador Arts. 715, 1841 CC & Art. 202-A Com C; El Salvador Arts. 661, 1676 CC & Art. 1038 Com C; Guatemala Art. 1834 CC; Mexico Art. 2312 CC; Paraguay Art. 780 CC; Peru Art. 1583 CC; Portugal Art. 934 CC; Venezuela Art. 1 LRTS.

36 Argentina: R. Compagnucci de Caso, Contrato de Compraventa 332 (2007); Colombia: E.G. Escobar Velez, La compraventa civil y comercial: los contratos de promesa de compraventa y la permuta 288 (1991).

37 Expressly stated in Bolivia Art. 585 (I) CC; Ecuador Art. 202-A para. 2 Com C; Guatemala Art. 1834 CC; Mexico Art. 2312 CC; Paraguay Art. 780 CC; Peru Art. 1583 CC; Venezuela Art. 1 LRTS; Brazil: O. Gomes, Contratos 316 (2008); Mexico: Vásquez del Mercado, *supra* note 6, at 202; Venezuela: Aguilar Gorrondona, *supra* note 19, at 291.

38 Such is expressly recognised in Bolivia Art. 585 CC; Ecuador Art. 202-A Com C; El Salvador Art. 1038 Com C; Guatemala Arts. 1834-1843 CC; Mexico Arts. 2312, 2310 CC; Portugal Art. 934 CC; Venezuela Art. 1 LRTS; Spain Supreme Tribunal, 13 May 1982,

complicated and cheaper for both parties than other means, such as payment through credit card, letters of credit, guarantors, *etc.*[39] However, this method may offer less security to the seller.

This type of agreement is not expressly governed by the Civil Codes of Argentina and Spain.[40] But the doctrine and the jurisprudence have recognised this modality of sale as valid,[41] since it does not contradict the law or the public order.[42]

On the other hand, under many laws only ascertained and identified goods can be subject to the title's retention.[43] Also some laws require the contract with retention of title to be in writing and registered, in order to be valid against third parties in the place where the goods are or at the buyer's domicile.[44]

In this type of sales, the contract is perfectly concluded at the time of the parties' meeting of the minds on the goods and the price. But the seller retains the title of property until the buyer fulfils the condition, namely- payment of the goods, and once the buyer do so he automatically becomes the owner of the goods.[45] Except in C2C sales under the laws of Chile, Ecuador and El Salvador, where there exists contradiction between the provisions on the General Obligations of the Civil Code allowing the retention of the

Id Cendoj: 28079110011982100041: applying Law No. 50/1965 on the sale of goods by installments, applicable to consumer transactions but also to traders who acquire goods in order to integrate them into a production process. The court recognised the effects of the retention of title clause when the buyer fails to pay the whole price; *see also* Brazil: Gomes, *supra* note 37, at 316; El Salvador: Miranda, *supra* note 9, at 298; Colombia: Escobar Vélez, *supra* note 36, at 289.

[39] Mexico: Vásquez del Mercado, *supra* note 6, at 202; Venezuela: Aguilar Gorrondona, *supra* note 19, at 292.

[40] Though there is in Spain the Law No. 50/1965 on the sale of goods by installments, applicable to consumer transactions but also to traders who acquire goods in order to integrate them into a production process.

[41] *See* Argentina Art. 1197 CC; Spain Art. 1255 CC; Spain Supreme Tribunal, 12 July 1996, *Id Cendoj:* 28079110001996100990; *see also* Argentina: Compagnucci de Caso, *supra* note 36, at 332.

[42] Venezuela Supreme Tribunal, *Cass civ*, 2 August 1967, *cited in* Venezuela: Aguilar Gorrondona, *supra* note 19, at 293.

[43] Colombia Art. 953 Com C; Ecuador Art. 202-B Com C; Guatemala Art. 1835 CC; Mexico Arts. 2312, 2310 CC; Venezuela Art. 1 LRTS.

[44] Bolivia Art. 39 Com C; Brazil Art. 522 CC; Colombia Art. 953 Com C; Ecuador Art. 202-C Com C: establishing in addition some details on the content of the contract; El Salvador Art. 1038 Com C; Guatemala Art. 1835 CC; Mexico Art. 2312 CC; Paraguay Art. 781 CC; Peru Art. 1584 CC; Venezuela Art. 5 LRTS; Mexico: Vásquez del Mercado, *supra* note 6, at 202.

[45] Bolivia Art. 585 CC; Brazil Art. 524 CC; Ecuador Art. 202-A para. 2 CC; Colombia Art. 952 Com C; Guatemala Art. 1834 CC; Mexico Art. 2313 CC; Peru Art. 1583 CC; Portugal Art. 934 CC; Venezuela Art. 1 LRTS; Argentina: Compagnucci de Caso, *supra* note 36, at 339; Mexico: Vásquez del Mercado, *supra* note 6, at 202.

ownership,[46] and the special provisions on sales negating it.[47] The result is that under such type of sales the property of the goods passes to the buyer though the reserve is made. This position has been sustained by the doctrine,[48] and the jurisprudence;[49] concluding that the only effect such agreement has is to entitle the seller to claim the price or alternative the avoidance of the contract.

5.2. Right of Stoppage in Transit

While the general right to withhold performance, under specific circumstances, is recognised in the Ibero-American laws,[50] the right to stop the goods in transit has no express equivalent under the Ibero-American laws. Contrary, under CISG Article 71(2) the seller may stop the delivery of the goods even if the goods are already loaded and on their way in the carrier who transports them to the place of delivery. The seller's right to stop the goods in transit requires the existence of evident risk of breach by the buyer after the goods have been dispatch. Accordingly, its importance in practice is limited to cases in which the buyer's capacity to fulfil the contract diminishes after the seller has sent the goods. In this sense, the right to stop the goods in transit means to suspend performance after performance.[51] Evidently, such a right distinguishes from the *Exceptio non adimpleti contractus* or right to withhold performance as provided in CISG Article 71(1).

46 Chile Art. 680 CC; Ecuador Art. 715 CC; El Salvador Art. 661 CC.

47 Chile Arts. 1873, 1874 CC; Ecuador Arts. 1840, 1841 CC; El Salvador Arts. 1675, 1676 CC.

48 El Salvador: Miranda, *supra* note 9, at 297.

49 Chile Supreme Court, RDJ, Vol. 24, Sec. 1, at 550 *cited in* Chile: Díez Duarte, *supra* note 9, at 123, n. 324.

50 *See generally* Ch. 48.

51 A. von Ziegler, *The Right of Suspension and Stoppage in Transit (and Notification thereof)*, 25 The Journal of Law and Commerce 353, at 366 (2005).

CHAPTER 43

TAKING DELIVERY

The Ibero-American laws contemplate the buyer's obligation to take delivery of the goods. Some laws expressly dictate that the buyer is obliged to receive the goods in the time determined by the contract or the local usage, and absent a usage or agreement on this issue, the buyer shall take delivery immediately after the conclusion of the contract.[1] Likewise, the obligation is implicit in the provisions under which the definitive refusal or the non-appearance of the buyer to take delivery of the goods, automatically amounts to avoidance of the contract in the seller's benefit.[2]

The Ibero-American laws do not explain what the obligation to take delivery consists of. Only Bolivia's law makes a brief reference. Under the national term of commerce CIF the buyer is obliged to accept the documents presented, to take over the goods upon their arrival, to pay and to take charge of any logistic manoeuvre required, to pay all the unloading charges, including any taxes or expenses at the place of arrival.[3] However, this rule is binding upon agreement of the parties in relation to the referred national term and do not contemplate a default obligation to the buyer.

On the other hand, the obligation to perform all the acts which could reasonable be expected to allow the seller to make delivery can be subtracted from Ibero-American law principles of cooperation and good faith.[4] Under

---

1 Argentina Art. 1427 CC; Bolivia Art. 846 Com C; Colombia Art. 943 Com C; Paraguay Art. 764 CC; Peru Art. 1565 CC; Bolivia: V. Camargo Marín, Derecho Comercial Boliviano 406 (2007).

2 Chile Arts. 1827, 1489 CC & Art. 153 Com C; Colombia Arts. 1546, 1883 CC; Ecuador Arts. 1794, 1532 CC; El Salvador Arts. 1630, 1360 CC; Spain Art. 1.505 CC; Venezuela Art. 1.531 CC & Art. 141 Com C; Costa Rica: D. Baudrit Carrillo, Los Contratos Traslativos del Derecho Privado – Principios de Jurisprudencia 43 (2000); Spain Supreme Tribunal, 1 July 1991, *Id Cendoj:* 28079110011991101272.

3 Bolivia Art. 860 Com C.

4 Spain: A. Cabanillas Sánchez, *in* L. Díez Picazo y Ponce De León, La Compraventa

these principles, the parties to a sales contract are not only obliged to perform their main obligations but also to cooperate so that the other party can fulfil his own obligations.[5]

In both the CISG and the Ibero-American laws, the reception of the goods has important consequences concerning the passing of risk. The buyer bears the risks of the goods and their conservation expenses from the moment the goods are at his disposal and he refuses with no reasonable justification to take over the goods.[6]

Besides, under the CISG the non-performance of this buyer's contractual duty amounts to breach of contract and, thus, gives the seller a right to any of the remedies contemplated in articles 61-65, including the avoidance of the contract.[7] In this regard, the Ibero-American laws have also acknowledged that the seller may exercise any other remedies granted by the law for the ordinary breach of contract, such as specific performance or alternative the avoidance of the contract, both entitling to damages.[8]

Internacional de Mecaderias – Comentario sobre la Convención de Viena Art. 60, II, at 488 (1998).

5 *See* Ch. 32, 3.

6 *See* Ch. 44, 3.4.

7 Schwenzer/Mohs, Art. 61, para. 4, p 869.

8 *See* Ch. 49, 1.1, Ch. 50, Ch. 52 & Ch. 53, 2.2.

Part 10

Passing of Risk

CHAPTER 44

THE PASSING OF RISK

1. General Remarks on the Passing of Risk

1.1. Notion of Risk

The Ibero-American laws, the CISG and the INCOTERMS place emphasis on a type of risk normally called 'price risk'. The legal notion of this type of risk refers to accidental injury to the goods.[1] This injury can be caused by theft, seizure, deterioration or damage. In some cases, the goods may be lost completely while in other cases partial harm may allow their restoration.

The exact time of the passing of risk under a sales contract is of crucial importance because it determines the party who bears the loss of or damage to the goods. The question of when the risk passes from the seller to the buyer, will determine which party will be discharged from having to perform his obligations, and which party remains obliged to perform his obligations.[2] For example, if goods are lost or damaged after the risk has passed to the buyer, the seller may be released from having to supply equivalent goods,[3] while the

---

[1] Chile Supreme Court, RDJ, Vol. 24, Sec. 1, at 484 *cited in* Chile: R. Díez Duarte, La Compraventa en el Código Civil Chileno 206, n. 566 (1993): defining risk as an uncertain event that can harm or even destroy a thing.

[2] P.M. Roth, *The Passing of Risk*, 27 American Journal of Comparative Law 291, at 291 (1979).

[3] Though in specific cases, the seller still needs to compensate the buyer for non-delivery, even if the loss was due to unforeseeable events. For example, when the goods have not been yet determined, or identified with distinctive marks or signals which prevent confusion, or when the seller had been already late in the delivering the goods, *etc.*, *see* on this Argentina Art. 894 CC; Brazil Art. 238 CC; Chile Art. 1670 CC *contrario sensu* & Art. 143(1)(3) Com C; Colombia Art. 1729 CC *contrario sensu*; Costa Rica Art. 459(a)(c) Com C; Ecuador Art. 1713 CC *contrario sensu* & Art. 188(1)(3) Com C; El Salvador Art. 1540 CC *contrario sensu*; Paraguay Art. 632 CC; Spain Art. 334(1)(3) Com C.

buyer is nevertheless bound to pay the price of the lost goods. On the other hand, if the risk is on the seller's side the buyer may not pay the price, or if already paid, this must be reimbursed,[4] and the seller will bear the total loss or damage of the goods.

In an interesting case submitted before an ICC Arbitral Tribunal, the seller of turbo compressors fulfilled his principal obligation consisting in their delivery CIF Quebec.[5] The seller also fulfilled his accessory obligation to supervise the installation of the said turbo-compressors in a designated oil-platform. Days after their installation, the oil platform, on which the turbo compressors were installed, sank in Brazilian waters due to undetermined causes not attributable to the parties. The buyer refused payment of the remaining price arguing that as the period of tests and the 12 months warranty had not yet expired, the seller would be unjustifiably enriched if the buyer paid the remaining price. The Tribunal dismissed the buyer's arguments upholding that the risk of the price has already passed to him far before the installation of the compressors and that the argument put forward was based on the premise that the goods furnished already presented defects. However, the evidence showed that as far as the tests on the compressors were performed, the goods did not present any problem that would require the implementation of the agreed warranty.[6]

Finally, the loss of or damage to the goods must be accidental. In other words, it must be due to an unexpected unintentional event, for which the other party does not share responsibility. Such is an important condition since the loss of or damage to the goods caused by the other party's own omission, misconduct or due to an inherent vice of the goods, shall be borne by that party.[7]

1.2. Different Domestic Systems for Passing of Risk

The basic principle in all the Ibero-American systems, as in the CISG is that the moment when the risk passes from the seller to the buyer, depends on the agreement of the parties.[8] Only absent an agreement the applicable law supplies the default rules regarding the allocation of the risk.[9]

---

[4] *See* expressly Spain Art. 335 Com C; Uruguay Art. 542 Com C: in Uruguay the price shall be reimbursed plus interests if the goods were lost because of seller's fault, misconduct or delay, *see* Uruguay Art. 543 Com C.

[5] ICC Final Award Case No. 13458 *Lex Contractus* Brazilian Law and INCOTERMS 2000.

[6] *Id.*

[7] *See for example* Art. 66 CISG; Argentina Arts. 1385, 892 CC; Brazil Arts. 234, 444 CC; Bolivia Art. 633 CC & Art. 851 Com C; Chile Art. 142 Com C; Ecuador Art. 187 Com C; Mexico Art. 377 Com C; Peru Arts. 1516-1518, 1567 CC; Spain Art. 1.182 CC & Art. 333 Com C; Uruguay Arts. 1682, 1438(I) CC.

[8] *See infra* 2.

[9] *See infra* 3.

The default rules for the allocation of risk vary from system to system. The rule changes depending on the national legal system, but also depending on the type of contract and goods. Certainly, the default rules may change in the same legal system depending on whether the goods are determined or undetermined at the time of the conclusion of the contract; on whether the contract is considered as a B2B or a C2C contract; or on whether the contract involves the carriage of the goods from one place to another.[10]

2. Contractual Allocation of Risk

2.1. General Remarks on the Agreed Allocation of Risk

Although it has not been expressly declared in either the CISG[11] or in most of the Ibero-American laws,[12] the parties can decide how to allocate the risk of the goods between them. This possibility is based on the principle of 'freedom of contract' since this is not an issue which opposes the national public order. Consequently, the primary rule is that the risk of loss of or damage to the goods passes from the seller to the buyer at the moment agreed by the parties.[13]

In addition, this freedom is impliedly recognised in the Ibero-American laws in which the default rule declares that the risk passes from the seller to the buyer at the time of delivery of the goods.[14] In these countries, as in the rest of the Ibero-American laws, the primary rule is that the time and place of delivery of the goods can be mutually agreed to by the parties.[15] Consequently, the parties are not only directly allowed to decide on the moment and place of delivery, but also indirectly have the choice to establish the point in time for the passing of the risk of the goods. Other types of provisions also impliedly support such a freedom. For example, an often found provision, permits the parties to postpone the passing of risk until the goods are examined by the buyer or the conformity of the goods is fulfilled.[16]

---

10 *See infra* 3.

11 The CISG is silent on the role of the parties' intention in the passing of risk, nevertheless, the freedom to allocate the risk emerges from the integral interpretation of the convention; *see for example* Art. 6 CISG.

12 With the following exceptions of provisions which expressly recognise such freedom Chile Art. 142 Com C; Ecuador Art. 187 Com C; Guatemala Art. 1813 CC; Uruguay Art. 541 Com C; also such freedom is expressly recognised in Guatemala Arts. 697-704 Com C; Bolivia Arts. 852– 862 Com C and Costa Rica Arts. 472-475 Com C as the last three countries' laws establish different terms of commerce that the parties can freely choose to allocate the risk of the goods.

13 Spain Supreme Tribunal, 3 October 1997, *Id Cendoj:* 28079110001997100230.

14 *See infra* 3.

15 *See* Ch. 35, 2.1 & 3.1.

16 *See for example* Costa Rica Art. 459(b) Com C; Spain Art. 334(2)(3) Com C.

Finally, the parties may consciously or unconsciously allocate the risk of the goods among themselves by inserting within their contract a selected national or international term of commerce.[17] Among the Ibero-American countries, Bolivia, Costa Rica, El Salvador and Guatemala have integrated into their laws the commercial terms known under the letters of FOB, CIF, C y F and FAS.[18] Also Ibero-American parties often adopt the more developed International Commercial Terms, or INCOTERMS.[19] These INCOTERMS distinguish between four different categories of terms depending on the place of the passing of risk, which is directly connected to the place in which the goods are placed at the buyer's disposal.

2.2. INCOTERMS and National TERMS

The general rule in all thirteen INCOTERMS is that the risk of loss of or damage to the goods passes from the seller to the buyer when the seller has fulfilled his obligation to deliver the goods. The same approach is followed by the national terms of commerce.[20] Additionally, all the INCOTERMS establish that the passing of risk may occur even before delivery, if the buyer does not take delivery as agreed, or fails to inform the seller about the time or place of delivery.

In this last point, the INCOTERMS are in concordance with the CISG and the Ibero-American laws. According to CISG article 69 (1) in cases not within articles 67[21] and 68,[22] the risk passes to the buyer when he takes over the goods, or if he fails to do so in time, when the goods are placed at his disposal and he commits breach of contract by failing to take delivery. Similarly, a group of Ibero-American laws expressly recognise that if the buyer refuses with no reasonable justification to take over the goods, or if he incurs delay, he shall bear the risks of the goods and their conservation expenses.[23]

17 Spain Supreme Tribunal, 3 October 1997, *Id Cendoj:* 28079110001997100230.

18 Bolivia Art. 852 *et seq.* Com C; Costa Rica Art. 473 *et seq.* Com C; El Salvador Art. 1030 *et seq.* Com C; Guatemala Art. 697 *et seq.* Com C.

19 ICC introduced the first version of Incoterms in 1936.

20 Bolivia Arts. 852 (EX), 853 (FOB), 854 (FAS), 855, 856 (C y F & CIF with the delivery of documents) Com C; Costa Rica Arts. 473, 474 (CIF & C y F), 475 (FOB) Com C; El Salvador Arts. 1033 (CIF), 1034 (C y F), 1035 (FOB) Com C; Guatemala Arts. 697 (FOB); 698 (FAS), 702 (CIF), 704 (C y F) Com C.

21 Art. 67 CISG relates to cases involving the carriage of the goods and the seller is not bound to hand them over at a particular place, the risk passes to the buyer when the goods are handed over to the first carrier for transmission. But if the seller is bound to hand the goods over to a carrier at a particular place, the risk does not pass to the buyer until the goods are handed over to the carrier at that place.

22 Art. 68 CISG relates to goods sold in transit where the risk passes to the buyer from the time of the conclusion of the contract.

23 *See* Ch. 43 & Ch. 44, 3.4.

However, the premature passing of risk, due to the buyer's failure to take delivery on time or to provide the necessary information for the seller to perform his obligation, only occurs if the goods have been duly appropriated to the contract or identified as intended for the buyer. This requirement is particularly important under EXW INCOTERM. Under this term the goods are delivered to the buyer when the seller places them at the buyer's disposal generally at the seller's premises.[24] However, it may happen that despite the goods are available for the buyer at the seller's premises thus, they are not duly appropriated to the contract.

In all other INCOTERMS the goods would normally be identified as intended for the buyer when measures have been taken for their dispatch or delivery at destination. However, there may be cases where the goods have been sent in bulk by the seller without identification of the quantity or weight for each buyer. Yet again, in these cases the passing of risk does not occur until the goods have been properly identified.

This requirement is in consonance with CISG Articles 67(2) and 69(3). In the two different situations covered by these articles, the risk does not pass to the buyer until the goods are clearly identified to the contract. Also, the Ibero-American laws have a similar requirement regarding the passing of risk of unascertained goods. The general principle about the unascertained goods is that the risk does not pass to the buyer until they are ascertained or identified, namely- once they have been measured, weighted or counted or identified to the contract.[25]

As has been previously mentioned,[26] the first INCOTERMS category, known with the letter 'E', is the term whereby the seller only makes the goods available to the buyer at the seller's own premises: *i.e. Ex works*; the second group whereby the seller is called upon to deliver the goods to a carrier appointed by the buyer is known with the letter 'F': *i.e. FCA, FAS*, and *FOB*; the third group or 'C' terms are those where the seller has to contract for the carriage but without assuming the risk of loss of or damage to the goods or additional cost due to events occurring after shipment or dispatch: *i.e. CFR, CIF, CPT* and *CIP*; and finally, the 'D' terms whereby the seller has to bear all cost and risk needed to bring the goods to the place of destination: *i.e. DAF, DES, DEQ, DDU* and *DDP*.

As a result the exact place and time for the passing of risk is as follows:

The Ex works INCOTERM into a contract causes that the seller must bear all risks of loss of or damage to the goods until he places the goods at the disposal of the buyer at the seller's premises or another named place *e.g.* works, factory, warehouse, *etc.*[27] If no specific point has been agreed within

24 Same approach under Bolivia Art. 852 (EX) Com C.

25 *See* 3.1.

26 *See* Ch. 35.

27 ICC, Incoterms 2000: ICC official rules for the interpretation of trade terms, at 155.

the named place, and there are several points available, the seller may choose the place he considers convenient.[28] Bolivia's national term of commerce called 'origin's point' or EX seems to extend the time of the passing of risk to the time the buyer takes possession of the goods at the place and at the time of delivery agreed.[29] However, under Bolivia's term of commerce it should be understood that if the buyer fails to take possession of the goods at the place and time agreed the risk of the goods shall be understood to have prematurely passed since the time the goods were at the buyer's disposal.

If the parties choose a Free Carrier delivery (FCA) INCOTERM, the seller bears all risk of loss of or damage to the goods until the seller delivers the goods to the carrier or another person nominated by the buyer at the named place.[30] If the Free alongside ship (FAS) INCOTERM has been chosen by the parties, the seller must bear all risk of loss of or damage to the goods until the seller places the goods alongside the vessel nominated by the buyer at the loading place named by the buyer at the named port of shipment.[31] The same point of passing of risk is established by the national term of commerce FAS which does not limit itself to vessels but includes any sort of transport.[32]

If the parties have chosen either the Free on board (FOB), the Cost and freight (CFR) or the Cost, insurance and freight (CIF) terms, the seller must bear all risk of loss of damage to the goods until the goods have been delivered at the named port of shipment and on board the vessel nominated by the buyer, as they have passed the ship's rail at the port of shipment.[33] A similar solution is provided by the FOB, C y F and CIF national terms of commerce according to which the risk passes to the buyer from the time the goods are placed on board of the means of transport concerned.[34] Except for Bolivia's national terms CIF and C y F, since the law expressly provides that under such terms the passing of risk passes from the time of the delivery of the documents representing the goods and their transport (and the insurance policy in the case of CIF).[35]

---

28 *Id.*, at 156.

29 Bolivia Art. 852 Com C.

30 ICC, *supra* note 27, at 164.

31 ICC, *supra* note 27, at 170.

32 Bolivia Art. 854 (FAS) Com C.

33 ICC, *supra* note 27, at 178, 186, 196; Spain Supreme Tribunal, 3 October 1997, *Id Cendoj:* 28079110001997100230: applying a CIF term the Supreme Tribunal upheld that the seller was release from bearing the risk when he handed over the goods to the first carrier contracted by the buyer; ICC Final Award Case No. 13458 *Lex Contractus* Brazilian Law and INCOTERMS 2000: upholding that the risk has already passed from the seller to the buyer at CIF Quebec and decided the buyer should pay the price of the goods that were lost after that point.

34 Bolivia Arts. 853 (FOB) Com C; Costa Rica Arts. 473, 474 (CIF & C y F), 475 (FOB) Com C; El Salvador Arts. 1035 (FOB), 1033 (CIF), 1034 (C y F) Com C; Guatemala Arts. 697 (FOB), 702 (CIF), 704 (C y F) Com C.

35 Bolivia Arts. 855, 856 (C y F & CIF with the delivery of documents) Com C.

In case the parties have included a Carriage paid to (CPT) INCOTERM or a Carrier and Insurance paid to (CIP) INCOTERM, the passing of risk takes place when the seller has delivered the goods to the carrier contracted or if there are subsequent carriers to the first carrier for transport to the agreed point at the named place.[36]

Finally, when the parties have agreed to insert into their contract one of the 'Delivery' terms the risk of loss of or damage to the goods shall pass from the seller to the buyer: (DAF) on the arriving means of transport not unloaded at the named place of delivery at the frontier; (DES) on board of the vessel at the unloading point referred to, in the named port of destination; (DEQ) on the named quay at the named port of destination; (DDU & DDP) or at that of any other person named by the buyer, on any arriving means of transport not unloaded at the named place of destination.[37]

3. Default Allocation of Risk

3.1. Default Rules

In Ibero-America, the default rules for the allocation of risk vary from one system to another. The rule changes depending on the national legal system, but also depending on the type of sale and goods. Certainly, the default rules may change in a same legal system depending on whether the goods are sufficiently ascertained and identified at the time of the conclusion of the contract;[38] on whether the contract is considered as a C2C or B2B sale;[39] or on whether the contract involves the carriage of the goods from one place to another.[40]

The general principle is that the risk does not pass to the buyer until the goods have been measured, weighted, counted or at least identified in some way to the contract.[41] With respect to ascertained goods which have been identified to the contract, some statutory laws establish that the risk passes

---

36 ICC, *supra* note 27, at 202, 210.

37 ICC, *supra* note 27.

38 For more about the concept of ascertained and ascertainable goods *see* Ch. 6, 1.2.2.2.

39 For general reference as to B2B contracts and C2C contracts distinction *see* Ch. 5, 1.

40 *See infra* 3.2.

41 Brazil Art. 492 (1) CC; Chile Art. 1821 (2) CC & Art. 143 (1) Com C; Colombia Art. 1877 (2) CC; Costa Rica Art. 459 (c) Com C; Ecuador Art. 1788 para. 2 CC & Art. 188 (1) Com C; El Salvador Art. 1624 CC; Paraguay Art. 761 part 2 CC; Peru Art. 1569 CC; Portugal Art. 472 Com C; Spain Art. 1.452 CC & Art. 334 (1) Com C; Uruguay Art. 1683 part 2 CC; Venezuela Art. 1.475 CC; Mexico: O. Vásquez del Mercado, Contratos Mercantiles 203 (2008).

from the seller to the buyer at the time of entering into the contract.[42] This was indeed the approach followed by Roman Law and *Las Siete Partidas*.[43]

The last rule is not very practical for international sales where the goods are still in the seller's possession at the contract conclusion. The rule is not appropriate because buyers are usually tempted to claim that sellers did not take due care of the goods, which creates serious controversies. This has caused that, under many jurisdictions which establish such default rule for C2C sales, a different approach is taken for B2B sales or sales requiring the transportation of the goods to a place different to that of contract conclusion.[44]

A second default rule dictates that the risk passes from the seller to the buyer at the time of the *tradittio* of the goods.[45] It must be noticed that the Civil Codes of Brazil and El Salvador distinguish between delivery and *tradittio* of the goods. *Tradittio* involves the transfer of effective ownership on the goods, while delivery only means to hand over the material goods. One can happen without the other.[46]

Although the Civil Codes of Chile, Colombia, Ecuador and El Salvador follow normally the same pattern,[47] El Salvador departs from the rest regarding the time for the passing of risk of the goods. Certainly, while in Chile, Colombia and Ecuador C2C sales, the risk of loss of or damage to the goods passes to the buyer at the time of contract conclusion, in El Salvador, the risk of individualised-determined goods passes from the seller to the buyer until the *tradittio* of the goods takes place.[48]

A third approach establishes that the risk passes from the seller to the buyer at the time of delivery of the goods.[49] This means that the party having

---

[42] A common provision dictates that any loss of or damage to or improvement in the goods shall be borne by the buyer, despite the fact that the goods had not yet been delivered: Bolivia Art. 600 CC (implied rule); Chile Art. 1820 CC & Arts. 142, 143 (1) Com C; Colombia Art. 1876 CC; Ecuador Art. 1787 CC & Arts. 187, 188 Com C; Mexico Art. 2014 CC; Paraguay Art. 761 CC; Uruguay Arts. 1682, 1438 (I) CC; Spain Arts. 1.182, 1.452 CC; Venezuela Art. 1.161 CC.

[43] *See* Las Siete Partidas del Rey Alfonso El Sabio, Cotejadas con varios Códices Antiguos por la Real Academia de la Historia, Tomo III, Partida Cuarta, Quinta, Sexta y Séptima (1807), Partida V, Title V, Law XXIII *in* Ch. 1, 2.2; *see also* Chile: Díez Duarte, *supra* note 1, at 210.

[44] *See infra* 3.2, other approaches as to the default rule to the passing of risk.

[45] *See* Brazil Arts. 237, 492 CC; El Salvador Art. 1624 CC; *see also* Brazil: O. Gomes, Contratos 281 (2008); El Salvador: A.O. Miranda, De la Compraventa 177-180 (1996).

[46] In this regard *see* Colombia: A. Tamayo Lombana, El Contrato de Compraventa su Régimen Civil y Comercial 121-123 (2004); El Salvador: Miranda, *supra* note 45, at 186, 187.

[47] Chile's Civil Code had an influence in Colombia, Ecuador, and El Salvador; *see* Ch. 1, 3.1.

[48] Since the enactment of the reforms made in 1902, *see* El Salvador: Miranda, *supra* note 45, at 22.

[49] Argentina Arts. 890, 892, 1430 CC (systematic interpretation); Bolivia Art. 837 Com C; Colombia Art. 929 Com C; Costa Rica Art. 461 Com C; Guatemala Art. 1813 CC; Mexico Arts. 377, 378 Com C; Peru Art. 1567 CC; Portugal Art. 796 CC; Spain Art. 333 Com C; Uruguay Art. 541 Com C. In Peru, the risk may pass to the buyer at the time of dispatch if the buyer

real or virtual control over the goods will be the one bearing the risk.[50] This approach is more reasonable since the party who possesses the goods is in a better position to keep the goods in conformity to the contract. This approach was developed exclusively for B2B contracts under some jurisdictions.[51]

For contracts subject to title retention the same default rule applies in many countries. The buyer bears the risk of the goods from the time he is in possession of the goods,[52] although the ownership may only be transferred until payment of the price.[53] However, the approach is not uniform in all Ibero-American countries. An opposite provision is found in some civil codes. If the goods are completely lost while the seller retains the ownership he shall bear any loss even though the goods were already at the buyer's possession; however, any improvement or minor deterioration of the goods during that time will belong to the buyer.[54]

3.2. Handing Over to Carriers

CISG article 67 (1) covers situations in which the contract of sale involves the carriage of the goods and the seller is not bound, the same as when he is bound, to hand them over at a particular place. In the first case, the risk shall pass to the buyer when the goods are handed over to the first carrier for transmission to him. In the second case, the risk does not pass to the buyer until the goods are handed over to the carrier at that particular place.

In addition, CISG article 67 (2) requires that the goods are clearly identified to the contract, so that the passing of risk takes place. This CISG requirement is in agreement with the INCOTERMS and the Ibero-American laws.[55] The general rule in all thirteen INCOTERMS is that the risk of the goods passes

---

requests the delivery of the goods at a different place from the one originally agreed, *see* Peru Art. 1570 CC.

[50] *See* Bolivia: V. Camargo Marín, Derecho Comercial Boliviano 405 (2007); Costa Rica Art. 461 Com C; Mexico Art. 377 Com C; Paraguay Art. 788 CC; all these provisions expressly contemplate the three types of delivery *i.e.* real, legal and virtual in the passing of risk; Mexico: Vásquez del Mercado, *supra* note 41, at 203; For the three types of delivery *see also* Ch. 35, 1.

[51] Colombia, Costa Rica, Mexico and Uruguay follow the rule according to which risk passes at the time of contract conclusion for C2C contracts and at the time of delivery for B2B contracts.

[52] Argentina: R. Compagnucci de Caso, Contrato de Compraventa 339 (2007); Brazil Art. 524 CC; Colombia Art. 952 Com C; Ecuador Art. 202-A Com C; Mexico Art. 2024 CC; Paraguay Art. 780 CC; Peru Art. 1583 CC; Venezuela Art. 1 LRTS. Although Colombia and Ecuador take a different for C2C sales, *see* Colombia Art. 1876 part 2 CC; Ecuador Art. 1787 part 2 CC.

[53] Mexico: Vásquez del Mercado, *supra* note 41, at 203.

[54] Chile Art. 1820 part 2 CC; Colombia Art. 1876 part 2 CC; Ecuador Art. 1787 part 2 CC; Chile: Díez Duarte, *supra* note 1, at 209. Although Colombia and Ecuador take a different approach for B2B sales, *see* Colombia Art. 952 Com C; Ecuador Art. 202-A Com C.

[55] *See supra* 3.1.

from the seller to the buyer at the time of delivery, provided that the goods have been duly identified to the contract.[56]

Similarly, under the Brazilian law if the buyer requests the delivery of the goods to a place other than the place where the goods were at the conclusion of the contract, the risk may pass to the buyer from the time the seller hands over the goods to the first carrier.[57] The Paraguayan law provides that if the goods have to be delivered to a place other than the place of contract conclusion the risk passes to the buyer when the seller gets released from the goods.[58] The expression 'to get released' may be understood as handing over the goods to the carrier who shall transport them to that other place.

Likewise, under the Portuguese law, the risk may pass to the buyer from the time the seller hands over the goods to the first carrier if the buyer requests the delivery of the goods to a place other than the place of contract performance.[59] The rule may be understood as, an exception for cases involving additional transportation of the goods after the place of delivery has been agreed. In such a case, the risk shall pass to the buyer when the seller hands over the goods to the first carrier.

Finally, under some Ibero-American laws if the sale involves the carriage of the goods and the seller hands over their insurance policy to the buyer or carrier, the risk passes to the buyer when the seller hands over the goods to the carrier.[60]

3.3. Goods Sold in Transit

The Ibero-American laws does not contain a special rule concerning the passing of risk for goods sold in transit. CISG article 68 does. The general rule of the risk on the goods sold in transit is that the risk passes to the buyer from the time of the conclusion of the contract.

3.4. Taking Over the Goods

Under the Ibero-American laws, the CISG and the INCOTERMS, if the buyer does not take delivery as agreed or fails to inform the seller about the time or place of delivery, the risk would prematurely pass to the buyer when the goods are placed at his disposal.[61] In the Ibero-American laws, the rule is drawn from the provisions stating that the party having real or virtual control

[56] *See supra* 2.
[57] *See* Brazil Art. 494 CC.
[58] Paraguay Art. 761 CC.
[59] Portugal Art. 797 CC.
[60] Costa Rica Art. 476 Com C; Bolivia Art. 851 Com C; Guatemala Art. 696 Com C.
[61] *See* Art. 69(1) CISG and *supra* 2.

over the goods will be the one bearing the risk.[62] Additionally, a group of Ibero-American laws expressly recognise that if the buyer refuses with no reasonable justification to take over the goods, or if he incurs delay, he shall bear the risk of the goods eventually destroyed or deteriorated as well as their conservation expenses.[63]

---

62 *See* Costa Rica Art. 461 Com C; Mexico Art. 377 Com C; Paraguay Art. 788 CC; all these provisions expressly contemplate the three types of delivery *i.e.* real, legal and virtual in the passing of risk.

63 Argentina Art. 1430 CC; Bolivia Art. 328 CC; Brazil Art. 492 (2) CC; Colombia Art. 929 Com C; Guatemala Art. 1830 CC; Peru Art. 1568 CC; Portugal Art. 807 CC; Venezuela Art. 1.265 CC; Bolivia: G. Castellanos Trigo & S. Auad La Fuente, Derecho de las Obligaciones en el Código Civil Boliviano 116-117 (2008).

Part 11

Transfer of Title

CHAPTER 45

GENERAL REMARKS ON TRANSFER OF TITLE

1. Applicable Law

The CISG does not provide specific rules regarding the transfer of title as it does for the passing of risk.[1] The question as to the transfer of title is therefore left to domestic law and, when it is necessary to determine which domestic law applies, one may refer to the rules of private international law.[2]

2. Contractual Determination of Title of Property

The basic rule in the Ibero-American laws is that the passing of property passes from the seller to the buyer at the time specified or intended in the contract of sale. In absence of agreement on this issue, the appropriate default provisions will determine at what moment the parties intended the property of the goods to pass from the seller to the buyer. This was indeed the position since the Roman law.[3]

The freedom of the parties to determine the specific moment for the transfer of title can be subtracted from the freedom to subject the sales contract to a *pactum reservati dominii.*[4] Under this type of sales, the parties can agree to

[1] Art. 4 CISG states that the CISG governs only the formation of the contract of sale and the rights and obligations of the seller and the buyer arising from such a contract, but it is not concerned with the effect which the contract may have on the property in the goods sold

[2] Art. 7(2) CISG establishes that questions do not governed by the CISG are to be settled in conformity with the law applicable by virtue of the rules of private international law.

[3] P.D.V. Marsh, Comparative Contract Law: England, France, Germany 239 (1994).

[4] Bolivia Art. 585 CC; Brazil Art. 521 CC; El Salvador Arts. 661, 1676 CC & Art. 1038 Com C; Colombia Art. 750 CC & Art. 952 Com C; Chile Arts. 680, 1874 CC; Ecuador Arts. 715, 1841 CC; Guatemala Art. 1834 CC; Mexico Art. 2312 CC; Paraguay Art. 780 CC; Peru Art. 1583 CC; Portugal Art. 934 CC; Venezuela Art. 1 LRTS.

postpone the transfer of title after the conclusion of the contract or the delivery of the goods.[5] In other words, the seller retains the title of ownership until the buyer completely meets the condition imposed, *e.g.* that he pays the price of the goods, that a period of time elapses or that other fact occurs.[6]

3. Different Default Systems

3.1. Title Passes upon the Conclusion of the Contract

3.1.1. Specific Goods

Under French law, the mere conclusion of the contract transfers the property of the goods without need of a separate delivery.[7] The French law had in this instance abandoned the Roman rules. Article 1583 of the French Civil Code states that the sale is perfect between the parties and the property is acquired in law by the buyer in respect to the seller from the moment when there is an agreement on the thing and the price, even if the thing has not yet been delivered nor the price paid.[8]

Following the French tradition, the passing of title of specific goods under many of the Ibero-American laws takes place, unless otherwise agreed, at the time the parties fully agreed on the essential elements of the sale.[9] The essential elements of the sales are normally the determined goods and the price, irrespective of whether the goods have been delivered or their price paid. The

---

[5] Argentina: R. Compagnucci de Caso, Contrato de Compraventa 332 (2007); Colombia: E.G. Escobar Velez, La compraventa civil y comercial: los contratos de promesa de compraventa y la permuta 288 (1991).

[6] For further details regarding this modality of sale, the requirements and effects *see* Ch. 42, 5.1.

[7] Marsh, *supra* note 3, at 238; Peru: M. Castillo Freyre, Comentarios al contrato de compraventa: análisis detallado de los artículos 1529 a 1601 del Código Civil 124, 125 (2002).

[8] About the foundations of the Roman-Germanic law v. the French law on the passing of ownership *see* R. Zimmermann, The Law of Obligations – Roman Foundations of the Civilian Tradition 271 (1990); Venezuela: J.L. Aguilar Gorrondona, Contratos y Garantias: Derecho Civil IV, 217 (2008).

[9] Bolivia Art. 584 CC; Guatemala Arts. 1791, 1790 CC; Mexico Art. 2014 CC & Art. 374 Com C; Paraguay Arts. 737, 2061, 2062 CC; Peru Arts. 1529, 947 CC; Portugal Arts. 879, 408 (1) CC; Venezuela Arts. 1 474, 1.161 CC; *see also* supporting this approach for each respective country Bolivia: W. Kaune Arteaga, Curso de Derecho Civil, Contratos, Vol. 2, 125 (1996); Costa Rica: D. Baudrit Carrillo, Los Contratos Traslativos del Derecho Privado – Principios de Jurisprudencia 48 (2000); Mexico: S. León Tovar, Los Contratos Mercantiles 152, 198 (2004); Mexico: O. Vásquez del Mercado, Contratos Mercantiles 200 (2008); Peru: Castillo Freyre, *supra* note 7, at 124-126; Portugal: L. De Lima Pinheiro, Dereito Comercial Internacional 285 (2005); Venezuela: Aguilar Gorrondona, *supra* note 8, at 217; ICC Final Award Case No. 11570 *Lex Contractus* Portuguese Law: confirming the rule.

rule was confirmed by the Costa Rican Supreme Court which sustained that even if the buyer had failed to pay one of the installments under the contract, the seller could not sell the goods to a third party, as the buyer was already the owner from the meeting of the minds on the thing and the price.[10]

However, there are some exceptions to this general default rule. These shall be reviewed subsequently.

3.1.2. Unascertained Goods

The Ibero-American laws have established a different moment for the passing of title regarding undetermined goods. Certainly, when the goods subject to the sales contract are of a type but have not yet been determined, the transfer of title does not take place until the goods have been determined by being appropriated in some apparent way to the contract.[11] Similarly, in cases where the goods are generally not sold in a lump but by weight, number or measure, title of property remains with the seller until they have been weighed, counted, or measured.[12]

In this regard, the Bolivian Civil Code establishes that when the goods are only determined by their type, the ownership is not transferred until they have been individualised as agreed by the parties.[13] The Mexican and the Portuguese Civil Codes establishes the same rule, but in addition requires that the buyer knows about the determination of the goods so that the transfer of property effectively takes place at that moment.[14]

However, an exception to the exception is found in some Ibero-American codes. If the goods are sold in a lump and the goods themselves are determined at the time of the sale but determining their price requires subsequent weighing, counting or measuring, the title of property passes as originally: when the parties' intent was exchanged.[15] For example, the parties agree on the sale of all the urea kept in Buenos Aires Port at $100 each tonne. In such case, though

---

[10] Costa Rica Supreme Court, Judgment 00212-98, *Segunda Sala Civil*, 19 August 1998: upholding that if the buyer fails to pay one of the installments, the seller cannot sell the goods to a third party, as the buyer was already the owner since the meeting of the minds on the thing and the price, neither can the seller retained the installment already paid, unless there is express agreement to do so by means of penalty clause or arrears, what proceeds is the specific performance or the avoidance of the contract.

[11] Bolivia Art. 586(1) CC; Guatemala Art. 1538 CC; Mexico Art. 2015 CC; Paraguay Art. 746 CC (deduced from integral interpretation of the code); Peru Art. 1532 CC (deduced from integral interpretation of the code); Portugal Art. 408(2) CC; *see also* Mexico: León Tovar, *supra* note 9, at 198; Mexico: Vásquez del Mercado, *supra* note 9, at 200.

[12] Venezuela Art. 1.475 CC.

[13] Bolivia Art. 586 (1) CC.

[14] Mexico Art. 2015 CC; Portugal Art. 408 (2) CC.

[15] Bolivia Art. 586 (2) CC; Paraguay Art. 746 CC (deduced from integral interpretation of the code); Venezuela Art. 1.476 CC.

it is necessary to determine how many tonnes are in the Port of Buenos Aires and to multiple them for the individual price per tonne, the transfer of property occurred since the conclusion of the contract.

Under Venezuela's Code of Commerce, the transfer of property of goods sold while in transit is not effective until the designated carrier reach the place of delivery. This means that the property of the goods does not pass from the seller to the buyer but upon that moment.[16]

Regarding future goods the title of property only passes to the buyer when such goods are manufactured, grown or otherwise come into existence and the buyer can take effective delivery of them, and when they have been ascertained.[17] Finally, in conditional sales, under most laws title passes when the condition is fulfilled.[18]

3.2. Title Passes by the Handing over of the Goods

3.2.1. To the Buyer

The Roman law rule regarding the transfer of property required a real physical transfer of the goods together with a will or intention to transfer ownership.[19] Also in German law the contract of sale alone does not cause the transfer of property. Under the principle of abstraction the property may be validly transferred even if the contract of sale is invalid.[20] The title is transferred under BGB article 929 (1) by a valid agreement that the property should be transferred,[21] together with the actual delivery of the goods. *Ordenanzas de Bilbao* followed the Roman thesis on the transfer of property and hence such approach made an impact on many of the Ibero-American laws.[22]

A Romanic-Germanic combined approach has been retained in some Ibero-American laws under which there must be both an agreement between the parties to transfer the property plus delivery of possession of the goods so that the property effectively passes to the buyer. Certainly, the general rule in many laws is that the ownership of the goods passes from the seller to

---

[16] Venezuela Art. 136 Com C. A similar rule is provided in Guatemala Art. 1802 CC, but contrary, the passing of property is not suspended until the goods arrival. Instead, the non-arrival in time and good manner may cause the avoidance of the contract.

[17] Bolivia Art. 594 CC; Guatemala Art. 1538 CC; Mexico Art. 2015 CC; Peru Art. 1534 CC; Portugal Art. 408 (2) CC.

[18] *See* Ch. 42, 5.1.

[19] Marsh, *supra* note 3, at 238; Chile: R. Díez Duarte, La Compraventa en el Código Civil Chileno 189 (1993).

[20] Marsh, *supra* note 3, at 241.

[21] German term *Einigung*.

[22] *See* Ch. Eleven Num XII Ordenanzas de la Ilustre Universidad y Casa de Contratación de la Villa de Bilbao, por el Rey Don Felipe Quinto (1737) in Ch. 1, 2.2.

the buyer with the *tradittio* of the goods.[23] *Tradittio* involves the transfer of effective ownership on the goods, while delivery only means to hand over the material goods.[24] One can happen without the other.[25] Thus, the contract of sale does not transfer the property of the goods by its mere conclusion.[26] In order to transfer the ownership of the goods the *tradittio* is needed.[27]

3.2.2. To Other Persons

Property title may also pass when the goods or the document representing them are handed over to third parties or persons related to the buyer. In some Ibero-American Codes of Commerce it has been expressly dictated that the dispatch or the reception of the goods by agents, managers or employees shall be considered executed by the principal.[28] Other laws establish that where no time or person was selected by the buyer to take delivery, the seller fulfils his

---

23 Argentina Arts. 1323, 577 CC; Though in Argentina, there is still doctrinal discussion as to whether the transfer of title is consensual or the *tradittio* is needed: on this Argentina: Compagnucci de Caso, *supra* note 5, at 37-41; *see also* Argentina National Civil Chamber, *Sala A*, *Monte Grande S.A. v. Mercado José M.*, 20 August 1985: "(…) The sales contract is not concluded by *tradittio*, if that was the case, the delivery of the goods would be necessary for the agreement to be concluded. This has not been sustained by scholars as it contradicts what articles 1140 C.C. (*et. al.*) state, which reflect the roman tradition consolidated in classical law, this is different from the case of the title that is acquired until the delivery of the goods (arts 577 and 2601 CC). Hence, what should be considered as an act of transfer of real property is the *tradittio*, as it is such which extinguishes title for the *tradens* and gives birth to title for the *accipiens*, but delivery relates to the way of acquiring and not to the title"; Brazil Art. 237 CC; Chile Arts. 1793, 1824, 1548, 675 CC interpretation supported by El Salvador: A.O. Miranda, De la Compraventa 22 (1996); Colombia Arts. 1849, 1880, 1605, 740 CC interpretation supported by Colombia: A. Tamayo Lombana, El Contrato de Compraventa su Régimen Civil y Comercial 123 (2004); Ecuador Arts. 1759, 1791, 1591, 710 CC interpretation supported by Miranda, *id.*, at 22; El Salvador Arts. 1597, 1627, 1419, 656 CC interpretation supported by Miranda, *id.*, at 14-16, 18-19; Spain Art. 906 CC, interpretation supported by Spain: M. Medina de Lemus, Derecho Civil: Obligaciones y Contratos II, Contratos en Particular, Vol. 2, 31 (2004) and Spain Supreme Tribunal, 14 May 2009, *Id Cendoj:* 28079110012009100320.

24 In this regard *see* Colombia: Tamayo Lombana, *supra* note 23, at 121-123; El Salvador: Miranda, *supra* note 23, at 186, 187.

25 *See for example* Colombia Art. 923 (3) para. 2 Com C.

26 Chile Supreme Court, RDJ, Vol. 28, Sec. 1, at 205 *cited in* Chile: Díez Duarte, *supra* note 19, at 198, n. 531: noting that the sale of goods is the title and the *tradittio* or delivery is the means to acquire the property. So that the contract of sale can exist without the *tradittio*; El Salvador Sentence in the third instance RJ 1-6, January to July 1936, at 153-160 *cited in* El Salvador: Miranda, *supra* note 23, at 388: noting that the *tradittio* of the goods shall be performed by one of the means established in Art. 665 CC, as the mere express agreement of the parties is not enough to constitute a real physical transfer of the goods possession.

27 El Salvador: Miranda, *supra* note 23, at 12; Spain: Medina de Lemus, *supra* note 23, at 31.

28 Argentina Art. 153 Com C; Bolivia Art. 94 Com C; Mexico Art. 324 Com C; Paraguay Art. 69 LM; Spain Art. 295 Com C.

obligation to deliver if he does at the buyer's domicile.[29] Also the rule can be deduced from other provisions of the Ibero-American laws, dictating that "in the performance or fault of the debtor it is included, the performance and the fault of those for who are under his responsibility."[30]

Accordingly, if certain acts performed by persons engaged or under the supervision of the buyer may make him liable, the same principle may be extended to the passing of title through the delivery of the goods or documents to other persons engaged or under the supervision of the buyer.

3.3. Documents of Title

The passing of title through the transfer of documents has been succinctly presented in the Ibero-American laws. This may be explained by the fact that in many Ibero-American laws the passing of title operates concurrently to the meeting of the minds on the goods and the price.[31]

The passing of title may take place by means of delivery of the bill of lading, the invoice, the representative documents or any other means established by the law or the usages, even if the goods are not materially delivered. The rule may be subtracted from the possibility to virtually deliver the goods recognised under all the Ibero-American laws.[32]

In countries like Spain, with no similar statutory provision, scholars and case law recognise that the delivery (*tradittio*) also takes place as soon as the seller allows the buyer to dispose of the goods by handing over the property titles in the time and the place agreed.[33] Such has been expressly recognised in other commercial laws where the delivery of goods can virtually take place

---

[29] *See* Argentina Art. 2386 CC & Art. 462 Com C; Uruguay Art. 528 Com C.

[30] Bolivia Art. 349 CC; Chile Art. 1679 CC; Colombia Art. 1738 CC; Ecuador Art. 1722 CC; El Salvador Art. 1549 CC; Peru Art. 1325 CC; Portugal Art. 791 CC; *see also* Bolivia: G. Castellanos Trigo & S. Auad La Fuente, Derecho de las Obligaciones en el Código Civil Boliviano 166 (2008).

[31] *See supra* 3.1.

[32] Argentina Art. 2385 CC & Arts. 461, 463(3)(4) Com C; Bolivia Arts. 850, 864 Com C; Chile Art. 149(1) Com C; Colombia Art. 923(1) Com C; Ecuador Art. 194(2) Com C; Guatemala Art. 695 para. 1 Com C; Mexico Art. 2284 para. 3 CC & Art. 378 Com C; *see also* Colombia Art. 923 Com C; Costa Rica Art. 466(b)(c)(f) Com C; Nicaragua Art. 355 Com C; Uruguay Art. 529(3)(4) Com C; Venezuela Art. 1.489 CC & Art. 149(2)(3) Com C; *see also* Argentina Art. 463(2) Com C; Chile Art. 149(2) Com C; Ecuador Art. 194(3) Com C; Uruguay Art. 529(2) Com C: under Argentina, Chile, Ecuador and Uruguay's Com C when the buyer marks the goods with his mark with the consent of the seller; Spain Supreme Tribunal, 22 November 2006, *Id Cendoj:* 28079110012006101175: applying Spain Art. 339 Com C upheld that the buyer was bound to pay the price from the time the seller placed the goods at the buyer's disposal; Mexico: León Tovar, *supra* note 9, at 151, 153; Venezuela: Aguilar Gorrondona, *supra* note 8, at 219.

[33] *See* Spain: E. Guardiola Sacarrera, La compraventa internacional: importaciones y exportaciones 64 (2001); Spain Supreme Tribunal, 22 December 2000, *Id Cendoj:* 28079110002000100627.

with the deliverance of the bill of lading, the invoice, or by any other means authorised by the trade usage.[34] Additionally, under Bolivia and Guatemala's laws the seller fulfils his obligation to deliver by handing over the documents or titles representing the goods, the transport and, if required, the insurance.[35]

In summary, the passing of title may take place with the delivery of the documents representing the property titles of the goods even if the latter have not been materially delivered.

[34] *See* Argentina Art. 2388 CC & Arts. 461, 463(4) Com C; Chile Art. 149(1) Com C; Colombia Art. 923 Com C; Uruguay Arts. 527, 529(4) Com C.

[35] Bolivia Arts. 850, 864 Com C; Guatemala Art. 695 Com C.

Chapter 46

Transfer of Title by a Non-Owner

1. General Remarks

In Ibero-American law there is no uniform answer as to whether the seller must be the owner of the goods in order to have a valid sale. The lack of uniformity comes from the fact that while some countries follow the French code approach under which the sale of goods by non-owners is voidable, some other laws follow the approach taken by Las *Siete Partidas*.[1] This medieval instrument based in Roman law,[2] did not require the seller to be the owner of the goods.[3]

2. Validity and Voidability under some Instances

In Spain, the law does not expressly require the seller to be the owner of the goods.[4] Therefore, the majority of the scholars consider that from the

[1] Argentina: R. Compagnucci de Caso, Contrato de Compraventa 256 (2007); *see below* in this Chapter, *for example*, the contradictions in Argentinean law which follows both approaches.
[2] In Roman law the seller should not necessary be the owner of the goods, *see* Ulpiano, Digest 18.1.23 *cited in* Argentina: Compagnucci de Caso, *supra* note 1, at 255; also *cited in* Peru: M. Castillo Freyre, Comentarios al contrato de compraventa: análisis detallado de los artículos 1529 a 1601 del Código Civil 73 (2002).
[3] *See* Partida V, Title V, Law XIX *in* Ch. 1, 2.2; *see also* Peru: Castillo Freyre, *supra* note 2, at 296; Peru: M. Castillo Freyre (Ed.), El bien materia del contrato de compraventa: algunas consideraciones preliminares sobre el contrato de compraventa y estudio del capitulo segundo de dicho contrato en el código civil 74 (1995); Spain: L.J. Gutierrez Jerez, *La obligacion de saneamiento por eviccion y la transmision del dominio en la compraventa*, *in* J. Aguirre Zamorano (Ed.), La Compraventa Ley de Garantías 13, at 18 (2006).
[4] Spain: M. Medina de Lemus, Derecho Civil: Obligaciones y Contratos II, Contratos en Particular, Vol. 2, 41 (2004).

systematic reading of the Spanish Civil Code, the sale of other people's goods are valid since the seller is not bound to transfer the uncontested property.[5] The Spanish jurisprudence has also recognised the validity of the sales by non-owners.[6]

In Chile, Colombia, Ecuador and El Salvador the contract of sale does not transfer the property of the goods by its mere conclusion. In order to transfer the ownership of the goods the tradition is needed.[7] Based on that fact, the sale by non-owners is valid,[8] and the buyer is bound to pay the price although the goods do not belong to the seller.[9] Although the sale by a non-owner is valid between the parties, it does not affect the legitimate ownership of the real owner; since the contract cannot defeat his rights as the legal owner.

In Bolivia and Paraguay, although the transfer of the property of the goods operates by the mere conclusion, the law allows the transfer of title by non-owners.[10] But the law also imposes the seller the duty to procure the goods from the original owner in favour of the buyer. The transfer of property does not take place until the moment when the original owner ratifies the sale or the seller acquires the goods from him.[11]

Castillo considers that for these systems,[12] the sale by non-owners is susceptible to be voided in case the seller fails to procure the goods for the buyer or in case the original owner does not ratify the sale, however, these codes do not consider the sale by non-owner as void in itself.[13]

In Argentina and Costa Rica B2B sales, the principle is that the sale by non-owners is valid, unless the buyer knew that the goods were other people's goods.[14] On the contrary, the solution for Argentina C2C sales is that in principle the sale by non-owners is void,[15] but susceptible to be revalidated

[5] Spain: Gutiérrez Jerez, *supra* note 3, at 14-20.

[6] Spain Supreme Tribunal, 14 April 2000 (ar. 3376); Supreme Tribunal, 11 November 1997 (ar. 7872); Supreme Tribunal, 7 March 1997 (ar. 1643).

[7] Chile: R. Díez Duarte, La Compraventa en el Código Civil Chileno 198 (1993); El Salvador: A.O. Miranda, De la Compraventa 12 (1996); *see also* Ch. 45, 3.2.

[8] Chile Art. 1815 CC; Colombia Art. 1871 CC & Art. 907 Com C; Ecuador Art. 1781 CC & Art. 169 Com C; El Salvador Art. 1619 CC.

[9] Such was the statement in the Chilean Jurisprudence Chile Supreme Court, RDJ, Vol. 21, Sec. 1, at 219; Supreme Court, RDJ, Vol. 78, Sec. 1, at 138, both *cited in* Chile: Díez Duarte, *supra* note 7, at 172.

[10] Bolivia Art. 595 CC; Paraguay Arts. 143, 759(b) CC.

[11] Bolivia Art. 595 CC; Paraguay Arts. 143, 759(b) CC.

[12] Bolivia, Paraguay. But he also refers to Chile, Colombia, Ecuador and El Salvador. However, scholars from Chile and el Salvador have a different view *see* El Salvador: Miranda, *supra* note 7, at 463: in no case the buyer would be legally allow to claim the rescission of the sales contract, since these codes have an express provision establishing the validity of the sale made by non-owners.

[13] Peru: Castillo Freyre, *supra* note 2, at 78-79.

[14] Argentina Art. 453 Com C; Costa Rica Art. 440 Com C.

[15] Argentina Art. 1329 CC.

if the original owner ratifies the sale.[16] However, other provisions within the Argentinean Civil Code add some uncertainty. The general provisions on contracts establish that other people's goods can be the object of a valid contract.[17] Considering the general system for the transfer of property based in Roman law, the doctrine has sustained that, regardless of the principle contained in Argentina's Civil Code Article 1329, the sale of goods by a non-owner is valid and, thus, the contract cannot be affected of nullity.[18]

In this regard, the Argentinean courts have sustained that although in principle goods totally or partially affected by third parties' ownership cannot be sold, the voidability can be overcome by the ratification of the sale made by the real owner of the goods, or when subsequently the seller becomes the owner of the goods.[19] Additionally, the agreement to sell goods encumbered, does not release the seller of all obligations, as it should be understood that the seller has assumed an obligation to obtain ratification by the real owner. This arises from the fact that all contracts should be interpreted and performed in good faith and that they create obligations in relation to all consequences arising therein.[20]

Guatemala Mexico, Portugal and Venezuela's Civil Codes expressly provide that the sale of goods by non-owners are void.[21] Mexico and Portugal grant the opportunity to the seller to revalidate the sale if he becomes the owner of the goods before the eviction takes place.[22] On the other hand, Portugal and Venezuela B2B sales allows the sale by non-owners provided that the seller acquires in due time the goods from the legitimate owner.[23]

The situation in Peru is not so clear. On the one hand, Peru's Civil Code states that the sale by non-owners can be rescinded at the buyer's choice if the seller does not acquire the goods before the notice of claim from the competent court,[24] but only when the buyer ignored that the goods did not belong to the seller.[25]

On the other hand, the Peruvian Supreme Court has sustained that the Peruvian law allows the sale of goods by non-owners provided the buyer knows such a situation, in which case the seller binds himself on behalf of the

---

16 Argentina Art. 1330 CC.

17 Argentina Art. 1177 CC.

18 Argentina: Compagnucci de Caso, *supra* note 1, at 261.

19 Argentina National Civil Chamber, *Sala* E, *García, Enrique A. O. y otro v. Canjalli de Cababié, Alegra M. y otros*, 12 October 2005, Lexis No. 35012125.

20 *Id.*

21 Guatemala Art. 1794 CC; Mexico Arts. 2269, 2270, 2271 CC; Portugal Arts. 893, 894 CC; Venezuela Art. 1483 CC; *see also* Mexico: S. León Tovar, Los Contratos Mercantiles 162-163 (2004).

22 *See* Mexico Arts. 2269, 2270, 2271 CC; Portugal Arts. 893, 894 CC. *Also* Mexico: León Tovar, *supra* note 21, at 162-163.

23 Portugal Art. 467 sole para. Com C; Venezuela Art. 133 Com C.

24 Peru Art. 1539 CC.

25 Peru Supreme Court, *Sala civil transitoria*, Resolution 001064-2003, 6 June 2003.

real owner, but under any other circumstance, the sale of goods by non-owners is voided.[26] However, in a subsequent decision, the same Court sustained that the sale of goods by non-owners could not be declared voided, even if the buyer ignored the fact, since for such sort of contracts the law does not require, as an element of validity, the seller to be the owner of the goods at the time of the sale conclusion.[27]

Finally, the Brazilian Civil Code establishes an independent liability of the seller for all debts or rights that encumber the goods up to the time of delivery,[28] with not specific provision as to the validity or voidability of the sale by non-owners. In Uruguay B2B sales by non-owners are valid, but a buyer may lose the price paid if the he knew that the goods belonged to others, unless otherwise agreed.[29]

3. Remedies

In the Ibero-American laws, the remedies to the buyer in a sale by non-owners differ to some extent. In Chile, Colombia, Ecuador an El Salvador, if a person sells the goods of others, the buyer has the following options: first, the original owner ratifies the sale and if such happens the buyer retroactively acquired all rights from the date of the sale;[30] second; that the non-owner acquires the goods from the original owner and in such case the buyer will be regarded as the owner of the goods from their *tradittio*.[31] The third possibility for the buyer is to claim damages whenever the non-owner fails to acquire the goods, though this is only expressly recognised for B2B sales under the Colombian and the Ecuadorian laws.[32]

The buyer will not legally be allowed to claim the rescission of the sales contract, since these codes have an express provision establishing the validity of the sale made by the non-owners.[33] Actually, neither the real owner can seek the voidability of the contract. As sustained by Salvadoran Supreme Court,

---

26 Peru Supreme Court, *Sala civil permanente,* Resolution 001017-1997, 19 October 1998.

27 Peru Supreme Court, *Sala civil permanente,* Resolution 002857-2001, 23 December 2002.

28 Brazil Art. 502 CC.

29 Uruguay Art. 518 Com C (But if the buyer was unaware of that fact, the seller shall reimburse the money paid by the buyer together with the monetary compensation for any damage and loss of profits caused, *see* Uruguay Art. 518 Com C.)

30 Chile Art. 1818 CC; Colombia Art. 1874 CC & Art. 908 Com C; Ecuador Art. 1785 CC; El Salvador Art. 1622 CC.

31 Chile Art. 1819 CC; Colombia Art. 1875 CC & Arts. 907, 908 Com C; Ecuador Art. 1786 CC & Art. 169 Com C; El Salvador Art. 1623 CC.

32 Colombia Arts. 907, 925 Com C; Ecuador Art. 169 Com C.

33 Chile Art. 1815 CC; Colombia Art. 1871 CC & Art. 907 Com C; Ecuador Art. 1781 CC & Art. 169 Com C; El Salvador Art. 1619 CC.

the real owner has an automatic right to recover the possession of the goods through a statutory revendication action with no need to previously claim the voidability of the sale.[34]

As to the possibility to seek the avoidance of the contract, in case the non-owner (seller) fails to acquire the goods, the doctrine is divided. While some sustain that the buyer can make resort to the remedy of contract avoidance,[35] others deny such a possibility.[36] Unless, as the Chilean Supreme Court has sustained, the seller had, by express agreement, bound himself to deliver the goods free of encumbrances, so that the buyer is able to make resort of the remedy of avoidance for ordinary breach of contractual agreements or, alternatively, may claim the specific performance of the contract, any of them conjunctively with damages and loss of profits.[37]

Under some laws, if the buyer at the time of the contract conclusion ignored that the goods were other people's goods, the buyer can make resort to the remedy of contract avoidance, unless the seller before the claim had acquired the property of the goods.[38]

Nevertheless, the Bolivian Supreme Court denied the avoidance of the contract to a buyer who knew at the conclusion of the contract that the goods belonged to a third party.[39] The Court found that, instead, the applicable remedy was provided by Article 598 of the Civil Code which establishes that if the buyer was aware that the goods were other people's goods and the seller failed to acquire the goods for him, the buyer may only ask for the restitution of the price paid in consideration for the goods.[40]

But also under the Bolivian law, if the seller by his own faulty conduct cannot acquire the goods for the buyer, the seller may compensate the damages caused to the buyer in addition to the reimbursement of the price. In addition, the seller may always compensate the improvement made to the goods by the buyer.[41] In the Paraguayan law if the loss of or damage to the goods was caused by the buyer, compensation to the original owner shall be deducted from the price paid.[42]

In Peru, the approach is slightly different. The sale by non-owners is not voidable but rescindable.[43] As has been previously stated, in practice

---

34 El Salvador Supreme Court, RJ, 7-12, 1935, at 384-390, *cited in* El Salvador: Miranda, *supra* note 7, at 463.

35 El Salvador: Miranda, *supra* note 7, at 12.

36 Chile: Díez Duarte, *supra* note 7, at 248.

37 Chile RDJ, Vol. 2, Sec. 1, at 53 *cited in* Chile: Díez Duarte, *supra* note 7, at 303, n. 827.

38 Bolivia Art. 596 CC; Paraguay Art. 744 CC.

39 Bolivia Supreme Court, *Francisco de Asis Perales v. Rolando Soliz Velásquez.*

40 *Id.*

41 Bolivia Art. 596 CC.

42 Paraguay Art. 744 part 2 CC.

43 Peru Supreme Court, *Sala civil permanente,* Resolution 002857-2001, 23 December 2002.

the effects are similar, except for the amount of damages recovered.[44] The rescission has a retroactive effect which means, that whenever it is possible the parties must be restored to the position they were, before the conclusion of the contract.[45] Thus, the parties can demand each other and must return their respective performances.[46] However, the reason why the drafters of the Peruvian Civil Code decided to grant the buyer a remedy of rescission is because of the applicable limitation period. The limitation period of 10 years to exercise the remedy of avoidance is longer than the limitation period of 2 years to claim the rescission of the contract based on defects of intent.[47]

Under the Guatemalan, the Mexican and the Venezuelan laws the seller must return the price, and compensate for the damage and loss of profits caused to the buyer if the seller has acted in bad faith, *i.e.* if the seller new that the goods were other people's goods, and did not disclose such fact.[48]

In Portugal the buyer in good faith, *i.e.* who ignored that the goods were other people's goods, has the right to claim the total restitution of the price, despite the fact that the goods had been lost, damaged or devaluated by any caused. But if the seller has gained from any the loss, damage or devaluation of the goods he shall compensate the buyer in the amount representing the profit made by the seller.[49] In Portugal and Venezuela B2B contracts, the seller will only compensate the buyer for any loss and damage derived from the seller's inability to acquire the goods from the real owner, regardless of whether he knew that the goods belonged to other people.[50]

---

[44] In rescission, the compensation is granted for the *reliance interest* while in avoidance of the contract the parties are entitled to compensation for his *expectation interest* in the performance of the contract, *see* for more details on this distinction Ch. 24, 4 & Ch. 50, 2.

[45] Argentina: M.U. Salermo, Contratos Civiles y Comerciales 243 (2007).

[46] This is, the buyer to a sales contract declared rescinded is under the obligation to return the goods to the seller, and the latter to reimburse the payment and to compensate for the damage caused to the buyer; *see* Peru Art. 1541 CC on the rescission of sales by non-owners.

[47] Peru: Castillo Freyre, *supra* note 2, at 83.

[48] Guatemala Art. 1794 CC; Mexico Art. 2270 CC; Venezuela Art. 1483 CC.

[49] Portugal Art. 894 CC.

[50] Portugal Art. 467 sole para. Com C; Venezuela Art. 133 Com C.

Part 12

Remedies for Breach of Contract

CHAPTER 47

GENERAL REMARKS ABOUT REMEDIES

1. Remedies System Under the Ibero-American Laws

In the Ibero-American laws, different remedies are available to the party who suffers the other party's breach of any default statutory warranty or of any contractual obligation. In this chapter, we explain how they are interrelated to each other and how they exclude their concurrent application. In the next chapters, we shall review in detail the elements and mechanisms to access these remedies, as well as their limitations.

In the context of the remedies available to the buyer for the seller's obligations breach, the Ibero-American laws establish different grounds for different remedies.[1] This differs from the CISG system of remedies that evades any type of categorisation regarding the grounds of breach. The CISG has a unitary breach of contract system that does not distinguish between remedies on the grounds of defect of title, non-conformity, delay or non-performance.[2] Under the CISG, the same remedies are always triggered regardless of the type of breach.

Regrettably, the same cannot be said of the Ibero-American system of remedies for the buyer. On the one hand, the general statutory warranty of *saneamiento* encompasses three actions or remedies available for two different types of breaches. First, the redhibitory action and the estimatory action, which are the available remedies for cases of delivery of goods with unnoticed and unknown defects affecting their natural or general use or

[1] Spain: A. Martínez Cañellas, *El incumplimiento esencial del contrato de compraventa internacional de mercaderías*, Doctoral thesis, Universitat de les Illes Balears, Facultat de Dret. Àrea de Dret mercantil Palma de Mallorca 285 (2001), http://www.tdx.cat/TDX-0308105-095856.

[2] Chile: A. Vidal Olivares, *La Noción de Incumplimiento Esencial en el Código Civil*, XXXII(1) Revista de Derecho de la Pontificia Universidad Católica de Valparaíso 221, at 233-235 (2009); Spain: Martínez Cañellas, *supra* note 1, at 285.

their agreed use or purpose. Except for Costa Rica,[3] a successful redhibitory action (*actio redhibitoria)*[4] normally results in the avoidance of the contract,[5] while the estimatory action (*quanti minoris*)[6] grants the buyer a remedy for the reduction of the price of the defective goods.[7] Second, when the goods delivered do not have a clear title and the buyer is defeated in trial by a third party holding a better right of property, use or exploitation over the goods, the Ibero-American laws grant the buyer a right of compensation against eviction.[8]

On the other hand, the breach of any of the obligations contracted under a *synallagmatic* contract grants three main remedies. These remedies are

---

[3] Under Costa Rican law the delivery of goods affected by hidden defects does not trigger the right to a redhibitory or estimatory action, but rather to the voidability of the sales contract if such defects in the goods indeed derived from one party's defective intent such as mistake or fraud, *see* Costa Rica Art. 1082 CC; Costa Rica: D. Baudrit Carrillo, Los Contratos Traslativos del Derecho Privado – Principios de Jurisprudencia 49-52 (2000); Costa Rica: M. Ramírez Altamirano, Derecho Civil IV, Vol. II, Los Contratos Traslativos de Dominio 75 (1991): both authors referring to the jurisprudence developed on the issue by the Costa Rican Supreme Court.

[4] An action instituted to avoid a sale on account of some vice or defect in the thing sold which renders it either absolutely useless, or its use so inconvenient and, imperfect, that it must be, supposed the buyer would not have purchased it, had he known of the vice. Source: Bouviers Law Dictionary 1856 Edition.

[5] However, some authors consider it a mistake to characterise the redhibitory action as resolutory or rescinding action (action for the avoidance of the contract under CISG) for three main reasons: 1) there is a shorter term to exercise the action; 2) because it does not affect third party rights in good faith; 3) it does not presuppose the breach of obligations, *see* on this Venezuela: J.L. Aguilar Gorrondona, Contratos y Garantias: Derecho Civil IV, 256 (2008).

[6] An *actio quanti minoris* is one brought for the reduction of the price of a thing sold, in consequence of defects in the thing which is the object of the sale. Source: Bouviers Law Dictionary 1856 Edition; *see also generally* Mexico: A. Muriá-Tuñón, *The Actio Quanti Minoris and Sales of Goods Between Mexico and the U.S.: An Analysis of the Remedy of Reduction of the Price in the UN Sales Convention, CISG Article 50 and its Civil Law Antecedents*, Pace database on the CISG and International Commercial Law (1998), http://www.cisg.law.pace.edu/cisg/biblio/muria.html#actio.

[7] *See* express references to these two legal actions: Bolivia Art. 632(I) CC & Art. 849 Com C; Brazil Art. 442 CC; Chile Art. 1860 CC; Colombia Art. 1917 CC; Ecuador Art. 1827 CC; El Salvador Art. 1662 CC; Guatemala Art. 1561 CC; Mexico Art. 2144 CC; Uruguay Art. 1720 CC; Venezuela Art. 1.521 CC; *also* Colombia: A. Tamayo Lombana, El Contrato de Compraventa su Régimen Civil y Comercial 175 Ley (2004); El Salvador: A.O. Miranda, De la Compraventa 248-250 (1996); Mexico: S. León Tovar, Los Contratos Mercantiles 157-160 (2004); Argentina Supreme Court, *Inversiones y Servicios S.A. v. Estado Nacional Argentino*, 19 August 1999; Brazil Tribunal of Justice of the State of Rio Grande do Sul, Civil Recourse 71000950527, published 28 September 2007.

[8] *See* Argentina: R. Compagnucci de Caso, Contrato de Compraventa 153 (2007); Bolivia: W. Kaune Arteaga, Curso de Derecho Civil, Contratos, Vol. 2, 139 (1996); Brazil: C.M. Da Silva Pereira, Instituçaoes de Dereito Civil, Vol. III, Contratos, Electrônica 90 (2003); Brazil: O. Gomes, Contratos 115-117 (2008); Chile: R. Díez Duarte, La Compraventa en el Código Civil Chileno 155 (1993).

available in case of the debtor's delay in performing, partially or totally, any of the obligations agreed in the contract.[9] The delay can be temporary or definitive, but delay is always a key element to access these remedies; namely, the specific performance, the avoidance of the contract or/and the compensation for damages.[10] Under the redhibitory and estimatory actions there is no such delay required since, usually the seller performs his main obligation consisting of the delivery of the goods. Thus, it cannot be claimed to be in delay. The redhibitory and estimatory actions focus on whether the already delivered goods are fit for the ordinary use or the particular agreed purpose.[11] Similarly, neither the redhibitory action nor the estimatory action grant a right to claim the specific performance based on defects of the goods, since they do not contemplate as such.[12] The reason goes back to the Roman law, where it was understood that if the goods were useless,[13] the only option was the termination of the contract or the reduction of the price but never the specific performance of the contract since the contract was conceived to be already performed.

Similarly, under the system of eviction, the loss or deprivation of the property, use or exploitation over the goods, suffered by the buyer, is not redressed with the avoidance of the contract or with an order for specific performance. Instead, a defeated buyer will usually be reimbursed the price and compensated for the costs of the contract conclusion, the improvements made on the goods, the costs of the trial, and the increased value of the goods up to the date of the eviction.[14]

The above being said, scholars and courts have sustained that when the seller has, by express agreement, bound himself to deliver the goods free of title and he fails to do so, the buyer may make resort of the remedy of avoidance for ordinary breach.[15] This approach can be extended to cases of non-conformity based on defective goods. Both eviction and redhibitory actions form part of

---

9 For details as to when a party is considered to be delayed *see* Ch. 52, 2.

10 *See* Chile: Díez Duarte, *supra* note 8, at 176.

11 *See* Ch. 37, 1.

12 *See* Ch. 49, 2.

13 And the means to repair them were not always available, *e.g.* hidden defects on slaves, livestock, *etc.*

14 *See for example*, Chile Arts. 1847, 1845, 1849, 1850, 1851 CC; Chile: Díez Duarte, *supra* note 8, at 159-160; *see also* Argentina: Compagnucci de Caso, *supra* note 8, at 154; Brazil: Gomes, *supra* note 8, at 115-117; Chile: Díez Duarte, *supra* note 8, at 156; Mexico: León Tovar, *supra* note 7, at 162; Venezuela: Aguilar Gorrondona, *supra* note 5, at 237, 238.

15 Chile: Vidal Olivares, *supra* note 2, at 235, 236; Bolivia Supreme Court, *Sala Civil, Francisco de Asis Perales v. Rolando Soliz Velásquez*: granted to a seller an additional 30 day period, from the date of the Judgment, to deliver the documents required by the buyer in order to register the contract of sale of a vehicle. The same Court confirmed that if the seller failed to do so, the buyer may declare the contract avoided; Chile Supreme Court, RDJ, Vol 2, Sec. 1, at 53 *cited in* Chile: Díez Duarte, *supra* note 8, at 303, n. 827.

a general statutory remedy called warranty of *saneamiento*.[16] So that if the parties expressly agreed on such warranty, the remedy available shall not be a statutory one, but instead, the remedies available for breach of contractual obligations, namely the specific performance or the avoidance of the contract.[17]

Additionally, the Ibero-American laws distinguish between the delivery of goods containing the mentioned defects (*redhibitory vices*) and the delivery of goods which are completely different to those agreed (*aliud pro alio*).[18] The delivery of different goods or *aliud pro alio* constitutes in itself a breach of the obligation to deliver.[19] As noticed, the distinction has an impact on the remedies available, on the standards of non-conformity required by the law for the avoidance of the contract,[20] and on the different limitation periods to file law suits.[21]

Examples of *aliud pro alio* have included the delivery of goods completely different such as corn and wheat, but also goods that although are of the same type required, are *totally* unfit for the use they were acquired for, causing an *objective* business frustration to the buyer.[22] For example, the delivery of olive oil which does not meet the import standards established in the contract, or the sale of an inaccurate type of cement installed by the seller which under the circumstances could not be subject to the system of defective goods.[23]

Besides, in ordinary breach of obligations, the law requires the existence of *negligence* for the remedy of avoidance, specific performance and damages.[24] *Negligence* by one of the parties also has an impact on the rules

---

16 The different names given are *e.g.* in Argentina *saneamiento por vicios redhibitorios* (warranty for redhibitory defects) *see* Argentina Art. 1414 CC and Argentina Compagnucci de Caso, *supra* note 8, at 205; In Brazil's Civil Code this sections has the name of *Dos Vícios Redibitórios* in Arts. 441-446.

17 Chile: Vidal Olivares, *supra* note 2, at 235, 236.

18 *See* in this regard Spain: E. Guardiola Sacarrera, La compraventa internacional: importaciones y exportaciones 75 (2001); Spain Supreme Tribunal, 20 November 2008 *Id Cendoj:* 28079110012008101062.

19 *See* Brazil Tribunal of Justice of the State of São Paulo, Appeal with Revision 965123400, published 12 April 2006: the Tribunal differentiated the delivery of goods containing hidden defects and delivery of different goods from the ones contractually established, avoiding a contract under which a label company produced a wrong label written 'language' instead of 'languages' for a school of languages; Spain Supreme Tribunal, 28 October 2008, *Id Cendoj:* 28079110012008100918.

20 *See* Ch. 53, 1.1.

21 *See* Ch. 60, 2.2 & 2.3.

22 Chile: Vidal Olivares, *supra* note 2, at 237; Spain Supreme Tribunal, 14 May 2009, *Id Cendoj:* 28079110012009100320.

23 Spain Supreme Tribunal, 22 October 2007, *Id Cendoj:* 28079110012007101093.

24 The term in Spanish is *culpa, see* Bolivia: R. Carrillo Aruquipa, Lecciones de Derecho Civil, Obligaciones 428 (2008); G.H. Treitel, *Remedies for Breach of Contract*, *in* A.T. von Mehren (Ed.), International Encyclopedia of Comparative Law, Vol. VII Contracts, Ch. 16, at 56, para. 78 (1999); The Ibero-American laws requirement of *culpa* (negligence) is unknown in common law countries, where negligence of the debtor is not a necessary element for compensation.

of impossibility, as the debtor may still be liable for damages and loss of profits if the impossibility was caused by his *negligence*.[25] The negligence referred to in the Ibero-American laws is objective.[26] Some laws expressly define negligence as the omission of those diligences that are required by the nature of the obligation according to the personal circumstances, the time and the place.[27] Other laws add that when no level of diligence has been agreed to perform the obligation, it shall be required a level of diligence corresponding to that of the *bonus pater familias*.[28] As noted by an author, the issue is not about the psyche of the debtor but about his conduct that deviates from the standard required by the law.[29]

The negligence of the debtor in breach is presumed.[30] Many Civil Codes expressly state that the debtor bears the burden to prove that he has acted with care and diligence, so that no negligent conduct can connect him with the events.[31] All the more since it is presumed that if the goods are lost in the debtor's possession, this is due to his conduct or negligence.[32]

The debtor's negligence is rather the measure of damages available to the buyer, *see Spain:* Martínez Cañellas, *supra* note 1, at 302 n. 762.

25 Argentina Arts. 513, 888, 889 CC & Art. 467 Com C; Brazil Art. 248 CC; Chile Art. 1547 paras. 1, 2 CC; Colombia Art. 1604 paras. 1, 2 CC & Art. 930 Com C; Ecuador Art. 1590 paras. 1, 2 CC; El Salvador Art. 1418 paras. 1, 2 CC; Mexico Art. 2111 CC; Peru Arts. 1317, 1321 CC; Portugal Arts. 546 part 1, 801 CC; Spain Art. 1.104 CC; Uruguay Art. 220 (2) Com C; Venezuela Art. 1.271 CC; *see also* Argentina: G.A. Borda, Manual de Contratos 140 (2004): noting that in Argentina the faulty debtor may be released from performing due to the impossibility but he is liable for damages and loss of profits; Argentina: R.L. Lorenzetti, Tratado de los Contratos Parte General 59 (2004): same opinion; Brazil: Gomes, *supra* note 8, at 213 same opinion; El Salvador: A.O. Miranda, Guía Para el Estudio del Derecho Civil III, Obligaciones 157; El Salvador Supreme Court, *Cass civ, Kereitz Medrano v. Liceo Centroamericano, S.A. de C.V.*, 11-C-2007, 17 November 2008: the alleged impediment should not result of the faulty conduct of the debtor.

26 Spain: A. López López, *in* L. Díez Picazo y Ponce De León (Ed.), La Compraventa Internacional de Mecaderias – Comentario sobre la Convención de Viena Art. 45, VI, at 411-414 (1998).

27 Argentina Art. 512 CC; Bolivia Art. 302(I)(II) CC; Peru Arts. 1319, 1320 CC; Spain Art. 1.104 CC; Uruguay Art. 221 Com C; Bolivia: G. Castellanos Trigo & S. Auad La Fuente, Derecho de las Obligaciones en el Código Civil Boliviano 48-50 (2008).

28 Bolivia Art. 302(I) CC; Spain Art. 1.104 *in fine* CC; *see also* Bolivia: Castellanos Trigo & Auad La Fuente, *supra* note 27, at 48; X. O'Callaghan (Ed.), Código Civil Comentado Art. 1.105, at 1075 (2004).

29 Argentina: Lorenzetti, *supra* note 25, at 603.

30 Spain: López López, *supra* note 26, Art. 45, VI, at 411-414.

31 Chile Art. 1547(3) CC; Colombia Art. 1604(3) CC; Ecuador Art. 1590(3) CC; El Salvador Art. 1418(3) CC.

32 Chile Art. 1671 CC; Colombia Art. 1730 CC; Ecuador Art. 1714 CC; El Salvador Art. 1541 CC; Spain Art. 1.183 CC; *see also* Argentina: Lorenzetti, *supra* note 25, at 602.

2. Contractual Modification or Limitation of Remedies

As parties are free to contractually define their obligations, they may also contractually regulate the remedies available for breach and the scope of their liability. This freedom is recognised in both the CISG[33] and the Ibero-American laws.

On the one hand, the Ibero-American law principle of freedom of contract allows the parties not only to extend, but also to reduce or to completely suppress, the statutory warranty for hidden or apparent defects on the goods.[34] Again, an agreement on this issue does not affect any public policy consideration. This has been expressly recognised in different Civil Codes. In most of them, the parties can restrict, renounce and extend their liability for any redhibitory defect provided that the seller does not act in bad faith.[35] A seller is considered to have acted in bad faith when he is in knowledge of the existence of defects in the goods and does not disclose them to the buyer.[36] The same applies regarding the statutory warranty against eviction. All the laws uphold the validity of limitation of the liability clauses of this type, unless the seller conceals the fact that the goods are affected by a third party's rights affecting their property, use or exploitation.[37] On this issue, tribunals have upheld that when the parties agree on a specific remedy or remedies available for breach of any of the obligations contracted, they might also be considered to have waived their rights to all default remedies established by law.[38]

33 Art. 6 CISG.

34 *See* Argentina: Compagnucci de Caso, *supra* note 8, at 219-220; Chile: Díez Duarte, *supra* note 8, at 170; Bolivia: Kaune Arteaga, *supra* note 8, at 153; Colombia: Tamayo Lombana, *supra* note 7, at 176, 177, 185-187; El Salvador: Miranda, *supra* note 7, at 262.

35 Argentina Art. 2166 CC; Bolivia Arts. 624(II), 628(I) CC & Art. 838 Com C; Chile Art. 1859 CC; Colombia Art. 1916 CC; Ecuador Art. 1826 CC; El Salvador Art. 1661 CC; Guatemala Art. 1544 CC; Mexico Art. 2158 CC; Paraguay Art. 1792 CC; Uruguay Art. 1719 CC; Venezuela Art. 1.520 CC.

36 Argentina Art. 2169 CC; Bolivia Art. 628(II) CC; Chile Art. 1859 CC; Colombia Art. 1916 CC; Ecuador Art. 1826 CC; El Salvador Art. 1661 CC; Paraguay Art. 1792 CC; Spain Art. 1485 CC; Uruguay Art. 1719 CC.

37 *See for example*, Argentina Arts. 2098, 2099 CC; Bolivia Arts. 624, 628(I)(II) CC; Brazil Arts. 448, 457 CC; Chile Arts. 1839, 1842 CC; Colombia Arts. 1895, 1898 CC; Ecuador Arts. 1806, 1809 CC; El Salvador Arts. 1641, 1644 CC; Mexico Arts. 2121, 2122 CC; Paraguay Art. 1763 CC; Peru Art. 1497 CC; Spain Art. 1476 CC; Venezuela Arts. 1505, 1506 CC.

38 ICC Final Award Case No. 11367 *Lex Contractus* Portuguese Law: the buyer was seeking a reduction of the purchase price by 31.5% (the difference between the contracted one and the real performance of the equipment, in accordance with his calculations). But according to the contract the buyer only had the option to reject the equipment, or to have it redone by another supplier, plus, in both cases, compensation for damages. The Contract, however, did not give the buyer the third option he was seeking, this is, to keep the equipment and to unilaterally reduce the price, in the same proportion as the alleged shortfall in capacity. The Sole Arbitrator upheld that the buyer had not proven that such a remedy was available under general Portuguese law. "But even if it were, Portuguese contractual law is dispositive, and the provision of specific

Parties may also limit their liability for damages with a limitation of liability clause of this type. The Ibero-American laws expressly grant the parties the possibility to agree on the amount and the mechanism of compensation for breach of contract within the limits established by law.[39] On this issue, tribunals have explained that the rules on damages established by the Civil Code have a subsidiary character *vis à vis* to the provisions agreed by the parties; so that there is no ground for the compensation of a certain type of damages when the agreement has excluded them.[40]

Additionally, even if the breach of contract never leads *ipso iure* to the avoidance of the contract, as such needs to be declared by the competent court, the parties can agree that failure to perform a specified obligation, albeit such obligation may be seen as an ancillary one, would automatically cause the avoidance of the contract.[41] However, the parties' freedom, to raise or to lower the standard of breach required for the avoidance may encounter a limit in the duty to act in good faith and the notion of abuse of right. Based on this, the courts and tribunals may have the possibility to moderate the effects of clauses allowing the avoidance of the contract for breach of obligations of minor importance to the whole economy of the contract.[42]

In addition, parties can freely agree that a party may not be discharged from his obligations and be released from his liability under the contract in case of breach, even if his failure to comply with the contract is due to events beyond his control or due to legitimate impediments.[43] The same applies regarding the allocation of the risk related to the impediment to perform.

On the contrary, parties may not exempt themselves from tort liability directly or indirectly related to the contract.[44] Similarly, a clause or agreement under which any of the parties purportedly waive a right to seek the invalidity of the illegal or immoral transaction is in itself considered illegal.[45] Likewise, as previously mentioned in this work,[46] under many laws, clauses that exclude or reduce the responsibility of the party who drafted the standard terms of an

remedies [under the contract] must be construed as an implicit waiver of any remedy provided for by law, which is not foreseen in the Contract."

39 Chile Art. 1558 para. 3 CC; Colombia Art. 1616 para. 3 CC; Ecuador Art. 1601 para. 3 CC; El Salvador Art. 1429 para. 3 CC; Mexico Art. 2117 CC; Peru Arts. 1329, 1328; Portugal Art. 800 (2) CC; Venezuela Art. 1.277 CC.

40 ICC Final Award Case No. 13918 *Lex Contractus* Spanish Law: the buyer was precluded from the already limited compensation established by the contract and from the compensation established by the law, since the parties had agreed to depart from the default rules.

41 Chile: Vidal Olivares, *supra* note 2, at 251, 252; *see* Ch. 53, 3.

42 *See* Spain: Martínez Cañellas, *supra* note 1, at 364, n. 865: referring to the jurisprudence of the Spanish Supreme Tribunal on the issue.

43 *See* Ch. 51, 1.2.

44 *See* Ch. 55.

45 *See* expressly Chile Art. 1469 CC; Ecuador Art. 1512 CC.

46 *See* Ch. 13, 1.2.

adhesion contract are considered invalid.[47] Clauses that grant an exclusive right to the drafter to avoid the contract or to change their conditions, or that in any way deprive the adherent party of some right without just cause are also invalid.[48] Similarly, clauses that impede the adherent party to sue the other party, or that impose on the adherent party the anticipated renounce of any right that could be found on the contract, or that impose a term or condition on the right of the adherent to raise a legal action, or that limits the right to raise exceptions, or the use of judicial procedures of which the adherent could make resort, are invalid.[49]

[47] Honduras Art. 727 Com C; Mexico Art. 90 CPL; Paraguay Art. 691 CC; Peru Art. 1398 CC.

[48] Honduras Art. 727 Com C; Mexico Art. 90 CPL; Paraguay Art. 691 CC; Peru Art. 1398 CC.

[49] Brazil Art. 424 CC; Honduras Art. 727 Com C; Mexico Art. 90 CPL; Paraguay Art. 691 CC; Peru Art. 1398 CC.

CHAPTER 48

SUSPENSION OF THE CONTRACT

1. *Exceptio non adimpleti contractus* – Right to Withhold Performance

1.1. General Remarks

The Ibero-American laws allow one of the parties to withhold performance of his obligations.[1] This possibility is known under the doctrine of *exceptio non adimpleti contractus* and has two different purposes. First, it aims to protect one party from incurring any loss caused by performing his own obligation without receiving the counter-performance from the other party. Second, it seeks to exercise some sort of pressure over the other party so that he performs

[1] The following provisions acknowledge the doctrine generally to all contracts: Argentina Art. 1201 CC; Bolivia Art. 576 CC; Brazil Arts. 476, 477 CC; Costa Rica Art. 425 Com C; Guatemala Art. 682 Com C; Paraguay Arts. 719, 720 CC; Peru Arts. 1426, 1427 CC; Portugal Arts. 428-431 CC; Venezuela Arts. 122, 123 Com C; Other provisions apply the doctrine to the contract of sale in specific: Argentina Arts. 1418, 1419, 1428 CC & Art. 464 Com C (*Exceptio* for seller) & Art. 1426 CC (*Exceptio* for buyer); Bolivia Art. 623 CC (*Exceptio* for seller) Art. 638 CC & Art. 862 C Com (*Exceptio* for buyer); Brazil Art. 495 CC (*Exceptio* for seller); Chile Art. 1826 CC & Arts. 147, 151, 155 Com C (*Exceptio* for seller) & Art. 1872 CC (*Exceptio* for buyer); Colombia Art. 1882 CC & Art. 926 Com C (*Exceptio* for seller) & Art. 1929 CC (*Exceptio* for buyer); Costa Rica Arts. 1072, 1073 CC (*Exceptio* for seller) & Art. 1089 CC (*Exceptio* for buyer); Ecuador Art. 1793 CC & Arts. 193, 196 Com C (*Exceptio* for seller) & Art. 1839 CC (*Exceptio* for buyer); El Salvador Art. 1629 CC (*Exceptio* for seller) & Art. 1674 CC (*Exceptio* for buyer); Mexico Arts. 2286, 2287 CC (*Exceptio* for seller) & Art. 2299 CC (*Exceptio* for buyer); Panama Arts. 1236, 1237 CC (*Exceptio* for seller) & Art. 1273 CC (*Exceptio* for buyer); Portugal Art. 468 Com C (*Exceptio* for seller); Spain Arts. 1.466, 1.467 CC (*Exceptio* for seller) & Art. 1.505 CC (*Exceptio* for buyer); Uruguay Art. 526 para. 2 Com C (*Exceptio* for seller); Venezuela Art. 1493 CC & Art. 148 Com C (*Exceptio* for seller) & Art. 1530 CC (*Exceptio* for buyer).

his obligations as agreed upon the contract.[2] The rule is clearly exposed in the Paraguayan and the Peruvian Civil Codes, according to which in contracts with reciprocal and simultaneous obligations, each of the parties has the right to suspend performance until the counter-performance has been fulfilled or guaranteed, unless one of the parties must perform first.[3]

Thus, simultaneous performance in the context of *exceptio non adimpleti contractus* infers that normally one of the parties has a well-founded fear that the other party will fail to perform one of his obligations, at the moment where both parties were expected to have their obligations performed, so that the first party can exercise his *right to withhold* performance.[4] As explained by an ICC Arbitral Tribunal, the exception of *non adimpleti contractus* can be raised only where the contract governs reciprocal obligations and does not determine which party must first give performance.[5]

Yet, the party withholding performance must be ready to perform.[6] A good example of the readiness to perform is cases of the retention of the letter of credit opened by the buyer until the seller delivers the goods.[7]

In a case relating to the transport of Gas LP, the Bolivian Supreme Court upheld that the respondent, a gas producer, could not raise the *exception* to pay for the non-executed transport services of the claimant since he was unprepared to perform, and indeed had failed to execute one of the ancillary obligations.[8] The contract called for the transportation of Gas LP in special containers to be provided by the respondent. In multiple occasions, the claimant had requested for the containers with no response from the respondent. On that basis, the

---

[2] Argentina: M. Iturraspe, *in* A. Bueres (Ed.), Código civil y normas complementarias: análisis doctrinario y jurisprudencial Art. 1201, at 57 (1995); G.H. Jones & P. Schlechtriem, *Breach of Contract (Deficiencies in a Party's Performance)*, *in* A.T. von Mehren (Ed.), International Encyclopedia of Comparative Law, Vol. VII Contracts, Ch. 15, 62, para. 86 (1999).

[3] Paraguay Art. 719 CC; Peru Art. 1426 CC. *See also* Portugal Art. 428 CC; Paraguay Supreme Court, Judgment 219, 17 May 2001, *Baúl De La Felicidad S.A. v. Pony Automotores–Mitsuservice Import S.R.L.*

[4] Bolivia: W. Kaune Arteaga, Curso de Derecho Civil, Contratos, Vol. 2, 134 (1996); Mexico: S. León Tovar, Los Contratos Mercantiles 154 (2004); Mexico Supreme Court, *Octava Época.* SJF I, First Part, January-June 1988, at 295: stating that the *Exceptio adimpleti* can only work on bilateral contracts where the performance of the obligations are simultaneous.

[5] ICC Final Award Case No. 14083 *Lex Contractus* Brazilian Law.

[6] Jones & Schlechtriem, *supra* note 2, at 65, para. 98: the party invoking the *Exceptio* must be willing and ready to perform. Interestingly, the Supreme Court of Chile has sustained that if both parties are reluctant to perform the contract is not avoided for ordinary breach but terminate for lack of intent to conclude the contact, *see* Chile Supreme Court, RDJ, Vol. 28, Sec. 1, at 689 *cited in* Chile: R. Díez Duarte, La Compraventa en el Código Civil Chileno 123, n. 237 (1993).

[7] *See for example* Bolivia Art. 865 Com C; Venezuela Art. 122 para. 1 Com C.

[8] Bolivia Supreme Court, Sala Civil 1, 25 October 2005, *Elizabeth Chávez Guzmán v. Yacimientos Petrolíferos Fiscales Bolivianos*.

Court recognised the legality of the damages awarded to the claimant by a lower instance Court and dismissed the *exceptio non adimpleti contractus* raised by the respondent.[9]

On the other hand, the practice of modern sales shows that the 'simultaneous performance rule' is usually derogated by the agreement of the parties.[10] Indeed, when a contractual clause or usages require that one of the parties fulfils first his obligation, the general principle is that such party cannot exercise his right to withhold performance based on the belief that the other party may not perform his future obligation.[11] As explained by an ICC Arbitral Tribunal, where performance is to be given successively, the contracting party which is bound to perform its obligation prior to the other party cannot refuse to carry it out on the assumption that the other party will not perform its obligation, as is the case in contracts of deferred execution which are similar to the supply of goods contracts.[12]

Hence, for example, if the parties have agreed in their contract that the buyer will pay the price of the remaining goods once the seller has delivered the whole of the goods, the seller cannot withhold performance of his own obligation, and seek the avoidance of the contract, alleging a supposed future buyer's breach to pay the price.[13] On the other hand, if under the contract the delivery of the goods would have to take place any time during a five month period at the option of the seller, and the price would have to be paid on the first day of the mentioned period against the invoice, then, it is evident that the seller preserves his right to withhold delivery of the goods after he handed over the invoice, as under the contract the price was to be paid before the delivery of the goods and the buyer cannot seek avoidance of the contract on that basis.[14]

Furthermore, the exceptio *non adimpleti contractus* can be raised only in relation to obligations which are mutually dependent. Where the obligations are not mutually dependent, the contracting parties cannot raise the exception. For example, a party cannot stop performing his main obligation on the

---

9 *Id.*

10 Jones & Schlechtriem, *supra* note 2, at 62, para. 91.

11 *See* expressly Costa Rica Art. 425 Com C; Jones & Schlechtriem, *supra* note 2, at 63, para. 91; Brazil: O. Gomes, Orlando, Contratos 110 (2008); Brazil: C.M. Da Silva Pereira, Instituçaoes de Dereito Civil, Vol. III, Contratos, Electrônica para. 215 (2003); ICC Final Award Case 12035 *Lex Contractus* Mexican Law: "In a bilateral agreement, *i.e.* a contract providing for mutual obligations of the parties, neither party may seek performance unless he has performed his own duties"; Mexico Supreme Court, *Octava Época*. SJF I, First Part, January-June 1988, at 295: declaring that in cases where one of the parties must perform first so that subsequently the other party fulfils the counter-performance none of the parties is entitled to raise the exception.

12 ICC Final Award Case No. 14083 *Lex Contractus* Brazilian Law.

13 Mexico Collegiate Tribunals, *Novena Época*, Registry 185'427, SJF XVI, December 2002, p 759.

14 Spain AT Pamplona, 15 December 1988.

grounds that the other party has failed to fulfil an ancillary obligation, unless such ancillary obligation was of considerable importance for the fulfilment of the whole contract.[15]

The interdependence requirement was discussed by an ICC Arbitral Tribunal in application of the Brazilian law. In the case at stake, the seller and buyer agreed on the sale/purchase of 240 wagons, with an initial payment of 20% of the price equivalent to 48 wagons which were to be delivered first, and the remaining 80% payment being dependent on the buyer's ability to obtain a loan from a bank. The buyer fulfilled his first obligation with the advance payment in respect of the price for the first 48 wagons; the seller did not deliver the 48 wagons in the manner and within the time limit agreed. Later on, when the buyer obtained the loan for the remaining 192 wagons, the buyer refused the 80% payment of the remaining price arguing that its refusal to complete the order was justified under the *exceptio non adimpleti contractus* principle. The Tribunal dismissed the claim on the basis that the buyer's obligation to complete the order, once the bank loan had been approved, was not dependent on, nor was it simultaneous with, the seller's obligation to deliver the first 48 wagons in the manner and within the time limit agreed.[16]

The above being said, the CISG and also many Ibero-American systems recognise an exception to the general principle. A party may have the right to withhold performance, even if he was required to perform first, in the event of deterioration of the other's party economic situation, or whenever other circumstances will evidently affect the performance of the contract.[17] Some laws recognise this special *exceptio* generally to all contracts,[18] while the rest of the codes contain a special exception in favour of the seller who may be under a duty to deliver before being paid.[19]

An ICC Arbitral Tribunal recognised this exception to the exception, explaining that it is true that, by way of exception, in contracts involving staggered performance, the *exceptio non adimpleti contractus* may be invoked if, once the contract is concluded, the other party's resources are diminished

---

15 ICC Final Award Case 11853 *Lex Contractus* Mexican Law; ICC Final Award Case 13524 *Lex Contractus* Mexican Law.

16 ICC Final Award Case No. 14083 *Lex Contractus* Brazilian Law.

17 Bolivia: Kaune Arteaga, *supra* note 4, at 134, 135; Brazil: Gomes, *supra* note 11, at 110; Chile: Díez Duarte, *supra* note 6, at 146, 147; El Salvador: A.O. Miranda, De la Compraventa 191-193 (1996); X. O'Callaghan (Ed.), Código Civil Comentado Art. 1.467, at 1475 (2004); Venezuela: J.L. Aguilar Gorrondona, Contratos y Garantias: Derecho Civil IV, 220-221 (2008); *see also* Art. 71(1)(a)(b) CISG.

18 Bolivia Art. 576 CC; Brazil Art. 477 CC; Paraguay Art. 720 CC; Peru Art. 1427 CC; Portugal Art. 429 CC; Venezuela Art. 123(1)(2) Com C.

19 Argentina Art. 1419 CC; Brazil Art. 495 CC; Bolivia Art. 623 (II) CC; Chile Art. 1826 para. 4 CC & Art. 147 Com C; Colombia Art. 1882 para. 4 CC & Art. 926 Com C; Costa Rica Art. 1073 CC; Ecuador Art. 1629 para. 4 CC & Art. 193 Com C; El Salvador Art. 1629 para. 4 CC; Mexico Art. 2287 CC; Panama Art. 1237 CC; Portugal Art. 468 Com C; Spain Art. 1.467 CC; Uruguay Art. 1688 CC & Art. 526 para. 2 Com C; Venezuela Art. 1493 CC.

in such a way that it jeopardises or throws doubt on the party's ability to carry out the obligation which it undertook.[20] In such a situation, the party which is obliged to carry out its obligation first may refuse to do so until such time as the other party performs the obligation incumbent on it, or gives the first party a sufficient guarantee that it will do so.

The Ibero-American codes mention specific threats such as bankruptcy or insolvency of the buyer.[21] Concerning the right of the buyer to suspend payment, some codes also specify the applicability of the defence upon specific threats such as perturbation of the property rights on the goods by third parties or a founded fear to be perturbed, giving the buyer the right to suspend payment.[22]

In countries like Chile, Colombia, Ecuador and El Salvador, the buyer has no right to retain the price as such, rather, he has to make deposit of the price in a competent court, and the price shall be kept within the court until the seller stops the third party claims or guarantees his performance and the cost of possible law suits.[23] However, this has been considered inequitable. Some have recognised the possibility of the buyer to keep under his custody the price since, on the other hand, the seller has indeed the right to retain the goods in cases of threats such as bankruptcy or insolvency of the buyer.[24]

Closer to the CISG approach, Paraguay and Peru's Civil Codes enlarge the scope of the right to withhold performance as they do not limit the right to specific cases but the defence applies to general threats and circumstances affecting the implementation of the contract.[25]

Interestingly, the Argentinean law has a provision allowing the exercise of the right to withhold performance in a case of partial fulfilment of the other party's obligation, also known with the Latin expression of *exeptio non rite adimpleti contractus*.[26] Argentina's Civil Code article 1426 establishes that the buyer can refuse payment if the seller did not deliver exactly what the

[20] ICC Final Award Case No. 14083 *Lex Contractus* Brazilian Law.

[21] Argentina Art. 1419 CC; Bolivia Art. 623 CC; Chile Art. 1826 CC; Colombia Art. 1882 CC; Costa Rica Art. 1073 CC; Ecuador Art. 1793 CC; El Salvador Art. 1629 CC; Mexico Art. 2287 CC; Panama Art. 1237 CC; Portugal Art. 468 Com C; Spain Art. 1.467 CC; Venezuela Art. 1.493 CC.

[22] Argentina Art. 1425 CC; Bolivia 638 (1) CC; Chile Art. 1872 CC; Colombia Art. 1929 CC; Ecuador Art. 1839 CC; El Salvador Art. 1674 CC; Mexico Art. 2299 CC; Panama Art. 1273 CC; Spain Art. 1.502 CC; Venezuela Art. 1.530 CC; *see also* Bolivia: Kaune Arteaga, *supra* note 4, at 157.

[23] Chile Art. 1872 CC; Colombia Art. 1929 CC; Ecuador Art. 1839 CC; El Salvador Art. 1674 CC; *see also* Chile: Díez Duarte, *supra* note 6, at 174, 175; El Salvador: Miranda, *supra* note 17, at 278-280.

[24] Colombia: A. Tamayo Lombana, El Contrato de Compraventa su Régimen Civil y Comercial 198-200 (2004); El Salvador: Miranda, *supra* note 17, at 280, 281.

[25] Paraguay Art. 720 CC; Peru Art. 1427 CC.

[26] Brazil: Gomes, *supra* note 11, at 110.

contract required. The buyer may also refuse payment if the seller intends to deliver goods of a different description, quantity or quality as required by the contract.[27]

In addition, an important example of partial performance, which is present in other Ibero-American countries,[28] involves the delivery of goods which are encumbered by third parties' property or intellectual property rights, and which also gives the buyer a right to withhold payment of the goods.[29] Indeed, some authors and the Venezuelan jurisprudence have maintained that, even though this provision expressly refers to threats or actual perturbation of the property rights; the general principles of the law would permit to withhold performance in the case of delivery of goods containing hidden defects.[30]

Finally, the right to suspend the performance is available in the sale of goods by installments. In the event that some installments have already been fulfilled, the suspension will operate for the outstanding installments.[31]

1.2. Standards and Conditions

Withholding performance may not be always so easily justified in every jurisdiction. On the one hand, under the Bolivian sales subject to payment against delivery, if the goods and their packages are not in apparent bad conditions the buyer shall not withhold or refuse payment at the time of delivery.[32]

On the other hand, the right to withhold performance requires that the party who intends to do so has a well-founded claim against the other party. These are objective facts, serious reasons and not mere suggestions, which are to be assessed by a competent court in due course.[33] For example, a Mexican Tribunal has sustained that the fact that the buyer had discovered in the Registry of Property that the immovable goods, which are the object to the contract, appeared to be the property of a different person than the seller, met

[27] *See* on this Argentina: G.A. Borda, Manual de Contratos 229 (2004).

[28] Bolivia Art. 638(1) CC; Chile Art. 1872 CC; Colombia Art. 1929 CC; Ecuador Art. 1839 CC; El Salvador Art. 1674 CC; Mexico Art. 2299 CC; Panama Art. 1273 CC; Spain Art. 1.502 CC; Venezuela Art. 1.530 CC.

[29] Mexico Collegiate Tribunals, *Novena Época*, Registry 195'846, SJF VIII, August 1998, at 838: applying Art. 2299 CC.

[30] *See* Venezuela: Aguilar Gorrondona, *supra* note 17, at 220, 221 and the Venezuelan Jurisprudence cited in the same work.

[31] Mexico Art. 2299 CC; Mexico Collegiate Tribunals, *Novena Época*, Registry 195'846, SJF VIII, August 1998, p 838; *see also* Jones & Schlechtriem, *supra* note 2, at 70, para. 110.

[32] Bolivia Art. 862 Com C.

[33] Argentina: Borda, *supra* note 27, at 229; O'Callaghan, *supra* note 17, Art. 1.467, at 1476.

the requirement of 'founded fear', which consecutively allowed the buyer to withhold payment of the price.[34]

In addition, a Mexican Collegiate Tribunal has explained that the foreseeable breach of one party's obligation is not enough, by itself, to justify the non-performance of the other party, since it is required that the breach is of such importance to leave unsatisfied the interest of the party withholding performance, taking into consideration the functional interdependence of the respective performances.[35] The Tribunal based its reasoning on the principle of good faith that aims to prevent *abuse of right* situations derived from foreseeable breaches of minor importance.

On this issue, the Peruvian Supreme Court has found, in two different occasions, that the non-performance of obligations categorised as collateral, such as the registry of the sale and the release of encumbrances, does not constitute an exception for performance of the buyer's obligation to pay the price, unless the parties had otherwise agreed,[36] all the more since the seller's main obligation was already performed.[37]

In all Ibero-American systems, the right to withhold performance also requires that the circumstances or the deterioration in the situation of the other party affecting the performance occurs subsequent to the conclusion of the contract.[38] However, the doctrine concurs that when such circumstances or deterioration existed prior to the contract, the party may still withhold performance if he ignored them at the conclusion of the contract.[39]

On the other hand, none of the Ibero-American laws contain the CISG express duty to give notice to the other party about one party's intent or actual suspension.[40] However, the same requirement should follow from the principle of good faith.[41] All the Ibero-American laws require contracts to be performed in good faith. Thus, the parties may be required to inform their counter-parts of any issue concerning the performance of the contract, if such follows from the nature of the contract, the equity or the usages.[42]

---

[34] Mexico Collegiate Tribunals, Registry 195'846, *Novena Época*, SJF VIII, August 1998, at 838: applying Art. 2299 CC.

[35] Mexico Collegiate Tribunals, *Novena Época,* Registry 183'878, SJF XVIII, July 2003, at 1061.

[36] Peru Supreme Court, *Sala civil transitoria*, Resolution 004010-2001, 17 May 2002.

[37] Peru Supreme Court, *Sala civil transitoria,* Resolution 000114-1998, 24 February 1999.

[38] *See* expressly Uruguay Art. 526 para. 2 Com C; Jones & Schlechtriem, *supra* note 2, at 63, para. 91.

[39] Argentina: G. Clusellas, *in* A. Bueres (Ed.), Código civil y normas complementarias: análisis doctrinario y jurisprudencial Art. 1419, at 601, para. 2 (1995).

[40] Art. 71(3) CISG imposes to the party who decides to exercise his right of suspension the duty to inform the other party about his intention to suspend performance.

[41] Portugal: L. De Lima Pinheiro, Dereito Comercial Internacional 323 (2005).

[42] *See* Ch. 32, 1 & 3.

1.3. Collateral Securities

As in the CISG,[43] most Ibero-American laws recognise that the party, against who the right of *exceptio* is intended to be exercised, can stop the insecurity defence by providing adequate collateral securities to the other party.[44]

1.4. Effects

If the prerequisites for the right to suspend performance are satisfied and the other party has not provided adequate collateral securities, the principle in the Ibero-American statutory laws[45] and in the jurisprudence[46] is that the party entitled to *exceptio* is not guilty of non-performance of his own obligation. In other words, that party does not breach the contract even if, and during the time in which, he has not formally invoked the exceptio.[47]

Indeed, the effects of the *exceptio* are that a party can withhold his performance until the danger to suffer the failure to counter-perform, in due manner and time, disappears.[48] This normally happens when the party corrects the deficiencies the goods, recovers his solvency, or provides adequate assurance of his performance depending on the case.[49]

---

43 Art. 71 CISG.

44 Chile Art. 147 Com C; Ecuador Art. 193 Com C; Guatemala Art. 684 Com C; Portugal Art. 468 Com C; Venezuela Art. 122 *in fine* CC. And also *in fine* of the following individual countries provisions: Argentina Art. 1419 CC; Brazil Art. 477 CC; Bolivia Arts. 576, 623, 638(1) CC; Chile Arts. 1826, 1872 CC; Colombia Arts. 1882, 1929 CC; Costa Rica Art. 1073 CC; Ecuador Arts. 1793, 1839 CC; El Salvador Arts. 1629, 1674 CC; Mexico Arts. 2287, 2299 CC; Panama Arts. 1237, 1273 CC; Paraguay Art. 720 CC; Peru Arts. 1426, 1427 CC; Portugal Art. 428(2) CC; Spain Arts. 1.467, 1.502 CC; Uruguay Art. 526 para. 2 Com C; Venezuela Arts. 1.493, 1.530 CC; Argentina: Borda, *supra* note 27, at 231; Portugal: De Lima Pinheiro, *supra* note 41, at 322.

45 Argentina Art. 510 CC; Chile Art. 1552 CC; Colombia Art. 1609 CC; Ecuador Art. 1542 CC; El Salvador Art. 1423 CC; Honduras Art. 1356 CC; Nicaragua Art. 1859 CC; Panama Art. 985 CC; Spain Art. 1.100 CC.

46 *See* Argentina National Civil Chamber, *Sala A*, LL, 1990-D-328 *cited in* Argentina: Iturraspe, *supra* note 2, Art. 1201, at 58.

47 Bolivia: Kaune Arteaga, *supra* note 4, at 157.

48 *See for example* Guatemala Art. 685 Com C: stating that the right to withhold performance does not cease even if the debtor has transferred the property of the goods retained. On this *see also* Venezuela Art. 122 para. 3 Com C.

49 Argentina: Borda, *supra* note 27, at 230; O'Callaghan, *supra* note 17, Art. 1.467, at 1476.

2. Anticipatory Breach

The Ibero-American laws do not have an independent concept of, or rules on, anticipatory breach, as it exists under the CISG.[50] Indeed, such possibility goes against the requirement of delayed performance for the avoidance of contracts referred to in chapter 47, 1 in fine. However, scholars agree on the validity of an agreement to avoid the contract, even before the time of performance, if it becomes apparent that one of the parties will not duly fulfil his obligations.[51]

CISG Article 72 establishes the following requirements. First, the foreseen breach must be fundamental under the concept established by the same CISG,[52] *e.g.* the expected non-delivery of the goods or the failure to pay the price of the goods. Second, such fundamental breach must be foreseeable, *i.e.* manifest or clear. On this, objectively known cases can include the total destruction of the seller's premises, the enactment of governmental regulations on the transfer of money abroad, the imposition of export or import embargos on the goods concerned, *etc.*[53]

[50] Paraguay: A. Sierralta Ríos, La Compraventa Internacional de Mercaderias y el Derecho Paraguayo n. 74 (2000); Portugal: De Lima Pinheiro, *supra* note 41, at 324; Jones & Schlechtriem, *supra* note 2, at 90, para. 140. CISG Art. 72 establishes that if prior to the date of performance of the contract it is clear that the other party will commit a fundamental breach of the contract, the other party may declare the contract avoided. The party who intends to avoid the contract must give reasonable notice to the other party, unless there is not time to do so or the other party has already declared that he will not perform his obligation.

[51] Paraguay: Sierralta Ríos, *supra* note 50, n. 74.

[52] Art. 25 CISG.

[53] Spain: A.-L. Calvo Caravaca, *in* L. Díez Picazo y Ponce De León (Ed.), La Compraventa Internacional de Mecaderias – Comentario sobre la Convención de Viena Art. 72, II, at 570 (1998).

CHAPTER 49

SPECIFIC PERFORMANCE

1. Specific Performance of Ordinary Obligations

Ibero-American scholars[1] and the jurisprudence[2] agree on the fact that the creditor of the contractual obligation shall first claim the specific performance or the avoidance of the contract, and subsidiary or conjunctively, may claim monetary compensation. The rule is commonly embodied in the following statutory provision of the Ibero-American laws: if one of the parties fails to fulfil his obligations, the other party may, at his choice, demand the specific performance of the obligation or the avoidance of the contract. Any of these actions may be claimed together with compensation for damages and loss of profits caused.[3] However, the aggrieved party has to prove that he had

[1] Argentina: G.A. Borda, Manual de Contratos 209 (2004); Argentina: R. Compagnucci de Caso, Contrato de Compraventa 141 (2007); El Salvador: A.O. Miranda, De la Compraventa 191 (1996); Mexico: S. León Tovar, Los Contratos Mercantiles 169, 170 (2004); Spain: A. Cabanillas Sánchez, *in* L. Díez Picazo y Ponce De León, La Compraventa Internacional de Mecaderias – Comentario sobre la Convención de Viena Art. 28, III, at 231 (1998); Uruguay: N. Rodriguez Olivera *et al.*, Manual de Derecho comercial uruguayo, v. 2: Obligaciones y contratos comerciales, t. 1: Régimen general de las obligaciones comerciales, compraventa y distribución mercantil 211 (2005); Spain: S. Herman, *Specific Performance: a Comparative Analysis*, 1 Edinburgh Law Review 1 (2003).

[2] Chile Supreme Court, RDJ, Vol. 10, Sec. 1, at 416; RDJ, Vol. 78, Sec. 2, at 1 *cited in* Chile: R. Díez Duarte, La Compraventa en el Código Civil Chileno 172 (1993); Costa Rica Supreme Court, Judgment 108, *Segunda Sala Civil*, 18 July 1989; Mexico Supreme Court, *Octava Época*, *Tercera Sala*. SJF I, p 283.

[3] Argentina Art. 1204 CC & Art. 216 Com C; Bolivia Art. 568 CC & Art. 845 Com C; Brazil Arts. 474, 475 CC; Chile Art. 1489 CC & Art. 156 Com C; Colombia Art. 1546 CC & Art. 870 Com C; Costa Rica Art. 463 Com C; El Salvador Art. 1360 CC; Ecuador Art. 1532 CC & Art. 199 Com C; Mexico Art. 1949 CC & Art. 376 Com C; Paraguay Art. 725 CC; Peru Art. 1429 CC; Portugal Arts. 817, 801(2) CC; Spain Art. 1.124 CC & Art. 330 Com C; Uruguay Art. 1431 CC & Art. 246 Com C; Venezuela Art. 1.167 CC; ICC Final Award Case No. 13127 *Lex*

performed or was ready to perform his obligations under the contract,[4] while the other party *negligently* breached his obligation under the contract.[5]

The rule is based on the civil law principle of *pacta sunt servanda.* Under this principle, the party suffering the breach of contract has, before all, the right to claim performance of the obligation contracted and not its equivalent.[6] A different approach would mean that any obligation would have a facultative character.[7] Consequently, no debtor is bound to concede the performance of an alternative obligation that was not in principle agreed.

Only when performance is impossible, or when it is possible but unreasonable, the creditor shall claim an equivalent performance,[8] namely monetary compensation.[9] For example, some laws would deny the enforced performance for cases where such is exceedingly onerous for the debtor.[10] Also a different legal remedy, such as damages, shall be granted to a buyer if the goods no longer exist, or are already the property of a third party.[11] The Bolivian Supreme Court denied specific performance in one case, instead, it declared the avoidance of a sales contract and, awarded damages to the buyer

---

Contractus Brazilian Law: the Tribunal uphold the two possibilities given by the Brazilian Law at the aggrieved party's choice; ICC Final Award Case No. 13663 *Lex Contractus* Spanish Law: the Tribunal uphold the two possibilities given by Spain Art. 1.124 CC at the aggrieved party's choice.

4 Paraguay Supreme Court, Judgment 219, 17 May 2001, *Baúl De La Felicidad S.A. v. Pony Automotores – Mitsuservice Import S.R.L.*; ICC Final Award Case No. 13882 *Lex Contractus* Spanish Law.

5 For the concept of negligence (*culpa*), its objective criteria and presumption *see* Ch. 47, 1.

6 *See* expressly stated in Paraguay Art. 557 CC: the debtor must deliver the same goods or perform the obligation that he was exactly bound to fulfil. The performance cannot be substituted with non-performance damages or by any other goods or act, regardless of the fact that these are of a similar or greater value. Similar provision in Costa Rica Art. 470 Com C; Costa Rica Supreme Court, Judgment 108, *Segunda Sala Civil*, 18 July 1989.

7 Spain: Cabanillas Sánchez, *supra* note 1, Art. 28, III, at 232; ICC Final Award Case No. 13882 *Lex Contractus* Spanish Law.

8 Expressly stated in Brazil Art. 461 CPC; Chile Art. 152 Com C; Ecuador Art. 197 Com C; Paraguay Art. 722 CC; Spain Art. 1.124 CC; Uruguay Art. 1431 CC & Art. 246 Com C; *see also* Argentina: Compagnucci de Caso, *supra* note 1, at 141.

9 Argentina Art. 471 Com C; Brazil Arts. 461, 287 CPC; Chile Art. 152 Com C; Paraguay Art. 722 CC; Uruguay Art. 544 Com C; ICC Final Award Case No. 13882 *Lex Contractus* Spanish Law: recognising the principle, though in the present case, the claimant did not prove that the specific performance was impossible, hence, the Sole Arbitrator refused to award the sum claimed as alternative compensation.

10 *See for example,* doctrinal support in Portugal and Spain: Portugal: L. De Lima Pinheiro, Dereito Comercial Internacional 293 (2005); Spain: Herman, *supra* note 1, at 1.

11 Argentina Art. 471 Com C; Chile Art. 152 Com C; Ecuador Art. 197 Com C; Uruguay Art. 544 Com C; *see also* Spain: Herman, *supra* note 1, at 1; Uruguay: Rodríguez Olivera *et al.*, *supra* note 1, at 211.

because the goods that the seller was expected to deliver were seized and auctioned by the State after the contract conclusion.[12]

1.1. Buyer's Breach

More to the point, the Ibero-American laws recognise, in favour of the seller, the remedy of specific performance.[13] If the buyer has failed to pay the price at the place and time agreed, the delay will not only generate interest in favour of the seller,[14] but it also gives the seller the right to require the buyer to pay the price due in consideration there-off or to declare the contract avoid.[15] In any case, the seller retains his right to be compensated for the damages and loss of profits caused.[16]

Also, if the buyer refuses or delays the reception of the goods, the seller may not only claim payment of the cost of deposit and care of the goods,[17] but additionally, the seller retains the right to other legal actions derived from the delayed performance, such as the specific performance plus monetary

---

[12] Bolivia Supreme Court, *Severo Vega Veizaga v. René Reyes Reyes y Rosa Rivas de Reyes,* 200003-Sala Civil-1-067.

[13] *See also* Argentina: Compagnucci de Caso, *supra* note 1, at 242; Chile: Díez Duarte, *supra* note 2, at 175; Colombia: A. Tamayo Lombana, El Contrato de Compraventa su Régimen Civil y Comercial 201 (2004); Colombia: E.G. Escobar Velez, La compraventa civil y comercial: los contratos de promesa de compraventa y la permuta 242 (1991); El Salvador: Miranda, *supra* note 1, at 283; Mexico: León Tovar, *supra* note 1, at 169, 170; Uruguay: Rodríguez Olivera *et al.*, *supra* note 1, at 214; Venezuela: J.L. Aguilar Gorrondona, Contratos y Garantias: Derecho Civil IV, 272 (2008).

[14] *See* Ch. 52, 1.

[15] Argentina Arts. 505, 3893 CC; Bolivia Arts. 636, 568 CC; Chile Arts. 1873, 1489 CC; Colombia Arts. 1930, 1546 CC; El Salvador Arts. 1675, 1360 CC; Ecuador Arts. 1840, 1532 CC; Guatemala Arts. 1825, 1535 CC; Mexico Art. 376 Com C & Arts. 2293, 1949 CC; Paraguay Arts. 763, 725 CC; Peru Arts. 1559, 1429 CC; Uruguay Art. 1731 CC; Venezuela Arts. 1527, 1.167 CC; Bolivia Supreme Court, *Sala Civil*, 6 December 2005, *Bartolomé Erland Rodríguez Álvarez v. Fabricio Ludwing Braner Ibáñez*: recognising that failure to pay the price by the buyer gives the seller the right to claim the specific performance or the avoidance of the contract, with any of them, damages; Costa Rica Supreme Court, Judgment 00212-98, *Segunda Sala Civil*, 19 August 1998: upholding that if the buyer fails to pay one of the instalments, the seller cannot sell the goods to a third party (as the buyer was already the owner with the meeting of the minds on the thing and the price), neither can the seller retained the instalment already pay, unless there is express agreement to do so by means of penalty clause or arrears, what proceeds is the specific performance or the avoidance of the contract.

[16] *See* Ch. 50.

[17] Argentina Art. 465 Com C; Bolivia Art. 846 Com C; Brazil Art. 400 CC; Chile Art. 1827 CC; Colombia Art. 1883 CC; El Salvador Art. 1630 CC; Ecuador Art. 1794 CC; Mexico Art. 2292 CC & Art. 387 Com C; Spain Art. 332 para. 3 Com C; Uruguay Art. 535 para. 2; *see also* Colombia: Escobar Vélez, *supra* note 13, at 242; El Salvador: Miranda, *supra* note 1, at 194.

compensation.[18] This has been recognised by scholarship[19] and sustained by courts.[20] The same rule would apply to the other main obligations of the buyer.

1.2. Seller's Breach

A remedy of specific performance for breach of the seller's duties is recognised in the Ibero-American laws.[21] The majority of the laws establish that if the seller does not deliver the goods at the time agreed, the buyer may claim the specific performance of the contract consisting in delivering the goods agreed, together with the compensation for damages and loss of profits.[22] Similarly, if the seller delivers a quantity of goods less than that agreed, the buyer can require the seller to deliver the rest.[23] The same rule applies to the seller's obligations to receive the price or to keep the goods in good condition until delivery.

---

[18] Argentina Art. 1430 CC; Bolivia Art. 846 Com C; Chile Arts. 1827, 1489 CC & Art. 153 Com C; Colombia Arts. 1546, 183 CC & Art. 943 Com C; Ecuador Arts. 1794, 1532 CC; El Salvador Arts. 1630, 1360 CC; Guatemala Art. 1830 CC; Paraguay Arts. 764, 725 CC; Peru Arts. 1565, 1429 CC; Spain Art. 332 Com C; Uruguay Arts. 535 para. 1, 246, 536 Com C: requires the legal interpellation of the buyer by the seller so that the buyer is effectively considered to be delayed in taking delivery; Spain Art. 1.505 CC; Venezuela Art. 1.531 CC: establishing that a refusal or the non-appearance of the buyer in due time to take delivery of the goods would amount to avoidance of the contract in the seller's benefit.

[19] *See for example* Chile: Díez Duarte, *supra* note 2, at 149; Colombia: Tamayo Lombana, *supra* note 13, at 201; Costa Rica: D. Baudrit Carrillo, Los Contratos Traslativos del Derecho Privado – Principios de Jurisprudencia 43 (2000); Peru: M. Castillo Freyre, Comentarios al contrato de compraventa: análisis detallado de los artículos 1529 a 1601 del Código Civil 170 (2002); Venezuela: Aguilar Gorrondona, *supra* note 13, at 266; Uruguay: Rodríguez Oliver, *et al.*, *supra* note 1, at 217.

[20] Spain Supreme Tribunal, 1 July 1991, *Id Cendoj:* 28079110011991101272; Chile Supreme Court, RDJ. Vol. 10, Sec. 1, at 416 *cited in* Chile: Díez Duarte, *supra* note 2, at 149.

[21] Bolivia: W. Kaune Arteaga, Curso de Derecho Civil, Contratos, Vol. 2, 133 (1996); Chile: Díez Duarte, *supra* note 2, at 147; El Salvador: Miranda, *supra* note 1, at 191-193; Venezuela: Aguilar Gorrondona, *supra* note 13, at 223; Uruguay: Rodríguez Olivera *et al.*, *supra* note 1, at 211.

[22] Argentina Art. 1412 CC & Arts. 467, 471 Com C; Bolivia Art. 622 CC & Art. 845 Com C; Chile Art. 1826 CC & Art. 156 Com C; Colombia Art. 1882 CC; El Salvador Art. 1629 CC; Ecuador Art. 1793 CC & Art. 199 Com C; Mexico Arts. 2283, 1949 CC; Peru Arts. 1549, 1429 CC; Paraguay Arts. 759, 725 CC; Spain Art. 1.096 CC & Art. 329 Com C; Uruguay Art. 1688 CC & Art. 534 Com C; Venezuela Arts. 1486, 1.167 CC; Peru Supreme Court, *Sala civil permanente,* Resolution 000119-1999, 27 March 2000: confirming that the buyer was entitled to require subsequent delivery of the goods that did not arrive at the date agreed plus damages caused by late performance.

[23] Argentina Art. 468 Com C; Chile Art. 157 Com C; Colombia Art. 927 Com C; Ecuador Art. 200 Com C; Spain Art. 330 Com C; Uruguay Arts. 537, 534 Com C.

2. Specific Performance, Substitution or Reparation of Defective Goods

The Ibero-American laws do not follow the CISG approach under which specific performance may be enforced by requiring the seller to deliver substitute goods or to repair the lack of conformity of the goods delivered.[24] In other words, the Ibero-American laws do not grant a default right to specific performance consisting of the delivery of substitute goods or the reparation of the goods affected by defects or non-conformity.[25]

As mentioned in chapter 47, if the goods received by the buyer are completely different to those agreed in the contract, one is in front of an *aliud pro alio* case. In the Ibero-American systems the delivery of completely different goods or *aliud pro alio* constitutes a breach to the obligation to deliver.[26] In such a case, the buyer may require, indeed, specific performance consisting of the delivery of the goods of the type that was originally agreed upon or may opt for the avoidance of the contract.[27]

However, if the goods delivered contain non-conformity defects, the aggrieved buyer has at his election one of the two available legal actions:[28] First, the redhibitory action (*actio redhibitoria)* which normally results in the avoidance of the contract.[29] Second, the estimatory action (*quanti minoris*) grants the buyer a remedy for the reduction of the price of the defective goods.[30] However, none of these two remedies allow the claim for the replacement or the reparation of the defective goods.

---

[24] Art. 46(2)(3) CISG.

[25] Statement sustained in Mexico: Leon Tovar, *supra* note 1, at 162.

[26] *See* in this regard Spain: E. Guardiola Sacarrera, La compraventa internacional: importaciones y exportaciones 75 (2001); Spain Supreme Tribunal, 20 November 2008, *Id Cendoj:* 28079110012008101062.

[27] Spain Supreme Tribunal, 20 November 2008, *Id Cendoj:* 28079110012008101062.

[28] In principle, the buyer can choose between the redhibitory action or the *actio quanti minoris* according to his own convenience. However, if the restitution of the goods is not possible the buyer may necessary opt for the readjustment of the price, *see for example* Bolivia Art. 633 CC; Bolivia: Kaune Arteaga, *supra* note 21, at 149; Guatemala Art. 1563 CC; Venezuela: Aguilar Gorrondona, *supra* note 13, at 259-261.

[29] However, some authors consider a mistake to characterise the redhibitory action as resolutory or rescinding action (action for the avoidance of the contract under CISG) for three main reasons: 1) there is a shorter term to exercise the action; 2) because it does not affect third party rights in good faith; 3) it does not presuppose the breach of obligations, *see* on this Venezuela: Aguilar Gorrondona, *supra* note 13, at 256.

[30] *See* express references to these two legal remedies in: Bolivia Art. 632(I) CC & Art. 849 Com C; Brazil Art. 442 CC; Chile Art. 1860 CC; Colombia Art. 1917 CC; Ecuador Art. 1827 CC; El Salvador Art. 1662 CC; Guatemala Art. 1561 CC; Mexico Art. 2144 CC; Uruguay Art. 1720 CC; Venezuela Art. 1.521 CC; and *see also* Colombia: Tamayo Lombana, *supra* note 13, at 175; El Salvador: Miranda, *supra* note 1, at 248-250; Mexico: León Tovar, *supra* note 1, at 157-160; Argentina Supreme Court, *Inversiones y Servicios S.A. v. Estado Nacional Argentino*,

Similarly, if the seller delivers goods affected by third party property rights and the buyer is defeated in trial, the Ibero-American laws grant the buyer a right of compensation against eviction.[31] The loss or deprivation suffered by the buyer is not redressed with an order for the substitution of the goods. Instead, a defeated buyer will usually be reimbursed the price of the goods and compensate for the cost of the contract conclusion, the improvements on the goods, the cost of the trial, and the increased value of the goods up to the date of the eviction.[32]

Mexican scholars have sustained that under B2B sales the lack of (quality agreed) would also constitute an ordinary breach of contract.[33] This would trigger a right to request from the seller the delivery of the goods agreed upon or to perform all the necessary acts, repairs and substitutions which are deemed necessary to redress the contract.[34]

However, the same scholar and generally the courts have recognised that, by default, the actions available against the seller, who delivers defective goods or goods affected by third party encumbrances, do not grant a right to claim the substitution or the reparation of the goods.[35] Except for the Portuguese law, where a similar CISG approach is adopted.[36] In the Portuguese law, the delivery of defective goods grants the buyer a remedy to claim for the replacement or reparation of the goods.[37]

The above being said, such does not mean that similar remedies are totally unavailable. Some Ibero-American laws expressly foresee the possibility of the parties on agreeing on a warranty clause regarding the fitness of the goods that normally gives to the buyer a remedy of reparation or substitution of the goods, plus compensation for damages.[38]

---

19 August 1999; Brazil Tribunal of Justice of the State of Rio Grande do Sul, Civil Recourse 71000950527, published 28 September 2007.

31 *See* Argentina: Compagnucci de Caso, *supra* note 1, at 153; Bolivia: Kaune Arteaga, *supra* note 21, at 139; Brazil: C.M. Da Silva Pereira, Instituçaoes de Dereito Civil, Vol. III, Contratos, Electrônica 90 (2003); Brazil: O. Gomes, Contratos 115-117 (2008); Chile: Díez Duarte, *supra* note 2, at 155.

32 *See for example*, Chile Arts. 1847, 1845, 1849, 1850, 1851 CC; Uruguay Arts. 552, 553, 554 Com C; Chile: Díez Duarte, *supra* note 2, at 156, 159, 160; *see also* Argentina: Compagnucci de Caso, *supra* note 1, at 154; Brazil: Gomes, *supra* note 31, at 115-117; Mexico: León Tovar, *supra* note 1, at 162; Venezuela: Aguilar Gorrondona, *supra* note 13, at 237, 238.

33 *See* Ch. 37, 2.3; Mexico: León Tovar, *supra* note 1, at 155.

34 Mexico: León Tovar, *supra* note 1, at 155.

35 Statement sustained in Mexico: Leon Tovar, *supra* note 1, at 162; El Salvador Tribunal Superior, RJ 1-12, January-December 1954, at 343-366, *cited in* El Salvador: Miranda, *supra* note 1, at 545.

36 Portugal: De Lima Pinheiro, *supra* note 10, at 293.

37 Portugal Arts. 817, 914 CC; Art. 46(1)(2) CISG; ICC Final Award Case No. 11367 *Lex Contractus* Portuguese Law.

38 *See for example*, Bolivia Art. 838 Com C; Costa Rica Art. 452 Com C; El Salvador Art. 1021 Com C; Paraguay Art. 753 CC; Portugal Art. 921 CC.

Moreover, the Chilean Supreme Court has sustained that when the seller has bound himself, by express agreement, to deliver the goods free of encumbrances and he fails to do so, the buyer may make resort of the remedy of specific performance or, alternatively, may claim the avoidance for ordinary breach of contractual agreements.[39] In this sense, the Chilean Supreme Court's approach could be extended to cases of defective goods. So that if the parties expressly agreed that the remedy available should not be the statutory one, but instead, the remedies available for breach of contractual obligations, or any other described remedy, the buyer may require the delivery of substitute clean goods, their reparation or the avoidance of the contract.[40]

Such possibility was actually deducted by the Argentinean National Civil Chamber, which explained that the fact that Article 2174 of the Civil Code exclusively provides for two actions – the redhibitory and the *quantity minoris*- does not imply that the buyer is not able to pursue the exact compliance of the obligation assumed by the seller when, once the goods were delivered, hidden defects arise making the goods unfit for the intended purpose or reducing considerably the use expected by the buyer.[41]

3. The Mechanism to Enforce Performance

The mechanisms to enforce performance of the seller's obligation to make delivery vary from one system to another. In addition, the attitude of the courts may be different depending on the type of goods or the circumstances of the case. In some countries, if the goods are determined and exist with no third party's encumbrance, for example a particular machine or product, a court may order the seller to give to the buyer the possession of the goods. If the seller does not comply with the judicial order, the court may make use of its powers to bind the seller to deliver the goods to the buyer.[42]

If the contract relates to generic or undetermined goods that may be available in the market, the buyer may resort to the two different options available. The buyer may demand specific performance by requiring the seller

39 Chile Supreme Court, RDJ, Vol. 2, Sec. 1, at 53 *cited in* Chile: Díez Duarte, *supra* note 2, at 303, n. 827.

40 ICC Final Award Case No. 10299 *Lex Contractus* Chilean Law: the Arbitral Tribunal sustained that only if a defect is not covered by the 'Representations and Warranties' clause, Chilean law principles on hidden defects (*vicios redhibitorios*) shall apply.

41 Argentina National Civil Chamber, *Sala* F, *González, Roberto v. Sáez, Federico C*, 7 November 2003, Lexis No. 1/1000184.

42 Argentina Art. 505 (1) CC; Portugal Art. 827 CC; *see also* Argentina: Borda, *supra* note 1, at 209; Spain: Herman, *supra* note 1, at 13.

to purchase substitute goods at the seller's expense,[43] or the buyer may acquire the goods and demand the reimbursement of the substitute goods.[44]

In other countries, the party suffering the breach may, at his election, demand: 1) that the other party performs his obligation; 2) that the court authorises him or a third party to perform the obligation due at the expenses of the breaching party; 3) that the breaching party compensates in money the breach of contract. Irrespective of the remedy elected, the suffering party has a right to be compensated for the delay in performing the obligation.[45]

Under Brazil's civil procedural code, the enforcement of specific performance or the equivalent compensation, allows the judge, by request or at his own initiative, to determine the necessary measures, such as the imposition of a fine for delay in performing, the search or seizure of the object in dispute and so on.[46] In relation to the performance consisting of the delivery of goods, the same statute establishes that the judge will fix a deadline for its fulfilment. If the obligation is not performed within the deadline established, the judge will grant an injunction for search or seizure of the goods and an order of delivery.[47]

---

43 Argentina Art. 1421 CC & Art. 467 Com C; the same rule is present in Uruguay Art. 544 Com C.

44 Argentina Art. 467 Com C; Spain Art. 1.096 CC; Argentina: Borda, *supra* note 1, at 209, 210; Argentina: Compagnucci de Caso, *supra* note 1, at 141; Spain: Herman, *supra* note 1, at 13.

45 Chile Art. 1553 CC; Colombia Art. 1610 CC; El Salvador Art. 1424 CC; Ecuador Art. 1596 CC; Peru Art. 1219 CC; *see* similar provision in Costa Rica Art. 429 Com C.

46 Brazil Art. 461 para. 5 CPC.

47 Brazil Art. 461-A para. 2 CPC.

CHAPTER 50

DAMAGES

1. General Remarks on Damages

1.1. Purposes of Damages

In the multiplicity of legal systems, contractual damages are often understood to have two different purposes. First, damages may seek to compensate the aggrieved party from the loss caused by the breach of contract. Second, damages may have the additional purpose of acting as a deterrence to or punishment for the conduct of the breaching party. The majority of the legal systems share the first purpose, including the Ibero-American laws. The second purpose operates in some Common Law systems but only in limited cases.

1.1.1. Compensation

The compensatory principle of damages is based on the assumption that there must be some injury to the interest of one of the parties to the contract, so that compensation for damages can be granted.[1] Thus, damages are based on the loss caused to the suffering party, and generally not on the gain obtained by the breaching party. If there is no loss, there is neither liability to prosecute.[2]

The function of the contractual damages in the Ibero-American system, is precisely to compensate the creditor of the obligation for the loss caused

[1] G.H. Treitel, *Remedies for Breach of Contract*, *in* A.T. von Mehren (Ed.), International Encyclopedia of Comparative Law, Vol. VII Contracts, Ch. 16, at 24, para. 42 (1999).

[2] Paraguay Supreme Court, Judgment 350, 27 June 2001, *Liberata Ibarrola Vda. De García v. Vilda Selva D'Ecclesis Y Otra.*

by the debtor's breach of contract.[3] Even in cases of late or non-performance the purpose remains the compensation of the damage caused. The Peruvian and the Portuguese Civil Codes establish that in case of late performance the creditor may refuse to claim subsequent specific performance if such is useless for him; instead, he may opt for the compensation through compensatory damages.[4]

The compensatory principle also means that damages will only be granted to one party if he can show that the loss in his patrimony resulted from the fact that the contract was not performed or performed defectively.[5] It may happen that the party has suffered loss due to different reasons despite of the fact that the contract was broken. As expressly dictated by some Ibero-American laws, there must be a causal link between the damages caused and the breach of contract.[6] The principle is presented in the Argentinean Civil Code which declares that "[I]n the compensation of the damages will only be included those that will be immediate and necessary consequence of the other party's failure to perform his obligation."[7] In other words, the duty to compensate presupposes that there is a *direct* relationship between the loss and the act that originates it.[8] And thus, a party cannot recover more than the loss directly caused by the breach.

[3] *See for example* Mexico Art. 2107 CC; Peru Art. 1321 CC; Portugal Art. 798 CC; *also* Spain: A. Soler Presas, La Valoracion del Daño en el Contrato de Compraventa 30 (1998).

[4] Peru Art. 1317 CC; Portugal Art. 808 CC.

[5] Paraguay Supreme Court, Judgment 350, 27 June 2001, *Liberata Ibarrola Vda. De García v. Vilda Selva D'Ecclesis Y Otra*; ICC Final Award Case No. 10299 *Lex Contractus* Chilean Law: explaining that in order to determine contractual liability the aggrieved party must prove that damages have ensued as a result of said breach.

[6] Argentina Art. 520 CC; Bolivia Art. 346 CC; Brazil Art. 403 CC; Mexico Art. 2110 CC; Peru Art. 1336 *in fine* CC; Uruguay Art. 223 para. 2 Com C; ICC Final Award Case No. 13685 *Lex Contractus* Paraguayan Law: upholding that the claimant may only recover the emerging damage having a causal link and direct relation with the performance of the contract. Thus, all those expenses that in the Tribunal's view do not have a casual link and are not considered related to the performance of the contract, such as expenses prior to the contract conclusion, shall not be reimbursed.

[7] Argentina Art. 520 CC.

[8] *See* Argentina Art. 901 CC: Spanish term *inmediato* in this context means *direct.*

The jurisprudence has recognised the principle.[9] In the more basic understanding the causal link means that if a party's breach of contract has not been proven, logically, the claimed damages cannot be awarded.[10]

In a strict standard of the causal principle, the Chilean Supreme Court held that the cost supposedly incurred by the buyer (natural person) to bring about the contract, *i.e.* expenses in order to repair the defective goods delivered by seller, but which were invoiced to a different entity other than the buyer, did not show that the buyer had indeed suffered the alleged incidental loss.[11]

In different circumstances though, an ICC Arbitral Tribunal granted the recovery of expenses invoiced by a subsidiary company of the claimant. In the Tribunal's point of view, although the subsidiary was not a party of the frustrated contract it certainly was involved in its performance. Thus, such expenses which show a casual link and direct relation to the performance of the contract and invoiced by the subsidiary should be reimbursed to the claimant.[12]

The casual link requirement establishes a high standard of proof that is borne by the aggrieved party. On this issue, the Peruvian Supreme Court dismissed a claim for damages since the claimant had failed to specify the specific amount demanded for each of the type of damages invoked *i.e.* emerging damage, prevented profits and non-pecuniary damages. The claimant had, instead, fixed a global amount for all the damages, a fact that the Court considered to be a clear ground for lack of causal link.[13]

The Supreme Court of Mexico has considered that the invoices of similar goods at a higher price paid by the claimant to other suppliers are not sufficient evidence of the causal relationship between breach of contract and the damages. For the Court the invoices only demonstrated that other purchases were made to other suppliers but not that they were caused by the

---

9 Brazil Tribunal of Justice of Rio de Janeiro, Appeal 2008.001.65722, published 29 January 2009: the buyer has not proven the causal link between the damages to the car and the seller's fault to comply with the contract; Mexico Collegiate Tribunals, *Novena Época,* Registry 195'143, SJF VIII, November 1998, at 555; Paraguay Supreme Court, Judgment 700, 16 December 1999, *Adalberto Walter Zierz v. Osmar Lautenschleiger E Isona Serenita Lautenschleiger*: requiring to prove the relationship between the breach and the loss caused; Peru Supreme Court, *Sala civil permanente*, Resolution 004289-2008, 6 March 2008: though breach of contract was found, the damages claimed were not linked directly and immediately to the breach of contract.

10 Mexico Supreme Court, *Quinta Época*, Registry 343989, SJF CIV, p 1652; Mexico Collegiate Tribunals, *Novena Época,* Registry 186'790, SJF XV, June 2002, p 649; ICC Final Award Case No. 10299 *Lex Contractus* Chilean Law: explaining that in order to determine contractual liability the aggrieved party must prove the breach of a contractual obligation; ICC Final Award Case No. 10044 *Lex Contractus* Portuguese Law.

11 Chile Supreme Court, *Rol* 3405-2001, (*Visto* 2), 12 August 2008.

12 ICC Final Award Case No. 13685 *Lex Contractus* Paraguayan Law.

13 Peru Supreme Court, *cass*, Resolution 001211-2005, 22 July 2005.

breach and that they intended to bring about the contract, particularly if some of the invoices were issued prior to the breach of contract.[14]

Finally, a consequence of the compensatory principle of damages is that deterring damages or punitive damages will not be awarded for breach of the contract. Subsidiary relief through punitive damages is unknown in the Ibero-American jurisdictions.

1.1.2. Deterrence

The concept and the practice of punitive damages have been developed in the common law jurisdictions, and remains unknown and unpractised in the Ibero-American systems based on the civil law tradition. Under Ibero-American laws, damages cannot be awarded to one party in order to deter the breach of future contracts by the other parties. Under many common law countries, this type of damages may be awarded in tort cases, not to compensate the suffering party but, to indicate the court's disapproval of the conduct and to punish the defendant.[15]

Indeed, even in Common Law jurisdictions the general rule is that punitive damages will not be awarded for breach of contract.[16] However, there have been casuistic exceptions. In a sales contract for example, punitive damages were granted against a party who induced the other party to buy a gelding by fraudulently representing that it was a colt.[17] In all the cases which departed from the general rule, it appears that there were tortious elements in the actions, besides the breach of contract.[18]

1.2. General Principles

1.2.1. Full Compensation

CISG Article 74 expresses the principle of full compensation with the statement "damages for breach of contract by one party consists of a sum equal to the loss, including loss of profit, suffered by the other party as a consequence

---

[14] Mexico Supreme Court, *Octava Época, Tercera Sala,* Registry 207549, SJF I, Part 1, January to June 1988, p 289.

[15] Treitel, *supra* note 1, at 25, para. 45.

[16] The principle is well established by the Uniform Commercial Code, *see* on this Treitel, *supra* note 1, at 26, para. 45.

[17] *See Grandi v. Le Sage*, 74 N.M. 799, 399 P2d 285 (1965) *in* Treitel, *supra* note 1, at 26, para. 45, n. 216.

[18] Treitel, *supra* note 1, at 26, para. 45.

of the breach."[19] The creditor has a right to be fully compensated for all the disadvantages suffered by the breach of contract.[20]

The full compensation principle is also expressed in the Ibero-American statutory laws.[21] Also the jurisprudence has acknowledged that the aggrieved party shall be compensated for the direct damage caused and the loss of profits due to the debtor's failure to duly perform his obligations.[22]

Full compensation covers possible forms of damages as result of breach such as non-performance loss, consequential loss, incidental loss, as well as loss of profits. These forms are briefly presented in the said order.

1.2.1.1. Forms of Damages

First, non-performance loss may occur when the creditor of the obligation takes reasonable measure to bring about the situation which would have existed if the contract had been duly perform, and to recover the cost of doing so from the debtor.[23] An example of this can be found in a decision from the Chilean Supreme Court that explained that the cost of importing replacement parts by the buyer in order to repair a machine sold by seller could have been deducted from the price of the goods, in order to compensate the incorrect performance.[24]

Second, incidental loss includes expenses incurred by the creditor of the obligation, not related with his expectation interest, but rather incurred to prevent any additional disadvantage, for example, the seller's expenses for taking care of or storing the goods in vain, costs incurred while arranging

[19] I. Schwenzer, *in* I. Schwenzer (Ed.), Schlechtriem & Schwenzer Commentary on the UN Convention on the International Sale of Goods Art. 74, para. 2, at 1000 (2010).

[20] *Id.*, Art. 74, para. 3, at 1000.

[21] Compensation may be granted for both the loss suffered and the profits prevented: Argentina Art. 519 CC; Bolivia Art. 344 CC & Art. 845 Com C; Brazil Art. 402 CC; Chile Art. 1556 CC; Colombia Art. 1613 CC; Ecuador Art. 1599 CC; El Salvador Art. 1427 CC; Mexico Arts. 2108, 2109 CC; Paraguay Art. 450 CC; Peru Art. 1321 CC; Spain Art. 1.106 CC; *see also* Bolivia: G. Castellanos Trigo & S. Auad La Fuente, Derecho de las Obligaciones en el Código Civil Boliviano 153-155 (2008); Spain: M. Medina de Lemus, Derecho Civil: Obligaciones y Contratos II, Contratos en Particular, Vol. 2, 152 (2004).

[22] ICC Final Award Case No. 13127 *Lex Contractus* Brazilian Law; Bolivia Supreme Court, *Sala Civil*, *Carlos Maida y Celinda Pinto de Maida v. Osvaldo Trigo Arispe*: noting that may not only be recovered the loss directly caused but also the lost profit that is an immediate consequence of the breach; Chile Supreme Court, No. 4303-05 (*Visto* 4), 24 de Julio 2007; Spain Supreme Tribunal, 05 June 2008, *Id Cendoj:* 28079110012008100535.

[23] Schwenzer, *supra* note 19, Art. 74, para. 21-26, at 1006-1008; Portugal Supreme Tribunal of Justice, *Revista* 2015/05, Rapporteur Justice: Silva Salazar, published 5 July 2005: in the case at hand, the immovable goods subject to the contract presented some defects that required the buyers to undertake several repairs. The Court then decided that the seller must compensate such expenses and also the Court awarded the buyer with non-pecuniary damages.

[24] Chile Supreme Court, *Rol* 3405-2001, (*Visto* 1), 12 August 2008.

the payment method, *etc.*[25] For example, an ICC Arbitral Tribunal granted damages to the seller related to out of pocket and opportunity costs incurred in warehousing and maintaining some finished products, the purchase-order for which had been cancelled by the buyer. The Tribunal found that the buyer, which breached the agreement by cancelling the orders, may not take advantage of the seller's first offer for free storage.[26] Moreover, the fact that the seller had space to store the products was irrelevant for the Tribunal since "[...] Space is precious in any business and has a cost."[27]

Third, consequential loss includes additional losses beyond the non-performance, such as the creditor's liability *vis a vis* third parties as a result of the breach, or harm caused to a third person or his patrimony due to defects of quality.[28] Finally, loss of profits is any increase in the assets which the creditor reasonably expected and that were prevented because of the breach of contract.[29]

1.2.1.2. Currency

A usual question regarding the principle of full compensation is whether the monetary compensation shall be granted in the currency established by the contract or in the currency in which the cost or loss was incurred. In an interesting decision of the Peruvian Supreme Court, it was established that the compensation of damages in foreign currency is available to the aggrieved party as far as such was the intention of the parties in their agreement. But in absence of such implied or expressed agreement, compensation for damages shall be calculated in national currency which, in the case at hand, was the national currency under the Peruvian law (applicable law).[30]

For the Spanish Supreme Tribunal, damages do not have to be paid in the currency agreed for payment of the price; as such agreement does not automatically extend to the recoverable damages.[31]

As to the damages compensating costs and expenses, an ICC Arbitral Tribunal has sustained that as a rule these must be awarded in the currency in which costs and expenses have been incurred.[32] The rule obeys to the

---

25 ICC Final Award Case No. 14024 *Lex Contractus* Spanish Law: the Sole Arbitrator admitted the claim for the rental cost of the buyer's premises where the goods were stored because the buyer extended the said rent from April to June as he reasonably expected that the supply agreement would continue for such time, although the seller did not supply the goods during such period.

26 ICC Final Award Case No. 11256 *Lex Contractus* Mexican Law.

27 *Id.*

28 Schwenzer, *supra* note 19, Art. 74, para. 32, at 1012.

29 *Id.*, Art. 74, para. 36, at 1014.

30 Peru Supreme Court, *cass*, Resolution 002454-2000, 12 January 2001.

31 Spain Supreme Tribunal, 12 May 1990, *Id Cendoj:* 28079110011990101070.

32 ICC Final Award Case No. 11404 *Lex Contractus* Argentinean Law.

full compensation principle. Nevertheless, a different ICC Arbitral Tribunal granted the currency conversion of expenses awarded as damages on the basis that the aggrieved party had so requested and the breaching party did not raise any objection to it.[33]

1.2.2. Overcompensation

One of the consequences of the compensatory principle is that there should not be overcompensation of the injury suffered. The compensation should not enrich the party suffering the breach.[34] In other words, the party who suffers the breach cannot recover more than his loss. Consequently, for example, no damages are recoverable if the party bringing the claim has suffered no loss.[35] Unless compensation had previously been agreed to by the parties in the form of a fixed sum, so that the aggrieved party is not bound to prove loss.[36]

1.2.3. Non-Pecuniary Damages

Some Ibero-American laws concede to the aggrieved party the possibility of awarding non-pecuniary damages[37] caused by the breach of contract.[38] While doing so, regard is to be had to the circumstances which generated the liability of the breaching party and other general circumstances of the case.[39]

An interesting provision of Mexico's Civil Code illustrates a specific situation. The judge may not take into consideration the affective price of the goods while calculating the amount of damages, unless it is proven that the debtor destroyed or damaged the goods with the intention of hurting the feelings or the affection that the owner had on them.[40] In addition, a related provision establishes that the increase of the compensation due to moral damages will be determined considering the injured rights, the degree of liability, the economic situation of the offender and the victim, and other related circumstances.[41]

The Spanish jurisprudence has also recognised the duty to compensate the non-pecuniary damages derived from breach of contractual obligations.[42] The Spanish Supreme Tribunal held that in principle mere annoyance, boredom

---

33 ICC Final Award Case No. 13685 *Lex Contractus* Paraguayan Law.

34 Treitel, *supra* note 1, at 25, para. 44.

35 *Id.*, at 26, para. 46.

36 *See infra* 5.1.1.

37 These are commonly known under the Spanish term of *daño moral*.

38 *See for example*, Argentina Art. 522 CC; Mexico Arts. 2116, 1916 CC; Paraguay Art. 451 CC; Peru Art. 1322 CC.

39 *See for example*, Argentina Art. 522 CC; Mexico Arts. 2116, 1916 CC; Paraguay Art. 451 CC.

40 Mexico Art. 2116 CC.

41 Mexico Art. 1916 CC.

42 *See* the series of court decisions *cited in* Spain: Medina de Lemus, *supra* note 21, at 153.

and anger caused by the breach of a contractual agreement are not sufficient to produce a *moral* damage. However, the same court recognised that situations producing grave affliction or perturbation of an entity derived from hours of annoyance, boredom and anger may amount to non-pecuniary damage.[43]

A Portuguese Supreme Tribunal sustained in one case, that the seller's delay to supply the shoes agreed to negatively affected the buyer's reputation so that the buyer was entitled to damages that comprised both pecuniary and non-pecuniary losses.[44] Similarly, the Portuguese Supreme Tribunal awarded compensation to a buyer based on the damages to its brand caused by defective goods supplied by the seller which caused the buyer to take its products out of the market for 6 months. The Tribunal stated that this forced absence from the market and the fact the company was not able to fulfil 99 deliveries harmed its reputation, giving rise to non-pecuniary damages.[45] Nevertheless, when the regular exercise of the rights under a contract give rise to moral damages, they cannot be claimed by the party. However, when in the framework of the contract such damages result from an illicit act they need to be compensated.[46]

Finally, other Ibero-American laws expressly deny the possibility to compensate the moral damages derived from breach of contractual duties.[47]

1.2.4. Loss of Goodwill

Pecuniary damages caused by the loss of goodwill are compensated by CISG article 74.[48] The recovery of loss of goodwill is supported by the full compensation principle. Nevertheless, the difficulties in establishing a shared notion of goodwill also makes difficult to prove and measure the pecuniary loss covered under such notion. As commented by the CISG-AC

> [L]oss of goodwill can simply refer to a loss of future lost profits. Loss of goodwill also has been defined as a decline in business reputation or commercial image, quantified by the retention of customers ... [B]ecause there is no uniform definition, some tribunals have required a higher level of proof for damages resulting from a loss of goodwill.[49]

---

43 Spain Supreme Tribunal, 31 May 2000, *Id Cendoj:* 28079110002000100800.

44 Portugal Supreme Tribunal of Justice, *Revista* 2411/04, Rapporteur Justice: Azevedo Ramos, published 30 September 2004.

45 Portugal Supreme Tribunal of Justice, *Revista* 1526/05, Rapporteur Justice: Ferreira Girão, published 22 June 2005.

46 Portugal Supreme Tribunal of Justice, *Revista* 2402/04, Rapporteur Justice: Moitinho de Almeida, published 23 September 2004.

47 *See for example* Ecuador Art. 1599 CC.

48 CISG-AC, Opinion No. 6, Calculation of Damages under CISG Article 74. Rapporteur: Professor John Y. Gotanda, Villanova University School of Law, Villanova, Pennsylvania, USA, Comment 7.1.

49 *Id.*, Comment 7.3.

The Supreme Tribunal of Portugal has been developing the right to compensate the loss of goodwill.[50] An ICC Arbitral Tribunal referring to the jurisprudence developed by the Portuguese Supreme Tribunal explained how the loss of clients may be compensated in situations where suppliers terminate the distributorship agreement and subsequently take over the clientele developed by the distributor: under the Portuguese law "clients' compensation is due according to the benefits that the supplier continues to obtain by dealing with the customers acquired by the distributor;"[51] so that even if the distributor sustains no damage, the supplier is still enriched, and compensation is justified.[52]

An ICC Sole Arbitrator has followed that same approach to compensate the loss of goodwill caused by the principal's breach to his sales agent.[53] The Sole Arbitrator explained that according to the Portuguese law of agency (which also applies to the distributorship contact),[54]

> [w]ithout prejudice of the indemnities for breach of contract, the agent may be entitled to a goodwill indemnity if the requirements set out in article 33 of the Agency Law are complied with.[55]

The Sole Arbitrator was satisfied that the requirement established by the Portuguese Law was met since the witness evidence and non-controverted accountancy figures indicate that the agent had effectively (1) obtained new clients for the principal during the eighteen years of its agency and, (2) substantially increased its turnover (although these two requirements are alternative, not cumulative, in Article 33(1)(a)). In addition, there was no doubt that (3) the principal benefited considerably, after the termination of the contract, from the activity carried out by its former agent, as he found himself in a position to negotiate directly with agents and members of the industry who had been previous clients of the agent. Finally, (4) it was not denied that the former agent, stopped receiving any remuneration from the clients he obtained.[56]

---

50 Portugal Supreme Tribunal of Justice, 4 May 1994 (P.83 376) "*A indemnizaçao de clientela e devida na concessao pelos benefícios que o principal continua a auferir pela clientela angariada.*"; Portugal Supreme Tribunal of Justice, 23 April 1998: "*Masmesmo que o agente nao sofra danos, haverá um enriquecimento do concedente que legitima e justifica a comensaçao.*".

51 ICC Final Award Case No. 10818 *Lex Contractus* Portuguese Law.

52 *Id.*

53 ICC Final Award Case No. 12853 *Lex Contractus* Portuguese Law.

54 Portugal Art. 33 Decree Law No. 118/93.

55 *Id.*

56 ICC Final Award Case No. 12853 *Lex Contractus* Portuguese Law.

1.2.5. Partial Non-Performance

As has been reviewed *supra* 1.2.1., the endorsement of the creditor's positive interest on the contract is guaranteed in the Ibero-American laws, regardless of the remedy or principal legal action undertaken. The creditor can opt for the specific performance, or the avoidance of the contract, or the reduction of the price, besides the recovery of damages to which he is entitled.[57]

Accordingly, some Ibero-American laws expressly state that damages can emerge either because the obligation has not been fulfilled, or it has been imperfectly or partially fulfilled, or it has been fulfilled with delay.[58] But logically, the amount of damages may differ depending on whether the creditor has been able to retain or to recover some of the value of his performance.[59] Hence, the laws may limit the recovery of the damages. Such has been recognised in the Peruvian Civil Code according to which the recovery of the damage may be reduced depending on the gravity or importance of the deriving consequences.[60] In the rest of the systems the principle has been developed by the jurisprudence[61] and is also implied from the rules on penalty clauses which limit the extent of the penalty depending on the degree of non-performance and the gravity of the failure to comply.[62]

2. Protected Interests

While measuring the extent of compensation, the law, the doctrine and the jurisprudence normally take a particular position between: on the hand one, restoring the economical situation that existed as if the contract had never been concluded, and; on the other hand, compensating the economical situation

[57] *See* Ch. 47.

[58] Argentina Art. 508 CC (impliedly stated); Bolivia Arts. 849, 850 Com C: granting damages for delay in the delivery of the goods bought by the buyer; Chile Art. 1556 CC; Colombia Art. 1613 CC & Art. 943 Com C; Ecuador Art. 1599 CC; El Salvador Art. 1427 CC; Mexico Art. 2112 CC; Portugal Arts. 802, 803 CC; Uruguay Art. 219 Com C.

[59] Spain: Soler Presas, *supra* note 3, at 82; Spain: Medina de Lemus, *supra* note 21, at 157; Paraguay Supreme Court, 27 December 2002, *Olegario Farrés y Otra v. Bancoplus S.A.I.F.*

[60] Peru Art. 1326 CC; Portugal Art. 803 CC.

[61] In case of late performance, the creditor is only allowed to claim the damages and loss of profits caused by the delayed performance, and remains bound to perform his obligation. Thus, the legally available damages are the delay damages and not the compensatory damages see: Mexico Supreme Court, *Quinta Epoca, Tercera Sala*, SJF LXXXVIII, p. 2590; Spain Supreme Tribunal, 21 December 1998, *Id Cendoj:* 28079110001998100061. Nevertheless, in some countries the aggrieved party may prove that the delay in payment has caused him more damages than the interests generated so that a supplementary compensation is granted: Portugal Art. 806 (3) CC; Mexico Collegiate Tribunals, *Novena Época*, Registry 174887, SJF XXIII, June 2006, at 1164.

[62] *See infra* 5.1.1.

that the party who suffered the breach would have if the contract had been properly fulfilled.[63] The first approach is known under the name of *reliance interest or negative interest*, while the second approach is known by the name of *expectation interest or positive interest.*

In the next paragraphs, both approaches, as well as the position that the Ibero-American laws have taken while measuring the extent of compensation due to cases of breach of contract, will be examined.

2.1. Reliance Interest

Under this approach, damages are calculated in order to restore the economic position that the creditor of the obligation had before the contract conclusion.[64] This is done by compensating him for expenses or other losses incurred in reliance of the contract.[65] In the context of *pre-contractual* liability, such approach is followed by the Ibero-American laws.[66] The affected party who had already incurred in some expenses in reliance of the negotiations and with views of reaching an agreement shall be compensated in the amount of money representing such expenses, and for the loss derived from other business opportunities missed in reliance of the expected contract.

However, in the context of contracts already concluded and never or defectively performed this approach is not followed by Ibero-American law. It is understood that the creditor has no interest to go back to the situation he had before the conclusion of the contract.[67] He rather has an interest to continue with the deal and to have the contract fully performed, so that the expected benefits of the business are reached.

2.2. Expectation Interest

Compensating the aggrieved party for loss of his expectation interest requires putting him into as good a financial position as that in which he would have been if the contract has been duly performed.[68] This interest is referred to in Ibero-American law as *interés positivo* or positive interests in the conclusion

[63] Spain: Soler Presas, *supra* note 3, at 82.
[64] *Id.*, at 82.
[65] Treitel, *supra* note 1, at 28, para. 50.
[66] About this *see* Ch. 28, 2.
[67] Conversely, in situations of invalidity or voidability of the contract the aggrieved party may indeed have an interest to go back to the situation he had before the conclusion of the contract and for such a reason the damages recovered are in reliance, *see* Ch. 24, 4.
[68] Treitel, *supra* note 1, at 27, para. 49.

of the contract; it guarantees that the creditor will obtain the economic benefits that would normally have been obtained through the performance of the contract.[69]

2.2.1. *Dannum Emergen*s and *Lucrum Cesans*

Following the same concept, it is not difficult to distinguish that two different expectations can arise, first, that of receiving the performance due in consideration; second, that of making a profit with the performance promised. For example, a merchant who buys a particular product for resale purposes will expect both: to get the products bargained for and to resell them at a profitable price.

The distinction between these two kinds of expectations is drawn by many civil law systems,[70] including the Ibero-American systems. A common rule in the Ibero-American laws dictates that compensation for damages may include the value of the direct damage caused and the loss of profits incurred by the creditor, due to the debtor's failure to perform duly his obligations.[71] In other words, damages may result in the decrease of the creditor's patrimony whether because of the loss suffered, known under the Latin term of *dannum emergens,* or whether because of the hindered profits, better known under the Latin term *lucrum cesans*.[72]

This approach is endorsed by many legal systems aiming to promote the conclusion of agreements.[73] Particularly in B2B sales where the law seeks to guarantee the benefits of the contract by conceding an amount of damages that would also take into consideration the parallel business opportunities failed because of the breach of contract.[74]

On this issue, the Argentinean Supreme Court has acknowledged that the deprivation of the goods allocated to a particular use gives rise to a loss of profits claim. This is even clearer in cases where the goods are used for a commercial activity, and such activity supposes an aim of profits that cannot be ignored.[75] The Brazilian Supreme Court stated that a unilateral breach of

[69] *See* definition of protected interests in Spain Supreme Tribunal, 5 June 2008, *Id Cendoj:* 28079110012008100535.

[70] Treitel, *supra* note 1, at 29, para. 51.

[71] Argentina Art. 519 CC; Bolivia Art. 344 CC & Art. 845 Com C; Brazil Art. 402 CC; Chile Art. 1556 CC; Colombia Art. 1613 CC; Ecuador Art. 1599 CC; El Salvador Art. 1427 CC; Mexico Arts. 2108, 2109 CC; Paraguay Art. 450 CC; Peru Art. 1321 CC; Spain Art. 1.106 CC; Uruguay Art. 222 Com C.

[72] Spain: Medina de Lemus, *supra* note 21, at 152; Treitel, *supra* note 1, at 29, para. 51; ICC Final Award Case No. 13127 *Lex Contractus* Brazilian Law.

[73] Spain: Soler Presas, *supra* note 3, at 82.

[74] Awarding damages for the loss in the volume of sales Spain Supreme Tribunal, 5 June 2008, *Id Cendoj:* 28079110012008100535.

[75] Argentina Supreme Court, *Expreso Hada S.R.L. v. San Luis, Provincia de y otros*, 28 May 2002.

contract before the stipulated deadline in the context of a commercial relation requires a compensation for loss of profits.[76] The same position has been sustained by other courts of the region.[77]

2.2.2. Lost Sales Volume

The Spanish Supreme Tribunal has recognised the loss of profits in a lost-volume-of-sales situation.[78] In a case concerning the sale of street cleaning machines, the buyer failed to perform its obligation to pay the price. A second instance tribunal upheld that lost profits could not possibly be awarded since the seller had resold the machine to another buyer and he had not proven that such a sale had been passed at a lower price than the one contracted with the breaching buyer. Thus, if the seller resold the goods at the same or higher price it was assumed that the seller suffered no damages. The Supreme Tribunal acknowledged that usually the seller's damages are measured by the difference between the contract price and the price at which the goods can be resold in the market.[79] However, in the case at stake, the seller diary sold his products to multiple buyers, which caused that the second transaction could not be considered a substitute for the first, but simply a second sale. Therefore, damages measured under the traditional formula would not be adequate to compensate the expectation interest and the aggrieved party should be able to recover damages for lost sales volume; which meant that damages should be awarded for the prevented profit of that sale.[80]

2.2.3. Limits

The positive interests of the creditor on the contract must be reasonable.[81] It may occur that the creditor had made unreasonable expenses or investments in relation to the contract or that his expectations on the performance of the contract are also unreasonable.[82] In such a case, the limitation known under the name of *quantum respondatur* impedes that the creditor is compensated for his failures or incorrect expectations.[83]

Another limitation to the debtor's liability is found in the principle requiring a causal link between the damages caused and the breach of contract. Such

[76] Brazil Superior Tribunal of Justice, REsp 704384/MG, Minister Ari Pargendler, published 1 April 2008.

[77] Chile Supreme Court, *Rol* 3405-2001, (*Visto* 1), 12 August 2008: *contrario sensus*.

[78] Spain Supreme Tribunal, 5 June 2008, *Id Cendoj*: 28079110012008100535.

[79] *See infra* 3.1.

[80] Spain Supreme Tribunal, 5 June 2008, *Id Cendoj*: 28079110012008100535.

[81] Spain: Soler Presas, *supra* note 3, at 82.

[82] Spain: Medina de Lemus, *supra* note 21, at 154.

[83] Spain: Soler Presas, *supra* note 3, at 82.

principle is recognised in both the CISG[84] and the Ibero-American laws.[85] The breaching party is only liable for the damages incurred by his failure to duly perform the contract.[86]

Also the requirement of foreseeability plays an important role in limiting the extent of the debtor's liability. As developed below, it has been upheld that damages that the party in breach of the contract shall compensate are those that are foreseeable or that the breaching party ought to have foreseen.[87]

3. Calculation of Damages

Once it is established the extent of recoverable damages that may be awarded to the aggrieved party, the following step is to deploy a method to translate such damages into money terms. There are two different ways of calculating the amount of damages aiming to compensate the expectation interest; *i.e.* of calculating the economic situation that the party who suffered the breaching conduct would have if the contract had been properly fulfilled. The amount of damages can be calculated either in *concreto* or in *abstracto*.

As some scholars have already commented, it is perfectly possible for an aggrieved party to be entitled to concrete calculation of emerging damage and to abstract calculation of loss of profits.[88] In addition, it should be noticed that neither method of calculation limits the amount of recovery, which according to the full compensation principle may also include the incidental loss or the consequential loss.[89]

3.1. Concrete Calculation

The concrete method of determination of the monetary amount of emerging damages and lost profits is the starting point in many legal systems,[90] including the Ibero-American ones. The compensable loss requires being real and effective. Such means that merely hypothetical or eventual loss that is not

---

84 Schwenzer, *supra* note 19, Art. 74, para. 40, at 1015.
85 *See for example* Argentina Art. 520 CC; Mexico Art. 2110 CC.
86 *See supra* 1.1.
87 *See infra* 4.
88 Treitel, *supra* note 1, 50, para. 72.
89 *Id.*, at 45, para. 69.
90 *Id.*, at 44, para. 69.

certain that will happen, are not compensable.[91] However, this requirement does not exclude the possibility to compensate for the future loss, which has not happened, provided there is no doubt that it will occur.[92]

Regarding compensation for non-performance loss, where the seller fails to deliver the goods, the concrete method of calculating the emerging damages will take into consideration the actual cost incurred by the buyer in procuring substitute goods.[93] In a case of a buyer's failure to take delivery and to pay the price of the goods, the concrete method of calculation will look to the amount of money for which the seller has actually resold the goods.[94]

Also a concrete calculation approach can be taken in order to asses the amount of recoverable loss of profits. This means the amount of gain that the creditor of the obligation would have been able to make with the subject matter of the promised performance.[95]

---

[91] Argentina Supreme Court, *Serradilla, Raúl Alberto v. Mendoza, Provincia de y otro,* 12 June 2007: there is no place for a claim of expenses which have not been duly demonstrated or that result from mere speculations; Costa Rica Supreme Court, Judgment 082-01, 25 November 2005: compensation for loss of profits may only take place when such is based in a real and existing situation at the moment the harm occurred; Mexico Supreme Court, *Quinta Epoca, Tercera Sala*, SJF XCVI, p 951: the amount of loss of profits is determined by the licit profit that the creditor should have obtained *in concreto* and not by the profit that he could simple have obtained *in abstracto*; Paraguay Supreme Court, 27 December 2002, *Olegario Farrés y Otra v. Bancoplus S.A.I.F.*: loss of profits cannot consist of hypothetical of revenues. The compensable loss requires being real and effective.

[92] Chile Supreme Court, No. 4303-05, 24 de Julio 2007.

[93] Treitel, *supra* note 1, at 44, para. 69; *see* expressly Venezuela Art. 142 para. 4 Com C: but the substitute purchase shall be at the regular-current price of the trade concerned and notice of the substitute transaction to the other party is required under the law; ICC Final Award Case No. 13478 *Lex Contractus* Venezuelan Law: noting that "[A]rticle 142 of the Venezuelan Commercial Code provides that if a seller breaches its obligations to sell, then a buyer has the right to go into the market place and purchase the goods there, and is entitled to claim damages from the seller including the difference in price."

[94] *See* expressly Venezuela Art. 142 para. 3 Com C: but the substitute sale shall be at the regular-current price of the trade concerned and notice to the other party of the substitute transaction is required under the law; Treitel, *supra* note 1, at 44, para. 69.

[95] Treitel, *supra* note 1, at 50, para. 72; ICC Final Award Case No. 13478 *Lex Contractus* Venezuelan Law: as a consequence of the seller's breach of the supply contract, the buyer was forced to seek alternative sources of Boscan oil suitable for refining asphalt at his refinery. Because seller's monopoly over the Boscan oil, the buyer was forced to purchase replacement oil. The buyer was also at the mercy of then current market prices and was not in the position to conclude long term arrangements which would likely have represented a better value. The replacement oil was purchased at higher prices than Boscan oil under the sales agreement and yielded less asphalt, which caused the buyer to make less profits with the same amount of crude. The Tribunal awarded the difference on money between the profits the buyer made on a barrel of alternate crude based on its actual cost and yield in comparison to the Boscan yields at the cost agreed under the contract.

As to the seller's recoverable profits, the Spanish Supreme Tribunal explained that in case of buyer's breach to pay the price of fungible goods, the prevented profits to the seller are determined by the difference between the price agreed and the lower price at which the seller was able to resell the goods.[96]

With precise figures, an ICC Arbitral Tribunal took into consideration the following elements in the calculation of the seller's lost profits caused by the buyer's cancellation of 208 purchase-orders. First, the Arbitral Tribunal fixed the gross sales' revenues that the seller could had made for 208 orders USD 4,200,352 (based on the gross sales revenues actually taken from previous orders). To such amount the following elements were subtracted: costs of materials USD 2,960,256; Direct and indirect costs of labour USD 179,296; other variable costs USD 114,608; Warranty and insurance USD 104,978; Delivery costs USD 109,200. Based on the mathematical result of such calculation the Tribunal upheld that the seller was entitled to an amount of USD 732,014 for loss of profit as damages.[97]

Equally, the Peruvian Supreme Court supported the decision of the Superior Court of Lima which had calculated the recoverable seller's lost profits caused by a buyer who failed to purchase the total number of goods agreed. The Tribunal considered the difference between the number of orders agreed for that year and those actually made by the buyer during the year of breach. The result was later multiplied by the percentage of profits actually obtained in the previous year according to accounting documents and witness experts reports, but discounting from such amount the cost production and administrative expenses that the seller had saved.[98]

As to the buyer's recoverable profits, in a case known by the Paraguayan Supreme Court, a seller and a buyer entered into a ten-year supply of goods contract. Some time after the second year of performance, the seller unjustifiably stopped the supply of the products. The Court found the seller in breach of his contractual duties and declared the avoidance of the contract in favour of the buyer. In order to establish the profits prevented, the Court agreed on basing the recoverable compensation on the percentage of profits obtained in the previous year before the buyer filed his claim. Such percentage was obtained by calculating the difference between the price paid for the goods and the total value of the resales made during that year, less the administrative expenses.[99]

In a dispute relating to a non-exclusive supply of goods agreement submitted to an ICC Arbitral Tribunal, the buyer claimed that his supplier (seller) had failed to supply him with the volume of products he was entitled to

---

[96] Spain Supreme Tribunal, 27 October 1992, *Id Cendoj:* 28079110001992100296.

[97] ICC Final Award Case No. 11256 *Lex Contractus* Mexican Law.

[98] Peru Supreme Court, *Sala civil permanente,* Resolution 005139-2007, 18 March 2008.

[99] Paraguay Supreme Court, Judgment 1313, 20 December 2007, *Casa Gagliardi Y Otro v. Firma Unilever Capsa Del Paraguay S.A.*

under the agreement, while giving to the buyer's competitors a most favoured treatment in the buyer's detriment.[100] The Tribunal found the supplier (seller) liable for the alleged breach of the non-exclusive supply of goods agreement. In the determination of the buyer's lost profits the Tribunal took into account the additional revenues that buyer could have obtained if he had received at least the supply of the products prognosticated by the agreement during the supplier's breach period. The Tribunal took the percentage of revenues that the buyer had in previous occasions obtained in reselling the products, and multiplied such percentage by the number of units the buyer was entitled to acquire during the specific period, less the cost of the resale that the buyer saved.[101]

3.2. Abstract Calculation

This method gives the value that the performance of the obligation would have according with the market.[102] Certainly, in a case of a seller who fails to deliver the goods, the abstract method of calculating the damages to the buyer will take into consideration the market price at which substitute goods could be obtained.[103] In a case of a buyer's failure to take delivery and to pay the price of the goods, the abstract method of calculation will look to the market price of the goods at which they could have been sold.[104] Where the abstract method is used, the damages are recoverable even if no substitute transaction has been performed.[105]

In Spain, the Supreme Tribunal, in cases of avoidance of contract for breach of the seller's duty to deliver the goods, has mainly sustained that the market substitution price is the general criteria to estimate the amount of damages.[106] The same is calculated by subtracting the cost of acquiring analogous goods available in the market from the price of the goods in the contract.

In addition, an abstract calculation can be made to asses the amount of money to compensate the loss of profits. This amounts to the gain that the creditor of the obligation would have been able to make with the subject matter of the promised performance.[107] The buyer may have bought goods in order to resell them or make a service with them, and the goods may have

---

[100] ICC Final Award Case No. 11853 *Lex Contractus* Mexican Law.

[101] *Id.*

[102] Spain: Soler Presas, *supra* note 3, at 82.

[103] Treitel, *supra* note 1, at 44, para. 69.

[104] *Id.*

[105] *Id.*, at 45, para. 69.

[106] *See* Spain Supreme Tribunal Judgments of 26 January 1978 on the sale of wine; 16 March 1975 on the sale of pork; 16 and 18 March 1977, on the sale of cereals, all *cited in* Spain: Soler Presas, *supra* note 3, at 107, 108, n. 56.

[107] Treitel, *supra* note 1, at 50, para. 72.

never been delivered or are delivered with defects, and as a consequence the buyer is unable to satisfy one or several sub-buyers or clients. An abstract calculation would give the buyer the money he could have obtained while exploiting the conforming goods in the market.

This method is generally rejected in Ibero-American law.[108] An interesting decision of the Chilean Supreme Court has confirmed this view.[109] The facts were as follows: The claimant declared that the machine bought to the defendant remained in reparation works for more than three months. The claimant further alleged that each work hour of a machine of the same type has a value in the market of $19.000- $25.000 and that is a usage that such machines are only rented for a minimum of 534 hours per month. Thus, according to the claimant the amount of profits he was prevented from receiving was $ 9.423.173. In order to support his claim the claimant submitted to the Court the declaration of two witnesses and an expert's report, and other market quotations for the rent of similar machines he had carried out himself. After considering these facts and the evidence of the case, the Supreme Court confirmed the decision of the appellate court. The Court held that the evidence did not prove the amount of the loss of profits; the claimant did not prove that the machine had been used, that its productivity was based on a hourly rate, that the amount of income that it generated, and that would have been prevented, was due to the defects of the machine. The Court sustained that the witnesses' declarations were rejected since they referred to a hypothetical form of leasing of a similar machine in the market and its value, but they do not witness that the machine was performing or was intended to perform that service before the machine was broken and the income that such generated.[110]

On the other hand, an ICC Arbitration Tribunal applying the Mexican law to a supply agreement of managerial services was prepared to abstractly determine the claimed loss of profits. The Arbitral Tribunal found the respondent liable for the unlawful termination in the first year of a ten year contract, and found the claimant to be entitled to the profits that he would have been able to earn if the respondent had not frustrated the agreement. However, the determination of the actual amount required making certain projections and assumptions on, for example, Rooms-Average-Annual-Occupancy-Average-Room-Rate. An expert's report presented by the claimant forecasted the claimant's financial results using comparable industry data for the damages period. The Tribunal found the economic assumptions used in the expert's report reasonable and agreed with the projections of the report regarding the Hotel's performance.

[108] *See for example*, Argentina Supreme Court, *Serradilla, Raúl Alberto v. Mendoza, Provincia de y otro,* 12 June 2007; Chile Supreme Court, No. 4303-05, 24 de Julio 2007; Mexico Supreme Court, *Quinta Época, Tercera Sala*, SJF XCVI, p. 951; Paraguay Supreme Court, 27 December 2002, *Olegario Farrés y Otra v. Bancoplus S.A.I.F.*

[109] Chile Supreme Court, *Rol* 3405-2001 (*Visto* 4-9), 12 August 2008.

[110] *Id.*

Thus, the Arbitral Tribunal found that the respondent should pay the claimant the sum established for lost profits based on the abstract calculation of the expert report.[111]

4. Fault and Foreseeability

The Ibero-American laws, as all civil law systems, start with the general principle that some degree of negligence (*culpa*)[112] or gross negligence (*dolo*)[113] in the non-performance or deficient performance of contract is a condition of damages. However, the said degree of negligence or gross negligence does not require an intention to damage or to cause harm to the other party.[114]

On the other hand, under most laws the seller who because of his expertise knew or ought to have known the defects in the goods is liable for damages and lost profits; but if the seller did not know and could not have known the defects, the buyer may only be able to get the price of the goods reduced through the estimatory action or the reimbursement of the price through the redhibitory action, excluding compensation for damages and lost profits.[115]

Also the Ibero-American laws contain a provision stating that the debtor of the obligation in good faith is only liable for the damages and loss of profits that he foresaw or could have foreseen at the conclusion of the contract.[116] As previously mentioned, the provision is one of a group that defines and limits the extent of the breaching party's liability. It must be read together with the

[111] ICC Final Award Case No. 11556 *Lex Contractus* Mexican Law.

[112] Bolivia: Castellanos Trigo & Auad La Fuente, *supra* note 21, at 153-154; Treitel, *supra* note 1, at 56, para. 78; regarding the concept of negligence (*culpa*), its objective criteria and presumption, *see* Ch. 47, 1.

[113] In this context, gross negligence (*dolo*) means the aware intention to breach the contract, *see* Bolivia: Castellanos Trigo & Auad La Fuente, *supra* note 21, at 153, 154.

[114] *Id.*

[115] Argentina Art. 2176 CC; Brazil Art. 443 CC; Chile Art. 1861 CC; Colombia Art. 1918 CC; Ecuador Art. 1828 CC; El Salvador Art. 1663 CC; Guatemala 1562 CC; Mexico Arts. 2145, 2148 CC; Panama Arts. 1254a, 1256 CC; Paraguay Art. 1795 (a) (b) CC; Peru Art. 1512 (5) CC; Spain Arts. 1485, 1486 CC; Uruguay Arts. 1721, 1719 CC; Venezuela Art. 1522 CC.

[116] Bolivia Art. 345 CC; Chile Art. 1558 CC; Colombia Art. 1616 CC; Ecuador Art. 1601 CC; El Salvador Art. 1429 CC; Peru Art. 1321 CC; Spain Art. 1.107 CC; Portugal Art. 798 CC; Uruguay Art. 223 para. 1 Com C; *see also* Spain: Soler Presas, *supra* note 3, at 44; ICC Final Award Case No. 14024 *Lex Contractus* Spanish Law: "Defendant's unlawful behaviour has undeniably exposed Claimant to immediate damage and to the loss of the profit." But "Defendant is to respond for foreseeable damages only. Its behaviour, although unlawful, was not characterized by the intention to damage Claimant or, at least, no evidence has been produced to that extent."

provision dictating that the breaching party is liable for both the emerging damage and the loss of profits,[117] and the provision exonerating the breaching party from indirect damage (lack of causal link).[118]

As has been commented,[119] the limitation of liability to "direct" damage (with causal link) must be distinguished from that to foreseeable damages; though the requirements of foreseeability and directness are sometimes confused in civil law countries. A debtor who with gross negligence (*dolo*) breaches the contract is liable to compensate the unforeseeable damages caused by his breach, but, of course, he is not liable for the damage that is indirect, *i.e.* where no causal link exist between the damage and the breach.[120] Hence, the causal link requirement is always needed regardless of whether the breach occurred by mere negligence (*culpa*) or by gross negligence (*dolo*) of the debtor.[121]

Some Ibero-American scholars understand foreseeable damages, as all those risks that the breach of a contract 'would' normally or necessary caused.[122] Such risks are considered general and known by all parties to a similar contract. So, it is presumed that the debtor should have been aware of them, unless otherwise can be interpreted from the contract. A similar reasoning was given by the Argentinean Supreme Court while stating that the deprivation of the goods allocated to a particular use results in a compensable loss of profits, which is even clearer in cases where the goods are used for a commercial activity, and such activity supposes an aim of profits that cannot be ignored.[123]

---

[117] Argentina Art. 519 CC; Bolivia Art. 344 CC & Art. 845 Com C; Brazil Art. 402 CC; Chile Art. 1556 CC; Colombia Art. 1613 CC; Ecuador Art. 1599 CC; El Salvador Art. 1427 CC; Mexico Arts. 2108, 2109 CC; Paraguay Art. 450 CC; Peru Art. 1321 CC; Spain Art. 1.106 CC.

[118] *See* for example Argentina Art. 520 CC; Bolivia Art. 346 CC; Brazil Art. 403 CC; Mexico Art. 2110 CC; Peru Art. 1336 *in fine* CC; Uruguay Art. 223 para. 2 Com C; *see* different opinions in Spain: Medina de Lemus, *supra* note 21, at 155.

[119] Treitel, *supra* note 1, at 59, para. 82.

[120] Such rule is expressly stated in Uruguay Art. 223 para. 2 Com C; *see also* Spain: Soler Presas, *supra* note 3, at 44; ICC Final Award Case No. 13478 *Lex Contractus* Venezuelan Law: explaining that "[U]nder the provisions of the Venezuelan Civil Code, Articles 1274-1275, damages for breach of contract are limited at law (save in cases of wilful misconduct) to damages that were foreseen or could have been foreseen at the time the parties entered into the contract. Even in the case of wilful misconduct, damages must be an immediate and direct consequence of the breaching party's failure to perform its obligations."

[121] Argentina Art. 521 CC; Brazil Art. 403 CC *contrario sensu*; Paraguay Art. 425 CC; Spain: Medina de Lemus, *supra* note 21, at 157; Argentina Supreme Court, *Isocrom SA. v. Banco Sudameris y Banco Central de la Rep Arg.*, 28 December 1989.

[122] Spain: Soler Presas, *supra* note 3, at 45.

[123] Argentina Supreme Court, *Expreso Hada S.R.L. v. San Luis, Provincia de y otros*, 28 May 2002.

The same understanding of the foreseeability requirement appeared in an ICC dispute, governed by the Venezuelan law.[124] The case concerned the sales of a type of oil used to produce asphalt known under the name of *Boscan* crude oil which is produced only in Venezuela. The seller had breached the agreement to sell at the price agreed under the contract. The Arbitral Tribunal had to decide on whether the damages caused by the seller's breach of contract met the foreseeability requirement under Venezuela's Civil Code Articles 1274-1275. The Tribunal considered that from the evidence provided by the buyer it was uncontradicted that, at the time of entry into the supply contract, the seller was aware that:

> (i) it was the only supplier of Boscan crude oil; (ii) Boscan is always priced at a discount to higher grades of crude oil; (iii) Boscan has a higher yield of asphalt than other crudes; (iv) using crude oils with a higher sulphur content than Boscan would require a more expensive maintenance schedule at the Refinery; and (v) the Boscan contracted for was destined for the Refinery, which in turn had been configured for the use of Boscan.

On this basis, the Tribunal found that seller could (and should) have foreseen that its failure to supply the quantity of Boscan required by the supply contract would lead directly to:

> (i) the losses caused to (buyer) by it having to purchase replacement crude oils at a higher price; (ii) the losses caused to (buyer) by it having to purchase additional volumes of crude oil than would otherwise have been necessary in order to provide the additional volume of asphalt that would have been produced had Boscan been available; and (iii) the additional costs incurred in the refining process (including the maintenance of the facility) by the forced use of crude oils other than Boscan.[125]

5. Contractual Stipulations

As parties are free to define contractually their obligations, they may also contractually regulate the scope of their liability. This freedom is recognised in both the CISG[126] and the Ibero-American laws. The parties may agree to a *penalty clause* in the sense given by the civil law[127] or they may limit their liability by a limitation liability clause.

[124] ICC Final Award Case No. 13478 *Lex Contractus* Venezuelan Law.

[125] *Id.*

[126] Art. 6 CISG.

[127] Clauses known under the name of *Cláusula Penal*. In principle such clauses are valid. The literal English translation of the Spanish term *Cláusula Penal i.e. penalty clause* in the Anglo-American law is normally used to refer to an invalid stipulation for the payment of a fixed sum in the event of default. Where the clause is valid in the Anglo-American law, it is referred to as a 'liquidated damage' clause, *see* Treitel, *supra* note 1, at 90, para. 119.

5.1. Fixed Sums

5.1.1. Penalty Clauses

5.1.1.1. Purposes

In the Ibero-American laws a penalty clause normally takes the form of an agreement requiring one or both of the parties to pay a fixed sum of money or any other performance in case of breach of specific obligations, in favour of the creditor or a third person.[128] But a contract with a penalty clause does not normally create an alternative obligation.[129] The rule impeding the debtor to discharge himself of performing his principal obligation by paying the penalty is expressed in the Argentinean, the Paraguayan and the Spanish Civil Codes.[130]

One of the purposes of a penalty clause is to fix in advance the damages payable in the event of non-compliance with the obligation contracted.[131] In this regard, the Spanish Civil Code establishes that in the obligation subject to a penalty clause, the penalty clause will substitute the compensation for the emerging damages and the loss of profits for breach of this obligation, unless otherwise agreed.[132]

Some Ibero-American codes have expressly provided that the purpose of the penalty clause is to ensure the fulfilment of an obligation by means of a penalty or fine in case of delay or total non-performance of an obligation.[133]

[128] Argentina Art. 653 CC; Brazil Art. 409 CC; Chile Arts. 1535, 1536 last para. CC; Colombia Arts. 1592, 1593 last para. CC; Costa Rica Art. 426 Com C; Ecuador Arts. 1578, 1579 last para. CC; El Salvador Arts. 1406, 1407 last para. CC; Mexico Arts. 1840, 1481 last para. CC; Paraguay Art. 454 CC; Peru Art. 1341 CC; Spain Art. 1.152 CC; Uruguay Art. 284 Com C; Venezuela Art. 1.257 CC.

[129] Treitel, *supra* note 1, at 94, para. 124.

[130] Argentina Art. 658 CC; Paraguay Art. 457 CC; Spain Art. 1.153 part 1 CC.

[131] Brazil Superior Tribunal of Justice, REsp 687285/SP, Minister Nancy Andrighi, published 25 September 2007: When the obligation is completely non-performed, the penalty clause serves as a fixed compensation; ICC Final Award Case No. 14083 *Lex Contractus* Brazilian Law: explaining that a penalty clause of this type is agreed, for two reasons: (i) to strengthen the binding nature of the contract by indicating to the parties in advance and in an unequivocal manner the consequences of a breach of contract, and (ii) to pre-establish the quantum of compensation owed by the parties in breach, prohibiting that amount from being accumulated with any other claims for compensation, even when the damage incurred exceeds the said quantum.

[132] Spain Art. 1.152 CC; ICC Final Award Case No. 13278 *Lex Contractus* Spanish Law: "Under Spanish law, the predominant function of a penalty clause is to liquidate damages beforehand and to replace the payment of damages accordingly, it being specified that a contrary agreement is admissible if it is unequivocal."

[133] Argentina Art. 652 CC; Chile Art. 1535 CC; Colombia Art. 1592 CC; Ecuador Art. 1578 CC; El Salvador Art. 1406 CC; Uruguay Art. 284 Com C; Venezuela Art. 1.257 CC.

Such provisions express a means of pressure on the debtor which force him to perform his obligation rather than ensuring a perfect development of the contract.

Another purpose of a penalty clause is simply to establish with some certainty the extent of liability of the breaching party. Though penalty clauses are not limitation clauses, in some cases they may have the same function.[134] The Peruvian and the Portuguese Civil Codes contain a provision stating that a penalty clause has the effect of limiting the compensation.[135] On this issue, Paraguay's Civil Code simply confirms that parties can agree a penalty for the case of total or partial non performance of the obligations or delay in its performance.[136]

Regardless of the specific purpose stated in the individual Civil Codes, one can say that all the penalty clauses share all of the purposes described.[137] What may be more important to bear in mind are characteristics, the requirements, the limits, and the effects of penalty clauses, as well as the slight differences existing between the Ibero-American laws.

5.1.1.2. Different types

Different types of penalty clauses can be agreed upon, depending on the breaching conduct. On the one hand, a penalty clause can be introduced in a contractual relation in order to compensate or penalise the delay in performing the agreed obligations. On the other hand, penalty clauses may establish compensation or penalties in cases of total non-performance of the whole of the obligations or of a special clause.[138]

An ICC Arbitral Tribunal enforced these different types of penalty clauses agreed in a single contract. On the one hand, the parties agreed that if the contract was terminated unjustifiably by the buyer, he should pay the seller a penalty corresponding to 20% of the total price of the goods. On the other hand, if the seller did not deliver the goods in accordance with the timetable stipulated in the contract two different penalties were imposed: (i) the payment to the buyer of a penalty equivalent to 0.27% of the unit price of the goods

[134] Mexico Collegiate Tribunals, *Novena Época,* Registry 187'461, SJF XV, March 2002, at 1405.

[135] Peru Art. 1341 CC; Portugal Art. 810 CC; confirmed by Peru Supreme Court, *Sala civil transitoria*, Resolution 001064-2003, 10 September 2003.

[136] Mexico Art. 1840 CC; Paraguay Art. 454 CC.

[137] Treitel, *supra* note 1, at 93, para. 122.

[138] *See* Brazil Art. 409 CC; *see* an example of special clause in ICC Final Award Case 13847 *Lex Contractus* Guatemalan law/*ex aequo et bono* per determination of the Arbitral Tribunal: purchaser decided to terminate the contract and supplier got payment of the a penalty for early termination of the contract and the penalty for not reaching the minimum volume of sales for the year.

per day of delay until such time as they were delivered and (ii) the payment to the buyer of a penalty corresponding to 20% of the price of the goods never delivered.[139]

5.1.1.3. Requirements

Failure to perform temporally or definitive is an essential element of contract liability and thus it must exist before the penalty clause can be exercised against the debtor. The Ibero-American Civil Codes use different statements to explain the requirement *e.g.* "penalty ... against the party who does not fulfil his obligation" or "in case the obligation is non performed" or "lack of performance."[140] If an ultimatum to perform or similar notice is required, for the purpose of putting the debtor in effective delayed or failure to perform, such must equally be given to put into effect a claim for a penalty clause.[141]

5.1.1.4. Limits

If performance of the obligation agreed becomes impossible due to an event for which the debtor is not responsible, *e.g.* acts of God or force majeure, fault of the creditor, or if the debtor has any other good excuse for not to perform, the default rule is that the debtor shall be discharged of any liability to pay the penalty clause.[142]

Additionally, the Spanish jurisprudence has developed the rule under which: when the basic assumptions upon which the parties agreed at the time of the conclusion of the contract are significantly altered, the penalty clause becomes ineffective.[143] Under this rule, it is no longer about alteration or impossibility of the principal obligation which breach of triggers the penalty, but rather the test is a change in circumstances related to the basic assumptions considered by the debtor when entering into the clause. Hence, "a change in circumstances pertaining to the economy of the contract is sufficient to make the penalty clause unenforceable."[144]

[139] ICC Final Award Case No. 14083 *Lex Contractus* Brazilian Law.

[140] Argentina Art. 654 CC; Brazil Art. 408 CC; Costa Rica Art. 426 Com C; Mexico Art. 1841 CC & Art. 88 Com C; Paraguay Art. 454 CC; Peru Art. 1341 CC; Spain Art. 1.152 CC & Art. 56 Com C; Uruguay Art. 284 Com C; Venezuela Art. 1.258 sentence 1 CC.

[141] Brazil Art. 408 CC; Chile Arts. 1537 sentence 1, 1538 CC; Colombia Arts. 1594 sentence 1, 1595 CC; Ecuador Arts. 1580 sentence 1, 1581 CC; El Salvador Arts. 1408 sentence 1, 1409 CC; Paraguay Art. 456 CC; *see also* Brazil Art. 405 CC; Guatemala Art. 1826 (3) CC; Portugal Art. 805 CC: unless there was a fixed date for performance; Spain Art. 1.109 CC.

[142] Argentina Art. 665 CC; Costa Rica Art. 428 Com C; Mexico Art. 1847 CC; Peru Art. 1343 sentence 2 CC; Uruguay Art. 290 para. 2 Com C; Mexico Collegiate Tribunals, *Novena Época,* Registry 173'722, SJF XXIV, December 2006, p 1378.

[143] *See* Spain Supreme Tribunal, 16 September 1996, *Id Cendoj:* 28079110011986100021; also referred in ICC Final Award Case No. 13278 *Lex Contractus* Spanish Law.

[144] ICC Final Award Case No. 13278 *Lex Contractus* Spanish Law: the Sole Arbitrator found

In addition, if the principal obligation or contract is declared invalid or voidable so is the penalty clause; but if the penalty clause is declared invalid or voidable the principal obligation remains valid.[145]

Termination of the contract by mutual agreement normally deprives the penalty clause of its effects, unless the clause provides for damages on termination.[146] On the question of whether termination has retrospective effects, some authors sustain that it should not be assumed that liability in damages is extinguished merely because termination operates retrospectively by bringing back the obligations already performed.[147]

5.1.1.5. Effects

One of the effects of penalty clauses is that the aggrieved party cannot claim both the penalty and further compensation for damages, unless otherwise agreed.[148] The penalty takes the place of the compensation for damages and loss of profits. However, if the agreed penalty clause was intended to penalise only the late performance or the non-performance of an specific duty, the aggrieved party is still entitled to claim further damages for the definitive and total non-performance of other obligations.[149]

Furthermore, under Brazil, Peru and Portugal's laws, if the incurred damages exceed the sum fixed in the penalty clause, the party could claim additional compensation if so was agreed.[150] In this case, the party must prove this surpassing loss.[151] Under the Costa Rican commercial law, an extra amount of damages can be recovered when the creditor of the obligations proves that the debtor fraudulently breached the contract.[152]

that respondents' arguments with respect to the alleged change of circumstances leading to the unenforceability of the penalty clause were without merit.

145 Argentina Art. 663 CC; Chile Art. 1536 para. 1 CC; Colombia Art. 1593 para. 1 CC; Ecuador Art. 1579 para. 1 CC; El Salvador Art. 1407 para. 1 CC; Mexico Art. 1841 CC; Paraguay Art. 455 CC; Peru Art. 1345 CC; Portugal Art. 810 para. 2 CC; Spain Art. 1.155 CC; Uruguay Art. 285 Com C.

146 Treitel, *supra* note 1, at 94, para. 123.

147 *Id.*, at 141, para. 179.

148 Argentina Art. 655 CC; Chile Art. 1543 CC; Colombia Art. 1600 CC; Costa Rica Art. 426 Com C; Ecuador Art. 1586 CC; El Salvador Art. 1414 CC; Mexico Art. 1840 CC; Paraguay Art. 454 para. 2 CC; Peru Art. 1341 part 1 CC; Spain Art. 1.152 CC; Uruguay Art. 288 para. 1 Com C.

149 ICC Final Award Case No. 12035 *Lex Contractus* Mexican Law: the Tribunal upheld that the 'sole remedy' limitation set forth in the delay penalty clause does not apply in the case of termination for definitive non-performance to the extent that additional compensation is foreseen under a different clause of the agreement.

150 Brazil Art. 416 sole para. CC; Peru Art. 1341 CC; Portugal Art. 811 (2) CC.

151 Brazil Art. 416 sole para. CC.

152 Costa Rica Art. 427 Com C.

Some laws provide that it is at the creditor's option to choose between the penalty and the compensation.[153] Nevertheless, a Mexican Collegiate Tribunal has denied such an option since one of the purposes of the penalty clause is to limit the liability of the debtor in case of breach.[154]

In addition, a general rule is that in cases of total non-performance of the obligation the aggrieved party cannot claim both the penalty clause and the performance.[155]

On the other hand, it is possible that the penalty, or part of it, is paid because of some partial failure or delay to perform. For these situations all Ibero-American countries contain provisions, exempting from the general rule, under which it is made possible to claim both the penalty clause for the particular breach and either performance or compensation for non-performance in respect of other breaches.[156] For example, to be entitled to the penalty agreed for late performance and further claim damages for incomplete or defective performance of one or more of several obligations agreed.[157]

It has also been stated, in all the Ibero-American laws, that the aggrieved party can recover the sum of the penalty without need to prove that he has indeed suffered loss.[158] Furthermore, a judgment may be granted for the penalty, even though the breaching party alleges or proves that the aggrieved party did not suffer any loss or that he has made profits or subtracted a benefit.[159] The rule embodies the immutability principle of penalty clauses.

[153] Chile Art. 1543 CC; Colombia Art. 1600 CC; Ecuador Art. 1586 CC; El Salvador Art. 1414 CC.

[154] Mexico Collegiate Tribunals, *Novena Época,* Registry 187'461, SJF XV, March 2002, p. 1405.

[155] Argentina Art. 659 part 1 CC; Brazil Art. 410 CC; Chile Art. 1537 sentence 2 CC; Colombia Art. 1594 sentence 2 CC; Costa Rica Art. 426 Com C; Ecuador Art. 1580 sentence 2 CC; El Salvador Art. 1408 sentence 2 CC; Mexico Art. 1846 sentence 1 CC & Art. 88 Com C; Paraguay Art. 458 part 1 CC; Peru Art. 1341 part 1 CC; Portugal Art. 811 (1) CC; Spain Art. 1.153 para. 2 CC & Art. 56 Com C; Uruguay Art. 288 para. 2 Com C; Venezuela Art. 1.258 part 2 CC; Mexico Collegiate Tribunals, *Novena Época,* Registry 186'339, SJF XVI, August 2002, p. 1252; Mexico Collegiate Tribunals, *Novena Época,* Registry 202'940, SJF III, March 1996, p. 923.

[156] Argentina Art. 659 part 2 CC; Brazil Art. 411 CC; Chile Art. 1537 *in fine* CC; Colombia Art. 1594 *in fine* CC; Costa Rica Art. 426 Com C; Ecuador Art. 1580 *in fine* CC; El Salvador Art. 1408 *in fine* CC; Mexico Art. 1846 *in fine* CC; Paraguay Art. 458 part 2 CC; Peru Art. 1342 CC; Portugal Art. 811 (1) CC; Uruguay Art. 288 para. 3 Com C.

[157] *See for example,* Costa Rica Art. 426 Com C; Mexico Collegiate Tribunals, *Novena Época,* Registry 186'339, SJF XVI, August 2002, p 1252.

[158] Argentina Art. 656 part 1 CC; Brazil Art. 416 *chapeau* CC; Costa Rica Art. 427 Com C; Mexico Art. 1842 CC; Paraguay Art. 454 last para. CC; Peru Art. 1343 sentence 1 CC; ICC Final Award Case No. 14083 *Lex Contractus* Brazilian Law: "A penalty clause dispenses the need to prove damage, which is presumed, and therefore the existence and extent of the said damage is not at issue."

[159] Argentina Art. 656 part 1 CC; Chile Art. 1542 CC; Colombia Art. 1599 CC; Ecuador Art. 1585 CC; El Salvador Art. 1413 CC; Mexico Art. 1842 CC; Paraguay Art. 454 last para. CC;

5.1.1.6. Reduction or Modification

However, under most Ibero-American laws, except for the Spanish and the Mexican, the judge has the faculty to equitably reduce the amount payable under the penalty clause; due consideration of the amount of loss actually suffered, the excessiveness of the penalty, the circumstances of the case, or the benefits already profited by the aggrieved party.[160]

Under some of these laws though, namely the Brazilian law or the Paraguayan law, it may be still controversial whether the faculty to reduce the penalty is discretional or whether the provision establishes an obligation to reduce the penalty, *ex oficio* or *ex parte*, whenever such appears excessive under the circumstances. The concern has already arisen in a dissenting opinion in an ICC case.[161] The dissenting arbitrator disagreed with the enforcement of the full amount of a penalty clause, as under the circumstances it appeared excessive. The majority of the arbitrators explained that the *ex oficio* reduction of the penalty clause would jeopardise the validity of the award on the grounds of lack of due process, since the issue of the excessiveness of the penalty clause had not been raised by the breaching party even when the Tribunal had invited the parties to comment on the clause. The dissenting arbitrator considered though that the Tribunal had an *ex oficio* faculty to reduced the penalty since article 459 of Paraguay's Civil Code employs the wording "the judge shall reduce equitably the penalty"[162] while other Civil Codes such as the Argentinean[163] employs the wording "the judges may reduce the penalty."[164]

ICC Final Award Case No. 14083 *Lex Contractus* Brazilian Law: "Even if the party in breach could produce incontrovertible proof that no damage was caused as a result of the breach and delay, the penalty is still owed as the legal dispensation of the need to prove damage is based on the absolute presumption that the failure to perform the obligation or the delay are, in themselves, damaging."

[160] Argentina Art. 656 para. 2 CC; Brazil Art. 413 CC; Chile Art. 1544 *in fine* CC; Colombia Art. 1601 *in fine* CC; Ecuador Art. 1587 *in fine* CC; El Salvador Art. 1415 *in fine* CC; Paraguay Art. 459 CC; Peru Art. 1346 CC; Portugal Art. 812 (1) CC; Argentina Camara Nacional de Apelaciones de lo Civil, *Tibiletti de Castillo Freyre Valeria Susana y Otro v. Lunasky Isabel Rosa*, 20 December 2006.

[161] ICC Final Award Case No. 13685 *Lex Contractus* Paraguayan Law.

[162] "El Juez reducirá equitativamente la pena." A similar wording is used in Art. 413 of Brazil's Civil Code "A penalidade deve ser reduzida eqüitativamente pelo juiz".

[163] Argentina Art. 656 "Los jueces podrán reducir las penas …": Similar wording is found in Chile Art. 1544 CC "se podrá rebajar la pena"; El Salvador Art. 1415 CC "se deja a la prudencia del Juez moderar la pena"; Peru Art. 1346 CC "El juez, a solicitud del deudor, puede reducir equitativamente la pena"; Portugal Art. 812 (1) CC "A cláusula penal pode ser reduzida."

[164] ICC Final Award Case No. 13685 *Lex Contractus* Paraguayan Law.

An Argentinean court explained that in order to determine whether a penalty clause is excessive the judge must consider the economic consequences of its strict application and the impact of the alleging party's conduct on the extension of the breach or damage.[165]

Also under most laws, including the Spanish and Mexican, the penalty may be reduced proportionally in cases of partial or defective performance.[166] The Spanish Supreme Tribunal has sustained that the Spanish law does not recognise the equitable reduction of the penalty clause for mere excessiveness but only the reduction of the penalty clause for partial breach.[167] Further, the Supreme Tribunal has repeatedly sustained that there is no possibility of reducing a penalty clause when this has been precisely agreed for partial breach.[168] In other words, the penalty clause can only be reduced when this has been agreed for a total breach of obligations but only part of them are non-performed.[169] For example, if a certain amount of money was agreed to be paid for each day of delay in the performance, the same shall be recognised and remained unmodified by the judge, as the penalty was agreed for that specific situation.

In both situations, the aggrieved party may have an advisable interest to prove that in fact, he has suffered loss and to what extent, even though law does not bind him.

5.1.1.7. Unenforcement

About its effective enforcement, in some legal systems penalty clauses are unenforceable if the penalty is higher than the value of the principal obligation.[170] On this issue, a Mexican Collegiate Tribunal has explained

[165] Argentina National Chamber of Appeals in Commercial Matters, *Juridica Pueyrredon S.R.L. v. Jara Marino,* 2 December 2008.

[166] Argentina Art. 660 CC; Brazil Art. 413 CC; Chile Art. 1539 CC; Colombia Art. 1596 CC; Ecuador Art. 1582 CC; El Salvador Art. 1410 CC; Mexico Arts. 1844, 1845 CC; Paraguay Art. 459 CC; Peru Art. 1346 CC; Portugal Art. 812 (2) CC; Spain Art. 1.154 CC; Uruguay Art. 291 Com C; Venezuela Art. 1.260 CC; Argentina National Chamber of Appeals in Civil Matters, *Tibiletti de Castillo Freyre Valeria Susana y Otro v. Lunasky Isabel Rosa*, 20 December 2006, MJ-JU-42526-AR; Mexico Supreme Court, *Tercera Sala,* Registry 271745, SFJ Part 4 XXVII, p 226; Mexico Supreme Court, *Tercera Sala,* Registry 271721, SJF Part 4 XXVII, p 138.

[167] Spain Supreme Tribunal, 20 December 2006, *Id Cendoj:* 28079110012006101363.

[168] Spain Supreme Tribunal, 1 June 2009, *Id Cendoj:* 28079110012009100394.

[169] ICC Final Award Case No. 13278 *Lex Contractus* Spanish Law: upholding that there was not partial or irregular performance in the case at hand. "Respondents terminated the Agreement at the end of the 2003 season, which is precisely the action the penalty clause sought to deter. Considering the nature of the action sought to be sanctioned, there is no room for partial or irregular performance."

[170] Bolivia Art. 534 CC; Brazil Art. 412 CC; Mexico Art. 1843 CC; Portugal Art. 811(3) CC; Mexico Supreme Court, *Novena Época, Primera Sala,* Registry 177'470, SJF XXII, August 2005, at 142; Bolivia: V. Camargo Marín, Derecho Comercial Boliviano 402 (2007).

that the relevant moment to calculate the value of the principal obligation is the time of conclusion of the contract and not afterwards. This is because in contracts of long duration, such as installments contracts, the value of the principal obligation may increase, which means that the penalty clause may become ineffective by the time the breach occurs.[171]

Finally, a provision of the Mexican Civil Code establishes that a penalty clause cannot be enforced when the debtor was unable to fulfil his obligations due to the conduct of the creditor.[172] This provision follows the principle that only the damage that is necessary and, inevitably the consequence of the harming act can be compensated,[173] and is in close relation with the topic of the breach of the debtor's obligations due to the conduct of the creditor[174] and the duty to mitigate damages.[175]

5.1.2. Arrears

Under some Ibero-American laws, a party may agree to pay in advance an amount of money, known under the name of *arrears*, to the other party in order to confirm his interest in the conclusion or performance of a contract.[176] The institute called 'arras' or 'signal' represents a warranty of the conclusion or execution of the contract of sale. As pointed out by the Bolivian Supreme Court,[177] according to the general interpretation given by the doctrine, and admitted with universal character, often in the form of statutory law, the following situations can arise from the arrears agreement:

i) If the contract has been performed, the *arrears* shall be returned to the performing party or they shall be deducted as part of the payment of the price due.[178]

ii) If the contract has not been performed, the *arrears* may have different endings depending of the case:

[171] Mexico Collegiate Tribunals, *Novena Época,* Registry 187'460, SJF XV, March 2002, at 1258.

[172] Mexico Art. 1847 CC; A similar provision is found in Peru Art. 1343 CC.

[173] *See supra* 1.1.1.

[174] *See* Ch. 51, 3.

[175] *See infra* 7

[176] Mexico: O. Vásquez del Mercado, Contratos Mercantiles 198 (2008).

[177] Bolivia Supreme Court, Sala Civil 2, 23 November 2004, *Augusto Valencia Sanabria y María Ruth Borda de Valencia v. José Luís Álvarez Cáceres.*

[178] Argentina Art. 475 Com C; Brazil Arts. 417, 418 CC; Bolivia Art. 537 (I) CC; Chile Art. 1804 CC; Colombia Art. 1861 CC; Ecuador Art. 151 Com C; Mexico Art. 381 Com C; Spain Art. 343 Com C; Uruguay Art. 558 Com C; Brazil Superior Tribunal of Justice, REsp 782999/ SP, Minister Castro Filho, published 16 April 2007.

a) If the party who gave the arrears failed to perform, the other party is entitled to abandon the contact and to keep the arrears received,[179] but he can always prefer the specific performance of the contract or, alternative, the avoidance of the contract conjunctively with the compensation of the effective damage.

b) If the party who received the arrears failed to perform, the other party, who gave the arrears, is entitled to claim back the exact amount of the arrears plus its equivalent, and to avoid the contract.[180] In this case, the arrears are similar to a penalty clause.

c) In case both of the parties have breach the obligation, it is interpreted that the party who had given the arrears will lose them, still with the possibility that the party who received the arrears has the obligation to give the same amount of money as damages.[181]

5.2. Limitation Clauses

Some Ibero-American laws expressly grant to the parties the possibility to agree on the amount and the mechanism of compensation for breach of contract, within the limits of the law;[182] provided the waiver to the right to compensation is made in such a manner that it is precise and leaves no doubt as to the right that the affected party is waiving.[183]

[179] Argentina Art. 475 Com C; Bolivia Art. 537(II) CC; Chile Arts. 1803, 1875 CC; Colombia Arts. 1859, 1932 CC; Uruguay Art. 558 Com C; Bolivia: Camargo Marín, *supra* note 170, at 404.

[180] Argentina Art. 475 Com C; Bolivia Art. 537(II) CC; Brazil Art. 420 CC; Chile Arts. 1803, 1875 CC; Colombia Arts. 1859, 1932 CC; Bolivia: Camargo Marín, *supra* note 170, at 404.

[181] Bolivia Supreme Court, *Sala Civil* 2, 23 November 2004, *Augusto Valencia Sanabria y María Ruth Borda de Valencia v. José Luís Álvarez Cáceres*: overturning the decision of the Court of Appeal which did not consider that not only the seller had failed to sell the goods but also the buyer has failed to pay the price.

[182] Chile Art. 1558 para. 3 CC; Colombia Art. 1616 para. 3 CC & Art. 936 Com C; Ecuador Art. 1601 para. 3 CC; El Salvador Art. 1429 para. 3 CC; Mexico Art. 2117 CC; Peru Arts. 1329, 1328 CC; Portugal Art. 800 (2) CC; Uruguay Art. 222 Com C; Venezuela Art. 1.277 CC; ICC Final Award Case No. 13918 *Lex Contractus* Spanish Law: explaining that the rules on damages established in Spain Arts. 1.101, 1.106 CC have a subsidiary character *vis à vis* the provisions agreed by the parties on this issue, so that there is no ground for the compensation of certain type of damages when the agreement has excluded them. The Sole Arbitrator found that as the buyer had failed to follow the procedure established by the contract with regards to the time limits, the form and requirements of the notice to raise any claim on the financial situation of the purchased company, the buyer was precluded from the already limited compensation established by the contract and from the compensation established by the law, since the parties had agreed to depart from the default rules; *see also* Bolivia: Castellanos Trigo & Auad La Fuente, *supra* note 21, at 167.

[183] Mexico Art. 7 CC; ICC Partial Award Case No. 12949 *Lex Contractus* Mexican Law.

Among the limitations, some laws establish that it is void to completely renounce the right or duty to compensate for breach contract, when the liable party has acted with gross negligence.[184] Also is void the agreement that exonerates or limits the liability when such violates public policy rules.[185]

The Supreme Court of Paraguay endorsed a decision of a Court of Appeal which had dismissed the buyer's claim for damages related to incidental losses caused by the seller's breach of a supply of goods agreement; such as the cost for the rent of a warehouse, expenses in publicity, training of personnel, cancellation of loans with banks. The denial of the Court of Appeal was based on the parties' express agreement on a limitation clause releasing the seller from any liability regarding cost of investments, loss of goodwill, labour obligations and other related losses derived from the termination of the contract.[186]

Similarly, in an ICC case the question arose about the validity of what was in the Sole Arbitrator's view a non-recourse clause limiting the seller's available remedy to the recovery of the goods. In the case at hand, the Sole Arbitrator found that "[T]he non-recourse provision is valid on the grounds of the principle of party autonomy and does not contravene public policy (*orden público*) under the Mexican law."[187] The Sole Arbitrator rejected the seller's argument as to the violation of law inasmuch as the clause contravened the obligation to pay a price (an essential clause), since in the sole arbitrator's view the fact of limiting the buyer's liability in the event of breach, does not suggest that the original obligation was eliminated. The original obligation to pay the price was still valid as it was the limited liability.[188]

Finally, some commercial laws expressly establish the possibility to extend, moderate or exonerate the seller's warranty to provide goods free of defects,[189] except when a seller at the conclusion of the contract remains silent, in bad faith, about the defects of the goods,[190] or when the defects result from the seller's acts or misconduct after the conclusion of the contract.[191]

---

[184] Bolivia Art. 350 (1) CC; Mexico Art. 2106 CC; Peru Art. 1328 CC; Spain Art. 1.102 CC; *see also* Bolivia: Castellanos Trigo & Auad La Fuente, *supra* note 21, at 167, 168.

[185] Bolivia Art. 350 (2) CC; Portugal Art. 800 (2) CC; Peru Art. 1328 CC; *see also* Bolivia: Castellanos Trigo & Auad La Fuente, *supra* note 21, at 167-168.

[186] Paraguay Supreme Court, Judgment 1313, 20 December 2007, *Casa Gagliardi Y Otro v. Firma Unilever Capsa Del Paraguay S.A.*

[187] The Sole Arbitrator referred to Mexico Art. 1839 CC: "the parties can insert into their contracts the clauses which may consider more convenient"; ICC Partial Award Case No. 12949 *Lex Contractus* Mexican Law.

[188] ICC Partial Award Case No. 12949 *Lex Contractus* Mexican Law.

[189] Colombia Art. 936 Com C; Costa Rica Art. 467 Com C; Mexico Art. 384 Com C; Spain Art. 345 Com C; Uruguay Arts. 549, 550 Com C.

[190] Colombia Art. 936 Com C.

[191] Uruguay Art. 550 Com C.

6. Questions of Proof

6.1. Burden of Proof

Under the CISG and the Ibero-American laws, since the creditor is the party who claims the existence of emerging damages, even though such may not exist, he bears the burden of proving that damages were caused.[192] This is not so difficult since most patrimony harm leaves a trace.[193] On the contrary, it is not always so easy to prove the loss of profits, as their determination is based on negative events that could often be confounded with fake expectations.[194]

In this regard, the Peruvian Civil Code dictates that the burden of proof on the existence and the sum of damages corresponds to the party suffering the complete, partial, late or imperfect performance of the obligation.[195] The Chilean Supreme Court,[196] the Mexican Supreme Court,[197] and the Paraguayan Supreme Court have sustained the same rule.[198] The latter had previously established that the claimant must also prove the authorship of the loss, since it is not enough to prove the loss caused, but also is needed to show the relationship between the breach and the prejudice incurred.[199]

In addition, the Spanish Jurisprudence has sustained that while considering the market price of substitute goods as the criteria to estimate the amount of damages, the party claiming damages has the duty to prove that the goods he has acquired are indeed of a substitute character.[200]

---

[192] *See* on this Schwenzer, *supra* note 19, Art. 74, para. 64, at 1025; Spain: Medina de Lemus, *supra* note 21, at 153; ICC Final Award Case No. 10299 *Lex Contractus* Chilean Law: stating that in order to determine contractual liability the aggrieved party must prove that damages have ensued as a result of the said breach; ICC Final Award Case No. 13478 *Lex Contractus* Venezuelan Law: noting that although the buyer's evidence and the methodology for calculating its losses was neither contradicted nor attacked by seller by presentation of alternative factual and/or expert evidence, the burden to persuade the Tribunal about the price of the goods had the contract not been breached, rests with buyer.

[193] However, such does not mean that any breach of a sale of goods contract having a profits' aim automatically causes damages, such shall be still proven in his amount, *see* Mexico Collegiate Tribunals, *Novena Época,* Registry 178'481, Tesis SJF XXI, May 2005, p 1448.

[194] Spain: Medina de Lemus, *supra* note 21, at 153; ICC Final Award Case No. 10044 *Lex Contractus* Portuguese Law: "In Portuguese law, the party claiming damages has to prove its loss on a balance of probabilities."

[195] Peru Art. 1331 CC.

[196] Chile Supreme Court, *Rol* 3405-2001 (*Visto* 10), 12 August 2008.

[197] Mexico Supreme Court, *Quinta Época, Tercera Sala*, SJF XCVI, p 951.

[198] Paraguay Supreme Court, Judgment 1199, 22 July 2003, *Fernando Bruno Román López v. Ideal S.A. De Seguros Y Reaseguros.*

[199] Paraguay Supreme Court, Judgment 700, 16 December 1999, *Adalberto Walter Zierz v. Osmar Lautenschleiger E Isona Serenita Lautenschleiger.*

[200] Spain Supreme Tribunal, 29 October 1995, *cited in* Spain: Soler Presas, *supra* note 3, at 114.

Under CISG Article 74, the burden of proof of demonstrating the foreseeability of the loss is on the aggrieved party.[201]

Finally, the debtor has the burden to prove that the failure to perform or the defecting performance was not due to his fault or negligence or that the failure was due to an impediment beyond his control.[202]

6.2. Standard of Proof

Some courts have required concrete evidence as to the amount of incurred loss. In an Argentinean case, the Supreme Court denied the avoidance of the contract and the award of damages since the claimant had failed to provide the court with trustworthy elements to determine with a degree of certainty the value of the non-performance.[203] In a different case, a claim for financial loss derived from the delay of the debtor was admitted, but the concrete expression of such loss was required.[204]

In Chile, the Supreme Court has also declared that the loss of profits shall be proven, and for that it must be shown the productivity of the specific goods before their damage, the productivity decrease and the loss of profits resulting from it.[205] Witnesses' declarations were rejected by the Court since they referred to a hypothetical form of leasing of a similar machine in the market and its value, but did not witness that the machine was performing or was intended to perform that service before the machine was broken and the income that such generated.

Conversely, other courts have expressed flexibility in relation to the exactness of the amount of loss in monetary terms. First, an interesting provision of Peru's Civil Code establishes that if the compensation for damages cannot be proven in its exact amount, the judge shall fix the recoverable damages based on an equitable calculation.[206]

Second, a Mexican Collegiate Tribunal explained that although the Supreme Court has sustained the *quantum* is an essential element of a claim for damages, such does not mean that the exact amount of the damage established in the memorandum of claim has to exactly match the amount

---

[201] Schwenzer, *supra* note 19, Art. 74, para. 64, at 1026.

[202] Chile Arts. 1547 (3), 1674 CC; Colombia Arts. 1604 (3), 1733 CC; Ecuador Arts. 1590 (3), 1717 CC; El Salvador Arts. 1418 (3), 1544 CC; Portugal Art. 799 (1) CC; Spain Art. 1.183 CC; Venezuela Art. 1.344 CC (3); *see also* Argentina: R.L. Lorenzetti, Tratado de los Contratos Parte General 602 (2004); X. O'Callaghan (Ed.), Código Civil Comentado Art. 1.105, at 1075 (2004); ICC Final Award Case No. 12755 *Lex Contractus* Argentinean Law.

[203] Argentina Supreme Court, Santa Fe, *Provincia de v. Empresa Nacional de Correos y Telégrafos S.A.* 11 July 2002.

[204] Argentina Supreme Court, *Calderas Salcor Caren S.A. v. Estado Nacional-Comisión Nacional de Energía Atómica y otra*, 24 September 1996.

[205] Chile Supreme Court, *Rol* 3405-2001 (*Visto* 4-9), 12 August 2008.

[206] Peru Art. 1332 CC.

proved by the claimant; since it would be totally unfair to dismiss a claim of damages based on difference between the amount claimed and the amount of damage actually proven to occur.[207] Similarly, the Paraguayan Supreme Court has sustained that article 452 of Paraguay's Civil code gives the judge a discretionary faculty to equitably fix the amount of compensation when the damages have been proven but not its *quantum*.[208]

Regarding the standard of proof of non-pecuniary damages, the Venezuelan Superior Tribunal of Justice has sustained that the only thing that shall be completely proven is the generating fact of the damage. This means, the group of circumstances that generates the *affliction* for which a *petitum dolores* is claimed.[209] Such approach was further supported by a subsequent decision establishing that while existence and the source of the loss of profits has to be specified and demonstrated, the non-pecuniary loss, due to subjective nature of the damage, are not subject to direct material verification, as such is impossible.[210]

Similarly, a Mexican Collegiate Tribunal explained that while regarding pecuniary damages the recovery is based on the equivalence between the loss and the reparation, in the non-pecuniary damages the recovery is based not on the equivalence but on the satisfaction of the aggrieved party, since pain and human feelings are not susceptible to have monetary equivalence.[211] For such a reason the judge has wide discretionary faculty to freely evaluate the amount of the compensation of non-pecuniary damages, which are not subject to the objective parameters on the compensation of pecuniary damages.[212]

7. Mitigation

In Ibero-American law, the duty to mitigate the damages has not been expressly stated as in the CISG.[213] Except for some statutory laws, according to which, damages are not due regarding losses that the creditor could have been able

---

207 Mexico Collegiate Tribunals, *Novena Época,* Registry 177'643, SJF XXII, August 2005, at 1883.

208 Paraguay Supreme Court, 27 December 2002, *Olegario Farrés y Otra v. Bancoplus S.A.I.F.*

209 Venezuela Supreme Tribunal, Judgment 340, *Cass civ,* file 99-1001 of 31 October 2000.

210 Venezuela Supreme Tribunal, Judgment 01210, *Sala Político Administrativa,* file 14728 of 8 October 2002.

211 Mexico Collegiate Tribunals, *Novena Época,* Registry 173'279, SJF XXV, February 2007, p. 1798.

212 Mexico Art. 1916 CC.

213 Under CISG article 77 the party entitled to damages is required to mitigate the loss. The specific effect of this rule is that loss resulting from a breach of contract, including the loss of profits, is not compensated to the extent that it could have been reduced by taking reasonable measures and that loss which could have been prevented entirely by taking the said measures cannot be recoverable at all, *see* Schwenzer, *supra* note 19, Art. 77, para. 1, at 1042.

to avoid using an ordinary diligence.[214] Nor has the topic been studied by the doctrine.[215] Nevertheless, the duty on the creditor exists and imposes certain limits to the amount of damages that can be claimed. As clarified by the Mexican Supreme Court, the damages that the party in breach of the contract shall compensate are those that necessary had to suffer the other party.[216]

The duty to mitigate the damages must be constructed on the basis of the principle of good faith.[217] Contracts are binding on the parties not only in what has been expressed in them but, also in all that emanates from the nature of the obligation, the law, the equity or the usages.[218] This can be broadly interpreted to indicate that the breaching party has a good faith duty to take all reasonable measures to prevent loss or to mitigate the extent of the loss caused by the debtor's breach of contract.[219]

---

[214] Bolivia Art. 348 CC; Peru Art. 1327 CC; *see also* Bolivia: Castellanos Trigo & Auad La Fuente, *supra* note 21, at 163-165.

[215] *See* recognising the absence of doctrinal studies on this issue Spain: Soler Presas, *supra* note 3, at 45.

[216] Mexico Supreme Court, *Quinta Época, Tercera Sala*, SJF XCVI, p 951.

[217] Spain: A. Soler Presas, *in* L. Díez Picazo y Ponce De León (Ed.), La Compraventa Internacional de Mecaderias – Comentario sobre la Convención de Viena Art. 77, II, at 622 (1998); Portugal: L. De Lima Pinheiro, Dereito Comercial Internacional 280 (2005).

[218] Argentina Art. 1198 CC; Bolivia Art. 803 Com C; Brazil Art. 422 CC; Chile Art. 1546 CC; Colombia Art. 1603 CC & Art. 863 Com C; Cuba Art. 6 CC; Ecuador Art. 1589 CC; El Salvador Art. 1417 CC; Guatemala Art. 17 JOL; Mexico Art. 1796 CC; Paraguay Art. 715 CC; Peru Art. 1362 CC; Portugal Art. 762 CC; Spain Art. 1258 CC & Art. 57 Com C.

[219] *See* Ch. 32, 3.

CHAPTER 51

IMPOSSIBILITY, HARDSHIP AND EXEMPTION

1. Impossibility

All the Ibero-American laws recognise the principle under which a party to a contract is released from his contractual obligation to perform if an impediment or impossibility occurs after the formation of the contract and cannot be considered to be the negligence of the debtor.[1]

1.1. Contract Terms

Determination of impossibility frequently starts within the specific contractual terms agreed by the parties. In other words, the question of whether one party's duty to perform has become impossible has a first answer in the characteristics of the obligations agreed.[2] A contract may call for the goods to have certain characteristics and the seller may fail to meet them because of events beyond his control. A contract could also require payment to be made upon a fixed

[1] Argentina Arts. 513, 888 CC (distinguishes between legally or physically impossible); Bolivia Art. 379 CC; Brazil Arts. 234, 248 CC; Chile Art. 1547 (2) CC; Colombia Art. 1604 (2) CC & Art. 930 Com C; Ecuador Art. 1590 (2) CC; El Salvador Art. 1418 (2) CC; Mexico Art. 2111 CC; Paraguay Art. 628 CC (distinguishes between legally or physically impossible); Peru Arts. 1314, 1315, 1316, 1317 CC; Portugal Art. 790 CC; Spain Arts. 1.105, 1.184 CC; *see also* Argentina: G.A. Borda, Manual de Contratos 140 (2004); Argentina: M.U. Salermo, Contratos Civiles y Comerciales 237 (2007); Argentina: R.L. Lorenzetti, Tratado de los Contratos Parte General 598 (2004); Brazil: O. Gomes, Contratos 211 (2008); El Salvador: A.O. Miranda, Guía para. el Estudio del Derecho Civil III, Obligaciones 156; X. O'Callaghan (Ed.), Código Civil Comentado Art. 1.105, at 1075 (2004); ICC Final Award Case No. 13967 *Lex Contractus* Bolivian Law and INCOTERMS 2000.

[2] G.H. Jones & P. Schlechtriem, *Breach of Contract (Deficiencies in a Party's Performance)*, *in* A.T. von Mehren (Ed.), International Encyclopedia of Comparative Law, Vol. VII Contracts, Ch. 15, 99, para. 158 (1999).

date, and though the buyer is ready to pay, some unanticipated incident may stop him from performing in due time.

But the contractual terms are even more relevant in respect of the understanding of subsequent impossibility and the legal consequences of the impossibility to perform.[3] The default rules of the Ibero-American laws establish what should be understood by impossibility and which party shall bear the consequences of the impossibility to perform. However, the same rules also acknowledge that the agreement of the parties on this issue is the ultimate law. Such freedom is subtracted from a recurrent provision stating that the party who fails to perform his obligations due to events beyond his control may still be bound to perform or may still be liable to pay damages, if that party has agreed to bear the consequences of such events.[4]

In this manner, it is common that parties contractually define the impossibility that may discharge them from performance. They may do so by giving examples of specific cases covered by the definition or by excluding other specific cases from the definition. For example, contractual clauses may exclude from the definition of impossibility any action generated from third parties that cannot be reasonably resisted, including, in this case, strikes, civic demonstrations, acts of the State or others of similar nature that have direct effects on the performance of the contract.[5]

In addition, parties may agree on the process and requirements for the termination of the contract on the basis of subsequent impossibility; for example, by requiring the party bearing the impossibility to communicate to the other party within a short period, and by fixing the time during which the impossibility should last before a party terminates the contract.[6]

The same applies regarding the allocation of the risk related to the impediment to perform. In most civil law systems, when the object of contract is lost or damaged, and this is not attributed to the fault of one of the parties, both parties are released from performing their obligations.[7] That is, damage

---

[3] Jones & Schlechtriem, *supra* note 2, at 99, para. 158.

[4] Argentina Arts. 513, 889 CC; Bolivia Art. 577 sentence 2 CC; Brazil Art. 393 CC; Chile Art. 1673 CC; Colombia Art. 1732 CC; Ecuador Art. 1716 CC; El Salvador Art. 1543 CC; Mexico Art. 2111 CC; Peru Art. 1317 CC; Portugal Art. 546 part 1 CC; Uruguay Art. 220 (1) Com C; Venezuela Art. 1.344 CC (2 para); *see also* ICC Final Award Case No. 12755 *Lex Contractus* Argentinean Law: upholding the validity of a clause in a sales contract preventing one of the parties to invoke the impossibility exemption in monetary obligations originating from the said contract; Mexico Collegiate Tribunals, *Novena Época,* Registry 197163, SJF VII, January 1998, at 1069; *see also* El Salvador: Miranda, *supra* note 1, at 158; O'Callaghan, *supra* note 1, Art. 1.105, at 1075.

[5] Such clause was analysed in ICC Final Award Case No. 13967 *Lex Contractus* Bolivian Law and INCOTERMS 2000.

[6] *Id.*

[7] *See* expressly stated in Argentina Art. 895 CC: stating that the debtor shall give back the performance already made by the creditor; *see also* Jones & Schlechtriem, *supra* note 2, at 114, para. 182.

or complete loss of the object discharges the debtor of the obligation because the impossibility is not due to his conduct, and the other party, as a matter of principle, is also discharged from counter-performing.[8] However, this basic legal configuration may be modified by the rules on the passing of risk of the goods subject to the sales contract.[9]

As mentioned before,[10] the exact time of the passing of risk under a sales contract is of crucial importance because it does not only determines the party who bears loss of or damage to the goods, but also which party is discharged from having to perform his obligations, and which party remains obliged to perform his obligations.[11] For example, if goods are lost or damaged after risk has passed to the buyer, the seller may be released from having to supply equivalent goods, while the buyer is nevertheless bound to pay the price of the lost goods. On the other hand, if the risk is at the seller's side, the buyer may not pay and the seller will bear the total lost or damage of the goods.[12]

1.2. Default Provisions

1.2.1. Notion

Most of the Ibero-American laws rely on the concepts of *Fortuitous Event* and *Force Majeure*[13] as the main sources of impediments to perform, and which result in the extinction of the debtor's obligation and release him from liability.[14] These two concepts are doctrinally distinguished, depending on the

---

8 Argentina: Lorenzetti, *supra* note 1, at 599.

9 *See* expressly provided in Argentina Art. 889 CC; Costa Rica Art. 459 *chapeau* CC; *see also* Jones & Schlechtriem, *supra* note 2, at 114, para. 182; Argentina: Lorenzetti, *supra* note 1, at 599; Brazil: Gomes, *supra* note 1, at 212.

10 *See* Ch. 44, 2 & 3.

11 P.M. Roth, *The Passing of Risk*, 27 American Journal of Comparative Law 291, at 291 (1979).

12 Though in specific cases, the seller must compensate the buyer for the non-delivery, even if the loss was due to unforeseeable events. For example, when the goods have not been yet determined, or identified with distinctive marks or signals which prevent confusion, or when the seller is been already late in delivering the goods, *etc*, *see* Argentina Art. 894 CC; Brazil Art. 238 CC; Chile Art. 1670 CC *contrario sensu* & Art. 143 (1) (3) Com C; Colombia Art. 1729 CC *contrario sensu*; Costa Rica Art. 459 (a) (c) Com C; Ecuador Art. 1713 CC *contrario sensu* & Art. 188(1)(3) Com C; El Salvador Art. 1540 CC *contrario sensu*; Paraguay Art. 632 CC; Spain Art. 334(1)(3).

13 Translation of *Caso Fortuito* and *Fuerza Mayor* in Spanish; *see* Argentina Art. 513 CC. In Portuguese *Caso Fortuito* and *Força Maior*; *see* Brazil: Gomes, *supra* note 1, at 212.

14 *See* Argentina: Borda, *supra* note 1, at 140; Argentina: Salermo, *supra* note 1, at 237; El Salvador: Miranda, *supra* note 1, at 156; O'Callaghan, *supra* note 1, Art. 1.105, at 1075; Mexico Collegiate Tribunals, *Novena Época,* Registry 197163, SJF VII, January 1998, at 1069.

cause that originates the event.[15] However, the definitions provided by Ibero-American authors are not uniform and confusion has been created.[16]

Fortunately, all the laws that rely on these concepts take them as synonyms, and define them as a single concept. For example, the Civil Codes of Chile, Colombia, Ecuador and El Salvador share a uniform definition of the two impediments. A provision reads:

> Force Majeure and Fortuitous Event is the unforeseen event that is impossible to resist, like a shipwreck, an earthquake, the capture of enemies, the acts of authority executed by a government official, *etc.*[17]

The Argentinean Civil Code dictates that *fortuitous event* is the one that cannot be foreseen, or if foreseen, cannot be evaded.[18] Similarly, Brazil's Civil Code establishes that a fortuitous event or force majeure is an inevitable event, the effects of which were not possible to avoid or prevent.[19] Finally, Peru's Civil Code conjunctively define these concepts as the non-imputable cause, consisting in an extraordinary event, unforeseeable and unavoidable, which impedes the performance of the obligation or causes a partial, delayed or defective breach.[20]

Other Ibero-American laws base the discharge of the debtor's obligation on the notion of impossibility due to unforeseen, and/or inevitable events, with no reference to the concepts of force majeure or fortuitous event.[21]

Whatever the case may be, all the Ibero-American laws concur on the necessary elements for the impossibility to discharge the debtor of his contractual obligations. As the Mexican Supreme Court has explained:

---

15 Mexico Collegiate Tribunals, *Novena Época*, Registry 197163, SJF VII, January 1998, p. 1069: explaining how scholars such as Bonnecase, García Goyena, Henri León Mazeaud y André Tunc distinguish three categories of impossibilities (force majeure or fortuitous events) depending on whether such derived from events of the nature, the human beings or government's acts.

16 While some authors consider as Fortuitous Event the unexpected incident that originates from the forces of nature, others define the same concept as events within the debtor's sphere of action that cannot be prevented. Similarly, while Force Majeure is understood to be the obstructive act coming from a third person, others consider the same concept to originate out of the scope of debtor's influence; *see* Chile: L. Acuña Tapia & G. Novoa Muñoz, *Cambio de Circunstancias en el Contrato*, Doctoral thesis, Universidad Católica de Temuco, Escuela de Derecho 7 (2004), http://biblioteca.uct.cl/tesis/luis-acuna/tesis.pdf; Spain: M. Medina de Lemus, Derecho Civil: Obligaciones y Contratos II, Teoria General Vol. 1, 145 (2004); *see also* a different definition of Fortuitous Event and Force Majeure in Mexico: R. De Pina, Elementos de Derecho Civil Mexicano, Contratos en Particular, Vol. IV, 342-358 (2007).

17 Chile Art. 45 CC; Colombia Art. 64 CC; Ecuador Art. 30 CC; El Salvador Art. 43 CC.

18 Argentina Art. 514 CC.

19 Brazil Art. 393 CC.

20 Peru Art. 1315 CC.

21 Argentina Art. 467 Com C; Bolivia Art. 577 CC; Paraguay Art. 628 CC; Portugal Art. 790 CC; Spain Art. 1.105 CC.

> Irrespective of the doctrinal understanding that may be adopted regarding the concepts of force majeure and fortuitous event, it cannot be denied that their essential elements and their effects are the same. They refer to incidents of the nature or human conduct, unknown by the debtor, that affect him in his legal relationships; that prevent him, temporally or definitively, to perform, partially or totally, an obligation; being such fact non-imputable, directly or indirectly, to his fault, and which effects cannot be avoided with the means that his social environment would provide him with, in order to prevent the event or to oppose it and resist it.[22]

1.2.2. Requirements

The Ibero-American laws require that the impossibility appear after the formation of the contract and from an unforeseeable event.[23] This means that if the performance of the obligation was already impossible before the contract's formation, this is a case of initial impossibility that renders the contract void.[24] It also means that within the ordinary understanding of an average man, it was not possible to foresee at that time that the event would occur.[25]

Third, it must be an event insurmountable or irresistible. This means that the same event or fact impedes the debtor or any other person to perform under all circumstances.[26] The Supreme Court of Chile has explained that an event is "irresistible when it is not possible to avoid its consequences, in a case where any person in the same circumstances could neither have foreseen it nor avoided it."[27]

On this issue, an ICC Arbitration Tribunal explained that acts of authority, such as the restriction of exports on the type of goods, constitute impossibility when such impede the performance of the obligation. In the present case, the excused seller was further able to prove that he had negotiated, in good faith, a mutually acceptable solution with the buyer and that he had assisted with efforts to provide substitution of the goods to the buyer.[28]

---

22 Mexico Supreme Court, *Séptima Época*, Registry 245709, SJF 121-126 Part VII, p. 81.

23 Brazil: Gomes, *supra* note 1, at 212; El Salvador: Miranda, *supra* note 1, at 156; Mexico Collegiate Tribunals, *Novena Época,* Registry 197'162, SFJ VII, January 1998, at 1069.

24 *See* express reference to this distinction in Portugal Arts. 401(1), 790(2) CC; *see also* Argentina: Lorenzetti, *supra* note 1, at 598; *see* Ch. 19.

25 O'Callaghan, *supra* note 1, Art. 1.105, at 1075; Chile Supreme Court, RDJ, Vol. 46, Sec. 1, at 533: sustained that an event is fortuitous when there is no grounded reason to believe it will occur; El Salvador Supreme Court, *Cass civ, Kereitz Medrano v. Liceo Centroamericano, S.A. de C.V.,* 11-C-2007, 17 November 2008: there is no force majeure when the debtor could have *reasonably* foreseen the event.

26 Argentina: Lorenzetti, *supra* note 1, at 598; Brazil: Gomes, *supra* note 1, at 212; El Salvador: Miranda, *supra* note 1, at 156; O'Callaghan, *supra* note 1, Art. 1.105, at 1075.

27 Chile Supreme Court, RDJ, Vol. 46, Sec. 1, at 533.

28 ICC Final Award Case No. 13385 *Lex Contractus* Argentinean Law: In February 2004, the Argentine Ministry of Energy issued several resolutions with respect to natural gas distribution.

In a different ICC arbitration governed by the Bolivian Law, a Bolivian seller was released from his obligation to deliver a type of hydrocarbon extracted from crude oil known by the name of *condensado* to a Brazilian buyer on the grounds of subsequent impossibility. In the case at hand, the seller stopped the delivery of *condensado* due to a Governmental Order requesting any national producer to furnish a compulsory quota of crude oil to the Bolivian refineries for the production of diesel oil for domestic consumption. The Government Order did not restrict the export of *condensado* but rather imposed great fines to those crude oil producers that did not comply with the Order. The Arbitral Tribunal found that the seller was able to prove that he did not have the crude oil production capacity to fulfil both his contractual obligations and the Government Order. Further, even if by paying the fine the impossibility could have disappeared, the huge amount of the fine (USD 1,000,000.00 per day) rendered impossible the equilibrium of the contract.[29]

In summary, a debtor may only be discharged from his duty to perform and be released from his liability for breach of contract if the impossibility has the mentioned characteristics. However, a debtor would still be liable for non-performance if he has agreed to bear the consequences of the impossibility.[30]

1.2.3. Limits

If the impossibility originates after the agreed time of performance, that is, during the time when the debtor is already in delay, he shall be accountable for the consequences of the non-performance,[31] unless the impossibility would still occur despite the goods being already delivered.[32]

In addition, many Ibero-American laws contain the basic rule under which the debtor shall be released from his obligation to deliver ascertained and identified goods if such are lost due to events beyond his control.[33] But if the obligation consists of the delivery of generic goods, only ascertained on its type, the performance will never be considered to be impossible and the debtor may be liable for damages caused by breach of contract.[34]

In May 2004, respondents decided to suspend gas exports, alleging force majeure, based on the resolutions of the government.

29 ICC Final Award Case No. 13967 *Lex Contractus* Bolivian Law and INCOTERMS 2000.

30 *See supra* 1.1.

31 *See* Spain Art. 1.182 CC *contrario sensu*; Uruguay Art. 220 (3) Com C; Venezuela Art. 1.344 CC; *see also* Brazil: Gomes, *supra* note 1, at 213; El Salvador: Miranda, *supra* note 1, at 157; O'Callaghan, *supra* note 1, Art. 1.105, at 1075.

32 Chile Arts. 1547(2), 1672 CC; Colombia Arts. 1604(2), 1731 CC; Ecuador Arts. 1590(2), 1715 CC; El Salvador Arts. 1418(2), 1542 CC; Uruguay Art. 220(3) Com C; Venezuela Art. 1.344 CC.

33 Argentina Arts. 890, 893 CC; Brazil Art. 238 CC; Chile Art. 1670 CC; Colombia Art. 1729 CC & Art. 930 Com C; Ecuador Art. 1713 CC; El Salvador Art. 1540 CC; Paraguay Art. 632 CC.

34 Argentina Art. 894 CC; Brazil Art. 238 CC; Chile Art. 1670 CC *contrario sensu* & Art. 143

1.2.4. Negligent Conduct

The debtor may still be liable for damages and loss of profits if the impossibility is caused by his negligence.[35] Some laws expressly define negligence as the omission of those diligences that are required by the nature of the obligation according to the personal circumstances, the time and the place.[36] The Bolivian and the Spanish Civil Codes add that when no level of diligence has been agreed to perform the obligation, it shall be required a level of diligence corresponding to that of the *bonus pater familias*.[37] As noted by a scholar, the issue is not about the psyche of the debtor but about his conduct that deviates from the standard required by the law.[38]

In relation to the issue, many Civil Codes expressly state that it is on the debtor to prove that he has acted with care and diligence, so that no negligent conduct can connect him with the events.[39] All the more since it is presumed that if the goods are lost in the debtor's possession, it is due to his conduct or negligence.[40] Similarly, the burden of proving the impossibility is on the debtor who claims it has been prevented to perform.[41] Also the debtor must

(1) (3) Com C; Colombia Art. 1729 CC *contrario sensu*; Costa Rica Art. 459 (a) (c) Com C; Ecuador Art. 1713 CC *contrario sensu*; El Salvador Art. 1540 CC *contrario sensu*; Paraguay Art. 632 CC.

[35] Argentina Arts. 513, 888, 889 CC & Art. 467 Com C; Brazil Art. 248 CC; Chile Art. 1547 paras. 1, 2 CC; Colombia Art. 1604 paras. 1, 2 CC & Art. 930 Com C; Ecuador Art. 1590 paras. 1, 2 CC; El Salvador Art. 1418 paras. 1, 2 CC; Mexico Art. 2111 CC; Peru Arts. 1317, 1321 CC; Portugal Arts. 546 part 1, 801 CC; Spain Art. 1.104 CC; Uruguay Art. 220 (2) Com C; Venezuela Art. 1.271 CC; *see also* Argentina: Borda, *supra* note 1, at 140: noting that in Argentina the negligent debtor may be released from performing due to the impossibility but he is liable for damages and loss of profits; Argentina: Lorenzetti, *supra* note 1, at 599: same opinion; Brazil: Gomes, *supra* note 1, at 213 same opinion; El Salvador: Miranda, *supra* note 1, at 157; Portugal: J. de M. Antunes Valera, Das Obrigações em Geral 403 (2003): in addition, the creditor has a right to avoid the contract; El Salvador Supreme Court, *Cass civ, Kereitz Medrano v. Liceo Centroamericano, S.A. de C.V.,* 11-C-2007, 17 November 2008: the alleged impediment should not result of the negligent conduct of the debtor.

[36] Argentina Art. 512 CC; Peru Arts. 1319, 1320 CC; Spain Art. 1.104 CC; Uruguay Art. 221 Com C.

[37] Bolivia Art. 302 (I) CC; Spain Art. 1.104 *in fine* CC; *see also* Bolivia: G. Castellanos Trigo & S. Auad La Fuente, Derecho de las Obligaciones en el Código Civil Boliviano 48 (2008); O'Callaghan, *supra* note 1, Art. 1.105, at 1075.

[38] Argentina: Lorenzetti, *supra* note 1, at 603.

[39] Chile Art. 1547 (3) CC; Colombia Art. 1604 (3) CC; Ecuador Art. 1590 (3) CC; El Salvador Art. 1418 (3) CC.

[40] Chile Art. 1671 CC; Colombia Art. 1730 CC; Ecuador Art. 1714 CC; El Salvador Art. 1541 CC; Spain Art. 1.183 CC; *see also* Argentina: Lorenzetti, *supra* note 1, at 602.

[41] Chile Arts. 1547 (3), 1674 CC; Colombia Arts. 1604 (3), 1733 CC; Ecuador Arts. 1590 (3), 1717 CC; El Salvador Arts. 1418 (3), 1544 CC; Portugal Art. 799 (1) CC; Spain Art. 1.183 CC; Venezuela Art. 1.344 CC (3); *see also* Argentina: Lorenzetti, *supra* note 1, at 602; O'Callaghan, *supra* note 1, Art. 1.105, at 1075; ICC Final Award Case No. 12755 *Lex Contractus* Argentinean Law.

prove that the goods would have still been lost, due to unforeseeable events, even if he had performed on time.[42]

1.2.5. Effects and Standards

Under the Ibero-American laws, the effect of a 'legitimate' impossibility discharges the debtor of his obligation to perform. The impossibility extinguishes the contracted obligations and releases the debtor from any liability for breach of contract;[43] including the agreed or legal liability for damages and lost profits.[44] On the basis of a contractual relationship, the unwinding of the contract operates automatically and retroactively. The restitution of the already performed obligations is then due and subject to the rules on unjustified enrichment.[45] Judicial intervention only takes place if one of the parties refuses to give back the received performance.[46]

In cases where the impossibility only affects part of the debtor's overall obligations under the contract, the question arises on, whether the creditor is aggrieved only in respect of that part of the performance, or whether the entire obligation, which may have already been performed in part, is affected by the partial impossibility.[47] Some Ibero-American laws present an express solution to this problem. In cases of partial impossibility to perform, the

[42] Argentina Art. 892 CC; Chile Art. 1674 CC; Colombia Art. 1733 CC; Ecuador Art. 1717 CC; El Salvador Art. 1544 CC.

[43] *See* expressly stated in Argentina Art. 895 CC & Art. 467 Com C; Bolivia Art. 379 CC; Brazil Art. 248 CC; Chile Art. 1567 (7) CC; Colombia Art. 1625 (7) CC & Art. 930 Com C; Ecuador Art. 1610 (8) CC; El Salvador Art. 1438 (6) CC; Peru Art. 1316 sentence 1 CC; Portugal Art. 790 CC; Spain Arts. 1.182, 1.105, 1.184 CC; Venezuela Art. 1.272 CC; ICC Final Award Case No. 13967 *Lex Contractus* Bolivian Law and INCOTERMS 2000; ICC Final Award Case No. 13530 *Lex Contractus* Brazilian Law; Mexico Supreme Court, *Séptima Época, Tercera Sala,* SJF 139-144, Part 4, at 80; Bolivia: Castellanos Trigo & Auad La Fuente, *supra* note 37, at 235-236; Jones & Schlechtriem, *supra* note 2, at 114, para. 182; Portugal: Antunes Valera, *supra* note 35, at 402; O'Callaghan, *supra* note 1, Art. 1.105, at 1075.

[44] *See* Costa Rica: D. Baudrit Carrillo, Los Contratos Traslativos del Derecho Privado – Principios de Jurisprudencia 44-48 (2000): discussing a Supreme Court Judgment upholding this effect; Mexico Art. 1847 CC: a penalty clause cannot be enforced, and other damages cannot be claimed, when the debtor was unable to fulfil his obligations under the contract due to fortuitous events or insurmountable force; confirmed by Jurisprudence Mexico Collegiate Tribunals, *Novena Época,* Registry 173722, SJF XXIV, December 2006, at 1378; *see also* Bolivia: Castellanos Trigo & Auad La Fuente, *supra* note 37, at 237-238; O'Callaghan, *supra* note 1, Art. 1.105, at 1075.

[45] Expressly stated in Argentina Art. 895 CC: stating that the debtor shall give back the performance already made by the creditor; Bolivia Art. 577 CC: same; Portugal Art. 795 (1) CC: subject to the rules on unjustified enrichment; Portugal: Antunes Valera, *supra* note 35, at 402; ICC Final Award Case No. 13530 *Lex Contractus* Brazilian Law.

[46] Brazil: Gomes, *supra* note 1, at 213; Portugal Art. 795(1) CC: through an action for unjust enrichment; ICC Final Award Case No. 13530 *Lex Contractus* Brazilian Law.

[47] *See* Jones & Schlechtriem, *supra* note 2, at 103, para. 163.

debtor of the obligation may perform the part of the obligation still possible,[48] when the creditor of the obligation manifests his will to receive the partial performance.[49] In Costa Rica, Spain and Brazil, for example, if the goods have been lost only in part [due to unforeseeable events borne by the seller] the buyer may opt to claim the delivery of the remaining goods or may decide to avoid the contract.[50] The CISG embodies the same rule in its article 51, according to which if the failure to make delivery completely amounts to a fundamental breach, the buyer may declare the contract avoided.[51]

As noted by some authors, the decisive criteria in these cases is whether or not the creditor has an interest in partial performance.[52] The Peruvian and the Portuguese Civil Codes expressly establish an objective criterion: the whole obligation extinguishes if partial performance is not useful to the creditor or if he would not *justifiably* have interest in the partial performance.[53]

A temporary impediment may also temporarily discharge the debtor from his obligation to perform.[54] When the impossibility ceases, the debtor may be called to perform unless time was of the essence and the creditor of the obligation had opted to abandon the contract.[55] The creditor of the obligation may *justifiably* lose interest in the contract, in cases where it can be inferred that the exact performance was relevant to satisfy the creditor's interest.[56]

---

48 *See* Bolivia Art. 832 CC: including defective performance; Paraguay Art. 630 CC; Portugal Art. 793 (1) CC.

49 Bolivia Arts. 382, 578, 600 CC.

50 Brazil Art. 235 CC; Costa Rica Art. 471 Com C; Spain Art. 1460 CC.

51 Art. 51 (2) CISG. A similar provision is embodied in Bolivia's Art. 572 CC: dictating that there is no ground for the avoidance of the contra if the breach by one of the parties is of little gravity or little importance considering the interest of the other party.

52 Jones & Schlechtriem, *supra* note 2, at 104, para. 163; Argentina: Salermo, *supra* note 1, at 237: noting that in case of death of the debtor, the creditor may declared the contract avoided for the remaining performances if the debtor's identity was of fundamental importance for the contract; Brazil: Gomes, *supra* note 1, at 212: noting that the creditor can have an interest in contracts that have as its object the performance of multiple-principal obligations or of a principal obligation with multiples accessories.

53 Peru Art. 1316 last para. CC; Portugal Art. 793 (2) CC.

54 Expressly in Bolivia Art. 380 CC; Paraguay Art. 628 para. 2 CC; Peru Art. 1316 part 2 CC; Portugal Art. 792(1) CC; Liberal interpretation of the following provisions (the creditor may claim the delivery of goods that had suddenly disappeared but were subsequently found): Bolivia Art. 381 CC; Chile Art. 1675 CC; Colombia Art. 1734 CC; Ecuador Art. 1718 CC; El Salvador Art. 1545 CC; Paraguay Art. 629 CC; *see also* Jones & Schlechtriem, *supra* note 2, at 112, para. 177; Argentian: Lorenzetti, *supra* note 1, at 600.

55 *See* Art. 79(3) CISG; expressly in Bolivia Art. 380 CC; Paraguay Art. 628 para. 2 CC; Peru Art. 1316 part 2 CC.

56 Expressly in Bolivia Art. 380 CC; Paraguay Art. 628 para. 2 CC; Peru Art. 1316 part 2 CC; Portugal Art. 792 (2) CC; *see also* Argentina: Lorenzetti, *supra* note 1, at 600; Brazil: Gomes, *supra* note 1, at 212.

1.2.6. Third Persons

According to CISG Article 79(2), if the party's failure is due to the failure of a third person who was engaged to perform the whole or a part of the contract, that party is exempt from liability only if he and the third person would be exempted under the Convention. The same principle can be deduced from Ibero-American law. For example, a rule among the provisions on lawful impossibility to perform states that "in the performance or negligence of the debtor, it is included the performance and the negligence of those for who he will be responsible."[57] In Peru's Civil Code a similar provision dictates that if the debtor engages third parties to perform his obligation, he shall be liable for their negligent conduct, unless otherwise agreed.[58]

Accordingly, if the debtor is liable for the deficient performance or the fault of those persons under his supervision, the debtor may also be released of any duty to perform or liability for breach of contract due to unexpected events which have impeded, to these same persons, the performance of related duties.

1.2.7. Notice to the other Party

Under CISG Article 79(4), the debtor of the obligation must give notice to the other party of the events that impede him to perform. If the debtor fails to do so within a reasonable time after he knew or ought to have known of the impediment, he shall be liable for any loss derived from his failure to give notice. None of the Ibero-American laws contain a similar rule. Nevertheless, similar liability derives from the Ibero-American laws' duty to inform the other party of any circumstances that may be relevant to such party. As developed before,[59] the duty to act in good faith comes together with the duty to inform.[60] The good faith principle includes every sort of values embraced by justice and which shall be protected by the parties to a contract.[61]

2. Hardship

In some Ibero-American laws, one of the general principles of contracts is that the circumstances that modify the economy of the contract do not

[57] Chile Art. 1679 CC; Colombia Art. 1738 CC; Ecuador Art. 1722 CC; El Salvador Art. 1549 CC.

[58] Peru Art. 1325 CC; similarly Portugal Art. 791 CC.

[59] *See* Ch. 32 2.

[60] Argentina: A.A. Alterini, Contratos civiles, comerciales, de consumo 330 (1998); Chile: J. Lopez Santa Maria, Los Contratos: Parte General, Vol. 2, n. 598 (2005); Colombia: J. Oviedo Alban, La Formación de Contrato: tratos preliminares, oferta, aceptación 17 (2008).

[61] A duty inferred from Argentina Art. 1056 CC according to Argentina: F. López de Zavalia, Teoria de los Contratos, Vol. 1, 299 (2003).

affect its validity or enforceability. In other words, the parties are bound by the obligations agreed upon during and until the complete fulfilment of the contract, irrespective of any change of the circumstances. The rule is taken from the inherited Roman law principle of *pacta sunt servanda*.[62] This principle is deeply rooted in countries like Mexico.[63]

However, a group of Ibero-American legal systems have integrated into their provisions on contracts an exception to this general principle, commonly known as *rebus sic stantibus* clause.[64] In Argentina, Bolivia, Brazil, Paraguay and Peru, as well as under Colombia, El Salvador and Guatemala B2B contracts, a contract may be adjusted or avoided by a court when an extraordinary and unforeseeable event makes one of the party's obligations to become excessively onerous.[65] Similarly, the Spanish Jurisprudence has acknowledged the possibility of adjusting or avoiding the contract under the *rebus sic stantibus* doctrine.[66]

2.1. Notion

Hardship distinguishes from objective impossibility. As already reviewed in this chapter, a *force majeure* or fortuitous event absolutely impedes the performance, while hardship or subsequent excessive onerosity only makes performance difficult.[67] In practice, the line dividing the two notions is not always clear. Often both will apply. As noted, many times the answer will reside in an objective evaluation as to whether the change of circumstances has been relevant and important enough to cause a real impossibility to perform

[62] *See for example* Costa Rica Supreme Court, Judgment 108, 18 July 1989: the contract is the law for the parties which are bound by the terms expressed in it.

[63] *See for example* Mexico Art. 1796 CC & Art. 78 Com C; All negating the applicability of the doctrine of hardship in national contracts: Mexico Supreme Court, *Séptima Época, Tercera Sala,* Registry 240782 SJF 139-144, part 4, at 29; Mexico Collegiate Tribunals, *Novena Época,* Registry 195622, SJF VIII, September 1998, at 1217; Mexico Collegiate Tribunals, *Novena Época,* Registry 195621, SJF VIII, September 1998, at 1149.

[64] Brazil: Gomes, *supra* note 1, at 214.

[65] Argentina Art. 1198 part 2 CC; Bolivia Arts. 581-583 CC; Brazil Arts. 478-480 CC; Paraguay Art. 672 CC; Peru Arts. 1440-1444 CC; Colombia Art. 868 Com C; El Salvador Art. 994 Com C; Guatemala Art. 688 Com C; ICC Final Award Case No. 13347 *Lex Contractus* Brazilian Law: noting that the interested party on the revision shall prove: 1) the excessive onerosity of the obligations owed; 2) the casual link between the excessive onerosity and the subsequent events to the conclusion of the contract; 3) the unforeseeablility of such events for both of the parties; 4) that the cause of the event is not attributable to him.

[66] Spain Supreme Tribunal, 15 March 1994, *Id Cendoj:* 28079110011994101643; ICC Final Award Case No. 11317 *Lex Contractus* Spanish Law: The Arbitral Tribunal noted that in the light of Spanish case-law on the so-called *rebus sic stantibus* clause, a contract may be terminated on the grounds of imbalance of the contractual services supplied. However, in the instant case, the required conditions were not met for terminating or revising the contract.

[67] Argentina: Lorenzetti, *supra* note 1, at 518, 519; Brazil: Gomes, *supra* note 1, at 214.

or whether, simply grave difficulties to perform have arisen.[68] As stated by an Arbitration Tribunal, even grave difficulties imposed by free market competition rules or control measures in the currency exchange market may not constitute impossibility to perform.[69]

Hardship also distinguishes from gross disparity because excessive onerosity originates after conclusion of the contract, while gross disparity is previous or simultaneous to the formation of the contract.[70] Also, in the case of gross disparity there exists a subjective element *i.e.*, the conduct of one of the parties that disrupted the equal relationship under the contract, an element which does not exist in subsequent excessive onerosity.[71]

2.2. Scope and Requirements

The scope of the application of the provisions on excessive onerosity is mostly the same in the Ibero-American laws. The adjustment of the contract because of excessive onerosity only applies to, first, contracts of deferred, periodic or continued execution;[72] though Peru's Civil Code expressly extends its application to contracts of immediate execution when the performance was deferred by events which are not attributable to the debtor.[73] Second, it only applies to bilateral commutative contracts, such as sales contracts.[74] Third, Argentina, Bolivia, Brazil, Paraguay and Peru apply the exception to both C2C and B2B contracts, as the provisions not establish a different treatment, while Colombia, El Salvador and Guatemala apply it only to B2B sales.

Moreover, the requirements for the adjustment or avoidance of the contract are not so different. First, the event must be an extraordinary one in contrast to ordinary events that would be expected to occur.[75] Second, the event must

68 Argentina: Borda, *supra* note 1, at 158.

69 ICC Final Award Case No. 12755 *Lex Contractus* Argentinean Law.

70 *See* Ch. 25, 1.

71 Argentina: Lorenzetti, *supra* note 1, at 518, 519.

72 Argentina Art. 1198 part 2 CC; Bolivia Art. 581 (1) CC; Brazil Art. 478 CC; Colombia Art. 868 Com C; El Salvador Art. 994 Com C; Guatemala Art. 688 Com C: for the same sort of contracts only permits the avoidance and not the adjustment; Paraguay Art. 672 CC: only mentions 'contracts of deferred execution'; Peru Art. 1440 CC.

73 Peru Art. 1440 (1) CC.

74 Argentina Art. 1198 part 2 CC; Bolivia Art. 581 (1) CC; Brazil Art. 478 CC; Colombia Art. 868 Com C; El Salvador Art. 994 Com C; Paraguay Art. 672 CC; Peru Art. 1440 CC; However, the Argentinean, Brazilian, Bolivian, Paraguayan and Peruvian Civil Codes expressly state that such provision may also apply to unilateral onerous contract and random contracts in special cases, *see* Argentina Art. 1198 CC; Bolivia Arts. 582, 583 CC; Brazil Art. 480 CC; Paraguay Art. 672 CC; Peru Arts. 1441 (2), 1442 CC.

75 Argentina Art. 1198 part 2 CC; Bolivia Art. 581 (1) CC; Brazil Art. 478 CC; Colombia Art. 868 Com C; El Salvador Art. 994 Com C; Guatemala Art. 688 Com C; Paraguay Art. 672 CC; Peru Art. 1440 CC; *see also* Brazil: Gomes, *supra* note 1, at 215; Spain Supreme Tribunal, 15 March 1994, *Id Cendoj:* 28079110011994101643; ICC Final Award Case No. 13518 *Lex*

be an unforeseeable one.[76] An event is unforeseeable when the parties have been unable to foresee it, even if acting with due diligence. Foreseeability is determined according to the information available at the time of contract conclusion and according to the concrete capacity of the parties to forecast.[77]

Third, the event must provoke the excessive onerosity of the performance.[78] The question arises as to whether the modification of the obligation should be considered from the perspective of the debtor or, whether the objective unbalance between the mutual performances should solely be considered.[79] As noted by some authors, the extraordinary and unforeseeable event causes an excess in the onerosity of one of the performances, only if, measured against the counter-performance; such is an objective relation.[80] Thus, the economic situation of the affected party ought not to be taken into consideration solely. The value of the performance in itself is not as crucial as is the relation of equivalence *vis à vis* the counter-performance; equivalence lost by the alteration of the basis of the business.[81]

2.3. Effect

The effect of a judicially established excessive onerosity or hardship are almost identical. Six of the eight Ibero-American laws contemplate the avoidance of the contract by the competent court acting *ex parte*, as the principal effect.[82] Although, an ICC Arbitral Tribunal applying Argentina's law has admitted

Contractus Argentinean Law by operation of the Conflict of Law Rules in Argentina's civil code.

76 Argentina Art. 1198 part 2 CC; Bolivia Art. 581 (1) CC; Brazil Art. 478 CC; Paraguay Art. 672 CC; Peru Art. 1440 CC; Colombia Art. 868 Com C; El Salvador Art. 994 Com C; Guatemala Art. 688 Com C; *see also* Brazil: Gomes, *supra* note 1, at 215; Spain Supreme Tribunal, 15 March 1994, *Id Cendoj:* 28079110011994101643.

77 Argentina: Lorenzetti, *supra* note 1, at 521; ICC Final Award Case No. 11317 *Lex Contractus* Spanish Law: the Tribunal considered that the devaluation of the Brazilian currency was not an unforeseeable event, given that, in the situation under consideration, the parties had made express provision in their contract for suitable measures to mitigate the impact of such events, including amending the method of making payments, deducting from the total amount to be paid a sum to which the respondent was entitled by virtue of contract, should the revenue from passengers be lower than that forecast.

78 Argentina Art. 1198 part 2 CC; Bolivia Art. 581 (1) CC; Brazil Art. 478 CC; Colombia Art. 868 Com C; El Salvador Art. 994 Com C; Guatemala Art. 688 Com C; Paraguay Art. 672 CC; Peru Art. 1440 CC; Spain Supreme Tribunal, 15 March 1994, *Id Cendoj:* 28079110011994101643.

79 Argentina: Lorenzetti, *supra* note 1, at 521.

80 *Id.*, at 522; Brazil: Gomes, *supra* note 1, at 214.

81 Argentina National Civil Chamber, *Sala E*, Rep L L, XXXVIII-397, sum. 127 *cited in* Argentina: Lorenzetti, *supra* note 1, at 522; Brazil: Gomes, *supra* note 1, at 214, 215.

82 Argentina Art. 1198 CC; Bolivia Art. 581 (I) (IV) CC; Brazil Arts. 478, 479 CC; Paraguay Art. 672 CC; Colombia Art. 868 Com C; El Salvador Art. 994 Com C; Guatemala Art. 688 Com C.

the revision of the contract as the primary effect, as such was established in a hardship clause agreed by the parties.[83]

It should be mentioned that the avoidance of the contract does not affect the obligations already performed by the debtor, but only applies to the obligations still pending and that have legitimately become excessively onerous.[84]

The same legal systems establish as secondary effect, the revision or adjustment of the contract at the option of the creditor of the obligation who may be interested in the continuation of the contract.[85] In such a case, the question arises as to whether the debtor can file a request for the adjustment of the contract in order to keep the contract alive. In a literal interpretation of the provision, the Argentinean Supreme Court has negated the possibility of the debtor to autonomously file an action for the revision or adjustment of the contract.[86] Notwithstanding, the majority of scholars consider that it is unreasonable to deprive the debtor (affected by hardship) from his interest to continue with the contract once the inequality is eliminated.[87] A Brazilian scholar supports this view showing that other provisions of Brazil's Civil Code expressly allow the debtor to claim the adjustment of the contract.[88]

On this issue, an ICC Arbitral Tribunal applying the Argentinean law admitted the adjustment of the contract as requested by the debtor, based on the contractual hardship clause which granted such possibility to both parties.[89]

In contrast, under Peru's Civil Code and Colombia's Code of Commerce, the primary effect is not the avoidance but rather the revision and adjustment of the contract derived from the debtor's request seeking to cease the hardship. Only when such is not possible due to the nature of the obligation, the circumstances or because the creditor has so requested, the judge may declare the termination of the contract.[90] Such is also the approach followed by the UNIDROIT PICC for cases falling under the scope of their hardship provisions.[91]

---

83 ICC Final Award Case No. 13518 *Lex Contractus* Argentinean Law by operation of the Conflict of Law Rules in Argentina's civil code.

84 Expressly stated in Argentina Art. 1198 CC; Guatemala Art. 688 para. 2 Com C; Peru Art. 1440 *in fine* CC; Argentina: Lorenzetti, *supra* note 1, at 525. *See also* Bolivia Art. 581(II) CC: it is for that reason that some laws expressly provide that the provisions on excessive onerosity do not apply to cases where the excessively onerous obligation has already been executed.

85 Argentina Art. 1198 CC; Bolivia Art. 581(I)(IV) CC; Brazil Arts. 478, 479 CC; Paraguay Art. 672 CC; Colombia Art. 868 Com C; El Salvador Art. 994 Com C.

86 Argentina Supreme Court, *Kamestein, Victor y otros v. Fried de Goldring, cited in* Argentina: Lorenzetti, *supra* note 1, at 527, n. 46.

87 Brazil: Gomes, *supra* note 1, at 215; Argentina: Lorenzetti, *supra* note 1, at 527, n. 48.

88 Brazil: Gomes, *supra* note 1, at 216: Brazil Arts. 317, 620, 770 CC.

89 ICC Final Award Case No. 13518 *Lex Contractus* Argentinean Law by operation of the Conflict of Law Rules of Argentina's Civil Code.

90 Peru Art. 1440 CC; Colombia Art. 868 Com C.

91 *See for example* Arts. 6.2.1, 6.2.2, 6.2.3 of the UNIDROIT PICC.

Regarding the adjustment of the contract, an ICC Arbitral Tribunal applying the Argentinean law has explained that such should not be arithmetically made. This is, the revision of the price should not seek to overcome all the prejudices caused by the unforeseeable events. Instead, it should seek to release the contract from any unfair situation, in terms that the debtor should not become the beneficiary of the unforeseeable events and the creditor's profits should not result in being abusive.[92]

Whether the parties can agree in advance to renounce to the default remedies of hardship is under discussion in some jurisdictions. The Peruvian Civil Code expressly declares that renunciation to the remedy for excessive onerosity of the obligation is inadmissible under the law.[93] In Argentina, the doctrine has discussed the issue concluding that renunciation of the hardship remedy is valid in contracts with parties of equal conditions, as the provisions of the Civil Code grant a right and not an obligation, thus, susceptible to be modified by the parties' agreement.[94] Finally, Guatemala's Code of Commerce expressly confers such possibility as it negates the avoidance when the contract is aleatory, this is, when the parties have taken the risk of the subsequent excessive onerosity of the performances.[95]

Finally, under the Peruvian law, the limitation period to raise the hardship exemption is three months from the date the events altering the balance of the respective performances occurred.[96] However, as supported by the Peruvian Supreme Court, in order to raise the hardship exemption the event that produces the change of the circumstances should be sufficiently identified so that the beginning of the limitation period of the hardship action can be established.[97]

2.4. Argentina's Law No. 25.561 Pesificacion[98] of Monetary Obligations Owed in American Dollars or Foreign Currency

In Argentina, an Emergency Legislation was enacted to face the economic crisis of 2002. The said legislation established that the monetary obligations in foreign currency contracted before January 6, 2002, should be paid in Argentinean pesos at the rate of exchange of USD 1 = 1 Peso.[99] The Emergency Legislation established that the parties should, by mutual negotiation, adjust

92 ICC Final Award Case No. 13518 *Lex Contractus* Argentinean Law by operation of the Conflict of Law Rules of Argentina's Civil Code.

93 Peru Art. 1444 CC.

94 Argentina: Lorenzetti, *supra* note 1, at 529.

95 Guatemala Art. 688 para. 3 Com C.

96 Peru Arts. 1445, 1446 CC.

97 Peru Supreme Court, *Sala civil transitoria*, Resolution 002924-2003, 16 December 2003.

98 Spanish word which stands for the conversion of debts to Pesos.

99 Argentina's Law No. 25.561 of 6 January 2002 as amended by Decree No. 214/02, the Decree No. 320/02, Decree No. 410/02 and Decree No. 704/02.

the amount of the converted payment obligations.[100] Failing an agreement by the parties, such new amount should be established by courts.

An ICC Arbitral Tribunal, after examining the several criteria set forth by the legislation (*i.e.*, principle of shared effort, equity, replacement value for imported goods)[101] and their application in the Argentinean case law, decided, for example, that respondent should support 85% of the difference between the current values of 1 Peso and 1 US Dollar, which amounts to 90% of the original US Dollar amount.[102] As a result, the respondent was ordered to pay to the claimants an amount of Pesos equivalent to USD 28,371,361.48, at the sales rate of exchange quoted by the Bank of Argentina on the day before the payment date, plus V.A.T.

3. Impact of Non-Breaching Parties Behaviour

In the Ibero-American legal systems, as under the CISG,[103] the rule of mutual release to perform in the event of the debtor's legitimate impossibility is modified in cases where the creditor has caused the impossibility, and the debtor is successful in showing the causal link between his failure to perform and the creditor's conduct.[104]

The clearest enactment of such a rule is found in the Portuguese Civil Code according to which if the impossibility to perform is attributable to the creditor, the obligation is considered to be fulfilled, unless the debtor prefers to perform an alternative obligation and to be compensated by the damages he has suffered due to the creditor's attributable conduct.[105]

---

[100] *See for example* ICC Award by Consent No. 13242 *Lex Contractus* Argentinean Law: respondent paid the contractual price in Argentinean pesos at the conversion rate of Argentinean peso per US dollar as provided by the Emergency Law. The Claimant requested for the equitable readjustment, allowed by the Law. After parallel negotiations to the proceedings, the parties requested the arbitral tribunal to render an Award by Consent based on the agreements reached in the said negotiations.

[101] *See* Argentina's Law No. 25.561 of 6 January 2002 as amended by Decree No. 214/02, the Decree No. 320/02, Decree No. 410/02 and Decree No. 704/02.

[102] ICC Final Award Case No. 11949 *Lex Contractus* Argentinean Law, Seat of Arbitration Buenos Aires, Argentina; ICC Final Award Case No. 12755 *Lex Contractus* Argentinean Law.

[103] Art. 80 CISG: a party may not rely on the other party failure to perform, to the extent that such failure was caused by the first party's act or omission.

[104] ICC Final Award Case No. 12035 *Lex Contractus* Mexican Law: in the case at hand the claimant failed to demonstrate that his delay in performing was due to the respondent's delay in providing some drawings since "[I]n any event, even if some drawings should have been delivered later than contractually agreed (which is not established), [respondent] would not be in a position to rely on these delays since the witnesses at the hearing testified that in fact [respondent] always had more drawings than it needed in order to continue the work on an uninterrupted basis."

[105] Portugal Arts. 547, 795 (2) CC; Portugal: Antunes Valera, *supra* note 35, at 403.

Besides this, a provision of the Mexican Civil Code establishes that a penalty clause cannot be enforced when the debtor was unable to fulfil his obligations due to the conduct of the creditor.[106] Similarly, another group of provisions require, to the extent that the contractual condition is not fulfilled, the creditor to refrain himself from all acts intended to prevent the obligation from being fulfilled correctly.[107] These provisions have been interpreted by a Mexican Tribunal in the context of *avoidance clauses* expressly agreed upon by the parties and which lead to the automatic avoidance of the contract as soon as a breach occurs.[108] According to the Tribunal, these provisions impose upon the parties the obligation of cooperating, by not impeding or obstructing the performance of the other party's obligation, since contrary conduct could cause the avoidance of the contract in favour of the latter.[109]

More examples on the impact of non-breaching parties' behaviour can be found throughout the civil codes.[110] Peru's Civil Code dictates that the debtor is still in delay, when the creditor's notice to trigger the delay was not possible due to an act attributable to the debtor.[111]

Under the same logic, the mere delay in the performance of obligations having a fixed date is not sufficient to place the debtor in delay.[112] In addition, it is required that such delay is attributed to the debtor's conduct.[113] For example, the seller's failure to collect the price at the agreed, or default, place or time, may prevent the seller from claiming the interest due in case of delay and the avoidance of the contract.

More precisely, an ICC Tribunal has denied interest, as compensation for delay in payment, because the only reason why payment was not actually made to the seller within thirty (30) days of each of the respective bill of lading dates was due to its own failure to draw down the letters of credit that the buyer had posted. The right to interest can only be relied upon where handling and

---

[106] Mexico Art. 1847 CC; A similar provision is found in Peru Art. 1343 CC.

[107] Mexico Arts. 1940, 1942, 1945 CC; *see also* ICC Final Award Case No. 10299 *Lex Contractus* Chilean Law: by reference to Chile Arts. 1485, 1481 CC the Tribunal explained that if the seller wants to succeed on the merits, this is, to be paid at the price he alleges the contract determined, the seller must establish either that the condition has occurred or, if such condition has not arisen, that the buyer directly or indirectly made the condition to fail.

[108] *See* Ch. 53, 3.

[109] Mexico Collegiate Tribunals, *Novena Época,* Registry 179'354, SJF XXI, February 2005, p 1661.

[110] *See for example* Bolivia Art. 348 CC: concurrent negligence of the creditor; Bolivia: Castellanos Trigo & Auad La Fuente, *supra* note 37, at 163-165.

[111] Peru Art. 1333 (4) CC.

[112] *See* Ch. 52, 2.

[113] *See* Argentina Art. 509 CC; ICC Final Award Case No. 12755 *Lex Contractus* Argentinean Law; Mexico Collegiate Tribunals, *Novena Época,* Registry 201'660, SJF IV, August 1996, p. 642: upholding that a buyer cannot be considered to be in delay when he was ready to pay but the seller failed to collect payment at the agreed place.

collection charges arise as a result of the buyer's wrongful conduct, not where the failure to collect the amounts owing was entirely due to the fault of the seller.[114]

Similarly, the Paraguayan Supreme Court has explained that there is no ground for compensation, through the payment of interest, if the parties had agreed that the seller would deliver the goods once the buyer so required by a notice addressed to the seller, and the buyer had failed to send the notice to the seller's address indicated in the contract.[115]

Hence, a party's liability disappears when the breach was due to an act or conduct of the other party. On this issue, the Argentinean National Civil Chamber explained that the buyer can request the exact compliance of the obligation assumed by the seller, provided that the buyer did not acted negligently and could not have been aware of the non-conformity of the goods by taking the necessary due diligence.[116]

Furthermore, in Chile, Colombia, Ecuador and El Salvador, the principle can be deduced from a provision in their Civil Code stating that:

> the destruction of the goods in the debtor's hands, after he had delivered the goods to the creditor and during the delay in taking delivery by the creditor, does not make the debtor liable.[117]

In addition, the non-breaching party behaviour has an impact on the amount of recoverable damages. Since only the loss that is necessary and inevitably the consequence of the breach can be compensated,[118] regard has to be made for the aggrieved party's conduct.[119] This element is closely related to the mitigation duties of the suffering party reviewed in chapter 50.[120] On this issue, an ICC Arbitral Tribunal applying the Chilean law, explained that in synallagmatic contracts *la mora purga la mora*, *i.e.* when the aggrieved party

[114] ICC Final Award Case No. 13478 *Lex Contractus* Venezuelan Law.

[115] Paraguay Supreme Court, 22 July 1999, *Jorge Ruckelshaussen v. Wilhelm Albrecht*.

[116] Argentina National Civil Chamber, *Sala* F, *González, Roberto v. Sáez, Federico C*, 7 November 2003, Lexis No. 1/1000184.

[117] Chile Art. 1680 CC; Colombia Art. 1739 CC; Ecuador Art. 1723 CC; El Salvador Art. 1550 CC.

[118] Argentina Supreme Court, *Hotel Internacional Iguazú S.A. v. Estado Nacional,* 10 December 1987; Mexico Supreme Court, *Quinta Epoca, Tercera Sala*, SJF XCVI, at 951: stating that the damages that the party in breach of the contract shall compensate are those that necessary had to suffer the other party.

[119] Brazil Art. 945 CC: if the victim has negligently participated to the event that caused the damage, the damages' compensation will be determined considering the seriousness of its negligence compared to the negligence of the author of the damage; Mexico Art. 1847 CC: a penalty clause cannot be enforced when the debtor was unable to fulfil his obligations under the contract due to the conduct of the creditor; Peru Art. 1343 CC; ICC Final Award Case No. 10299 *Lex Contractus* Chilean Law: explaining that in order to determine contractual liability the aggrieved party must prove that the breach is not an excusable breach and is imputable to the breaching party.

[120] *See* Ch. 50, 7.

is also in breach, it cannot get compensation for the other party's breach, assuming that this breach is the result of contractual negligence.[121]

A different ICC Arbitral Tribunal, referring to article 945 of Brazil's Civil Code and the Brazilian doctrine, explained that the above-mentioned principle requires an assessment between the faults of both the author and victim of the damage. Thus, in the principle of joint negligence, it is essential to identify the causal link between the author of the conduct, the act and the assessment of the contribution of the victim to the damage occurred.[122]

Finally, the principle of good faith in contract performance is still present in the Ibero-American legal systems in order to balance the liability of the parties in a breach of contract.[123]

[121] ICC Final Award Case No. 9984 *Lex Contractus* Chilean Law.

[122] ICC Final Award Case No. 13870 *Lex Contractus* Brazil by operation of the Conflict of Laws Rules in Brazil's Introductory Law to the Civil Code.

[123] Argentina Art. 1198 CC; Bolivia Art. 803 Com C; Brazil Art. 422 CC; Chile Art. 1546 CC; Colombia Art. 1603 CC & Art. 863 Com C; Cuba Art. 6 CC; Ecuador Art. 1589 CC; El Salvador Art. 1417 CC; Guatemala Art. 17 JOL; Mexico Art. 1796 CC; Paraguay Art. 715 CC; Peru Art. 1362 CC; Portugal Art. 762 CC; Spain Art. 1258 CC & Art. 57 Com C.

Chapter 52

Interest

1. General Remarks on Interest

Many Ibero-American laws expressly provide that the rules on awarding interest due to late performance of obligations are applicable to the sales contracts; specifically the payment of the price made in delay by the buyer.[1] Nevertheless, the same rule is extended to any monetary and matured debt derived from the performance or lack of performance of the contract of sales.[2] In addition, some laws also expressly provide for the payment of interest based on the value of the goods which delivery has been delayed.[3]

The awarding of interest is understood as a type of compensation for damages and loss of profits.[4] As expressly mentioned by some Ibero-American Civil Codes, compensation can emerge either because the obligation has not

---

[1] Argentina Arts. 1423, 622 CC; Bolivia Art. 637 CC; Brazil Art. 389 CC; Chile Arts. 1873, 1875, 1559 CC; Colombia Arts. 1930, 1932, 1617 CC; Ecuador Arts. 1840, 1942, 1602 CC & Art. 202 Com C; El Salvador Arts. 1675, 1677, 1430 CC; Guatemala Art. 1826 CC; Mexico Art. 2296 CC; Peru Art. 1541 CC; Spain Art. 1.501 CC & Art. 341 Com C; Uruguay Art. 532 Com C; Venezuela Art. 1.529 CC & Art. 108 Com C; Argentina: G.A. Borda, Manual de Contratos 228, 229 (2004).

[2] *See infra* 2 & 3. These rules are established in the Civil Codes general provisions on obligations of monetary sums and are, thus, applicable to any matured debt irrespective of the source.

[3] Argentina Arts. 1423, 622 CC; Guatemala Art. 678 Com C; Argentina: Borda, *supra* note 1, at 228, 229.

[4] G.H. Treitel, *Remedies for Breach of Contract*, *in* A.T. von Mehren (Ed.), International Encyclopedia of Comparative Law, Vol. VII Contracts, Ch. 16, 54, para. 75 (1999): noting that "in civil law countries is common to distinguish between damages for various kinds of faults. Thus the French law draws a sharp distinction between 'moratory' and 'compensatory' damages [...] Moratory damages are assessed on the same principles as compensatory damages: this should not be obscured by the fact that often moratory damages are sought for delay in paying money (default in *obligation pécunaire*) in which case only interest is recoverable." *See also*

been fulfilled, or it has been imperfectly or partially fulfilled, or it has been fulfilled with delay.[5] Depending on the particular case, the laws may limit the compensation and also may establish the means to compensate. Interest is the legally available means of compensation for delayed performance and not the traditional mechanism of the compensatory damages.[6]

The above being said, the Supreme Court of Chile has sustained, in cassation on the merits, that although interest is the legally available means of compensation for delayed performance, such does not preclude the creditor to claim, in addition, the loss of profits caused due to the monetary depreciation occurred during the delay in payment.[7] Similarly, a Mexican Collegiate Tribunal has sustained that the delayed damages or damages awarded for late performance are different to the compensatory damages to which the aggrieved party still has a right.[8] Thus, as also expressly provided by the Guatemalan law, the seller may be able to recover further compensatory damages,[9] which may be related to the incidental loss, consequential loss or lost profits.

Also, in Portugal, and similar to the CISG, the creditor can prove that the delay in payment has caused him more damages than the interest generated so that he can recover a supplementary compensation which would fully compensate him.[10]

Argentina: A.A. Alterini, Contratos civiles, comerciales, de consumo 601 (1998); Portugal: L. De Lima Pinheiro, Dereito Comercial Internacional 313 (2005).

5 Argentina Art. 508 CC impliedly stated; Chile Art. 1556 CC; Colombia Art. 1613 CC; Ecuador Art. 1599 CC; El Salvador Art. 1427 CC; Portugal Arts. 802, 803 CC.

6 Bolivia Art. 347 CC; Brazil Art. 395 CC; Chile Art. 1559 CC; Colombia Art. 1617 CC; Ecuador Art. 1602 CC; El Salvador Art. 1430 CC; Guatemala Art. 678 Com C; Mexico Art. 2117 *in fine* CC; Peru Art. 1324 CC; Portugal Art. 806 CC; Spain Art. 1.108 CC; Uruguay Art. 225 Com C; Venezuela Art. 1.277 CC; Bolivia Supreme Court, *Sala Civil*, 10 March 2008, *Banco Unión S.A. v. Shuei Higa Nakandakari y otros*; Mexico Supreme Court, *Quinta Epoca, Tercera Sala*, SJF LXXXVIII, p 2590; Spain Supreme Tribunal, 21 December 1998 (ar. 9649); Spain Supreme Tribunal, 23 April 1998 (ar. 2988); Spain Supreme Tribunal, 19 May 1991 (ar. 3717); ICC Final Award Case No. 13743 *Lex Contractus* Spanish Law: stating that Article 1108 of the Spanish Civil Code provides that, "If the obligation consists in the payment of an amount of money, and the debtor is delayed in its payment, the damages due, unless the parties otherwise agreed, shall consist in the contractually agreed interest or, failing such an agreement, in the legal interest."

7 Chile Supreme Court, cass, Sociedad Agricola Ganadera José Montes con Corporación de la Reforma Agraria, *cited in* Chile: R. Díez Duarte, La Compraventa en el Código Civil Chileno 184, n. 487 (1993).

8 Mexico Collegiate Tribunals, *Novena Época*, Registry 174887, SJF XXIII, June 2006, at 1164.

9 Guatemala Art. 678 Com C.

10 Portugal Art. 806(3) CC.

2. Preconditions for Interest

As mentioned, under the Ibero-American laws, as under CISG, liability to pay interest is triggered only if the debtor of the obligation is 'in delay' in paying the sum owed.[11] This is, when the debtor has a matured debt. Thus, the question of when the debt is in reality a matured one, is very important.

The general rule under most Ibero-American laws is that a party to the contract which has a fixed date to perform, namely a fixed time for payment of the price or other related sums of money, is 'in delay' if he does not perform on the fixed date established.[12] However, if no fixed date to perform can be determined from the contract, the creditor shall first compel the debtor to pay the sum either by means of judicial claim or with notice made through a public notary, so that the debtor of the obligation is placed 'in delay', and the debt becomes a matured one.[13]

The said notice is not required to be so detailed, since the notice does not have a recognition function of the facts or elements of the breach, in the sense that further things which were not contained in the notice could not be alleged

[11] Argentina Arts. 622, 508 CC; Chile Art. 1557 CC; Colombia Art. 1614 CC; Ecuador Art. 1600 CC & Art. 202 Com C; El Salvador Art. 1428 CC; Mexico Art. 380 Com C; Paraguay Art. 423 CC; Peru Art. 1336 CC; Portugal Art. 804 CC; Spain Arts. 1.100, 1.501 CC; Uruguay Art. 532 Com C; Venezuela Art. 108 Com C. Under CISG Art. 78 interest is owed for any due money debt originating from the contract of sale. Not only for the payments of the price, but also for the reimbursement of the incurred expenses on one the other party's account, from the moment the claim legitimately originates, *see* Spain: F.P. Prieto, *in* L. Díez Picazo y Ponce De León (Ed.), La Compraventa Internacional de Mecaderias – Comentario sobre la Convención de Viena Art. 78, III, at 632 (1998).

[12] Argentina Art. 509 CC; Brazil Art. 397 CC; Chile Art. 1551(1) CC; Colombia Art. 1608(1) CC; Costa Rica Art. 418(a) Com C; Ecuador Art. 1594(1) CC & Art. 202 Com C; El Salvador Art. 1422(1) CC; Guatemala Art. 677 Com C; Mexico Art. 85(I) Com C; Paraguay Art. 424 CC; Portugal Art. 804(2) CC & Art. 4(1) Law No. 3/2004 integrating EC Directive 2000/35/EC; Spain Art. 63(1) Com C & Art. 4(1) Law 32/2003, of 17 March 2003 integrating EC Directive 2000/35/EC; Venezuela Art. 1.269 CC; ICC Final Award Case No. 12755 *Lex Contractus* Argentinean Law; ICC Final Award Case No. 13417 *Lex Contractus* Argentinean Law; ICC Final Award Case No. 13967 *Lex Contractus* Bolivian Law and INCOTERMS 2000; ICC Final Award Case No. 14083 *Lex Contractus* Brazilian Law: applying Brazil Art. 397 CC; El Salvador Supreme Court, *Cass civ*, *Sagicar S.A. de C.V. v. Empresa Electrónica de Oriente S.A. de C.V*, 18-C-2006, 19 February 2008; ICC Final Award Case No. 11367 *Lex Contractus* Portuguese Law.

[13] Brazil Art. 397 sole para. CC; Costa Rica Art. 418(b) Com C; Guatemala Art. 1826(3) CC; Mexico Art. 85(II) Com C; Paraguay Art. 725 CC; Portugal Art. 805 CC; Spain Arts. 1.100, 1.109 CC & Art. 63(2) Com C; El Salvador Supreme Court, *Cass civ*, *Sagicar S.A. de C.V. v. Empresa Electrónica de Oriente S.A. de C.V*, 18-C-2006, 19 February 2008; Mexico Collegiate Tribunals, *Novena Época,* Registry 186'633, SJF XVI, July 2002, at 1272: interpreting Mexico Arts. 2080, 2082 CC.

later.[14] Thus, it is enough that the notice states the grounds for the breach, with no need to enter into the details, so that it accomplishes its objective of placing the debtor in delay.[15]

Conversely, under, Bolivia, Peru and Spain's laws, the general rule is that there is a need for a request to perform, by means of notice made to the debtor, unless the parties have agreed in advance that such a notice is not necessary to place the debtor in delay.[16] Confirming the rule, an ICC Arbitral Tribunal, applying Bolivian Law, sustained that the payment of interest of the unpaid invoices started to be owed 15 days after the delivery of the invoices as agreed upon in the contract with no need of further notice. While the payment of interest for the price of the goods delivered but never invoiced, started to be owed after 15 days from the date of the notice requiring the payment.[17]

In addition, some exceptions have been established to the notice rule. Under some Civil Codes there is no need for the notice to perform when, because of the nature of the obligation and the circumstances of the case, a period of time to pay was an essential reason to enter into the contract.[18]

Moreover, the Bolivian and Peruvian Civil Codes dictate that the debtor is in delay, without requirement of notice, when he declares in writing that he will not perform his obligation,[19] or when the notice to trigger the delay was not possible due to an act attributable to the debtor.[20]

The above being said, the mere delay in the performance may not be sufficient to place the debtor in delay. It is additionally required that such delay be attributed to the debtor of the sum.[21] For example, the seller's failure to collect the price at the agreed or default place or time of payment may prevent the seller from claiming the interest and resulting in the avoidance of the contract.[22]

---

[14] ICC Final Award Case No. 11853 *Lex Contractus* Mexican Law.

[15] *Id.*

[16] Spain Art. 1.100(1) CC; Bolivia Art. 341 (1) CC; Peru Art. 1333 (1) CC; Bolivia Supreme Court, *Sala Civil, Boliviana de Ingeniería S.R.L v. Compañía La Boliviana CIACRUZ de Seguros y Reaseguros S.A.*: upholding that damages and loss of profits for the breach of contract (monetary obligation to pay insured goods) was fixed to 6% annual of the sum due, paid from the date when the debtor was placed in delay until the enforcement of the decision; Bolivia: G. Castellanos Trigo & S. Auad La Fuente, Derecho de las Obligaciones en el Código Civil Boliviano 148, 149 (2008).

[17] ICC Final Award Case No. 13967 *Lex Contractus* Bolivian Law and INCOTERMS 2000.

[18] Chile Art. 1551(2) CC; Colombia Art. 1608(2) CC; Ecuador Art. 1594(2) CC; El Salvador Art. 1422(2) CC; Paraguay Art. 424 CC; Spain Art. 1.100(1) CC; *also* Peru Art. 1333(2) CC (but only for performance of non-monetary obligations).

[19] Bolivia Art. 341(3) CC; Peru Art. 1333(3) CC.

[20] Peru Art. 1333(4) CC.

[21] *See* Argentina Art. 509 CC; ICC Final Award Case No. 12755 *Lex Contractus* Argentinean Law; El Salvador Supreme Court, *Cass civ, Sagicar S.A. de C.V. v. Empresa Electrónica de Oriente S.A. de C.V*, 18-C-2006, 19 February 2008.

[22] ICC Final Award Case No. 13478 *Lex Contractus* Venezuelan Law; Paraguay Supreme

Finally, interest is calculated from the time the debtor is 'in delay' in paying the monetary sum, either by failure to pay at the fixed date or after the notice required,[23] to the effective date of payment.[24] Unless the party entitled to them requests its calculation within a shorter period of time.[25]

Nevertheless, some codes expressly provide that payment of interest is due from the moment the goods were delivered, though the debtor is not in delay, when, for example: 1) so has been agreed in the contract or; 2) if the goods have been delivered to the buyer and they generate utilities and revenues.[26] This rule is based on the belief that it is unfair that the buyer can profit from the utilities and revenues generated by the goods without it being possible for the seller to profit from the interest naturally generated by the price.[27]

Interestingly, the Peruvian Civil Code specifically differentiates between the payment of sums of money which are required to be determined by judicial judgment. The debtor is only in delay from the date he receives notice of the claim filed by the creditor at the court, except when the delay has caused some harm to the debtor, in which case the debtor has a matured claim from the time the damage occurred.[28]

Court, 22 July 1999, *Jorge Ruckelshaussen v. Wilhelm Albrecht*; Mexico Collegiate Tribunals, *Novena Época,* Registry 201'660, SJF IV, August 1996, p 642.

23 Bolivia Art. 347 CC; Brazil Arts. 406, 407 CC; Chile Art. 1559 CC; Colombia Art. 1617 CC; Ecuador Art. 1602 CC & Art. 202 Com C; El Salvador Art. 1430 CC; Mexico Art. 2117 *in fine* CC; Peru Art. 1324 CC; Portugal Art. 806 CC; Spain Art. 1.108 CC; Venezuela Art. 1.277 CC; *see also* ICC Final Award Case No. 13417 *Lex Contractus* Argentinean Law; ICC Final Award Case No. 11818 *Lex Contractus* CIG and Spanish Law as supplementary law; Mexico Supreme Court, *Quinta Época, Cuarta Sala,* Registry 359076, SJF XLVII, at 4990; Mexico Collegiate Tribunals, *Séptima Época,* Registry 248381, SJF 199-204 VI, at 51; Paraguay Supreme Court, *Sala Civil,* Judgment 08, 2 February 2005, *Adriano Ayala Cano v. Reinaldo Pavia Maldonado, David Pavia Vega Y Pablo Dario Zaracho*; Bolivia: V. Camargo Marín, Derecho Comercial Boliviano 400 (2007).

24 Peru Supreme Court, *Sala civil transitoria,* Resolution 000476-2006, 18 August 2006; ICC Final Award Case No. 11317 *Lex Contractus* Spanish Law; ICC Final Award Case No. 11818 *Lex Contractus* CIG and Spanish Law as supplementary law; ICC Final Award Case No. 13478 *Lex Contractus* Venezuelan Law.

25 ICC Final Award Case No. 13743 *Lex Contractus* Spanish Law: the Sole Arbitrator explained that as Claimant had limited its interest claim to a period running from February 2004 to August 2005, any decision granting interest beyond 31 August 2005 could be characterised as *ultra petita* and would endanger the validity of the Final Award. For this reason, "the Sole Arbitrator is not entitled to award interest, for instance, until full payment is made by respondent."

26 Mexico Art. 2296 CC; Spain Art. 1.501 CC; Venezuela Art. 1.529 CC; *see also* Venezuela: J.L. Aguilar Gorrondona, Contratos y Garantias: Derecho Civil IV, 268 (2008); Argentina: Borda, *supra* note 1, at 228, 229; Mexico: B. Perez Fernandez del Castillo, Contratos Civiles 124 (2008); Spain: M. Medina de Lemus, Derecho Civil: Obligaciones y Contratos II, Contratos en Particular, Vol. 2, 64 (2004).

27 *See* on this Venezuela: Aguilar Gorrondona, *supra* note 26, at 268.

28 Peru Arts. 1334, 1985 CC.

3. Rate of Interest

As mentioned, in the civil law countries, the interest is the legally available means of compensation for late performance. There is a good reason for such an approach. According to the traditional rules on the burden of proof,[29] the creditor, who is the party claiming the existence of damages, bears the burden of proving either of two things: 1) that if the sum had been paid in time, he would have made a profit and its amount, or 2) that as a consequence of the non-payment or the lack of liquidity, he has been forced to seek or maintain financial services.[30]

In both cases, the difficulty to prove the causal relation between delays in payment and the loss incurred blocks the claim.[31] This difficulty together with the belief that the late delivery of assets, clearly productive as money, must unquestionably cause some loss,[32] as well as the need to facilitate the payment of matured debts, caused the Civil Codes of the nineteenth century to include a legal fixed rate of interest payable by the debtor, discharging the creditor from the high burden of proving the loss.[33]

Even though all the Ibero-American laws establish a flexible reference for the judge to determine the applicable rate or at least a fixed legal rate of interest, the primary rule is that the rate of interest is the one agreed upon by the parties.[34] However, the freedom of the parties to agree on the payable rate of interest has certain limits and must meet some conditions.

For example, under the Civil Codes of Chile, Colombia and Venezuela the rate of interest agreed cannot exceed 50% of the current legal rate at the time

---

[29] *See* Ch. 50, 6.

[30] *See* on this Spain: A. Soler Presas, La Valoracion del Daño en el Contrato de Compraventa 236 (1998).

[31] *See id.*, at 236.

[32] Argentian: Alterini, *supra* note 4, at 601; Mexico: S. León Tovar, Los Contratos Mercantiles 43 (2004).

[33] *See* expressly Uruguay Art. 225 para. 2 Com C; Argentina: Alterini, *supra* note 4, at 601; Spain: Soler Presas, *supra* note 30, at 236.

[34] Argentina Art. 622 CC; Bolivia Art. 410 CC; Brazil Art. 406 CC; Chile Art. 2206 CC; Colombia Art. 2230 CC; Ecuador Art. 2135 CC; El Salvador Art. 1963 CC; Guatemala Art. 691 Com C; Mexico Arts. 2394, 2395 CC; Paraguay Art. 475 CC; Peru Arts. 1243, 1245 CC; Portugal Art. 806(2) CC & Art. 102(1) Com C; Spain Art. 1.108 CC; Venezuela Art. 1.746 CC; ICC Final Award Case No. 11404 *Lex Contractus* Argentinean Law; ICC Final Award Case No. 13967 *Lex Contractus* Bolivian Law and INCOTERMS 2000: following the agreed interest rate established by the parties; ICC Final Award Case No. 14653 *Lex Contractus* Brazilian Law: confirming the applicability of the indexation rate agreed by the parties in their agreement; ICC Final Award Case No. 9400 *Lex Contractus* Colombian Law: the arbitrator orders payment of the sums owed, plus interests at the rates agreed in the respective agreements; ICC Final Award Case 11853 *Lex Contractus* Mexican Law: interpreting the agreement of the parties, the applicable rate was the one determined by the Bank of Mexico and published in Official Federal Gazette on the date of the award; *see also* Bolivia: Camargo Marín, *supra* note 23, at 400.

of the agreement.[35] The case being that, the judge shall reduce the agreed rate to the legal rate at the time of the agreement.[36] In Venezuela, the rule changes for B2B contracts with a yearly 12% of the capital debt as the maximum.[37] In Ecuador, the interest rate agreed upon shall not exceed the maximum fixed by the law, under the penalty of being reduced by the judge with no need for the debtor's request.[38]

In Brazil, the agreed interest may not be higher than the rate of 1% per month, without being compounded and with an annual monetary correction in line with the NCPI/BGSI index, in accordance with the Brazilian Decree-Law No. 22626/33.[39] In Bolivia the agreed interest rate cannot be higher than a monthly rate of 3%, any higher rate being automatically reduced to 3%.[40] Similarly, the Mexican Civil Code fixes an annual 9% percent as the legal interest rate, which can always be exceeded by an agreed upon interest rate. However, when such is excessively out of proportion, that makes one believe that the creditor has abused the debtor's need, inexperience or ignorance, the judge may equitably reduce the agreed upon interest, by request of the debtor and in consideration of the special circumstances of the case.[41]

---

35 The current interest rate in Chile is fixed by the Bank and Finance Corporations Superintendence that establishes a differential interest rate for operations in one or more foreign currencies, *see* Chile Art. 6 Law No.18.010; in Colombia the legal interest rate is the default annual interest rate at six percent according to Colombia Art. 1617(1) CC; in Venezuela the law establishes an annual three percent legal interest rate for C2C contracts in Venezuela Art. 1.746 CC.

36 Chile Art. 2206 CC; Colombia Art. 2231 CC; Venezuela Art. 1.746 CC (noting that in Colombia and Venezuela reduction is undertaken by the judge if the debtor so requests); ICC Final Award Case No. 9984 *Lex Contractus* Chilean Law: the Arbitral Tribunal subtracted the rule from Chile's Law No. 18.010 published in the Official Journal on 27 June 1981, which reads in its article 6 "(…) It is not possible to stipulate an interest rate that exceeds in more than 50% the ordinary interest applicable at the moment of the agreement, whether the rate is fixed or variable. This interest limit is called maximum conventional interest."

37 Venezuela Art. 108 Com C; ICC Final Award Case No. 13478 *Lex Contractus* Venezuelan Law: upholding that "having regard to the provisions of Article 1159 of the Venezuelan Civil Code and Article 108 of the Code of Commerce, which make it clear that parties may contract for the payment of a market rate of interest (in the event of non-payment) which does not exceed twelve (12%) per cent per annum, (…) the contract rate should apply."

38 Ecuador Art. 2136 CC.

39 ICC Final Award Case No. 11317 *Lex Contractus* Spanish Law and Brazilian Law: the Tribunal sustained that the interest due should be "calculated having regard to the limits laid down by Brazilian legislation: that is to say i) at the rate of 1% per month, without being compounded and with an annual monetary correction in line with the NCPI/BGSI index, in accordance with the Brazilian Decree-Law No. 22626/33, with effect from the date of the request for arbitration (…); ii) in line with the SELIC Rate (…). This criterion has been recently adopted in cases before the Brazilian High Court of Justice (STJ, 1ª T., Ag.Rg in Edcl in REsp 556068/PR, Rel. Ministro Francisco Falcao, judg. 08.06.2004, publ. DJ 16.08.2004)."

40 Bolivia Art. 409 CC. *See also* Bolivia Art. 411 CC: requiring as a condition for the validity of the agreed interest rate that such is in writing.

41 Mexico Art. 2395 CC.

Paraguay's Civil Code declares that the parties may not agree on an interest rate higher than the maximum interest rate established by the Central Bank of Paraguay, under the penalty of considering such agreement void.[42] Likewise, the Central Reserve Bank of Peru fixes a maximum limit for the agreed upon interest.[43]

The CISG does not contemplate the payment of interest over the interest already incurred.[44] This question may be left to the domestic applicable law. Some Ibero-American Civil Codes expressly prohibit what is known under the term of compound interest or anatocism, *i.e.* the payment of interest over the interest already incurred.[45] Parties are expressly barred from agreeing on the payment of compound interest in the laws of Bolivia, Chile, Colombia and Ecuador.[46]

In other jurisdictions payment of compound interest or anatocism is permitted under certain circumstances. In Argentina, compound interest is due if the parties have expressly agreed on the periodicity to accumulate the interest on the capital.[47] Also, interest may be capitalised, for example, when the judge refers to the interest rate charged by public banks, and this is a short term interest rate shorter that the period of delay of payment, in which case the creditor can claim the interest as the bank taken into reference would do.[48]

In Guatemala, the capitalisation of interest is permitted in B2B contracts, provided that the interest rate agreed upon is not superior to the average interest rate charged by banks in the period concerned.[49] In Peru, such an agreement is valid for B2B contracts, but invalid for C2C contracts if it was made at the time of the contract conclusion.[50]

In Mexico, payment of compound interest has raised some discussion. The Supreme Court does not recognise the integration of anatocism in the Mexican Law, but has failed to decide on the validity of such agreement.[51] However, some authors consider that from an integral interpretation of Article 2397 of Mexico's Civil Code and Article 363 of the Code of Commerce, the result is

---

42 Paraguay Art. 475 CC.

43 Peru Art. 1243 CC.

44 Spain: Prieto, *supra* note 11, Art. 78, III, at 632.

45 The Spanish term used by the statutory law and the jurisprudence in Ibero-America is *Anatocismo.*

46 Bolivia Art. 412 CC; Chile Art. 1559 (3) CC; Colombia Art. 1617 (3) CC; Ecuador Arts. 1602 (3), 2140 CC; *see* Bolivia: Camargo Marín, *supra* note 23, at 401.

47 Argentina Art. 623 CC.

48 Argentina National Commercial Chamber, Chamber, *Uzal S.A. v. Moreno Enrique*, 2 October 1991 cited and applied in ICC Final Award No. 11114 *Lex Contractus* Argentinean Law.

49 Guatemala Art. 690 Com C.

50 Peru Art. 1249 CC; *see also* Peru Art. 1250 CC: establishing that in non-commercial contracts the agreement is valid if made in writing one year after the debt is matured.

51 Mexico Supreme Court, *Novena Época,* SJF VIII, October 1998, p. 381.

that payment of compound interest is binding if the parties have agreed on them once the debt has matured, but that such an agreement is invalid prior to the debt being matured.[52]

Absent an agreement, some Ibero-American laws establish a flexible reference for the judge to determine the applicable rate, while other countries have a fixed legal rate of interest expressed in the law. On the one hand, in most countries an annual interest rate, also called legal interest rate, is periodically established by a governmental institution and such rate constitutes the reference for the judge to calculate the interest due for delay in performing pecuniary obligations. For example, in Argentina, though Article 622 of the Civil Code makes reference to the interest rate fixed by the judge, the jurisprudence has developed the rule according to which such interest mentioned by the Civil Code are those charged by the National Bank of Argentina.[53]

In Brazil, the interest for delay of performance is calculated based on the rate fixed by the Brazilian Central Bank's SELIC.[54] In Ecuador, the delay interest is determined in accordance with the rate established by the Monetary Council.[55] In Chile, the ordinary interest is the non-compound interest for re-adjustable operations determined by the Banks and Finance Corporations Superintendence pursuant to Law n°18.010.[56] In Peru and Paraguay, the legal interest rate is fixed periodically by their respective Central Banks.[57]

In Portugal and Spain, the legal interest rate is established following the guidelines of the EC Directive Combating Late Payment in Commercial Transactions.[58] Accordingly, Portugal enacted Law No. 32/2003 under which the legal interest rate will be periodically and conjunctively established by the Ministries of Finance and Justice,[59] which must not be lower than the interest rate applied by the European Central Bank to its most recent main refinancing operation carried out before the first calendar day of the half-year

---

[52] *See* Mexico: León Tovar, *supra* note 32, at 31-33.

[53] Argentina National Commercial Chamber, *Sala E*, Judgment 91.185, T 1993, cited and applied in ICC Final Award No. 11114 *Lex Contractus* Argentinean Law. *See also* ICC Final Award Case No. 13417 *Lex Contractus* Argentinean Law.

[54] SELIC stands for *Sistema Especial de Liquidação e Custodia*, that is, Special System for Settlement and Custody, being a daily adjusted average, based on federal bonds, adopted for calculating default interest in Brazil by Law 8.981 of 20 January 1995, by Law 9.065 of 20 June 1995 and by the new Civil Code, *see* ICC Final Award Case No. 13458 *Lex Contractus* Brazilian Law and INCOTERMS 2000.

[55] Ecuador Art. 2136 CC.

[56] *See* Chile Art. 6 Law No. 18.010; ICC Final Award Case No. 9984 *Lex Contractus* Chilean Law: the Arbitral Tribunal condemned the respondent to pay on the owed invoices non-compound ordinary interests calculated as provided in Article 6 of the Chilean law No. 18.010.

[57] Peru Art. 1244 CC; Paraguay Art. 475 CC.

[58] Directive 2000/35/EC of the European Parliament and of the Council of 29 June 2000.

[59] *See* Art. 6 of the Law Decree No. 32/2003, of 17 March 2003 integrating into the national law Art. 3(1)(d) of the EC Directive 2000/35/EC Combating Late Payment in Commercial Transactions, which amends Art. 102 of the Portuguese Code of Commerce.

in question, plus at least seven percentage points. The Spanish law offers two solutions. On the one hand, the application of Article 7 of Law No. 3/2004, which incorporates the EC Directive,[60] or the application of an annual interest rate resulting from the guidelines provided by the Spanish national budget law. According to scholars and case law, this second solution has prevailed during the last years.[61]

On the other hand, there are legal systems, such as the Bolivian and the Colombian, that fix the default annual interest rate at 6%.[62] In Mexico, an annual 9% is fixed for B2B obligations while an annual 6% applies to C2C obligations.[63] The Venezuelan law establishes an annual 3% legal interest rate for C2C contracts,[64] and the current interest in the trade concerned for B2B contracts.[65]

---

[60] Corresponding to Art. 3(1)(d) of the EC Directive 2000/35/E: the level of interest for late payment ('the statutory rate'), which the debtor is obliged to pay, shall be the sum of the interest rate applied by the European Central Bank to its most recent main refinancing operation carried out before the first calendar day of the half-year in question (the reference rate), plus at least seven percentage points (the margin), unless otherwise specified in the contract.

[61] *See* Spain: P. Perales Vizcasillas, *Late Payment Directive 200/35 and the CISG*, 19 Pace International Law Review 125, at 140 (2007); ICC Final Award Case No. 13743 *Lex Contractus* Spanish Law: found that "the Spanish legal interest rate of 4% per annum shall apply in this case" since "[T]he Spanish Law 2/2004 of 27 December 2004 on the General Budget of the State for 2005 (period in which interest is awarded to Claimant), in its additional provision N° 5, establishes that the legal interest rate in force until 31 December 2005 shall be 4% per annum."

[62] Colombia Art. 1617 (1) CC; Bolivia Art. 414 CC; Bolivia Supreme Court, *Sala Civil, Boliviana de Ingeniería S.R.L v. Compañía La Boliviana CIACRUZ de Seguros y Reaseguros S.A.*: upholding that damages and loss of profits for the breach of contract (monetary obligation to pay insured goods) was fixed to 6% annual of the sum due paid from the date when the debtor was placed on delay until the enforcement of the decision.

[63] Mexico Art. 362 Com C & Art. 2395 CC. However, it seems to be disputable whether the 6% annual rate established by Mexico's Code of Commerce regarding the contract of loan applies to compensate the delay of payment of monetary obligations relating to other commercial contracts such as the sales contract. On the one hand, Mexico: León Tovar, *supra* note 32, at 44, 45 denying the possibility based on the decision by the Collegiate Tribunals in Administrative Matters of the First Circuit, *Octava Epoca*, SJF XI, January 1993, at 274, on the other hand, ICC Final Award Case No. 11256 *Lex Contractus* Mexican Law: upholding that the applicable legal rate of 6% per year is to be found in article 362 of the Code of Commerce, which even if it relates to loan agreements, it is applied by analogy to other agreements and to damages, based on decision of Collegiate Tribunals in Civil Matters of the First Circuit of 31 January 1996, SJF III, May 1996, at 647, which states that although Art. 362 of the Code of Commerce is to be found in the chapter on the Loan Agreement and applies expressly to interests to be paid on this kind of debt, it is established that "this rule must be applied by analogy when moratory interests are claimed as from the date when damages were caused"; *see also* ICC Final Award Case 12035 *Lex Contractus* Mexican Law: applying the 6% interest rate for owed sums derived from a B2B contract of works.

[64] Venezuela Art. 1.746 CC.

[65] Venezuela Art. 108 Com C.

Finally, it is important to remember that many laws establish special interest rates for obligations agreed to be paid in foreign currency such as American dollars. In Argentina, for example, the judge would charge the active interest rate established by the Central Bank of Argentina for operations in dollars.[66] In Chile, the Banks and Finance Corporations Superintendence establishes a differential interest rate for operations in one or more foreign currencies.[67]

On the other hand, in Spain the jurisprudence has developed the rule according to which the Spanish legal interest rate for national currency obligations also applies to foreign currency obligations.[68]

66 ICC Final Award No. 11114 *Lex Contractus* Argentinean Law; ICC Final Award Case No. 13417 *Lex Contractus* Argentinean Law.

67 Chile Art. 6 Law No. 18.010.

68 ICC Final Award Case No. 13743 *Lex Contractus* Spanish Law: citing the following Spain Supreme Tribunal's decisions: Civil Chamber, decision No. 106/1986 of 20 February 1986; Civil Chamber, decision No. 767/1987 of 26 November 1987; Civil Chamber, decision No. 958/1991 of 21 December 1991 and Civil Chamber, decision of 5 April 2005.

CHAPTER 53

AVOIDANCE OF THE CONTRACT

1. Fundamental Breach

The Ibero-American laws ignore the notion of fundamental breach as understood under the CISG.[1] However, some comparable standards of breach or non-conformity may limit the possibility to avoid the contract.

1.1. Defective Goods

In the case of defective goods, a particular standard limits the remedy of contract avoidance based on a redhibitory action. In order to achieve a successful redhibitory, action the buyer must show that the defects of the goods make them improper for, or reduce, the function they are usually given.[2] It must be noticed that for this objective requirement, the defects must be in the goods themselves and must impede them to accomplish, totally or partially, the purpose for which they were created.

---

1 Under CISG Arts. 49 and 64 the parties may only declare the contract avoided if the failure by the other party to perform any of his obligations amounts to a fundamental breach of contract. According to CISG Art. 25, a breach by one of the parties is fundamental when such substantially deprives the other party of what he is entitled to expect under the contract. The CISG does not refer to the extent of the damage caused but rather to the importance such breach has on the interests that the contract actually creates for the affected party, *see* U.G. Schroeter, *in* I. Schwenzer (Ed.), Schlechtriem & Schwenzer Commentary on the UN Convention on the International Sale of Goods Art. 25, para. 21, at 409 (2010).

2 Argentina Art. 2164 CC; Brazil Art. 441 CC; Chile Art. 1858(2) CC; Colombia Art. 1915(2) CC; Ecuador Art. 1825 (2) CC; El Salvador Art. 1660(2) CC; Guatemala Art. 1559 CC; Mexico Art. 2142 CC; Paraguay Art. 1789 CC; Portugal Art. 913(2) CC; Spain Art. 1484 CC; Uruguay Art. 1718 CC; Venezuela Art. 1.518 CC.

Hence, a change in the use for which the goods were intended does not legitimate the buyer to claim the avoidance because of defects.[3] For example, the purchase of automobiles intended to transport people but later prove to be unsuccessful for the transport of merchandise or farming does not constitute sufficient grounds for the avoidance of the contract. Additionally, defects cannot result from the seller's *business puffery* regarding the characteristics of the goods. Such is normal language in national or international trade and is considered as *dolus bonus* accepted in all Ibero-American legal cultures, specially in the sale of goods.[4]

In addition, scholars and courts agree that the defects on the goods must be grave and important.[5] The defects must be important up to the extent that if the buyer had known them he would not have acquired the goods or he would have only offered a lower price.[6] This standard is equal to the one established for the breach of agreed obligations further reviewed, and which, on the other hand, is similar to the standard required under the CISG.[7]

The El Salvadorian Supreme Court explains that in countries where the same rule operates, upper level Courts have a tendency to declare the avoidance of the contract as far as the defects are enough to impede the use and exploitation of the goods sold, causing considerable damages to the aggrieved buyer.[8] For example, a buyer of an industrial machine used in the drying of sugar canes was granted the avoidance of the contract because the seller has failed to deliver an important element of the machine (a band) required for

[3] Colombia: A. Tamayo Lombana, El Contrato de Compraventa su Régimen Civil y Comercial 178 (2004).

[4] *See* in this regard R. Compagnucci de Caso, Contrato de Compraventa 212 (2007).

[5] *Id.*, at 208, 217; Bolivia: W. Kaune Arteaga, Curso de Derecho Civil, Contratos, Vol. 2, 149 (1996); Chile: R. Díez Duarte, La Compraventa en el Código Civil Chileno 167 (1993); Colombia: Tamayo Lombana, *supra* note 3, at 177; Argentina National Civil Chamber, *Sala* C, *Mariani, José A. y otros v. Consorcio Ática I S.R.L.* 30 June 2000: stating that "redhibitory defects are those hidden defects which deteriorates the essence of the goods as it existed at the moment of the sale, and if those defects were known by the buyer, the buyer would not have entered into the sales agreement or he would have had paid an inferior price"; Argentina National Civil Chamber, *Sala C, De Elizalde, Jorge E. y otro v. López Lecube, Marta*, 3 September 2001.

[6] Argentina Art. 2164 CC; Chile Art. 1858 (2) CC; Colombia Art. 1915 (2) CC; Ecuador Art. 1825 (2) CC; El Salvador Art. 1660 (2) CC; Guatemala Art. 1559 CC; Mexico Art. 2142 CC; Paraguay Art. 1789 CC; Spain Art. 1.484 CC; Uruguay Art. 1718 CC; Venezuela Art. 1.518 CC; Paraguay Art. 1790 CC states there is not basis for compensation when the decrease in the value or quality is few.

[7] *See infra* 1.2.

[8] El Salvador Superior Tribunal, RJ 1-12, January to December 1954, at 343-366, *cited in* El Salvador: A.O. Miranda, De la Compraventa 549 (1996).

his proper installation. After some weeks of use, the machine was heavily damaged because of the improper installation to a point that it could no longer be used.[9]

Finally, the same 'grave and important' standard must apply when a particular purpose or use is expressly or impliedly agreed and the goods do not appear to serve for such special purpose or use.[10]

1.2. Breach of Obligations

Concerning the ordinary breach of obligations, the law requires the negligence of one of the parties.[11] If the presumed negligence is not controverted by the breaching party, the judge may decide on whether the avoidance of the contract is awarded to the aggrieved party with all the consequences of the avoidance.[12] Under the CISG, in contrast, it is irrelevant whether the failure to perform is intentional or due to legitimate impossibility.[13] Under the CISG, however, for a breach to be fundamental the breaching party has to have foreseen, and a reasonable person of the same kind in the same circumstance would have also foreseen, the importance of the obligation breached and his significance to the other party.[14]

Most statutes rarely distinguish between different levels or degrees of breaches.[15] A literal reading of these statutes gives the impression that any breach triggers the right of avoidance despite whether the obligation breached

---

[9] *Id.*

[10] *See* expressly Peru Art. 1505 CC; Portugal Art. 913(1) CC; To evaluate the conformity of goods bought for a particular use the same objective requirements for the goods intended for ordinary purposes shall apply; *see* Colombia: Tamayo Lombana, *supra* note 3, at 179.

[11] *See* Ch. 47, 1.

[12] *See* Ch. 57.

[13] M. Müller-Chen, *in* I. Schwenzer (Ed.), Schlechtriem & Schwenzer Commentary on the UN Convention on the International Sale of Goods Art. 49, para. 4, at 748 (2010); Schroeter, *supra* note 1, Art. 25, para. 19, at 408.

[14] Schroeter, *supra* note 1, Art. 25, para. 27, at 412: It is not required the foreseeability of the detriment which substantially deprived the other party of what he is entitled to expect under the contract. Only when the particular importance or interest of the breached obligation cannot be subtracted from the contract or was not clearly point out during the negotiations, the foreseeability element may become relevant.

[15] *See* how there is no distinction in Argentina Art. 1204 CC & Art. 216 Com C; Bolivia Art. 568 CC; Brazil Arts. 474, 475 CC; Chile Art. 1489 CC; Colombia Art. 1546 CC & Art. 870 Com C; Costa Rica Art. 463 Com C; El Salvador Art. 1360 CC; Ecuador Art. 1532 CC; Mexico Art. 1949 CC & Art. 376 Com C; Paraguay Art. 725 CC; Peru Art. 1428 CC; Portugal Arts. 817, 801 (1) CC; Spain Art. 1.124 CC & Art. 330 Com C; Uruguay Art. 1431 CC & Art. 246 Com C; Venezuela Art. 1.167 CC.

is principal or accessory,[16] or whether the breach is of much or of less importance. However, some standards can still be found in other statutes and in the jurisprudence.[17]

On the one hand, the Bolivian and the Paraguayan Civil Code establish that there is no place for the avoidance of the contract if the breach by one of the parties is of little gravity or of scarce importance, taking into consideration the other party's interest.[18] On the other hand, under the Peruvian Civil Code, allegations of partial or defective performance do not entitle the creditor to avoid the contract. In the Peruvian Supreme Court understanding, only total non-performance under Article 1428 may cause the avoidance of the contract.[19]

Under the Portuguese Civil Code, the breach is definitive, *i.e.* produces fully effects, if the creditor loses his interest in the performance or the debtor does not perform within the supplementary period granted to comply.[20] But the creditor's loss of interest in the performance shall be appreciated objectively.[21] Additionally, under the Venezuelan Code of Commerce, the deterioration suffered by the goods in transit avoid the contract only if the goods are deteriorated in such a way that they are useless for the use that they are intended for.[22]

Similarly, the jurisprudence has established certain levels of breach in order to limit the possibility to avoid the contract. As a starting point, courts and tribunals have required, among other things, that the aggrieved party

[16] El Salvador Superior Tribunal, RJ 1-12, January to December 1954, at 343-366, *cited in* El Salvador: Miranda, *supra* note 8, at 549; Paraguay Supreme Court, Judgment 350, 27 June 2001, *Liberata Ibarrola Vda. De García v. Vilda Selva D'Ecclesis Y Otra:* stating that a contractual breach is any disruption between the conduct due and the behaviour of the bound party; and this can consist, thus, in a total or partial breach or in a defective performance, since who does not perform as it should, does not fulfil as he has to.

[17] Bolivia Art. 572 CC; Paraguay Art. 725 CC; Peru Art. 1151 CC; Paraguay Art. 782 CC: establishes that when the price has to be paid in installments, there is no ground for the avoidance of the contract, if the buyer has already paid 25% of the price, or if he has made improvements to the goods up to the mentioned percentage. Avoidance is also denied if the sum of the already paid price and the improvement make the 25% percent of the contract price; Portugal Art. 808(1) CC; Venezuela Art. 140 Com C.

[18] Bolivia Art. 572 CC; Paraguay Art. 725 CC.

[19] Peru Supreme Court, *Sala civil transitoria,* Resolution 002290-2002, 20 August 2002. Otherwise, the general rules on obligations grant the following remedies for partial or defective performances: a) the specific performance by the debtor or a third party on the account of the debtor, or; b) the right to consider the obligation as never performed, if the creditor proves that the same has been useless, or; c) the right to destroy the object, if it results hazardous, or; d) the right to reduce the value of the counter-performance, *see* Peru Art. 1151 CC.

[20] Portugal Art. 808(1) CC.

[21] Portugal Art. 808(2) CC; ICC Final Award Case No. 12853 *Lex Contractus* Portuguese Law: the issue at dispute was the breach of an Agency Sales Agreement. The Sole Arbitrator explained that "the breach must be serious or repeated so many times that it is no longer reasonable to ask the innocent party to continue to perform and to keep the contract in being."

[22] Venezuela Art. 140 Com C.

proves that he had performed or was ready to perform his obligations under the contract,[23] and that the breaching party was in permanent or temporary delay in performing his obligations.[24]

Additionally, the doctrine and the jurisprudence have limited the right of avoidance to the breach of main obligations under the contract or when the breach, in itself, is grave enough to frustrate the parties' interest in concluding the contract.[25] Accordingly, the Spanish Supreme Tribunal has sustained that delayed performance of an ancillary obligation does not constitute sufficient

---

[23] El Salvador Supreme Court, *Cass civ*, *Castillo de Lopez v. Iraheta Flores*, 1195-2000, 28 August 2000; El Salvador Supreme Court, *Cass civ*, *Funes Castillo v. Agropecuaria "La Cabaña"*, 141-C-2004, 13 December 2004; Mexico Collegiate Tribunals, *Novena Época,* Registry 191'011, SJF XII, October 2000, at 1280; Paraguay Supreme Court, Judgment 219, 17 May 2001, *Baúl De La Felicidad S.A. v. Pony Automotores – Mitsuservice Import S.R.L.*; Spain AT Pamplona, 15 December 1988; ICC Final Award Case No. 13882 *Lex Contractus* Spanish Law.

[24] El Salvador Supreme Court, *Cass civ*, *Castillo de Lopez v. Iraheta Flores*, 1195-2000, 28 August 2000; El Salvador Supreme Court, *Cass civ*, *Funes Castillo v. Agropecuaria "La Cabaña"*, 141-C-2004, 13 December 2004; ICC Final Award Case No. 11853 *Lex Contractus* Mexican Law: explaining that the delay in performing is a requirement for the avoidance of the contract, for both the avoidance by one party's declaration when permitted by the law or by the agreement of the parties and the traditional avoidance as declared by the competent court; ICC Partial Award Case No. 12296 *Lex Contractus* Mexican Law: explaining that for the avoidance to operate, Mexican law requires the prior failure of a party to comply with its contractual obligations; Mexico Collegiate Tribunals, *Novena Época,* Registry 196'579, SJF VII, March 1998, at 775: explained that the seller who failed to deliver the property titles was prevented from resorting to the avoidance action based on lack of payment by the buyer, since it was understood that the buyer would need the property documents to get a loan from a bank in order to fulfil his obligation to pay the price; Spain Supreme Tribunal, 15 November 2006, *Id Cendoj:* 28079110012006101110: explained that the buyer's refusal to pay the last two instalments of the price does not give the seller the right to avoid the contract, since such refusal was justified by the seller's breach of the implied obligation to deliver clean property documents.

[25] Chile: A. Vidal Olivares, *La Noción de Incumplimiento Esencial en el Código Civil*, XXXII(1) Revista de Derecho de la Pontificia Universidad Católica de Valparaíso 221, at 238-240 (2009); Spain: A. Martínez Cañellas, *El incumplimiento esencial del contrato de compraventa internacional de mercaderías*, Doctoral thesis, Universitat de les Illes Balears, Facultat de Dret. Àrea de Dret mercantil Palma de Mallorca 293-294 (2001), http://www.tdx.cat/TDX-0308105-095856; Mexico Collegiate Tribunals, *Novena Época,* Registry 183'878, SJF XVIII, July 2003, at 1061: stating that it is not enough to prove the breach of one of the obligations contracted by one of the parties so that the avoidance of the contract can be justified, since it is needed that such breach is of such importance so that the interest of the creditor on the performance of the contract is left unsatisfied, considering the functional interdependence of the correlated obligations in the agreement; Paraguay Supreme Court, Judgment 350, 27 June 2001, *Liberata Ibarrola Vda. De García v. Vilda Selva D'Ecclesis Y Otra*: even in cases of reciprocal breach, it should be evaluate the nature and importance of such mutual breaches in order to decide whether the contractual breaches from the one and the other party have a causal link and to asses the proportionality necessary for the avoidance of the contract in favour or against any of the parties.

breach to trigger the right to avoid the contract, since it is required that the breach affects the essential elements of the contract, so that it frustrates the contractual main cause.[26]

Nevertheless, as sustained by some scholars, delayed performance may constitute enough grounds for the avoidance, when it frustrates the other party's interest in concluding the contract.[27] In a particular case covered by the rules of the Code of Commerce, the Spanish Supreme Tribunal acknowledged that the seller did not properly perform his obligation when he shipped the goods with delay because the goods were not any longer useful for the economic purpose pursued by the buyer. The profitable aim was frustrated, giving rise to the avoidance of the sale in the buyer's favour.[28]

Finally, we may bear in mind that the delivery of different goods or *aliud pro alio* also constitutes a breach of the obligation to deliver.[29] In such a case, the buyer may terminate the contract through the avoidance remedy for ordinary breach, and not according to the rules of the redhibitory action for defects.[30] But Courts might not declare the avoidance of the contract on the grounds of *aliud pro alio*, unless the seller delivers goods completely different such as oil and gas. Or when although they are of same type required, the goods are *totally* unfit for the use they were acquired for, causing the frustration of buyer's business objective.[31] For example, if the seller delivers olive oil which does not meet the import standards established in the contract.[32]

Scholars have pointed out that the Ibero-American jurisprudence developed on this point, introduces an element which is close to the standard required under the CISG. That is, the requirement to establish the importance or gravity of the breach in the economy of the contract in order to justify the avoidance.[33] In other words, the characterisation of obligations as principal or as ancillary, or the nature of the defects on the goods may become irrelevant to determine the attaching interest of one of the parties, and thus, to determine whether a breach can lead to the avoidance. On the other hand, the circumstances of the

[26] Spain Supreme Tribunal, 27 November 1992, *Id Cendoj:* 28079110011992103416.

[27] *See* Chile: Vidal Olivares, *supra* note 25, at 239; Spain: J. Moxica Román, La compraventa mercantil e instituciones afines: análisis de doctrina y jurisprudencia, formularios 149 (2000).

[28] Spain Supreme Tribunal, 29 January 1991, *Id Cendoj:* 28079110011991101451.

[29] *See* in this regard Spain: E. Guardiola Sacarrera, La compraventa internacional: importaciones y exportaciones 75 (2001).

[30] Spain Supreme Tribunal, 20 November 2008, *Id Cendoj:* 28079110012008101062.

[31] Chile: Vidal Olivares, *supra* note 25, at 240; Spain Supreme Tribunal, 14 May 2009, *Id Cendoj:* 28079110012009100320.

[32] Spain Supreme Tribunal, 22 October 2007, *Id Cendoj:* 28079110012007101093.

[33] Chile: Vidal Olivares, *supra* note 25, at 245-254: referring to the Chilean Jurisprudence and statutory provisions that equal the understanding of 'grave breach' to the concept of 'fundamental breach' under the CISG; Spain: Martínez Cañellas, *supra* note 25, at 286, 294, 295 referring to jurisprudence developed by the Spanish Supreme Tribunal on Spain Art. 1.124 CC & Art. 330 Com C.

case and the intention of the parties as assumed from the contract are more relevant to establish the importance or gravity of the breach in the economy of the contract.

However, the standard developed by the Ibero-American jurisprudence may still be lower than the standard contained in Article 25 CISG.[34] For example, a Spanish court considered that the jurisprudential doctrine of *aliud pro alio* was applicable to a non-conformity case, and was compatible with CISG Article 25,[35] in its three grounds: (1) the delivery of goods different to the ones agreed; (2) the delivery of goods totally unfit for the use to which they are intended; (3) the objective dissatisfaction of the buyer.[36] Although in the case at hand it was evident that the buyer was substantially deprived of what he was entitled to expect under the contract,[37] the delivery of different goods to those agreed may not always be enough to avoid the contract under Article 49 (1) (a) and 25 CISG.[38] In the opinion of the CISG-Advisory Council,

> one has to take into account whether the buyer can be required to retain the goods because he can be adequately compensated through damages or through a price reduction. The substantiality of the detriment to the buyer may be ascertained by having regard to the terms of the contract, the purpose for which the goods are bought and finally, by the question of whether it is possible to remedy the defect.[39]

[34] *See* R.F. Henschel, *Conformity of Goods in International Sales Governed by Article 35 CISG: Caveat Venditor, Caveat Emptor and Contract Law as Background Law and as a Competing Set of Rules*, Nordic Journal of Commercial Law (2004): "[T]he relevance of the concept of insignificant defects has been rejected both in theory and in practice, since any variance at all from the agreed description of the goods is assumed to mean that the goods do not conform to the contract. The significance of the defect for the buyer is then decided according to the rights of the buyer in the event of lack of conformity of the goods, and this will typically involve compensation or a reduction in the price, although a minor defect will also amount to a fundamental breach in some cases."

[35] Audiencia Provincial de Palencia, Sec. 1, 26 September 2005. The Court also held that the doctrine of *aliud pro alio* was compatible with Arts. 30, 35 (1) (2) CISG.

[36] *Id.*

[37] A requirement for the avoidance under Art. 25 CISG, *see* Spain: P. Perales Vizcasillas, *CISG Case Law in Spain (2004-2006), in* C. Andersen & U. Schroeter (Ed.), Sharing International Commercial Law across National Boundaries: Festschrift for Albert H Kritzer on the Occasion of his 80th Birthday, 377, at 383 (2008).

[38] Perales Viscasillas, *supra* note 37, at 383.

[39] CISG-AC, Opinion No. 5, The buyer's right to avoid the contract in case of non-conforming goods or documents 7 May 2005, Badenweiler (Germany). Rapporteur: Professor Dr. Ingeborg Schwenzer, LL.M., Professor of Private Law, University of Basel, Comment 4.1.

1.3. Additional Period to Perform-Nachfrist

Some laws expressly declare that by means of notice,[40] the creditor may require the breaching party to comply with his obligation under the contract within a minimum 15-day period, so that if the debtor fails to perform again, the contract is automatically avoided.[41]

On this point, scholars have explained that the additional 15-day period is not a requirement when the obligation has an essential fixed time to be performed and later performance appears useless.[42] On the other hand, the Peruvian Supreme Court has clarified that the notice to the other party to perform does not constitute a *sine qua non* requirement in order to subsequently be able to appear before a court to claim the avoidance of the contract. The notice to perform within an additional period is an optional right of the aggrieved party to achieve the specific performance or, alternatively, the automatic avoidance of the contract in case of reiterated breach. But failure to give notice to perform does not prevent the aggrieved party from seeking the avoidance of the contract by means of the court's judgment.[43]

2. Breach of Contract

2.1. Seller's Breach

2.1.1. Non delivery

Under the Ibero-American laws, the avoidance of the contract for breach of the seller's duties is recognised as a remedy for the buyer.[44] Subject to the above mentioned standards,[45] most laws establish that if the seller does not deliver the goods at the time agreed within the contract, the buyer may claim

---

40 The Bolivian and Peruvian Civil Codes require such notice to be made through a notary public, *see* Bolivia Art. 570 CC; Peru Art. 1429 CC.

41 Argentina Art. 1204 CC & Art. 216 Com C; Bolivia Art. 570 CC; Paraguay Art. 728 CC; Peru Art. 1429 CC; Portugal Art. 808(1) CC: with no reference to the 15 day-period; Peru Supreme Court, *Sala civil permanente,* Resolution 000225-2002, 9 April 2003.

42 Argentina: R.L. Lorenzetti, Tratado de los Contratos Parte General 662 (2004).

43 Peru Supreme Court, *Sala civil transitoria,* Resolution 002838-2001, 25 January 2002.

44 *See* doctrine Argentina: Compagnucci de Caso, *supra* note 4, at 139, 217, 243; Brazil: O. Gomes, Contratos 203-206 (2008); Bolivia: Kaune Arteaga, *supra* note 5, at 133; Chile: Díez Duarte, *supra* note 5, at 147; El Salvadoor: Miranda, *supra* note 8, at 191-193; Mexico: O. Vásquez del Mercado, Contratos Mercantiles 204 (2008); Portugal: L. De Lima Pinheiro, Dereito Comercial Internacional 292 (2005); Uruguay: N. Rodriguez Olivera *et al.*, Manual de Derecho comercial uruguayo, v. 2: Obligaciones y contratos comerciales, t. 1: Régimen general de las obligaciones comerciales, compraventa y distribución mercantil 211 (2005); Venezuela: J.L. Aguilar Gorrondona, Contratos y Garantias: Derecho Civil IV, 223 (2008).

45 *See supra* 1.1.

the avoidance of the contract or, at his choice, the specific performance of the contract.[46] The same rule applies to other main obligations of the seller, such as, the duty to receive the price or to keep the goods in good condition until delivery.

The above mentioned rule is the confirmation of the remedy of avoidance, which is implicit in bilateral contracts.[47] This rule is commonly embodied in the general provisions on obligations: "in contracts with reciprocal performances, one of the parties may demand the avoidance of the contract if the other party fails to fulfil his obligations."[48] The remedy of avoidance, may include cases where 1) the goods are not delivered, are not going to be delivered in future, 2) the delivery is simply delayed; and 3) the delivery is made incomplete or executed without its accessories.[49]

2.1.2. Non Conforming Goods or Documents

Under the Ibero-American laws, except for Portugal,[50] if the goods delivered are affected by defects unknown to the buyer, he may make resort of a redhibitory action, but not to an action for ordinary breach of contract.[51] Subject to the

[46] Argentina Arts. 1412, 1420 CC & Arts. 467, 216 Com C; Brazil Arts. 474, 475 CC; Bolivia Art. 622 CC & Art. 845 Com C; Chile Art. 1826 CC & Art. 156 Com C; Colombia Art. 1882 CC; El Salvador Art. 1629 CC; Ecuador Art. 1793 CC & Art. 199 Com C; Mexico Arts. 2283, 1949 CC; Peru Art. 1556 CC; Paraguay Arts. 759, 725 CC; Spain Art. 1.124 CC & Art. 329 Com C; Uruguay Art. 1688 CC & Art. 534 Com C; Venezuela Arts. 1486, 1.167 CC & Art. 141 Com C; Peru Supreme Court, *Sala civil transitoria*, Resolution 002838-2001, 25 January 2002: upheld that failure to deliver the goods immediately after the contract's conclusion entitled the buyer to seek the avoidance of the contract, even though the seller had already performed other accessory obligations, as the clearance of title encumbrances and the payment of related taxes.

[47] *See* doctrine Argentina: Compagnucci de Caso, *supra* note 4, at 139; Brazil: Gomes, *supra* note 44, at 2005; Bolivia: Kaune Arteaga, *supra* note 5, at 133; Chile: Díez Duarte, *supra* note 5, at 147; El Salvador: Miranda, *supra* note 8, at 191-193; Portugal: De Lima Pinheiro, *supra* note 44, at 292; Spain: M. Medina de Lemus, Derecho Civil: Obligaciones y Contratos II, Teoria General Vol. 1, 173 (2004); Uruguay: Rodríguez Olivera *et al.*, *supra* note 44, at 211; Venezuela: Aguilar Gorrondona, *supra* note 44, at 223.

[48] Argentina Art. 1204 CC & Art. 216 Com C; Bolivia Art. 568 CC; Brazil Arts. 474, 475 CC; Chile Art. 1489 CC; Colombia Art. 1546 CC & Art. 870 Com C; El Salvador Art. 1360 CC; Ecuador Art. 1532 CC; Mexico Art. 1949 CC & Art. 376 Com C; Paraguay Art. 725 CC; Peru Art. 1428 CC; Portugal Arts. 817, 801 (1) CC; Spain Art. 1.124 CC & Art. 330 Com C; Uruguay Art. 1431 CC & Art. 246 Com C; Venezuela Art. 1.167 CC; ICC Final Award Case No. 13127 *Lex Contractus* Brazilian Law: the Tribunal uphold the two possibilities given by Brazilian Law at the aggrieved party's choice; ICC Final Award Case No. 11722 *Lex Contractus* Mexican Law; ICC Final Award Case No. 13663 *Lex Contractus* Spanish Law: the Tribunal uphold the two possibilities given by Spain Art. 1.124 CC at the aggrieved party's choice.

[49] *See* expressly Spain Art. 330 Com C; El Salvador: Miranda, *supra* note 8, at 191.

[50] *See* Portugal's Civil Code section called *Venda de coisas defectuosas* in Arts. 913-922: the sale of defective goods according to the contract or the law constitutes a breach of contract *per se* which does not need commencement of a particular legal action.

[51] *See* Ch. 47, 1.

above mentioned standards required to trigger the remedy,[52] a redhibitory action may have the same effect as that of the avoidance of the contract,[53] but it does not work exactly as the avoidance of the contract for breach of ordinary contractual duties.[54] This approach is clearly expressed in the Civil Codes of Chile, Colombia, Ecuador and El Salvador which define the term "redhibitory action" as the buyer's right to avoid the sale.[55] The redhibitory action has a concurrent action called estimatory action having as an effect the reduction of the price. The exercise of one of these actions excludes the exercise of the other.[56]

2.2. Buyer's Breach

Under the Ibero-American laws, failure to pay the price in due course, does not only generate interest in favour of the seller,[57] but it might also give him the right to claim the avoidance of the contract.[58] Yet again, the delay of the

[52] *See supra* 1.1.
[53] *See for example*, expressly recognised in Peru Art. 1511 CC.
[54] Some authors consider it a mistake to characterise the redhibitory action as resolutory or rescinding action (action for the avoidance of the contract under CISG) for three main reasons: 1) there is a shorter term to exercise the action; 2) because it does not affect third party rights in good faith; 3) it does not presuppose the breach of obligations, *see* on this Venezuela: Aguilar Gorrondona, *supra* note 44, at 256.
[55] The mentioned Civil Codes use the verb *rescindir* which literary means rescission. But such is a mistake of the drafters, since the appropriate verb was *resolver* which means to avoid, the remedy for breach of contract; this view is supported by El Salvador: Miranda, *supra* note 8, at 250.
[56] *See for example*, Guatemala Art. 1573 CC; Uruguay Art. 1720 CC.
[57] *See* Ch. 52.
[58] Argentina Arts. 505, 3893 CC: though avoidance cannot be claimed in sales by credit. The seller may only recover the interest of the due payment, *see* Argentina Art. 1429 CC; Bolivia Art. 639 CC; Chile Arts. 1873, 1489 CC; Colombia Arts. 1930, 1546 CC; El Salvador Arts. 1675, 1360 CC; Ecuador Arts. 1840, 1532 CC; Guatemala Arts. 1825, 1535 CC; Mexico Art. 2300 CC; Paraguay Arts. 763, 725 CC; Peru Arts. 1559, 1428 CC; Uruguay Art. 1731 CC & Art. 535 Com C; Venezuela Arts. 1527, 1.167 CC & Art. 141 Com C; *see also* Argentina: Compagnucci de Caso, *supra* note 4, at 243; Chile: Díez Duarte, *supra* note 5, at 175; Colombia: Tamayo Lombana, *supra* note 3, at 201; Colombia: E.G. Escobar Velez, La compraventa civil y comercial: los contratos de promesa de compraventa y la permutaa 242 (1991); El Salvador: Miranda, *supra* note 8, at 281; Mexico: S. León Tovar, Los Contratos Mercantiles 168, 169 (2004); Uruguay: Rodríguez Olivera *et al.*, *supra* note 44, at 214; Venezuela: Aguilar Gorrondona, *supra* note 44, at 274; Bolivia Supreme Court, *Sala Civil*, 6 December 2005, *Bartolomé Erland Rodríguez Álvarez v. Fabricio Ludwing Braner Ibáñez:* recognising that failure to pay the price by the buyer gives the seller the right to claim the specific performance or the avoidance of the contract, and with both of them damages; Chile Supreme Court, RDJ, Vol. 65, Sec. 1, at 314 *cited in* Chile: Díez Duarte, *supra* note 5, at 175, n. 467; Costa Rica Supreme Court, Judgment 00212-98, *Segunda Sala Civil*, 19 August 1998: upholding that if the buyer fails to pay one of the installments, the seller cannot sell the goods to a third party (as the buyer was already the owner with the meeting of the minds on the thing and the price), neither

buyer to perform is the key element for the ordinary remedy of avoidance of the contract.[59] Delay in performance can be partial or total, temporary or definitive. If the buyer is not in delay, then the remedy is not actionable.[60] Temporary delays in payment may only trigger the right of avoidance, if such affects the essential elements of the contract, so that it frustrates the economic purpose of the contract.[61]

Under the Peruvian law, in cases of the sale of goods being not yet delivered, the seller is allowed to dispose of the goods, and thus to automatically avoid the contract, in case the buyer fails to pay the whole or part of the price.[62]

In addition to delay or refusal to pay the price, if the buyer refuses or delays the reception of the goods, the seller may not only claim payment of the cost of deposit and care of the goods,[63] but also retains the right of avoidance of the contract.[64] Such has been recognised by some scholars[65] and sustained by some courts.[66] The same rule would apply to other obligations of the buyer.

can the seller retain the installment already paid, unless there is express agreement to do so by means of penalty clause or arrears, what proceeds is the specific performance or the avoidance of the contract; Mexico Collegiate Tribunals, *Novena Época,* Registry 185'801, SJF XVI, October 2002, p 1347; Peru Supreme Court, *Sala civil transitoria,* Resolution 000114-1998, 24 February 1999; Spain Supreme Tribunal, 12 May 1990, *Id Cendoj:* 28079110011990101070; Spain Supreme Tribunal, 5 June 2008, *Id Cendoj:* 28079110012008100535; ICC Final Award Case No. 11826 *Lex Contractus* CISG and Mexican Law: the outstanding payments for the goods delivered to the buyer allowed the seller to declared the contract avoided under both the CISG and the Mexican Law.

59 *See* Portugal: De Lima Pinheiro, *supra* note 44, at 311.

60 For an explanation of the meaning of 'to be in delay' *see* Ch. 52, 2.

61 *See supra* 1.2.

62 Peru Art. 1564 CC; Peru Supreme Court, *Sala civil transitoria,* Resolution 001584-2002, 2 July 2002: stating that the rule is not applicable in cases where the buyer has already paid some of the price.

63 *See for example* Argentina Art. 465 Com C; Brazil Art. 400 CC; Chile Art. 1827 CC & Art. 153 Com C; Colombia Art. 1883 CC; El Salvador Art. 1630 CC; Ecuador Art. 1794 CC & Art. 198 Com C; Mexico Art. 2292 CC & Art. 387 Com C; Spain Art. 332 para. 3 Com C; *see also* Colombia: Escobar Velez, *supra* note 58, at 242; El Salvador: Miranda, *supra* note 8, at 194; Mexico: Vásquez del Mercado, *supra* note 44, at 207.

64 *See for example* Bolivia Art. 846 Com C; Chile Art. 153 Com C; Costa Rica Art. 477 Com C; Ecuador Art. 198 Com C; Paraguay Arts. 764, 725 CC; Peru Arts. 1565, 1428 CC; Uruguay Arts. 535 para. 1, 246 Com C (Uruguay Art. 536 Com C requires the legal interpellation of the buyer so that the buyer is effectively considered to be delayed in taking delivery); Spain Art. 1.505 CC & Art. 332 Com C; Venezuela Art. 1.531 CC.

65 *See for example* Chile: Díez Duarte, *supra* note 5, at 149; Colombia: Tamayo Lombana, *supra* note 3, at 201; Costa Rica: D. Baudrit Carrillo, Los Contratos Traslativos del Derecho Privado – Principios de Jurisprudencia 43-47 (2000); Peru: M. Castillo Freyre, Comentarios al contrato de compraventa: análisis detallado de los artículos 1529 a 1601 del Código Civil 170 (2002); Venezuela: Aguilar Gorrondona, *supra* note 44, at 266; Uruguay: Rodríguez Olivera *et al., supra* note 44, at 217.

66 Chile Supreme Court, RDJ, Vol. 10, Sec. 1, at 416 *cited in* Chile: Díez Duarte, *supra* note 5, at 149.

3. Process of Avoidance

For most Ibero-American laws, the avoidance of the contract needs to be declared by the competent court so that it produces full effects on the parties' contractual relationship.[67] The judgment rendered by the competent court does not only have a declarative effect but also has an exequatur effect; it orders the restitution of the parties' respective performances and their fruits.[68]

Nevertheless, there are some countries that follow a different approach. In the Portuguese law, the default rule declares that the avoidance of the contract can be made by declaration to the other party.[69] If there is no agreed time limit to effectuate the declaration of avoidance the other party can establish a reasonable time limit so that the creditor exercises his right.[70]

Under the Bolivian, Spanish and the Venezuelan law, the avoidance is automatic for all sales of goods if the buyer does not take delivery of the goods or does not pay their price as agreed in the contract.[71] Such *ipso iure* avoidance for lack of payment has been expressly denied under Mexican Jurisprudence.[72]

In Brazil and Bolivia, the avoidance of the contract may also work automatically in contracts which establish a critical term for performance without which the aggrieved party would not have entered into the transaction.[73] Finally, Bolivia's Civil Code establishes that in the sale of food and perishable

[67] *See* expressly dictated in Bolivia Art. 568 CC; Peru Art. 1428 CC; Chile Supreme Court, RDJ, Vol. 77, Sec. 2, at 77, *cited in* Chile: Díez Duarte, *supra* note 5, at 333, n. 930; Mexico Collegiate Tribunals, *Novena Época,* Registry 195'050, SJF VIII, December 1998, at 1030; ICC Final Award Case No. 11722 *Lex Contractus* Mexican Law: explaining the possibility to avoid the contract as far as the other party is in breach, but if the Tribunal finding is that the other party was not in breach the contract remains existing and being valid; *see also* Bolivia: R. Carrillo Aruquipa, Lecciones de Derecho Civil, Obligaciones 428 (2008); Bolivia: Kaune Arteaga, *supra* note 5, at 159; Brazil: Gomes, *supra* note 44, at 208; El Salvador: Miranda, *supra* note 8, at 283; Peru: Castillo Freyre, *supra* note 65, at 162: notes that once the declaration is made by the competent court the effects work retroactively to the breach.

[68] *See* Ch. 57, 1.1 & 1.2.

[69] Portugal Art. 436 (1) CC; ICC Final Award Case No. 10818 *Lex Contractus* Portuguese Law: the Tribunal upheld that by letter dated 00.00.000, the seller terminated the Agreement as of 00.00.0000. The termination complied with the requirements of the Agreement and was therefore valid; ICC Final Award Case No. 12853 *Lex Contractus* Portuguese Law: the issue at dispute was the breach of an Agency Sales Agreement. The Sole Arbitrator explained that "the termination of the contract can be done through a declaration directed to the other party."

[70] Portugal Art. 436(2) CC.

[71] Bolivia Art. 846 Com C; Spain Art. 1505 CC; Venezuela Art. 1.531 CC & Art. 141 Com C.

[72] Mexico Collegiate Tribunals, *Novena Época,* Registry 195'050, SJF VIII, December 1998, p. 1030: upholding that lack of payment does not automatically render the contract avoided, neither it produces the *ipso iure* avoidance, since the court declaration is needed.

[73] Bolivia Art. 571 CC; Brazil: Gomes, *supra* note 44, at 211; Bolivia Supreme Court, *Sala Civil*, 3 September 2002, *Jorge Arze Murillo y otra v. Aerolínea Varig.*

products, the avoidance works automatically, with no need of notice from the seller, if the buyer does not take delivery or does not pay the price in the time agreed in the contract.[74]

In some of the countries which followed the above-mentioned court declaration approach, the first exception comes into play when the parties have previously agreed that failure to perform X's or Y's obligations would automatically cause the avoidance of the contract.[75] This agreement is usually called *avoidance clause*.[76] With this clause, the avoidance has full effect since the debtor of the obligation is considered to be in delay or in definitive non-performance of the obligation agreed, with no need of a court judgment.[77]

Under some laws, notice of avoidance to the other party is required so that the agreed *avoidance clause* effectively causes the automatic avoidance of the contract.[78] The aggrieved party must communicate to the other party his intention to avoid the contract.

On this issue, the Peruvian Supreme Court sustained that such a rule must be interpreted in accordance with the aim and effect of the unilateral declaration of avoidance. First, the notice of avoidance cannot be replaced by a declaration of a different type, such as that requiring the breaching party to perform in a supplementary period of time. Second, the notice has a receptive character, where the declaration must not only be addressed to the breaching party, but it must also be intended to be known by that party. It is understood that the breaching party knows of the declaration of avoidance when it reaches his domicile. However, the Court acknowledged that nothing prevents the parties from agreeing that the notice or declaration of avoidance would gain full effect from the moment it was dispatched by the aggrieved party, as such an agreement does not conflict with the public order of the Peruvian law.[79]

---

[74] Bolivia Art. 640 CC.

[75] Argentina Arts. 1204 (3), 1375 CC & Art. 216 Com C; Bolivia Art. 569 CC; Brazil Art. 474 CC; Chile Arts. 1877-1880 CC; Colombia Arts. 1935-1938 CC; Ecuador Arts. 1844-1846 CC; Mexico Arts. 1940, 1941 CC; Mexico Supreme Court, *Novena Época, Primera Sala,* Registry 189'425, SJF XIII, June 2001, p 165; Mexico Collegiate Tribunals, *Novena Época*, Registry 199'343, SJF V, February 1997, p 769; *see also* Brazil: Gomes, *supra* note 44, at 209.

[76] Known in Spanish as *Pacto Comisorio* or *Cláusula Resolutoria.*

[77] ICC Final Award Case No. 11853 *Lex Contractus* Mexican Law; ICC Final Award Case No. 13524 *Lex Contractus* Mexican Law: the Arbitral Tribunal referred to a good number of decisions constructing the principle under Mexican Law.

[78] Argentina Art. 1204(3) CC & Art. 216 Com C; Bolivia Art. 569 CC; Paraguay Art. 726 CC; Peru Art. 1430 CC; Mexico Collegiate Tribunals, *Novena Época*, Registry 199'343, SJF V, February 1997, at 769; Paraguay Supreme Court, Judgment 219, 17 May 2001, *Baúl De La Felicidad S.A. v. Pony Automotores – Mitsuservice Import S.R.L.*: in dissenting opinion of one of the three Supreme Court Judges who decided this case, it was established that the declaration of avoidance based on the avoidance clause lack of effects since the person who executed it was not authorised as representative of the company; Bolivia: Carrillo Aruquipa, *supra* note 67, at 429.

[79] Peru Supreme Court, *Sala civil transitoria,* Resolution 000050-2005, 10 January 2006.

Nevertheless, as explained by an ICC Arbitral Tribunal, the automatic avoidance agreed to by the parties in the form of an avoidance clause is part of the wider avoidance right granted by (Brazilian) law. Consequently, the mere insertion of the avoidance clause in a contract, or the failure to comply with the preconditions for the automatic avoidance established by the same clause, as the notice requirement, does not prevent the aggrieved party from seeking the declaration of avoidance of the contract by means of a judicial claim before a competent court.[80]

[80] ICC Final Award Case No. 13127 *Lex Contractus* Brazilian Law.

Chapter 54

Set-off

1. General Remarks on Set-Off

Under the Ibero-American laws, the set-off of obligations is generally understood to take place when two parties reciprocally acquire the character of creditors and debtors to each other, irrespective from the source of the debts.[1] The set-off[2] constitutes one of the means for the extinction of obligations.[3] In the words of the Venezuelan Supreme Tribunal, the effect of a set-off judgment must be regarded as means of payment of the reciprocal debts recognised by the judge.[4] Except in Portugal where the effect is not the extinction, but rather the discharge of the obligations as in the UNIDROIT PICC.[5]

A frequent question in sales contracts is whether and under which circumstances one party may set-off an already matured obligation he has, against another obligation that his counterparty owes to him. For example,

---

1 Argentina Art. 818 CC; Bolivia Art. 363 CC; Brazil Art. 373 CC; Mexico Collegiate Tribunals, *Novena Época,* Registry 185'809, SJF XVI, October 2002, at 1341; *see also* Bolivia: G. Castellanos Trigo & S. Auad La Fuente, Derecho de las Obligaciones en el Código Civil Boliviano 199, 200 (2008): referring to Argentinean and Paraguayan scholars.

2 Known under the Spanish name of *Compensación* or the Portuguese word of *Compensação*.

3 Argentina Art. 724 para. 3 CC; Bolivia Art. 351 (5) CC; Brazil Art. 368 CC; Chile Art. 1567 (5) CC; Colombia Art. 1625 (5) CC; Ecuador Art. 1610 (6) CC; El Salvador Art. 1438 (4) CC; Mexico Art. 2186 CC; Peru Art. 1288 CC; Spain Art. 1.156 CC; Venezuela Art. 1.331 CC; Mexico Collegiate Tribunals, *Novena Época,* Registry 185'809, SJF XVI, October 2002, at 1341.

4 Venezuela Supreme Tribunal, Judgment 62, *Cass soc*, file 01-262 of 14 February 2002.

5 Portugal Art. 847 (1) CC. Under the UNIDROIT PICC, where two parties owe each other an obligation arising from a contract or any other cause of action, each party may set-off his obligation against the obligation of the other party. By mutual compensation, both parties are discharged from their obligations up to the amount in value of the lower obligation, *see* M.J. Bonell, The Unidroit Principles in Practice: Caselaw and Bibliography on the Unidroit Principles of International Commercial Contracts Art. 8.1, p. 432, para. 1 (2006).

a buyer may seek to set-off his own obligation to pay $ 1000 for the goods delivered by the seller, against the seller's obligation to pay him $ 9000 in compensation for damages derived from the non- conformity of the goods of the same contract. The answer to this question will be reviewed below.

2. Requirements

All the Ibero-American laws acknowledge, though with some exceptions and variances, the same legal requirements for the set-off of obligations. As described by the jurisprudence, these are: 1) Simultaneity: obligations must exist at the same time, though they may have been born in different moments; 2) Homogeneity: the debt owed must have the same object or similar object as the debt to set-off; 3) Liquidity: the credit to set-off must be liquid, that is, it should be exactly known what is owed and its exact amount; 4) Executability: the obligations must be due.[6]

In the following paragraphs, the variances in the mechanism of set-off in the Ibero-American laws and the UNIDROIT PICC will be compared and examined in order to establish the availability of set-off of obligations derived from the contract of sales.

According to the Article 8.1 of the UNIDROIT PICC, and the Ibero-American laws on the set-off of obligations, a first requirement is that each party is the creditor and the debtor of each other.[7] Consequently, set-off is not possible if one party has an obligation to the other party in his own name but is the debtor of the other party in another capacity.[8] In this regard, some Ibero-American laws establish, for example, that the principal debtor cannot claim the set-off of what he owes to the creditor against what the creditor owes to the principal debtor's guarantor.[9] Also, while in some countries compensation of reciprocal debts of solidary debtors and creditors are available to set-off,[10] others expressly forbid it.[11] As pointed out by Bonell, in practice, the

[6] ICC Final Award Case No. 9984 *Lex Contractus* Chilean Law; Mexico Collegiate Tribunals, *Novena Época,* Registry 191'160, SJF XII, September 2000, at 721; Venezuela Supreme Tribunal, Judgment 00559, file 15666 of 3 April 2001.

[7] Argentina Arts. 818, 826, 827, 828 CC (providing different examples); Bolivia Art. 363 CC; Brazil Art. 368 CC; Chile Art. 1657 sentence 1 CC; Colombia Art. 1716 sentence 1 CC; Ecuador Art. 1700 sentence 1 CC; El Salvador Art. 1527 sentence 1 CC; Guatemala Art. 1469 CC; Mexico Art. 2185 CC; Paraguay Art. 615 CC; Peru Art. 1288 CC; Spain Arts. 1.195, 1.196 (1) CC; Venezuela Art. 1.331 CC.

[8] Bonell, *supra* note 5, Art. 8.1, para. 2, at 433.

[9] Argentina Art. 829 CC; Brazil Art. 371 CC; Chile Art. 1657 para. 2 CC; Colombia Art. 1716 para. 2 CC; Ecuador Art. 1700 para. 2 CC; El Salvador Art. 1527 para. 2 CC; Guatemala Art. 1475 CC *contrario sensu*; Mexico Art. 2199 CC; Peru Art. 1291 CC *contrario sensu*; Venezuela Art. 1.336 CC.

[10] Argentina Art. 830 CC; Mexico Art. 1991 CC.

[11] Paraguay Art. 620(c) CC: unless an agreement of all the persons involved.

most common situation would be that of the buyer who wants to set-off his obligation to pay the price to a subsidiary company against a proportional monetary debt owed by the parent company to the buyer, since parent and subsidiary companies are different persons.[12]

Under the UNIDROIT PICC, the reciprocally compensable obligations must be in money or in other performances of the same kind.[13] The Ibero-American laws have a similar requirement. Set-off is only possible when the owed obligations consist of money or of fungible goods "of the same kind and quality."[14] The specificity of being 'fungible goods' and of the 'same kind and quality' narrows the scope of the compensable obligations, while the concept of 'performances of the same kind' is broader. As pointed out by one commentator, non-monetary obligations may be of the same kind but may not be fungible goods [of the same kind and quality].[15] "Two obligations to deliver wine of the same vineyard but not of the same year may be obligations of the same kind, but would not be fungible."[16] Finally, a few Ibero-American laws expressly provide that the obligation to execute acts or services is not available for set-off.[17]

Similarly, the right to set-off reciprocal obligations may only be available if parties' obligations are ascertained both as to its existence and as to its amount.[18] The existence of the obligation is meant to be ascertained when the obligation itself cannot be contested by the other party.[19] For example, if the obligation derives from a valid contract or a final non-appealable judgment or arbitration award. Besides its uncontested existence, the obligation shall be ascertained as to its amount or value.

The Ibero-American laws acknowledge the same requirement. The debts must be liquid.[20] Thus, in most countries it is not possible to exercise the right to set-off if one of the owed amounts has not been determined, even if

---

[12] *See* illustration in Bonell, *supra* note 5, Art. 8.1, para. 2, at 433.

[13] UNIDROIT Principle Art. 8.1 (1); The only Ibero-American law sharing the approach is Paraguay Art. 615 CC.

[14] Argentina Art. 820 CC (or consisting in unascertained non-fungible goods, only by their species, as long as the choice belongs respectively to both debtors); Bolivia Art. 366 CC; Brazil Arts. 369, 370 CC; Chile Art. 1656 (1) CC; Colombia Art. 1715 (1) CC; Ecuador Art. 1699 (1) CC; El Salvador Art. 1526 (1) CC; Guatemala Art. 1470 CC; Mexico Art. 2187 CC; Peru Art. 1288 CC; Portugal Art. 847 (1) (b) CC; Spain Art. 1.196 (2) CC; Venezuela Art. 1.333 CC.

[15] Bonell, *supra* note 5, Art. 8.1, para. 3, at 433,.

[16] *Id.*

[17] Argentina Art. 825 CC; Guatemala Art. 1473 (3) CC.

[18] Art 8.1 (1) (b) PICC.

[19] Bonell, Art. 8.1, para. 5, *supra* note 5, at 435.

[20] Argentina Art. 819 CC; Bolivia Art. 366 CC; Chile Art. 1656 (2) CC; Colombia Art. 1715 (2) CC; Ecuador Art. 1699 (2) CC; El Salvador Art. 1526 (2) CC; Guatemala Art. 1470 CC; Mexico Art. 2188 CC; Paraguay Art. 615 CC; Peru Art. 1288 CC; Spain Art. 1.196 (4) CC; Venezuela Art. 1.333 CC. Mexico Art. 2189 CC defines 'liquid debt' as the one whose amount has been determined or can be determined within the term of nine days.

the existence of the debt is not disputed.[21] Except in Portugal, where the non-liquidity of the debt does not prevent the set-off of obligations.[22] Similarly, in Bolivia and Paraguay, a judge can declare the set-off, of non liquidated but easily and quickly ascertained debts, to the amount that the other party recognised such, and suspend the debts effects until the judge determines the existence and the amount of the compensable debts.[23]

This requirement answers one of the most recurrent questions in the set-off of sales contracts. In the Ibero-American laws, except for the mentioned countries,[24] one party may not be available to set-off his own obligation under the sales contract, against the other party's obligation derived from the same contract, *e.g.* to compensate him for damages arising from the same contract, as far as a judgment or arbitral award had not been rendered asserting the exact amount of the indemnity due by the other party. However, such does not mean, as occurred in many instances, that the judge or the arbitrator cannot determine in a single judgment or award, firstly, the buyer's recoverable damages for the seller's breach, secondly, the buyer's duty to pay the upstanding invoices to the sellers and, subsequently, proceeds to set-off the sums determined under such concepts.[25]

Under the UNIDROIT PICC, the conditions to set-off a contract are modified on this point when the obligations arise from the same contract. Certainly, if the obligations of the parties stem from the same contract, the first party is allowed to set-off his own obligation against the other party's obligation even if the other party's obligation is still not ascertained as to its existence or its amount.[26] In such a case, even if the liability to pay damages may be contested as to its existence or as to its amount, the other party can exercise his right to set-off because both obligations arise from the same contract and can be identified.

As pointed out, even if judicial intervention may be necessary to identify that the conditions are met,[27] the quick set-off of obligations belonging to the same contract is a very useful way to facilitate the settlement of this kind of

---

[21] ICC Final Award Case No. 14088 *Lex Contractus* Spanish Law: the Sole Arbitrator considered that whether the claimant breached the contract by not providing two out of several major obligations and whether the respondent had any right for a set-off under Spanish Law is immaterial because respondent never substantiated the amount it wished to set-off against the claimed amount. The respondent did not persuade the Sole Arbitrator that the amount which respondent wanted to set off against the claimed amount was sufficiently evidenced.

[22] Portugal Art. 847 CC.

[23] Bolivia Art. 367 CC; Paraguay Art. 616 CC.

[24] Bolivia Art. 367 CC; Paraguay Art. 616 CC; Portugal Art. 847 CC.

[25] ICC Final Award Case No. 11853 *Lex Contractus* Mexican Law: applying Mexico Art. 2185 *et seq.* CC; ICC Final Award Case No. 13478 *Lex Contractus* Venezuelan Law: concluded that Arts. 1333-1335 of Venezuela's Civil Code do allow the set-off under these circumstances.

[26] Art. 8.1 (2) PICC.

[27] Argentina Art. 831 CC.

disputes which are very common in national and international commerce.[28] As noted by the Venezuelan Supreme Court, through the set-off of obligations, the parties avoid the useless transfer of money, the related risk and expenses.[29]

Additionally, both parties' obligations must be due in both the UNIDROIT PICC and the Ibero-American laws.[30] Obligations are due when the parties are reciprocally entitled to request their respective performances, and any of them have a legitimate defence to refuse performance.[31] A legitimate denial to perform would be available, for instance, if the fixed date for payment of the debt has not yet elapsed.

For example, X supplies some (not a substantial part) of the materials that Y needs for the production of electronic circuits. Y has unpaid invoices for USD 1.000.000 with X whose date of payment has already elapsed. On the other hand, among Y's clients is X to whom last week he has delivered USD 900.000 in merchandise with a 30 day credit. Y may not be currently able to compensate his debt with X since X still has some 20 days so that his obligation becomes due.

Finally, in recognition of the principle of freedom of contract, the parties can agree on the set-off of their respective obligations and achieve its effects even if the above-mentioned conditions are not met.[32] Parties can also voluntarily exclude the possibility to set-off their obligations, since such agreement does not disturb the public order.[33]

3. Foreign Currency Set-off and Debts to Be Paid in Different Places

Under the UNIDROIT PICC, the set-off of obligations to pay money in different currencies is available, provided that they are both freely convertible, and the parties had not previously agreed that the first party shall only pay in a specified currency.[34] The reason for this last requirement is that as the value of a currency, which is not freely convertible, cannot be readily ascertained

---

28 Bonell, *supra* note 5, Art. 8.1, para. 7, at 436.

29 Venezuela Supreme Tribunal, Judgment 00559, file 15666 of 3 April 2001.

30 Art 8.1(1)(a)(b) PICC; Argentina Art. 819 CC; Bolivia Art. 366 CC; Chile Art. 1656(3) CC; Colombia Art. 1715(3) CC; Ecuador Art. 1699(3) CC; El Salvador Art. 1526(3) CC; Guatemala Art. 1470 CC; Mexico Art. 2188 CC; Paraguay Art. 615 CC; Peru Art. 1288 CC; Portugal Art. 847(1)(a) CC; Spain Art. 1.196(3)(4) CC; Venezuela Art. 1.333 CC.

31 *See* expressly Mexico Art. 2190 CC.

32 *See* expressly stated in Bolivia Art. 375 CC; Mexico Art. 2188 CC; Peru Art. 1289 CC; *see also* Bonell, *supra* note 5, Art. 8.1, para. 8, at 437.

33 *See* expressly stated in Brazil Art. 375 CC; Mexico Art. 2197 CC; Peru Art. 1288 CC.

34 Art 8.2 PICC.

as generally required to compensate, set-off cannot be used to impose the payment in such a currency on the other party.[35]

The Ibero-American laws do not have a similar provision. However, the laws seem to indicate that the set-off of obligations payable in foreign currency is available, provided the cost of the remittance is taken into account. This rule can be deduced from a frequent provision dictating that when the debts are to be paid in different places, the expenses of transportation, or the cost of the remittance, shall be taken into consideration in the set-off.[36]

4. Process of Set-off

Under the UNIDROIT PICC, the right to set-off is exercised by giving notice to the other party.[37] The first party must inform the other party that it will discharge its owed obligation by set-off, and the notice must meet certain conditions. First, the notice must specify the obligations to which it relates.[38] The other party receiving the notice must understand the mechanism of the set-off, *i.e.* which obligation is set-off against which obligation(s) and the amount compensated. If there are two or more obligations that could be set-off, and the first party has not specified the obligations he wants to compensate, the other party may choose, within reasonable time, which of the first party's obligations he would like to be discharged of.[39]

On the other hand, if the other party fails to choose and communicate to the first party which of the several first party's obligations he would like to set-off, all the obligations of the first party will be discharged by proportional set off, up to the value of the first party's obligation.[40]

Similarly in Portugal, set-off shall only be effective with the declaration made by the interested party to the other.[41] In the Guatemalan, the Paraguayan and the Peruvian laws, the interested party is not exactly required to declare

---

[35] Bonell, *supra* note 5, Art. 8.2, para. 1, at 439.

[36] Expenses of transportation: Bolivia Art. 368 CC; Brazil Art. 378 CC; Guatemala Art. 1476 CC; Mexico Art. 2204 CC; Paraguay Art. 618 (a) CC; Spain Art. 1.199 CC; Venezuela Art. 1.338 CC. Cost of the remittance: Chile Art. 1664 CC; Colombia Art. 1723 CC; Ecuador Art. 1707 CC; El Salvador Art. 1534 CC; Mexico Art. 2204 CC; Paraguay Art. 618 (a) CC; Spain Art. 1.199 CC; Venezuela Art. 1.338 CC; similar solution in Portugal Art. 852 CC; *see also* Bolivia: Castellanos Trigo & Auad La Fuente, *supra* note 1, at 210, 211.

[37] Art. 8.3 PICC.

[38] Art. 8.4(1) PICC.

[39] Art. 8.4(2) PICC.

[40] *Id.*

[41] Portugal Art. 848(1) CC: but the credits-debts are considered as extinguished since the moment they satisfied the conditions of the law of set-off *see* Portugal Art. 854 CC.

the set-off, but at least he must raise the set-off as an exception to the payment, so that it produces effects.[42] However, these laws are silent as to the way of raising the set-off.

For the rest of the Ibero-American laws, the set-off operates automatically,[43] even without the recognition of the debt-credit by,[44] or knowledge of,[45] the other party, and even if, by general usage or by one of the parties, is conceded a supplementary period of time for performance.[46]

In cases of multiples debts, the Ibero-American laws on set-off arrive to a different result. In Chile, Colombia, Ecuador and El Salvador the party who seeks the set-off of the obligation (first party under UNIDROIT PICC) may choose the debt he wishes to compensate. If the first party does not prefer any debt in particular, the other party may chose among the obligations the first party owes to him. If none of the parties have made a choice as to the compensable debt, it would be prefer the oldest debt in time.[47]

In the rest of the countries, absent a choice by the interested party, the higher debt shall be preferred to the lower; if all the debts have the same value, then the oldest debt in time would be preferred, and if all the debts have the same maturity, then the set-off shall be applied proportionally to all of them.[48]

---

[42] Guatemala Art. 1471 CC; Paraguay Art. 615 para. 2 CC: though extinction of the obligation goes back to the time when all of the conditions were met; Peru Art. 1288 CC: the extinction effect take place when the interested party raised the set-off.

[43] Argentina Art. 831 CC; Bolivia Art. 364 CC; Chile Art. 1656 CC; Colombia Art. 1715 CC; Ecuador Art. 1699 CC; El Salvador Art. 1526 CC; Mexico Art. 2186 CC; Venezuela Art. 1.332 CC; ICC Final Award Case No. 9984 *Lex Contractus* Chilean Law: "Chilean law ignores the concept of set-off by the judge (*compensación judicial*), with the exception of what is sometimes called *compensación reconvencional*, which occurs when the judge having granted both claims and counterclaims, only condemns one party to the balance of them. However, this is only a judicial practice and not a right that a debtor of a liquid and matured debt may invoke as an excuse not to pay such debt because it has a claim on its own, to be decided by a judge or an arbitrator."

[44] Argentina Art. 831 CC; Paraguay Art. 615 para. 2 CC.

[45] Chile Art. 1656 CC; Colombia Art. 1715 CC; Ecuador Art. 1699 CC; El Salvador Art. 1526 CC; Spain Art. 1.202 CC; Venezuela Art. 1.332 CC.

[46] Bolivia Art. 365 CC; Brazil Art. 372 CC; Chile Art. 1656 *in fine* CC; Colombia Art. 1715 *in fine* CC; Ecuador Art. 1699 *in fine* CC; Paraguay Art. 617 CC; Portugal Art. 849 CC; Venezuela Art. 1.334 CC.

[47] *See* Chile Arts. 1613, 1596, 1597 CC; Colombia Arts. 1722, 1654, 1655 CC; Ecuador Arts. 1706, 1639, 1640 CC; El Salvador Arts. 1533, 1466, 1467 CC.

[48] Brazil Arts. 379, 352, 355 CC; Guatemala Arts. 1477, 1404, 1406 CC; Mexico Arts. 2196, 2092, 2093 CC; Paraguay Arts. 622, 591 CC; Peru Arts. 1293, 1259 CC; Portugal Arts. 855, 784 CC; Spain Arts. 1.201, 1.172, 1.174 CC; Venezuela Arts. 1.339, 1.305 CC; ICC Final Award Case No. 11853 *Lex Contractus* Mexican Law: in application of Mexico Arts. 2093, 2196 CC the Tribunal set-off the seller's liability for damages against the buyer's debt for outstanding invoices beginning from the oldest invoices.

5. Effects

Under the Ibero-American laws, if the conditions to set-off established by the applicable law are satisfied, the obligations of both parties are extinguished.[49] Or as expressed by the UNIDROIT PICC with different words but with the same function: the set-off discharges the parties from their obligations.[50] Following the same legal logic, if the obligations that are intended to be set-off differ in their amount, the set-off will discharge or extinguish the obligations only up to the amount of the lesser obligation.[51]

Finally, while under the UNIDROIT PICC the set-off becomes effective at the time of notice to the other party.[52] In the Ibero-American laws, the extinction of the obligation goes back to the time when all of the conditions established by the law, or by the parties, are satisfied.[53] Except in Peru, where the extinction effect takes place until the interested party raises the set-off.[54]

As noted by one author, UNIDROIT PICC's approach is consistent with the necessity to know when exactly the set-off occurred.[55] Such determines, for example, up to when the monetary interest or fruits are owed.

---

49 *See* Argentina Art. 818 CC; Bolivia Art. 363 CC; Brazil Art. 368 CC; Chile Art. 1655 CC; Colombia Art. 1714 CC; Ecuador Art. 1698 CC; El Salvador Art. 1525 CC; Guatemala Art. 1471 CC; Mexico Arts. 2186, 2194 CC; Paraguay Art. 615 para. 2 CC; Peru Art. 1288 CC; Portugal Art. 854 CC; Spain Art. 1.202 CC.

50 Art. 8.5(1) PICC.

51 Art. 8.5(2) PICC; Argentina Art. 818 CC; Bolivia Art. 364 CC; Brazil Art. 368 CC; Guatemala Art. 1471 CC; Mexico Arts. 2186, 2194 CC; Paraguay Art. 615 para. 2 CC; Peru Art. 1288 CC; Portugal Art. 847 (2) CC; Mexico Collegiate Tribunals, *Novena Época,* Registry 185'809, SJF XVI, October 2002, at 1341.

52 Art. 8.5(3) PICC.

53 Argentina Art. 818 CC; Bolivia Art. 364 CC; Chile Art. 1656 CC; Colombia Art. 1715 CC; Ecuador Art. 1699 CC; El Salvador Art. 1526 CC; Guatemala Art. 1471 CC; Mexico Art. 2194 CC; Paraguay Art. 615 para. 2 CC; Portugal Art. 854 CC; Venezuela Art. 1.332 CC.

54 Peru Art. 1288 CC.

55 Bonell, *supra* note 5, Art. 8.5, para. 2, at 444.

Chapter 55

Concurrent Remedies

1. General Remarks on Concurrent Remedies

Under the Ibero-American laws, when the breach of a contract by defective performance occurs at the same time as a tort or a crime,[1] the aggrieved party can discretionarily opt to file a claim under contractual liability or under extra-contractual liability.[2] The option is available for either torts or crimes, since both of them are extra-contractual acts. However, as pointed out by a Mexican Tribunal, certain preconditions have to be met in order to establish tort liability in contractual parties' conduct. This task may not be easy as criminal intent occurring previously or during the contract has to be evidenced, otherwise, the available legal actions would be ordinary liability for breach of contract.[3] In addition, tortious or criminal conduct must be imputable to the party in breach of the contract.[4]

[1] Venezuela Supreme Tribunal, Judgment 1100, *Cass pen*, file C00-0156 of 1 August 2000: recognising that in the performance of contracts, as has been confirmed in many occasions, crimes of various categories can be committed.

[2] Argentina Arts. 1107, 1109 CC; Bolivia Art. 984 CC; Brazil Arts. 186, 187, 927 CC; Chile Arts. 2314, 1437 CC; Colombia Arts. 2341, 1494 CC; Ecuador Arts. 1480, 2241 CC; El Salvador Arts. 2065, 1308 CC; Guatemala Arts. 1645, 1646 CC; Mexico Arts. 1910, 1915 CC; Paraguay Art. 1833 CC; Peru Arts. 1969, 1970, 1985 CC; Portugal Arts. 483, 483 CC; Venezuela Art. 1.185 CC; *see also* Argentina: R.L. Lorenzetti, Tratado de los Contratos Parte General 591 (2004).

[3] Mexico Collegiate Tribunals, *Novena Época,* Registry 202'973, SJF III, March 1996, at 948.

[4] Argentina Art. 1111 CC; Chile Art. 1437 CC; Colombia Art. 1494 CC; Ecuador Art. 1480 CC; El Salvador Art. 1308 CC; Guatemala Art. 1645 CC; Mexico Art. 1910 CC; Paraguay Art. 1836 CC; Spain Art. 1.887 CC; Spain: M. Medina de Lemus, Derecho Civil: Obligaciones y Contratos II, Teoria General Vol. 1, 462 (2004).

In addition, while some courts recognise the possibility of filing a claim under contract liability and a subsidiary claim under tort liability or *vice versa*,[5] for others, the categories of contractual parties and third parties linked by tort liability are incompatible. As a contractual party is not a third party, there must be a choice between one or the other, the contractual liability excludes *ipso iure* the tort or criminal liability.[6]

Also under all laws, if the breach causes a harm to a third person, there is no option any more, since there may only be contractual liability of the debtor in favour of the creditor, and tort liability against the debtor in favour of the third party.[7] This may be the case, for example, of the sale of defective goods which have produced some harm to sub-buyers or consumers. Although, as further described, the line separating tort liability and contractual liability is, in some cases, almost imperceptive.[8]

2. Differences Between Contractual Liability and Tort Liability

In the Ibero-American civil law system, obligations and liability can arise from two sources, namely- contractual relations and illicit acts or events.[9] Though in modern times, the doctrine and the jurisprudence have reduced the differences towards unification.[10] We shall briefly review such differences emphasising the main functional distinctive elements.

On the one hand, tort or crime liability derives from a generic social duty consisting of refraining from causing injury to other people in which the negligence or the intention must be proven by the aggrieved party, while contractual liability originates from the breach of a pre-existing agreement in which the negligence of the breaching party is presumed.[11] Thus, as the contract is considered a private instrument, the agreed provisions normally

---

5 *See for example*, Chile Supreme Court, *Sala* 1, *Rol* 3076-03, 18 August 2004.

6 Venezuela Supreme Tribunal, Judgment 72, *Cass civ*, file 99-973 of 5 May 2002.

7 *See for example* Argentina Art. 1110 CC; Chile Art. 2315 CC; Colombia Art. 2342 CC; Ecuador Art. 2242 CC; El Salvador Art. 2066 CC; *see also* Argentina: A.A. Alterini, Contratos civiles, comerciales, de consumo 612 (1998).

8 *See infra* 3.

9 *See* expressly dictated in Chile Art. 1437 CC; Colombia Art. 1494 CC; Ecuador Art. 2250 CC; El Salvador Art. 1308 CC; Spain Arts. 1.089, 1.902 CC; *see also* Brazil: F. Noronha, Direito das Obriga¢ões, Vol. 1, 417-419 (2007); Spain: Medina de Lemus, *supra* note 4, at 461.

10 *See for example* Cuba Art. 294 CC: declaring that the rules on tort liability are applicable, when such is pertinent, to the breach of obligations; Argentina: Alterini, *supra* note 7, at 611.

11 Bolivia: R. Carrillo Aruquipa, Lecciones de Derecho Civil, Obligaciones 473, 474 (2008); *see also* ch. 47, 1. in fine.

establish the standard of breach, while liability from tort or crime is based on the collective values of welfare embodied in the law.[12]

On the other hand, contractual liability is restricted by the mechanism of delay in performing, which does not exist in tort or crime liability.[13] Under tort liability, the non-material injury or moral damage is compensable,[14] while under contractual liability only some countries concede to the aggrieved party such possibility, and in doing so regard has to be had to the facts that generate the liability of the breaching party and the circumstances of the case.[15]

Concerning the limitation of actions periods, in many countries contractual liability offers a longer term to exercise any legal claim derived from the breach of contract, such limitation period can go up to ten years depending on the jurisdiction.[16] The limitation periods to exercise tort actions are generally shorter and start running from the time the harm occurred or was noticed.[17]

As to the competent jurisdiction, contractual legal claims can be taken to the forum agreed upon by the parties,[18] or to the competent court according to *lex fori* conflicts of jurisdiction rules on contracts; which normally lead to the jurisdiction of a court at the place of performance, at the defendant's domicile or at the place of the contract's conclusion. Conversely, most conflict of laws rules for tort cases lead by default to the place where the injuring act or event occurred, and alternatively, to the place where the tortious act produces effects.[19]

Finally, there is also a difference as to the legal capacity of natural persons, which in the case of tort liability age is reached before that of contract.[20] Though, this difference is susceptible to have little impact in sales contracts.

---

[12] Indeed, tort liability has been divided in objective tort liability, or extra-contractual liability derived from dangerous activities with harming results legally relevant, and subjective extra-contractual liability, derived from intentional acts which require the following three elements, misconduct, intention, and causal link between the misconduct and the damages produced, *see* Costa Rica Supreme Court, Judgment 2006-01022, *Segunda Sala Civil,* 8 November 2006.

[13] *See* Bolivia: Carrillo Aruquipa, *supra* note 11, at 473; Ch. 52, 2.

[14] *See for example* Bolivia Art. 994 (II) CC; Ecuador Art. 2258 CC; Mexico Art. 1916 CC; Paraguay Art. 1835 CC; Peru Art. 1984 CC; Portugal Art. 496 CC; Venezuela Art. 1.196 CC.

[15] *See* Ch. 50, 1.2.3.

[16] *See for example* Argentina Art. 4023 CC (ten years); Chile Art. CC (three years); El Salvador Art. 2254 CC (up to twenty years); Peru Art. 2001 (1) CC (ten years). For more details *see* Sec. 60, B, III.

[17] *See for example* Argentina Art. 4037 CC (two years); Bolivia Art. 1508 CC (three years); Chile Art. CC (four years); Ecuador Art. 2259 CC (four years); El Salvador Art. 2083 CC (three years); Guatemala Art. 1673 CC (one year); Mexico Art. 1934 CC (two years); Paraguay Art. 663 (f) CC (two years); Peru Art. 2001 CC (4) (two years); Portugal Art. 498 CC (three years).

[18] *See* Ch. 26.

[19] Bolivia: Carrillo Aruquipa, *supra* note 11, at 473.

[20] *See* Argentina Arts. 921, 127 CC (ten years old for tort liability); Chile Art. 2319 CC (ten years old for tort liability); Colombia Art. 2346 CC (ten years old for tort liability); Ecuador Art. 2246 CC (seven years old for tort liability); El Salvador Art. 2070 CC (ten years old for tort liability); Guatemala Art. 1660 CC (fifteen years old for tort liability); Portugal Art. 488 (2)

3. Liability for Injuries Caused by Products

The line dividing contractual liability and tort liability is almost imperceptible or nonexistent for injuries caused by products under special laws.[21] Most Ibero-American consumer protection laws establish a sort of contractual-tort relationship between parties which are not necessarily directly related.

Thus, for example, a manufacturer shall not only guarantee the quality and safety of his consumable products to his direct buyer, but also to final consumers. Final consumers are generally entitled to claim from the manufacturer, the importer, the seller, or the retailer the warranties granted by consumers' laws.[22] Likewise, if a consumer suffers personal damage or injury because of the defects or the danger of the products, the manufacturer, the importer, distributor, retailer, or whoever has marked the product shall be conjunctly liable.[23]

As can be noticed, such rule deviates from the general causal link requirement of contractual and tortious liability, as these actors acquire shared responsibility for both the characteristics of the goods and the injuries caused.[24] And although all of these actors have available contractual remedies against their counterparts involved in the breach, or against any party who has caused them tort, the burden of proof has shifted and, only the party who proves to be unconnected to the breach or injury shall be released from the solidary responsibility.[25]

CC (seven years old tort liability). For details on the minimum ages to enter into contracts *see* Ch. 21.

21 Argentina: Alterini, *supra* note 7, at 611.

22 Argentina Art. 13 CPL; Brazil Art. 12 CPL; Chile Arts. 20, 21 CPL; Colombia Arts. 23, 29 CPL; Ecuador Arts. 20, 28, 71 CPL; Mexico Arts. 79, 82 CPL; Peru Art. 32 CPL; Spain Arts. 4, 10, 13 CPL; Venezuela Art. 52 CPL.

23 Argentina Art. 40 part 1 CPL; Brazil Arts. 18, 12, 13 CPL; Chile Arts. 20, 21 CPL; Colombia Arts. 23, 29 CPL; Costa Rica Art. 35 CPL; Ecuador Art. 2256 (5) CC & Art. 28 CPL; Guatemala Arts. 45, 46 CPL; Mexico Arts. 79, 82 CPL; Peru Art. 32 CPL.

24 Argentina Art. 40 part 2 CPL; Brazil Arts. 12, 13, 18 CPL; Ecuador Art. 28 CPL; Mexico Art. 79 CPL; Peru Art. 32 CPL; Venezuela Arts. 52, 12 CPL & Art. 1.195 CC.

25 Argentina Art. 40 part 2 CPL; Chile Arts. 20, 21 CPL; Colombia Arts. 23, 29 CPL; Ecuador Art. 28 CPL; Peru Art. 32 CPL; Venezuela Art. 1.195 CC.

Part 13

Unwinding of the Contract

Chapter 56

General Remarks on the Unwinding of the Contract

Under the Ibero-American law, the unwinding of a sales contract has different sources. Depending on the source, different set of rules may become applicable and different effects on the parties' performances may take place. Scholars consider that the main events causing the unwinding of the sales contract are the impossibility to perform, the rescission and the avoidance of the contract.[1] In all these cases, the purpose of the law is to place the parties back in the position they were before the contract conclusion. However, the mechanism of restitution is not absolute, as there are cases where it may be legally or physically impossible to restore the respective performances. In such cases, different rules attempt to strike a balance between the interests of each party and the allocation of risks.[2]

A sales contract may be unwound on the grounds of permanent impossibility to perform. As previously mentioned, the impossibility extinguishes the contracted obligations and releases the debtor from any liability for breach of contract.[3] On the basis of a contractual relationship, the unwinding of the contract operates automatically and retroactively. The restitution of the other party's already performed obligations is then due, and judicial intervention only takes place if one of the parties refuses to give back the received performance.[4]

1 Argentina: G.A. Borda, Manual de Contratos 140 (2004); Bolivia: R. Carrillo Aruquipa, Lecciones de Derecho Civil, Obligaciones 424-431 (2008).

2 *See* Ch. 57, 3 & Ch. 24.

3 *See* Ch. 51, 1.2.5.

4 *Id.*

The rescission also unwinds the contract. As reviewed, the declaration of rescission on the grounds of invalidity or voidability stops the effects originally wanted by the parties and, when lawfully and materially possible, situates the parties in the position they were before the contract.[5]

Finally, the declaration of avoidance also unwinds the contract.[6] As mentioned, the avoidance may only be granted when the standard of breach of contract established by the law is attained.[7] The effects of the avoidance are further reviewed in the next chapter.

---

[5] *See* Ch. 24.

[6] Bolivia Supreme Court, *Auto Supremo* No. 29, 1 March 2006, *cited in* Bolivia: G. Castellanos Trigo & S. Auad La Fuente, Derecho de las Obligaciones en el Código Civil Boliviano 50 (2008).

[7] *See* Ch. 53, 1.

Chapter 57

The Effects of Avoidance

1. General Consequences

1.1. Effects *ex tunc*

The avoidance of contracts under the Ibero-American laws acts retrospectively,[1] in that, the avoidance situates the parties in the position they were before the conclusion of the contract.[2] The parties must return to each other their respective performances,[3] except when this is legally or physically impossible.[4] This corresponds to the same effect as the rescission of the contract because of questions of validity[5] or of the voluntary termination before the contract is fulfilled.[6]

---

1 *See* expressly dictated in Bolivia Art. 574 (I) CC; Paraguay Art. 729 CC; Portugal Art. 434 (1) CC.

2 Brazil: O. Gomes, Contratos 210 (2008); Chile: R. Díez Duarte, La Compraventa en el Código Civil Chileno 176 (1993); Peru: M. Castillo Freyre, Comentarios al contrato de compraventa: análisis detallado de los artículos 1529 a 1601 del Código Civil 162 (2002); Spain: M. Medina de Lemus, Derecho Civil: Obligaciones y Contratos II, Teoria General Vol. 1, 173 (2004); Venezuela: J.L. Aguilar Gorrondona, Contratos y Garantias: Derecho Civil IV, 275 (2008).

3 Bolivia Supreme Court, *Sala Civil,* 6 December 2005, *Bartolomé Erland Rodríguez Álvarez v. Fabricio Ludwing Braner Ibáñez*: noting that the avoided contract has retroactive effect (*ex tunc*) in the case of the buyer who failed to pay the price, he has to return the goods; *see infra* 2.1.

4 *See infra* 3.

5 *See* Ch. 24. However, there is difference on the amount of damages susceptible to be recovered. While the rescission of the contract allows the aggrieved party to recover his *reliance interest*, the avoidance of the contract allows the aggrieved party to recover his *expectation interest*; *see* differences between these two types of *interests* in Ch. 50, 2.1.2.

6 *See* Mexico Collegiate Tribunals, *Novena Época,* Registry 182'002, SJF XIX, March 2004, at 1534. In line with the CISG consensual termination, *see* CISG-AC. Opinion No.

1.2. Effects *ex nunc*

However, the avoidance of the contract does not have any effect on the performances that have already been fulfilled as agreed to in the contract.[7] As already explained by courts and tribunals, if the transaction involves continuous or periodic execution, as it is the case in a supply of goods contract, the fulfilment of the condition that would terminate the contract have effect *ex nunc*.[8] This is, the contractual effects already produced being preserved.

For example, in an ICC case, the purchase of the remaining 80% (192 wagons) was subject to the granting of a line of credit by a Bank, the buyer was unable to get the loan on time and the supply of goods' contract was automatically terminated, nevertheless the already performed 20% remained valid.[9]

2. Restitution

2.1. Of Performance

Under both the CISG and the Ibero-American laws, parties are entitled to restitution of their respective performances when the avoidance of the contract takes place.[10] If both parties are bound to make restitution they are bound

---

9, Consequences of Avoidance of the Contract, Rapporteur: Professor Michael Bridge, London School of Economics, London, United Kingdom, Comment 3.5: "Where the parties consensually terminate the contract, the position is governed by their termination agreement in accordance with the Convention."

7 *See* expressly Argentina Art. 1204 (2) CC & Art. 216 Com C; Bolivia Art. 574 (I) CC: the avoidance does not affect the obligations already performed in a contract of successive or periodic execution; Paraguay Art. 729 CC; Portugal Art. 434 (2) CC: unless there is a link between the already performed obligation and the breach that justifies the restitution of all performances; Brazil: Gomes, *supra* note 2, at 210.

8 El Salvador Supreme Court, *Cass, León v. Urbina,* 1998; Spain Supreme Tribunal, 30 October 1997, *Id Cendoj:* 28079110001997100226: applying the Law No. 50/1965 on the sale of goods by instalments, applicable to consumer transactions but also to traders who acquire goods in order to integrate them into a production process; ICC Final Award Case No. 11779 *Lex Contractus* Spanish Law: the Arbitral Tribunal indicated that, under Spanish law, an indivisible contract (which is for a global object, not capable of partial performance) does not fall within the category of exceptions recognised under Spanish law that would give effect to the termination only for the future *i.e. ex nunc*, but rather the termination has effects *ex tunc.*

9 ICC Final Award Case No. 14083 *Lex Contractus* Brazilian Law.

10 *See* expressly Bolivia Arts. 574 (I), 547 CC; Chile Arts. 1487, 1489 CC; Colombia Arts. 1544, 1549 CC & Art. 942 Com C; Costa Rica Art. 457 Com C; Ecuador Arts. 1530, 1532 CC; El Salvador Arts. 1358, 1360 CC; Mexico Art. 2311 CC; Mexico Collegiate Tribunals, *Novena Época,* Registry 194'993, SJF VIII, December 1998, at 1028; Mexico Supreme Court, *Novena Época, Primera Sala,* Registry 177'470, SJF XXII, August 2005, p. 142; Peru Supreme

to do so concurrently.[11] However, when the underlying circumstances have changed, for example, regarding the goods, restitution may only be possible under certain conditions.[12]

Peru's Civil Code literally establishes that the effects of the avoidance, *i.e.* the restitution of the reciprocal performances, are effective from the moment when the cause of the avoidance took place.[13] This literally means that the effects of avoidance would only take place from the date when, for example, the buyer breached his obligation to pay the price, and that the goods which had been delivered before the breach could not be given back to the seller.

The Peruvian Supreme Court has realised the unfair results, and the unjustified enrichment situation, caused by a literal meaning of the provision.[14] In view of that, the Court, in an axiological interpretation of the provision and the rules on contacts, has sustained that the rule only applies to contracts of continued performance, such as installments contracts, where effectively the effects of the avoidance could be understood to take place at the time of breach. However, in instantaneous contracts as is generally the case with the sale of goods, the effects of the avoidance should be understood to take place retroactively, being from the moment the legal relation is created.[15]

In conclusion, under the Ibero-American laws the effects of the avoidance entitle the buyer to recover the price he has paid, while the seller shall be able to take back the goods delivered.[16]

Courts have already sustained that payment of the price of the goods shall not be reimbursed in the nominal amount agreed but according to the intrinsic value that the money had at the time of contract conclusion.[17] So that if the price was agreed in foreign currency, the reimbursement shall be made according to the intrinsic value, such currency had at the time of contract conclusion.[18]

Court, *Sala civil transitoria,* Resolution 000476-2006, 18 August 2006: confirming the effect of avoidance.

[11] Art. 81(1) CISG.

[12] Arts. 82-84 CISG.

[13] Peru Art. 1372 paras. 2, 3 CC.

[14] Peru Supreme Court, *Sala civil permanente*, Resolution 001977-2001, 26 June 2002.

[15] *Id.*

[16] Argentina Art. 1420 CC; Chile Art. 1875 para. 2 CC; Colombia Art. 1932 para. 2 CC; Costa Rica Art. 457 Com C; Ecuador Art. 1842 para. 2 CC; El Salvador Art. 1677 para. 2 CC; Mexico Art. 2311 CC; Peru Art. 1236 CC; Spain Art. 1295 sentence 1 CC; Venezuela Art. 1.499 CC; *see also* Venezuela: Aguilar Gorrondona, *supra* note 2, at 275.

[17] Peru Supreme Court, *Sala civil permanente,* Resolution 001949-2002, 30 October 2002: confirmed the valorism approach contained in article 1236 of Peru's Civil Code.

[18] Mexico Collegiate Tribunals, *Novena Época*, Registry 196'579, SJF VII, March 1998, at 775: the Tribunal upheld the validity of a clause requiring reimbursement of the price to be made in foreign currency.

The Mexican Civil Code establishes that the price of the goods shall be that at the time they were given back to the owner.[19] Additionally, the code dictates that in determining the damages for deteriorated goods, regard is to be had not only to the decrease in their value but also of the expenses incurred in repairing them.[20]

2.2. Of Fruits of Performance

2.2.1. Interest on the Price Paid

Under the Ibero-American laws, as under the CISG, the seller shall refund the price with the interest generated from the time of payment.[21]

2.2.2. Calculation Period

In this regard, the Peruvian Supreme Court has sustained that if the money paid in consideration of the goods has to be reimbursed to the buyer, interest on the price is to be calculated from the date of payment, to the date of effective reimbursement of the price (and not to the time of breach of contract nor to the date of avoidance declaration).[22]

2.2.3. Goods Fruits

In the Ibero-American laws, the parties are also entitled to take back the fruits or revenues produced by their respective performances.[23] Some Civil Codes expressly establish that the avoidance of the contract for lack of payment

---

[19] Mexico Art. 2114 CC.

[20] Mexico Art. 2115 CC.

[21] *See* expressly stated in Argentina Art. 1420 CC; Colombia Art. 942 Com C: or to retain the fruits generated by the goods; Mexico Art. 2311 CC; Peru Arts. 1556, 1512(2) CC; Spain Art. 1295 sentence 1 CC; *see also* Brazil: Gomes, *supra* note 2, at 210; El Salvador: A.O. Miranda, De la Compraventa 286 (1996); Venezuela: Aguilar Gorrondona, *supra* note 2, at 275; Mexico Supreme Court, *Novena Época, Primera Sala,* Registry 189'166, SJF XIV, August 2001, at 170; ICC Final Award Case No. 13530 *Lex Contractus* Brazilian Law. Under CISG Art. 84 if the contract is avoid, the seller not only has an obligation to reimburse the price he received, but also he must pay interest on the purchase price from the date of payment.

[22] Peru Supreme Court, *Sala civil transitoria,* Resolution 002128-2002, 10 December 2002; Peru Supreme Court, *Sala civil transitoria,* Resolution 000476-2006, 18 August 2006.

[23] Argentina Arts. 1052, 1054, 1420 CC; Bolivia Arts. 637, 83(III), 84 CC; Chile Art. 1875 para. 1 CC; Colombia Art. 1932 para. 1 CC; Ecuador Art. 1842 para. 1 CC; El Salvador Art. 1677 para. 1 CC; Mexico Art. 2311 CC; Paraguay Art. 751 CC; Peru Art. 1563 CC; Spain Art. 1295 CC; Venezuela Art. 1563 para. 1 CC; *see also* Argentina: G.A. Borda, Manual de Contratos 243 (2004); Brazil: Gomes, *supra* note 2, at 210; Chile: Díez Duarte, *supra* note 2, at 176; Peru: Castillo Freyre, *supra* note 2, at 163.

of the price entitles the seller to recover the fruits generated by the goods proportionally to amount of the price paid.[24]
As pointed out by a CISG commentator, "[I]rrespective of which party caused or declared the avoidance of the contract, neither party should retain any benefits."[25] Such benefits may include the natural fruits *i.e.* the products derived from the goods themselves; or the indirect fruits of the goods, *e.g.* the money earned out of hiring or licensing the reproduction of the goods.[26]

2.2.4. Depreciation and Deterioration (Risk) of the Goods

The Ibero-American laws establish that the seller is entitled to be compensated for the normal use (depreciation) and also for the deterioration (risk) of the goods caused by the buyer from the time he received the goods.[27] The Spanish Supreme Tribunal has explained the difference between depreciation and deterioration in the following way: the deterioration is not presumed since it could not necessarily exist: the seller shall prove its existence and amount. It regards the damage to the functional or physic integrity of the goods, while the depreciation is based on the market forecast of goods of the same type.[28]

Besides, the buyer may still be liable to pay for damages and prejudices caused by the breach of contract.[29]

2.2.5. Calculation of Goods Fruits and Deterioration

The Peruvian Supreme Court, upholding the appeal decision rendered by the Superior Tribunal of Lima, explained that compensation for the use of the

---

24 Chile Art. 1875 para. 1 CC; Colombia Art. 1932 para. 1 CC & Art. 950 Com C; Ecuador Art. 1842 para. 1 CC; El Salvador Art. 1677 para. 1 CC; Venezuela Art. 1563 para. 1 CC.

25 C. Fountoulakis, *in* I. (Ed.), Schlechtriem & Schwenzer Commentary on the UN Convention on the International Sale of Goods Art. 84, para. 23, at 1138, 1139 (2010).

26 Fountoulakis, *supra* note 26, Art. 84, para. 26, at 1139.

27 *See* expressly Colombia Art. 950 Com C; Costa Rica Art. 457 Com C; Chile: Díez Duarte, *supra* note 2, at 176; Venezuela: Aguilar Gorrondona, *supra* note 2, at 275; Mexico Supreme Court, *Novena Época, Primera Sala,* Registry 177'470, SJF XXII, August 2005, p 142; Mexico Supreme Court, *Novena Época, Primera Sala,* Registry 189'166, SJF XIV, August 2001, at 170; Peru Supreme Court, *Sala civil permanente,* Resolution 001427-2006, 17 May 2006.05.17: confirming that unless otherwise agreed, the seller is entitled to compensation for the use of the goods and for further damages and loss of profits incurred; Spain Supreme Tribunal, 30 October 1997, *Id Cendoj:* 28079110001997100226: the seller is entitled to 10% of the instalments already performed by the buyer as compensation for use of the goods. The Superior Tribunal applying the Law No. 50/1965 on the sale of goods by instalments, applicable to consumer transactions but also to traders who acquire goods in order to integrate them into a production process.

28 Spain Supreme Tribunal, 30 October 1997, *Id Cendoj:* 28079110001997100226.

29 *See for example* expressly declared in Argentina Art. 1420 CC; Colombia Art. 946 Com C; *see also* Brazil: Gomes, *supra* note 2, at 210; *see generally* Ch. 50.

goods did not need to be established with mathematical precision.[30] The seller of a fishery boat declared the contract avoided for lack of payment. Although no evidence of the works carry out by the boat, neither of the net profits derived from his economic exploitation, was available to the Judge of Appeals, the Supreme Court sustained that prudential calculation of the compensation was still legally correct due to circumstances surrounding the case: 1) the delay in payment by the buyer had been reclaimed since the claim was filled (since 13 years from the Supreme Court knowledge of the case); 2) the buyer had been using and exploiting the goods since the date of delivery; 3) the material condition of the goods and the value of USD 78.200 at the date of purchase, was far from being the optimal, all the more considering that three years after the delivery of the goods already showed some deteriorations.[31]

3. Effects of Impossibility to Restore

The mechanism of restitution may not always be absolute, as there may be cases in which it is impossible to restore the respective performances. The seller may only be able to recover the goods sold when they are in the buyer's possession, but such is not always possible when the goods have already be sold or transfer to third parties.

Some Ibero-American codes expressly state that the avoidance of the contract because of lack of payment does not entitle the seller to recover the goods or to claim any property right against third parties who in good faith had acquired the goods from the buyer in breach.[32] As a general rule, third parties acquiring or subscribing any property rights over goods subject to the sales contract should not be molested, if such third parties ignored the fact that the buyer in the first contract still owed the price of the goods.[33] The seller may, nevertheless, turn to his buyer in order to claim the restitution in money and the compensation for the damages and loss of profits caused.[34] But if the third party had knowledge of the buyer's debt, the seller may successfully vindicate his ownership before the competent court.[35] If the third party in bad faith is

---

30 Peru Supreme Court, *Sala civil transitoria,* Resolution 000476-2006, 18 August 2006.

31 *Id.*

32 *See* Bolivia Art. 966 CC; Chile Arts. 1876, 1490 CC; Colombia Arts. 1933, 1547 CC; Ecuador Arts. 1843, 1533 CC; El Salvador Arts. 1678, 1361 CC; Mexico Arts. 1951, 2300 CC; Paraguay Art. 729 CC; Portugal Art. 435 (1) CC; Spain Art. 1295 part 2 CC; Venezuela Art. 794 CC.

33 Mexico Art. 1886 CC; Chile: Díez Duarte, *supra* note 2, at 177; El Salvador: Miranda, *supra* note 21, at 286; Venezuela: Aguilar Gorrondona, *supra* note 2, at 275.

34 Expressly stated in Bolivia Arts. 968 (I), 969 (I) CC; Spain Art. 1295 *in fine* CC.

35 *See* Ch. 59.

unable to return the goods, the seller may be able to recover from him the compensation due for the damages and loss of profits incurred.[36]

Finally, if the specific goods subject to the contract are lost on the buyer's side, the buyer may restore the monetary value that the goods had at the time of the breach.[37]

36 *See* Bolivia Art. 968 (II) CC; Spain Art. 1298 CC; *see also* Venezuela: Aguilar Gorrondona, *supra* note 2, at 275.

37 *See* Bolivia Art. 969 (III); Peru: Castillo Freyre, *supra* note 2, at 162.

CHAPTER 58

UNJUSTIFIED ENRICHMENT

1. Unjustified Enrichment and the Unwinding of the Contract

1.1. Rescission, Avoidance and Voluntary Termination

In the Ibero-American legal systems, the rules on unjustified enrichment are not needed in the unwinding of the sales contract. The rules on rescission and avoidance are designed to situate the parties in the position they were as if the contract has never been concluded,[1] so that it is understood that any already performed obligation falls automatically back to the party concerned. Additionally, the effects of the avoidance cause the property of the goods and the price to fall back to the seller and the buyer respectively and entitle them to claim back the fruits or revenues produced by their respective performances,[2] since a different solution would create an unjustified enrichment of the parties.[3]

1.2. Interruption of the Formation of the sales contract

Only in cases where the formation of the contract has been interrupted and one of the parties has already performed his obligations, the legal action of

---

1 *See generally* Ch. 24 & Ch. 57; *see also* Brazil: O. Gomes, Contratos 210 (2008); Chile: R. Díez Duarte, La Compraventa en el Código Civil Chileno 176 (1993); Peru: M. Castillo Freyre, Comentarios al contrato de compraventa: análisis detallado de los artículos 1529 a 1601 del Código Civil 162 (2002); Spain: M. Medina de Lemus, Derecho Civil: Obligaciones y Contratos II, Teoria General Vol. 1, 173 (2004); Venezuela: J.L. Aguilar Gorrondona, Contratos y Garantias: Derecho Civil IV, 275 (2008).

2 *See* Ch. 57, 2.2.

3 *See* Brazil: Gomes, *supra* note 1, at 210; Chile: Díez Duarte, *supra* note 1, at 176.

unjustified enrichment may be relevant. For example, when a suspensive condition is required for the contract to produce effects and such is not fulfilled, one of the parties must reimburse any payment of the price already performed, together with the interest generated, as no legitimate legal cause exists to justify the enrichment of that party. In case of refusal, the creditor may consider claiming back the money paid through an unjustified enrichment action.[4] Relevant examples may contemplate the sale of future crops or vintages that never came into existence. Also common in practice, is the purchase of a complete future production of goods from a manufacturer.

In the following paragraphs we briefly consider the notion, requirements and characteristics of the unjustified enrichment actions in the Ibero-American civil codes.

2. Notion and Requirements

2.1. Notion

The unjustified enrichment action is based on the idea that any displacement or movement of wealth must have a determined cause or reason.[5] Thus, if there is not justified reason or cause for such a movement of wealth, the same must be restored through the relevant legal action, usually called unjustified enrichment or undue payment action.[6]

The doctrine of unjustified enrichment or undue payment is based in the notion of equity. It is irrelevant whether the unjustified enrichment occurred intentionally, with fault, or in bad faith.[7] Its purpose is merely to redress the property unbalance between two persons not always linked.

2.2. Requirements

Accordingly, the doctrine and the jurisprudence have integrated four main requirements: first, the enrichment of the defendant must be unjustified, such can be represented by the augment of his patrimony or the non-decrease of the same; second, the impoverishment of the claimant, which can be represented

[4] El Salvador: A.O. Miranda, De la Compraventa 132 (1996); Paraguay Supreme Court, Judgment 996, 11 December 2001, *Fernando Ayala v. Nicolas G. Luthold Feldmann.*

[5] Spain: Medina de Lemus, *supra* note 1, at 449.

[6] Bolivia Art. 951 CC; Mexico Art. 1882 CC; Paraguay Art. 1817 CC; Peru Art. 1954 CC; Portugal Art. 473 CC; Spain Art. 1895 CC; Spain: Medina de Lemus, *supra* note 1, at 449.

[7] Spain Supreme Tribunal, 5 October 1985, *Id Cendoj:* 28079110011985100180; Spain Supreme Tribunal, 25 November 1985, *Id Cendoj:* 28079110011985100202; Paraguay Supreme Court, Judgment 996, 11 December 2001, *Fernando Ayala v. Nicolas G. Luthold Feldmann*: in Paraguay the cause of enrichment shall be licit.

by a positive damage or a prevented profit; third, a causal link between the unjustified enrichment and the impoverishment; fourth, the non-existence of a specific legal provision that excludes the application of this remedy to the specific case.[8]

2.3. Requirement Preventing the Action in the Unwinding of the Contract

The last requirement prevents a claim of unjustified enrichment to be exercised collaterally to the rescission or the avoidance of the contract. As has been pointed out by some Courts, the unjustified enrichment action is subsidiary, in the sense that when the law grants a specific legal action for a case specifically regulated, there is no place for unjustified enrichment.[9] The available actions are the ones that must be filed; neither their lack of efficacy before a court, nor the failure to exercise them, legitimates a party to collaterally claim an unjustified enrichment.[10]

3. Change of Position

The party who is unjustifiably enriched may raise the objection that his position has changed, in other words, that the first requirement is not met since he is no longer enriched. This situation is likely to occur in the context of interrupted sales where the goods have been consumed, destroyed, lost or simply transfer to third parties. The position expressly taken by some Ibero-American statutes is that the party who transfers or loses the performance in bad faith or being aware of the obligation to restore it shall be bound to wholly restore the performance either with a substitute one or in money value.[11] The party in good faith shall only give back what remains from the performance unjustifiably received including any compensation or payment received for it.[12]

[8] *See* the last requirement in Bolivia Art. 952 CC; Paraguay Art. 1818 CC; Portugal Art. 474 CC; Peru Art. 1955 CC; all requirements in Mexico Collegiate Tribunals, *Novena Época,* Registry 194'119, SJF IX, April 1999, at 579; Paraguay Supreme Court, Judgment 996, 11 December 2001, *Fernando Ayala v. Nicolas G. Luthold Feldmann*; Portugal: J. De M. Antunes Valera, Das Obrigações em Geral 480-492 (2003); Spain: Medina de Lemus, *supra* note 1, at 449; plus the requirement that the cause must be licit.

[9] El Salvador Supreme Court, *Cass civ*, *Martínez de Magaña v. Gálvez Rojas,* 601-2000, 11 October 2000.

[10] Spain Supreme Tribunal, 19 February 1999, *Id Cendoj:* 28079110001999100087.

[11] Bolivia Art. 969(II) CC; Mexico Arts. 1883, 1884 CC; Paraguay Arts. 1822 (2), 1824 CC; Peru Art. 1276 CC; Portugal Art. 480 CC; Spain Arts. 457, 1896 CC.

[12] Bolivia Art. 969(I)(III) CC; Mexico Arts. 1883, 1887 CC; Paraguay Arts. 1822 (1), 1823

A change in position may also take place when the enriched party has incurred some expenses on the performance unjustifiably received while believing the contract was effective or valid. This is likely to happen, for example, when the buyer makes some improvements to the goods or when the seller has incurred in financing services related to the price received. The position expressly taken by some Ibero-American laws is that the enriched party in good faith shall still give back the performance unjustifiably obtained preserving the right of reimbursement of all necessary expenses and useful improvements made over the performance.[13] The party in bad faith may only be reimbursed the expenses needed for the conservation of the goods.[14]

CC; Peru Art. 1276 CC; Portugal Art. 479 (2) CC; Spain Arts. 457, 1897 CC; Portugal: Antunes Valera, *supra* note 8, at 515.

13 Bolivia Arts. 972, 95, 97 CC; Mexico Art. 1889 CC; Peru Art. 917 CC; Spain Arts. 453, 454 CC.

14 Bolivia Art. 97 CC; Spain Art. 455 CC; Venezuela Art. 792 CC.

CHAPTER 59

REVENDICATION ACTION AND RULES OF PROPERTY

1. Revendication Action and the Unwinding of Contracts

Generally under the Ibero-American laws, the *revendication action* is not the appropriate legal action to recover the goods delivered in a later rescinded contract (on the grounds of invalidity (void) or voidability) or a later avoided contract. Under those countries that follow the approach under which the property of the goods passes by the mere conclusion of the contract,[1] as soon as the essential elements for the existence of the sale are evidenced, the relationship established between the parties is a *personal* one.[2] The legal available action is a *personal action* for invalidity, voidability or for breach of the terms agreed between individuals, contrary to the *real action* which derives from the relationship between a person and an object.[3] The same relationship is established if the *tradittio* of the goods effectively occurs under those countries where *tradittio* required for the transfer of property.[4] Unless the *tradittio* as understood in these laws do not take place and the buyer is in possession of the goods, the *revendication action* would be the available remedy for the seller who is legally considered to be the owner.

Once the competent court or tribunal acknowledge the avoidance of the contract based on the breach of (personal) agreed obligations, the rules on avoidance are designed to situate the parties in the position they were before the contract.[5] This involves that the property and the possession of the goods fall automatically back to the seller.

1 *See* Ch. 45, 3.1.
2 Mexico Collegiate Tribunals, *Novena Época,* Registry 195'963, SJF VIII, July 1998, p. 347.
3 In the civil law systems different types of remedies are granted depending on the relationship which exists between individuals and objects; Mexico Collegiate Tribunals, *Novena Época,* Registry 195'963, SJF VIII, July 1998, p. 347.
4 *See* Ch. 45, 3.2.
5 *See* Ch. 57, 1 & 2.

Only in cases where the formation of the contract has been interrupted and the buyer was already in possession of the goods the *revendication action* may be relevant. For example, when a suspensive condition is required for the contract to produce effects and such is not fulfilled, the seller may bind the buyer to deliver back the goods through a *revendication action*. This may occur in the sales of goods subject to title retention under which the buyer is already in possession when the breach to pay the complete price occurs. Also in sales under which it is a usage to try or degust, in the sale of goods subject to the buyer's satisfaction or subject to trial or test. Under these modalities of sale, the existence of the contract is definitively suspended while the buyer is already in possession of the goods.[6]

2. Rules on Property and the Unwinding of the Contract

The Rules of Property Law may become relevant to complement the effects of the unwinding of the contract. Certainly, as previously established,[7] the seller is entitled to be compensated for the deterioration of the goods caused by the buyer from the time he received the goods.[8] This is because under certain Property Rules, the buyer is considered to be a possessor of the goods in bad faith, as he is believed to be negligent in not paying the price.[9] Also, according to Property Rules the buyer in bad faith may only be reimbursed the expenses of conservation of the goods.[10] The buyer may only be able to change his status to a good faith possessor if he proves that he has, unintentionally, suffered a loss in his fortune, so great that it was impossible for him to perform the contract.[11]

Similarly, as the effects of the avoidance can be limited when third party's have the possession of the goods, the seller may only be able to recover the goods when a third party had knowledge of the buyer's debt *vis à vis* the seller.[12] The recovery of the goods in possession of such parties is made by means of a revendication action before the competent court.[13]

---

6 *See* Ch. 14, 1-4.

7 *See* Ch. 57, 2.2.

8 Chile: R. Díez Duarte, La Compraventa en el Código Civil Chileno 176 (1993); Venezuela: J.L. Aguilar Gorrondona, Contratos y Garantias: Derecho Civil IV, 275 (2008).

9 Chile Art. 1875 para. 3 CC; Colombia Art. 1932 para. 3 CC; Ecuador Art. 1842 para. 3 CC; El Salvador Art. 1677 para. 3 CC.

10 *See for example* Bolivia Art. 97 CC; Spain Art. 455 CC; Venezuela Art. 792 CC; Venezuela: Aguilar Gorrondona, *supra* note 8, at 275.

11 *See* Chile Art. 1875 para. 3 CC; Colombia Art. 1932 para. 3 CC; Ecuador Art. 1842 para. 3 CC; El Salvador Art. 1677 para. 3 CC.

12 *See* Chile Arts. 1876, 1490 CC; Colombia Arts. 1933, 1547 CC; Ecuador Arts. 1843, 1533 CC; El Salvador Arts. 1678, 1361 CC; Mexico Arts. 1951, 2300 CC; Paraguay Art. 729 CC; Portugal Art. 435(1) CC; Spain Art. 1295 part 2 CC; Venezuela Art. 794 CC.

13 *See* Mexico Art. 1885 CC.

Part 14

Limitations of Actions

Chapter 60

Limitation Periods

1. Procedural or Substantive Approach

The Ibero-American substantive laws, namely the Civil Codes, refer to diverse limitation periods depending on the specific legal action. Different periods are established for actions based on the voidability of the sales contract due to defects in the formation process, such as error, fraud and duress. Also, limitation periods are provided for remedies derived from the non-conformity of the goods. Finally, specific limitation periods are found for claims based on ordinary breach of contract seeking specific performance, or alternatively, the avoidance of the contract. As a substantive law matter, the expiration of such periods deprives the parties of the specific remedies granted by the substantive law.[1]

2. Select Domestic Rules

2.1. Limitation Periods for the Rescission of the Contract Due to Defects of Intent

Voidability for defects of intent must be invoked within a certain period of time. The limitation periods contained in the Ibero-American systems are diverse. With regards to mistake, some laws establish that the period begins running from the time the mistake was discovered, or discoverable. The limitation period after the discovery of the mistake or after the moment in which the mistaken party should have known of the mistake varies from country to

---

1 Argentina: G.A. Borda, Manual de Contratos 225 (2004); Bolivia: W. Kaune Arteaga, Curso de Derecho Civil, Contratos, Vol. 2, 152 (1996); Venezuela: J.L. Aguilar Gorrondona, Contratos y Garantias: Derecho Civil IV, 261 (2008).

country.[2] In Mexico, for example, a sixty-day period is established,[3] while in Portugal a one-year period is allowed.[4] Under most other laws a fixed limitation period starts running from the conclusion of the contract, irrespective of the fact the mistaken party knew or should have known the mistake.[5]

Regarding fraud, the Ibero-American Civil Codes also have established two different approaches. Some laws fix the starting point in conjunction with a future event such as the time of discovery of the deception,[6] while others refer to a past event such as the conclusion of the contract,[7] regardless of any future contingency. The length of the limitation period also varies from country to country. Some Ibero-American Civil Codes establish an absolute time limit ranging from two years to four years from the conclusion of the contract[8] or from the time the fraud was discovered.[9]

In relation to duress, all codes establish a relative limitation time period which starts to run from the moment the duress ceases.[10] The term can go from six months as in the case of Mexico to four years as established by the Spanish Civil Code.[11]

---

[2] Argentina Art. 4.030 CC (two years); Bolivia Art. 556 (1) (2) CC (five years); Venezuela Art. 1.346 CC (five years).

[3] Mexico Art. 2236 CC; ICC Final Award Case No. 13184 *Lex Contractus* CISG and Mexican Law as supplementary law: the Tribunal agreed with the respondent on that "in any event an action for voidability for mistake is prescribed pursuant to Article 2236 of the Federal Civil Code because the prescription period for this action is sixty days from the date the mistake was known."

[4] Portugal Art. 287 CC.

[5] Brazil Art. 178 CC (four years); Chile Art. 1691 para. 1 CC (four years); Colombia Art. 1750 para. 1 CC (four years); Ecuador Art. 1735 para. 1 CC (four years); El Salvador Art. 1562 para. 1 CC (four years); Guatemala Art. 1312 CC (two years); Peru Art. 2001 (4) CC (two years); Spain Art. 1301 CC (four years).

[6] Argentina Art. 4.030 CC; Venezuela Art. 1.346 CC.

[7] Brazil Art. 178(II) CC; Chile Art. 1691 para. 1 CC; Colombia Art. 1750 para. 1 CC; Ecuador Art. 1735 para. 1 CC; El Salvador Art. 1562 para. 1 CC; Guatemala Art. 1312 CC; Spain Art. 1301 CC.

[8] Brazil Art. 178 para. 2 CC (four years); Chile Art. 1691 para. 1 CC (four years); Colombia Art. 1750 para. 1 CC (four years); Ecuador Art. 1735 para. 1 CC (four years); El Salvador Art. 1562 para. 1 CC (four years); Guatemala Art. 1312 CC (two years); Peru Art. 2001(4) CC (two years); Spain Art. 1301 CC (four years).

[9] Argentina Art. 4.030 CC (two years); Bolivia Art. 556 (1) (2) CC (five years); Venezuela Art. 1.346 CC (five years).

[10] Argentina Art. 4030 CC (two years); Bolivia Art. 556 (1) (2) CC (five years); Brazil Art. 178 para. (I) CC (four years); Chile Art. 1691 para. 1 CC (four years); Colombia Art. 1750 para. 1 CC (four years); Ecuador Art. 1735 para. 1 CC (four years); El Salvador Art. 1562 para. 1 CC (four years); Guatemala Art. 1313 CC (one year); Venezuela Art. 1.346 CC (five years).

[11] Mexico Art. 2237 CC (six months); Spain Art. 1301 para. 1 CC (four years).

2.2. Limitation Periods Derived from Defects on the Goods

In absence of an express agreement as to the extent of the warranty,[12] the default rule establishing the limitation period for redhibitory and estimatory actions varies depending on the country or the nature of the transaction.

For B2B sales some Codes of Commerce follow the general six months[13] or one year[14] expiration period for *hidden* defects. On the other hand, the laws of Bolivia, Mexico and Spain grant a limitation period of 6 six months to file a legal claim based on defective goods.[15] The laws of Chile, Colombia, Ecuador and El Salvador distinguish between the caducity for redhibitory action, oriented towards the termination of the contract, and that of the estimatory action, namely- the remedy of readjustment of the price.[16] The time limit for the remedy of termination is six months, while the time limit to rely on the remedy of readjustment of the price is of one year.[17] Thus, if the six months time limit to activate the remedy of termination expiries, the buyer can still claim the readjustment of the price within the following six months.[18]

---

[12] The default rule is not mandatory since a different agreement of the parties overrides it; *see* El Salvador: A.O. Miranda, De la Compraventa 63 (1996).

[13] Argentina Art. 473 Com C: establishes (for hidden defects) that the court shall decided the caducity period but this shall never exceed six months from the date of delivery; Chile Art. 154 para. 2 Com C; Colombia Art. 938 Com C; Ecuador Art. 191 Com C extends the limitation period to one year for international sales; El Salvador 192 Com C: extends the limitation period up to one year for international sales; Argentina Supreme Court, *Inversiones y Servicios S.A. v. Estado Nacional Argentino*, 19 August 1999.

[14] Bolivia Art. 849 Com C.

[15] Bolivia Art. 635 CC; Mexico Art. 2149 CC; Spain Art. 1.490 CC; Bolivia Supreme Court, *Sala Civil*, 6 December 2005, *Bartolomé Erland Rodríguez Álvarez v. Fabricio Ludwing Braner Ibáñez:* confirmed the six-month limitation period for the *redhibitory* and *estimatory* actions based on defects of the goods and dismissed the allegations raised by respondent and the Court of Appeal Judgment which wrongly considered that the action raised by the claimant (buyer) for ordinary breached (lack of payment of the goods) shall prescribed after the six months; Spain Supreme Tribunal, 7 December 2006, *Id Cendoj:* 28079110012006101236: explaining that there are different limitation periods depending on whether the claim is for hidden defects (six months) or ordinary breach of contract (fifteen years); Spain Supreme Tribunal, 6 June 2006, *Id Cendoj:* 28079110012006100524: confirming the six-month limitation period for the estimatory or redhibitory actions.

[16] *See* Chile: R. Díez Duarte, La Compraventa en el Código Civil Chileno 170 (1993); Colombia: A. Tamayo Lombana, El Contrato de Compraventa su Régimen Civil y Comercial 189-191 (2004); Ecuador: L. Navarro Moreno, Compraventa internacional y conflictos de leyes: aspectos jurídicos de la contratación internacional 138 (2002); El Salvador: Miranda, *supra* note 12, at 64.

[17] Chile Arts. 1866-1869 CC & Art. 154 Com C; Colombia Arts. 1923-1926 CC; Ecuador Arts. 1833-1836 CC & Art. 191 Com C; El Salvador Arts. 1668-1671 CC; ICC Final Award Case No. 10299 *Lex Contractus* Chilean Law: dismissing the buyer's claim as the price readjustment claim was time-barred in accordance with Chile's Statute of Limitations as applied to *quanti minoris i.e.*, one year for personal property.

[18] *See* Chile: Díez Duarte, *supra* note 16, at 170; Colombia: Tamayo Lombana, *supra* note 16,

In Argentina, Peru and Venezuela's Civil Codes, the limitation period of a redhibitory or estimatory actions is of three months for the sale of goods.[19] Under the Portuguese law it can go up to 2 years.[20]

Depending on the countries' laws, the limitation periods start running from: the date of delivery of the goods,[21] the date of effective real delivery of the goods,[22] the date when the defects became apparent[23] or the date of the conclusion of the contract.[24]

2.3. Limitation Periods for Claims based on Ordinary Breach of Contract

Regarding the limitation periods for claims based on ordinary breach of contract seeking the specific performance or the avoidance of the contract, the elapsing times are not uniform. While some countries offer long terms that can go up to ten or twenty years to raise any legal claim derived from the breach of contract, others only give a few years.[25]

at 189, 191; Ecuador: Navarro Moreno, *supra* note 16, at 138; El Salvador: Miranda, *supra* note 12, at 64.

[19] Argentina Art. 4041 CC; Peru Art. 1514 CC; Venezuela Art. 1.525 CC.

[20] Portugal Art. 929 CC.

[21] Argentina Art. 473 Com C; Bolivia Art. 635 CC & Art. 849 Com C; Peru Art. 1514 CC; Spain Art. 1.490 CC; Venezuela Art. 1.525 CC.

[22] Chile Art. 1866 CC & Art. 154 Com C; Colombia Art. 1923 CC; Ecuador Art. 1833 CC & Art. 192 Com C; El Salvador Art. 1668 CC.

[23] This is the case in Argentina civil sales, except when the defects were apparent the caducity term shall start counting from the date of delivery *see* on this Argentina: Borda, *supra* note 1, at 225.

[24] Portugal Art. 929 (2) CC.

[25] *See for example* Argentina Art. 4023 CC (ten years); Bolivia Arts. 1507, 1493 CC (five years from the time the right could have been exercised or from the time the holder of the right gave up the exercise of the right); Chile Art. CC (three years); Colombia Art. 2536 CC (ten years); El Salvador Art. 2254 CC (up to twenty years) but Art. 995 Com C (two years); Mexico Arts. 1047 (ten years), 1040 Com C: the time limit (whatever its duration) within which a party must bring a claim for breach of a commercial contract starts counting from the date on which the action could be legally exercised; Peru Art. 2001(1) CC (ten years); Portugal Art. 309 CC (twenty years); Spain Art. 1. 964 CC (fifteen years); ICC Partial Award Case No. 13741 *Lex Contractus* CISG and Italian Law, but also referring to the Colombian Law: confirming that the ordinary time limit of ten years would have to be applied to claim the ordinary breach of contract pursuant to Article 2536 of the Colombian Civil Code; ICC Final Award Case No. 12296 *Lex Contractus* Mexican Law: noting that "according to article 1047 of the CCo, the legal statute of limitations for filing a claim for breach of a commercial contract is 10 years; and it might be argued that under Mexican law this term is peremptory and cannot be modified by contract"; ICC Final Award Case No. 12853 *Lex Contractus* Portuguese Law: stating that "[t]he general terms of Portuguese civil law determine that the time limit for the claim for damages is 20 years (Código Civil, art. 309)"; Bolivia Supreme Court, *Sala Civil*, 6 December 2005, *Bartolomé Erland Rodríguez Álvarez v. Fabricio Ludwing Braner Ibáñez:*

3. The UN Limitation Convention

Argentina, Cuba, Mexico, Paraguay and Uruguay are among the 20 member States of the UN Convention on the Limitation Period in the International Sale of Goods of 1974.[26] The rules of this Convention shall apply if, at the time of the conclusion of the contract, the place of business of the parties to a contract of international sale of goods are in Contracting States; or if the rules of private international law make the law of a Contracting State applicable to the contract of sale.[27]

In principle, all claims resulting from an international sales contract, or referring to a breach, cancellation or invalidity of such a contract are subject to a four-year limitation period.[28] According to Article 9 of the Limitation Convention, the limitation period starts counting from the date on which a claim accrues. In order to dispel any uncertainty as to the due date of certain categories of claims, Article 10 contains special provisions for claims arising from breaches of contract, from a defect or lack of conformity, and for claims based on fraud.[29]

Under the first paragraph of Article 10 the limitation period of a claim arising form a breach of contract commences on the date of such a breach. A breach of contract is defined as the "failure of a party to perform the contract or any performance not in conformity with the contract."[30]

On the other hand, the four-year limitation period of a claim arising from a defect or other lack of conformity commences on the date on which the goods

---

confirmed the five-year limitation period for ordinary breach of contract and dismissed the allegations raised by respondent and overturned the Court of Appeal Judgment which wrongly considered that the action raised by the claimant (buyer) for ordinary breached (lack of payment of the goods) shall prescribed after the six-month limitation period for action for redhibitory and estimatory actions based on defects of the goods; El Salvador Supreme Court, *Cass civ, Caja De Credito Rural De Olocuilta v. Tochez Arévalo Y Tochez,* 1574-Cas.S.S., 28 July 2003: distinguishing between the limitation period for actions under El Salvador Art. 2254 CC (up to twenty years) and Art. 995 Com C (two years); Spain Supreme Tribunal, 7 December 2006, *Id Cendoj:* 28079110012006101236: the Tribunal confirmed the fifteen-year limitation period established by Art. 1964 CC for breach of obligation *aliud pro alio* as the seller delivered goods containing defects that make them improper for the use they were intended, dismissing the allegations of the buyer who understood the case as a hidden defects one with a six-month limitation period.

26 Argentina entry into force 1 August 1988; Cuba entry into force 10 June 1995; Mexico entry into force 1 August 1988; Paraguay entry into force 1 March 2004; Uruguay entry into force 1 February 1997; *see* in http://www.uncitral.org/uncitral/en/uncitral_texts/sale_goods/1974Convention_status.html (accessed on 20 March 2009).

27 Limitation Convention Art. 3 (1) (a) (b).

28 Limitation Convention Art. 8; *see also* M. Müller-Chen, *in* I. Schwenzer (Ed.), Schlechtriem & Schwenzer Commentary on the UN Convention on the International Sale of Goods Art. 8 Limitation Convention 1974, para. 2, at 1227 (2010).

29 *See* Müller-Chen, *supra* note 28, Art. 10 Limitation Convention 1974, para. 2, at 1230.

30 *See* Art. 1(3)(d) Limitation Convention.

are actually handed over to, or their tender is refused by, the buyer.[31] Lack of conformity includes discrepancies in the quantity or quality of the goods and their defective packaging. Defects in property title fall within the scope of such limitation period.[32] Goods are actually handed over when they are physically transferred to the buyer, but the limitation period will only commence when the buyer is able to actually inspect the goods.[33]

The four year standardised limitation period of a claim based on fraud begins running on the date on which the fraud was or, reasonably could have been discovered.[34] As noted by one scholar, "whether, under the particular circumstances, the deceived party could reasonably be expected to perceive a deceit should not be judge too strictly."[35]

31 Art. 10(2) Limitation Convention.
32 Müller-Chen, *supra* note 28, Art. 10 Limitation Convention 1974, para. 4, at 1231.
33 Müller-Chen, *supra* note 28, Art. 10 Limitation Convention 1974, para. 5, at 1231.
34 Art. 10 (3) Limitation Convention.
35 Müller-Chen, *supra* note 28, Art. 10 Limitation Convention 1974, para. 8, at 1232.

Chapter 61

Limitations Due to a Party's Behaviour

The Ibero-American courts have interrupted or extended the limitation periods for claims related to contracts relaying on the doctrine of *venire contra factum proprium*.[1] Certainly, under the Ibero-American laws the limitation period prescribed shall cease to run when the debtor acknowledges his obligation to the creditor.[2] Accordingly, courts have upheld that the acknowledgement of the obligation and the renouncing of the right of having the limitation period expired, may be expressed or implied from conduct, such as the notice of avoidance made after the expiration of the limitation period or the spontaneous performance of the obligation, which are clear enough to cause the reliance of the other party.[3] The Supreme Tribunal also explained that the limitation periods are not based on strict principles of justice, but the law gives to the judge the power to carefully consider any element affecting their duration.[4]

---

[1] For the notion of *venire contra factum Proprium see* Ch. 33, 1.

[2] *See for example* Chile Art. 2518 CC; Colombia Art. 2539 CC; El Salvador Art. 2257 CC; Mexico Art. 1041 Com C; Peru Art. 1996 (1) CC; Spain Art. 1973 CC.

[3] Mexico Collegiate Tribunals, *Novena Época,* Registry 202'182, SJF III, June 1996, p. 908; Spain Supreme Tribunal, 2 July 2008, *Id Cendoj*: 28079110012008100595.

[4] Spain Supreme Tribunal, 2 July 2008, *Id Cendoj*: 28079110012008100595.

Court Judgments

Argentina

Court	*Sala*	*Parties*	*Date*
Supreme Court		*Serradilla, Raúl Alberto v. Mendoza, Provincia de y otro*	12 June 2007
Supreme Court		*Santa Fe, Provincia de v. Empresa Nacional de Correos y Telégrafos S.A.*	11 July 2002
Supreme Court		*Expreso Hada S.R.L. v. San Luis, Provincia de y otros*	28 May 2002
Supreme Court		*Inversiones y Servicios S.A. v. Estado Nacional Argentino*	19 August 1999
Supreme Court		*Calderas Salcor Caren S.A. v. Estado Nacional - Comisión Nacional de Energía Atómica y otra*	24 September 1996
Supreme Court		*Autolatina Argentina S.A. v. Resolución N° 54/90 Subsecretaría de Transportes Marítimos y Fluviales*	19 December 1991
Supreme Court		*Isocrom SA. v. Banco Sudameris y Banco Central de la Rep Arg*	28 December 1989
Supreme Court		*Roco, Juan C. y otra v. Provincia de Santa Fe*	9 November 1989 (*Fallos* 312:2152)
Supreme Court		*Cía. Azucarera Tucumana SA. v. Estado Nacional*	21 September 1989
Supreme Court		*Hotel Internacional Iguazú S.A. v. Estado Nacional*	10 December 1987
Supreme Court		*Florencio, Madero y Cía. v. Lezama, Gregorio*	1873 (T. 14, at 102)
National Chamber of Appeals in Civil Matters		*Tibiletti de Castillo Valeria Susana y Otro v. Lunasky Isabel Rosa*	20 December 2006 (MJ-JU-42526-AR)

National Chamber of Appeals in Federal Administrative Matters	*Sala* IV	*Wal Mart Argentina S.A. v. Dirección Nac. de Comercio Interior*	13 April 2004
National Chamber of Appeals in Commercial Matters		*Juridica Pueyrredon S.R.L. v. Jara Marino*	2 December 2008
National Commercial Court of Appeals		*Bravo Barros, Carlos Manuel Del Corazón De Jesus v. Martinez Gares, Salvador S.A.*	31 May 2007
National Commercial Court of Appeals		*Cervecería y Maltería Paysandú S.A. v. Cervecería Argentina S.A.*	21 July 2002
National Commercial Court of Appeals		*Mayer Alejandro v. Onda Hofferle GmbH & Co.*	24 April 2000
National Commercial Court of Appeals	*Sala* E	*Farley, Omar D. v. LR1 - Radio El Mundo*	5 June 1996
National Commercial Court of Appeals		*Quilmes Combustibles, S.A. c. Vigan, S.A.*	15 March 1991
National Commercial Court of Appeals	*Sala* B	*Muraro, Heriberto v. Eudeba, S.E.M.*	7 February 1989
National Commercial Court of Appeals	*Sala* A	*Pelisch, Juan y otro v. Imago Producciones, S.R.L. y/u otro*	11 June 1974
National Civil Chamber	*Sala* E	*García, Enrique A. O. y otro v. Canjalli de Cababié, Alegra M. y otros*	12 October 2005, (Lexis Nº 35012125)
National Civil Chamber	*Sala* F	*González, Roberto v. Sáez, Federico C*	7 November 2003, (Lexis Nº 1/1000184)
National Civil Chamber	*Sala* C	*De Elizalde, Jorge E. y otro v. López Lecube, Marta*	3 September 2001
National Civil Chamber	*Sala* C	*Mariani, José A. y otros v. Consorcio Ática I S.R.L.*	30 June 2000
National Civil Chamber	*Sala* A	*Municipalidad de Buenos Aires v. Consorcio Colombres 1175/77*	10 August 1988
National Civil Chamber	*Sala* D	*Adyco S.A. v. Mizrahi Aldo R.*	4 August 1986 (JA 1987-II-535)
National Civil Chamber	*Sala* A	*Monte Grande S.A. v. Mercado José M.*	20 August 1985
National Commercial Chamber		*Sala* D, *Castelar S.A. v. Maralc SRL*	11 April 1990 (JA 1990-IV-165)

National Commercial Chamber	*Sala* C	*Pandemonium v. Thinkercorp S.A.*	13 November 1985
National Commercial Chamber	*Sala* D	*Expreso los Angeles c. Fábrica de Muebles*	3 March 1984
National Commercial Chamber	*Sala* D	*Chiarini, Roberto L. v. Leoco Industrieanlagen GmbH & Cia. KG*	unknown

Bolivia

Court	*Sala*	*Parties*	*Date*
Supreme Court	*Sala Civil*	*Banco Unión S.A. v. Shuei Higa Nakandakari y otros*	10 March 2008
Supreme Court	*Sala Civil*	*Empresas Agrícolas Ganaderas San Jorge y Rincón Chuchío v. CITIBANK N.A. Sucursal Bolivia*	6 February 2007
Supreme Court	*Sala Civil*	*Bartolomé Erland Rodríguez Álvarez v. Fabricio Ludwing Braner Ibáñez*	6 December 2005
Supreme Court	*Sala Civil* 1	*Elizabeth Chávez Guzmán v. Yacimientos Petrolíferos Fiscales Bolivianos*	25 October 2005
Supreme Court	unknown	*Empresa DICA S.R.L. v. José Fernando Cadima Camacho*	28 July 2005
Supreme Court	unknown	*Alejandro Ramírez Mamani v. Guillermo Franco Gómez*	15 February 2005
Supreme Court	*Sala Civil* 2	*Augusto Valencia Sanabria y María Ruth Borda de Valencia v. José Luís Álvarez Cáceres*	23 November 2004
Supreme Court	*Sala Civil* 1	*Marcial Xavier Pérez y otra v. Teddy Mercado Mendoza*	29 September 2004
Supreme Court	*Sala Civil*	*Juan Pablo Prudencio Borda v. Servicio Prefectural de Caminos Chuquisaca*	10 April 2003
Supreme Court	*Sala Civil*	*Bárbara Tapia vda. de Casas v. Petrona Cazas vda. de Mayta*	22 April 2003
Supreme Court	*Sala Civil*	*Carla Cecilia Chacón de Pino v. Luis Iriondo Angola*	11 March 2003
Supreme Court	*Sala Civil*	*Jorge Arze Murillo y otra v. Aerolínea Varig*	3 September 2002
Supreme Court	*Sala Civil*	*Jaime Roger Lema Gonzáles v. Bo. Gunnar Byren Johansson*	10 June 2002
Supreme Court	*Sala Civil*	*René Jorge Rojas y Sonia Veliz de Jorge v. Celia Veliz de Aranda*	11 March 2002
Supreme Court	*Sala Civil*	*Guillermo Farwig Guillén v. Sociedad Bol-Art S.A.*	6 March 2002
Supreme Court	unknown	*Antonio Ivar Perales Guerrero v. Deysi Alvarez vda. de Perales*	unknown

Supreme Court	unknown	*Benedicto Coronel v. Edgar Marcelo Coronel Gutiérrez*	unknown
Supreme Court	unknown	*Estudio Jurídico Moreno Baldiviezo v. Prefectura de Tarija*	unknown
Supreme Court	unknown	*Felipe Orozco Cabrera v. Hugo Aguirre Calderón y María Paz Villalba de Aguirre*	unknown
Supreme Court	unknown	*Julio Ramiro Saniz Balderrama v. Galindo S.A.*	unknown
Supreme Court	*Sala Civil*	*Boliviana de Ingeniería S.R.L v. Compañía La Boliviana CIACRUZ de Seguros y Reaseguros S.A.*	unknown
Supreme Court	*Sala Civil*	*Carlos Maida y Celinda Pinto de Maida v. Osvaldo Trigo Arispe*	unknown
Supreme Court	*Sala Civil*	*Erwin Antelo Justiniano v. Luis Fernando Antelo López*	unknown
Supreme Court	*Sala Civil*	*Francisco de Asis Perales v. Rolando Soliz Velásquez*	unknown
Supreme Court	*Sala Civil*	*Gladys Pedriel Ribera v. Dora Barroso vda. de Rivero*	unknown
Supreme Court	*Sala Civil*	*Javier Hinojosa Huarachi v. Elsa Claros Soto y Luciano Rojas Pérez*	unknown
Supreme Court	*Sala Civil*	*Julia Fernández Aparicio v. Isidro Soruco Fernández*	unknown
Supreme Court	*Sala Civil*	*NOVA S.R.L. v. Consorcio Minero S.A.*	unknown
Supreme Court	*Sala Civil*	*Rosalina Rodríguez Vega de Villarroel v. Félix Tapia Villarroel y otros*	unknown
Supreme Court	*Sala Civil*	*Severo Vega Veizaga v. René Reyes Reyes y Rosa Rivas de Reyes* 200003- -1-067	unknown

Brazil

Court	*Identification Number*	*Date of Publication*	*Ministry or Justice*
Superior Tribunal of Justice	REsp 3.035/EX, Registy 2008/0044435-0	20 May 2009	Minister Fernando Gonçalves
Superior Tribunal of Justice	REsp 704384/MG	1 April 2008	Minister Ari Pargendler
Superior Tribunal of Justice	REsp 782999/SP	16 April 2007	Minister Castro Filho
Superior Tribunal of Justice	REsp 687285/SP	25 September 2007	Minister Nancy Andrighi
Superior Tribunal of Justice	RO 39/MG	March 2006	Minister Jorge Scartezzini
Superior Tribunal of Jutisce	AgRg no Ag 637639/RS	9 May 2005	Minister Aldir Passarinho Junior

Superior Tribunal of Justice	REsp 151079/SP	29 November 2004	Minister Barros Monteiro
Superior Tribunal of Justice	REsp 222148/SP	30 June 2003	Minister Cesar Asfor Rocha
Tribunal of Justice of the State of Rio de Janeiro	Appeal 2008.001.65722	29 January 2009	unknown
Tribunal of Justice of the State of Rio Grande do Sul	Civil Recourse 71000950527	28 September 2007	unknown
Tribunal of Justice of the State of Rio Grande do Sul	Civil Appeal 70019324029	23 August 2007	unknown
Tribunal of Justice of the State of Rio Grande do Sul	Civil Appeal 70012118220	9 September 2005	Justice Marilene Bonzanini Bernardi
Tribunal of Justice of the State of Santa Catarina	Civil Appeal 2008.042773-6	18 December 2008	unknown
Tribunal of Justice of the State of São Paulo	Appeal with Revision 1057296004	26 December 2007	unknown
Tribunal of Justice of the State of São Paulo	Appeal with Revision 1104540009	19 November 2007	unknown
Tribunal of Justice of the State of São Paulo	Civil Recourse 71001411644	23 October 2007	Justice Eduardo Kraemer
Tribunal of Justice of the State of the São Paulo	Civil Recourse 71001123140	4 May 2007	unknown
Tribunal of Justice of the State of São Paulo	Appeal with Revision 965123400	12 April 2006	unknown
Appeal Tribunal of São Paulo	1.247.070-7	18 December 2003	unknown

Chile

Court	*Source*	*Date*
Supreme Court *Sala* 1	*Rol* 1782-2007	22 September 2008
Supreme Court	*Rol* 3405-2001	12 August 2008
Supreme Court	*Rol* 4303-05	24 July 2007
Supreme Court	*Rol* 239-04	18 May 2006
Supreme Court	*Rol* 1120-04	26 January 2006
Supreme Court	*Rol* 3076-03	18 August 2004
Supreme Court	*Rol* 228-03	9 November 2004

Supreme Court	*Rol* 4989-02	10 June 2004
Supreme Court	RDJ XCVIII, Sec. 1, at 99, 100	9 May 2001
Chile Supreme Court	RDJ Vol. 27, Sec. 1, at 365	10 June 1929
Supreme Court	RDJ Vol. 46, Sec. 1, at 533	unknown
Supreme Court	RDJ Vol. 36, Sec. 1, at 362	unknown
Supreme Court	RDJ Vol. 44, Sec. 1, at 397	unknown
Appeal Court of Santiago	unknown	13 September 2006

Colombia

Court	*Date*	*Source*
Supreme Court	19 December 1952	GJ LXXIII, at 751
Supreme Court	24 March 1947	GJ LXII, at 84

Costa Rica

Court	*Judgment*	*Sala*	*Date*
Supreme Court	2006-01022	*Segunda Sala Civil*	8 November 2006
Supreme Court	082-01	unknown	25 November 2005
Supreme Court	00212-98	*Segunda Sala Civil*	19 August 1998
Supreme Court	226	*Segunda Sala Civil*	14 July 1995
Supreme Court	167	*Segunda Sala Civil*	26 May 1995
Supreme Court	108	unknown	18 July 1989

El Salvador

Court	*Sala*	*Parties*	*Number*	*Date*
Supreme Court	*Cass civ*	*Kereitz Medrano v. Liceo Centroamericano S.A. de C.V.*	11-C-2007	17 November 2008
Supreme Court	*Cass civ*	*Sagicar S.A. de C.V. v. Empresa Electrónica de Oriente S.A. de C.V.*	18-C-2006	19 February 2008
Supreme Court	*Cass civ*	*Sociedad Antonio Comandari Hijos Y Compañía v. BENDECK et al.*	93-C-2006	14 March 2007
Supreme Court	Civil Appeal	*Cuéllar Vásquez v. Estado de El Salvador como sucesor de ANTEL*	46-AP-2005	5 December 2006
Supreme Court	*Cass civ*	*Barahona de Renderos v. Paredes Medrano*	80-C-2005	18 October 2005
Supreme Court	*Cass civ*	*Contreras Castro v. Garza Heredia*	247 –C -2004	5 May 2005

Supreme Court	*Cass civ*	*Instituto de Previsión Social de la Fuerza Armada v. Cooperativa de la Fuerza Armada Limitada o COOPEFA*	Ca.29-C-2004	14 March 2005
Supreme Court	*Cass civ*	*Funes Castillo v. Agropecuaria "La Cabaña"*	141-C-2004	13 December 2004
Supreme Court	Civil Appeal	*Edificadora. Salvadoreña S.A. de C.V. v. Estado de El Salvador*	1612 S.S	7 July 2004
Supreme Court	*Cass civ*	*Cuenca Rodríguez v. Banco Ciscatlan S.A.*	1732 S.S.	19 June 2004
Supreme Court	*Cass civ*	*Pineda Solis v. Henández Landa Verde*	1593 S.S.	11 May 2004
Supreme Court	*Cass civ*	*"Caja De Credito Rural De Olocuilta" v. Tochez Arévalo Y Tochez*	1574-Cas.S.S.	28 July 2003
Supreme Court	*Cass civ*	*Aseguradora Salvadoreña Compañía de Seguros v. American International Group, Inc.*	1466 S.S.	31 March 2003
Supreme Court	*Cass civ*	*Alvarenga Bonilla v. Hsien Tang*	1530 S.S.	30 September 2002
Supreme Court	Civil Appeal	*Landaverde v. Estado y Gobierno de El Salvador Agricultura y Ganadería*	1507 S.S	19 August 2002
Supreme Court	*Cass civ*	*Ortíz de Hernández v. Campos Rivera*	1346-2001	24 July 2002
Supreme Court	*Cass civ*	*Daglio y Compañía S.A. C.V. v. Sociedad Regional de Inversiones S.A. de C.V.*	1294-2001	19 August 2001
Supreme Court	*Cass civ*	*Trujillo Lopez v. De Paz Ayala*	1219-2001	9 February 2001
Supreme Court	*Cass civ*	*Alberto Zelaya y Zaldivar Gallardo v. Montenevado Comercial S.A. De C.V.*	1198-2001	30 January 2001
Supreme Court	*Cass civ*	*Martínez de Magaña v. Gálvez Rojas*	601-2000	11 October 2000
Supreme Court	*Cass civ*	*Castillo de Lopez v. Iraheta Flores*	1195-2000	28 August 2000
Supreme Court	*Cass civ*	*León v. Urbina*	unknown	1998
Supreme Court	*Cass civ*	*Estadios Deportivos de El Salvador S.A.de C.V. v. Asociación de Clubes de Liga Mayor*	CCS1041.96	unknown
Supreme Court	*Cass civ*	*Inversiones J. R, S.A. de C.V. v. Industrial de Alimentos S.A. de C.V.*	CCS1118.98	unknown

Mexico

Court	*Period*	*Registry*	*Source*
Supreme Court	*Ninth*	172'566	SJF XXV, May 2007, at 251
Supreme Court	*Fifth*	343989	SJF CIV, at 1652
Supreme Court	unknown	271745	SJF Part 4 XXVII, at 226
Supreme Court	unknown	271721	SJF Part 4 XXVII, at 138
Supreme Court	*Seventh*	No. 241287	SJF 87 Part 4, at 17
Supreme Court	unknown	240'067	SJF IV, at 14
Supreme Court	*Eighth*	207549	SJF I Part, 1 January to June 1988, at 289
Supreme Court	*Ninth*	189'425	SJF XIII, June 2001, at 165
Supreme Court	*Ninth*	189'166	SJF XIV, August 2001, at 170
Supreme Court	*Ninth*	177'470	SJF XXII, August 2005, at 142
Supreme Court	*Eighth*	unknown	SJF I First Part, January-June 1988, at 295
Supreme Court	*Ninth*	unknown	SJF VIII, October 1998, at 381
Supreme Court	*Eighth*	unknown	SJF I, at 283
Supreme Court	*Seventh*	unknown	SJF Part 4, Vol. 6, at 18
Supreme Court	*Seventh*	unknown	SJF 139-144, Part 4, at 80
Supreme Court	*Fifth*	unknown	SJF XCVI, at 951
Supreme Court	*Fifth*	unknown	SJF XCVI, at 951
Supreme Court	*Fifth*	unknown	SJF CXIX, at 775
Supreme Court	*Fifth*	unknown	SJF LXXXVIII, at 2590
Collegiate Tribunals	*Ninth*	172'151	SJF XXV, June 2007, at 1170
Collegiate Tribunals	*Ninth*	172234	SJF XXV, June 2007, at 1048
Collegiate Tribunals	*Ninth*	173'279	SJF XXV, February 2007, at 1798
Collegiate Tribunals	*Ninth*	173722	SJF XXIV, December 2006, at 1378
Collegiate Tribunals	*Ninth*	174'773	SJF XXIV, July 2006, at 1169
Collegiate Tribunals	*Ninth*	174887	SJF XXIII, June 2006, at 1164
Collegiate Tribunals	*Ninth*	177'052	SJF XXII, October 2005, at 2318
Collegiate Tribunals	*Ninth*	177'335	SJF XXII September 2005, at 1436
Collegiate Tribunals	*Ninth*	177'643	SJF XXII, August 2005, at 1883
Collegiate Tribunals	*Ninth*	178'481	SJF XXI, May 2005, at 1448
Collegiate Tribunals	unknown	177'198	SJF XXII, September 2005, at 1532
Collegiate Tribunals	unknown	177335	SJF XXII, September 2005, at 1436

Collegiate Tribunals	*Ninth*	179'354	SJF XXI, February 2005, at 1661
Collegiate Tribunals	*Ninth*	182'002	SJF XIX, March 2004, at 1534
Collegiate Tribunals	*Ninth*	182'396	SJF XIX, January 2004, at 1535
Collegiate Tribunals	unknown	181'356	SJF XIX, June 2004, at 1425
Collegiate Tribunals	*Ninth*	183'410	SJF XVIII, August 2003, at 1831
Collegiate Tribunals	*Ninth*	183'878	SJF XVIII, July 2003, at 1061
Collegiate Tribunals	unknown	182'003	SJF XIX, March 2004, at 1533
Collegiate Tribunals	*Ninth*	184'840	SJF XVII, February 2003, at 1103
Collegiate Tribunals	*Ninth*	185'427	SJF XVI, December 2002, at 759
Collegiate Tribunals	*Ninth*	185'801	SJF XVI, October 2002, at 1347
Collegiate Tribunals	*Ninth*	185'809	SJF XVI, October 2002, at 1341
Collegiate Tribunals	*Ninth*	186'243	SJF XVI, August 2002, at 1306
Collegiate Tribunals	*Ninth*	186'332	SJF XVI, August 2002, at 1256
Collegiate Tribunals	*Ninth*	186'339	SJF XVI, August 2002, at 1252
Collegiate Tribunals	*Ninth*	186700	SJF XVI July 2002 at 1231
Collegiate Tribunals	*Ninth*	186'790	SJF XV, June 2002, at 649
Collegiate Tribunals	*Ninth*	187'228	SJF XV, April 2002, at 1261
Collegiate Tribunals	*Ninth*	187'461	SJF XV, March 2002, at 1405
Collegiate Tribunals	*Ninth*	187'474	SJF XV, March 2002, at 1395
Collegiate Tribunals	unknown	186'287	SJF XVI, August 2002, at 1279
Collegiate Tribunals	*Ninth*	191'011	SJF XII, October 2000, at 1280
Collegiate Tribunals	*Ninth*	191'033	SJF XII, October 2000, at 1279
Collegiate Tribunals	*Ninth*	191'160	SJF XII, September 2000, at 721

Collegiate Tribunals	*Ninth*	194'119	SJF IX, April 1999, at 579
Collegiate Tribunals	*Ninth*	194'993	SJF VIII, December 1998, at 1028
Collegiate Tribunals	*Ninth*	195'050	SJF VIII, December 1998, at 1030
Collegiate Tribunals	*Ninth*	195'143	SJF VIII, November 1998, at 555
Collegiate Tribunals	*Ninth*	195'846	SJF VIII, August 1998, at 838
Collegiate Tribunals	*Ninth*	196'579	SJF VII, March 1998, at 775
Collegiate Tribunals	*Ninth*	197'122	SJF VII, January 1998, at 1097
Collegiate Tribunals	*Ninth*	197'162	SFJ VII, January 1998, at 1069
Collegiate Tribunals	*Ninth*	197163	SJF VII, January 1998, at 1069
Collegiate Tribunals	*Ninth*	195'508	SJF VIII, September 1998, at 1154
Collegiate Tribunals	*Ninth*	199'343	SJF V, Feburary 1997, at 769
Collegiate Tribunals	*Ninth*	199'602	SJF V, January 1997, at 442
Collegiate Tribunals	*Ninth*	201'660	SJF IV, August 1996, at 642
Collegiate Tribunals	*Ninth*	202'182	SJF III, June 1996, at 908
Collegiate Tribunals	*Ninth*	202'940	SJF III, March 1996 at 923
Collegiate Tribunals	*Ninth*	202'973	SJF III, March 1996, at 948
Collegiate Tribunals	*Ninth*	204'714	SJF II, August 1995, at 319
Collegiate Tribunals	*Ninth*	205'193	SJF I, May 1995, at 349
Collegiate Tribunals	*Eighth*	unknown	SJF IX, February 1992, at 137
Collegiate Tribunals	*Eighth*	222109	SJF VIII, August 1991, at 165
Collegiate Tribunals	*Seventh*	248381	SJF 199-204 VI, at 51
Collegiate Tribunals	*Seventh*	249211	SJF VI, at 139
Collegiate Tribunals	*Fifth*	385712	SJF CXIII, at 696

Paraguay

Court	*Judgment*	*Date*	*Parties*
Supreme Court	250	18 May 2008	unknown
Supreme Court	1313	20 December 2007	*Casa Gagliardi Y Otro v. Firma Unilever Capsa Del Paraguay S.A.*
Supreme Court, *Sala Civil*	08	2 February 2005	*Adriano Ayala Cano v. Reinaldo Pavia Maldonado, David Pavia Vega Y Pablo Dario Zaracho*
Supreme Court	1345	5 October 2004	*Angel Anibal Nuñez Ortiz v. La República Compañía Paraguaya De Seguros Generales S.A.*
Supreme Court	1199	22 July 2003	*Fernando Bruno Román López v. Ideal S.A. De Seguros Y Reaseguros*
Supreme Court	unknown	27 December 2002	*Olegario Farrés y Otra v. Bancoplus S.A.I.F.*
Supreme Court	996	11 December 2001	*Fernando Ayala v. Nicolas G. Luthold Feldmann*
Supreme Court	878	19 November 2001	*Martín Ma. Del Puerto J. Y Osvaldo López v. Cirila Rojas Vda. De Aguirre*
Supreme Court	350	27 June 2001	*Liberata Ibarrola Vda. De García v. Vilda Selva D'Ecclesis Y Otra*
Supreme Court	224	18 May 2001	*Diego Pizziolo v. Nereo Tiso Y Otros*
Supreme Court	219	17 May 2001	*Baúl De La Felicidad S.A. v. Pony Automotores – Mitsuservice Import S.R.L.*
Supreme Court	700	16 December 1999	*Adalberto Walter Zierz v. Osmar Lautenschleiger E Isona Serenita Lautenschleiger*
Supreme Court	unknown	22 July 1999	*Jorge Ruckelshaussen v. Wilhelm Albrecht*
Supreme Court	45	unknown	*Bartolome Sánchez v. El Estado Paraguayo*

Peru

Court	*Sala*	*Resolution*	*Date*
Supreme Court	*Sala civil transitoria*	005192-2006	21 July 2008
Supreme Court	*Sala civil permanente*	004913-2008	29 April 2008
Supreme Court	*Sala civil permanente*	005211-2007	27 March 2008
Supreme Court	*Sala civil permanente*	005139-2007	18 March 2008
Supreme Court	*Sala civil permanente*	004289-2008	6 March 2008
Supreme Court	*Sala civil transitoria*	002380-2007	12 December 2007
Supreme Court	*Sala civil transitoria*	002534-2006	2 April 2007
Supreme Court	unknown	002752-2006	17 October 2006
Supreme Court	*Sala civil transitoria*	000476-2006	18 August 2006
Supreme Court	*Sala civil permanente*	001427-2006	17 May 2006

Supreme Court	*Sala civil transitoria*	000050-2005	10 January 2006
Supreme Court	*Sala civil permanente*	001253-2004	9 August 2005
Supreme Court	*cass*	001211-2005	22 July 2005
Supreme Court	*Sala civil transitoria*	002924-2003	16 December 2003
Supreme Court	*Sala civil transitoria*	001656-2003	25 November 2003
Supreme Court	*Sala civil transitoria*	001064-2003	10 September 2003
Supreme Court	*Sala civil transitoria*	001010-2003	26 August 2003
Supreme Court	*Sala civil transitoria*	001064-2003	6 June 2003
Supreme Court	*Sala civil permanente*	000225-2002	9 April 2003
Supreme Court	*Sala civil permanente*	002857-2001	23 December 2002
Supreme Court	*Sala civil transitoria*	002128-2002	10 December 2002
Supreme Court	*Sala civil permanente*	001949-2002	30 October 2002
Supreme Court	*Sala civil transitoria*	002290-2002	20 August 2002
Supreme Court	*Sala civil permanente*	002671-2001	12 August 2002
Supreme Court	*Sala civil transitoria*	001860-2002	19 July 2002
Supreme Court	*Sala civil transitoria*	001584-2002	2 July 2002
Supreme Court	*Sala civil permanente*	001977-2001	26 June 2002
Supreme Court	*Sala civil transitoria*	004010-2001	17 May 2002
Suprema Corte	*Sala civil transitoria*	000070-2001	25 April 2002
Supreme Court	*Sala civil transitoria cass*	002670-2001	unknown
Supreme Court	*Sala civil transitoria*	000028-2001	23 August 2001
Supreme Court	*Sala civil permanente*	000045-2001	24 July 2001
Supreme Court	*Sala civil permanente*	000119-1999	27 March 2000
Supreme Court	*cass*	002454-2000	12 January 2001
Supreme Court	*Sala civil transitoria*	002838-2001	25 January 2002
Supreme Court	*Sala civil transitoria*	000114-1998	24 February 1999
Supreme Court	*Sala civil permanente*	001017-1997	19 October 1998
INDECOPI	unknown	422-2003/TDC-INDECOPI	unknown

Portugal

Court	*Date*	*Rapporteur Justice*	*Source*
Supreme Tribunal of Justice	22 May 2008	unknown	unknown
Supreme Tribunal of Justice	13 March 2008	unknown	unknown
Supreme Tribunal of Justice	19 February 2008	unknown	unknown
Supreme Tribunal of Justice	27 November 2007	unknown	unknown
Supreme Tribunal of Justice	13 March 2007	unknown	unknown
Supreme Tribunal of Justice	21 June 2006	unknown	unknown

Supreme Tribunal of Justice	4 April 2006	unknown	unknown
Supreme Tribunal of Justice	5 July 2005 published	Rapporteur Justice: Silva Salazar	*Revista* 2015/05
Supreme Tribunal of Justice	22 June 2005 published	Rapporteur Justice: Ferreira Girão	*Revista* 1526/05
Supreme Tribunal of Justice	30 September 2004 published	Rapporteur Justice: Azevedo Ramos	*Revista* 2411/04
Supreme Tribunal of Justice	23 September 2004 published	Rapporteur Justice: Moitinho de Almeida	*Revista* 2402/04
Supreme Tribunal of Justice	12 March 2002	unknown	unknown
Supreme Tribunal of Justice	4 October 2001	unknown	unknown
Supreme Tribunal of Justice	23 January 2001	unknown	unknown
Supreme Tribunal of Justice	23 April 1998	unknown	unkown
Supreme Tribunal of Justice	4 May 1994	unknown	unknown
Supreme Tribunal of Justice	2 May 1981	unknown	unknown

Spain

Court	*Date*	*Source*
Supreme Tribunal	1 June 2009	*Id Cendoj:* 28079110012009100394
Supreme Tribunal	14 May 2009	*Id Cendoj:* 28079110012009100320
Supreme Tribunal	4 February 2009	*Id Cendoj*: 28079110012009100039
Supreme Tribunal	23 January 2009	*Id Cendoj:* 28079110012009100016
Supreme Tribunal	24 April 2009	*Id Cendoj:* 28079110012009100358
Supreme Tribunal	20 November 2008	*Id Cendoj:* 28079110012008101062
Supreme Tribunal	20 November 2008	*Id Cendoj:* 28079110012008101099
Supreme Tribunal	28 October 2008	*Id Cendoj:* 28079110012008100918
Supreme Tribunal	9 July 2008	*Id Cendoj:* 28079110012008100731
Supreme Tribunal	2 July 2008	*Id* Cendoj: 28079110012008100595
Supreme Tribunal	5 June 2008	*Id Cendoj:* 28079110012008100535
Supreme Tribunal	22 October 2007	*Id Cendoj:* 28079110012007101093
Supreme Tribunal	12 July 2007	*Id Cendoj:* 28079110012007100879
Supreme Tribunal	10 January 2007	*Id Cendoj:* 28079110012007100999
Supreme Tribunal	20 December 2006	*Id Cendoj:* 28079110012006101363
Supreme Tribunal	7 December 2006	*Id Cendoj:* 28079110012006101236
Supreme Tribunal	22 November 2006	*Id Cendoj:* 28079110012006101175
Supreme Tribunal	15 November 2006	*Id Cendoj:* 28079110012006101110
Supreme Tribunal	18 October 2006	*Id Cendoj:* 28079110012006101032

Supreme Tribunal	8 June 2006	*Id Cendoj:* 28079110012006100603
Supreme Tribunal	6 June 2006	*Id Cendoj:* 28079110012006100524
Supreme Tribunal	6 April 2006	*Id Cendoj:* 28079110012006100366
Supreme Tribunal	22 December 2000	*Id Cendoj:* 28079110002000100573
Supreme Tribunal	22 December 2000	*Id Cendoj:* 28079110002000100627
Supreme Tribunal	31 May 2000	*Id Cendoj:* 28079110002000100800
Supreme Tribunal	14 April 2000	(ar 3376)
Supreme Tribunal	27 January 2000	AC 462/2000
Supreme Tribunal	31 December 1999	(ar 9386)
Supreme Tribunal	25 June 1999	*Id Cendoj:* 28079110001999100407
Supreme Tribunal	11 May 1999	*Id Cendoj:* 28079110001999100864
Supreme Tribunal	19 February 1999	*Id Cendoj:* 28079110001999100087
Supreme Tribunal	21 December 1998	*Id Cendoj:* 28079110001998100061
Supreme Tribunal	11 November 1997	(ar 7872)
Supreme Tribunal	30 October 1997	*Id Cendoj:* 28079110001997100226
Supreme Tribunal	3 October 1997	*Id Cendoj:* 28079110001997100230
Supreme Tribunal	7 March 1997	(ar 1643)
Supreme Tribunal	5 December 1996	unknown
Supreme Tribunal	16 September 1996	*Id Cendoj:* 28079110011986100021
Supreme Tribunal	12 July 1996	*Id Cendoj:* 28079110001996100990
Supreme Tribunal	30 May 1996	unknown
Supreme Tribunal	13 December 1994	AC 341/1995
Supreme Tribunal	2 April 1994	*Id Cendoj:* 28079110011994103098
Supreme Tribunal	15 March 1994	*Id Cendoj:* 28079110011994101643
Supreme Tribunal	15 March 1994	*Id Cendoj:* 28079110011994101643
Supreme Tribunal	13 May 1993	*Id Cendoj:* 28079110011993101284
Supreme Tribunal	26 March 1993	unknown
Supreme Tribunal	12 March 1993	unknown
Supreme Tribunal	27 November 1992	*Id Cendoj:* 28079110011992103416
Supreme Tribunal	27 October 1992	*Id Cendoj:* 28079110001992100296
Supreme Tribunal	14 May 1992	*Id Cendoj:* 28079110011992103723
Supreme Tribunal	1 July 1991	*Id Cendoj:* 28079110011991101272
Supreme Tribunal	29 January 1991	*Id Cendoj:* 28079110011991101451
Audiencia Provincial de Lérida	16 January 1991	unknown
Supreme Tribunal	12 May 1990	*Id Cendoj:* 28079110011990101070
Supreme Tribunal	26 November 1987	*Id Cendoj:* 28079110011987101175
Supreme Tribunal	25 November 1985	*Id Cendoj:* 28079110011985100202
Supreme Tribunal	5 October 1985	*Id Cendoj:* 28079110011985100180
Supreme Tribunal	20 November 1984	*Id Cendoj:* 28079110011984100596
Supreme Tribunal, *Sala 6*	2 May 1984	RJA 1984, No 2950
SupremeTribunal	13 May 1982	*Id Cendoj:* 28079110011982100041
Supreme Tribunal	21 December 1981	*Id Cendoj:* 28079110011981100141
Supreme Tribunal	15 November 2006	*Id Cendoj:* 28079110012006101110
Supreme Tribunal	21 February 1990	AC 515/1990

Audiencia Provincial de Palencia	26 September 2005	unknown
Audiencia Provincial Zaragoza	20 January 1999	unknown
Audiencia Provincial Bacelona	20 June 1997	unknown
Audiencia Provincial Vitoria	6 April 1985	unknown
AT Pamplona	15 December 1988	unknown
AT Albacete	11 July 1980	unknown
AT Toledo, Sec. 1	18 October 1996	unknown

Venezuela

Court	*Judgment*	*Sala*	*File*	*Date*
Supreme Tribunal	01210	*Sala Político Administrativa*	14728	8 October 2002
Supreme Tribunal	72	*Cass civ*	99-973	5 May 2002
Supreme Tribunal	319	*Cass civ*	99-044	17 July 2002
Supreme Tribunal	82	*Cass*	00-423 2	8 February 200
Supreme Tribunal	72	*Cass civ*	99-973	5 February 2002
Supreme Tribunal	62	*Cass soc*	01-262	14 February 2002
Supreme Tribunal	363	*Cass soc*	01-474	19 December 2001
Supreme Tribunal	00559	unknown	15666	3 April 2001
Supreme Tribunal	340	*Cass civ*	99-1001	31 October 2000
Supreme Tribunal	323	*Cass civ*	00-254	6 October 2000
Supreme Tribunal	1100	*Cass pen*	C00-0156	1 August 2000
Supreme Tribunal	202	*Cass civ*	99-458	14 June 2000
Supreme Tribunal	81	*Cass civ*	99312	30 March 2000

United States

Court	*Date*	*Number*	*Source*
US Court of Appeals for the Fifth Circuit	11 June 2003	02-20166	CLOUT Abstract No 575

Arbitral Awards

ICC Awards Applying Incoterms, CISG, UNIDROIT PICC

Institution	*Type of Award*	*Case Number*
ICC Ct Arb	Final Award	14633

ICC Awards from CLOUT

Institution	*Type of Award*	*Case Number*	*Source*
ICC Ct Arb	Final Award	7565	CLOUT Abstract No. 300
ICC Ct Arb	Final Award	6653	CLOUT Abstract No. 103

Lex Contractus Argentinean Law

Institution	*Type of Award*	*Case Number*
ICC Ct Arb	Final Award	13518
ICC Ct Arb	Final Award	13417
ICC Ct Arb	Final Award	13385
ICC Ct Arb	Award by Consent	13242
ICC Ct Arb	Final Award	12755
ICC Ct Arb	Preliminary Award on the Jurisdiction	12231
ICC Ct Arb	Final Award	11949
ICC Ct Arb	Final Award	11520
ICC Ct Arb	Final Award	11404
ICC Ct Arb	Final Award	11114

Lex Contractus Bolivian Law and INCOTERMS 2000

Institution	*Type of Award*	*Case Number*
ICC Ct Arb	Final Award	13967

Lex Contractus Brazilian Law

Institution	*Type of Award*	*Case Number*

ICC Ct Arb	Final Award	14653
ICC Ct Arb	Final Award	14375
ICC Ct Arb	Final Award	14083
ICC Ct Arb	Final Award	13870
ICC Ct Arb	Final Award	13530
ICC Ct Arb	Final Award	13458
ICC Ct Arb	Final Award	13347
ICC Ct Arb	Final Award	13127
ICC Ct Arb	Final Award	11911

Lex Contractus Chilean Law

Institution	*Type of Award*	*Case Number*
ICC Ct Arb	Final Award	10299
ICC Ct Arb	Final Award	9984

Lex Contractus Colombian Law

Institution	*Type of Award*	*Case Number*
ICC Ct Arb	Final Award	13741
ICC Ct Arb	Final Award	9400

Lex Contractus Guatemalan Law

Institution	*Type of Award*	*Case Number*
ICC Ct Arb	Final Award	13847

Lex Contractus Mexican Law

Institution	*Type of Award*	*Case Number*
ICC Ct Arb	Final Award	13751
ICC Ct Arb	Final Award	13524
ICC Ct Arb	Final Award	13184
ICC Ct Arb	Partial Award	12949
ICC Ct Arb	Partial Award	12296
ICC Ct Arb	Final Award	12035
ICC Ct Arb	Final Award	11853
ICC Ct Arb	Final Award	11826
ICC Ct Arb	Final Award	11722
ICC Ct Arb	Final Award	11556
ICC Ct Arb	Final Award	11256

Lex Contractus Paraguayan Law

Institution	*Type of Award*	*Case Number*
ICC Ct Arb	Final Award	13685

Lex Contractus Portuguese Law

Institution	*Type of Award*	*Case Number*
ICC Ct Arb	Final Award	12853
ICC Ct Arb	Final Award	11570
ICC Ct Arb	Final Award	11367
ICC Ct Arb	Final Award	10818
ICC Ct Arb	Final Award	10044

Lex Contractus Spanish Law

Institution	*Type of Award*	*Case Number*
ICC Ct Arb	Final Award	14088
ICC Ct Arb	Final Award	14024
ICC Ct Arb	Final Award	13918
ICC Ct Arb	Final Award	13882
ICC Ct Arb	Final Award	13743
ICC Ct Arb	Final Award	13678
ICC Ct Arb	Final Award	13663
ICC Ct Arb	Final Award	13542
ICC Ct Arb	Final Award	13435
ICC Ct Arb	Final Award	13278
ICC Ct Arb	Final Award	11818
ICC Ct Arb	Final Award	11779
ICC Ct Arb	Final Award	11317

Lex Contractus Venezuela Law

Institution	*Type of Award*	*Case Number*
ICC Ct Arb	Final Award	13750
ICC Ct Arb	Final Award	13478

Bibliography

Abarca Junco, Ana Paloma, Derecho Internacional Privado Vol. I, Madrid, Colex: Universidad Nacional de Educación a Distancia (4th ed. 2003).

Acuña Tapia L. & G. Novoa Muñoz, *Cambio de Circunstancias en el Contrato*, Doctoral thesis, Universidad Católica de Temuco, Escuela de Derecho (2004), http://biblioteca.uct.cl/tesis/luis-acuna/tesis.pdf.

Aguilar Gorrondona, José Luis, Contratos y Garantias: Derecho Civil IV, Caracas, Universidad Católica Andrés Bello (17th ed. 2008).

Aguilar Guerra, Vladimir, El Negocio Jurídico, Guatemala, Serviprensa (4th ed. 2004).

Albornoz, María Mercedes, *El derecho aplicable a los contratos internacionales en el sistema interamericano*, Portal Jurídico Peruan (2008), http://www.ciberjure.com.pe/index.php?option=com_content&task=view&id=3531&Itemid=9.

Alterini, Atilo Aníbal, Contratos civiles, comerciales, de consumo, Buenos Aires, Abeledo-Perrot (1998).

Alvarado Herrera, Lucia, *in* David Morán Bovio (Ed.), Comentario a los Principios de Unidroit para. los Contratos del Comercio Internacional, Navarra, Thomson-Aranzadi (2003).

Álvarez Vigaray, R. & R. De Aymerich, La Resición por Lesión en el Derecho Civil Español Común y Floral, Granada, Comares (1989).

Antunes Valera, João De Matos, Das Obrigações em Geral, Coimbra, Almeida (10th ed. 2003).

Arce Gargollo, Javier, Contratos Mercantiles Atípicos, México, Editorial Porrúa (12th ed. 2007).

Barrera Graf, Jorge, El Derecho Mercantil en la América Latina, México, Universidad Nacional Autonoma de Mexico (1963).

Barriuso Ruiz, Carlos, La Contratacion Electronica, Madrid, Dykinson (2006).

Basadre Ayulo, Jorge, Derecho Internacional Privado, Lima, Grijley (2000).

Baudrit Carrillo, Diego, Los Contratos Traslativos del Derecho Privado – Principios de Jurisprudencia, San José, Juricentro (2nd ed. 2000).

Bernal Gutierrez, Rafael, *El Código de Comercio Colombiano (Historia y Proyecciones)*, *in* Instituto de Investigaciones Jurídicas (ed.), Centenario del Código de comercio, Mexico, Universidad Nacional Autónoma de México 85-108 (1991).

Bialostosky de Chazán, Sara, *La buena fe de los contratos*, 1970(79-80) Revista de la Facultad de Derecho de México 1104-1112.

Blanc-Jouvan, Xavier, Worldwide Influence of the French Civil Code of 1804, on the Occasion of its Bicentennial Celebration, Ithaca, New York, Cornell Law School (2004).

Boggiano, Antonio, Derecho Internacional Privado Vol. II, Buenos Aires, LexisNexis Abeledo-Perrot (5th ed. 2006).

Bomchil Group, Doing Business en Latin America, Bomchil Group, 2006, http://www.bomchilgroup.org/doing_business_in_latin_america/index.html.

Bonell, Michael Jochim, The Unidroit Principles in Practice: Caselaw and Bibliography on the Unidroit Principles of International Commercial Contracts, New York, Transnational Publishers (2nd ed. 2006).

Borda, Guillermo A., Manual de Contratos, Buenos Aires, LexisNexis Abeledo-Perrot (20th ed. 2004).

Brenes Cordoba, Alberto, Gerardo Trejos & Marina Ramírez, Tratado de los Contratos, San José, Editorial Juricentro (5th ed. 1998).

Cabanillas Sánchez, Antonio, *in* Luis Díez Picazo y Ponce De León, La Compraventa Internacional de Mecaderias – Comentario sobre la Convención de Viena, Madrid, Civitas (1998).

Calvo Caravaca, Alfonso-Luis, *in* Luis Díez Picazo y Ponce De León (Ed.), La Compraventa Internacional de Mecaderias – Comentario sobre la Convención de Viena, Madrid, Civitas (1998).

Camara, Hector, *Código de Comercio de la República Argentina*, *in* Instituto de Investigaciones Jurídicas (Ed.), Centenario del Código de comercio, Mexico, Universidad Nacional Autónoma de México 109-129 (1991).

Camargo Marín, Victor, Derecho Comercial Boliviano, La Paz (3rd ed. 2007).

Carcamo Tercero, Hernan, Eficacia e Ineficacia de los Contratos en Materia Civil, Tegucigalpa, Editorial Universitaria (2001).

Carrillo Aruquipa, Ramiro, Lecciones de Derecho Civil, Obligaciones, La Paz, Temis (2008).

Castellanos Trigo, G. & S. Auad La Fuente, Derecho de las Obligaciones en el Código Civil Boliviano, Tarija, Bolivia (2008).

Castillo Freyre, Mario (Ed.), El bien materia del contrato de compraventa: algunas consideraciones preliminares sobre el contrato de compraventa y estudio del capitulo segundo de dicho contrato en el código civil, Lima, Pontíficia Universidad Católica del Perú – Fondo Editoria (2nd ed. 1995).

Castillo Freyre, Mario, Tratado de la Teoria General de los Contratos Vol. I, Lima, Pontifícia Universidad Católica del Perú (2002).

Castillo Freyre, Mario, Comentarios al contrato de compraventa: análisis detallado de los artículos 1529 a 1601 del Código Civil, Lima, Gaceta Jurídica (2002).

Cevallos Vásquez, Víctor, Contratos Civiles y Mercantiles Vol. I, Quito, Editorial Jurídica del Ecuador (2005).

CISG-AC, Opinion No. 4, Contracts for the Sale of Goods to Be Manufactured or Produced and Mixed Contracts (Article 3 CISG), 24 October 2004. Rapporteur: Professor Pilar Perales Viscasillas, Universidad Carlos III de Madrid.

CISG-AC, Opinion No. 5, The buyer's right to avoid the contract in case of non-conforming goods or documents 7 May 2005, Badenweiler (Germany). Rapporteur: Professor Dr. Ingeborg Schwenzer, LL.M., Professor of Private Law, University of Basel.

CISG-AC, Opinion No. 6, Calculation of Damages under CISG Article 74. Rapporteur: Professor John Y. Gotanda, Villanova University School of Law, Villanova, Pennsylvania, USA.

CISG-AC. Opinion No. 9, Consequences of Avoidance of the Contract, Rapporteur: Professor Michael Bridge, London School of Economics, London, United Kingdom.

Clusellas, G., *in* Alberto Bueres (Ed.), Código civil y normas complementarias: análisis doctrinario y jurisprudencial, Buenos Aires, Hammurabi (1995).

Compagnucci de Caso, Rubén, Contrato de Compraventa, Buenos Aires, Hammurabi (2007).

Cornejo Fuller, Eugenio, *El Código de Comercio Chileno y sus Principales Reformas*, *in* Instituto de Investigaciones Jurídicas (Ed.), Centenario del Código de comercio, Mexico, Universidad Nacional Autónoma de México 131-141 (1991).

Da Silva Pereira, Caio Mário, Instituçaoes de Dereito Civil, Vol. III, Contratos, Electrônica, Rio de Janeiro (2003).

Dam, Kenneth W., *Legal Institutions, Legal Origins, and Governance*, 38961, University of Chicago Law & Economics, Olin Working Paper No. 303.

De la Puente y Lavalle, Manuel, El contrato en general: comentarios a la sección primera del libro VII del Código civil, Vol. I, Lima, Palestra Editores (2nd ed. 2001).

De Lima Pinheiro, Luís, Dereito Comercial Internacional, Ediçoes Almeida (2005).

De Pina, Rafael, Elementos de Derecho Civil Mexicano, Contratos en Particular, Vol. IV, México, Editorial Porrúa (2007).

Delgado Barreto, Cesar, *et al.*, Introducción al Derecho Internacional Privado, Vol. I, Lima, Pontificia Universidad Católica del Perú – Fondo Editorial (2002).

Díez Duarte, Raul, La Compraventa en el Código Civil Chileno, Santiago, Editorial Jurídica ConoSur Ltda. (2nd ed. 1993).

Dolganova, I. & M. Boff, *A Case for Brazil's Adhesion to the 1980 UN Convention on Contracts for the International Sale of Goods*, 13(2) The Vindobona Journal of International Commercial Law and Arbitration, 351 372 (2009).

Dos Santos, Olga María, Contratos Internacionales en el Ordenamiento Jurídico Venezolano, Caracas, Vadell Hermanos Editores (2000).

Elías Azar, Edgar, La Contratacion por Medios Electronicos, México, Editorial Porrúa (2005).

Escobar Velez, Edgar Guillermo, La compraventa civil y comercial: los contratos de promesa de compraventa y la permuta, Medellín, Ed. Jurídica de Colombia (1991).

Fajardo Fernandez, Javier, La Compraventa con Precio Determinable, Madrid, Editorial EDIJUS (2001).

Farina, Juan M., Contratos Comerciales Modernos, Buenos Aires, Astrea de A. y R. Depalma (2nd ed. 1999).

Fernández Rozas, J.C., Sánchez Lorenzo, S., Curso de Derecho Internacional Privado, Madrid, Editorial Civitas (3rd ed. 1996).

Ferrer Correia, A., Lições de direito internacional privado, Coimbra, Almedina (2005).

Fountoulakis, Christiana, *in* Ingeborg Schwenzer (Ed.), Schlechtriem & Schwenzer Commentary on the UN Convention on the International Sale of Goods, New York, Oxford University Press (3rd ed. 2010).

Gambaro, Antonio, *Causa y Contrato*, *in* El Contrato en el Sistema Jurídico Latinoamericano, Vol. I, Bogotá, Universidad de Externado de Colombia 159-198 (1998).

Garcia Rubio, Ma. Paz, La Responsabilidad precontractual en el Derecho Español, Madrid, Tecnos (1991).

Garro, Alejandro M., *Unification and Harmonization of Private Law in Latin America*, 40 American Journal of Comparative Law 587-616 (1992).

Giral Pimentel, José Alfredo, *La teoría de las vinculaciones*, Publicaciones Juridicas Venezolanas (1999), http://www.zur2.com/fcjp/117/giral.htm.

Gomes, Orlando, Contratos, São Paulo, Forense (26th ed. 2008).

Gonçalves, Carlos Roberto, Dereito Civil Brasileiro, Vol. III, Contratos e Atos Unilateralais, São Paulo, Saraiva (2004).

Gonzalez, José María Miguel, *in* Luis Díez Picazo y Ponce De León (Ed.), La Compraventa Internacional de Mecaderias – Comentario sobre la Convención de Viena, Madrid, Civitas (1998).

Guardiola Sacarrera, Enrrique, La compraventa internacional: importaciones y exportaciones, Barcelona, Bosch (2nd ed. 2001).

Gutierrez Jerez, Luiz Javier, *La obligacion de saneamiento por eviccion y la transmision del dominio en la compraventa*, *in* José Aguirre Zamorano (Ed.), La Compraventa Ley de Garantías, Madrid, Consejo General del Poder Judicial 13-59 (2006).

Guzman Brito, Alejandro, Historia de la Codificación civil en Iberoamerica, Navarra, Thomson Aranzadi (2006).

Henschel, René Franz, *Conformity of Goods in International Sales Governed by Article 35 CISG: Caveat Venditor, Caveat Emptor and Contract Law as Background Law and as a Competing Set of Rules*, 1 Nordic Journal of Commercial Law 1-27 (2004).

Herman, Shael, *Specific Performance: a Comparative Analysis*, 1 Edinburgh Law Review 1-26 (2003).

Hernandez Fernandez, Lisette, *La oferta y la aceptación. Especial referencia a los contratos celebrados por medios electrónicos*, 2004 (23-24) Revista Cubana de Derecho 78-91.

Herrera Espinoza, Jesús Jusseth, *et al.*, Contratos Civiles y Mercantiles, Managua, Universidad Centroamericana (2006).

Hionestrosa, Fernando, *Validez e Invalidez del Contrato en el Derecho Latinoamericano*, *in* El Contrato en el Sistema Jurídico Latinoamericano, Vol. I, Bogotá, Universidad de Externado de Colombia 199-221 (1998).

ICC, Incoterms 2000: Die offiziellen Regeln der ICC zur Auslegung von Handelsklauseln = ICC official rules for the interpretation of trade terms; gültig ab 1. Januar 2000. Köln: ICC Deutschland Vertriebsdienst.

ICC, UCP 600 Drafting Group, International Chamber of Commerce, & ICC Banking Commission, 2007, Commentary on UCP 600: Article-by-article analysis. Paris, France: International Chamber of Commerce.

Infante Ruiz, F. & F. Oliva Blázquez, *Los Contratos Ilegales en el Derecho Europeo*, 3 InDret 1-58 (2009).

Iturraspe, M., *in* Alberto Bueres (Ed.), Código civil y normas complementarias: análisis doctrinario y jurisprudencial, Buenos Aires, Hammurabi (1995).

Jijena Leiva, Renato, Comercio Electronico, Firma Digital y Derecho, Santiago, Editorial Jurídica de Chile (2nd ed. 2005).

Jones, G.H. & P. Schlechtriem, *Breach of Contract (Deficiencies in a Party's Performance)*, *in* Arthur T. von Mehren (Ed.), International Encyclopedia of Comparative Law, Vol. VII Contracts, Ch. 15, Tübingen, Mohr Siebeck (1999).

Kaune Arteaga, Walter, Curso de Derecho Civil, Contratos, Vol. 1 & 2, La Paz, Temis (4th ed. 1996).

Kramer E.A. & T. Probst, *Defects in the Contracting Process*, *in* Arthur T. von Mehren (Ed.), International Encyclopedia of Comparative Law, Vol. VII Contracts, Ch. 11, Tübingen, Mohr Siebeck (1999).

La Porta, Rafael, *et al.*, *The Economic Consequences of Legal Origins*, 46(2) Journal of Economic Literature, American Economic Association 285-332 (2008).

Lagarde, P. & M. Giuliano, *Report on the Convention on the law applicable to contractual obligations*, Journal Official n° C 282 du 31 October 1980, 1-50.

Las Siete Partidas del Rey Alfonso El Sabio, Cotejadas con varios Códices Antiguos por la Real Academia de la Historia, Tomo III, Partida Cuarta, Quinta, Sexta y Séptima, Madrid en la Imprenta Real (1807).

León Tovar, Soyla, Los Contratos Mercantiles, México, Oxford University Press (2004).

Llobet I Aguado, Josép, El Deber de Información en la Formación de los Contratos, Madrid, Marcial Pons (1996).

López de Zavalia, Fernando, Teoria de los Contratos, Vol. 1, Buenos Aires, Zavalia Editor (4th ed. 2003).

López López, Angel, *in* Luis Díez Picazo y Ponce De León (Ed.), La Compraventa Internacional de Mecaderias – Comentario sobre la Convención de Viena (1998).

Lopez Santa Maria, Jorge, Los Contratos: Parte General, Vol. 2, Santiago, Editorial Jurídica de Chile (4th ed. 2005).

Lorenzetti, Ricardo Luis, Tratado de los Contratos Parte General, Santa Fe, Robinzal-Culzoni Editores (2004).

Marsh, P.D.V., Comparative Contract Law: England, France, Germany, Aldershot Hampshire England, Brookfield Vt. USA: Gower, cop. (1994).

Martínez Cañellas, Anselmo, *El incumplimiento esencial del contrato de compraventa internacional de mercaderías*, Doctoral thesis, Universitat de les Illes Balears, Facultat de Dret. Àrea de Dret mercantil Palma de Mallorca (2001), http://www.tdx.cat/TDX-0308105-095856.

Medina de Lemus, Manuel, Derecho Civil: Obligaciones y Contratos II, Teoria General Vol. 1, Madrid, Editorial Dilex (2004).

Medina de Lemus, Manuel, Derecho Civil: Obligaciones y Contratos II, Contratos en Particular, Vol. 2, Madrid, Editorial Dilex (2004).

Mélich-Orsini, José, Doctrina General del Contrato, Caracas, Académia de Ciencias Politicas y Sociales – Centro de Investigaciones Jurícicas (4th ed. 2006).

Miranda, Adolfo Oscar, De la Compraventa, San Salvador, Editorial Delgado Universidad 'Dr. José Delgado' (1996).

Miranda, Adolfo Oscar, Guía para. el Estudio del Derecho Civil III, Obligaciones, San Salvador (1996).

Mohs, Florian, *in* Ingeborg Schwenzer (Ed.), Schlechtriem & Schwenzer Commentary on the UN Convention on the International Sale of Goods, New York, Oxford University Press (3rd ed. 2010).

Moisset de Espanés, Luis, *El Método del Código Civil*, Academia Nacional de Derecho y Ciencias Sociales de Córdoba (2003), http://www.acaderc.org.ar/doctrina/articulos/artelmetododelCódigocivil/?searchterm=explicativa.

Moldes Ruibal, Victor *et al.*, Contratos civiles y comerciales: técnica y práctica, Vol. 1, Motevideo, B de f (2006).

Monroy Cabra, Marco Gerardo, *El Arbitraje Internacional en Colombia*, Sevilex (1999), http://www.servilex.com.pe/arbitraje/congresopanama/b-07.php.

Morales Hernandez, Alfredo, *Evolución Histórica y Tendencias de la Legislacion Mercantil Venezolana*, *in* Instituto de Investigaciones Jurídicas (Ed.), Centenario del Código de Comercio, Mexico, Universidad Nacional Autónoma de México 273-306 (1991).

Morales Moreno, Antonio Manuel, *in* Luis Díez Picazo y Ponce De León (Ed.), La Compraventa Internacional de Mecaderias – Comentario sobre la Convención de Viena, Madrid, Civitas (1998).

Moreira Alves, Juan Carlos, *Aspectos de la Formacion de los Contratos Obligatorios en las Fuentes Romanas y en algunos Paises Latinoamericanos*, *in* El Contrato en el Sistema Jurídico Latinoamericano, Vol. I, Bogotá, Universidad de Externado de Colombia 121-146 (1998).

Moreno Ródriguez-Alcalá, Roberto, *Paraguay*, *in* Dennis Campbell (Ed.), Remedies for International Sellers of Goods, Vol. III, Yorkhill Law Publishing 63-80 (2008).

Moxica Román, José, La compraventa mercantil e instituciones afines: análisis de doctrina y jurisprudencia, formularios, Navarra, Thomson Aranzadi (2000).

Müller-Chen, Markus, *in* Ingeborg Schwenzer (Ed.), Schlechtriem & Schwenzer Commentary on the UN Convention on the International Sale of Goods, New York, Oxford University Press (3rd ed. 2010).

Muriá-Tuñón, Arnau, *The Actio Quanti Minoris and Sales of Goods Between Mexico and the U.S.: An Analysis of the Remedy of Reduction of the Price in the UN Sales Convention, CISG Article 50 and its Civil Law Antecedents*, Pace database on the CISG and International Commercial Law (1998), http://www.cisg.law.pace.edu/cisg/biblio/muria.html#actio.

Murillo, María Luisa, *The Evolution of Codification in the Civil Law Legal Systems: Towards Decodification and Recodification*, 11(1) Journal of Transnational Law & Policy 1-20 (2001).

Navarro Moreno, Lenín, Compraventa internacional y conflictos de leyes: aspectos jurídicos de la contratación internacional, Quito, Corporación de Estudios y Publicaciones (2002).

Neumayer, Karl H., Catherine Ming & François Dessemontet (Eds.), Convention de Vienne sur les contrats de vente internationale de marchandises: commentaire, Lausanne, Centre du droit de l'entreprise (1993).

Neumayer, Karl H., *Contracting Subject to Standard Terms and Conditions*, *in* Arthur T. von Mehren, International Encyclopedia of Comparative Law, Vol. VII Contracts, Ch. 12, Tübingen, Mohr Siebeck (1999).

Noronha, Fernando, Direito das Obriga¢ões, Vol. 1, São Paulo, Editora Saraiva (2nd ed. 2007)

O'Callaghan, Xavier (Ed.), Código Civil Comentado, Madrid, La Ley (2004).

Obando Peralta, Juan José, *Los Contratos Electrónicos y Digitales*, 39 AR: Revista de Derecho Informático (2001), http://www.alfa-redi.org/rdi-articulo.shtml?x=819.

Olivera Garcia R. & S. Rippe, *Evolucion y Panorama del Derecho Mercantil Uruguayo*, *in* Instituto de Investigaciones Jurídicas (Ed.), Centenario del Código de Comercio, Mexico, Universidad Nacional Autónoma de México 303-337 (1991).

Ordenanzas de la Ilustre Universidad y Casa de Contratación de la Villa de Bilbao, por el Rey Don Felipe Quinto (1737) Reimpresión en Madrid (1775).

Orrego Acuña, Juan Andrés, De la Responsabilidad Precontractual (2009), http://www.juanandresorrego.cl/trabajos_publicados/pfd/articul_entheos_de_la_responsabilidad_precontractual.pdf.

Ovando Ovando, Jaime, Sociedades Comerciales, Doctrina y Legislación Nacional, La Paz, Plural (2008).

Oviedo Alban, Jorge, La Formación de Contrato: tratos preliminares, oferta, aceptación, Bogota, Temis (2008).

Oviedo Albán, Jorge, Usos y Costumbres en el Derecho Privado Contemporáneo (2001), http://www.derecho-comercial.com/Doctrina/oviedo01.pdf.

Pangrazio, Miguel Angel (Ed.), Código Civil Paraguayo Comentado, Asunción, Intercontinental (2nd ed. 1990).

Perales Vizcasillas, Pilar, *in* David Morán Bovio (Ed.), Comentario a los Principios de Unidroit para. los Contratos del Comercio Internacional, Navarra, Thomson-Aranzadi (2003).

Perales Vizcasillas, Pilar, *Late Payment Directive 200/35 and the CISG*, 19 Pace International Law Review 125-142 (2007).

Perales Vizcasillas, Pilar, *CISG Case Law in Spain (2004-2006)*, *in* C. Andersen & U. Schroeter (Ed.), Sharing International Commercial Law across National Boundaries: Festschrift for Albert H Kritzer on the Occasion of his 80th Birthday, London, Wildy, Simmonds & Hill Publishing 377-392 (2008).

Perez Fernandez del Castillo, Bernardo, Contratos Civiles, Mexico, Editorial Porrúa (12th ed. 2008).

Pereznieto Castro, Leonel, Derecho Internacional Privado, Parte General, México, Oxford University Press (8th ed. 2005).

Pereznieto Castro, Leonel, *Introducción a la Convención Interamericana sobre Derecho Aplicable a los Contratos Internacionales*, 13-14-15 Revista de Derecho Privado, 137-149 (1994).

Pisano, Beatriz, *La autonomía de la voluntad en el Derecho Internacional Privado Paraguayo*, Blog del CEDEP (2009), http://cedep.wordpress.com.

Prieto, Fernando Pantaleón, *in* Luis Díez Picazo y Ponce De León (Ed.), La Compraventa Internacional de Mecaderias – Comentario sobre la Convención de Viena, Madrid, Civitas (1998).

Ramírez Altamirano, Mariana, Derecho Civil IV, Vol. II, Los Contratos Traslativos de Dominio, San José, Juricentro (1991).

Ramirez Necochea, Mario, Derecho Internacional Privado, Santiago, LexisNexis (2005).

Ramírez, Roberto, *Codificación Mercantil en la República de Honduras*, *in* Instituto de Investigaciones Jurídicas (Ed.), Centenario del Código de Comercio, Mexico, Universidad Nacional Autónoma de México 425-436 (1991).

Rodriguez Olivera, Nuri *et al.*, Manual de Derecho comercial uruguayo, v. 2: Obligaciones y contratos comerciales, t. 1: Régimen general de las obligaciones comerciales, compraventa y distribución mercantil, Montevideo, Fundación de Cultura Universitaria (2005).

Rodriguez Russo, Jorge, La Interpretacion del Contrato, Montevideo, Fundación de Cultura Universitaria (2006).

Rodriguez, Luis Alberto, Comentarios sobre: Contratos, Caracas, Editorial Livrosca (2nd ed. 2007).

Rojo, Angel, *La Codificación Mercantil Española*, *in* Instituto de Investigaciones

Jurídicas (Ed.), Centenario del Código de Comercio, Mexico, Universidad Nacional Autónoma de México 475-494 (1991).

Roth, P.M., *The Passing of Risk*, 27 American Journal of Comparative Law 291-310 (1979).

Saldias Collao, Osvaldo, El Contrato de Compraventa Internacional en el Comercio Chile-Union Europea, Santiago, Ediciones Metropolitana (2006).

Salermo, Marcelo Urbano, Contratos Civiles y Comerciales, Buenos Aires, Editorial de la Universidad Católica de Argentina (2007).

Sánchez Medal, Ramón, De los contratos civiles: teoría general del contrato, contratos en especial, registro público de la propiedad, Mexico, Editorial Porrúa (19th ed. 2002).

Schlechtriem, Peter, *Non-Material Damages – Recovery Under the CISG?*, 19 Pace International Law Review 89-102 (2007).

Schlechtriem, Peter, *in* Ingeborg Schwenzer (Ed.), Schlechtriem & Schwenzer Commentary on the UN Convention on the International Sale of Goods, New York, Oxford University Press (3rd ed. 2010).

Schlechtriem, Peter, *The Seller's Obligations Under the United Nations Convention on Contracts for the International Sale of Goods*, *in* Nina M. Galston & Hans Smit (Eds.), International Sales: The United Nations Convention on Contracts for the International Sale of Goods, Matthew Bender, Ch. 6, 6-1 to 6-35, http://www.cisg.law.pace.edu/cisg/biblio/schlechtriem10.html.

Schroeter, Ulrich G., *in* Ingeborg Schwenzer (Ed.), Schlechtriem & Schwenzer Commentary on the UN Convention on the International Sale of Goods, New York, Oxford University Press (3rd ed. 2010).

Schwenzer, I. & P. Hachem, *in* Ingeborg Schwenzer (Ed.), Schlechtriem & Schwenzer Commentary on the UN Convention on the International Sale of Goods, New York, Oxford University Press (3rd ed. 2010).

Schwenzer, I. & B. Leisinger, *Ethical Values and International Sales Contracts*, *in* Ross Cranston, Jan Ramberg & Jacob Ziegel (Eds.), Commercial Law Challenges in the 21st Century; Jan Hellner in memorium, Stockholm Centre for Commercial Law Juridiska institutionen 249-275 (2007), http://www.cisg.law.pace.edu/cisg/biblio/schwenzer-leisinger.html.

Schwenzer, Ingeborg, *in* Ingeborg Schwenzer (Ed.), Schlechtriem & Schwenzer Commentary on the UN Convention on the International Sale of Goods, New York, Oxford University Press (3rd ed. 2010).

Sierralta Ríos, Aníbal, La Compraventa Internacional de Mercaderias y el Derecho Paraguayo, Asución, Intercontinental Editora (2000).

Sierralta Ríos, Aníbal, La Compraventa Internacional y El Derecho Peruano, Lima, Pontificia Universidad Católica del Perú (1997).

Solarte Rodríguez, Arturo, *La buena fe contractual y los deberes secundarios de conducta*, 108 Vniversitas 282-315 (2004).

Soler Presas, Ana, La Valoracion del Daño en el Contrato de Compraventa, Pamplona, Aranzadi Editorial (1998).

Soler Presas, Ana, *in* Luis Díez Picazo y Ponce De León (Ed.), La Compraventa Internacional de Mecaderias – Comentario sobre la Convención de Viena, Madrid, Civitas (1998).

Sozzo, Gonzalo, Antes del contrato: los cambios en la regulación jurídica del período precontractual (2005).

Stringer, Dana, *Choice of Law and Choice of Forum in Brazilian International Commercial Contracts: Party Autonomy, International Jurisdiction, and the Emerging Third Way*, 44(33) Columbia Journal of Transnational Law 959-991 (2006).

Tamayo Lombana, Alberto, El Contrato de Compraventa su Régimen Civil y Comercial, Bogota, Ediciones Doctrina y Ley (2004).

Torres y Torres Lara, Carlos, *La Codificación Comercial en el Peru de un Código 'Formal' a un Código 'Real'*, *in* Instituto de Investigaciones Jurídicas (Ed.), Centenario del Código de Comercio, Mexico, Universidad Nacional Autónoma de México 583-596 (1991).

Treitel, G.H., *Remedies for Breach of Contract*, *in* Arthur T. von Mehren (Ed.), International Encyclopedia of Comparative Law, Vol. VII Contracts, Ch. 16 (1999).

Valdivieso Bermeo, Carlos, Tratado de las Obligaciones y Contratos, Loja, Offset Grafimundo: Comisariato del Estudiante (2005).

Vásquez del Mercado, Oscar, Contratos Mercantiles, Mexico DF, Porrúa (2008).

Vázquez Barros, Sergio, Contratos de compraventa y permuta: comentarios, formularios, jurisprudencia: legislación básica y bibliografía, Madrid, Editorial Tecnos (2003).

Vidal Olivares, Alvaro, *La Noción de Incumplimiento Esencial en el Código Civil*, XXXII(1) Revista de Derecho de la Pontificia Universidad Católica de Valparaíso 221-258 (2009).

Von Ziegler, Alexander, *The Right of Suspension and Stoppage in Transit (and Notification thereof)*, 25 The Journal of Law and Commerce 353-374 (2005).

Widmer, Corine, *in* Ingeborg Schwenzer (Ed.), Schlechtriem & Schwenzer Commentary on the UN Convention on the International Sale of Goods, New York, Oxford University Press (3rd ed. 2010).

Woodward, Ralph, *The New Consulados de Comercio in the Spanish Empire 1778-1829*, Tulane University (1999), http://www.tulane.edu/~woodward/newcons.htm.

Yrarrázaval A., Ovalle G., *Chile*, *in* Dennis Campbell (Ed.), Remedies for International Sellers of Goods, Vol. I, Yorkhill Law Publishing 297-316 (2008).

Zimmermann, Reinhard, The Law of Obligations – Roman Foundations of the Civilian Tradition, Cape Town, Juta (1990).

Zuloaga Rios, Isabel Margarita, Teoría de la responsabilidad precontractual: aplicaciones en la formación del consentimiento de los contratos, Santiago, LexisNexis (2nd ed. 2007).

International Commerce and Arbitration (Series Editor: Ingeborg Schwenzer)

Volume 1: Mariel Dimsey, The Resolution of International Investment Disputes: Challenges and Practical Solutions, ISBN 978-90-77596-52-4

Volume 2: Sarah E. Hilmer, Mediation in the People's Republic of China and Hong Kong (SAR), ISBN 978-90-77596-74-6

Volume 3: Christina Knahr, Christian Koller, Walter Rechberger and August Reinisch (Eds.), Investment and Commercial Arbitration – Similarities and Divergences, ISBN 978-90-77596-81-4

Volume 4: Markus Jäger, Reimbursement for Attorney's Fees, ISBN 978-90-77596-98-2

Volume 5: Olivier Luc Mosimann, Anti-Suit Injunctions in International Commercial Arbitration, ISBN 978-90-77596-99-9

Volume 6: Edgardo Muñoz, Modern Law of Contracts and Sales in Latin America, Spain and Portugal, ISBN 978-94-90947-03-3